OCCUPATIONAL PRESTIGE
IN COMPARATIVE
PERSPECTIVE

This is a volume of

Quantitative Studies in Social Relations

Consulting Editor: Peter H. Rossi, University of Massachusetts, Amherst, Massachusetts

A complete list of titles in this series is available from the publisher.

OCCUPATIONAL PRESTIGE IN COMPARATIVE PERSPECTIVE

DONALD J. TREIMAN

Department of Sociology
University of California, Los Angeles

ACADEMIC PRESS   New York   San Francisco   London

A Subsidiary of Harcourt Brace Jovanovich, Publishers

ACADEMIC PRESS, INC.
111 Fifth Avenue, New York, New York 10003

United Kingdom Edition published by
ACADEMIC PRESS, INC. (LONDON) LTD.
24/28 Oval Road, London NW1

HT
675
, T73

Library of Congress Cataloging in Publication Data

Treiman, Donald J
  Occupational prestige in comparative perspective.

  (Quantitative studies in social relations series)
  Bibliography: p.
  Includes indexes.
  1.   Occupational prestige.   I.   Title.
HT675.T73   301.5'5   76-50405
ISBN 0−12−698750−5

For my parents

Contents

I
INTRODUCTION

II
SETTING THE STAGE: DATA, METHODS, AND BASIC RESULTS

V
CONCLUSION

List of Figures

List of Tables

Preface

This book is a study of the nature of inequality in human society. Although ostensibly concerned simply with describing and accounting for societal similarities and differences in occupational prestige hierarchies, the book actually speaks to a much broader issue. I argue that stratification is inevitable in complex societies because they are characterized by a highly developed division of labor into distinct occupational roles, and occupational role differentiation inherently gives rise to inequalities in power, privilege, and prestige. Moreover, all complex societies have fundamentally similar occupational status hierarchies because occupational differences in power, and hence in privilege and prestige, are rooted in the division of labor and are thus everywhere the same.

These conclusions derive from a comparative analysis of occupational hierarchies in over 60 societies, both past and present, based on popular evaluations of the prestige of occupations drawn from sample surveys and on data on occupational skill and wealth levels drawn from census records and other sources. The mode of analysis, in which societies are the units of observation and patterns of systematic covariation among various societal characteristics are identified, reflects a particular conception of the purpose of comparative analysis: to discover the invariant properties of human social systems. To do this we must move away from the case study approach that dominates comparative analysis. It is not enough to analyze a single society or even a handful of societies; rather, we must obtain data from a sufficiently large and diverse set of societies to be able to distinguish between those elements of social organization that are characteristic of all societies, those that are characteristic of particular types of societies, and those that are unique to specific societies at specific points in their histories.

This, however, raises a practical difficulty. It is not ordinarily possible for a single investigator to collect primary data from a large enough sample of societies to sustain an analysis of this sort. This means that data must be pieced together from studies conducted by different investigators, and such data will typically be drawn from diverse samples assessed with a variety of procedures. Hence, to achieve even reasonable confidence in the validity of one's conclusions requires devoting a great deal of effort to problems of data comparability. Even so, the conclusions of this sort of analysis must necessarily be tentative, given the fragmentary nature of the data. But knowledge based on some evidence, however fragmentary, from a wide variety of societies is surely better than extrapolation from detailed studies of a few special cases. I contend that now, and for the foreseeable future, wide ranging secondary analysis of existing data is the only way we will have of achieving a valid comparative sociology.

This study is conceived as a contribution to such an effort in two respects. First, it serves as an example of the sort of comparative analysis that can be carried out solely on the basis of preexisting data. Second, an important conclusion of the analysis—that occupational prestige hierarchies are fundamentally invariant across all complex societies—has made it possible to develop a cross-nationally valid occupational prestige scale that can be used as a standard measure of occupational status in future comparative research.

Acknowledgments

This book had its origin more than 10 years ago, at the National Opinion Research Center of the University of Chicago in the summer of 1964, when Pete Rossi suggested to Bill Hodge that they update the paper that Rossi had done with Alex Inkeles comparing the prestige hierarchies of eight industrialized countries (Inkeles and Rossi, 1956) and Hodge invited me to work with him on it. The paper (Hodge, Treiman, and Rossi, 1966) begat my Ph.D. dissertation, defended in 1967, and the dissertation begat the present monograph, albeit with many digressions and other devotions in the intervening years.

The research reported here can probably best be described as an attempt at the making of silk purses from sows' ears, dependent as it has been on the piecing together of data from diverse sources for the purpose of effecting systematic cross-national comparisons. Whether the effort was successful is for the reader to judge. But the attempt would not have been possible without the generosity and support of a large number of people, at several universities and research centers.

The substantial support and aid I received in preparing the Ph.D. dissertation that served as a springboard for the present analysis has already been acknowledged in the dissertation itself. Here I would like to single out for special thanks those who contributed to the subsequent analysis.

First, the development of the ideas presented here profited enormously from extensive discussion with my colleague Jonathan Kelley, now at Yale; Kelley also read and tore apart parts of several drafts of the manuscript, which are clearly better for his attentions. Others who provided helpful suggestions are David Featherman and Hal Winsborough, University of Wisconsin; Dudley Duncan, University of Arizona; Judah Matras, Hebrew University of Jerusalem; and Jonathan Cole, Si Goode, Jack Hammond, Eugene Litwak, Andy Beveridge, Herb Klein, Amitai Etzioni, and Bernard Barber, Columbia University.

Many research assistants had a hand in the preparation of the materials presented here. Thanks are due to Gretchen Condran, Harry Travis, Mark Evers, and Louise Turner at the University of Wisconsin; Vincent Covello, Kermit Terrell, Thomas Di Prete, and Betty Sheets at Columbia University; and J. L. P. Thompson, Jo Lea Gaddis, and Patricia A. Roos at UCLA. Michael Freeman and Walter Harrison at the Center for Policy Research and Richard Alba at Columbia University carried out various specialized computer programming tasks. Ulla Colgrass and Candy Howes at the Center for Policy Research and Bunny Levitt at UCLA ably and cheerfully typed various drafts of a complicated manuscript, and generally kept me sane. Judith Herschman prepared the index.

A project such as this depends heavily upon the cooperation of other researchers. Many individuals went out of their way to furnish me with unpublished data and to respond to my inquiries of one sort or another. Thanks are due Athol Congalton, Allen Eister, Frederick Gulliksen, Archibald O. Haller, Eugene Hammel, George Helling, David Herlihy, Keith Hope, Iwao Ishino, Michael Katz, Jonathan Kelley, Gerhard Kleining, David Lewis, Tom Lux, Fabio Metelli, Clyde Mitchell, Wade Pendleton, Valdo Pons, Carlo Remondino, Theodore Riccardi, and Paul Siegel.

I wish to acknowledge permission from the University of Chicago Press to quote from Marc Bloch, Feudal Society, 1964, pp. 337–339; from E. P. Dutton to quote from Raymond Firth, Primitive Economics of the New Zealand Maori, 1929, pp. 206–207; from Harvard University Press to quote from H. Kent Geiger, The Family in Soviet Russia, 1968, p. 57; from Oxford University Press to quote from John H. Goldthorpe and K. Hope, The Social Grading of Occupations, 1974, p. 5; from the American Sociological Association to quote from Eva Rosenfeld, "Social stratification in a 'classless' society," American Sociological Review 16 (December, 1951), p. 769; and from Cambridge University Press to quote from Edward Shils, "Deference," in J. A. Jackson (ed.), Social Stratification, 1968, pp. 107–108.

The research reported here has been supported at various stages by National Science Foundation Grant GS-2487 to the University of Wisconsin, National Science Foundation Grant 28050 to Columbia University, and National Institute of Mental Health Grant MH26606 to the Center for Policy Research. The administrative assistance of Stephanie Clohesy of the Center for Policy Research is particularly appreciated.

Acknowledgments would not be complete without mention of my very special debt to Stanley Holwitz, Sponsoring Editor at Academic Press, who nursed this creation through an excessively long gestation and did what no one else could—got me to let go.

Finally, there are Judith, Noah, and Ethan. I cannot honestly say that they facilitated production of the book—sometimes they were helpful and sometimes they weren't. But life would have been far less rich, and far less happy, without them.

I

INTRODUCTION

1

The Division of Labor and Occupational Stratification

Men are known by their work. It is no accident that when strangers meet, a standard opening gambit is the question, "What sort of work do you do?," for this information provides the best single clue to the sort of person one is. It marks a person as "someone to be reckoned with" or as one who can be safely ignored, one to whom deference is due or from whom deference can be expected. Moreover, it permits at least crude inferences regarding attitudes, experiences, and style of life. In short, occupational roles locate individuals in social space, thereby setting the stage for their interaction with one another.

This is possible because people in all walks of life share understandings about occupations—how much skill they require, how physically demanding they are, whether they are considered men's work or women's work, and so on—but particularly about their prestige. Every adult member of society ordinarily is able to locate occupations on a hierarchy of prestige. These perceptions form part of the *conscience collective*. This permits one to rank oneself and others with respect to the social honor derived from occupational status. Of course, occupational prestige is not the only basis of rank, but it is an important one in all societies with any substantial degree of occupational role differentiation.

It is therefore important to understand the nature of occupational prestige systems: What determines the relative prestige ordering of occupations? Do the same factors operate in all societies? If not, what accounts for the differences that do exist? This book addresses these questions by studying occupational prestige hierarchies in a large number of societies, both past and present. I propose a theory that argues that prestige ultimately is rooted in power relations, and then draw upon data from diverse sources to

1

test the theory. In doing this I have two goals: first, to show that the theory applies to all complex societies and is not restricted to any one society or any particular type of complex society; and, second, to account for the observed similarities and differences in the prestige hierarchies of different societies.

This study reflects a particular conception of the purposes of comparative research. It seems to me that if we are to arrive at an adequate understanding of the nature of human society, we must replicate the studies made in any particular society in a large sample of societies in order to distinguish three classes of phenomena: those that are universally characteristic of human social systems; those that systematically covary across societies; and those that are unique to particular times and places. In the present context, this amounts to (*1*) establishing the extent of similarity in prestige hierarchies throughout the world, and accounting for it; (*2*) determining whether and in what way differences between societies in prestige evaluations are related to differences in other aspects of social structure, such as the level of industrialization; and (*3*) relating any idiosyncratic differences in prestige evaluations to other idiosyncratic societal characteristics, such as those associated with specific cultural patterns.

ORGANIZATION OF THE VOLUME

This book argues a particular thesis—that the relative prestige of the social roles known as occupations is essentially invariant in all complex societies, past and present, and that this must be so as a consequence of inherent features of the division of labor as it exists in all societies. Competing hypotheses—that the prestige hierarchy of each society reflects idiosyncratic cultural values, that worldwide similarity exists but only because a Western system of occupational evaluation has diffused throughout the world as an adjunct to Western hegemony, or that worldwide similarity is a consequence of the constraints imposed by an industrial structure and industrial technology—are considered and rejected.

In the remainder of the present chapter I lay the groundwork for the subsequent analysis by developing a *structural* theory of prestige determination and contrasting it to the competing *cultural* and *diffusion* theories just alluded to. The structural theory argues that the division of labor creates inherent differences in the power associated with various occupational roles wherever they are found, that these differences, in turn, create differences in privilege, and that power and privilege beget prestige. Since a similar complement of occupational roles tends to arise in all complex societies, the resulting prestige hierarchies will also be similar.

In Chapters 2–4 I establish that there is indeed a question to study, by documenting that there is a single worldwide occupational prestige hierarchy.

Chapter 2 introduces the basic data, which consist of 85 occupational prestige studies from 53 countries. This chapter will be of interest principally to those concerned with the adequacy of the data and the procedures utilized to effect comparisons. I first address the question of whether or not data generated by popular evaluations of the prestige of occupations are valid indicators of prestige in its classical sociological sense, and I conclude that they are. I then consider and reject the possibility of bias due to various noncomparabilities in the data and inadequacies in the procedures utilized to effect comparisons. Finally, I describe the procedures for coding the data and effecting the comparisons upon which the remainder of the analysis is based.

Chapter 3 reviews the evidence regarding subgroup variations in prestige evaluations within societies and concludes that there is remarkable consensus in the perceptions of members of any single society. There is virtually no evidence of systematic variation in occupational prestige evaluations on the basis of the rater's occupation, ethnicity, sex, or the date the study was conducted. In particular, students are no different from and no more Western than other groups in nonindustrialized societies. The lack of subgroup variation in prestige perceptions is important both from a substantive point of view—reinforcing the perception of prestige as a manifestation of the *conscience collective*—and from a practical standpoint, since it permits us to utilize data from nonrepresentative samples to characterize entire societies. The single exception to the overwhelming evidence of internal consensus is that in some nonindustrialized countries there appear to be regional differences in the way occupations are evaluated. In view of this, data from nonindustrialized countries that show regional variations of this sort are sometimes treated separately; as a result we have data from 60 places, rather than 53.

Chapter 4 presents the basic data comparing occupational prestige hierarchies across societies. The key finding is that occupational evaluations are fundamentally the same throughout the world, which argues against the cultural theory of prestige determination. The average intercorrelation of prestige ratings across pairs of countries is .79, with a standard deviation of .14. This level of intersocietal agreement is very high, although somewhat lower than that found by previous investigators; this is hardly surprising considering that a much larger and much more diverse set of countries is included in the present analysis. The results are extremely robust in the sense that they hardly change when various subsets of countries are considered. The same pattern holds when white-collar and blue-collar occupations are considered separately, although intersocietal agreement in the rating of white-collar jobs is greater than in the rating of blue-collar jobs; this difference reflects the greater intersocietal variation in the social organization of manual than of nonmanual work.

Chapter 5 provides a partial test of the theory proposed in Chapter 1, showing that in all societies for which data are available, both past and present, occupational hierarchies are similar with respect to not only prestige but also education (an aspect of power) and income (an aspect of privilege). These characteristics are strongly intercorrelated across countries and are also strongly correlated within countries. Because past societies exhibit the same relationships among occupational characteristics as do present societies, the structural theory of prestige determination and prestige similarity proposed in Chapter 1 is strongly supported and the diffusionist theory rejected.

Chapters 6 and 7 take up the possibility that within the context of general intersocietal similarity in prestige evaluations there exist systematic intersocietal differences. The structural theory of prestige determination would suggest that differences in the social organization of work resulting from industrialization create differences in occupational prestige evaluations, and the analysis presented in Chapter 6 provides modest support for this view: More highly industrialized countries tend to be more similar to the United States in their pattern of prestige evaluations than less industrialized nations; among pairs of countries the greater the similarity in level of industrialization, the greater the similarity in prestige rankings. These patterns tend to be stronger with respect to the evaluation of manual occupations than of nonmanual occupations, which reflects the fact that the process of industrialization creates greater differences in the organization of manual than of nonmanual work. In Chapter 7 I consider the possibility that particular occupations are differentially evaluated in different societies. There is no evidence that differences in cultural values create differences in the prestige accorded particular occupations or particular types of occupations. However there is some evidence suggesting that variations in social organization that create differences in the power or privilege associated with a particular occupation in different societies create corresponding differences in prestige. So once again we have a confirmation of the structural theory of prestige determination.

Because of the basic similarity of prestige evaluations in all societies, it has been possible to construct a Standard International Occupational Prestige Scale that can be validly used to assign prestige scores to occupations in any country. Chapter 8 describes the construction and validation of the Scale, while Chapter 9 describes procedures for its use.

Chapter 10 summarizes the thesis of the book and goes on to discuss the inevitability of occupational stratification, drawing upon evidence from societies that have deliberately tried to abolish status distinctions based on occupational roles.

The book also includes four appendixes for the convenience of research workers. Appendix A presents the Standard International Occupational Prestige Scale; Appendix B is an alphabetical index to the Scale; Appendix C provides scale scores for the occupational categories of the first edition of the International Standard Classification of Occupations and for the United States Census detailed occupational classifications of 1950, 1960, and 1970; and Appendix D presents the basic prestige data from each country utilized in the analysis. Chapter 9 discusses the Appendixes and their uses in detail.

A THEORY OF OCCUPATIONAL PRESTIGE

In this section I outline what I referred to earlier as the structural theory of prestige determination, which predicts that the prestige ordering of occupations will be fundamentally invariant in all complex societies, past or present. The theory consists of four propositions, which are outlined here and elaborated below.

First, the similarity in the "functional imperatives" faced by all societies results in a basic similarity in the specific functions that have to be accomplished. This, together with inherent limitations in possible organizational forms, results in a basically similar configuration of occupational roles in all societies beyond those of the most rudimentary size and organizational complexity. That is, a division of labor will necessarily develop and, moreover, will develop in a similar way in all societies.

Second differentation inherently implies stratification. Specialization of functions carries with it inherent differences in the control over scarce resources, which is the primary basis of stratification. These resources include skill, authority, and property, each of which functions in a somewhat different way. Together they create differential power, in the most general sense of that term. Thus, the division of labor creates a characteristic hierarchy of occupations with respect to power exercised.

Third, the power resulting from control over scarce resources creates the opportunity for, and almost invariably results in, the acquisition of special privilege; thus the basic similarity among all complex societies in the relative power exercised by various occupations creates a corresponding similarity with respect to occupational differences in privilege.

Fourth, power and privilege are everywhere highly valued, and hence powerful and privileged occupations are highly regarded in all societies.

Thus, since the division of labor gives rise to characteristic differences in power, and power begets privilege, and power and privilege beget prestige, there should be a single, worldwide occupational prestige hierarchy. The remainder of this chapter will be devoted first to elaborating this argument and then to considering alternative explanations for the observed prestige ordering of occupations in the contemporary world.

The Division of Labor and Occupational Specialization. Here I address the question of why a division of labor arises at all and why a basically similar configuration of occupational roles arises in all complex societies. The basic factor promoting the division of labor is its efficiency. Relative to unspecialized labor, specialized labor is far more efficient. There are several reasons for this.

First, some tasks can be more efficiently performed by individuals with particular personal traits—great strength, height, agility, speed, stamina, sharpness of eyesight, intelligence, tenacity, aggressiveness, and so forth. Sporting events provide a good illustration. No crew that expected to win would allow the coxswain and the oarsman to trade roles; the one is chosen for his small size and light weight and the other for his strength. Differences in the physical traits demanded by various kinds of work are recognized by all societies in a division of labor based on age and sex; some tasks are performed exclusively by women and others exclusively by men in virtually every known society (Murdock, 1937); similarly, some activities are rigidly age stratified virtually everywhere. But physical differences are not the only ones that come into play in determining occupational capabilities. Personality differences, differences in talent, and differences in general capacity, all of which are probably as much a matter of socialization as of genetic endowment, are also important in occupational performance.

Second, most tasks require learned skills, many of which take considerable time to master. Hence, individuals ordinarily can only learn one or a few skills. This is recognized in the adage, "jack of all trades and master of none." Beyond the apprenticeship required for learning a skill, the experience gained in continuously performing it will serve to reinforce the skill. Weekend craftsmen can hardly expect to be as expert as those who perform a craft on a full-time basis; but weekend craftsmen will be more skilled than those with only intermittent and sporadic practice.

For these reasons, virtually all societies develop at least a rudimentary occupational specialization beyond the division of labor based on age and sex—even societies based on subsistence economies where the bulk of the population is engaged in agriculture or in hunting and gathering will ordinarily include some specialists, if only on a part-time basis. For example, in an isolated Mexican Mayan agricultural community where all adult males were corn farmers, there were three part-time specialized roles (Cancian, 1965): political officials, religious officials, and "curers" (traditional healers). Among the aboriginal Maori of New Zealand, a people who lived mostly by fishing,

> Specialization in industry, though not highly developed, indubitably existed. In every Maori community there were a number of people who, through inborn skill or special training, possessed greater ability than their fellows in certain types of work. A man of this kind became a specialist, in that while not necessarily devoting the whole of his time to the one craft he made it his major interest, and was peculiarly expert therein. Such people were valuable, and were called upon by others less skilled to perform work for them. The transmission of technical and magical knowledge in closely guarded fashion, as from father to son, also tended to favor the creation of specialized crafts.
>
> A point of interest is that specialization in primitive economy cannot occur so readily in the seasonal crafts. A man who is skilled in the snaring of birds, for instance, may devote himself largely to this work, but it cannot be practiced all the year round, so he must find other occupations to support himself for the remainder of the time. It is in the constant employment, for the product of which there is a continual and steady demand, that the most favorable opportunity offers for specialization. Hence it is natural to find that among the Maori the persons who really did devote the major portion of their time to one craft were makers of stone adzes, wood-carvers, house and canoe builders, and above all, perhaps, tattooers [Firth, 1929:206–207; see Udy, 1959, for additional examples from other societies].

Firth's observation about seasonal crafts permitting only limited specialization illustrates a more general point—the division of labor is limited by the ability of the social system to support specialized activity. This is, of course, the basis of Durkheim's famous theorem about the division of labor increasing with the dynamic density of a society (Durkheim, 1933:256–262). Obviously, small societies, or populations that are so loosely connected that the effective social system is the family or the hamlet, cannot support an extensive division of labor simply because there would not be enough work to occupy a specialist full-time, or enough of a surplus to provide for his sustenance. However, larger, more highly integrated societies can support an extensive division of labor. The same point is confirmed by recent work on organizational size and organizational complexity (Blau, 1973:258–270, and the studies cited therein). Large-scale organizations are able to support a much more highly developed division of labor than are small organizations.

To sum up, specialization of tasks is efficient, and for this reason a division of labor develops in all social systems large enough to support specialists. The crucial next question is whether or not, and to what extent, a *similar* set of occupational roles develops in all societies with substantial role differentiation, that is, in all complex societies.

There are two main reasons why roughly the same complement of occupational roles is found in all complex societies. First, all societies, of any level of complexity, face the same *functional imperatives*, the same needs that must be met if the society is to survive (Aberle *et al.*, 1950). Second, complexity carries its own *organizational imperatives;* some social roles require others and some depend upon others—for example, complex organization is not possible without specialized managerial and clerical roles.

If we accept as a minimal definition of complex societies the presence of an extensive division of labor in a territorially organized state the following functional roles necessarily emerge. First, food must be grown or gathered. In most societies, both historical and contemporary, the provision of food has occupied most of the population most of the time; complex societies have only been possible when a large enough surplus could be created by the food producers to sustain nonproducers. Second, tools, clothing, housing, and other goods must be manufactured. As we have seen, these functions often require substantial skill and hence come to be performed by specialists, although in the simplest societies each family manufactures its own goods. Third, whenever there is a division of labor that extends beyond single families or local hamlets, institutionalized mechanisms for the exchange of goods and services must exist, and this gives rise to commercial or trading specialists. Fourth, societies are also cultures, with shared norms and a shared system of beliefs, lore, and knowledge about the world. In all but the simplest societies, specialized roles develop concerned with systematizing, expanding, utilizing, and transmitting the cultural heritage. In simple societies these functions tend to be restricted to interpreting the relationship between the people and the gods, passing on the lore of the tribe to successive generations, and healing the sick, and these activities tend to be performed on a part-time rather than a full-time basis. In complex societies, such roles occupy individuals full-time, and others are added: scientists and scholars, engineers, lawyers, and so on—in short, what we now refer to as the professions. Finally, all societies beyond the simplest will develop political roles to coordinate the activities of their members and to keep order. However, order implies control over the use of force, and specialized roles will ordinarily develop to enforce the authority of the political leadership against the threat of both internal and external challenges. In many societies no distinction is made between the internal (policing) function and the external (military) function, but whether or not such a distinction exists, the leadership roles are usually performed by full-time specialists.

Thus, we have in all complex societies the following sorts of roles: agriculturalists (hunting and gathering, fishing, and herding societies cannot ordinarily generate enough of a surplus to sustain complex social organization); craftsmen; traders, intellectual and cultural specialists, including clergy; political leaders; and military specialists. But social organization of this degree of complexity generates its own pressure toward further specialization, creating two additional types of roles: managers and clerks.

Management is an inherent aspect of social organization. Wherever tasks that require the cooperation of more than one individual are to be performed, there is need for a coordinator who will see that the necessary specialists are assembled, will assign tasks, and will ensure that everything is done in the proper order. However, management is a special talent; some are clearly better at it than others. As Udy notes (1959:91), quoting from Ray's study of the Sanpoil (1933:77–82):

> Among the Sanpoil, anyone could theoretically organize a hunt, "but in each community certain men were reputed to be good hunting leaders and usually only these instigated trips. Others would have found it difficult to get followers." Preparations for the trip, starting time, and deployment of the forces were subject to the leader's direction. He selected men for each post, according to whether they were good shots or good runners.

Because management is a special talent, specialized managerial roles develop in all societies. As we shall see later, there is a natural tendency for those in positions of leadership to consolidate and institutionalize their authority, becoming firmly identified with the role. Still, in the simplest societies there is not enough demand to support full-time managerial specialists. In complex societies, however, the problems of coordination are sufficiently great that a class of full-time managers emerges. It is impossible to manage a complex territorial state without a well-developed bureaucracy, consisting of local administrators in addition to the central political authorities. Large-scale construction of palaces, temples, fortifications, and other edifices likewise requires extensive coordination of effort, as does mining, and manufacture not restricted to small local workshops. Large-scale bureaucracies also require extensive records—to ensure that taxes (in kind or in cash) are collected, that everyone does his required labor or military service, and so on. But efficient record keeping requires clerical specialists, and hence clerks are found in all complex societies.

Not only are the same broad categories of occupational roles found in all complex societies, but there are organizational imperatives that create strong tendencies for work to be similarly organized everywhere.

First, the greater efficiency of specialization tends to create a "horizontal" division of labor to the extent that the population base and social structure are sufficient to support it. Thus, in very small societies there may be house-building specialists, but in larger societies house builders will become specialized into carpenters, roofers, masons, plumbers, electricians, and so on. Among the Maori, a seagoing people, "the making of a large canoe required the services of a carpenter, flax-dresser, painter, caulker, carver, and sail-maker," but agricultural activities were not similarly specialized (Firth, 1929:207).

Second, the greater efficiency of specialization together with a tendency for those in power to try to improve their situation—indeed, for everyone to try, but for those in power to succeed—tends to create a "vertical" division of labor insofar as the social system can support it. There is a strong tendency in complex societies to separate skilled from unskilled aspects of a given functional task into different roles. For example, hod carriers become distinguished from masons, carpenters' helpers from carpenters, registered nurses from practical nurses, and practical nurses from nursing aides. This is clearly efficient from the standpoint of the employer who must pay a higher price for the labor of the skilled specialist than for that of the semiskilled or unskilled assistant, and hence would prefer that the highly skilled specialist not perform tasks that could be performed more cheaply by others. It is also desirable from the standpoint of the skilled specialist, who is thereby freed from what is ordinarily less interesting and less pleasant work. The fact that it is less desirable from the standpoint of those who end up doing the unskilled work is of little consequence.

So far I have argued that there is a basically similar division of labor in all complex societies, as a consequence of both the functional imperatives that all societies face and the organizational imperatives common to all complex social systems; but it must be noted that this similarity holds unequivocally only with respect to general categories of work and not with respect to specific occupations. It is obvious that the specific occupations included in the labor force and the exact tasks performed in these occupations vary enormously from place to place and have changed radically over time, particularly as a consequence of technological advances in the twentieth century. For example, the wide variety of jobs dependent upon the use of electrical power simply did not exist before 1900. How, then, is it possible to talk about a uniform division of labor in all complex societies, past and present?

The answer comes in two parts. First, for any given level of technology there is a limited number of ways of accomplishing particular functions. That is, the technology itself, together with the sorts of organizational constraints discussed above, determines the number and the content of the occupational roles involved in the performance of any given function. In building an American-style house, for example, a variety of things need to be done: preparing a foundation, putting up a frame, putting on the roof, finishing the exterior and interior walls, laying the floor, putting in the plumbing and wiring. At the most rudimentary level, one or a few men may do everything. More commonly, as we have seen, the tasks are divided among specialists. At a minimum there would be a mason, an electrician, a plumber, and a carpenter. If need be, the mason might also be the cement setter, and might even build the necessary wooden forms for his work, but one would never expect a single specialist to do both the masonry and the plumbing—the skills are too different. Similarly, the carpenter might do the roofing and lay the floorboards, but he would not do the masonry. The point is that there are only so many ways to build a house, given a particular technology, and a characteristic division of labor emerges from the nature of that technology. The same is true of farming, of fishing, of canoe building, of craft manufacture, even of science and commerce. For example, let us consider commerce. First, there is a distinction between small-scale trading and vending and large-scale wholesale trade with respect both to the activities entailed and the resources required. This produces several classes of traders, ranging from peddlers to merchant princes. Second, there is a distinction in the organization of activity depending upon the product being traded. Not only is a specialized knowledge of a particular type of goods required, but the organization of the activity varies depending upon the nature of the product. Real estate agents face one set of problems and constraints and cattle buyers quite another, but the tasks of a cattle buyer in, say, Mexico are not likely to be much different from those of a cattle buyer in Denmark. And the same is true of real estate agents in the two countries. Of course, different societies do have different needs. Fishing is not a big industry in Tibet, for example. The claim, however, is not that every occupation exists in every place, but simply that work is organized in a similar way everywhere it is performed at all.

But what about technological differences? How can we reconcile the claim of basic similarity in occupational structure with the obvious changes in technology that have been occurring continuously over time and at an accelerated pace in recent years? The answer is that the main effect of technological changes is not to introduce new functions but rather new procedures for accomplishing old functions. For example, when truck drivers replace wagon drivers, they are still performing the function of transporting goods. Although articled clerks have been replaced by junior managers, candlemakers by electrical assemblers, and copyists by typists, the division of labor, seen in a broad sense, has remained remarkably uniform.

Furthermore, when new occupational roles develop in response to technological changes, they tend to be incorporated into the occupational prestige hierarchy at a level similar to that of existing occupations entailing a comparable degree of skill, authority, or responsibility. For example, electricians, nonexistent before the turn of the century, entered the occupational prestige hierarchy in the position they retain today, alongside other highly skilled workers (Counts, 1925; Hodge, Siegel, and Rossi, 1964). Similarly, nuclear physicists almost from the first took their place among other scientists (as soon as the public realized in even a vague way what a nuclear physicist did; see Hodge and Hodge, 1964); computer programmers and television cameramen among other technicians; telephone solicitors among routine clerical and sales workers; trailer truck drivers among semiskilled workers; and elevator operators among unskilled service workers (Siegel, 1971:Table 2).

All this is, of course, not to say that there have been no changes in the organization of work and no transformations in the type of skill required to accomplish particular functions. Indeed, there have been, with an attendant transformation of the status of the occupations involved. The shift from a craft to a factory mode of production has resulted in a bifurcation of the production force, a transformation from a system of master craftsmen, journeymen, and apprentices engaged in the production of particular products from beginning to end—which by its organization held out the promise to individual workers of eventually gaining superior status as master craftsmen—to a two-class system of highly skilled machine setters and fixers, on the one hand, and semiskilled machine tenders on the other hand. But this does not vitiate the main point—which is that the relative status position in the division of labor of highly skilled craftsmen, be they shoemakers or silversmiths or machine setters and fixers in shoe or jewelry factories, remains unchanged; and similarly, that the status of semiskilled workers, be they factory operatives or workers in handicraft shops, or for that matter teamsters or truck drivers, remains essentially constant over time.

Moreover, despite enormous technological changes, especially in this century, the organization of many functions remains relatively similar to what it was in preindustrial civilizations. A comparison of the ancient Egyptian bureaucracy (Erman, 1894:328–329) with the bureaucracy, both public and private, of mid-century America is instructive. In both cases a similar range of positions exists, from the highest ranking policymaking officials down to the most minor functionaries; and in both cases a similar range of supporting clerical roles also exists, ranging from "scribes" with considerable responsibility and independent authority, equivalent to confidential clerks or executive secretaries, down to mere copyists, equivalent to routine typists and file clerks. In the organization of work, as in architecture, form follows function.

Occupational Specialization and Differential Command of Resources. Specialization of functions into distinct occupational roles inherently gives rise to differential control over scarce and valued resources. These differences are inherent because they arise from the very nature of occupational roles, and for this reason they tend to be relatively constant in all societies where the roles are found at all. High priests tend to be powerful in all societies and peasants not to be powerful in any society. But the claim of a relatively invariant power hierarchy is not limited to the extremes; all occupations, by their very nature, entail greater or lesser control over valued resources, and hence greater or lesser power.

There are three types of resources which in combination create differences in power, defined as the ability to achieve whatever ends are desired (Weber, 1947:152). These are (1) knowledge and skill relevant to the performance of socially valued tasks; (2) control over economic resources; and (3) authority, or legitimate control over the activities of others. These all function in somewhat different ways, and hence need to be considered one by one.

Take knowledge and skill first. As we have seen above, occupations differ with respect to the amount of knowledge, training, or talent required for their performance. Some jobs can be done by almost anyone, with little or no preparation or training time. Others require special training or special talent. These differences are not accidental, but arise from the definition of occupational roles. One cannot be a lawyer without knowing the law, which in any complex society is complex and requires extensive training. One cannot be a clerk without being literate; an illiterate clerk is a definitional absurdity. Distinctions in the skill required to do various jobs are embedded in the language used to describe them, as in the distinction between "skilled," "semiskilled," and "unskilled" manual workers, between "certified" and "uncertified" professionals, and so on. Because differences in skill inhere in the definition of occupations, they tend to be relatively constant from place to place. Jewelers are everywhere regarded as skilled craftsmen, and porters are regarded as unskilled in all societies. But the stability of occupational differences in skill requirements is much more general than this, as will be confirmed in Chapter 5.

As Bacon noted, *"Nam et ipsa scientia potestas est."* Knowledge itself is power. In what sense is this so? How do occupational differences in knowledge and skill requirements create differences in power? First, since specialized knowledge is a scarce resource, holders of such knowledge have an advantageous market position. They are able, in one way or another, to insist upon a higher than ordinary price for their labor. This point will be pursued in greater detail in the next section. Second, and of more direct interest at the moment, knowledge enhances mastery over the world, both physical and social. The greater one's store of knowledge, the greater one's ability to manipulate the world to one's own advantage.[1] In this respect, general knowledge is far more valuable than specialized knowledge, because general knowledge creates the ability to cope with new and unexpected situations. For this reason, elite education is always general education; and professional and executive positions, which entail extensive high-order decision making, tend to require a broad general education, only sometimes supplemented by specific vocational training.

But specific skills, as well as general education, can also be utilized to advantage. Cancian (1965:20) notes that among the Mayan corn farmers he studied

> Within the community, according to informants, there has been a series of political leaders. Most reports indicate that there were usually two or three men who held great political power in the community. These were usually men who could speak Spanish and manipulate the Ladino world as well as maintain the respect of Zinacantecos.

Here the fact of being able to communicate with the authorities of the "outside world," the Ladinos, itself created political power, the power that derives from control of information. In this case, specialized knowledge (of Spanish) enabled certain men to assume political leadership roles. Often the position itself creates a monopoly on knowledge, and with it the power of decision making based on that knowledge, as when, for example, a priest is charged with reading the omens and deciding when they are auspicious for the beginning of the planting season or the start of the harvest.[2] The power of decision making based on expert knowledge should not be underrated, for it permeates contemporary life.

Just as occupations can be differentiated with respect to the knowledge or skill required to perform them, so too can they be differentiated with respect to the economic power their incumbents wield. Obviously, owner-

[1] For this reason, in feudal societies access to education was often restricted to the upper classes. For example, among the ancient Incas the "greatness [of the nobility] arose not merely from place and from political power, but also from superior education. When the Inca Roca founded the *Yacha-huasi* or College at Cuzco, he enunciated a great social principle, namely, "that the children of the common people should not learn the sciences, which should be known only by the nobles, lest the lower classes should become proud and endanger the commonwealth' [Means, 1936:305]."

Consistent with this, Weber (1958:351–352) notes that the principal basis of priestly power in feudal societies was the monopolization of education by the priesthood. Where this monopolization was broken, as in ancient China and classical Greece, priestly religion was eliminated as an important institution.

[2] Chinua Achebe, in *Arrow of God* (1969), provides a vivid account of what happens in an Ibo village when a chief attempts to defy the gods by delaying the planting season. Even priestly power has its limits.

ship of land or capital carries with it enormous power, at least if the holdings are large enough; the greater the size of the holdings, the greater the power. But even small holders are powerful relative to the landless, because they are relatively free from the domination of others. In feudal societies control over land and its produce is the principal basis of the power of the aristocracy. In capitalist' societies the large landowner or capitalist can manipulate the system to his own advantage, buying and selling goods and services only when terms are particularly advantageous, underselling competition to gain monopolistic control and then fixing prices, buying labor in the same self-advantageous way, and even buying, through gifts, bribes, or pressure, advantageous legislation to promote his own interests. Managers, like owners, have similar powers; indeed, it was Berle and Means' (1933) insight that in the modern world, management of the means of production has much the same consequences as ownership. Even low-level managerial decisions are concerned with the allocation of scarce resources to one sort of activity rather than another, and many occupations that are not formally classed as managerial positions also involve allocation decisions of various sorts. Purchasing agents, for example, are in a position to wield economic influence by deciding from which firm to make purchases. Even professors, by their choice of assigned textbooks and their control of research grants, wield some measure of economic power, albeit not a great deal.

Just as occupational roles differ in their control over economic resources, they tend to differ in their intrinsic authority, if authority is defined as the ability to legitimately control the behavior of other individuals. In part this derives from differences in expertise and economic power, but only in part. Political officials, for example, have important, albeit usually indirect, authority (and in some times and places have had very direct authority). Employers exercise control over the behavior of their employees, as do supervisors over their subordinates. In contrast to control over capital or material resources, which tends to be concentrated in relatively high-status positions, authority in varying degrees is relatively well spread throughout the occupational system: For example, laborers' foremen exercise some authority, because they control the activities of a gang of laborers. Similarly, truck drivers have authority over truck drivers' helpers, bricklayers over hod carriers, and so on. And of course policemen exercise substantial authority over the general population in the course of carrying out their duties. Just as with skill and economic power, the greater the authority, the greater the ability of incumbents of a position to accomplish their goals; and, just as with the other two forms of power, authority differentials are inherent in the definitions of occupations.

To sum up, I have argued that the division of labor gives rise to differences among occupations with respect to knowledge and skill, economic control, and authority. Because these differences derive from the definition of occupational roles—the nature of the functions to be fulfilled and the tasks required to fulfill them—they will be relatively invariant across societies. We can expect that in all societies intellectual or "professional" roles will require the greatest skill and knowledge and achieve the greatest monopoly of crucial expertise, that owners and managers of land or capital will exercise the greatest economic power, and that political officials, together with managers of other enterprises, will exercise the greatest direct authority over the actions of others. In consequence, in all societies these positions enjoy the greatest privilege, as we shall see in the following section.

Power and Privilege.   There are two major processes by which occupational differences in skill, authority, and economic control give rise to corresponding differences in privilege. First, these aspects of power affect the position of occupations in the labor market, driving up the price for some kinds of work relative to others. Second, differential control over scarce resources permits favored groups to maximize their own advantage, either by directly allocating to themselves an unequal share of the surplus (Lenski, 1966:44–46) or by manipulating the system to promote their special interests.

Consider market position first. Occupations that require unusual skill or talent ordinarily command superior income, simply because such skill and talent is in scarce supply relative to demand, and competition drives up its price. In addition, there tends to be great competition to secure competent personnel in those occupations requiring the exercise of great authority or involving control over substantial material resources. The more powerful an occupation, the more important that it be performed well, since the consequences of competent or incompetent performances are more telling in such occupations. For example, if a chain store manager makes a poor business decision it may cost a firm a few hundred or at the most a few thousand dollars; but a poor decision on the part of a major executive can run into millions. In the same way, the performance of lawyers is ordinarily far more consequential than the performance of law clerks. Thus law firms will compete more strenuously for lawyers than for law clerks, and will pay well enough to attract a competent staff of lawyers. The general demand for competence in fields where the consequences of performance are great drives up the average level of reward, and this in turn serves to attract individuals who might otherwise choose to do other work. The result of this process is to create a close connection between occupational power and privilege in all societies.

Of course, other factors do enter into the determination of rewards, so the relationship between power and privilege is not perfect. Some functions are in greater demand than others, depending upon the needs of society at any particular time; and some functions are in greater demand in some societies than in others, depending upon both structural and cultural factors. For example, hunting skills will be of less importance, and hence will tend to be less well rewarded, in agricultural societies than in hunting and gathering societies. And in commercial economies, law is of particularly great importance and hence lawyers are likely to be especially highly rewarded. During wartime the military competence of generals is crucial, so good military strategists are more likely to be quickly promoted than in peacetime.

Often the willingness to pay a high price to secure particular services will depend upon the profit these services are expected to yield, as when the owner of a basketball team pays an exorbitant bonus for a star player in expectation that his presence will draw sufficiently large crowds to more than offset the bonus price. But the willingness to pay well may also involve public policy decisions to subsidize particular activities because of their "importance" to the system, as when the Soviet Union subsidizes champion chess players without regard to their purely economic value but rather to enhance Soviet prestige. To be sure, these examples may seem to be somewhat esoteric and to apply to only a small fraction of all occupations, but other examples can be found as well. Coal miners are much more highly paid relative to other occupations in Eastern Europe than in Western Europe or the United States (see footnote 4, Chapter 7), which apparently reflects a policy decision about their relative importance in these countries. Similarly, forestry workers are more highly paid relative to other positions in Sweden than they are in the United States (computed from data reported in Table 5.2), which presumably reflects the greater economic importance of logging activity in Sweden than here. In sum, because of differential demand arising from cultural values and structural conditions, we must expect some intersocietal variation in the rewards enjoyed by different occupational groups. But these differences will be relatively minor compared to those differences in occupational requisites and perquisites which are inherent in the definition of jobs and are therefore stable across time and space.[3]

The second major source of differences in the material rewards accruing

---

[3] The reader will note the similarity in the above argument about demand to that of Davis and Moore (1945) on the functional importance of occupations as a criterion of differential rewards. However, while there are affinities between the two notions, I want to stress that demand is ultimately an economic commodity and refers to the willingness of a social system (via its personnel who make wage decisions) to pay a higher or lower price for a particular sort of labor. While that willingness may sometimes reflect the "importance" of the function for society, it need not. For example, in capitalist societies it may reflect purely individual interests in profit maximization.

to occupational groups is that differential control over resources puts favored groups in a superior position to maximize their own advantage. They may do this in a number of ways. The principal mechanism is manipulation of the political system to secure special rights or privileges. In feudal societies, for example, differential privileges for various occupational groups are customarily embedded in law; these typically include monopoly rights over the practice of particular crafts and the sale of particular goods, differential tax bases, and even the right to claim a share of the labor and product of others. In feudal estates, the serfs typically owed the lord so many days of labor per year as well as a portion of the product of their labor; at the extreme, the special privilege of the lord included the notorious "right of the first night" with the bride of a serf. In modern society, men are held to be equal under the law and distinctions tend not to be made on ascriptive grounds. But the special privileges of occupational groups continue to exist, principally in the form of tax breaks that benefit some more than others and in the form of restrictions on competition by tariff and licensing arrangements. Obviously, the more powerful an occupational group, the greater the likelihood that it will be able to ensure that advantages are institutionalized in the law. For example, the strict licensing requirements for physicians adopted by most states may be seen as a device for restricting competition from foreign doctors as much as a procedure to ensure the maintenance of medical standards.

Second, in capitalist societies at least, control over capital ordinarily creates opportunities to accumulate personal wealth; it takes money to make money. As we have seen above, large capitalists are in a superior position to manipulate the economic system to their own advantage. But even middle-level managers often have access to wealth-enhancing information and opportunities from which ordinary workers are entirely excluded.[4]

---

[4] Even apart from "inside dope," which creates superior investment opportunities, executive personnel often have advantageous consumption possibilities that serve to increase their effective income—expense accounts, subsidized travel, discount purchasing privileges, and the like. This is as true in socialist as in capitalist systems. Geiger (1968:157) notes:

> As any reader of the Soviet press is aware, the privileges, and temptations, of upper class social position in the USSR are often buttressed by high political office. There are frequent complaints about government and party officials who use their influence to make special purchases, get their sons and daughters admitted to universities, and otherwise obtain exceptions to rules and favorable personal treatment. Not rarely, we may suppose, a good part of the pressure upon them comes from their families. The case of Sergei, a high official in the party and district executive committee is a good example. In the course of a short period, his wife or his mother made the following specific requests of him: (1) speak to the director of the agricultural experimental station about buying some currants that

Furthermore, executives are often in a position to negotiate the level and form of their own compensation, something lower-level personnel are almost never able to do. Of course, ordinary workers may seek to overcome their individual powerlessness by collective bargaining. Indeed, collective bargaining developed explicitly in recognition of the fact that the power of the individual worker was low relative to that of management, by virtue of management's command of capital and authority. But, even so, the relative power of occupational groups in collective bargaining situations differs depending upon their political influence, their economic power (the ability to sustain a lengthy strike), and their monopoly of essential skills. Doctors' and policemen's strikes are much more likely to be successful than garbagemen's or farm workers' strikes, simply because the former cannot be replaced by substitute labor while the latter can.

In short, occupational groups are able to convert their command of scarce resources—skill and knowledge, economic power, and authority—into material advantage both by virtue of the superior market position command of these resources provides and by virtue of the ability to directly manipulate the system that such power creates. For this reason, there is a general consistency in the skill, economic control, authority, and material reward hierarchies of occupations in all societies, and a similarity in these hierarchies across societies. As we shall see in the next section, this consistency extends to the prestige hierarchy as well.

Power, Privilege, and Prestige.   Before considering the nature of the connection between power, privilege, and prestige, we must first consider what is meant by prestige. As numerous writers have recognized (Veblen, 1919:22–34; Parsons, 1954:386–392; and Shils, 1968:104–105, come to mind), man is an evaluative animal, holding some objects, ideas, and attributes to be more worthy than others; the propensity for invidious distinctions is a fundamental aspect of human nature. By *invidious* I mean exactly what Veblen (1919:34) meant,

> as describing a comparison of persons with a view to rating and grading them in respect of relative worth or value—in an aesthetic or moral sense—and so awarding and defining the relative degrees of complacency with which they may legitimately be contemplated by themselves and by others. An invidious comparison is a process of valuation of persons in respect of worth.

---

were bigger, firmer, available in thick clusters, and cheaper than those bought through the usual channels; (2) telephone the manager of a store about the purchase of a wool blouse for his wife, to avoid the "frightful queue," (3) telephone the director of the theater for the favor of seats without previous purchase of tickets; (4) arrange an exception to the hospital rule so his wife could stay there with their sick daughter.

Of course, invidious comparisons need not be limited to persons but may be made with respect to any sort of attribute or object.[5] The important point is that the evaluation is a *moral* one, carrying a connotation of the relative *worthiness* of the attribute being judged, and is not simply a matter of taste or preference. As such, invidious comparisons reflect shared norms and values regarding the relative position of attributes in hierarchies of value. The currency of moral worth is *prestige,* known synonymously as honor, regard, respect, standing, and esteem.

But what is the basis of prestige? There is apparently a limited number of attributes that confer prestige in human societies. Shils (1968:106) defines these attributes as "deference-entitlements" and notes:

> Deference-entitlements include: occupational role and accomplishment, wealth (including types of wealth), income and the mode of its acquisition, style of life, level of educational attainment, political or corporate power, proximity to persons or roles exercising political or corporate power, kinship connections, ethnicity, performance on behalf of the community or society in relation to external communities or societies, and the possession of "objective acknowledgements" of deference such as titles or ranks.
>
> It is on the basis of the perception of these entitlements that individuals and classes or more or less anonymous individuals who are believed to possess some constellation of these entitlements are granted deference; it is on the basis of the possession of these properties that they grant deference to themselves and claim it from others. It is on the basis of simultaneous assessments of their own and others' deference-entitlements that they regulate their conduct toward others and anticipate the deferential (or derogatory) responses of others.

This list is instructive in that it includes occupational role as a separate attribute, "one of the most significant entitlements to deference [1968: 107]." Occupational roles are considered to be deference-entitlements for two reasons, according to Shils (1968:107–108).
First,

> The most esteemed occupations . . . are those which are in their internal structure and in their functions closest to the *centres.* The centres of society are those positions which exercise earthly power and which mediate man's relationship to the order of existence—spiritual forces, cosmic powers, values and norms—which legitimates or witholds legitimacy from the earthly powers or which dominates earthly existence. The highest "authorities" in society—governors, judges, prime ministers and presidents and fundamental scientists—are those whose roles enable them to control society or to penetrate into the ultimate laws and forces which are thought to control the world and human life. Occupational roles are ranked in a

---

[5] Kleining (1973) has shown that people are quite capable of rating the "prestige" (*sozialer status*) of foods, plants, animals, and the like, and, moreover, display considerable consensus regarding the relative prestige of the members of each of these classes.

sequence which appears approximately to correspond with the extent to which each role possesses these properties.

But Shils goes on to acknowledge a second basis for differential occupational prestige (1968:108):

> Of course, occupational roles and their incumbents are also deferred to on account of certain highly correlated deference-entitling properties such as the income which the practice of the occupation provides, the educational level of its practitioners, the ethnic qualities of its incumbents, etc. . . . Nonetheless, occupational role is an independent entitlement to deference.

Actually, the deference-entitlements are probably the *primary* bases of occupational differentiation, and the charismatic qualities a *secondary* basis, if only because relatively few occupational roles entail much charisma. The charismatic basis is useful in explaining deviations from the prestige expected on the basis of the power and privilege associated with the occupation, although those occupational roles that entail great charisma also tend to involve great power and privilege.

But why should power and privilege be deference-entitlements, that is, why should they confer prestige? The answer is simple—power and privilege are universally valued in all societies. There is no society where power is not accorded respect.[6] Even in utopian societies that deny the ordinary bases of stratification there is an inexorable tendency for the leadership to be deferred to (Rosenfeld, 1951). Evidence from observations of children's games and experiments on the process of structuring newly formed groups show the same pattern (Kimberly, 1970; Leik *et al.*, 1975). This is because, as Shils notes (1968:110–111), "the exercise of power . . . is determinative of the life chances of the persons over whom it is exercised; therewith it shares in the charisma which is inherent in the control of life." Privilege is also valued in all societies, and its acquisition provides evidence of "prepotence and success [Veblen, 1919:4]." Moreover, wealth is usually a necessity for participating in the style of life that manifests central cultural values. Finally, education is inherently valued, not only as an aspect of power but because education implies acceptance and command of the central values of the society: "The educated person is one who has received the culture of beliefs and appreciations which are central in the society [Shils, 1968:110]."

If, then, occupational hierarchies of power and privilege are relatively invariant in all societies, then occupational prestige hierarchies will also be relatively invariant. Of course, prestige hierarchies will not be perfectly

---

[6] Interestingly, Weber (1958:78) notes that a major motivation for acquiring power is to enjoy the prestige it confers.

invariant, just as power and privilege hierarchies are not. First, insofar as the power and privilege associated with particular occupations vary across societies, so will their prestige. We will take up these "exceptions that prove the rule" in Chapter 7. Second, as we noted just above, other features of occupations in addition to power and privilege also confer prestige, and these are not necessarily invariant across societies. Still, the theory proposed here would lead us to expect substantial similarity among all complex societies in the hierarchical ordering of occupations with respect to their power, privilege, and hence prestige.[7]

ALTERNATIVE POSSIBILITIES

Before accepting the theory of occupational prestige determination just proposed, we must of course verify it empirically. This requires, first, that we show that observed data on occupational prestige hierarchies are consistent with the theory and, second, that we are able to reject alternative explanations for the observed patterns. Three main alternatives to the structural theory must be considered.

First, the prestige ordering of occupations may reflect idiosyncratic cultural values and hence may vary substantially from society to society; this is the cultural hypothesis suggested by Inkeles and Rossi (1956). While the evidence available to date (Hodge, Treiman, and Rossi, 1966) indicates a high degree of agreement between the occupational prestige hierarchy of the United States and those of a number of foreign countries, it is possible that data from a larger and more representative sample of world cultures would exhibit substantially more variation. Moreover, there has been some suggestion that residues of traditional stratification systems may influence contemporary occupational evaluations in the more traditional sectors of modern societies (Lewis and Haller, 1964). Hence, our first order of business must be to establish that there are not, in fact, substantial subcultural or cross-cultural variations in occupational prestige hierarchies.

Second, even if we establish that the occupational prestige hierarchies of

---

[7] It is important to distinguish occupational roles from their institutional settings. The prestige of individuals may arise from either or both, but the two are not the same. We may know that the church has greater prestige than the military, but this does not mean that a parish priest will outrank a general. Similarly, the fact that the formal class structure of ancient China distinguished four estates—gentry, farmers, craftsmen, and merchants—does not mean that an agricultural laborer enjoyed greater prestige than a wholesale trader. In this book, we are concerned solely with accounting for the relative prestige of *occupational* roles without regard to other bases of social differentiation.

all contemporary societies are fundamentally similar it is possible that this simply reflects the diffusion of a Western pattern of occupational evaluation alongside the diffusion of other aspects of Western culture. After all, there is hardly a country that has not been profoundly affected by the political and economic hegemony of the North Atlantic nations. Perhaps Euro-American perceptions of occupations were acquired along with Euro-American dress, language, and values. If this were so, it would be manifest in a pattern of worldwide similarity in occupational prestige evaluations without a corresponding similarity in hierarchies of occupational power and privilege. Some support for this possibility is to be found in the observation that even nonindustrialized countries in the contemporary world appear to evaluate occupations in the same way as highly industrialized Western nations such as the United States (Hodge, Treiman, and Rossi, 1966:320).

Third, there is an alternative diffusionist explanation. Perhaps what diffused throughout the world was not just a Western value system but a Western system for organizing production, that is, a Western division of labor and organization of work roles (Inkeles and Rossi, 1956). Indeed, we know that this is true. Virtually every nation in the world is industrializing as rapidly as it can muster the resources to do so, following the model first developed in Western Europe and the United States in the nineteenth century. The constraints in social organization created by the industrial system have led some scholars to argue that all industrial societies are basically alike (Kerr *et al.,* 1960; Inkeles, 1960; but see the critical response in Halmos, 1964). Whether or not this is so, a Western pattern of industrial organization surely would create a characteristic set of occupational roles and therefore—if we accept the argument outlined above—a characteristic hierarchy of occupations in terms of power. But differences among occupations with respect to power should, again by the above arguments, lead to concomitant differences in privilege, and hence in prestige. So the observed result would be substantial similarity in occupational hierarchies of power, privilege, and prestige in all contemporary societies, albeit greater similarity among the most industrialized societies. The contrast between this possibility, which we might label a *structural diffusion* hypothesis, and the preceding one, which we might label a *cultural diffusion* hypothesis, is in the prediction of similarity in the power and privilege hierarchies as well as the prestige hierarchy; and, further, dependence of prestige similarity upon similarity with respect to power and privilege.

Of course, the fourth possibility is the one we entertained at great length, which argues that all complex societies, and not merely industrial societies, are similar with respect to the relative power, privilege, and prestige accorded occupations. If this is true, then past societies should exhibit the same pattern as contemporary societies; hence comparison of past and present societies provides a basis for deciding between the third and fourth hypotheses.

These hypotheses are framed in such a way as to permit at least a partial evaluation on the basis of currently available data, and such an evaluation appears in Chapters 4 through 7. First, however, it is necessary to establish the adequacy of the data, and this is the concern of Chapters 2 and 3, to which we now turn.

II

SETTING THE STAGE: DATA, METHODS, AND BASIC RESULTS

2

Problems of Method in Comparing Occupational Prestige Systems

In the period since World War II there have been some 85 studies of occupational prestige conducted in nearly 60 countries throughout the world, ranging from highly industrialized societies such as the United States to traditional societies such as peasant India and Thailand, northern Nigeria, and New Guinea. While these studies vary somewhat in their specific details, they all utilize the same basic procedure: A sample of the population is asked to rate or rank a set of occupational titles with respect to their prestige or social standing. These ratings are then aggregated into mean scores (or other measures of central tendency) and the scores are treated as indicators of the relative prestige of the evaluated occupations. The amount of intersocietal agreement in prestige evaluations can be assessed by matching occupational titles across countries, for example, "physician" in the United States with "doctor" in Australia, "*médicin*" in Mauritania, "*medico*" in Argentina, "*laege*" in Denmark, "*lekarz internista*" in Poland, and so on, and then computing product moment correlations between the scores associated with matching titles in each pair of countries.

Taken together, these studies potentially constitute a rich body of data with which to address the issues raised in the previous chapter—provided it can be established that the data yield valid measurements of the true prestige of occupations in each of the populations to which they pertain. The question of validity turns on two issues: First, do occupational prestige studies actually measure what we mean conceptually by prestige? Second, if we accept the first premise, are the data at hand of adequate quality to provide accurate estimates of the average prestige accorded occupations in each society? This and the following chapter will deal with these issues. In the present chapter I first address the conceptual issue and then, having disposed of it, turn to a description of the data available for analysis and an evaluation of their quality and of possible biases that could affect the validity of the analysis. I conclude the chapter with a discussion of coding procedures and other technical matters. In the following chapter I address an issue which has both substantive and methodological implications—the extent of *intra*societal variation in occupational prestige evaluations. By showing that consensus within each society regarding the prestige hierarchy is on the whole very high, I legitimate the use of ratings by nonrepresentative samples of raters for the purpose of *inter*societal comparisons.

DO "OCCUPATIONAL PRESTIGE" STUDIES ACTUALLY MEASURE PRESTIGE?

In accordance with the theory of occupational prestige proposed in the previous chapter, prestige must be understood as a deference-entitlement in Shils' (1968) sense. Perhaps the best statement of this interpretation of prestige, and its implications, is provided by Goldthorpe and Hope (1974:5). They note that

> if "prestige" is to be understood in any way approximating to its established sense within the sociological tradition, then it must refer to the position of an individual or group within a structure of relationships of deference, acceptance and derogation, which represents a distinctive, "symbolic" aspect of social stratification. Relative advantage and power in terms of prestige stem from the ability of an actor to exploit and benefit from *meanings* and *values*—rather than, say, economic resources, authority or physical force. From this standpoint, therefore, occupational prestige must derive from certain symbolic significance, relevant to ideas of social superiority or inferiority, which the incumbency of an occupational role or membership of an occupational collectivity conveys. *And so a measure of occupational prestige is to be regarded as valid to the extent that one may correctly infer from it the relative chance that a member of an occupational category has of experiencing deference, acceptance or derogation in his relations with members of other categories* [Italics in last sentence added].

Although Goldthorpe and Hope (1972, 1974) argue strongly that prestige in this sense is not measured by occupational prestige studies, their argument is not persuasive. Moreover, evidence they do not cite confirms that occupational prestige studies do, indeed, measure the deference accorded occupational categories.

First, let us deal with their objections. They rest their argument on two main points: First, when respondents who have performed a prestige-rating task have been asked what criteria they mainly had in mind when assessing the occupations presented to them, only a few have indicated "social prestige" or some synonymous term; more commonly, respondents named skill requirements, income returns, and the like. While Goldthorpe and Hope regard this sort of result as indicating that people evaluate occupations in terms of their "desirability" rather than their "prestige" in the strict sense, I would suggest that this evidence must be discounted as a linguistic artifact. Most respondents no doubt failed to name "prestige" because they thought it synonymous with the criterion of evaluation, "social standing";[1] indeed, it is surprising that *any* respondents named prestige. The second point that Goldthorpe and Hope make is that since prestige ratings are not socially structured—that is, since there are no appreciable subgroup variations in occupational evaluations (a point that will be documented exhaustively in the following chapter)—such ratings must actually involve the desirability of occupations rather than their prestige. Inexplicably, Goldthorpe and Hope believe that the things people regard as desirable about jobs will be invariant from place to place and group to group while the degree to which occupations command deference will strongly reflect differences in values. This view is particularly odd since they themselves cite evidence (e.g., Hyman, 1953) showing that perceptions of what makes occupations desirable—that is, what people value in occupations—are themselves structured by social position. In short, desirability assessments are socially structured while prestige evaluations are not.

In light of the weakness of these two points, Goldthorpe and Hope's objections cannot be regarded as persuasive.

Moreover, there is persuasive evidence that "deference" *is* highly correlated with prestige. First, let us define deference, again following Goldthorpe and Hope (1972:23–24):

> As a provisional statement, a prestige hierarchy might be one in which actors
> (i) *defer to* their superiors—that is, acknowledge by speech or other action their own social inferiority—and seek, or at least appreciate, association with superiors;
> (ii) *accept* their equals as partners, associates etc. in intimate social interaction—entertainment, friendship, courtship, marriage, etc.;
> (iii) *derogate* their inferiors, if only by accepting their deference and avoiding association with them other than where their own superiority is confirmed.

---

[1] For example, in the 1947 NORC study (Reiss et al. 1961:19), respondents were asked to evaluate occupations in terms of "*your own personal opinion* of the *general standing* that such a job has." After completing their rating task they were then asked: "When you say that certain jobs have excellent standing, what do you think is the *one main* thing about such jobs that gives them this standing? [p. 31]" Of the responses, 14% were coded as referring to "social prestige," compared to 18% coded as "pays well," 14% coded as "education, hard work, money," and 16% coded as "service to humanity, essential," the other leading responses. One might well conclude that the question simply was not very successful at eliciting criteria of evaluation, even leaving aside the ambiguity always associated with the coding of open-ended material.

How, then, are occupational prestige differences manifested?

First, people clearly seek association with their occupational superiors and avoid association with their inferiors. A study by Laumann (1965:31) shows that when individuals are asked to indicate whether they would desire association of varying degrees of intimacy with incumbents of 17 occupations, they strongly prefer association with incumbents of high-prestige occupations. Laumann used Duncan's (1961) index as a surrogate for a prestige index and obtained a correlation of .89 between mean social distance scores and Duncan scores; when I computed the correlation substituting pure prestige (Standard Scale) scores (see Chapter 8), the correlation increased to .95. Moreover, the strong association holds for each of five occupational groups with only a slight diminution for the lowest-status groups. A similar pattern holds for Germany (Laumann and Senter, 1976).

Second, occupational prestige appears to be a major determinant of the social standing of individuals, which bolsters the idea that prestige ratings represent moral evaluations and not simple cognitive judgments about the desirable features of occupations. Duncan and Artis (1951:26) showed that in a small town in the United States the prestige of families as judged by local residents was strongly predicted by the prestige of the heads' occupations as rated in the 1947 National Opinion Research Center (NORC) study. Warner (1960:131–138, 168) obtained a similar result, although his occupation scale is only nominally a prestige scale. However, it obviously is not legitimate to generalize from small towns where everyone knows everyone else to the society at large. Thus it is particularly useful to have national data that show the same pattern. In a 1965 NORC study (see Klatsky, 1970, for a description of the data set), respondents were asked to rate the "social standing" of a set of 16 relevant others ("father," "spouse's oldest brother," etc.); approximately 15,000 ratings were obtained. Siegel (1967) divided these according to the occupation of the person being rated and computed the mean social standing rating for each occupational category containing at least 25 cases; 113 occupations out of 296 could be scored in this way. The correlation between these scores and prestige scores derived in the usual way (Siegel, 1971:Table 5) is approximately .7. This is strikingly high (keeping in mind that an individual-level correlation would not be nearly as high as the aggregate one under discussion) and shows that occupational prestige strongly influences the social standing of concrete individuals.

Third, the prestige of occupations appears to be one of the major dimensions underlying the differential association of members of occupational groups, an important criterion of prestige *stricto sensu* mentioned by Goldthorpe and Hope (1974:10). Studying the friendship choices of members of 16 occupational groups by means of smallest space analysis, Laumann (1973:79–80) found that a two-dimensional solution fit the data quite well.

One of the dimensions, which Laumann labeled "educational status," can be shown to be highly correlated with the relative prestige of occupational groups, scored with the Standard Scale described in Chapter 8 (r = .75). Stewart, Prandy, and Blackburn (1973) found a similar pattern among white-collar workers in England.

Finally, other "relational" aspects of occupational structure, such as patterns of residential segregation (Duncan and Duncan, 1955), assortative mating (Laumann, 1966:74–77), and commensalism (Dumont, 1970:83–89) also can be shown to follow a prestige gradient.

Thus we can conclude that, despite the reservations of Goldthorpe and Hope, occupational prestige studies do indeed appear to tap an aspect of occupational differentiation that conforms to a classical meaning of prestige, involving deference and derogation and differential associational intimacy. Thus, we can proceed with confidence to ask whether and why the prestige evaluation of occupations is much the same throughout the world.[2] But first we must address the more mundane question of whether or not the prestige data available to us are, on strictly technical grounds, equal to the task.

DATA AND DATA QUALITY

On the basis of a reasonably exhaustive search of the literature through 1971, I was able to locate 85 occupational prestige studies conducted in 60 societies;[3] these studies, described in Table 2.1, provide the basic data for

[2] Concluding that what prestige studies really measure is the general desirability of occupations, Goldthorpe and Hope (1974:13) dismiss as theoretically unexciting the question of why there appears to be universal agreement across time and space in occupational prestige assessments. On the contrary, I would suggest that if one were to accept their position there would be all the more reason to wonder why there is such uniform consensus about what constitutes desirable features of occupations. The two perspectives are not, in fact, as different as Goldthorpe and Hope make them out to be, and both lead to the same interesting questions about the extent of and reasons for consensus in subjective hierarchical evaluations of occupations.

[3] These actually represent 51 nations; however, for reasons that will be made clear in the following chapter, India, Nigeria, and Indonesia are represented by two studies each, and Brazil and Thailand by three studies each. In addition, Guam and Puerto Rico are treated as separate countries just as are the overseas territories of European nations. Following this convention, West Irian probably should have been treated as a separate country rather than as part of Indonesia (although its status is somewhat ambiguous). Countries are listed in Table 2.1 in alphabetical order, on the basis of the names by which they were popularly known as of 1971. However, two errors crept in (so much for memories based on boyhood stamp collecting!): The Republic of South Africa is listed as the Union of South Africa, and Rhodesia is listed as Southern Rhodesia. I did not consider it worth the effort to correct these errors since country names change so often these days that the list would shortly be out of date in any event.

the bulk of the analysis. In addition, a few data sets found subsequently are discussed in later chapters. Although prestige ratings are more readily available for highly industrialized nations, it has been gratifying to discover data for a relatively large number of nonindustrialized countries in many parts of the world. Of the 56 places for which both prestige and GNP data are available,[4] well over half (33) are below the worldwide mean in per capita GNP and about 40% (22) are below the median (Ginsburg, 1961:Table 3). The 60 societies for which we have prestige data are distributed throughout the world as follows:

Western Europe and Anglo-Saxon countries	15
Eastern Europe	4
Africa	11
Asia and Oceania	17
Latin America and the Caribbean	13

Since the countries for which prestige data are available are reasonably representative of the world's nations, the conclusions of this analysis can be viewed as a valid description of the worldwide pattern—provided of course that the quality of the data can be shown to be adequate.

Estimates of data quality are reported in the right-hand column of Table 2.1. These scores represent my subjective judgments of the quality of the data contained in each study. My primary criterion was the quality of the sample. These studies are based on four types of samples: representative (probability or quota) samples of national populations, representative samples of local populations, casual samples of general populations, and samples of special groups, such as students. In the absence of other factors, the assigned score corresponded to the quality of the sample, ranging downward from 4 points for representative national samples. However, data based on ratings of stimuli other than prestige were judged to be of low quality (scored 1). For example, some studies involved evaluations of occupations in terms of their "desirability," which, as we have seen in the previous section, is not synonymous with prestige; the Swedish, Nigerian (Bornu), and Yugoslav studies all utilized this criterion. The Czechoslovak study was different still, involving evaluations of "ideal income." Finally, marked idiosyncrasies in the rating procedure were penalized. This resulted in the assignment of a low quality rating to the Grenadan study, although in some

---

[4] In the case of the seven countries for which data for two or three places are included, each of the places is scored with information representing the country as a whole. This is tantamount to treating all places within a country as separate societies, each with the same characteristics. While this introduces a certain amount of error, it is in principle no different from tagging a particular city with the characteristics of the whole country, which I have also done *faute de mieux*.

TABLE 2.1

Summary of Sample and Rating Characteristics of Studies Used to Form Basic Data Set

Country (Source)	Date of Data Collection[a]	Numbers of Occupations Rated	Sample Size	Sample Characteristics	Prestige Rating Procedure (Language of Interview or Questionnaire)	Measure Utilized in Comparison	Data Quality Estimate
(1a) United States (Hodge et al., 1964:290–292)	1963	90	651	Stratified national quota sample.	Occupations rated on 5-point scale according to "your own personal opinion of the general standing that such a job has." (English)	Mean rating.	4
(1b) United States (Siegel et al., 1974)	1964	203	923	Stratified national area probability sample.	Occupations rated on 9-point scale according to their "social standing." (English)	Linear transformation of mean rating, with logical range 0–100.	4
(1c) United States (same as 1b)	1965	201	1500	Stratified national block quota sample divided into 3 subsamples; one third of titles rated by each subsample.	Same as 1b.	Mean rating.	4
(2) Argentina (Cucullu de Murmis, 1961: 8)	1959	30	500	Members of 5 occupational groups, 100 respondents per group. All respondents residents of Buenos Aires.	Occupations rated on 5-point scale according to their "prestige or social position." (Spanish)	Mean rating.	2
(3a) Australia (Congalton, 1962:Table 1)	1962	135	303	Quota sample of Sydney residents, with quotas for sex, 4 age groups, and 4 occupational groups.	Occupations rated on 7-point scale according to their "social standing in the community." (English)	Median rating.	3
(3b) Australia (Congalton, 1965:128)	1965	33	443	Quota sample of population of unnamed Australian city, with quotas for sex, 4 age groups, and 4 occupational groups.	Respondents asked to divide occupations on basis of "social standing" into as many groups as they thought appropriate. Median category computed for each scale, then converted to 7-point metric. (English)	Weighted mean of medians for various scale types.	3
(4) Belgium (Gulliksen, 1964:87–88)	1964	31	337	Students completing secondary school; results available for Flemish ($N = 195$) and French-speaking ($N = 142$).	Modified paired comparisons; occupational titles presented in 31 sets of 6 and within each set ranked according to "which occupation has the better social standing." (Flemish, French)	Normalized mean score.	1

TABLE 2.1 *(Continued)*

Country (Source)	Date of Data Collection[a]	Numbers of Occupations Rated	Sample Size	Sample Characteristics	Prestige Rating Procedure (Language of Interview or Questionnaire)	Measure. Utilized in Comparison	Data Quality Estimate
(5) Brazil (Açucena) (Haller et al., 1972)	1967	71	100	Random subsample of random sample of households in most isolated and mountainous sector of *município* of Açucena, State of Minas Gerais.	Occupations rated on 5-point scale according to prestige. (Portuguese)	Mean rating.	3
(6) Brazil (Bezerros) (same as 5)	1968	75	121	Household heads: 35 city dwellers, 28 large farmers, 39 small farmers, and 19 farm tenants.	Same as 5.	Mean rating.	2
(7a) Brazil (São Paulo) (Hutchinson, 1957: 1970)	1955	30	500	Representative sample of first-year students at the University of São Paulo.	Occupations rated on 6-point scale according to their "general social standing," then ranked within groups. (Portuguese)	Mean of median ranks for sex - SES - IQ subgroups.	1
(7b) Brazil (São Paulo (Castaldi, 1956: Tables 1-3)	1956	30	180	Italian immigrants to São Paulo and their descendants, from 3 age groups.	Same as 7a.	Weighted mean of median ranks for 3 age groups.	1
(8) Canada (Pineo and Porter, 1967:36-40)	1966	208	793	Stratified national area probability sample.	Same as 7b. (English, French)	Same as 1b.	4
(9) Ceylon (Green, 1953:488)	1953	37	?	Graduate teachers.	Unknown. (Unknown)	Rank order.	1
(10a) Chile (Barilari and Oxley, 1966:43)	1959	91	379	Representative sample of twelfth-grade male students in schools in Greater Santiago.	Occupations rated on 5-point scale according to prestige. (Spanish)	Mean rating.	1
(10b) Chile (Carter and Sepulveda, 1964:21)	1963	16	230	Area probability sample of residents of Santiago.	"Level of prestige" of occupations rated on 5-point scale. (Spanish)	Mean rating.	3
(11) Congo (Kinshasa) (Xydias, 1956:492)	1956	30	72	Upper form students in African secondary and trade schools in Kisangani (Stanleyville).	Occupations open to Africans ranked "in order of the social standing which most people granted them." (French?)	Mean rank.	1

Country / Reference	Year	N occupations	N respondents	Description	Method	Rating
(12) Costa Rica[b]	1960	80	118	Male high school students in the town of Turrialba (population about 6,500).	"Prestige" of occupations rated on 5-point scale. (Spanish)	Mean rating.	1
(13) Czechoslovakia (Brenner and Hrouda, 1969)	1966	30	1399	Representative national sample?	Respondents asked to specify "ideal salary" for each occupation. (Czech, Slovak)	Mean salary.	1
(14) Denmark (Svalastoga, 1959:80ff.)	1953	75	3128	Stratified national probability sample, females undersampled.	Respondent handed card with occupational title, amount of education incumbent normally has, and number of people supervised, and asked to rate "prestige" of occupation on 5-point scale. (Danish)	Mean rating.	4
(15) France (same as 4)	1964	31	1200	14- and 15-year-old boys in highest grade of public elementary school.	Same as 4. (French)	Same as 4.	1
(16) French Guiana (Bone, 1962: 48–51)	1962	80	?	School teachers in city of Cayenne.	Occupations of students' fathers rated on 4-point scale according to "the amount of prestige attached to each occupation by the society." (French)	Mean rating.	1
(17a) Germany (Bolte, 1959: 42)	1952	38	133	Total of 1612 respondents, including university students, apprentice school students (industrial and commercial) and adults from a number of towns in Schleswig-Holstein. Only results for adults used here.	Occupations ranked according to their social standing (soziales anschen," "einschatzung," "gasellschaftliche stellung." (German)	Mean rank.	2
(17b) Germany (Bolte, 1959: 58)	1953	47	103	Adult males from 3 isolated rural villages: 31 farm owners, 31 farm laborers, 31 artisans, 10 village school teachers.	Occupations ranked according to their social standing; actual ranking done by interviewer on basis of responses to open-ended interview. (German)	Mean rank.	2
(17c) Germany (Bolte, 1959: 103–104)	1953	20	100	University students: 40 males, 60 females.	List of occupations restricted to those commonly performed by women; ranked according to their social standing. (German)	Mean rank.	1

TABLE 2.1 *(Continued)*

Country (Source)	Date of Data Collection[a]	Numbers of Occupations Rated	Sample Size	Sample Characteristics	Prestige Rating Procedure (Language of Interview or Questionnaire)	Measure Utilized in Comparison	Data Quality Estimate
(17d) Germany (Wurzbacher, 1954:33)	1950	17	156	Random sample of small community.	Occupations ranked according to their "prestige." (German)	Mean rank.	3
(17e) Germany (Mayntz, 1956: 61)	1956?	18	315	Unknown.	Occupations rated as "upper class," "middle class," or "working class." (German)	Mean rating 5-point scale).	1
(17f) Germany (Kunde and Dawes, 1959: 351)	1952	23	341	High school students in Berlin, Hamburg, and Stuttgart.	Occupations ranked according to their social status. (German)	Median rank.	1
(18) Ghana (Foster, 1965: 268–275)	1961	25	775	Fifth-form males in 23 secondary schools; sample encompassed 45% of all fifth-form males in Ghana at this time.	"Prestige" of occupations rated on 5-point scale. (English)	Mean rating.	1
(19) Grenada (Smith, 1965: 114–115)	1953	35	19	"Knowledgable" members of Grenadian elite, purposively chosen to be as representative of the elite as possible; mostly native-born males over 40.	Individuals listed in *The Grenada Handbook and Directory* (a compendium of occupationally prominent persons; *N*=388) and known to respondent ranked or rated according to "position you think they hold in Grenada today" (the number of categories up to the respondent). (English)	Mean rating, computed after each rater's scale transformed to standard metric.	1
(20a) Great Britain (Moser and Hall, 1954: 39)	1949	30	1399	Questionnaires distributed through adult education and other organizations.	"Social standing" of occupations rated on 5-point scale, then ranked within categories. (English)	Mean rating.	2
(20b) Great Britain (Butcher and Pont, 1968:273)	1965	15	300	Random subsample of sample of Scottish secondary school students likely to attend university.	Occupations rated on 5-point scale according to prestige. (English)	Mean rating.	1
(21) Guam (Cooper et al., 1962: 268)	1962	25	144	Seniors at Guam's largest high school.	Unknown; apparently evaluated according to prestige. (English)	Rank order.	1

	Year					
(22) Guyana (Graham and Beckles, 1968: 368ff.)	1965	40	142	Random subsample of random sample of male household heads in Greater Georgetown.	Occupations rated on 5-point scale according to their "general standing," then ranked within categories. (English)	Mean rank.	3
(23a) India (Peasant) (D'Souza, 1964: 37)	1961	18	235	All household heads in village of Chincholi, East Khandesh District, State of Maharashtra; majority of households are tribal.	All occupations practiced in village ranked according to prestige. (Marathi)	Weighted mean of median rankings by various caste groups.	3
(23b) India (Peasant) (D'Souza, 1964: 34)	1961	7	79	All household heads in village of Bhumas, Kaira District, State of Gujarat.	Same as 23a. (Gujarati)	Same as 23a.	3
(23c) India (Peasant) (D'Souza, 1964: 41)	1961	16	114	Household heads in village of Kotur, Dharwar District, State of Mysore. Due to coding error, only 114 of 306 questionnaires usable, but two groups similar on variables not affected by error.	Same as 23a. (Kannada)	Same as 23a.	3
(23d) India (Peasant) (Singh, 1967: 382)	1967	18	40	Stratified probability sample of household heads, stratified by caste, in village of Mohali (located on Rupar-Chandigarh road).	Same as 23a. (Unknown)	Median ranking.	3
(24) India (University Students) (D'Souza, 1962: 149)	1959	30	214	Students at Bombay University: undergraduates, master's candidates in statistics and social science, and students in business management course (working business executives); mostly Marathi and Gujarati speaking.	Occupations ranked according to "social standing." (English)	Median rank.	1

TABLE 2.1 (Continued)

Country (Source)	Date of Data Collection [a]	Numbers of Occupations Rated	Sample Size	Sample Characteristics	Prestige Rating Procedure (Language of Interview or Questionnaire)	Measure Utilized in Comparison	Data Quality Estimate
(25) Indonesia (Java) (Thomas and Soeparman, 1963: 431)	1961	30	939	Students from 6 Bandung, Java, high schools.	Occupations ranked "according to their prestige." (Unknown)	Rank order.	1
(26) Indonesia (West Irian) (Van Der Veur, 1966:109)	1962	34	774	Papuan secondary school students; mostly students from small villages attending missionary boarding schools.	Occupations open to Papuans rated on 5-point scale according to prestige. (Dutch and Bazaar Malay; neither is mother tongue of respondents.)	Mean rating.	1
(27) Iraq (Alzobaie and El-Ghannam, 1968:232-233)	1968	62	225	Students in the College of Education and the Girl's College of the University of Baghdad.	Occupations rated on 7-point semantic differential scale of "social desirability." (Arabic)	Mean rating.	1
(28a) Israel (Lissak, 1964: 495-496, 1965:58)	1959	27	450	Males (apparently urban) age 16-25.	Unknown; occupations apparantly evaluated according to prestige society accords them. (Hebrew)	Rank order.	2
(28b) Israel [c]	1966	31	251	Israel army personnel, equally divided between men and women.	Same as 4. (Hebrew)	Same as 4.	2
(29) Italy [d]	1964	31	416	Female high school students from Turin (N = 218) and students from the University of Padua--male (N = 75) and female (N =123).	Same as 4. (Italian)	Simple average of scores for the three groups; scores derived by same procedure as in 4.	1
(30) Ivory Coast (Clignet & Foster, 1966: 146-152)	1963	25	259	Students in eight secondary schools preparing for the baccalaureat examination, part 1; sample encompassed 82% of student at this level in the Ivory Coast at this time.	"Prestige" of occupations rated on 5-point scale. (French)	Mean rating.	1

	Year		N	Sample	Method	Scoring	
(31a) Japan (Nisihira, 1968:549)	1964	98	622	Probability sample of Tokyo residents, divided into 2 subsamples each of which rated about half the titles.	Occupations rated on 5-point scale according to their "importance." (Japanese)	Mean rating.	3
(31b) Japan (Japan Sociological Society, 1954:426)	1952	30	899	Stratified probability of males age 20-69 in the 6 largest cities of Japan.	Occupations ranked according to social status and prestige. (Japanese)	Mean rating.	3
(31c) Japan (Ramsey and Smith, 1960:477)	1958	23	536	Seniors in 2 Tokyo and 2 small city (20,000 population) high schools.	"Prestige of occupations rated on 5-point scale. (Japanese)	Mean rating.	1
(32) Mauritania (Bonis, 1964:386)	1964	42	?	Berber industrial workers in Port Etienne; about half are literate.	Unknown. (Indigenous language?)	Rank order.	2
(33) Mexico (Wilkerson, 1967:63-64)	1967	50	109	One-third of the student body of the Faculty of Humanities, University of Veracruz.	Occupations rated on 5-point scale with respect to prestige (10 occupations per category) then ranked within categories. (Spanish)	Mean rank.	1
(34a) Netherlands (van Heek and Vercruijsse, 1958:25-26)	1952	57	500	Stratified national probability sample.	Occupations ranked according to their standing ("aanzien"). (Dutch)	Mean rank.	4
(34b) Netherlands (Tobi and Luyckx, 1950:32-35)	1959	116	100	Purposive sample of males, distributed across five industry categories according to the total labor force distribution; appears to be well distributed according to occupation.	Occupations rated on 5-point scale according to their "rank" ("rangstand"). (Dutch)	Mean rating.	2
(34c) Netherlands (van Hulten, 1953:23-24)	**1950**	**71**	**50**	**Employees of Philips works at Endhoven or members of their families, drawn from 3 status groups.**	**Occupations rated on 5-point scale according to their "standing." (Dutch)**	Score is percentage of ratings in highest category minus percentage in lowest category plus 100.	2

TABLE 2.1 *(Continued)*

Country (Source)	Date of Data Collection[a]	Numbers of Occupations Rated	Sample Size	Sample Characteristics	Prestige Rating Procedure (Language of Interview or Questionnaire)	Measure Utilized in Comparison	Data Quality Estimate
(34d) Netherlands (Kuiper, 1954: 49–52)	1951	163	100	**Purposive sample of residents of town of Zwolle, distributed according to 1947 census figures for occupation and religion for Zwolle; 50 men and 50 women.**	Occupations rated on 3-point scale "according to the social prestige of these occupations as (the rater) saw it." (Dutch)	Mean rating.	2
(35) New Britain (Epstein, 1967: 114–115)	1960	30	334	Students in five Rabaul secondary schools. Most are Tolai from the Gazelle Peninsula.	Occupations rated on 5-point scale with respect to prestige. (English)	Mean rating.	1
(36a) New Zealand (Congalton and Havighurst, 1954:15ff.)	1954	116	73	University students.	Occupations rated on 7-point scale according to "the status which each occupation carries in the community." (English)	Median rating.	1
(36b) New Zealand (Vellekoop, 1966:46)	1966	15	196	Sociology students at a university in Christ-church.	Occupations rated (?) with respect to prestige. (English)	Rank order.	1
(37) Nigeria (Bornu) (Cohen, 1970: 251–252)	1957	55	81	Kanuri secondary school boys.	Occupations ranked in order "as if God had given you power to do anything you liked." (Kanuri)	Mean rank.	1
(38) Nigeria (Kano) (Armer, 1968: 31)	1964	16	591	All 17-year-old boys within wards selected on basis of area probability sample of Kano City, Northern Nigeria.	Occupations rated on 5-point scale according to their positions relative to the "social positions of all people in this city." (Hausa)	Mean rating.	3
(39a) Norway (same as 4)	1964	31	275	18 to 20-year old men in military service.	Same as 4. (Norwegian)	Same as 4.	2
(39b) Norway (Øyen, 1964:149)	1964	20	12	University students.	201 occupations (127 male occupations, 74 female occupations) rated on 7-point scale with respect to prestige. Only 20 titles matching the Danish titles (see 14 above) reported. (Norwegian)	Median rating.	1

	Year		Sample size	Sample	Method/Scale	Rating	
(40) Pakistan[e]	1965	52	129	University students from various parts of Pakistan.	Same as 1a. (English)	Mean rating.	1
(41a) Philippines (Tiryakian, 1958:394)	1954	30	606	Quota samples of residents of a Manila suburb and four rural communities.	Occupations ranked "in order of social standing." (Tagalog and English)	Rank order, derived from mean rank.	3
(41b) Philippines (Castillo, 1962:147-157)	?	25	476	Seniors from six high schools.	Occupations rated on 5-point scale according to prestige. (Unknown)	Mean rating.	1
(41c) Philippines (same as 17f)	1954	23	510	Juniors at a state university.	Same as 17f. (English)	Same as 17f.	1
(42a) Poland (Sarapata and Wesołowski, 1961:585)	1958	29	763	Stratified quota sample of Warsaw residents.	"Social prestige" of occupations rated on 5-point scale. (Polish)	Mean rating.	3
(42b) Poland[c]	?	31	369	Students: 169 high school students, 200 "advanced" students.	Same as 4. (Polish)	Same as 4.	1
(43) Puerto Rico (Koppel, 1964:15)	1964	50	734	Quota samples (by socioeconomic status) of three metropolitan areas and five rural areas chosen to encompass different types of	Occupations rated on 5-point scale according to "social standing or prestige." (Spanish)	Rank order.	3
(44) South West Africa (Kelley and Pendleton, 1975)	1968	47	384	Census of South-West Africa secondary school students (single secondary school, located in Windhoek).	Occupations rated with respect to prestige. (Afrikaans)	Mean rating.	1
(45) Southern Rhodesia (Mitchell, 1966: 260-261)	1966	56	1485	Secondary school students.	Occupations open to Africans rated on 5-point scale according to their prestige. (English?)	Mean rating.	1
(46) Spain (de Miguel, 1967:53)	1960	39	?	Representative national sample of youth, age 16-21.	Occupations rated on 5-point scale with respect to "position"; income mentioned as criterion. (Spanish)	Mean rating.	4
(47) Surinam (Same as 16)	1962	55	?	Teachers in training.	Same as French Guiana. (Dutch)	Mean rating.	1

TABLE 2.1 (Continued)

Country (Source)	Date of Data Collection[a]	Numbers of Occupations Rated	Sample Size	Sample Characteristics	Prestige Rating Procedure (Language of Interview or Questionnaire)	Measure Utilized in Comparison	Data Quality Estimate
(48) Sweden (Carlsson, 1958: 148)	1958	26	1700	Stratified national probability sample divided into two subsamples, each rating about half the titles.	Occupations rated on 5-point scale with respect to how parents in general would view desirability for son. (Swedish)	Mean rating.	1
(49) Switzerland (Tofigh, 1964: 54-55)	1964	110	21	Adults.	Occupations rated on 5-point scale according to their prestige. (French)	Mean rating.	1
(50) Taiwan (Marsh, 1970 156)	1963	36	507	Systematic multi-stage area sample of male Taiwanese household heads living in Taipei City.	Same as la. (Chinese)	Mean rating.	3
(51) Thailand (Peasants) (Treiman et al., 1969)	1966	104	99	Almost all adult residents of village of Buan Muy, Udornthani Province, Northeastern Thailand.	Occupations rated on 5-point scale according to social standing. (North East Thai dialect)	Mean rating.	3
(52) Thailand (Teachers' College students) (same as 51)	1966	104	150	Students at Udornthani Teachers' College, Northeastern Thailand.	Same as 51. (Thai)	Mean rating.	1
(53) Thailand (University students) (same as 51)	1966	104	150	Students in the Faculty of Political Science, Chulalongkorn University, Bangkok.	Same as 51. (Thai)	Mean rating.	1
(54) Turkey (Helling, n.d.)	1955	63	310	Mostly students from rural, town, and city high schools in provinces of Ankara, Icel, Izmir, and Kayseri; 230 males, 80 females.	Occupations rated on 7-point scale in terms of the "honor or importance" accorded them. (Turkish)	Mean ratings.	1

	Date[a]			Sample	Procedure	
(55) Uganda[f]	1959	89	141	Kampala residents: 114 men, 27 women.	Occupations rated on 5-point scale according to social standing. (Unknown) Mean rating.	2
(56) Union of South Africa (Kuper, 1965:436)	1960	16	?	362 African primary and secondary school students in Durban; only scores for secondary school students (N unknown) used for analysis.	Occupations ranked according to their prestige. (English) Rank order.	1
(57) USSR (Vodzinskaia, 1969:39-61)	1964	80	100	Seniors in five Leningrad secondary schools.	Occupations rated on 10-point scale according to prestige. (Russian) Mean rating.	1
(58) Uruguay (Rama, 1960: 193-201)	1960	26	?	Upper-middle-class residents of a small city of about 20,000.	Procedure unclear. Apparently occupations ranked according to their "prestige." (Spanish) Rank order.	1
(59) Yugoslavia (Hammel, 1970:Table 1)	1966	100	100	Workers in motor and machine factory and in construction firm (50 each); both white- and blue-collar workers at various skill levels.	Occupations rated on 5-point scale in terms of their desirability "if you had all opportunities in your life to become whatever you wanted." (Serbian) Rank order.	1
(60) Zambia (Mitchell and Irvine, 1966: 48-49)	1959	42	298	Illiterate recruits to the copper mines (N = 96); "advancees" in the mines--senior mine workers (N = 55); secondary school students (N = 147)	Occupations open to Africans rated on a 5-point scale according to their prestige. (Unknown) Mean rating.	2

[a] Date of data collection given if known, otherwise date of publication.

[b] Unpublished data provided by Professors Archibald O. Haller, David Lewis, and Iwao Ishino.

[c] Unpublished data provided by Professor Frederick Gulliksen.

[d] Unpublished data collection by Professors Fabio Metelli and Carlo Remondino and provided by Prof. Frederick Gulliksen.

[e] Eister, 1965:68, plus unpublished data provided by Professor Eister.

[f] Unpublished data provided by Professor Valdo Pons.

respects it is particularly valuable.[5] With the benefit of hindsight it is clear that studies involving idiosyncratic stimuli should not have been included in the analysis at all; but this was, of course, impossible to know in advance. As we shall see, they are rather poor substitutes for conventional occupational prestige ratings.

Not surprisingly, the quality of the data tends to be highest in the more industrialized countries. When per capita GNP estimates are converted to ranks[6] and correlated with quality ratings, a modest positive correlation is obtained ($r = .27$). The varying quality of the data for countries at different levels of industrialization makes it mandatory to examine possible biases in the data and to consider the potential effects of such biases for the results of the analysis. The problem of nonrepresentativeness of samples of raters, the main source of differential quality, is serious enough to deserve a separate chapter. In the present chapter I consider the effect of variation in the rating task and show it to be inconsequential, which allows us to combine data from different studies conducted in the same country. I then consider problems of comparing occupational data across countries and outline procedures for doing this.

VARIATION IN THE RATING TASK

One potential source of bias is variability in the nature of the rating task. Occupations were rated (on 3-, 5-, 7-, or 9-point scales) in terms of their "social standing," "prestige," "respect," "desirability for one's son," "desirability for oneself," and so forth. Scores computed on the basis of these ratings or rankings include means, medians, simple ranks, and yet more prolix averages. Moreover, while in most cases occupational titles alone served as stimuli in the rating task, in a few instances additional characteristics of occupations, such as educational requirements, average income, and supervisory span, were included as well as the title itself.

---

[5] Whereas in most of the studies utilized here the stimuli for evaluation are occupational titles, in the Grenadan study concrete individuals were rated in terms of their prestige. I derived scores for occupations by computing the mean prestige of individuals in them. While the correlation between these scores and conventional occupational prestige scores would probably be reasonably high, judging from the Siegel study reported above, it cannot be assumed to be high enough for these scores to be taken as valid substitutes for conventional occupational prestige scores; this is especially true considering that the sample of individuals being evaluated was decidedly biased toward high-status persons and that many occupations had very few incumbents and hence unreliable mean prestige scores.

[6] The country with the lowest per capita GNP was given a score of 1, the country with the next lowest GNP a score of 2, and so on. This was done to correct for the marked skewness in the data, which would have resulted in an artificially inflated correlation had the GNP values themselves been used. Quality ratings are for the highest quality study from each country.

Fortunately, all the available evidence suggests that alternative ways of conducting the rating task make almost no difference in the results, so long as "prestige" or some synonymous term, such as "respect" or "social standing," is specified as the ordering criterion. In Holland, for example, five occupational prestige studies have been conducted: a local community study in 1942, two other local studies in 1951 and 1959, a study conducted at the Phillips works at Endhoven in 1950, and a survey of a national probability sample of the population in 1952 (for a description of the 1942 study, see van Heek, 1945:180–181; for the other four studies see Table 2.1). The procedures used in these various studies to develop prestige scores included (*1*) ranking occupations on the basis of their social standing ("*aangien*") and computing mean ranks; (*2*) rating occupations on a 5-point scale according to their rank ("*rangstand*") and computing mean scores; (*3*) rating occupations on a 3-point scale according to their standing and computing scores by subtracting the percentage placing the occupation in the lowest category from the percentage placing it in the highest category; and (*4*) rating occupations on a 3-point scale according to their "*prestige*" and computing mean scores. The number of occupations rated ranged from 57 to 163. Despite the wide variations in the rating task, the scoring procedures, and the sample characteristics, when correlations were computed between the national study and each of the four local studies, no correlation dropped below .94 and all but one were above .97. Since a certain portion of the variation from study to study doubtless may be attributed to real differences in the way occupations were rated from group to group, we can conclude that even radical variations in the rating task do not seriously affect the resulting scores. Similar evidence can be found in the generally high correlations between pairs of studies conducted in the same country. In all but 7 comparisons out of a total of 31, the correlations exceeded .95 despite considerable variation in both the rating task and the characteristics of raters.

Even substantial variations in the design of the rating task make little difference. In the Philippines 30 occupations were rated by urban and rural samples. The urban raters were given a set of cards containing occupational titles and asked to put them in order according to their social standing. The rural raters were given a set of 30 photographs depicting the same occupations and asked to order them in the same way. The correlation between the two sets of ranks was .96, which was probably less than unity due to real differences in the perceptions of urban and rural raters and not to differences in method (the largest discrepancies were in the ratings of "fisherman" and "factory worker," Tiryakian, 1958:395).

There is also some evidence that providing respondents with information about additional characteristics of occupations, such as average income, does not affect the way they are evaluated. The Brazilian study using

University of São Paulo students as raters (Hutchinson, 1957:183) asked one set of students to rate a set of 30 occupational titles; another set of students was asked to rate the same occupations in a task that included as part of the stimulus a given monthly income for each occupation. The rank correlation between the two sets of ratings was .99, while the rank correlation of prestige scores with the incomes shown with the titles was only .76.

On the other hand, using criteria of evaluation that are not precisely synonymous with prestige produces somewhat greater variability in ratings. For example, available data for Poland include ratings of occupations with respect to both "prestige" (Sarapata and Wesołowski, 1961) and "just remuneration," that is, the income respondents think is appropriate for each occupation (Sarapata, 1963). The correlation between these two sets of ratings for 20 matching occupations is .88 which, while still quite high, is substantially lower than the typical correlation of prestige ratings from two studies within a single country. Inspection of the scatterplot indicates that the largest discrepancy between prestige and just remuneration involves priests, who are regarded as deserving considerably lower remuneration than incumbents of other occupations of comparable prestige; presumably this reflects recognition of their lack of family responsibility and hence their need for less money. On the other hand, "farm laborer," the occupation displaying the next largest discrepancy, is thought to deserve more income than a number of occupations with higher prestige. Clearly, the factors that determine the prestige of occupations, although similar, are not identical to those that determine perceptions of just remuneration. Hence, ratings of just remuneration are only a moderately acceptable substitute for ratings of the prestige of occupations; specifically, this implies that caution must be exercised in the interpretation of Czech data, which use an "ideal income" measure rather than a prestige measure.[7]

Although we have no basis for directly evaluating other nonprestige criteria such as "desirability" (because we have no studies containing both prestige and desirability ratings), it will be clear from material presented in Chapter 4 and in Chapter 8 that such criteria of evaluation are not synonymous with prestige. Ratings of occupations "as if God had given you power to do anything you liked" (in Nigeria (Bornu); a similar phrase was used in Yugoslavia), or in terms of "what parents in general would think of the indicated occupation as an occupation for a son of theirs" (Sweden) seem to be tapping a somewhat different dimension of occupational evaluation than ratings of occupations in terms of "prestige," "respect," or "social standing," at least judging from the fact that nonprestige ratings are substantially

---

[7] Czech prestige data acquired after the main analysis was completed confirm the inadequacy of the ideal income data as a prestige substitute. The prestige data are far more similar to the worldwide average than are the ideal income data (see Tables 8.2 and 8.3).

less highly correlated with the worldwide average than are prestige ratings. For this reason, the five data sets (Czechoslovakia, Grenada, Nigeria (Bornu), Sweden, and Yugoslavia) not utilizing conventional prestige criteria will be excluded from some parts of the subsequent analysis.

COMBINING SEVERAL STUDIES FROM ONE COUNTRY

The fact that characteristics of the rating task do not appear to affect the resulting prestige scores makes it possible to combine studies for those countries where more than one study of occupational prestige has been conducted. The purpose of amalgamating studies is to increase the number of occupations in a given country for which prestige ratings are available, thus improving the quality of the cross-national comparisons. For example, by combining four Dutch studies, I was able to increase the number of occupations available for comparison from 57 to 215. After combining studies, the average number of occupational titles per county was 62.

The following procedure was used to amalgamate occupational titles from several studies:

1. The best study for a given country was chosen (based on the quality of its sample and extensiveness of its coverage of occupational titles),

2. If another study was available for that country, occupational titles contained in the two studies were matched,[8]

3. The regression and associated correlation of the scores from the best study on those of the other study were computed, using all matching occupational titles,

4. If the correlation between the two sets of scores was $\geq .95$, the regression equation was used to convert scores for all titles rated in the second study, but not in the best study, to the metric of the best study. If the correlation was $< .95$, the second study was not used. In a few instances (described in Chapter 3), the second study was regarded as representing a separate society within the same nation and was hence treated as an additional case.

5. Steps 1 through 4 were repeated for all additional studies from that country. If a new title appeared in more than one of the secondary studies, its score was estimated either from the best secondary study or, in the case where no secondary study was superior to the others, from the average predicted value.

---

[8] Matching of occupational titles within any society is quite straightforward because meanings of job titles and understandings about the organization of work are culturally determined and hence shared by members of a given culture. The question of whether occupations are genuinely comparable does not arise here as it does, with force, when it comes to matching occupational titles across countries.

It should be clear that this procedure depends upon the assumption that the prestige ratings in all studies from a given country reflect the same universe of prestige evaluations and hence that any of the added titles would have received the same score as that predicted by the regression equation had it actually been included in the primary study. Given the absence of important *intra*national subgroup variations or temporal changes in the ratings accorded occupations (documented in Chapter 3), as well as the stability of ratings generated by a variety of different procedures, this seems to be a reasonable assumption. Requiring a correlation of at least .95 between ratings of common titles as a criterion for utilizing a secondary study to supplement the primary one minimizes the potential for errors of the sort that could seriously bias the subsequent analysis.[9]

COMPARING OCCUPATIONAL TITLES ACROSS COUNTRIES

The most serious difficulty in comparing occupational prestige data across countries is to accurately match corresponding occupational titles for different societies. The basic procedure for assessing the degree of cross-cultural similarity in the prestige evaluation of occupations is to match occupational titles for pairs of countries and then to correlate the prestige scores for matching occupations. Thus, errors in the matching of titles will create invalid results. In the previous chapter I argued at length that the organization of work is sufficiently similar in all complex societies to sustain a comparison of occupational structures; here I spell out operational procedures for actually effecting such a comparison. In order to carry out the matching of occupational titles across countries, two basic decisions had to be made: (*1*) an occupational classification scheme had to be settled upon, to provide a framework for the matching process; and (*2*) criteria as to what would constitute an acceptable match had to be devised.

Occupational Classification. The very large number of occupational titles involved in the study required the development of some sort of classification scheme, simply to keep track of occupations both during the coding

---

[9] In one case, that of Australia, a different procedure was used to combine studies. Two good studies were available for Australia, the second of which was deliberately designed (for reasons which remain obscure) to include *no* titles rated in the first study. Hence, titles could not be matched between studies in the usual way. Therefore, in order to avoid losing the data contained in one of the studies, I treated the two studies initially as coming from two countries, matched titles from each of the studies with those evaluated in the United States' studies, regressed the United States' scores separately upon each of the Australian sets, used the resulting equations to convert both sets of Australian scores into a standard metric, and then combined the two sets of scores.

and in the course of the subsequent analysis. For a variety of reasons it seemed preferable to utilize an extant classification system rather than developing one de novo; the enormous amount of work entailed would have been reason enough, but the desirability of facilitating comparison with other bodies of data was an important additional consideration. For this reason I adopted as a coding frame the revised version of the *International Standard Classification of Occupations* (ISCO) developed by the International Labor Office (1969a). The ISCO scheme has been utilized by a large number of census bureaus throughout the world as a basis for their occupational classification schemes. Hence, analysis of the relation between prestige and various occupational characteristics reported in census statistics, as well as the ability to assign prestige scores to occupational data reported in foreign sample surveys and coded according to local census classification schemes, is greatly facilitated by the use of the ISCO scheme as a basis for classifying occupations.

To classify occupations, I followed almost exactly, down to the unit group level, the Revised ISCO scheme,[10] which consists of a four-level nested set of titles: "major groups," "minor groups," "unit groups," and "occupations" (a few minor exceptions are indicated later). Although it would have been possible to make use of the ISCO "occupations," this was not done for several reasons. First, the number of separate occupations identified in the ISCO (1506) is far too large for our needs and would have resulted in many occupations remaining unmatched. Second, occupational distinctions within ISCO unit groups are often made on the basis of industry group, without regard to status distinctions, whereas for our needs distinctions had to be made in such a way as to increase homogeneity within categories with respect to prestige. Hence, instead of using the ISCO individual occupations, I devised my own occupational classification within the ISCO unit groups (the fifth digit of the modified ISCO codes designates these occupations).[11] This coding scheme resulted in the distinction of some

---

[10] The Revised ISCO was used because it includes a more complete set of occupational titles and a more consistent set of distinctions than does the earlier version. However, since the 1960 round of population censuses mostly followed the original ISCO scheme, a conversion between the two versions had to be made for the purpose of relating prestige to other attributes of occupations. See Chapters 5 and 9 and Appendix C.1 for further discussion of this point.

[11] To facilitate data processing by computer, the format of the code numbers utilized in the ISCO manual was modified slightly. A five-digit code was created by (*1*) expanding the first digit in the ISCO manual to two digits to permit numerical coding of occupations not in the labor force; (*2*) dropping the hyphen separating the major group designation from the minor and unit group designations; and (*3*) adding a digit on the right to designate individual occupations. In addition, where a major group is referred to in the ISCO manual by more than one digit, as in major group 0/1, only the first digit was used. Comparison of the ISCO format (International Labor Office, 1969a) with the format of Appendix A should make clear the basic correspondence.

509 separate "occupations" within the ISCO unit groups.[12] Of course, the distribution of occupations within unit groups is dependent upon which particular titles happened to be rated in the occupational prestige studies that form the raw data for this analysis. This resulted in a somewhat uneven distribution of occupational titles across the ISCO unit groups, with some groups being entirely unrepresented by rated titles and others encompassing as many as nine distinguishable occupation lines.

Criteria for Matching Occupations.   Although occupational roles are roughly similar from place to place, occupational titles do not correspond perfectly from country to country. However, to effect comparisons, some basis for establishing a correspondence must be found. Given that we are faced with matching specific occupational titles, and not full-fledged job descriptions, three possible criteria suggest themselves.

One method would be simply to match those jobs with identical titles. This, however, turns out to be an unsatisfactory approach (*1*) because, for historical reasons, the same words are used to describe different jobs in different countries, and (*2*) because of difficulties in literal translation.[13]

---

[12] Two modifications were made to the ISCO scheme to facilitate the classification of occupational prestige data. These involved the creation of three additional unit groups. (*1*) Minor group "020 LEGISLATIVE OFFICIALS AND GOVERNMENT ADMINISTRATORS," was modified by creating three unit groups to replace the two provided by the ISCO. The ISCO includes unit groups "2-01 Legislative Officials," and "2-02 Government Administrators." In practice it proved impossible to distinguish consistently between the two categories in the coding of particular occupational titles. For example, the ISCO classification, as best I understand it, would include "mayor of a city" under legislative officials and "city manager" under government administrators, whereas both of these are from my point of view "local government heads." Problems of this kind led me to form three new groups out of the two ISCO groups, to wit: "0201 Heads of Governmental Jurisdictions," "0202 Members of Legislative Bodies," and "0203 High Administrative Officials." (*2*) The ISCO minor group "9-9 LABORERS n.e.c. [not elsewhere classified]" was expanded to include three unit groups rather than the single one in the ISCO classification, and the category name was changed to "MANUAL WORKERS n.e.c." The two additional groups are "0995 Skilled Workers n.e.c."and "0997 Semiskilled Workers n.e.c." The original unit group, "0999 Laborers n.e.c.," is thus now considered to include only unskilled laboring titles not elsewhere classified. While the authors of the ISCO are probably correct in assuming that only unskilled workers are labeled as "Laborers" without further specification in job descriptions returned by individuals, many occupational prestige studies include such gross titles as "skilled worker," and the modification in the code is made in order to be able to include these.

[13] For example, "machinist" may have three different meanings, depending on the country. In the United States a machinist is a highly skilled worker who sets up and operates a variety of metal-working machines and fits and assembles parts to make or repair metal tools or machines. In Australia, by contrast, the term "machinist" apparently refers to any machine operator in a factory, and hence describes a semiskilled job. In Holland, the term *machinist* used alone refers to what we would call a locomotive engineer. Similarly, in English-speaking countries the title "company director" refers to a member of a board of directors whereas elsewhere the literally equivalent title (e.g., *"director de compania"*) refers to the head of a firm.

A second criterion for making the matches would be to match those jobs involving the same tasks. This approach has several difficulties, however. First, no adequate description of occupational tasks is available for most countries. Second, many jobs in the United States, and presumably in other countries as well, are heterogeneous with respect to the tasks performed by their incumbents. Chemists, for example, may teach courses, do routine analysis in a laboratory, or administer large research projects, and still go under the title of chemist. Finally, to match jobs according to either the tasks performed or the organization of work is, in an important sense, to beg the question of just what it is that produces agreement or disagreement in the prestige evaluation of occupations.

The third alternative, which is the one utilized here, is to consider two jobs the same if they fulfill the same function in the division of labor, even if they involve different tasks. From the standpoint of the theoretical concerns that motivate this study, this is the most satisfactory procedure, even though the decision about whether or not titles refer to functionally similar occupations can be extremely arbitrary at times. The advantage of defining occupational similarity by similarity in function is that this permits the investigation of whether other characteristics of occupations, such as the skill required to perform them or the context in which they are performed, are associated with variations in their prestige. Thus, for example, operators of trucking firms would be matched in the United States and in Holland, even though in Holland such firms are ordinarily much smaller.

However, there is an important limitation on the decision to match jobs strictly on the basis of the function they perform. Many investigators have attached modifying terms to their job titles, such as "*country* doctor," "*self-employed* tailor," "manager of a *small* store in the *city*," and so forth, apparently because of the (somewhat misguided) notion that it is helpful to respondents to attach a particular concrete image to whatever job they are rating. It can be argued that such procedures defeat the point of occupational prestige studies, which presumably are concerned with how people hierarchically evaluate occupations per se, without detailed qualifying information.

A notorious example of the way explanatory information attached to an occupational title can modify the way it is evaluated is provided by ratings of the title "tenant farmer" in the United States. In the 1963 study, this occupation was listed as "tenant farmer—one who owns livestock and machinery and manages the farm," and received an average rating, in a 0 to 100 metric, of 43.9. By contrast, when the title was rated in 1964 without the modifying description attached, the average score dropped over 20 points, to 21.5. It seems clear that the image evoked by the phrase "tenant farmer" when that term is unmodified is of a low-status position—in the eyes of many Americans, a tenant farmer is a subsistence-level operator, scraping a living for himself and his family; even if he does own a few cows or pigs and maybe even a wagon or an old tractor, he is still a poor man, of lowly station. However, when the respondent is told explicitly that a tenant farmer *owns* livestock and machinery and *manages* a farm, additional evaluative factors come into play that, in this case, result in a substantial increment in prestige. Apparently, when modifying terms connoting differences in power or privilege are attached to occupational titles, their presence affects the rating of the whole stimulus phrase. As another example, being self-employed is generally more highly regarded than working for wages. Similarly, playing a leadership role in (managing or owning) a large enterprise brings higher status than does the same role in a small enterprise.

Since so many titles are modified in some way, it was necessary to utilize criteria that allowed matching as many of them as possible. While it would have been preferable to match titles only in the case of *exact* agreement (as nearly as exactness can be defined given the variation in the languages in which the studies were conducted), to have done so would have resulted in the loss of too many observations, leaving too few matches to support a viable analysis. For example, one result would probably have been the elimination of many of the matches in the middle of the range, where ambiguity is greatest, and hence an artificial increase in the size of the correlations between countries. The best that could be done was to try to guess which modifications of titles would affect the status position of an occupation, that is, which would evoke additional criteria of evaluation, and to define these as separate titles. In order to save cases, however, wherever it was possible to make a judgment about the typical condition of a given occupation, a modifier that defined the occupation as typical was ignored. For example, "electrician, wages" was matched with "electrician" on the assumption that since most electricians are wageworkers, people are thinking of wageworking electricians when they rate the title "electrician."

Some evidence that minor modifications of the stimuli do not affect ratings so long as they do not include the addition of hierarchically evaluated modifying terms is provided by the inclusion of several alternative descriptions of occupations in the United States' studies. "Funeral director" was included in the 1964 survey to test whether this presumably more favorable wording—for which the industry has campaigned incessantly in recent years—would be more highly evaluated than "undertaker," which was rated in 1963. For the same reason, "soda jerk" was included in 1964, whereas "soda fountain clerk" had been rated in 1963. In both cases, the 1963 scores are within one standard error of the 1964 scores, indicating that even invidious wordings of occupational titles have little effect on their prestige evaluation so long as they are not encumbered with modifying terms that are manifestly laden with status connotations.

Similarly, the sex of the incumbent ordinarily has no effect on the prestige accorded occupations. Bose (1973:119) has shown, for a sample of 108 occupations rated by residents of an American city (Baltimore), that the correlation between the average prestige of occupations identified as having a male incumbent and the same occupations identified as having a female incumbent is .97. Moreover, the departure from unity is apparently due to random fluctuations rather than to systematic differences in the ratings of particular types of occupations. Data for other countries are less systematic, but what data exist tend to show the same pattern. Ratings of "barmaid" and "barman" in Australia, of "laundress" and "clothes presser in a laundry" in Canada, of "*serveerster*" and "*kellner*" in the Netherlands, of "*sangster*" and "*sanger*" in South-West Africa, and of "*winkelclerk, m.*" and "*winkelclerk, v.*" in South-West Africa are all virtually identical; neither male nor female incumbents are more highly regarded. However, in South-West Africa a number of servile occupations traditionally performed by women (cooking, sewing, cleaning, and serving) are downgraded when performed by men (Kelley and Pendleton, 1975: Table 1). Also, for reasons that are unclear, in the Netherlands male hospital directors ("*directeur van een zeikenhuis*") have higher prestige than female hospital directors ("*directress van een zeikenhuis*"). Since women doing "men's work" or men doing "women's work" does not affect prestige evaluations in the United States but does in South-West Africa, it is unclear how general the tendency for nontraditional sex role performances to be downgraded is. In any event, the number of occupations for which such a distinction is made is too small to justify separate treatment. Hence, I made no distinction between male and female incumbents when matching occupational titles across countries.

Even having settled upon "functional similarity" as the basic criterion for matching occupational titles across countries, the matching procedure remained highly arbitrary. In particular, the question of how precise the matches should be was extremely vexing. Unfortunately, it is ordinarily not possible in situations of this kind to ascertain the consequences of making one sort of decision rather than another, short of repeating the procedure both ways. Thus it is particularly advantageous that part of the present analysis consists of a replication of work done in 1967 (Treiman, 1968). Subsequent to the initial analysis, 36 additional studies have been located. Since I decided to change the occupational classification for the present analysis from the 1960 United States Census classification to the ISCO, the original data had to be entirely recoded. By comparing the original and revised codings of the data used in the 1967 analysis, it is possible to get some sense of how robust the results of the analysis are under alternative coding schemes. The results are, indeed, robust. They are reported in detail later, particularly in Chapter 4.

In the 1967 analysis, I deliberately decided to make matches of occupations across countries as precise as possible. It seemed to me that one of the weaknesses of earlier studies, particularly the most notable of them (Inkeles and Rossi, 1956), was that the identification of matching occupations across countries was too crude.[14] In consequence, while it was possible to conclude generally that there is a high degree of intercountry similarity in prestige evaluations, it was not possible to make any valid statements about differences among countries in the *degree* of similarity. By restricting my matches to precisely equivalent occupational titles, I hoped to be able to analyze the *relative* degree of intercountry similarity. Indeed, the expectation was fulfilled, since I was able to show a modest correlation between intercountry similarity with respect to level to industrialization and intercountry similarity in occupational prestige evaluations.

However, this decision had its cost. Obviously, the more precise the requirement for matching occupational titles, the fewer the matches that can be made. As a result, many pairs of countries had almost no occupations in common. Hence, for the current analysis, I deliberately changed the procedure to reduce the number of discrete occupational categories. This involved not so much a change in criteria as a change in the way the criteria were applied. Two differences are particularly important.

First, modifying adjectives carrying status connotations typically were grouped into two classes for each occupation: positive modifiers and negative modifiers. Then, taking these together with titles not containing modifiers, three categories were formed—for example, "large farmer," "farmer," and "small farmer." More detailed status distinctions were not preserved.

Second, industry distinctions were not preserved. Thus, for example, salesclerks were matched across countries regardless of what they sold. This is a major source of reduction in the total number of separate occupations. Furthermore, subspecialities that are not recognized by the ISCO scheme were matched. Thus, for example, "mechanical engineer" and "aeronautical engineer" were matched, because they are both classified as mechanical engineers in the ISCO unit group classification. Similarly, "nuclear physicist" was matched with "physicist." To be sure, these decisions sometimes resulted in occupations that have somewhat different prestige being combined. For example, in the United States "aeronautical

---

[14] For example, Inkeles and Rossi (1956) matched "accountant for a large business" (U.S.) with "bookkeeper" (USSR); "bookkeeper" (USSR) with "company office clerk" (Japan); and the following with "machine operator in a factory" (U.S.): *maschinen-schlosser-geselle* (Germany); composite of "fitter," "carpenter," "bricklayer," "tractor driver," and "coal hewer" (Britain and New Zealand); "latheman" (Japan); and "rank-and-file worker" (USSR).

engineer" has a score of 71.1 while "mechanical engineer" has a score of 62.3. The United States' entry for the line "mechanical engineer" (the generic line) is then the mean of the two, or 66.7. Similarly, "clergyman" (71.8), "minister" (69.0), "priest" (73.2), and "rabbi" (68.0), are all combined under the generic title "clergyman" to make the United States' entry, with a score of 70.5 (the mean of the four). Although it makes little difference in this case, because the component scores are so similar, this procedure sometimes resulted in fairly large changes in prestige scores. Nonetheless, I felt it preferable to make such combinations in the interest of improving the ability to make cross-national comparisons, despite the loss of distinctions that are important for particular countries.[15] Obviously, the needs of the two sorts of analysis—single-country analysis versus cross-national comparisons—are not fully compatible. It might have been desirable, however, to take account of the relative representativeness of the occupations that happened to be rated and to combine them with a weighted mean. For instance, in the above example it might have been possible to weight the various clerical titles by the proportion of the American population adhering to each religious group. However, this possibility was rejected on the ground that it was unfeasible for foreign data since my knowledge of foreign situations was so limited that I would be as likely to err as not, to make distinctions where they were not warranted and to fail to make them when they were. Hence, a simple mechanical weighting procedure was adopted which, although crude, has the virtue of being simple and easily summarized.

The Basic Data Matrix.   To accomplish the matching task, occupational titles for each country were compared to the ISCO scheme and assigned a code. The obvious advantage of matching the titles for each country against a standard classification scheme rather than pair by pair (aside from the sheer impossibility of matching 1770 (= 60 × 59/2) pairs of occupation lists), is that the temptation to make inconsistent judgments in an attempt to capture nuances of differences among national occupational structures is precluded (recall footnote 14).

Although the highly arbitrary character of the coding procedure seemingly provided a great deal of leeway for biases of various kinds to creep in, the sheer magnitude and complexity of the coding task effectively minimized this possibility. There is no denying the subconscious temptation to resolve ambiguities in favor of one's hypothesis. However, in my case the

---

[15] Some indication of the magnitude of the distortion produced by this sort of collapsing can be gained by examining the titles in Appendix D, since both the scores of the component titles and the resulting category scores are shown.

TABLE 2.2

Illustrative Matches of Occupational Titles from Individual Countries to
the Standard Categories[a]

Standard Category	Standard Occupational Title	Matching Occupational Title(s)	Country
00131	Geologist	Nauchnyi rabotniki v oblasti: geologii	USSR
		Inzhener geolog	
00410	Airline Pilot	Airline pilot	Canada
00610	Physician	Médecin	Mauritania
00710	Professional Nurse, Nurse	Nurse (special certificate)	Indonesia (West Irian)
01101	Professional Accountant	Accountant for a large business	United States
01310	University Professor	University professor	Canada
01330	Teacher, Primary Teacher	Elementary school teacher	Israel
01410	Clergyman	Rabbijn	Netherlands
		Predikant	
		Pastoor	
		Geestelijke	
01590	Journalist	Newspaper reporter	Indonesia (Java)
01712	Musical Entertainer	Praise-singers and drummers	Nigeria (Kano)
01924	Social Scientist, nec	Nauchnyi rabotniki v oblasti:filosofii	USSR
02021	Member Upper House	Member of the U. S. Senate	United States
02111	Head of Large Firm	Fabrikbesitzer	Germany (West)
02116	Building Contractor	Building contractor	Canada
03101	Middle Rank Civil Servant	Wage-employed executive in government and agriculture	Grenada
		Government-employed executive	
03310	Bookkeeper	Bookkeeper	Israel
03700	Mail Carrier	Mailman	United States
		Mail carrier	
		Railway mail clerk	
03930	Office Clerk	Office employee in a large company	Japan
		Office employee in a private company	
		Office employee in a large spinning mill	
04100	Shop Keeper	Owner of a small grocery and parlour	Guyana
04210	Sales Manager	Commercial specialist, 4 years college	Yugoslavia
04510	Sales Clerk	Department store salesman	Japan
		Shop clerk	
		Supermarket sales clerk	
		Hardware store clerk	
		Salesman in a bookstore	
		Sales clerk in a green grocery	

Code	Title	Examples	Country
04521	Street Vendor, Peddler	Seller of fresh food in market place / Peddler with a cart / Food peddler	Thailand (Teachers' College Students)
05312	Cook's Helper	Buffet- en keukenpersoneel (behalve kok)	Netherlands
05510	Janitor	Janitor	Australia
05820	Policeman	Carabinero / Policeman	Chile
05990	Medical Attendant	Office nurse in a dentist's office / First aid nurse / Hospital attendant	United States
06111	Large Farmer	Grossbauer (100 Ha.)	Germany (West)
06210	Farm Hand	Farm labourer, established	Australia
07000	Foreman	Feitor ou capataz	Brazil (Açucena)
07540	Weaver	Weaver	India (Peasant)
07910	Tailor	Tailor with his own workshop	Poland
08340	Machine Operator in Factory	Machine operator in a factory	United States
08490	Mechanic, Repairman	Mechanic / Locomotive repairman / Air conditioning mechanic / Cash register repairman / Repairman / Operator of a fixit shop	United States
08710	Plumber	Plumber	Germany (West)
09290	Printing Worker, nec	Graphiste	Switzerland
09540	Carpenter	Carpenter	Puerto Rico
09712	Porter	Water-carrier	India (peasant)
09852	Taxi Driver	Taxi Driver	Southern Rhodesia
09950	Skilled Worker	Industrielfacharbeiter (z.b. schlosser, dreher usw.) / Gerlernter arbeiter	Germany (West)
09998	Road Construction Laborer	Roadworker	New Britain
13000	Lives off Stock - Bond Income	Someone who lives off stocks and bonds	United States

a Systematic 1% sample of titles. In cases where several titles from a country were combined to match one ISCO category, all titles are shown within a bracket.

effect of alternative coding decisions on the outcome of the analysis was never clear. Hence, I can be confident that my coding decisions have not even inadvertently or subconsciously biased my results. To provide the reader with a feel for the basic data, Table 2.2 presents the matches for a 1% systematic sample of the occupational titles appearing in the studies utilized here. From a list of titles ordered by their ISCO code numbers and alphabetically by country within the ISCO categories, every 100th title was selected. Titles are shown as they appeared in the original studies.

In the course of carrying out the matching task, I constructed a basic matrix consisting of 60 × 509 cells (509 being the total number of different occupations identified). Entries in the matrix consist of both the title and the prestige score for any occupation rated in any given country, and blanks otherwise; obviously, this procedure resulted in a matrix with a large number of blank cells. This basic data matrix was then prepared for processing by computer.

For the convenience of the reader interested in utilizing the prestige scores for specific occupations in particular countries, Appendix D presents the data for each of the 60 places included in the basic data set. The Appendix includes the code designating the ISCO category to which each title was matched, the exact wording of the title used in the rating task (if known), translation of the title into English, if necessary,[16] the prestige score of the title expressed in the metric of the United States' studies (the range of possible scores is approximately 0 to 100—see Chapter 8 for a description of the conversion procedure), and a score representing the deviation of the prestige rating in that place from the generic rating for the occupation (the Standard Scale score—see Chapters 8 and 9 for further discussion of these scores).

---

[16] Titles listed in the Appendix for each of the foreign studies are given exactly as published. This both enables the user to check for himself the quality of the matches and avoids the temptation to make the translation in such a way as to introduce more comparability between titles than existed in the original studies. In some cases studies were actually conducted in foreign languages, but are reported only in English. In such cases I am forced to present the English translations but recognize that they may not be as exact as my own translations. In any case where both English and foreign language versions of the occupational titles were provided by the original author, I utilized the language in which the questionnaire was actually administered to make the matches. In most cases involving foreign language titles (and in a few cases involving unfamiliar English language titles) I asked nationals from the countries in question (mostly graduate students at various American universities) to review my matching decisions. Moreover, in cases where nuances of meaning were ambiguous, I sought assistance from the staffs of foreign consulates located in New York City. No doubt, some errors of interpretation of foreign titles remain; I would appreciate being informed of them.

SUMMARY

This chapter has considered some of the problems entailed in the comparative study of occupational prestige systems. It was argued that the data generated by popular evaluations of the prestige of occupations are valid indicators of relative prestige in the classical sociological sense. Data from 60 societies were described and evaluated with respect to quality. It was shown that differences in rating procedures do not have much effect on the resulting ratings, making it possible to combine data from different studies where more than one study is available for a society. Finally, procedures for matching occupational titles across countries in order to compare prestige hierarchies were outlined. In the following chapter the remaining important methodological issue will be considered—can casual samples of raters be used to represent entire societies? If there is high societal consensus in prestige evaluations they can, but otherwise they cannot.

3

Intrasocietal Consensus in
Occupational Prestige Evaluations

One of the most striking features of occupational prestige systems in almost all societies is the lack of subgroup variation in prestige ratings. On the average, people in all walks of life, rich and poor, educated and ignorant, urban and rural, male and female, view the prestige hierarchy in the same way. With minor exceptions, there is extraordinary consensus throughout each society regarding the relative prestige of occupations. The prestige hierarchy appears to be a genuine Durkheimian social fact that exists independently of the particular values and attitudes of raters. Regardless of their views about what the prestige hierarchy ought to be, people are generally capable of reporting what it actually is. Those in low-prestige occupations correctly perceive their own low status and those in high-prestige occupations correctly perceive their own high status. Blacks perceive the same hierarchy as whites despite their severely disadvantaged position, and women perceive the same hierarchy as men.

This, of course, need not be so. Other sorts of prestige evaluations do not display such consensus. For example, ratings of the prestige of 20 religious denominations in the United States conform to a "social distance" rather than a "prestige" model. Raters tend to accord the highest prestige to their own religion and the least prestige to religions that are theologically and organizationally farthest removed from their own.[1] The contrast between the consensus that characterizes occupational prestige evaluations and the lack of consensus that characterizes the evaluation of other social categories is striking and serves to bolster a conception of occupational prestige

---

[1] Unpublished analysis of data from a 1964 National Opinion Research Center survey conducted in conjunction with the project "Occupations and Social Stratification."

ratings as peculiarly collective perceptions of social reality rather than expressions of personal values. In this conception, occupations *have* prestige and people learn the prestige hierarchy along with the other lore and knowledge they acquire as part of their socialization to adult roles. As I argued in the first chapter, the prestige of occupations is rooted in the structure of relationships of power and privilege that arises from the division of labor. These relationships produce a society-wide system of evaluations of occupations, which are known more or less well by every fully socialized member of society.

Of course, all individuals need not and do not share identical perceptions of the prestige hierarchy. There is, indeed, a relatively large idiosyncratic component in the prestige ratings made by each individual, so that the typical correlation in the ratings made by any pair of individuals is about .6. The point is that differences in perceptions of the prestige hierarchy are not socially structured; it is very hard to find systematic differences among subgroups of the population with respect to the way they hierarchically order occupations. While it is possible to locate isolated instances of differences in the evaluation of particular occupations, these exceptional cases are too few to seriously discredit the claim of near-perfect consensus across population subgroups in the prestige evaluation of occupations.

This chapter will review the evidence supporting the claim of intrasocietal consensus in occupational prestige evaluations. I will show that prestige judgments are not importantly affected by the occupational status, ethnic status, or sex of raters, either in the United States or in other societies. Furthermore I will show that prestige ratings by students in nonindustrialized countries are not particularly deviant and are no more Western than ratings by nonstudents, which means that it is valid to use data from student samples to estimate the prestige hierarchies of countries for which no better data are available. Finally, I will show that the prestige hierarchy tends to be extremely stable over time, even in countries undergoing rapid industrialization or other social change. Thus we need not be concerned about the fact that the available data span nearly a quarter of a century; they can be taken as representing the range of societies in the contemporary world.

The one exception to the pattern of consensus in prestige evaluations within each society is that within some—but by no means all—nonindustrialized countries, geographically distinct groups differ enough to warrant treatment as different populations (recall from Chapter 2 that the criterion for combining several studies from a single country was that the correlation between prestige ratings be at least .95). Not surprisingly, the level of sociocultural integration of some nonindustrialized countries is rather low, and it is probably reasonable to regard them as composed of several societies connected only by an overarching polity.

SUBGROUP VARIATIONS IN PRESTIGE RATINGS

Occupation of Raters. One of the most striking manifestations of societal consensus in prestige evaluations is the lack of variation in the ratings made by different occupational subgroups; for if any single characteristic could be expected to influence the way individuals perceive the occupational hierarchy, it is the sort of work they do. Not only does one's occupational position structure exposure to the patterns of deference and derogation that are manifest in prestige evaluations, but occupational groups are uniquely the objects of their own prestige perceptions. It would thus not be surprising to find that individuals perceive their own occupations more favorably than others do, a propensity for self-aggrandizement being an apparently universal aspect of the human condition. However, they do not, or at least not to any appreciable degree. In the United States, prestige ratings of "my family's main earner" average only about 3 points (about one standard error) higher than ratings of the actual occupations of family heads. And in Denmark (Svalastoga, 1959:105), ratings of 11 occupations by incumbents or others with very similar occupations are only a little higher than ratings of these occupations by those with dissimilar occupations (the largest differences, involving ratings of the title "agricultural laborer" by incumbents and by other male raters, is less than a third of a point on a 5-point scale).

Nor are perceptions of the occupational hierarchy as a whole importantly structured by the occupational position of raters. When respondents to the 1963 NORC survey are divided into four categories (upper white-collar, lower white-collar, upper blue-collar, and lower blue-collar)[2] on the basis of their own (or their main earner's) occupation—and correlations are computed between the average ratings accorded by each of these groups to 49 white-collar occupations, the lowest correlation is .973; and when corresponding correlations are computed for 30 blue-collar titles, the lowest correlation is .968.[3]

However, when finer distinctions are made among groups of raters, slightly larger differences emerge between extreme groups, although the

---

[2] Unpublished tabulations provided by Paul M. Siegel. Unfortunately, no information was available for respondents who were farmers. Unless otherwise indicated, the subgroup correlations reported here and below either appeared in the publications cited in the notes to Table 2.1 or were computed by me from these sources.

[3] Although the rank order of occupations appears substantially invariant across subgroups of raters, some tendency exists for people to make finer distinctions regarding occupations immediately surrounding their own, and to compress the scores accorded occupations differing substantially from theirs. Different people seem to use the scale of social standing in different ways—much as if it were a "rubber ladder" in which one part could be expanded and another part compressed (cf. Hodge and Siegel, 1965).

average intergroup correlation is virtually as high. Correlations of average prestige ratings of 200 occupations made by each of 9 major occupation groups in 1964 (all but farm laborers, for which there were too few cases to analyze) drop as low as .90 (between farmers and professionals), although the average intergroup correlation is .96. When these groups of raters are arranged in order of their own socioeconomic status, intergroup correlations decrease consistently as a function of the socioeconomic distance between groups. Hence, there may be small but real differences in the prestige evaluation of occupations by various occupational groups in the United States. However, they are not large enough to vitiate the basic conclusion of overwhelming intrasocietal consensus regarding the prestige evaluation of occupations. This is especially true considering that it proves impossible to detect any systematic differences in the evaluation of particular occupations by different subgroups; the deviation from perfect consensus appears rather to be the product of a large number of small and random differences.

For other Western countries a similar pattern emerges. In a large representative sample of the Danish population, the lowest intergroup correlations between mean prestige ratings of 75 occupations made by male raters grouped on the basis of occupation into 11 categories are .96 (between academic professionals and, respectively, small holders and rural laborers). Prestige scores for subgroups of raters divided on the basis of occupation are available for Argentina, Australia, and Spain; for Holland, scores are available for three socioeconomic groups. In no case is the correlation between ratings made by different occupational or socioeconomic status groups lower than .95, indicating that for these countries substantial agreement exists in the perception of the occupational hierarchy regardless of where people are located in it.

Thus far, we have considered evidence only from relatively urbanized and industrially developed countries. One might suppose that consensus across subgroups would not be so striking in less developed countries, since in such countries communication among different sectors of the population is generally less extensive. This, however, appears not to be the case. Data from four countries—the Philippines, Guyana, Zambia, and the Congo (Zaire)—exhibit consensus across occupational groups as high or nearly as high as in countries with well-developed mass communication systems and mass cultures. The most complete data come from Tiryakian's study in the Philippines. Tiryakian (1958) collected information from 566 respondents drawn from a suburb of Manila and 4 rural communities located within 100 miles of Manila. Many of his rural respondents were illiterate and were asked to order according to their prestige a set of pictures depicting occupational tasks. Tiryakian divided his sample into 10 occupational groups and computed rank correlations over the 30 occupational titles in his study. The lowest correlation between any two occupational groups was .92, and the average correlation for the 45 pairs was .96.

Although the differences are hardly overwhelming, the greatest lack of consensus in the evaluation of occupations seems to be between farmers and other sectors of the population. In the Philippines, omitting correlations involving ratings by farmers increases the lowest correlation from .92 to .96.[4] Similar observations can be made for the American, Danish, and Spanish data: Omitting correlations involving respondents in farming occupations increases the size of the lowest correlation from .90 to .93 for the United States, from .96 to .97 for Denmark, and from .968 to .974 for Spain.

The remaining data for nonindustrialized societies are all from urban areas. They also show high agreement among different occupational groups. The data for Guyana, drawn from a representative sample of the population of Greater Georgetown, the nation's capital, are unusually good. Prestige ratings of 40 occupations were available for 5 groups of raters but I combined Groups I and II into a general category of professionals and managers because there were only 8 Group I respondents. The lowest correlation between these groups was .98, between the professional–managerial group and the unskilled laboring group.

A 1959 Zambian study includes prestige ratings of 42 occupations open to Africans by "advancees" in the copper mines (highly skilled African mine workers with long seniority who had moved into mining jobs formerly restricted to Europeans) and raw recruits to the mines who were mostly illiterate and being trained for unskilled jobs. The correlation between ratings made by these two groups is .90, which is low as such correlations go. However, this may simply reflect the fact that the mine recruits were still ignorant of the nature and function of many of the jobs they were asked to rate; it is possible that their departure from the evaluations made by advancees represented not a difference in the evaluation of jobs, but simply error about what the social evaluation of jobs was. This should give rise to larger variances in the ratings made by recruits than by advancees. Unfortunately we do not have the data with which to assess this possibility. However, we can observe that there was considerably more agreement in the ratings of advancees and secondary school students ($r = .96$) than between the recruits and either of the other two groups.

One final example will complete our survey of occupational subgroup variation in prestige evaluations. In 1955, Xydias obtained prestige rankings for 12 occupations from three groups of adult males working in Kisangi

---

[4] In making this comparison, "laborers (including farm)" was counted as a farm category.

(Stanleyville), Congo—clerks, drivers, and unskilled laborers—by having them order a set of pictures of people performing these occupations. She reports rank order correlations between each of these groups. While these correlations tend to be somewhat lower than those reported above for other countries, they still indicate a relatively high degree of intergroup consensus. The matrix of correlations is given here:

	Drivers	Laborers
Clerks	.93	.79
Drivers		.87

Obviously, laborers show the greatest deviation from the other groups. Inspection of the raw data suggests that this deviation stems from the fact that laborers rank skilled manual occupations higher than do other groups; however, when so few occupations are rated, a difference in the rank of a single occupation can have a substantial effect on the size of the correlation, so these data should be treated with caution.

In sum, there appears to be substantial consensus in the evaluation of occupations by respondents who differ in their own occupational position, not only in industrially developed countries but in nonindustrialized countries as well, although the degree of agreement is somewhat less in two African societies than elsewhere and is slightly less for farmers than for other occupational groups. The data reviewed in support of these conclusions are summarized in Table 3.1.

Ethnicity of Raters. Another possible source of variation in prestige evaluations is ethnic group membership. In many countries ethnic groups differ substantially in their social and geographic distribution, and such differences are often associated with variations in occupational experience. Ethnic restrictions on pariah occupations provide an obvious case,[5] but the phenomenon is far more general. In many multiethnic societies there is occupational specialization by ethnicity, ranging from a division between farming and shopkeeping activities to quite complex patterns of monopolization of specific crafts. Moreover, some countries, such as Canada and Belgium, are split by ethnic frictions that have their roots in intergroup competition and attendant feelings of resentment about differential occupational opportunities (Lieberson, 1970). As a consequence of the different occupational experiences of members of various ethnic groups and resulting differences in perception of occupational opportunities, we

[5] Indeed, the word *pariah* is from the Tamil for "hereditary drummer" and initially referred to one of the low castes of Southern India that was associated with that occupation (Onions, 1955:1433).

TABLE 3.1

Summary of Correlations between Prestige Ratings by Occupational Subgroups within Countries

	Average Correlation	Lowest Correlation	Pair with Lowest Correlation	Number of Subgroups	Number of Occupations Rated
Industrialized countries					
U.S. 1963					
white–collar occupations	.98	.97	Upper white-collar – lower blue-collar	4	49
blue–collar occupations	.98	.97	Upper white-collar – lower blue-collar	4	30
U.S. 1964[a]	.96	.90	Professionals – farmers	9	200
Argentina[a]	.96	.95	Liberal professionals – skilled workers	4	30
Australia[a]	.99	.99	Group A (highest prestige) – Group D (lowest prestige)	4	134
Denmark	.98	.96	Academic professionals – {small holders {rural laborers	11	75
Netherlands[a]	.99	.99	High SES – low SES[b]	3	57
Spain	.97	.97	Nonmanual – peasant	3	39
Nonindustrialized countries					
Congo[a]	.86	.79	Clerks – unskilled laborers	3	12
Guyana	.98	.98	Group 1 (professional and managerial) – Group 5 (unskilled labor)	14	40
Philippines[a]	.96	.92	Farm tenants – managers; shop keepers and clerical – sales; laborers – managers	10	30
Zambia	.90	.90	Mine "advancees" – mine recruits	2	42

[a] Rank order correlations.

[b] SES = socioeconomic status.

might well expect relatively low interethnic consensus in occupational prestige evaluations. This, however, is not the case. Just as with occupational group membership, there are no important ethnic group differences in occupational evaluations for any of the places for which data are available. The correlation between ratings made by French and English Canadians is .95 and that between Flemish- and French-speaking Belgians is also .95. Thus, even in situations where considerable cleavage develops regarding political–economic issues, consensus in the evaluation of occupations is unaffected. Siegel (1970), in an analysis of racial differences in occupational prestige evaluations in the United States, found a correlation of .95 between ratings by whites and by blacks. He went on to consider whether the two racial groups use different criteria in making their prestige evaluations, but rejected this possibility on the basis of an analysis of the relationship of prestige to other characteristics of occupations. Data for Puerto Rico yield similar results: correlations between ratings by whites, blacks, and mulattoes all exceed .95. Czechoslovak ratings of the "ideal income" of 30 occupations likewise exhibit almost no ethnic differentiation: the correlation between the mean ratings made by representative samples of Czechs and Slovaks is .99. Finally, data for South-West Africa, a country with very sharp traditional ethnic divisions, show nearly the same degree of consensus: correlations between ratings of 40 occupations by members of 5 ethnic groups are never lower than .93. Hence, in sum, there seems to be no basis for expecting any bias in occupational evaluations as a result of the ethnic group membership of raters.[6]

Sex of Raters. There are two reasons for suspecting that women perceive the occupational prestige hierarchy differently from men. First, in almost all societies women have a weaker attachment to the labor force

---

[6] There is, however, one piece of evidence that seemingly contradicts the conclusion of interethnic consensus in occupational evaluations. This is a Zambian study that presents ratings of 118 occupations made by 25 African and 33 European third formers in a multiracial secondary school in 1965 (Hicks, 1967:208–211). The rank order correlation between the mean ratings of the two groups is only .80, which is substantially lower than any of the correlations reported above. However, there are several factors that tend to invalidate conclusions based on this data set. First, the occupations were deliberately chosen to induce maximum ethnic differentiation in ratings. Second, the number of raters was very small, leading to large sampling error. Third, the third form in the Zambian school system corresponds roughly to our ninth grade; hence raters were, by and large, young adolescents and may not yet have formed completely adult perceptions of the occupational structure. For these reasons this study was excluded from the basic data set when it failed to meet the criterion required for merger with the main Zambian study. For the same reasons the lack of consensus between African and European raters reported by Hicks cannot be regarded as particularly damaging to the basic claim of interethnic consensus in occupational evaluations.

than do men. They work less outside the home and are less exposed to the full panoply of occupations. Hence, they might be expected to know less about occupations and have greater difficulty making prestige judgments at all. To the extent this is true, it should be manifest in higher percentages of "don't know" responses by female than by male raters and also a tendency on the part of women to put less variance into their ratings than do males. Second, the fact that in most societies occupational opportunities for women are restricted to a relatively small number of jobs could result in an upgrading of "women's work" by women and a downgrading of such jobs by men, producing nontrivial differences in the evaluation of particular jobs by male and female raters.

Despite these theoretical expectations, the sex of raters has virtually no effect on ratings in any society for which pertinent data are available. First, in the United States at least, women are as willing to rate occupations as are men (Reiss, 1961:13–14, 196) and give as wide a range of ratings as men (Bose, 1973:50). Second, the correlations between the mean ratings by men and women are near unity in both industrialized and nonindustrialized societies. In the United States, the correlation is .98 (Reiss, 1961:189); in Denmark it is .99; both in the Philippines and in Zambia (Hicks, 1969) the rank correlation is .98; and in South-West Africa the correlation is .94. The relatively lower correlation in South-West Africa may be due to the slightly greater tendency for men than for women to downgrade male incumbents of traditionally female service occupations (recall the discussion in the previous chapter). But the overall pattern is one of striking agreement between men and women in their perceptions of the relative prestige of occupations. Indeed, in Denmark the correlation between the standard deviations of male and female ratings is .82.

In sum, occupational prestige evaluations are not importantly structured by occupational position, ethnic group membership, or sex, despite the relationship of these factors to differential life chances. There is, however, one group that requires special consideration because of its unique position in the social structure of all societies, but especially in that of developing societies. This is the student group.

HOW REPRESENTATIVE ARE STUDENTS IN THEIR OCCUPATIONAL EVALUATIONS?

In societies such as the United States, where most of the population gets at least a secondary education, we would expect students to perceive the occupational prestige structure in the same way as the general population does. And indeed they do. By early adolescence, children in the United

States have acquired adult prestige perceptions (Simmons, 1962: Table 5; Gunn, 1964) and high school students are indistinguishable from adults in their occupational evaluations (Siegel *et al.*, 1974:Table 5.2). This also appears to be true for Brazil (São Paulo), Chile, Germany, Great Britain, Japan, the Netherlands, Norway, the Philippines, and Poland, since for all of these places it was possible to combine prestige data from student and nonstudent samples (recall that the criterion for combining data sets is a correlation of at least .95).

However, in nonindustrialized countries one cannot assume that students are similar to nonstudents in their prestige perceptions. First, educational opportunities are generally very limited in such places so that only a small fraction of the population obtains secondary schooling. Hence, secondary students must be regarded as constituting the incipient elites of their countries. Second, in many nonindustrialized countries higher education (including secondary schooling) follows a Western model. Often the teachers are Europeans or are locals who have gone abroad for their own advanced schooling. Hence, the norms and values imparted along with instruction may promote a pattern of occupational evaluation that is more similar to that of the industrialized nations of the West than is that of the remainder of the population. Insofar as this is true, the use of prestige ratings by students to represent the prestige hierarchies of nonindustrialized societies may result in an overstatement of the degree of worldwide similarity in prestige evaluations.

Fortunately, the available evidence suggests that the "Western bias" of student prestige evaluations, insofar as it exists at all, is rather small. If we regard the United States as epitomizing advanced industrial societies, we can use the degree of agreement with United States' prestige ratings as a measure of bias toward prestige perceptions of industrialized Western societies. If such bias exists, the prestige ratings of students should be more similar to American prestige ratings than are the ratings of nonstudents from the same societies. Table 3.2 presents pertinent data for four societies: the Congo, Nigeria (Kano), Spain, and Zambia. The Nigerian data are particularly valuable because they were designed explicitly to address the issue that concerns us here. The data are from an area probability sample of 17-year-old boys in Kano, a traditional Moslem city in Northern Nigeria. Prestige rankings of 16 occupations are available for three groups of raters: those with no formal schooling, those with primary schooling only, and those with at least some secondary schooling. For the 13 occupations that could be matched, the correlations with United States' ratings are uniformly low, but the secondary school students are only a little more like Americans in their prestige perceptions than are those with no schooling at all, and those with primary education are least like Americans. Thus, there

TABLE 3.2

Similarity to the U.S. in Prestige Ratings by Students and
Various Occupational Groups, for Selected Countries

Country and Subgroups	Correlation with U. S.	Number of Raters
Congo (males in Stanleyville; 11 occupations)		
Unskilled laborers	.37	41
Drivers	.55	41
Clerks	.60	33
Secondary and technical students	.62	72
Nigeria (Kano) (representative sample of 17 year-old boys; 13 occupations)		
No schooling	.66	312
Primary school only	.61	210
Some secondary school	.70	69
Spain (representative sample of youth age 16 – 21; 32 occupations)		
Peasants	.74	--[a]
Manual workers	.80	--[a]
Nonmanual workers	.80	--[a]
Students	.81	--[a]
Zambia (Copperbelt towns; 25 occupations)		
Mine recruits	.82	96
Mine "advancees"	.91	55
Secondary students	.90	147

[a]Not available.

is virtually no evidence in the Nigerian data for a Western bias in the prestige evaluations of secondary school students.

The other three data sets include ratings by secondary school students and members of various occupational groups. All three show a similar pattern: Students are similar to most, but not all, of the occupational groups in the extent of their agreement with American prestige evaluations. In each case the lowest-status occupational group exhibits substantially less similarity to the United States' evaluations than the students or the other groups. But even here caution is in order. The Congolese correlations are based on 11 occupations, so minor fluctuations in rankings can have large effects on the size of the correlations. And in the Zambian case, as was pointed out above, the mine recruits were largely new arrivals in the Copperbelt who may not yet have learned the prestige structure of the mining area.

But even accepting the validity of these occupational differences, the data provide striking evidence of consensus in the prestige perceptions of students and nonstudents within each society. First, the correlations between the prestige ratings of students and nonstudents are, with three exceptions, all above .96. The exceptions are the correlation between those with no education and those with primary or secondary education in Kano (.92); the correlation between students and unskilled laborers in the Congo (.86); and the correlation between students and mine recruits in Zambia (.92). Second, there is almost no overlap between countries in the degree of prestige similarity to the United States displayed by various subgroups. The conclusion that the Congo, Nigeria (Kano), Spain, and Zambia display increasingly great similarity to the United States would, with a single minor exception, hold regardless of which subgroup was used to represent the prestige hierarchy of each country. The differences between countries in the degree of prestige similarity to the United States are much larger than the differences among subgroups within each country.

Taken together, these results give us considerable confidence that the use of student samples, or for that matter other samples of unrepresentative population groups, will not seriously distort conclusions regarding the extent of cross-cultural similarity in occupational prestige evaluations.

URBAN–RURAL AND REGIONAL VARIATIONS

Thus far our examination of subgroup variations in occupational prestige ratings has been restricted to comparisons of groups residing together and participating in or at least exposed to a common occupational structure.

The consequence, as we have seen, is consensus regarding the relative prestige of the occupations forming that structure. Now we must consider whether the same consensus holds for people living in different places within particular countries. Because of differences in the kinds of work done in large cities, small towns, and rural areas, people from these places might be expected to be familiar with different kinds of jobs and hence to acquire different perceptions of their social standing. Moreover, many nonindustrialized countries cannot be thought of as having national cultures. Given the limited amount of geographical mobility and the absence of an effective system of mass communications that often characterizes such countries, regional differences of all sorts are likely to be more pronounced than in highly industrialized countries. In consequence, local differences in occupational prestige evaluations may be greater in such countries than in more industrialized nations. Recall that even in industrialized countries, farmers were more deviant in their occupational evaluations than any other group.

In industrialized countries, the prestige hiearchy is essentially invariant across places of different size. For the United States, Denmark, Germany, Japan, and the Netherlands, prestige scores are available for respondents living in different-size places,[7] and for none of these countries does any correlation between size-of-place groups fall below .96.[8]

The evidence for nonindustrialized countries is somewhat less consistent.

[7] Sources: for the United States, Reiss, 1961:189, Table VIII.1; for Denmark, Svalastoga, 1959:91; for Germany, computed from Bolte, 1959:42, Table 5 and 1959:58, Table 10; for Japan, computed from Nisihira, 1968:549, Table 1, and Ramsey and Smith, 1960:477; for the Netherlands, van Heek and Vercruijsse, 1958:37–38, Table 12.

[8] For Japan, however, there is one body of data that appears to refute the notion that prestige evaluations are similar in rural areas, small towns, and large cities. Haller and Lewis (1966) administered a questionnaire containing 80 of the 90 NORC titles to Japanese schoolboys living in 5 communities ranging from 250,000 inhabitants to fewer than 6500. They found a systematic inverse relationship between the proportion of the population engaged in agriculture and the size of the rank order correlation with the 1947 NORC scores. However, at least two factors substantially weaken the credibility of this result. First, the three correlations for the rural communities—and it is these three correlations that establish the relationship—are all based on an extremely small number of junior high school boys (N = 23, 39, and 24, respectively). Hence, just as was argued in footnote 6, it is quite possible that these small correlations (−.4, .48, and .52, respectively) are simply a reflection of the unstable occupational views of children and have little or nothing to do with the fact that they live in rural areas. Of course, rural children might learn the national prestige hierarchy more slowly than urban children, but there is· no reason to believe that adults in rural areas view occupations differently from adults in urban areas. My suspicion about these data is strengthened by the fact that even in the most urban community, the correlation between the schoolboy ratings and the NORC ratings was only .84, which is substantially lower than the correlation of .93 between the ratings made by a representative sample of the Japanese population and a representative American sample, reported in the following chapter.

Two such countries exhibit a high degree of consensus between urban and rural raters or between raters from different parts of the country, while five do not, and the evidence for India is internally inconsistent (see footnote 9).

In both the Philippines and Puerto Rico, place of residence appears to have little effect on occupational evaluations: The rank order correlations between ratings by urban and rural respondents for the two places are, respectively, .96 and .95. However, it could be argued that these two countries do not provide an adequate test of the hypothesis of invariance in occupational ratings across geographic locales because the rural raters have too much exposure to urban experiences: Puerto Rico is a relatively small island (approximately 40 by 110 miles) and the Philippine sample was drawn from villages all located within 100 miles of Manila. This makes it particularly important to examine additional evidence.

For five nonindustrialized countries (Brazil, India, Indonesia, Nigeria, and Thailand), prestige ratings by different samples of raters proved different enough to require treating them as representing different populations. Table 3.3 gives the intercorrelations among ratings by the various groups within each country as well as correlations between each group and the United States. Two main conclusions may be drawn from these data.

First, the degree of consensus within these countries is on the whole rather low, suggesting that nonindustrialized countries should not be regarded as integrated societies. However, most of the very low correlations are based on an extremely small number of cases, which casts considerable doubt on the validity of these correlations. This is especially true considering that the Thai data yield a rather different conclusion. This study, which involved the evaluation of over 100 occupations chosen to match the categories of the Thai census of 1960, includes ratings by all the adult residents of an isolated rural village in Northeastern Thailand, by students at a provincial teacher's college in northeastern Thailand, and by students at Chulalongkorn University in Bangkok, the leading university in the country. Since we have already seen that student ratings can legitimately be taken as representative of the general population of a locale, we may regard these data as representing ratings by rural, town, and metropolitan populations. The correlation between the rural and metropolitan raters (the peasants and university students) is .86, which is low by the standards of industrialized societies, but considerably higher than the urban–rural correlations for Brazil, India, and Indonesia. Because of the superior quality of the Thai data, the Thai correlation should probably be regarded as the best estimate of the actual level of agreement between urban and rural areas in nonindustrialized countries.

Second, there is a slight tendency for more urban areas to exhibit greater similarity to the United States than less urban places in the same country.

TABLE 3.3
Intergroup Correlations and Similarity to
the U.S. in Prestige Ratings by Geographic Subgroups
for Countries Lacking National Consensus[a]

Country and Subgroups[b]	Intergroup Correlations		Similarity with U.S.
Brazil	B	S	
Açucena	.93(67)	.57(11)	.82(53)
Bezerros		.85(14)	.88(57)
São Paulo			.86(26)
India		U	
Villagers		.62(10)	.19(24)
University Students (Bombay)			.93(27)
Indonesia		B	
West Irian		.61(10)	.78(23)
Bandung, Java			.85(33)
Nigeria		K	
Bornu		.90(10)	.74(30)
Kano			.74(13)
Thailand	T.C.	U	
Peasants (northeast village)	.92(103)	.86(103)	.80(78)
Provincial Teachers' College Students		.94(103)	.84(78)
University Students (Bangkok)			.85(78)

[a] Number of matching occupations for each correlation given in parentheses.

[b] For each country, subgroups are arranged in order of increasing urbanization.

But, with the exception of India,[9] these differences are not large. Thus, they permit some confidence that the use of urban samples from nonindustrialized countries will not seriously overstate the degree of prestige similarity among the nations of the world.

VARIATION OVER TIME

Having established that the degree of consensus among different population groups is sufficient to permit the use of data from nonrepresentative samples for cross-national comparisons, one further task remains. We must show that prestige hierarchies remain stable over time. The data at our disposal cover a quarter of a century, dating from the end of the Second World War. Thus, if the prestige hierarchies of individual countries changed sharply in the short run, the use of such data to characterize prestige evaluations in the contemporary world would be questionable. Fortunately, systems of occupational prestige evaluations appear to be remarkably persistent over time. Wherever prestige data are available for two or more periods, the prestige hierarchy appears to be virtually unchanged. In the United States, the correlation between prestige ratings of 29 occupations in 1925 and 1963 is .94 (Hodge *et al.,* 1964); in the Netherlands the correlation between ratings of 24 titles in 1942 and 1952 is .94; and in Japan the correlation between 1952 and 1964 ratings of 23 titles is .98.

But less stability might be expected in societies undergoing rapid social change, especially change that affects the class structure, such as the communist revolutions of Eastern Europe or the achievement of independence in African countries. We have data from one country, Zambia, with which to assess this possibility. Zambia (formerly Northern Rhodesia) was com-

---

[9] The Indian data are something of an anomaly. The village data are an amalgam of prestige ratings from four villages located in widely varying parts of India. In each case, all the occupations practiced in the village were evaluated. Although the number of occupations being rated in each village was rather small, it was possible to match titles between the village with the largest number of occupations and each of the others; in each case a correlation of at least .95 was obtained between matching titles, which provides some evidence for similarity in occupational prestige evaluations throughout village India. The low correlation with the United States is mainly due to the fact that all agricultural occupations were rated above all nonagricultural occupations; this, apparently, represents a genuine difference between the rural Indian prestige hierarchy and that of the rest of the world. On the other hand, the Indian student ratings probably overstate the extent to which urban Indians are similar to Americans in their occupational evaluations. Not only are university students a far more elite group than the secondary students from whom ratings are available in most nonindustrialized countries, but Bombay University is a Catholic institution, which makes it particularly deviant and particularly Western in the Indian context.

pletely dominated by a white minority until the 1950s, when Africans began, in a limited way, to move into skilled manual jobs formerly reserved for whites. But until independence, in 1964, Africans continued to be denied access to most professional and managerial jobs and to many other occupations as well. With independence, the entire occupational structure opened up to the African population. In light of this, it is instructive to compare prestige ratings made in 1954 and 1967. In preindependence British Africa, it is asserted (Hicks, 1967), clerical positions were particularly highly regarded because (*1*) they required literacy, (*2*) they were situated close to the center of power occupied by the British, and (*3*) they were the highest positions open to Africans. Manual occupations, by contrast, paid very poorly and were very poorly regarded. After independence, however, professional and managerial positions became open to Africans, which might have been expected to downgrade the prestige of routine clerical workers. Also, the pay of skilled manual workers, especially mine workers, improved enormously as a consequence both of independence and of the rise in copper prices in 1965 (Beveridge, 1974). Hence, we might expect an upward shift in the prestige of skilled manual workers and a downward shift in the prestige of routine nonmanual workers between 1954 and 1967. Unfortunately, the available data are not really adequate to support a serious investigation of this hypothesis, since only nine occupations match between the two studies available for these years, surveys of secondary students training for both manual and nonmanual jobs (Mitchell and Epstein, 1959; Hicks, 1969). There are two matches involving routine clerical workers, and these are only approximate ("typist" with "clerical assistant" and "office messenger" with "office orderly"). In the first case, prestige appears to have dropped substantially since independence, but in the second case it rose substantially.[10] Similarly, the prestige of two matching skilled manual occupations, "garage mechanic" and "bricklayer," moved in opposite directions over the period. (The data are shown in Table 3.4.) Overall, the correlation between the two years is rather low as such correlations go—.88—but this is probably more a reflection of unreliability of the data than of systematic social change.

Actually, the data are interesting mainly for the vivid sense they give of the process by which occupational structures change while prestige hierarchies remain constant. A principal thesis of this book is that the *relative* prestige of occupations is essentially constant wherever the occupations are found. New occupations enter the prestige hierarchy at a level appropriate

---

[10] Scores are given in the 1954 metric. The 1967 scores were converted to the 1954 metric by regressing the 1954 scores on the 1967 scores for the nine occupations rated in common and using the resulting equation as a conversion equation.

TABLE 3.4
Zambian Student Occupational Prestige Ratings
before and after Independence[a]

Occupation Title[b]	Mean prestige[c]	
	1954	1967[d]
Scientist	--	5.27
Engineer	--	5.18
Cabinet minister	--	5.08
Lawyer	--	4.99
Medical doctor	--	4.89
African education officer	4.82	--
Technician (engineer)	--	4.79
Secondary school teacher/Teacher (secondary)	4.53	4.70
Technician (scientific)	--	4.60
Electrician	--	4.51
Headmaster	4.48	--
African police inspector	4.46	--
Administrative officer	--	4.41
African welfare officer	4.37	--
Agricultural officer	--	4.32
African minister of religion/Clergyman	4.48	4.12
Medical orderly	--	4.28
Trade union branch secretary	4.22	--
Political assistant	--	4.22
Senior clerk (mines)	4.09	--
Senior clerk (government)	4.06	--
Accountant	--	3.98
Technical assistant (agriculture)	--	3.98
Railway fireman	--	3.84
Carpenter	3.78	--
Primary school teacher/Teacher (primary)	3.80	3.64
Garage mechanic/garage mechanic	3.31	3.74
African constable/Police constable	3.40	3.55
Tribal chief	--	3.45
Typist/Clerical assistant	3.57	3.17
Bookkeeper	--	3.36
Crop demonstrator	--	3.26
Bricklayer/Bricklayer	3.48	2.97
Plumber	3.22	--
Contractor's capitão	3.22	--
Boss boy (mines)	3.20	--
Shop assistant	--	3.07
Painter	2.98	--
Lorry driver	2.97	--
Medicine man	--	2.78
Boma messenger	2.73	--
Machine boy	2.72	--
African dancer	--	2.69
Office messenger/Office orderly	2.32	2.88
Hunter	--	2.59
Building laborer	--	2.50
Domestic servant/Domestic servant	2.29	2.40
Farm laborer	--	2.30
Hotel waiter	2.21	--
Station boy	2.20	--
Petrol pump boy	1.90	--
Wood cutter	1.90	--

TABLE 3.4 (*Continued*)

| Occupation Title[b] | Mean prestige[c] | |
	1954	1967[d]
Garden boy	1.36	--
Scavenger	1.31	--

[a]Sources: 1954 ratings, Mitchell and Epstein, 1959; 1967 ratings, Hicks, 1969.

[b]Where two titles are shown the first is from the 1954 study and the second from the 1967 study.

[c]Occupations are listed in order of their prestige. Occupations rated in both years are located on the basis of the average of the two scores.

[d]Scores are shown in the 1954 metric. A conversion equation was derived by regressing the 1954 scores on the 1967 scores for the nine occupations rated in common.

to their position in the division of labor and once in it hardly change their prestige position. Occupations become obsolete and drop from the occupational structure, leaving the relative positions of the remaining occupations unchanged. Table 3.4 illustrates such a process, at least if we can assume that the occupations appearing in the 1954 and 1967 prestige studies represent the range of occupations extant at each date. In 1954 hardly any professional occupations were open to Africans, whereas extremely servile occupations were well represented, as they constituted an important part of the labor force. By 1967 the situation had changed; many professional occupations were included in the prestige study and relatively few service occupations. The result is that the 1967 prestige structure includes five occupations with higher prestige than any of those rated in 1954 while the 1954 prestige structure includes six occupations lower than any of those rated in 1967.[11] It is not that the existing structure shifted in any systematic way, but

[11] It must be recognized that this assertion rests on the assumption that the *absolute* prestige of occupations existing in both 1954 and 1967 did not, on the average, change during this period; such an assumption is implicit in the regression procedure used to relate the two sets of scores. An alternative conception would be to regard the maximum prestige level as fixed and hence to consider the prestige of an "African education officer" in 1954 to be the same as that of a "scientist" in 1967. In this case we would have to regard the prestige of all occupations rated in both 1954 and 1967 as having dropped during the intervening period. Considering that independence created opportunities for Africans in jobs previously reserved for Europeans, it is much more plausible to regard absolute prestige levels as constant and the structure of occupational opportunities as changing.

simply that new occupations assumed their natural place in the 1967 hierarchy. All in all, the data in Table 3.4 appear to represent a single hierarchy, but one in which some new occupations were added and some old ones eliminated in the transition from Northern Rhodesia to Zambia.

SUMMARY

Our review of the evidence regarding subgroup variations in prestige evaluations has shown remarkable internal consensus within almost all societies: Prestige ratings are apparently not systematically affected by the rater's occupation, ethnicity, or sex. In particular, students are no different from other groups in their occupational evaluations, so we can now lay to rest the old bugaboo about student samples producing a Western bias in prestige evaluations. The only exception to the pattern of general consensus is that in a few nonindustrialized countries there appear to be regional differences in the way occupations are evaluated, reflecting the generally low level of sociocultural integration of such places.

The lack of subgroup variations in prestige evaluations is important for two reasons. First, from a substantive point of view it provides strong evidence against a cultural theory of prestige determination. If prestige evaluations simply reflected cultural values we would expect substantial lack of consensus within each society across class and ethnic groups since these are the main cleavage lines of other forms of value differences. Second, from a practical standpoint the lack of subgroup variation permits us to utilize data from nonrepresentative samples to characterize entire societies with considerable confidence that the results of the projected analysis will not be seriously affected by the quality of the data.

4

The Extent of Intersocietal
Similarity in Occupational Prestige
Hierarchies

In this chapter I will show that there is general agreement throughout the world in the hierarchical ordering of occupations. A single prestige dimension appears to underlie the observed prestige hierarchy of every society, although some societies conform more closely to the generic hierarchy than do others. Also, intersocietal agreement is stronger with respect to the prestige ordering of nonmanual occupations than of manual occupations.

EXTENT OF PRESTIGE SIMILARITY

Previous researchers have found a very high level of agreement in prestige evaluations both between the United States and foreign countries and among small numbers of foreign countries and have taken this as evidence of fundamental uniformity throughout the world. The two best known earlier studies are those by Inkeles and Rossi (1956) and Hodge, Treiman, and Rossi (1966). Inkeles and Rossi found an average correlation of .94 between United States' prestige ratings and those of five relatively industrialized countries, and an average correlation of .91 across all pairs of countries; and Hodge, Treiman, and Rossi (1966) found an average correlation of .91 between United States' ratings and those of 23 other nations.

In order to assess the validity of the claim of fundamental intersocietal uniformity in prestige evaluations in the light of the newly available data described in Chapter 2, I computed correlations between prestige scores for all 60 places included in the present analysis. These correlations are presented in Table 4.1. Correlations were computed only between countries with at least 10 occupational titles in common on the ground that correlations based on fewer than 10 common titles would be extremely unreliable (omitted correlations are replaced by asterisks). Admittedly, the choice of 10 cases as the cutoff point is entirely arbitrary; some would argue that it should have been higher, but to have made it higher would have resulted in too much missing data. With this cutoff, coverage is reasonably complete: Of 1770 ($= 60 \times 59/2$) pairs of countries included in Table 4.1, 1386 (78%) met the criterion of 10 common cases.

The data in Table 4.1 tell us a number of things. First, the size of these correlations confirms that there is substantial uniformity in occupational prestige evaluations throughout the world; the average correlation between pairs of countries is about .8. Although intersocietal agreement is by no means perfect, it is clear that a very strong common dimension underlies the manifest prestige structure of all societies.[1] It is reasonable to think of the prestige hierarchy of each society as reflecting both the common dimension and idiosyncratic structural and cultural features that affect the evaluation of particular occupations.[2] Chapter 5 will attempt to account for the presence of the large common factor in prestige evaluations throughout the world while Chapters 6 and 7 will concentrate on understanding intersocietal differences in prestige evaluations. Chapters 8 and 9 will use the worldwide similarity in prestige evaluations to develop a Standard International Occupational Prestige Scale that can be used in any country.

The second point to be noted from these correlations is that agreement across countries, although high, is not quite as high as had been supposed. The average correlation between the prestige hierarchy of the United States

[1] It is important to stress that what is claimed here and elsewhere in the book is that the *relative* prestige of occupations is more or less invariant over time and space. The correlational methodology adopted here precludes any assessment of variation in the *absolute* prestige of particular occupations, if indeed it is even sensible to think in terms of amounts of prestige in the way one thinks of amounts of income or education. Comparing the amount of prestige enjoyed by an occupation at two different times or two different places would require that prestige be measured in the same metric in both samples; but this is almost never the case with respect to the data at hand, and even if it were, questions would arise regarding cultural variations in the propensity to make distinctions and in the tendency to make positive or negative evaluations. Hence, we are limited to assessments of the degree of correlation between populations in the prestige ordering of occupations.

[2] Of course, error cannot be discounted as a strong factor in the lack of perfect intercountry agreement in prestige rankings. First, as we saw in the previous chapters, many data sets derive from small, nonrepresentative samples and hence many scores treated here as point estimates probably have large standard errors. Second, there are, no doubt, substantial numbers of errors in the matches across countries; indeed, had I it to do over again I would change a number of my coding decisions. Thus, the observed average intercountry correlation of .8 may be taken as a lower bound for the true worldwide agreement in occupational prestige evaluations.

TABLE 4.1

INTERSOCIETAL CORRELATIONS OF OCCUPATIONAL PRESTIGE RATINGS, COMPUTED OVER ALL MATCHING TITLES (THE NUMBER OF OCCUPATIONS RATED IN EACH COUNTRY IS GIVEN IN THE DIAGONAL AND THE NUMBER OF OCCUPATIONS COMMON TO EACH PAIR OF COUNTRIES IS GIVEN BELOW THE DIAGONAL; THE CORRELATION IS NOT SHOWN WHERE THERE ARE FEWER THAN 10 COMMON TITLES)

	(1)	(2)	(3)	(4)	(5)	(6)	(7)	(8)	(9)	(10)
(1) UNITED STATES	333	.895	.924	.923	.824	.877	.887	.980	.879	.902
(2) ARGENTINA	23	30	.947	***	.887	.906	.957	.835	***	.962
(3) AUSTRALIA	116	23	145	.927	.798	.916	.939	.936	.862	.943
(4) BELGIUM	27	7	31	31	.836	.891	***	.922	***	.937
(5) BRAZIL-ACUCENA	53	20	34	12	67	.928	.614	.758	***	.746
(6) BRAZIL-BEZERROS	57	12	38	15	67	71	.849	.864	.896	.859
(7) BRAZIL-SAO PAOLO	25	14	23	8	12	15	30	.875	***	.876
(8) CANADA	176	20	82	23	34	38	25	185	.918	.903
(9) CEYLON	21	6	15	5	9	11	5	15	33	.899
(10) CHILE	76	20	60	19	31	35	22	58	13	89
(11) CONGO (ZAIRE)	22	6	16	10	13	13	9	15	5	17
(12) COSTA RICA	77	18	53	16	32	35	18	58	10	48
(13) CZECHOSLOVAKIA	25	8	21	8	8	11	8	18	6	21
(14) DENMARK	49	16	40	16	22	26	18	38	13	34
(15) FRANCE	27	7	20	31	12	15	8	23	5	19
(16) FRENCH GUIANA	46	12	38	18	13	15	14	35	12	32
(17) GERMANY (WEST)	64	18	49	20	23	27	17	48	12	40
(18) GHANA	19	9	16	12	8	12	9	16	5	16
(19) GRENADA	24	6	20	7	7	10	11	16	7	20
(20) GREAT BRITAIN	31	21	28	7	17	20	19	26	6	23
(21) GUAM	19	7	14	15	6	9	7	17	3	14
(22) GUYANA	30	8	27	11	12	13	8	24	7	22
(23) INDIA-PEASANT	24	6	16	9	13	14	8	13	4	17
(24) INDIA-UNIVERSITY STUDENT	27	18	24	8	10	13	17	24	5	19
(25) INDONESIA-JAVA	33	9	22	14	11	14	10	26	9	23
(26) INDONESIA-WEST IRIAN	23	4	13	9	5	6	7	18	4	14
(27) IRAQ	55	13	42	17	16	20	15	45	8	31
(28) ISRAEL	40	11	31	30	15	19	12	32	7	31
(29) ITALY	27	7	20	31	12	15	8	23	5	19
(30) IVORY COAST	21	7	20	10	9	13	9	19	5	17

	(1)	(2)	(3)	(4)	(5)	(6)	(7)	(8)	(9)	(10)
(31) JAPAN	67	12	45	17	19	22	14	49	8	38
(32) MAURITANIA	31	7	25	9	12	13	10	21	7	18
(33) MEXICO	41	13	35	17	14	17	13	34	7	31
(34) NETHERLANDS	120	25	77	21	37	41	25	75	19	62
(35) NEW BRITAIN	22	6	20	9	6	7	9	19	6	17
(36) NEW ZEALAND	85	22	101	17	27	30	22	63	13	48
(37) NIGERIA-BORNU	30	6	18	10	9	10	10	21	4	20
(38) NIGERIA-KANO	13	7	11	7	3	5	8	10	4	9
(39) NORWAY	37	9	28		16	19	12	31	6	27
(40) PAKISTAN	44	14	39	31	14	17	15	32	8	34
(41) PHILIPPINES	49	15	38	13	15	18	13	37	7	36
(42) POLAND	42	13	34	23	18	21	15	36	7	31
(43) PUERTO RICO	39	14	34	30	14	17	12	33	7	32
(44) SOUTHERN RHODESIA	44	11	33	13	14	18	11	31	10	25
(45) SOUTH WEST AFRICA (NAMIBIA)	36	5	26	10	9	10	9	24	6	24
(46) SPAIN	31	8	25	8	10	13	10	27	3	20
(47) SURINAM	64	14	45	19	19	22	18	50	15	39
(48) SWEDEN	22	7	16	8	10	11	8	17	5	13
(49) SWITZERLAND	79	17	55	16	17	21	19	55	13	42
(50) TAIWAN	29	11	24	10	15	17	16	21	4	23
(51) THAILAND-PEASANT	78	17	55	22	19	22	18	60	11	44
(52) THAILAND-TCHRS COL STUDENT	78	17	55	22	19	22	18	60	11	44
(53) THAILAND-UNIVERSITY STUDENT	78	17	55	22	19	22	18	60	11	44
(54) TURKEY	45	9	32	20	20	24	12	33	8	33
(55) UGANDA	58	13	44	18	21	25	16	43	16	37
(56) UNION OF SOUTH AFRICA	12	5	12	9	6	9	6	11	4	12
(57) U.S.S.R.	56	10	33	15	14	16	11	40	7	28
(58) URUGUAY	21	13	20	11	10	13	17	18	7	18
(59) YUGOSLAVIA	54	15	39	15	17	21	18	46	4	31
(60) ZAMBIA	30	7	22	10	14	16	9	22	8	18

	(11)	(12)	(13)	(14)	(15)	(16)	(17)	(18)	(19)	(20)
(1) UNITED STATES	.543	.909	.603	.927	.702	.831	.876	.926	.691	.942
(2) ARGENTINA	***	.949	***	.874	***	.837	.921	***	***	.939
(3) AUSTRALIA	.409	.917	.557	.950	.629	.749	.934	.949	.564	.976
(4) BELGIUM	.449	.887	***	.921	.710	.790	.846	.818	***	***
(5) BRAZIL-ACUCENA	.497	.812	.417	.865	.822	.802	.754	***	***	.787
(6) BRAZIL-BEZERROS	.561	.898	***	.876	.549	.857	.827	.776	.853	.919
(7) BRAZIL-SAO PAOLO	***	.891	.478	.907	***	.881	.946	***	.655	.908
(8) CANADA	.394	.911	***	.923	.701	.831	.925	.903	.637	.964
(9) CEYLON	***	.920	.483	.807	***	.737	.779	***	***	***
(10) CHILE	.721	.938	***	.936	.687	.861	.918	.950	.767	.937
(11) CONGO (ZAIRE)	28	***	.570	.497	.298	.715	.765	***	***	***
(12) COSTA RICA	6	79	***	.901	.612	.845	.914	.886	***	.874
(13) CZECHOSLOVAKIA	6	16	30	.616	***	.344	.450	.638	***	.233
(14) DENMARK	13	27	15	66	.532	.786	.944	.939	.578	.926
(15) FRANCE	10	16	8	16	31	.798	.540	.442	***	***
(16) FRENCH GUIANA	16	21	13	23	18	54	.811	.671	.638	.958
(17) GERMANY (WEST)	12	31	15	32	20	27	82	.803	.709	.954
(18) GHANA	7	12	12	13	12	10	12	25	***	.970
(19) GRENADA	7	8	6	12	7	13	14	7	36	***
(20) GREAT BRITAIN	5	23	11	14	7	11	17	10	9	40
(21) GUAM	6	14	5	11	15	11	19	7	5	7
(22) GUYANA	9	16	9	15	11	15	21	8	11	9
(23) INDIA-PEASANT	12	9	4	9	9	14	14	8	7	7
(24) INDIA-UNIVERSITY STUDENT	8	19	8	16	8	12	17	11	9	20
(25) INDONESIA-JAVA	10	20	11	21	14	18	23	13	8	8
(26) INDONESIA-WEST IRIAN	8	8	4	8	9	12	11	7	7	5
(27) IRAQ	12	27	16	22	17	27	26	14	14	12
(28) ISRAEL	12	25	15	24	30	23	26	14	10	10
(29) ITALY	10	16	8	16	31	18	20	12	7	7
(30) IVORY COAST	7	16	8	12	10	10	15	16	6	9

	(11)	(12)	(13)	(14)	(15)	(16)	(17)	(18)	(19)	(20)
(31) JAPAN	14	35	17	30	17	24	31	17	12	16
(32) MAURITANIA	11	11	6	14	9	16	12	7	9	6
(33) MEXICO	14	26	12	25	17	20	25	14	9	12
(34) NETHERLANDS	22	46	20	46	21	37	60	18	30	27
(35) NEW BRITAIN	9	13	4	11	9	10	12	7	5	6
(36) NEW ZEALAND	14	40	18	34	17	27	44	15	18	30
(37) NIGERIA-BORNU	12	13	7	13	10	15	16	7	12	9
(38) NIGERIA-KANO	5	7	5	9	7	10	9	8	6	7
(39) NORWAY	11	22	11	28	31	21	25	12	9	9
(40) PAKISTAN	8	30	15	27	13	21	26	13	13	14
(41) PHILIPPINES	13	29	14	23	23	22	34	17	10	15
(42) POLAND	13	25	19	23	30	26	29	15	10	11
(43) PUERTO RICO	12	27	11	16	13	19	22	14	9	14
(44) SOUTHERN RHODESIA	10	22	8	11	10	13	21	10	5	11
(45) SOUTH WEST AFRICA (NAMIBIA)	12	18	7	14	10	15	20	8	5	7
(46) SPAIN	4	20	10	27	8	12	15	8	9	8
(47) SURINAM	19	28	15	18	19	52	31	11	15	13
(48) SWEDEN	5	12	7	32	8	10	13	6	3	5
(49) SWITZERLAND	11	34	18	19	16	30	31	13	18	21
(50) TAIWAN	11	19	12	31	10	16	21	11	10	13
(51) THAILAND-PEASANT	18	36	18	31	22	33	39	17	16	18
(52) THAILAND-TCHRS COL STUDENT	18	36	18	31	22	33	39	17	16	18
(53) THAILAND-UNIVERSITY STUDENT	18	36	18	26	22	33	39	17	16	18
(54) TURKEY	10	26	14	29	20	23	25	12	16	8
(55) UGANDA	19	27	15	10	18	27	33	16	7	14
(56) UNION OF SOUTH AFRICA	6	8	5	17	9	9	11	10	7	6
(57) U.S.S.R.	11	23	17	15	15	26	26	10	10	13
(58) URUGUAY	7	15	6	24	11	13	15	7	7	14
(59) YUGOSLAVIA	13	23	17	11	15	23	30	13	7	12
(60) ZAMBIA	11	15	6		10	11	16	6	5	9

	(21)	(22)	(23)	(24)	(25)	(26)	(27)	(28)	(29)	(30)
(1) UNITED STATES	.917	.886	.188	.930	.846	.785	.853	.931	.929	.936
(2) ARGENTINA	***	***	***	.957	***	***	.975	.931	.952	***
(3) AUSTRALIA	.872	.883	.646	.957	.925	.836	.897	.915	.952	.942
(4) BELGIUM	.915	.935	***	***	.780	***	.912	.894	.949	.945
(5) BRAZIL-ACUCENA	***	.773	.555	.850	.572	***	.900	.813	.807	***
(6) BRAZIL-BEZERROS	***	.872	.388	.923	.791	***	.908	.779	.843	.940
(7) BRAZIL-SAO PAOLO	***	***	***	.938	.885	***	.857	.865	***	***
(8) CANADA	.895	.904	.355	.917	.876	.782	.855	.913	.909	.934
(9) CEYLON	***	***	***	***	***	***	***	***	***	***
(10) CHILE	.879	.899	.687	.951	.913	.903	.916	.935	.959	.910
(11) CONGO (ZAIRE)	***	***	.521	***	.678	***	.810	.454	.227	***
(12) COSTA RICA	.886	.855	***	.908	.925	***	.937	.920	.884	.893
(13) CZECHOSLOVAKIA	***	***	***	***	.769	***	.696	.589	***	***
(14) DENMARK	.933	.932	***	.914	.890	***	.941	.922	.949	.970
(15) FRANCE	.746	.872	***	***	.595	***	.644	.797	.692	.557
(16) FRENCH GUIANA	.767	.797	.492	.653	.732	.773	.788	.786	.805	.752
(17) GERMANY (WEST)	.822	.869	.678	.889	.883	.557	.855	.850	.841	.907
(18) GHANA	***	***	***	.955	.907	***	.838	.839	.894	.913
(19) GRENADA	***	.820	***	***	***	***	.686	.648	***	***
(20) GREAT BRITAIN	***	***	***	.963	.791	***	.884	.897	***	***
(21) GUAM	22	***	***	***	.791	***	.879	.969	.890	.899
(22) GUYANA	7	41	***	.724	***	***	.882	.913	.938	***
(23) INDIA-PEASANT	7	5	32	.620	***	***	.354	.458	***	***
(24) INDIA-UNIVERSITY STUDENT	9	11	10	30	.928	***	.859	.852	***	***
(25) INDONESIA-JAVA	12	10	6	10	37	.610	.916	.820	.787	.851
(26) INDONESIA-WEST IRIAN	7	7	6	7	10	32	.582	.771	***	***
(27) IRAQ	15	16	15	13	17	11	60	.876	.877	.899
(28) ISRAEL	17	14	11	10	22	11	25	48	.935	.924
(29) ITALY	15	11	9	8	14	9	17	30	31	.905
(30) IVORY COAST	9	11	6	9	13	7	16	12	10	24

85

	(21)	(22)	(23)	(24)	(25)	(26)	(27)	(28)	(29)	(30)
(31) JAPAN	12	17	13	16	22	11	24	23	17	17
(32) MAURITANIA	7	11	8	7	12	9	16	13	9	7
(33) MEXICO	13	15	12	16	19	13	27	22	17	13
(34) NETHERLANDS	15	27	20	23	33	19	39	31	21	20
(35) NEW BRITAIN	7	10	5	8	8	9	13	10	9	9
(36) NEW ZEALAND	13	24	13	23	18	12	33	23	17	18
(37) NIGERIA-BORNU	8	11	13	8	10	7	16	14	10	11
(38) NIGERIA-KANO	4	5	4	8	8	3	10	8	7	7
(39) NORWAY	16	12	10	9	17	10	21	32	31	11
(40) PAKISTAN	12	16	10	13	17	7	23	17	13	16
(41) PHILIPPINES	21	17	11	17	23	13	27	27	23	16
(42) POLAND	17	14	10	12	19	12	23	33	30	12
(43) PUERTO RICO	11	16	11	17	16	12	26	18	13	15
(44) SOUTHERN RHODESIA	8	10	7	13	11	10	19	12	10	12
(45) SOUTH WEST AFRICA (NAMIBIA)	7	11	11	9	10	8	16	11	10	10
(46) SPAIN	8	7	3	7	9	8	15	12	8	8
(47) SURINAM	13	19	15	14	18	15	34	24	19	12
(48) SWEDEN	2	7	4	7	9	4	15	11	8	5
(49) SWITZERLAND	11	15	11	18	19	10	32	26	16	13
(50) TAIWAN	11	11	9	11	15	7	21	17	10	11
(51) THAILAND-PEASANT	18	22	18	18	26	19	36	31	22	18
(52) THAILAND-TCHRS COL STUDENT	18	22	18	18	26	19	36	31	22	18
(53) THAILAND-UNIVERSITY STUDENT	18	22	18	18	26	19	36	31	22	18
(54) TURKEY	13	15	10	8	20	11	28	29	20	12
(55) UGANDA	10	20	18	18	19	16	31	22	18	19
(56) UNION OF SOUTH AFRICA	6	6	6	7	8	5	10	10	9	8
(57) U.S.S.R.	8	16	8	8	14	8	20	23	15	9
(58) URUGUAY	9	8	7	8	8	6	11	14	11	7
(59) YUGOSLAVIA	11	13	12	12	16	7	23	24	15	14
(60) ZAMBIA	8	10	7	8	8	10	14	12	10	9

	(31)	(32)	(33)	(34)	(35)	(36)	(37)	(38)	(39)	(40)
(1) UNITED STATES	.899	.811	.866	.882	.573	.912	.744	.740	.825	.889
(2) ARGENTINA	.885	***	.935	.927	***	.956	***	***	***	.906
(3) AUSTRALIA	.853	.867	.888	.929	.693	.990	.723	.728	.952	.894
(4) BELGIUM	.899	***	.862	.839	***	.905	.696	***	.826	.716
(5) BRAZIL-ACUCENA	.829	.948	.746	.686	***	.740	.752	***	.764	.849
(6) BRAZIL-BEZERROS	.882	.973	.750	.826	***	.903	.732	***	.759	.741
(7) BRAZIL-SAO PAOLO	.887	.762	.902	.931	***	.940	.691	***	.826	.741
(8) CANADA	.902	.799	.877	.922	.549	.906	.691	.689	.802	.860
(9) CEYLON	***	***	***	.727	***	.906	***	***	***	***
(10) CHILE	.886	.905	.903	.893	.525	.945	.796	***	.905	.844
(11) CONGO (ZAIRE)	.703	.732	.694	.511	***	.412	.665	***	.297	***
(12) COSTA RICA	.857	.880	.895	.906	.607	.891	.739	***	.817	.863
(13) CZECHOSLOVAKIA	.520	***	.668	.598	***	.482	***	***	.311	.806
(14) DENMARK	.931	.902	.861	.950	.718	.951	.765	***	.921	.887
(15) FRANCE	.710	***	.682	.499	***	.539	.649	***	.674	.731
(16) FRENCH GUIANA	.790	.845	.784	.727	.318	.726	.805	.883	.780	.769
(17) GERMANY (WEST)	.824	.696	.817	.924	.277	.919	.845	***	.783	.860
(18) GHANA	.920	***	.761	.878	***	.947	***	***	.838	.729
(19) GRENADA	.797	***	***	.676	***	.570	.376	***	***	.320
(20) GREAT BRITAIN	.874	***	.856	.934	***	.978	***	***	***	.701
(21) GUAM	.893	***	.930	.790	***	.827	***	***	.886	.695
(22) GUYANA	.949	.792	.856	.890	.628	.844	.760	***	.898	.927
(23) INDIA-PEASANT	.257	***	.582	.507	***	.617	.798	***	.622	.886
(24) INDIA-UNIVERSITY STUDENT	.840	***	.902	.906	***	.973	***	***	***	.709
(25) INDONESIA-JAVA	.817	.744	.852	.898	***	.929	.656	***	.778	.896
(26) INDONESIA-WEST IRIAN	.859	***	.596	.690	***	.820	***	***	.820	***
(27) IRAQ	.918	.832	.855	.925	.604	.887	.634	.713	.781	.845
(28) ISRAEL	.916	.864	.859	.851	.712	.904	.779	***	.858	.871
(29) ITALY	.925	***	.782	.837	***	.931	.706	***	.888	.754
(30) IVORY COAST	.946	***	.738	.932	***	.903	.848	***	.807	.797

	(31)	(32)	(33)	(34)	(35)	(36)	(37)	(38)	(39)	(40)
(31) JAPAN	88	.915	.822	.899	.609	.857	.832	***	.906	.890
(32) MAURITANIA	16	40	.839	.793	.623	.851	***	***	.919	.784
(33) MEXICO	28	10	49	.857	.749	.903	.746	***	.718	.883
(34) NETHERLANDS	42	27	37	177	.478	.913	.715	.669	.749	.833
(35) NEW BRITAIN	11	14	13	22	28	.636	***	***	***	.000
(36) NEW ZEALAND	35	24	27	61	20	107	.733	***	.944	.847
(37) NIGERIA-BORNU	17	9	13	26	5	17	43	.895	.875	.870
(38) NIGERIA-KANO	8	4	9	13	4	9	10	16	***	***
(39) NORWAY	20	10	21	29	9	24	12	8	44	.842
(40) PAKISTAN	29	13	18	36	12	30	13	8	18	50
(41) PHILIPPINES	36	14	32	39	14	33	13	9	26	22
(42) POLAND	24	14	19	34	11	28	12	8	31	22
(43) PUERTO RICO	29	9	42	35	12	26	12	9	16	19
(44) SOUTHERN RHODESIA	15	13	18	30	18	29	9	5	11	14
(45) SOUTH WEST AFRICA (NAMIBIA)	16	9	20	25	15	22	12	7	12	16
(46) SPAIN	17	10	11	24	8	16	5	4	12	19
(47) SURINAM	25	17	24	50	15	32	17	11	23	24
(48) SWEDEN	13	6	13	21	6	13	2	4	12	11
(49) SWITZERLAND	34	17	22	54	16	45	14	12	24	27
(50) TAIWAN	18	12	15	26	9	21	15	6	14	16
(51) THAILAND-PEASANT	37	17	35	62	15	47	21	8	25	29
(52) THAILAND-TCHRS COL STUDENT	37	17	35	62	15	47	21	8	25	29
(53) THAILAND-UNIVERSITY STUDENT	37	17	35	62	15	25	18	8	25	29
(54) TURKEY	26	13	24	40	10	25	18	6	23	17
(55) UGANDA	27	19	25	53	20	39	24	11	21	26
(56) UNION OF SOUTH AFRICA	9	4	11	13	3	11	7	7	11	8
(57) U.S.S.R.	25	13	14	35	8	25	11	5	17	14
(58) URUGUAY	13	8	10	22	7	20	8	4	13	14
(59) YUGOSLAVIA	25	17	17	44	11	33	12	8	21	20
(60) ZAMBIA	11	12	14	24	18	19	6	2	10	8

	(41)	(42)	(43)	(44)	(45)	(46)	(47)	(48)	(49)	(50)
(1) UNITED STATES	.880	.771	.932	.846	.853	.791	.834	.831	.872	.854
(2) ARGENTINA	.909	.838	.906	.883	***	***	.853	***	.935	.948
(3) AUSTRALIA	.914	.728	.915	.866	.893	.887	.825	.913	.876	.871
(4) BELGIUM	.905	.838	.932	.950	.773	.865	.865	***	.876	.776
(5) BRAZIL-ACUCENA	.802	.560	.833	.830	***	.383	.721	.518	.575	.869
(6) BRAZIL-BEZERROS	.865	.633	.856	.919	.765	.532	.930	.500	.832	.782
(7) BRAZIL-SAO PAOLO	.920	.823	.909	.892	***	.918	.837	***	.923	.753
(8) CANADA	.889	.726	.928	.798	.843	.825	.836	.877	.899	.861
(9) CEYLON	***	***	***	.717	***	***	.776	***	.537	***
(10) CHILE	.923	.684	.939	.879	.840	.810	.897	.832	.876	.856
(11) CONGO (ZAIRE)	.693	.414	.781	.734	.950	***	.669	***	.408	.491
(12) COSTA RICA	.910	.762	.897	.879	.789	.902	.866	.895	.900	.854
(13) CZECHOSLOVAKIA	.382	.706	.560	***	***	.659	.352	***	.608	.881
(14) DENMARK	.920	.738	.903	.932	.824	.864	.836	.871	.896	.831
(15) FRANCE	.573	.747	.732	.568	.167	***	.582	***	.456	.882
(16) FRENCH GUIANA	.785	.607	.894	.837	.858	.526	.932	.660	.720	.868
(17) GERMANY (WEST)	.864	.739	.855	.774	.861	.821	.828	.919	.903	.861
(18) GHANA	.910	.810	.889	.864	***	***	.746	***	.857	.813
(19) GRENADA	.891	.334	***	***	***	***	.759	***	.595	.353
(20) GREAT BRITAIN	.928	.698	.919	.931	***	***	.956	***	.825	.750
(21) GUAM	.908	.857	.956	***	***	***	.832	***	.810	.831
(22) GUYANA	.863	.807	.910	.925	.909	***	.789	***	.861	.926
(23) INDIA-PEASANT	.354	.302	.546	***	.722	***	.394	***	.018	***
(24) INDIA-UNIVERSITY STUDENT	.915	.778	.949	.912	.751	***	.775	***	.842	.723
(25) INDONESIA-JAVA	.843	.633	.855	.850	***	***	.724	***	***	.916
(26) INDONESIA-WEST IRIAN	.947	.525	.871	.870	***	***	.901	***	.388	***
(27) IRAQ	.817	.778	.851	.858	.775	.893	.809	.841	.873	.840
(28) ISRAEL	.901	.810	.894	.919	.836	.756	.832	.789	.897	.865
(29) ITALY	.942	.780	.879	.951	.798	***	.889	***	.879	.787
(30) IVORY COAST	.926	.885	.943	.918	.618	***	.811	***	.912	.889

	(41)	(42)	(43)	(44)	(45)	(46)	(47)	(48)	(49)	(50)
(31) JAPAN	.881	.751	.914	.885	.840	.868	.861	.837	.848	.908
(32) MAURITANIA	.877	.564	***	.960	***	.549	.888	***	.719	.830
(33) MEXICO	.794	.854	.891	.740	.767	.643	.735	.767	.871	.850
(34) NETHERLANDS	.860	.706	.889	.837	.686	.714	.812	.827	.842	.819
(35) NEW BRITAIN	.724	.396	.738	.622	.684	***	.432	***	.497	***
(36) NEW ZEALAND	.901	.709	.911	.828	.868	.929	.787	.896	.894	.841
(37) NIGERIA-BORNU	.881	.642	.916	***	.581	***	.799	***	.627	.807
(38) NIGERIA-KANO	***	***	***	***	***	***	.849	***	.730	.896
(39) NORWAY	.879	.689	.842	.917	.833	.824	.819	.789	.787	.899
(40) PAKISTAN	.792	.765	.823	.629	.647	.815	.685	.913	.844	.847
(41) PHILIPPINES	57	.656	.938	.942	.866	.934	.853	.659	.891	.846
(42) POLAND	25	51	.746	.568	.668	.734	.616	.640	.752	.848
(43) PUERTO RICO	31	16	49	.934	.890	.825	.880	.852	.920	.685
(44) SOUTHERN RHODESIA	16	14	19	53	.919	***	.845	***	.744	.651
(45) SOUTH WEST AFRICA (NAMIBIA)	19	13	19	19	39	***	.659	***	.704	.637
(46) SPAIN	13	14	11	6	5	39		***	.796	.747
(47) SURINAM	24	28	23	18	18	13	77	.398	.771	***
(48) SWEDEN	11	10	11	6	7	8	10	25	.797	.719
(49) SWITZERLAND	25	24	19	21	16	17	37	16	98	
(50) TAIWAN	22	16	15	12	12	10	20	7	17	36
(51) THAILAND-PEASANT	39	30	32	25	23	19	36	14	39	21
(52) THAILAND-TCHRS COL STUDENT	39	30	32	25	23	19	36	14	39	21
(53) THAILAND-UNIVERSITY STUDENT	39	30	32	25	23	19	36	14	39	21
(54) TURKEY	23	25	20	15	14	14	26	11	25	16
(55) UGANDA	23	25	25	33	26	12	33	10	30	16
(56) UNION OF SOUTH AFRICA	11	10	11	11	11	5	10	2	9	7
(57) U.S.S.R.	18	25	14	11	8	15	27	9	29	12
(58) URUGUAY	13	16	8	11	13	12	14	7	16	11
(59) YUGOSLAVIA	20	26	15	15	15	20	27	10	32	15
(60) ZAMBIA	14	14	14	31		6	15	5	15	10

	(51)	(52)	(53)	(54)	(55)	(56)	(57)	(58)	(59)	(60)
1) UNITED STATES	.800	.838	.848	.941	.904	.910	.789	.926	.669	.905
2) ARGENTINA	.772	.945	.953	***	.871	***	.872	.972	.911	***
3) AUSTRALIA	.733	.845	.898	.915	.934	.927	.712	.928	.741	.882
4) BELGIUM	.564	.814	.768	.898	.918	***	.703	.851	.777	.719
5) BRAZIL-ACUCENA	.819	.874	.801	.902	.773	***	.611	.794	.654	.753
6) BRAZIL-BEZERROS	.755	.897	.857	.839	.866	***	.726	.847	.753	.840
7) BRAZIL-SAO PAOLO	.742	.890	.923	.839	.809	***	.611	.921	.694	***
8) CANADA	.740	.811	.814	.925	.899	.893	.767	.927	.685	.860
9) CEYLON	.819	.807	.824	***	.902	***	***	***	***	***
10) CHILE	.831	.890	.900	.935	.929	.944	.664	.899	.815	.832
11) CONGO (ZAIRE)	.715	.731	.646	.810	.830	***	.287	***	.623	.867
12) COSTA RICA	.793	.885	.925	.914	.926	***	.754	.917	.803	.907
13) CZECHOSLOVAKIA	.316	.451	.418	.844	.681	***	.754	***	.610	***
14) DENMARK	.817	.905	.901	.916	.911	.953	.747	.929	.791	.864
15) FRANCE	.700	.759	.643	.832	.572	***	.495	.402	.680	.108
16) FRENCH GUIANA	.742	.754	.719	.862	.766	***	.541	.753	.646	.849
17) GERMANY (WEST)	.661	.806	.868	.831	.850	.926	.664	.945	.807	.898
18) GHANA	.807	.863	.844	.876	.956	.909	.856	***	.737	***
19) GRENADA	.255	.458	.462	.586	.772	***	***	.768	***	***
20) GREAT BRITAIN	.892	.949	.950	***	.962	***	.837	.947	.806	***
21) GUAM	.514	.804	.789	.948	.857	***	***	***	.837	***
22) GUYANA	.893	.899	.871	.871	.932	***	.522	***	.761	.816
23) INDIA-PEASANT	.430	.440	.515	.540	.683	***	***	***	.729	***
24) INDIA-UNIVERSITY STUDENT	.757	.922	.928	.901	.922	***	.716	.920	.695	***
25) INDONESIA-JAVA	.678	.805	.894	.840	.920	***	***	.816	***	***
26) INDONESIA-WEST IRIAN	.902	.798	.682	.936	.865	***	***	***	***	.829
27) IRAQ	.753	.869	.912	.936	.909	.747	.856	.957	.856	.942
28) ISRAEL	.796	.865	.830	.944	.909	.831	.685	.849	.754	.779
29) ITALY	.658	.825	.801	.923	.907	***	.631	.842	.728	.728
30) IVORY COAST	.674	.790	.832	.897	.881	***	***	***	.828	***

		(51)	(52)	(53)	(54)	(55)	(56)	(57)	(58)	(59)	(60)
(31)	JAPAN	.846	.868	.893	.955	.915	***	.830	.855	.772	.753
(32)	MAURITANIA	.846	.778	.692	.967	.851	***	.534	***	.688	.664
(33)	MEXICO	.738	.832	.858	.868	.835	.837	.807	.965	.781	.782
(34)	NETHERLANDS	.736	.831	.855	.896	.854	.860	.609	.902	.690	.871
(35)	NEW BRITAIN	.740	.639	.533	.847	.631	***	***	***	.081	.574
(36)	NEW ZEALAND	.781	.850	.913	.925	.911	.932	.661	.930	.726	.848
(37)	NIGERIA-BORNU	.865	.817	.770	.778	.760	***	.631	***	.787	***
(38)	NIGERIA-KANO	***	***	***	***	.756	***	***	***	***	***
(39)	NORWAY	.722	.795	.784	.866	.842	.935	.446	.812	.743	.707
(40)	PAKISTAN	.815	.921	.947	.877	.784	***	.808	.677	.884	***
(41)	PHILIPPINES	.723	.843	.856	.942	.922	.976	.742	.865	.756	.892
(42)	POLAND	.641	.785	.700	.804	.705	.677	.738	.882	.833	.745
(43)	PUERTO RICO	.823	.874	.889	.934	.921	.945	.791	.924	.714	.859
(44)	SOUTHERN RHODESIA	.796	.886	.846	.870	.900	***	.842	***	.641	.943
(45)	SOUTH WEST AFRICA (NAMIBIA)	.721	.808	.720	.788	.878	***	.387	***	.451	.941
(46)	SPAIN	.709	.832	.924	.667	.914	***	.819	.860	.873	***
(47)	SURINAM	.780	.782	.720	.911	.819	.801	.509	.622	.634	.736
(48)	SWEDEN	.780	.866	.827	.760	.774	***	***	***	.612	***
(49)	SWITZERLAND	.537	.745	.771	.862	.791	***	.905	.877	.813	.818
(50)	TAIWAN	.894	.892	.893	.922	.806	***	.759	.676	.837	.664
(51)	THAILAND-PEASANT	103	.915	.855	.867	.819	***	.646	.676	.568	.906
(52)	THAILAND-TCHRS COL STUDENT	103	103	.942	.924	.883	***	.724	.912	.735	.924
(53)	THAILAND-UNIVERSITY STUDENT	103	103	103	.916	.882	***	.711	.896	.777	.898
(54)	TURKEY	35	35	35	60	.912	***	.757	.887	.835	.785
(55)	UGANDA	42	42	42	31	79	.835	.696	.894	.768	.920
(56)	UNION OF SOUTH AFRICA	8	8	8	8	11	16	***	***	***	***
(57)	U.S.S.R.	31	31	31	19	18	8	75	.590	.764	.591
(58)	URUGUAY	18	18	18	12	12	6	13	26	.800	.946
(59)	YUGOSLAVIA	29	29	29	24	26	9	33	14	70	.615
(60)	ZAMBIA	18	18	18	14	23	5	10	10	13	38

and those of the 59 foreign places in the sample is .83, with a standard deviation of .12 (recall that the correlation obtained by Hodge *et al.* was .91). Thus, there is substantial variation in the extent to which other countries are similar to the United States in occupational evaluations. In fact, the correlations range from a low of .19 between the United States and peasant India[3] to a high of .98 between the United States and Canada. Moreover, when all the correlations between countries are examined, the average correlation (for the 1386 pairs with at least 10 cases in common) is .79 (compared to Inkeles and Rossi's correlation of .91) and the standard deviation is .14. It is clear that inclusion of a larger and more diverse set of countries in prestige comparisons increases observed intercountry differences in occupational evaluations. This is hardly surprising. In the first place, the 60 places for which prestige data are currently available are considerably more heterogeneous in social and economic characteristics than the 6 countries studied by Inkeles and Rossi. Second, considering the full matrix rather than the single row of correlations with the United States to which Hodge *et al.* restricted themselves allows more freedom for fluctuation. Third, the use of larger samples of occupations more precisely matched than in previous cross-national comparisons probably results in greater variation in the correlations between pairs of countries.[4] For these reasons, the present correlations probably represent the *true* degree of agreement in the prestige hierarchies of each pair of countries more accurately than the coefficients reported in previous studies.

Third, these results can be used to assess the effect of alternative occupational coding schemes, as promised in Chapter 2. Recall that the circumstances under which this study was conducted resulted in occupations for some countries being classified according to two alternative coding

[3] It would be unwise to make too much of this low correlation considering that no other correlation with the United States is less than .5, and only two (excluding three based on nonprestige criteria) are less than .7. Furthermore, evidence from a pre-1930 ethnographic study of an Indian village (in Uttar Pradesh), which I located after completing the main correlation analysis, yields somewhat different results. Dumont (1970:99–102) provides a rank ordering of caste groups, whose names correspond to occupational categories. Although unfortunately I was able to match only 10 of the 24 titles to United States' occupational categories, the correlation between the position of these categories in the United States and India is .85. Finally, Hodge, Treiman, and Rossi (1966:318) cite a correlation of .87 between Indian and American prestige ratings. Clearly, the prudent course is to withhold judgment on whether the traditional Indian occupational prestige hierarchy is truly anomalous until superior data are available.

[4] For example, Inkeles and Rossi found an average correlation of .91 and a range from .74 to .97 between the United States, Germany, Great Britain, Japan, New Zealand, and the USSR, using data sets with an average of 38 occupations. Using expanded data sets from the same countries (with an average of 121 occupations) and more precise coding procedures I found an average correlation of .85 and a range from .66 to .97.

schemes, one based on the 1960 United States Census detailed occupational classification and the other—the basic coding scheme for the present analysis—derived from the International Standard Classification of Occupations, Revised Edition (International Labor Office, 1969a). For 27 of the 60 places included in the present analysis, an identical set of occupations was coded according to both schemes, and for another 6 places additional occupations were included and the expanded list coded according to the new scheme. As a way of assessing the comparability of the two coding schemes, I computed the correlation between the degree of association with United States' ratings estimated under the alternative coding procedures, for all countries for which both procedures had been used. That is, I correlated the correlation coefficients in the top line of Table 4.1 with the corresponding correlation coefficients computed for the same data coded according to the alternative category scheme. The resulting correlation was .94, indicating a high degree of stability in the *pattern* of intercountry prestige similarity under alternative coding schemes. Results including the six countries for which additional data had been added are even more encouraging; the correlation between the two estimates of prestige similarity to the United States is .92, which is almost as high as before. Hence, we can safely conclude that the results obtained here are not sensitive to idiosyncracies of coding procedures, so long as care is taken to obtain precise matches between occupational titles (cf. footnote 14, Chapter 2).

Fourth, the pattern of intercountry correlations provides evidence that criteria of occupational evaluation other than prestige tend to produce lower correlations than would otherwise be expected, and hence are probably best excluded from analytic computations. Of the 60 places appearing in Table 4.1, data for 5—Czechoslovakia, Grenada, Nigeria (Bornu), Sweden, and Yugoslavia—are based on evaluative criteria other than prestige. In three cases, the "desirability" of jobs was used as a criterion, in one case "ideal income" was used, and in one case the average social standing of incumbents of each position was used to generate prestige scores (see Chapter 2 for details). As a way of assessing possible bias resulting from the use of these data, we can inspect the top line of the table. Note that the average correlation with the United States for these five countries is .71, a full 14 points below the average correlation for the remaining countries. Moreover, this cannot be attributed to other characteristics of the five countries. They are not, on the whole, among the least industrialized nations of the world, for which low correlations with the United States might be expected. Indeed, the correlation involving Sweden is 5 points below the average for the two other Scandinavian countries, and the average of the correlations involving Czechoslovakia and Yugoslavia is 14 points below the average of that for the two other Eastern European countries. Thus, despite claims made by the original investigators and others that such criteria of occupational evaluation can be considered as synonymous with prestige as it is ordinarily measured, there seems to be sufficient discrepancy in the results from what would be expected from a pure prestige stimulus to warrant separate treatment. Hence, the subsequent analysis (except where otherwise specified) is restricted to the 55 places with data based strictly upon a prestige stimulus. It should be mentioned that the omission of these five countries from the basic data set hardly affects the mean or the standard deviation of the intercountry correlations; they are, respectively, .81 and .13, based on 1202 pairs of countries—that is, almost identical to the figures for the full 60 countries. The minor impact on these coefficients probably results from the fact that the correlations involving the five countries are only a small fraction of the total number of correlations upon which the mean and standard deviation were computed.

For some purposes I will restrict the set of countries even further, omitting as well the other 28 places for which only poor data are available (data quality estimated as 1 in Table 2.1).[5] For the 27 remaining countries the average intercorrelation over the 308 pairs with at least 10 common occupations is .82, about the same as the average correlation computed over 55 places; the standard deviation is, likewise about the same, .12.

One obvious source of difficulty with the prestige correlations under review here is that they are based on whatever occupations happen to be common to a given pair of countries. It is thus possible that variations in the degree of correlation between countries may simply reflect differences among countries in the particular occupations being compared, some pairs of countries primarily including occupations rated in relatively standard ways throughout the world and other pairs including occupations rated in highly idiosyncratic ways from place to place. To assess this possibility, I created a special matrix, restricted to occupations rated in at least 20 places. Fifty of the 509 initial occupation lines were included in this matrix, which contained data for all 60 societies. Performing computations similar to those described above yields reassuring results. Both the average correlation and the standard deviation of the correlations, computed over the 1174 pairs based on at least 10 common occupations (out of the set of 50), are approximately the same as in the corresponding larger matrix based on all 509 occupation lines. For this subset of occupations, the mean intercorrelation is .80 and the standard deviation is .14. Moreover, the correlation between the two sets of intercountry prestige correlations—those based on all occupations and those based on the special subset of 50 occupations—is

---

[5] The two data sets for São Paulo, Brazil are treated as together constituting good data (data quality estimated as 2).

.94, indicating that the estimates of agreement in prestige evaluations between pairs of countries are not substantially affected by the inclusion of relatively uncommon occupations that may be peculiar to a limited set of countries. Thus, there is ample justification for using all available occupations for each pair of countries to establish the intercountry correlations.

We must also assess the converse problem. It has sometimes been claimed that the reason intersocietal similarity in prestige hierarchies appears to be so great is that comparisons necessarily are restricted to those occupations rated in pairs of countries. Thus the very occupations that are principally responsible for creating differences among societies in occupational structures and hence, presumably, in occupational prestige hierarchies, never enter the comparisons and as a result the true degree of intersocietal similarity is overstated. How can this claim be assessed? If we assume that the occupations that strongly affect the prestige hierarchy of a society are at least as likely as other occupations to be included among the titles rated in prestige studies, we can use the number of occupations uniquely rated in each country as a measure of uniqueness of occupational structures. By this criterion, occupational structures are remarkably similar throughout the world. Only about 5% of the more than 3700 titles analyzed here are unique to particular societies, and about half of these are from the United States. Only in the United States, Japan, and Switzerland are as many as four titles unique. Thus, we can proceed with assurance that our comparisons are not distorting reality or overstating cross-cultural similarity by omitting important components of the occupational structure of each country.

In sum, all available evidence points to the same conclusion: *There is high agreement throughout the world regarding the relative prestige of occupations.* The average intercountry correlation of about .8 remains essentially unchanged when the data are restricted in various ways to assess the effects of including idiosyncratic studies and occupational titles (the statistics yielded by these alternative specifications are summarized in Table 4.2).

So far we have concentrated on establishing the degree of cross-cultural similarity in occupational prestige hierarchies without considering which occupations are ranked high and which low. We must continue to defer this topic, only noting here that throughout the world occupational prestige evaluations conform to the general expectations developed in Chapter 1— occupations entailing the greatest power and privilege tend to have the highest prestige, as will be documented in Chapter 5. This produces a hierarchy in which professional and higher managerial occupations share the top positions, followed by technical, semiprofessional, and lower managerial occupations, then by lower white-collar and skilled blue-collar jobs,

TABLE 4.2
Summary of Intersocietal Similarity in Occupational
Prestige Hierarchies, for Selected Data Sets

Correlations	Mean Correlation	*SD* of Correlations	Pairs of Countries with at Least 10 Occupations in Common	
			Number	Percentage of Total
60 societies	.79	.14	1386	78
55 societies (non-prestige stimuli excluded)	.81	.13	1202	81
27 societies (poor data excluded)	.82	.12	308	88
60 societies, based on 50 common occupations	.80	.14	1174	66
60 societies, non-manual occupations	.80	.13	742	42
60 societies, manual and farm occupations	.63	.22	493	28

and finally by unskilled service and laboring jobs. In Chapter 8 I will take up the nature of the generic worldwide prestige hierarchy in greater detail, in the course of describing a Standard International Occupational Prestige Scale that represents the generic hierarchy. Readers desiring an intuitive feel for the prestige ordering of individual occupations may wish to consult Tables 3.4, 7.2, and 8.2, all of which contain listings of occupations ranked in order of their prestige.

REGIONAL AND CULTURAL VARIATIONS

One argument often made to account for differences among countries in prestige hierarchies is that cultural norms and values determine the deference and respect accorded various activities and occupations. To the extent this is true we would expect countries that are culturally similar also to be similar in their patterns of occupational evaluation. While it is not completely clear how to group countries into culturally homogeneous categories, Table 4.3 divides the 55 societies for which prestige data exist into 8 categories on the basis of geography, immigration patterns, and ideology. The average within-category correlations are on the whole hardly larger than the worldwide average, and for a few groups they are actually smaller. Only the anglo-American countries appear to display substantially greater than ordinary within-group similarity in prestige evaluations, while the South Asian and Eastern European groups each appear to have even less in

TABLE 4.3
Average Correlations for Various Regions and Culture Areas[a]

Region or Culture Area	Mean Correlation within Area	Number of Correlations	Number of Societies
Continental Western Europe, except Spain	.802	28	8
Eastern Europe	.738	1	2
Anglo-American Countries[b]	.950	10	5
Hispanic America[c] and Spain	.849	42	10
Non-Hispanic South America	.839	3	3
Africa	.861	23	10
South Asia and Middle East[d]	.759	14	10
East Asia and Oceania	.810	39	7
Average within area correlation	.831	160	--
Average between area correlation	.807	1042	--
Worldwide average	.810	1202	55

[a]Excludes five nonprestige data sets.
[b]U.S., Australia, Canada, Great Britain, and New Zealand.
[c]Includes Brazil.
[d]Includes Israel and Turkey.

common than pairs of countries chosen at random. Still, the basic pattern is one of uniformity across regions in the degree of intercountry agreement in prestige evaluations; there is little real evidence of cultural differences in occupational prestige evaluations, at least as measured in this crude way.

Additional evidence supporting the same point comes from an attempt to locate clusters of countries with especially similar prestige hierarchies via a multidimensional scaling procedure (Shepard, Romney, and Nerlove, 1972). This proved a complete failure. Using the correlations reported in Table 4.1 for the 55 countries with prestige data, I was unable to fit even a five-dimensional space (the stress coefficient remained greater than .4 through several attempts). Inspecting various two-dimensional plots, it was evident that the general pattern is one in which countries close to the worldwide average in their pattern of prestige evaluations (see Table 8.3) cluster near the center of the plot while those deviating from that average scatter around the center in a series of concentric circles. While this pattern might be interpreted as evidence for a convergence theory of prestige evaluations, it is equally likely that it is simply a reflection of differences in data quality between industrialized and nonindustrialized countries. I shall have more to say about this issue in Chapter 8. In any event, it is obvious that the world cannot be divided into discrete clusters of countries sharing patterns of prestige evaluation and differing from one another. Rather, there is a single dimension representing a worldwide pattern, from which individual societies deviate to a greater or smaller degree. Whether, how much, and in what way these deviations are structured we leave for later chapters.

RATINGS OF NONMANUAL AND MANUAL OCCUPATIONS

There is no reason to suppose that the degree of cross-cultural similarity in prestige evaluations holds equally for all types of occupations. Some occupations vary from society to society much more than others—in the skill they require, the rewards they command, their position relative to other occupations, and so on. Manual jobs, in particular, are more likely than nonmanual jobs to vary from country to country in the way they are organized and in the tasks entailed in performing them, being more dependent upon variations in the technology and social organization of production than nonmanual jobs. Thus the manual prestige hierarchy should be more variable from country to country than the nonmanual hierarchy.

Of course, the degree of cross-cultural similarity in prestige evaluations should vary along other dimensions as well. The prestige of agricultural occupations is probably more variable across countries that than of nonagricultural occupations, because of the enormous differences across countries in the social organization of agriculture. Similarly, traditional jobs might be expected to vary more from country to country than those imported from the West as a legacy of colonialism or as an adjunct of industrialization. Examination of these possibilities will be deferred to Chapter 7, where I consider intersocietal variations in the evaluation of particular occupations. They cannot be considered within the analytic framework of this chapter because there simply are not enough agricultural occupations rated in most countries to support a correlational approach to intercountry comparisons; and to assess how similar countries are with respect to the evaluation of "traditional" as against "modern" occupations requires that the same occupations be defined as traditional and as modern in all societies, which makes no sense at all. Thus, I restrict my attention in the present chapter to a comparison of the degree of intersocietal similarity in the prestige evaluation of nonmanual and manual occupations.

Aside from its theoretical interest, the division of the labor force into nonmanual and manual sectors has several practical advantages. First, this distinction reflects a division of labor that is recognized throughout the world, despite various ambiguities and exceptions in the classification of specific occupations. Second, given the form in which occupations were coded here, it is a relatively easy distinction to make,[6] in contrast, for example, to a distinction among skill levels within the manual sector. Finally, separate consideration of the nonmanual and manual sectors provides an opportunity to determine whether the correlations between countries are spuriously high due to correlation of extreme observations, a difficulty frequently encountered in occupational prestige comparisons in the past. Although these sectors do overlap substantially in prestige, nonmanual occupations, on the average, have more prestige and the range over each of the two sectors is substantially attenuated compared to the range over all occupations, although this is particularly true of manual occupations.

Any fears about the effect of correlating extremes prove unjustified, however. In contrast to previous studies (cf. Hodge, Treiman, and Rossi, 1966), there is no evidence in the present analysis that the high intercorrelations over all occupations are due to the correlation of extreme observations. On the contrary, the correlations over nonmanual occupations are actually slightly higher than the correlations over all occupations. The average intercorrelation of nonmanual occupational titles over 742 pairs of countries is .80 (compared to .79 for all occupations), while the standard deviation is .13 (compared to .14 for all occupations).[7] However, the average intercorrelation of manual occupational titles over 493 pairs of countries is only .63, and the standard deviation is .22.

It is hard to know to what extent the attentuation in intersocietal agreement in the evaluation of manual occupations compared to nonmanual occupations reflects actual variations in social structure and not simply statistical properties of the data. The variance in the prestige of manual occupations tends to be relatively small compared to the variance in the prestige of nonmanual occupations, and this in itself would reduce the correlations—the converse of the correlation of extremes. However, as indicated above, there are substantive reasons for expecting greater variation

---

[6] Nonmanual titles are defined here as ISCO major groups 0–4: Professional, Technical and Related Workers; Administrative and Managerial Workers; Clerical and Related Workers; and Sales Workers. Manual titles are defined as ISCO major groups 5–9: Service Workers; Agricultural, Animal Husbandry and Forestry Workers, Fishermen and Hunters; and Production and Related Workers, Transport Equipment Operations and Laborers. Exclusion of agricultural workers from the manual category has little effect on the results, but does reduce the number of pairs of countries meeting the minimum criterion for comparison—10 titles in common. Hence, agricultural occupations are included with nonagricultural manual occupations.

[7] The mean and standard deviation of the correlations over all occupations are based on 1386 pairs, as noted previously.

across societies in the prestige evaluation of manual occupations than of nonmanual occupations. First, the functional imperatives and organizational constraints common to all complex societies may impose greater limitations on the structure of white-collar than of blue-collar work. As Hodge, Treiman, and Rossi point out (1966:318):

> Major institutional complexes serving central societal needs which exist in all societies, and the common bureaucratic hierarchy imposed by the nation state, act to insure (despite vast differences in level of economic development) similarity between nations in the white collar prestige hierarchy of doctors, scientists, teachers, public officials, and clerks, but these factors cannot be expected to induce a corresponding degree of prestige similarity at the blue collar level.

Second, when European nations acquired colonial territories in other parts of the world, they tended to overlay the existing occupational structure with an imported administrative hierarchy long before a full-fledged industrial economy developed; in fact, in many of these countries a modern industrial system has not yet developed even today. Because of this, the white-collar sector of the occupational system may be more similar throughout the world than is the blue-collar sector, which would tend to induce corresponding similarity in the prestige hierarchies. Finally, the greater dependency of the organization of manual than nonmanual work upon the level of industrialization may create greater intersocietal variation in the relative power and privilege and hence prestige of manual than of nonmanual occupations. As we shall see in Chapter 6, the extent of intersocietal agreement in the prestige accorded manual occupations is more closely linked to similarity in level of industrialization than is true for nonmanual occupations.

The impression that somewhat different factors determine the similarity between countries in their evaluation of white-collar occupations and their evaluation of blue-collar jobs is strengthened by the fact that the correlation between the nonmanual and manual prestige correlations is quite low: $r = .25$ (computed over 386 pairs of countries). This is, however, substantially greater than the correlation reported by Hodge, Treiman, and Rossi (1966:319), relating similarity to the United States in the evaluation of white-collar occupations to similarity in the evaluation of blue-collar occupations. That correlation, computed over 23 foreign countries, was .06. Taken seriously, this would imply that completely different factors account for agreement between countries in the evaluation of white-collar occupations and in the evaluation of blue-collar occupations. It is more likely that the low correlation reported in that study is simply a reflection of unreliability in the data. Results such as that once again point up the crucial necessity of exercising extreme care in the matching of occupations across countries.

SUMMARY

This chapter has presented the basic evidence regarding the degree of agreement in occupational evaluations across societies. All in all, these results raise more questions than they answer. The general level of intersocietal agreement in the prestige evaluation of occupations appears to be very high, and there are no important tendencies for the level of agreement to be greater within particular regions or culture areas than across regions. This provides strong additional evidence against the cultural theory of prestige determination. However, the level of cross-national similarity in the prestige evaluation of blue-collar occupations is somewhat weaker than for white-collar occupations. This result is consistent with both of the diffusion theories (structural and cultural) and is not inconsistent with the pure structural theory elaborated in Chapter 1. Hence, we must turn to other evidence to evaluate these competing theories. This we do in the following chapter.

III

ISSUES OF SUBSTANCE

5

Explaining the Worldwide
Similarity in Prestige Hierarchies

On the basis of the material presented in the previous chapters, we now know that occupational prestige hierarchies are substantially similar throughout the world. In all societies, ranging from highly industrialized nations like the United States to peasant villages in up-country Thailand, the basic pattern of occupational evaluations is the same—professional and higher managerial positions are most highly regarded, lower white-collar and skilled blue-collar jobs fall in the middle of the hierarchy, and unskilled service and laboring jobs are the least respected. The question is, then, what accounts for the worldwide uniformity in occupational evaluations.

In Chapter 1, I proposed a *structural* theory of occupational prestige, arguing that occupational systems are essentially similar in all complex societies because the division of labor creates characteristic differences among occupations in the extent of power exercised, that differences in power give rise to differences in privilege, and that differences in power and privilege give rise to differences in prestige; thus, intersocietal prestige similarities reflect intersocietal similarities in occupational power and privilege. I also considered two alternative explanations for the worldwide similarity in prestige evaluations in the contemporary world: (*1*) a *cultural diffusion* theory, which argues that a Western pattern of occupational evaluation diffused throughout the world as a consequence of the colonial expansion and economic hegemony of Western nations, but without a corresponding diffusion of a Western occupational system; and (*2*) a *structural diffusion* theory, which argues that what diffused throughout the world was a Western division of labor and organization of work, which then gave rise to a Western pattern of prestige evaluations via the processes posited in Chapter 1. How can we distinguish among these alternatives?

First, we can distinguish between the structural and cultural explanations by asking whether the structure of occupational hierarchies is similar throughout the world. If it can be shown that not only prestige hierarchies, but also hierarchies of power and privilege are essentially uniform throughout the world, this would provide powerful support for a structural explanation and against a cultural one. This is especially so if it can be shown that the same pattern of connections between power, privilege, and prestige exists everywhere, that is, that the same model of prestige determination holds in all societies. Thus, our first task is to amass data on occupational hierarchies of power, privilege, and prestige for as many societies as possible. As we shall see, a structural explanation is supported.

Thus, our second task is to distinguish between a *pure structural* explanation and a *structural diffusion* explanation. To do this requires examination of evidence for past societies, before the advent of industrialization. If it can be shown that the same pattern of occupational differentiation with respect to power, privilege, and prestige holds for nonindustrial societies, and especially for past societies that were not attempting to industrialize, then a pure structural theory would be supported; for the unique division of labor created by the industrial system did not exist before the nineteenth century at the earliest. If, on the other hand, only contemporary societies, and especially industrialized societies, display a strong connection between occupational power, privilege, and prestige hierarchies, a structural diffusion explanation will be supported. As we shall see, the available evidence favors a pure structural explanation.

This strategy of successive theory testing allows us to divide our empirical analysis into two sections: (*1*) an examination of data for contemporary societies, as a basis for deciding between cultural and structural explanations; and, given the outcome of the first, (*2*) an examination of data for past societies, as a basis for deciding between pure and diffusionist structural theories.

DETERMINANTS OF PRESTIGE IN
CONTEMPORARY SOCIETIES

As is so often the case in comparative analysis, empirical data that can be used to assess the alternative theories presented above are extremely sparse. Of the three types of power discussed in Chapter 1, only one, skill, can be measured at all, and that only imperfectly and for only a limited number of societies. No measures of occupational differences in authority or economic control that are valid across nations are available at all. With respect to privilege the situation is only slightly better. For a number of countries, average incomes of occupational incumbents are available. But we have no systematic data on other forms of privilege. Thus, in sum, limited comparative data on three attributes of occupations, one measure of power, one measure of privilege, and, of course, a measure of prestige, are available. With these we will proceed as best we can. First, I will examine the extent of intersocietal similarity with respect to skill and income, the available indicators of power and privilege. Second, I will show how skill, income, and prestige are related to one another. Before beginning the analysis, however, it is necessary to describe the pertinent data.

Skill. The amount of skill and training required by an occupation is most conveniently indexed by the amount of formal education attained by its incumbents, and this is the measure I have adopted. It must be noted that such a measure has serious deficiencies. In the first place, it fails to take account of on-the-job training, which in some occupations constitutes the principal mode of learning the trade. In some countries with limited systems of formal education, differences in the level of skill required by different occupations may not be reflected in differences in the length of formal schooling. Second, in countries with complex educational systems that route students to specialized schools early in their careers, it is often difficult to devise a satisfactory scoring system for the amount of education completed, since the completion of different types of education usually carries different social meanings. On the other hand, there are two advantages in using such a measure to index skill differences.

First, as I argued in Chapter 1, those who possess generalized skills and knowledge—however these are defined by the particular culture—tend to be better able to manipulate the environment—both physical and social—than those lacking such skills: the greater the generalized knowledge, the greater the ability to discover the solutions to particular problems as they occur. Thus, while specialized knowledge should be valued over lack of knowledge, generalized knowledge should be valued over specialized knowledge, and the possession of both generalized knowledge and specialized knowledge should be valued most of all. Since how far one advances in the formal educational system is probably the best single indicator of the acquisition of general skills, occupational differences in the average level of educational attainment of incumbents are probably reasonably adequate indicators of occupational skill differences.

The second advantage of utilizing formal educational attainment as an indicator of skill requirements is that standardized data are reasonably widely available. Many countries collect information on formal schooling and publish tabulations of educational attainment by detailed occupation as part of their census statistics. In the absence of data of this sort it is essentially impossible to compare skill requirements for various jobs within a single country, much less across countries. Hence, census data are utilized wherever available to scale occupations with respect to educational attainment. Various summary measures are used, including mean years of school completed, percentage leaving school at the minimum age, percentage attaining a given level, and so on. While it seems to be the case that intercountry correlations are not strongly affected by variations in measurement procedures,[1] it would be unwise to interpret small differences in the size of correlations involving level of educational attainment.

Income. In contrast to skill, income is fairly easily measured. Since the concept is itself expressed in operational terms there is no difficulty in this regard. The main difficulty is the lack of data for the majority of countries. Income data are collected as part of the census inquiry in a few countries, and the best data derive from such sources. Even in such cases, however, there is some reason to doubt the accuracy of the data, since individuals not only forget many sources of income, but in many countries they are none too eager to reveal its extent for fear that information given to the census will find its way to the tax office. Nonetheless, census tabulations of income by detailed occupation are preferable to the alternative sources, which principally include enterprise wage surveys. While the accuracy of the information reported is probably greater than that collected directly from individuals, the coverage is typically relatively poor. Only individuals working for large enterprises are included, and this practice can mean excluding the bulk of the labor force in some occupations; and even for those working in covered enterprises, only wages paid by the enterprise are reported. Hence, sources of income other than the main job are omitted. Given this, census data on the average incomes of incumbents of detailed occupational categories are probably to be preferred and are used here wherever possible.

Data. Of the 53 nations for which occupational evaluations are available—and for these purposes we include the 5 places for which the criterion of occupational evaluation was something other than prestige—data on the relative educational achievements of incumbents of various occupations are available for 15 and data on average incomes are available for 11; for only 5 countries are there data for both variables.

[1] For Great Britain, data are available for two different summary measures of educational attainment—percentage leaving school at age 15 and mean school-leaving age (Great Britain General Register Office, 1956:Table 46). The correlation between the two measures is .87, and the average correlation of each of these measures with measures of educational attainment for other countries is virtually identical (.79 and .80, respectively), indicating that the same general conclusion would emerge from the use of either measure.

In order to assess the degree of intercountry similarity in occupational hierarchies with respect to income and education, it was, of course, necessary to match occupational categories across countries. This proved to be a difficult task. Census tabulation schemes are by no means comparable throughout the world, and even when they are founded on the same basic principles they tend to be idiosyncratic with respect to level of aggregation. In keeping with specific national needs, some parts of the category scheme are broken into finely detailed groups while other parts are highly aggregated. Fortunately, a fairly large number of countries based their 1960 occupational classification schemes on the category system of the first edition of the International Standard Classification of Occupations (International Labor Office, 1958a). Hence, by adopting the categories of the ISCO first edition, a reasonably adequate matching of census categories across countries could be effected.

The basic procedure was to match the lines from each detailed census classification of occupations to the categories of the ISCO. Excluding armed forces occupations, which are included in a separate major group of the ISCO scheme and not further differentiated, the ISCO first edition includes 198 separate lines, or "unit groups." Many countries had less detailed classifications than these and rather than omit a match altogether in such cases, the more highly aggregated lines of the individual country census were matched to each of the component ISCO lines. This resulted in each of the component ISCO lines being assigned the same value on the education or income variable, which amounts to assuming that the component occupational categories are identical with respect to their education or income distributions. This assumption is clearly false to at least some degree, as is clear from inspection of the distributions for those countries that do make fine distinctions. However, it seemed preferable to approximate the "true" education or income level for as many ISCO categories as possible by use of more highly aggregated averages than to forego matches altogether. The consequence of the procedure used here is that the true correlations between attributes of occupations both within and across countries will tend to be somewhat underestimated. Hence, the correlations reported here should be taken as minimum estimates of the correlations that would obtain if more precise matching had been possible. Of course, sometimes the individual country classifications were more detailed than the ISCO classification, and in this case the individual country lines were collapsed to match a single ISCO line. In this case, the same sort of error is not introduced, since the collapsing was done by taking a weighted average of the values of the component scores, with the weights representing the number of cases in each component category. The only difficulty entailed in collapsing individual country lines occurred when an ISCO line included part of but not all of an individual country line. This, however, is a standard difficulty of any occupational matching procedure.

To permit computation of correlations between education and income measures on the one hand, and prestige scores on the other, still another adjustment of the data was required. Recall that the matching of titles used in prestige studies across countries was effected by adapting and expanding the revised edition of the ISCO scheme while the education and income measures were coded according to the original edition. As was indicated above, the original edition was used to code census data because many national census classifications were based upon it, while the revised edition was used to code titles used in prestige studies because it is considerably more extensive than the original edition and, moreover, is likely to form the basis for subsequent census tabulations and hence provided a superior framework for the Standard International Occupational Prestige Scale (discussed in detail in Chapter 8). Because of the use of different coding schemes for the two sets of data, the two sets had to be brought into correspondence to enable the computation of correlations between prestige and the other characteristics. To accomplish this I made use of the conversion table provided in the revised edition of the ISCO manual (International Labor Office, 1969a) to map the 509 occupation lines generated in the course of the prestige coding into the 198 original edition ISCO categories. A simple average of the prestige scores of all occupations falling into any ISCO category was then computed, generating a matrix of 198 occupational categories by 60 places. This matrix was then combined with the census data coded for all available countries and the appropriate correlations were computed.

Undoubtedly, the crude averaging procedure adopted here does some violence to the accuracy of the prestige scores assigned to given lines. However, the alternative, equally arbitrary, would have been to introduce some judgmentally based weighting procedure for the occupational titles entering into each average. Since there was no good basis for arriving at weights, that alternative was abandoned. Finally, it should be noted that while the revised ISCO categories were for the most part mapped into a single original ISCO line, some exceptions were made. In particular, the original edition of the ISCO made industrial distinctions within the managerial category which neither the revised ISCO nor my modification of it preserved. Hence, in this instance my titles were distributed over several original edition ISCO categories.

Intercorrelations of Occupational Characteristics. Recall that the first proposition of the theory of prestige determination outlined in Chapter 1 is that occupational positions are inherently differentiated and hierarchically ordered with respect to, among other attributes, the skill it takes to perform them. A corollary of this is that the skill hierarchy of occupations should be more or less invariant across societies. If each job has a characteristic skill level associated with it that is inherent in the nature of the job, then despite differences in the organization of work from place to place, the relative skill of incumbents of each position should be much the same across societies.

Then if, as argued above, educational attainment can be taken as an adequate indicator of skill differentials, the average level of educational attainment of incumbents of various occupations should be highly correlated across societies. Table 5.1 is a matrix of such intercorrelations for the 15 countries for which data are available. The size of these intercorrelations is striking: The average correlation across all pairs of countries is .76, almost as high as the average intercountry prestige correlation reported in Chapter 4. These results can be taken as providing strong support for the idea that occupations are more or less invariant across societies with respect to relative skill requirements.

Moreover, it is possible to argue that the average intercountry correlation is even higher, and that unreliable data for Taiwan and Zambia pulled it down. With the exception of these two countries, all the education data are from national census statistics, and hence can be considered as reliable as any other data available for such countries. For Taiwan and Zambia, however, data are from surveys of enterprises. The Taiwan data are restricted to workers in manufacturing and service industries, and even within these categories coverage is incomplete. The Zambian data are restricted to occupations with large proportions of incumbents having at least some secondary education. Thus, a large fraction of the labor force, concentrated particularly in low-prestige jobs, is excluded from the survey, attenuating the range of educational attainment and probably reducing the correlations with other countries from what they would otherwise be. Some evidence supporting the assumption that the Zambian correlations, at least, are too low is to be found in a comparison of data from Ghana. Ghana, similar to Zambia in level of development (as measured by such indicators as per capita GNP, school enrollments per population, percentage of the labor force in agriculture, etc.), exhibits correlations with the other countries included in Table 5.1 that are markedly higher than those for Zambia and not much different from the intercorrelations among the remaining countries. Hence, it is questionable whether the low correlations involving Zambia should be taken as evidence of a deviant educational hierarchy of occupations or simply as evidence of unreliability in the data. Excluding Taiwan and Zambia, the average of the remaining correlations increases to .81, identical to the mean intersocietal prestige correlation.

Let us turn now to the second determinant of prestige for which we have

TABLE 5.1

Intercorrelations of Education Levels of Occupations[a]

Country[b]	(1)	(2)	(8)	(17)	(18)	(20)	(23)	(28)	(31)	(34)	(39)	(50)	(57)	(59)	(60)
(1) United States	*166*	.90	.93	.86	.75	.85	.89	.92	.85	.85	.74	.78	.84	.66	.55
(2) Argentina	125	*144*	.94	.91	.77	.85	.88	.90	.87	.94	.75	.75	.74	.65	.66
(8) Canada	149	124	*164*	.89	.81	.87	.91	.93	.94	.91	.78	.80	.84	.68	.56
(17) Germany (West)	89	75	80	*93*	.78	.80	.88	.89	.78	.89	.76	.68	.78	.84	.69
(18) Ghana	161	133	157	90	*182*	.72	.82	.78	.75	.74	.69	.74	.75	.63	.43
(20) Great Britain	148	127	146	84	160	*170*	.81	.92	.81	.86	.66	.75	.80	.75	.61
(23) India	49	44	47	32	55	55	*61*	.88	.84	.84	.76	.74	.85	.75	.38
(28) Israel	112	101	115	89	125	120	50	*137*	.90	.86	.73	.84	.78	.82	.57
(31) Japan	129	117	125	68	137	134	49	99	*146*	.85	.79	.73	.81	.67	.54
(34) Netherlands	138	121	130	91	140	133	45	107	114	*150*	.74	.68	.73	.67	.57
(39) Norway	123	102	113	80	127	117	42	90	100	123	*134*	.71	.70	.54	.46
(50) Taiwan	44	38	44	35	52	49	25	41	40	39	36	*53*	.53	.59	.34
(57) USSR	110	101	112	67	124	122	51	95	110	106	95	41	*135*	.72	.46
(59) Yugoslavia	109	94	105	61	110	108	34	77	98	96	88	31	82	*117*	.64
(60) Zambia	166	144	164	93	182	170	61	137	146	150	134	53	135	117	*198*

[a]Number of occupations entering each correlation given in lower triangle; diagonal gives total number of occupations for each country. Country numbers correspond to their ordering among all 60 places, to facilitate comparisons across tables. See Table 4.1 for a convenient listing of countries.

[b]Sources: Data for (2), (17), (34), (39), and (59) from Horowitz et al., 1966; other sources are (1) U.S. Bureau of the Census, 1963: Table 9; (8) Canada Dominion Bureau of Statistics, 1963a: Table 17; (18) Ghana Census Office, 1964: Table 8; (20) Great Britain General Register Office, 1956: Table 46; (23) India Cabinet Secretariat, 1970: Table 7.1; (28) Israel Central Bureau of Statistics, n.d.; (31) Japan Bureau of Statistics, 1963: Table 9; (50) Taiwan Labor Force Survey Research Institute, 1968: Table 16; (57) USSR Tsentral'noye Statistichyeskoye Oopravlyeniye, 1962: Tables 47, 51; (60) Zambia Office of National Development and Planning, 1966: Table C-1.

data, occupational income. Since income is posited to depend upon a number of factors, some of which may vary from place to place, intersocietal similarities with respect to the relative income of various jobs would not be expected to be as great as in the case of educational levels. For example, capitalist and socialist countries might be expected to exhibit somewhat greater divergences with respect to occupational income levels than countries with similar economic systems.

Table 5.2 presents intercorrelations in occupational income levels for 11 countries. The average intercountry correlation is .65. This is strikingly high, although, as predicted, not as high as that for education. However, the notion that socialist countries are different from capitalist countries with respect to occupational income levels does not hold up, at least when Yugoslavia is taken as socialist and compared with the other 10 countries (obviously, this is less than a perfect comparison, since many of the remaining countries have partially socialized economies). The average of the correlations with Yugoslavia is actually higher (.69) than the average across all countries. Costa Rica and Taiwan, by contrast, appear to have somewhat deviant income distributions. However, whether this reflects actual idiosyncracies in their income structures or inadequacies in the data is not clear. Hence, not too much should be made of those differences; rather, attention should be focused on the high average intercorrelation.

Apart from the census materials just reported, one additional body of data on occupational income distributions permitting cross-national comparsons exists—monthly wage rates for 41 industrial occupations, collected from enterprise censuses for 27 of the countries in our sample (International Labor Office, 1958b). The advantage of these data is that they are available for a far larger number of countries than are census data on occupational income distributions. However, they have two disadvantages: They are based on a much more restricted set of occupations than the census data, heavily concentrated in the skilled blue-collar range; and because they are based on enterprise surveys they do not take account of other sources of income, which are to some extent correlated with and derive from occupational position. Both of these factors can be expected to reduce the correlations across countries by attenuating the variance of the income distributions. Nonetheless, for the 306 pairs of countries with information for at least 10 occupations in common, the average intercountry correlation is .51, indicating a substantial degree of similarity in the relative wage rates of industrial occupations.

Relation of Prestige to other Occupational Characteristics. The next task is to examine directly the relationship between the prestige of occupations and their other characteristics. In light of the theory proposed above,

TABLE 5.2

Intercorrelations of Income Levels of Occupations[a]

Country[b]	(1)	(8)	(9)	(12)	(23)	(36)	(40)	(47)	(48)	(50)	(59)
(1) United States	*166*	.87	.68	.51	.81	.67	.64	.68	.82	.44	.72
(8) Canada	151	*166*	.65	.45	.76	.69	.72	.65	.77	.53	.75
(9) Ceylon	130	132	*151*	.53	.77	.65	.69	.73	.65	.55	.69
(12) Costa Rica	166	166	151	*198*	.50	.50	.41	.45	.53	.42	.65
(23) India	49	48	46	60	*60*	.72	.87	.84	.81	.57	.72
(36) New Zealand	166	166	151	198	60	*198*	.73	.65	.77	.56	.68
(40) Pakistan	74	74	67	86	43	86	*86*	.75	.74	.67	.57
(47) Surinam	98	99	91	117	42	117	65	*117*	.66	.53	.58
(48) Sweden	151	146	136	173	55	173	78	104	*173*	.45	.78
(50) Taiwan	87	87	80	102	38	102	61	71	91	*102*	.72
(59) Yugoslavia	105	108	96	117	38	117	53	64	103	57	*117*

[a]Number of occupations entering each correlation given in lower triangle; diagonal gives total number of occupations for each country.

[b]Sources: (1) U. S. Bureau of the Census, 1963: Table 25; (8) Canada Dominion Bureau of Statistics, 1963a: Table 21; (9) Ceylon Department of Census and Statistics, 1962: Table 1; (12) Costa Rica Direccion General de Estadistica y Censos, 1966: Table 39; (23) India Cabinet Secretariat, 1970: Table 8.1; (36) New Zealand Department of Statistics, 1964: Table 5; (40) Hashmi et al., 1964: Table 4.03; (47) Surinam Algemeen Bureau voor de Statistiek, 1962: 58-78; (48) Sweden Statistiska Centralbyrån, 1965: Table 26; (50) Taiwan Labor Force Survey Research Institute, 1968: Table 27, and Taiwan Provincial Government, 1969: Table 20; (59) Yugoslavia Savezni Zavod za Statistiku, 1965: Table 121.13.

education and income levels of occupations should be highly correlated with their prestige. Of course, as before, the correlations cannot be expected to be perfect, since other determinants of prestige, in particular amount of authority and economic power, are unmeasured. Nonetheless, if the theory is correct, correlations between prestige and, respectively, education and income should be uniformly high across societies.

The pertinent correlations are given in Table 5.3. First, we observe that both the education and the income correlations are strikingly high. The mean correlation of education with prestige is .72, and only three correlations fall below .6, those for peasant India, the USSR, and Zambia. The mean correlation of income with prestige is .69, and only two correlations fall below .6, those for Costa Rica and peasant India. Since we have already noted the anomalous nature of the prestige data from peasant India, and since the Indian income and education data refer to the nonagricultural population, the low correlations for India are hardly surprising. Similarly, the inadequate character of the education data for Zambia has been noted above. This leaves us with two true anomalies, the Soviet correlation between the percentage of middle school graduates and the prestige of occupations, and the Costa Rican correlation between mean income and prestige. Clearly, these deviations from the expected pattern require further study.

However, it is of interest to note that it is the prestige hierarchy and not the educational hierarchy of the USSR that deviates from the standard pattern. The relative educational attainments of incumbents of various occupations in the USSR are highly correlated with those in other countries (Table 5.1) as well as with the generic worldwide occupational prestige hierarchy represented by the Standard Scale, but are much more modestly correlated with the Soviet occupational prestige hierarchy. This informs us where to look in trying to understand the idiosyncratic features of the occupational structure of the Soviet Union, a topic we will return to in Chapter 7.

The final task in this section is to consider the joint effect of education and income on prestige. Data for both education and income levels are available for only five countries—the United States, Canada, India, Taiwan, and Yugoslavia, and for the latter three countries the data are deficient in various ways discussed earlier. Nonetheless, we can use them to make a tentative assessment of the determinants of occupational prestige hierarchies. Table 5.4 presents the results of the regression of prestige on income and education for each of these places; India is represented by two equations because we have two sets of prestige data for India. Two observations can be made about these results. First, with the exception of peasant India and Taiwan, for which the data are clearly poor, in each case at least two-thirds of the variance in the prestige of occupations can be attributed to

TABLE 5.3

Intercorrelations of Occupational Education, Income, and Prestige, and
Correlations with the Standard International Occupational Prestige Scale [a,b]

Country	Correlations within Countries — Education-Income r	N	Education-Prestige r	N	Income-Prestige r	N	Correlations with Standard Scale — Education r	N	Income r	N
(1) United States	.73	166	.85	135	.79	135	.83	166	.78	166
(2) Argentina	--	--	.60	19	--	--	.82	144	--	--
(8) Canada	.73	164	.87	94	.78	96	.84	164	.83	166
(9) Ceylon	--	--	--	--	.77	18	--	--	.70	151
(12) Costa Rica	--	--	--	--	.46	58	--	--	.53	198
(17) Germany (West)	--	--	.67	36	--	--	.86	93	--	--
(18) Ghana	--	--	.84	21	--	--	.79	182	--	--
(20) Great Britain	--	--	.82	34	--	--	.82	170	--	--
(23) India (Peasant)	.84	59	.48	14	.35	13	.83	61	.70	60
(24) India (Student)			.76	13	.81	13				
(28) Israel	--	--	.94	31	--	--	.87	137	--	--
(31) Japan	--	--	.81	46	--	--	.82	146	--	--
(34) Netherlands	--	--	.84	85	--	--	.82	150	--	--
(36) New Zealand	--	--	--	--	.73	67	--	--	.69	198
(39) Norway	--	--	.78	38	.77	30	.75	134	--	--
(40) Pakistan	--	--	--	--	.61	54	--	--	.67	86
(47) Surinam	--	--	--	--	.74	23	--	--	.60	117
(48) Sweden	--	--	--	--	.70	19	--	--	.77	173
(50) Taiwan	.71	53	.72	13	--	--	.66	53	.62	102
(57) USSR	--	--	.47	46	--	--	.79	135	--	--
(59) Yugoslavia	.85	87	.83	32	.80	34	.76	117	.86	117
(60) Zambia	--	--	.17	29	--	--	.55	198	--	--
Mean	.77		.72		.69		.79		.70	

[a] Sources: See footnotes to Tables 5.1 and 5.2.
[b] See Chapter 8 for a description of the Scale.

TABLE 5.4
Results of Regression of Prestige on Education and Income

Country	Net Regression Coefficients in Standard Form		Coefficient of Determination (R^2)
	Education	Income	
(1) United States	.58	.37	.78
(8) Canada	.63	.32	.80
(23) India (Peasant)	.63	.18	.37
(24) India (Student)	.27	.58	.68
(50) Taiwan	.45	.38	.59
(59) Yugoslavia	.56	.32	.73
Mean	.52	.36	.66

variance in occupational education and income levels (the remaining variance presumably is due in large part to aspects of power and privilege that we are unable to measure). Second, with the exception of Indian university students, the influence of education is substantially stronger than the influence of income, which is not surprising considering that educational requirements are an intrinsic feature of occupations while income differences are influenced by a host of exogenous as well as intrinsic factors. Together, these results provide substantial support for the notion that there is a uniform occupational structure throughout the world.

The similarity between the occupational structure of Yugoslavia and those of the United States and Canada is particularly striking, not only because Yugoslavia, in contrast to the United States and Canada, is a newly industrializing socialist country with strong aspects of central planning, but also because the criterion variable for Yugoslavia is not prestige but "desirability." Recall that for this reason Yugoslavia was excluded from the bulk of the analysis and only reintroduced here because of the paucity of other data. The similarity between the equations for the United States, Canada, and Yugoslavia is added testimony to the robustness of the relationship between education, income, and prestige.

To sum up, the results of this and the previous section clearly favor a structural model of occupational prestige determination. Wherever we have data we find basic intersocietal similarity in the relative education required to perform various occupations and in the relative income returned to them. Second, for the most part the connections between educational requirements, income gained, and prestige are similar throughout the world. Thus, it cannot be the case that occupational prestige hierarchies are similar merely as a consequence of the imposition of a Western value system on the non-Western world. Rather, it is evident that to a large degree occupational prestige hierarchies are similar throughout the world because occupational skill and hence income hierarchies are similar throughout the world and these features of occupations determine their prestige.

OCCUPATIONAL STRUCTURES IN PAST SOCIETIES

Having shown that occupational structures are essentially similar throughout the contemporary world, we now ask whether this is the consequence of the homogenizing effect of industrialization or whether occupational structures are similar in all complex societies, industrialized or not. To decide between these alternatives we examine data from past societies. Since industrialization is, at best, about 150 years old (the rapid expansion of industry known as the "industrial revolution" first occurred in Great Britain during the period 1750–1825, in the United States and Western Europe during the nineteenth century, and elsewhere still later, if at all: Hughes, 1968), demonstration of substantial similarity in occupational structures between pre-nineteenth-century societies and the present will constitute strong evidence for a pure structural theory of occupational prestige.

As usual, appropriate data are extremely sparse. Not only are there no data on authority or economic power, but there are no data for past societies on skill levels of occupations. I have, however, located systematic data on the wealth or income of occupational incumbents for six past societies and "prestige" data for two past societies. Let us consider the prestige data first.

In 1395 a rank ordering of castes was promulgated by Raja Jayastihi Malla of Nepal (Wright, 1958:111–112). Since this was the official ordering of castes and since fourteenth-century Nepali occupations were almost exclusively organized on the basis of caste membership (in fact, at the time castes were named by the occupations of their members), it seems reasonable to interpret such a caste ranking as an occupational prestige ranking. Similar data are available for fifteenth-century Florence, in the form of a ranking of guilds. An official rank order of guilds was maintained by the Florentine Commune, and a history of the guilds of Florence interpolates various subguilds and individual occupations into the official list (Staley, 1906:61–62). The rank order of guilds as of 1427 was used here to correspond to wealth data described below.

The wealth data consist of estimates, of varying quality, of either the average wealth held by incumbents of various occupations or the average income returned to particular occupations. Data are available for fifteenth-century Florence, late-seventeenth-century England, late-eighteenth-century

America, mid-nineteenth-century Philadelphia, mid-nineteenth-century Hamilton, Ontario, and late-nineteenth-century London.[2]

In order to assess the stability over time in the ordering of occupations with respect to income or wealth and prestige, it was necessary to match occupational titles from each of the historical data sets to the standard categories described in Chapter 2. Since these categories were developed inductively from mid-twentieth-century data the ease with which the matches could be made itself constitutes a partial test of the claim (see Chapter 1) that despite the proliferation of new jobs as a result of changes in technology, and despite the massive and ubiquitous shift in the distribution of labor forces associated with industrialization (out of agricultural and laboring jobs and into nonmanual jobs), the organization of functions into specific occupations has remained strikingly stable. Most of the differences between occupational structures, I claim, represent greater or lesser subdivision of functions into separately named occupational titles; they do not represent differences in the actual distribution of functions among occupational categories.

Furthermore, differences in the degree of differentiation of occupations tend to reflect the relative importance of specific functions in particular economies. Thus, in fifteenth-century Florence, fine distinctions were made between various kinds of wool workers; and in medieval Nepal several varieties of priests were distinguished. But since highly specialized subcategories of occupations tend to be relatively homogeneous with respect to their economic or prestige status, little precision is lost by aggregating such categories for comparative purposes.

The best evidence for the stability of occupational categories over time is the very fact that it was possible to carry out the task described here. In very few instances did it prove difficult or impossible to find a match between the historical data and contemporary titles. (And, for the most part, those difficulties that did arise resulted from vaguely defined titles, e.g., "agent," which are as common to contemporary data as to the historical material analyzed here.) Nearly all the lists of occupations include high government officials, clergy, lawyers, physicians, teachers, large merchants, shopkeepers, artisans of various sorts—smiths, masons, carpen-

---

[2] The data for Florence are from Professor David Herlihy's collation: "Census and Property Survey (*Catasto*) of Selected Italian Cities, 1427." They were made available, with Professor Herlihy's permission, by the Data and Program Library Service of the University of Wisconsin. The data for seventeenth-century England are Gregory King's estimates, first published in 1696. The version used here is that in Forster (1969:239–240). The data for eighteenth-century America were compiled by me from the narrative material presented in Main (1965: Chapter 3). The data for Philadelphia are from Blumin (1969: Table 1); those for Hamilton are from Katz (1971: Table II.42); and those for London are from Booth (1889, 1895).

ters, and so on—and unskilled laborers. Although specific occupational titles are present in some of the data sets and not in others, the extent to which the basic categories remain the same is striking. Even in medieval Nepal, by far the most nearly unique society under consideration here, the occupational categories are generally quite recognizable and are surprisingly comparable to occupations in the modern world. The matches between the Nepali and Florentine prestige data and the Standard Scale (Appendix A) are shown in Tables 5.5 and 5.6; space limitations preclude displaying the wealth data but they are available from me upon request. These materials are also more fully described in Treiman (1976).

Let us now consider how stable occupational status hierarchies have been over time. Table 5.7 presents intercorrelations of wealth and prestige levels among the eight historical data sets, as well as correlations with the generic prestige hierarchy of the contemporary world (Standard Scale). The size of these correlations is striking. For each historical period, going back to fifteenth-century Florence, the relative levels of occupational wealth or income are strongly related to the contemporary worldwide average occupational prestige hierarchy. In fact, the historical correlations are approximately as strong as the contemporary ones. For past societies the average correlation of occupational wealth (or income) levels with the Standard Scale is .75, whereas the corresponding average correlation for contemporary societies is only .70.[3] Similarly, the average intercorrelation of occupational wealth levels over the four and one-half centuries between 1427 and 1890 is .75, suggesting that the intertemporal stability of occupational structures within Europe is possibly greater than the intersocietal similarity within the contemporary world. Lending support to this view is the striking demonstration by Brown and Hopkins (1955) of stability in the relative wages of building craftsmen and laborers in England for more than 5 centuries:

> after [about 1410] there was no sustained change until the First World War. In the fifteenth century the craftsman got half as much again as the labourer, 6d. a day to his 4d.; in the 1890's he got half as much again, 7½d. an hour to his 5d.; he got half as much again, or within a halfpenny of it, in every settled period in between [Brown and Hopkins, 1955:202].

Finally, in our own data there is no evidence whatsoever that the industrial

[3] It may seem anomalous that the average correlation for the historical data is actually slightly higher than that for the contemporary data, but the difference is not large enough to be meaningful. Moreover, the historical average is obviously slightly inflated by the correlation between the 1688 British data and the Standard Scale, which is excessively high due to a correlation of extremes. Omitting this correlation, the average correlation for the historical data drops to .72.

TABLE 5.5

Matches of Caste Titles for Nepal (ca.1395) to Standard Scale, together with Rank Order of Nepali Castes Listed in Decreasing Order

Rank	Nepali Caste Title	Standard Scale Code	Standard Scale Title	Standard Scale Score
63	*Bhupa, raja, narendra* or *chhetri* (ruler or warrior)	10000	High Armed Forces Officer	73
62[a]	*Lekhaka* (scribe) (62) *Kayastha* (scribe) (61)	02033	High Civil Servant, Dept. Head	71
59[a]	*Mantrin* (state official, minister) (60) *Saciva* (state official, minister) (59) *Amatya* (state official, minister) (58)	03100	Middle Rank Civil Servant	66
59[a]	*Dwija, bipra* or *brahmana* (priest) (64) *Pujita* (temple priest) (57) *Acarya* (Hindu priest) (55)	01410	Clergyman	60
56[a]	*Deva cinta* (God thinker)	01490	Religious Teacher	56
53[a]	*Grahacintaka* (astrologer) (54) *Jyotisa* (astrologer) (53) *Ganika* (astrologer) (52)	01991	Diviner	37
51	*Daivajna* (lower caste priest?)[b]	--	--	--
50	*Alama* (?)	--	--	--
49	*Srichante* (?)	--	--	--
48	*Sajakara* (tailor)	07910	Tailor	40
47	*Supika* (soup cook?)	--	--	--
46	*Cichaka* (?)	--	--	--
45	*Marikara* (confectioner)	07760	Baker	33
44	*Silpikara* (craftsman)	09950	Skilled Worker	42
43	*Bharika* (bearer)	09712	Porter	17
42	*Napika* (barber)	05700	Barber	30
41	*Lepika* (plasterer)	09550	Plasterer	31
40	*Daukara* (wood carver)	0819[c]	Cabinetmakers and related woodworkers, nec	31
39	*Taksaka* (carpenter, house measurer)	09540	Carpenter	37

119

TABLE 5.5 (Continued)

Rank	Nepali Caste Title	Standard Scale Code	Standard Scale Title	Standard Scale Score
38	*Srinkhari* (?)	--	--	--
37	*Ksetrakara* (surveyor, gov't land measurer)	00310	Surveyor	58
36	*Kumbhakara* (potter)	08920	Potter	25
35	*Tuladhara* weigher--trading)	04520	Market trader	36
34	*Karnika* (weaver)	07540	Weaver	30
33	*Kansyakara* (bell maker)	07240	Metal Caster	33
32	*Suvarnakara* (goldsmith)	08800	Jeweler, Goldsmith	43
31	*Tamrakara* (copper smith)	08731	Copper, Tin Smith	32
30	*Gopaka* (cowherd)	06240	Livestock Worker	26
29	*Bhayala - chanchu* (?)	--	--	--
28	*Kanjikara* (?)	--	--	--
27	*Tayoruta* (?)	--	--	--
26	*Tankadhari* (?)	--	--	--
25[a]	*Vimari* (?)	0629[c]	Agricultural and Animal Husbandry Workers nec	14
24[a]	*Surppakara* (winnower) (24) *Natebaruda* (winnower) (23)	--	--	--
22	*Bathaḥom* (?)	01712	Musical Entertainer	32
21	*Gayane* (bard singer)	09310	Building Painter	31
20	*Citrakara* (painter)	--[c]	--	--
19	*Surabija* (?)	0599[c]	Other Service Workers	29
18	*Natijiva* (actor who lives by prostituting his wife)			

#	Nepali title	Code[b]	Standard Scale / Occupation	Score[a]
17	Mandhurda (oil presser)	0779[c]	Food and Beverage Processors nec	34
16	Vyanjanakara (cook)	05310	Cook	31
15	Mali (gardener)	06270	Gardener	21
14	Mansabikri (butcher)	07730	Butcher	31
13	Kirata (hunter)	06491	Hunter	6
12	Badi (?)	--	--	--
11	Dhanyamari (?)	--	--	--
10	Tandukara (weaver?)	--	--	--
9	Nadichedi (umbilical cord cutter? vein cutter?)	--	--	--
8	Kundakara (ivory carver)	09491	Ivory Carver	33
7	Lohakara (blacksmith)	08310	Blacksmith	34
6	Ksatrikara (?)	--	--	--
5	Dhobi (washerman)	05600	Launderer	22
4	Ravaka (dyer)	07560	Cloth Dyer	25
3	Niyogi (?)	--	--	--
2	Matangi (elephant driver)	09860	Animal Driver	18
1	Charmakara (leather worker)	08030	Leather Worker	22

Source: Wright (1958:111-112). Professor Theodore Riccardi, Jr., Department of Middle East Cultures and Languages, Columbia University, was consulted regarding translations.

[a] Average of component scores (individual scores are given at the end of each component Nepali title).

[b] Titles with doubtful or unknown translations were not matched to Standard Scale. These are indicated by a "?" following the title.

[c] Matched to a "unit group" category in the Standard Scale rather than to an "occupation" category; hence excluded from the correlations reported in the Table 5.7. See Appendix A.

121

TABLE 5.6

Matches of Occupational and Guild Titles for fifteenth-Century Florence to Standard Scale, together with Fifteenth-Century Florentine Protocol Rank Listed in Decreasing Order

Rank	Florentine Title	Standard Scale Code	Standard Scale Title	Standard Scale Score
34	Knights[a]	10000	High Armed Forces Officer	73
32[c]	Judges	01220	Judge	78
32[c]	Doctors of law (university degree holders)[a] (33)	01210	Lawyer, Trial Lawyer	71
	Notaries (30)			
27[c]	Bankers and money changers	02114	Bankers	67
27[c]	Doctors of medicine (university degree holders)[a] (31)	00610	Physician	78
	Physicians[b] - surgeons (23)			
25[c]	Goldsmiths	08800	Jeweler, Goldsmith	43
23[c]	Master merchants (guild of Calimala or merchants in foreign cloth) wholesale (29)	04106	Wholesale Distributor	58
	Wool manufacturers and merchants - wholesale (28)			
	Master silk manufacturers and merchants - wholesale (26)			
	Linen manufacturers and merchants - wholesale and retail (10)			
22[c]	Wool manufacturers. See above (28)	02112	Head of Firm	63
	Master silk manufacturers. See above (26)			
	Silk makers and merchants - retail (10)			
	Linen manufacturers. See above (10)			
22	Apothecaries	00670	Pharmacist	64
21	Agents and brokers	04104	Broker	55
20	Painters (miniatures)[b]	01610	Artist	57
19	Stationers, perfumers, mercers and veil makers[b]	—[d]	--	-
18	Furriers and skinners - wholesale	07920	Fur Coat Tailor	35

17	Silk makers and merchants - retail (24) / Linen manufacturers and merchants - wholesale and retail (10)	04101	Large Shop Owner	58
17	Butchers - wholesale livestock dealers	07732 / 04105	Master Butcher (45) / Livestock Broker (40)	42[c]
16	Butchers - retail	07730	Butcher	31
15	Blacksmiths	08310	Blacksmith	34
14	Shoemakers	08010	Shoemaker, Repairer	28[c]
13	Master Builders, stonemasons, and wood workers	09510 / 09594	Mason (34) / Skilled Construction Worker (46)	40[c]
11	Tailors	07910	Tailor	40
9	Wine makers and merchants (9) / Retail cloth dealers and retail traders (including small industries) (12) / Oil merchants - general provision dealers (grocers) (6)	04100	Shop Keeper	42
8	Innkeepers	05102 / 05104[e]	Hotel Operator (46) / Pub Keeper (33)	40
7	Tanners	0761	Tanners and Fellmongers	22
5	Saddlers	08030	Leather Worker	22
4	Locksmiths, precision metal workers	08390	Locksmith	40
3	Armourers	08730	Sheet Metal Worker	36
2	Carpenters	09540	Carpenter	37[c]
1	Millers and bakers	07710 / 07760	Grain Miller (33) / Baker (33)	33[c]

Source: Staley (1906:61-62).

[a] Not a guild; occupational category placed in protocol ordering by Staley.

[b] Guild that is a subsidiary of one of the 21 official guilds.

[c] Average of component scores (individual scores are given at the end of each component title).

[d] No matching occupation in Standard Scale.

[e] Matched to a "unit group" category in the Standard Scale rather than to an "occupation" category; hence, excluded from computation of correlations reported in Table 5.7. See Appendix A.

TABLE 5.7

Intercorrelations of Occupational Wealth and Prestige Levels for Past Societies, and Correlations with Standard International Occupational Prestige Scale[a]

Past Societies	Standard Scale	Nepal Prestige	Florence Prestige	Florence Wealth	England Income	U.S. Income	Phila-delphia Wealth	Hamilton Wealth	London Income
Standard Scale	_509_	.73	.82	.69	.91	.74	.73	.75	.69
Nepal, 1395, caste rank	33	_33_	--	-.13	--	--	--	.35	.60
Florence, ca.1427, guild rank	30	8	_30_	.45	--	.70	.75	.60	.78
Florence, 1427, total wealth (log)	55	16	24	_55_	_15_	.84	.87	.80	.44
England, 1688, income (log)	15	3	4	5	_15_	.90	--	--	--
U.S., ca.1776, income (log)	43	8	12	19	12	_43_	.68	.88	.83
Philadelphia, 1860, wealth (log)	44	7	14	21	4	17	_44_	.75	.66
Hamilton, Ontario, 1860, wealth	49	11	18	25	7	20	25	_49_	.60
London, ca.1890, income (log)	169	21	16	35	7	25	29	33	_169_

Sources: See pp. 116-117 for details on sources.

[a]Number of occupations for which data available given in diagonal and number of matching occupations upon which correlation based shown below diagonal; correlations based on fewer than 10 cases not shown.

revolution had any impact on the relative privilege of occupational groups or on the relation between privilege and prestige. The correlations of occupational wealth levels with the Standard Scale prestige scores are equally high for the three preindustrial societies as for the three nineteenth-century cities. If industrialization had an impact, surely it would be manifest in the occupational structure of London. But there is no evidence for that in these data.

The "prestige" data for Florence and Nepal are equally striking. As would be expected, the correlation with the Standard Scale is substantially higher for Florence than for Nepal. (Nepal, in fact, resembles the least industrialized contemporary societies in the extent of deviation from the standard occupational prestige hierarchy—see Table 8.3). Since Florence was a major mercantile center, it is not surprising that its occupational prestige hierarchy is closer than Nepal's to the generic hierarchy of the modern world. It must be noted, however, that the Florentine hierarchy is still more idiosyncratic than are most contemporary societies regardless of their levels of industrialization. Nonetheless, as was true of the wealth hierarchy, the most striking point about the prestige hierarchy is that it is relatively stable over time.

On the basis of the theory of prestige developed in Chapter 1, there is every reason to believe that were data available for skill hierarchies they would be even more stable over time than income or wealth hierarchies, just as is generally true in the contemporary world. This, then, provides the basis for an additional test of the theory at such time as suitable data become available for past societies.[4] If occupational skill hierarchies for past societies can be shown to be as uniform as occupational wealth and prestige hierarchies, and, further, if the connections between skill, wealth, and prestige can be shown to be as strong for past societies as for present ones, a pure structural theory of prestige could be said to be firmly verified. However, for the present we must content ourselves with a somewhat more limited confirmation of the theory on the basis of fragmentary data. In addition to the evidence presented above, there are various impressionistic accounts of the class structure of past societies.

For example, Gideon Sjoberg's analysis of preindustrial cities includes an explicit discussion of the characteristic features of the social class systems of such societies. On the basis of data from feudal realms in traditional China, Japan, India, the Middle East, Europe, and Mesoamerica he asserts

---

[4] I would be extremely interested to be informed of any data of this sort. In particular, I am interested in locating cross-tabulations of occupation by literacy, the amount of schooling received, or skill levels, for any past society, or, for that matter, for any society not already included here.

(1960:108–109):

> Preindustrial cities across cultures display strong consistency in their class structure—in the kinds of criteria that are highly valued and the manner in which these are assigned in determining class position. Thus specific kinds of occupations are rated highly, and these are closely associated with certain kinds of achievements, greater power and authority, the "desirable" possessions, a particular kind of kinship position, and special moral and personal attributes. So too, the kinds of criteria that are devalued are very similar for cities from one culture to the next.

Sjoberg then goes on to identify the occupational groups that comprise the two major classes he sees as characteristic of preindustrial cities: a small upper class and a large lower class. He also recognizes status distinctions within each of these classes. Although his discussion is in narrative form and does not easily lend itself to a definitive rank ordering of occupational groups, I have attempted to translate Sjoberg's description (1960:118–123) into an occupational hierarchy for the purpose of comparing it to the standard prestige hierarchy of the contemporary world. Table 5.8 shows the occupational groups mentioned by Sjoberg, listed in the order implied by his narrative account. Occupational categories treated by Sjoberg as having similar status are grouped together within brackets. The only real ambiguity in Sjoberg's account is with respect to the highest lower-class group—he may not have considered low-level government, religious, and military personnel to have higher status than other lower-class categories. The right-hand column represents my matches of contemporary occupational titles (Standard Scale categories) to Sjoberg's categories.

Two features of this match are striking. First, there was no difficulty in effecting the matches, with the exception of large merchants. The category "general managers" is probably a poor match, both because it includes personnel who are not merchants and because it is not restricted to those involved in large enterprises. Nonetheless, it includes bankers, heads of large firms, and other titles comparable to the merchant princes Sjoberg intended to include as having equivocal upper-class status. The difficulty in effecting a match probably reflects an inadequacy of the Standard Scale more than a true lack of comparable occupational groups in preindustrial and contemporary industrial societies. Thus, once again, we have confirmation of the similarity of the occupational structure in all complex societies, industrial or preindustrial.

Second, the status hierarchies are remarkably similar. High-status occupational groups in preindustrial societies have the greatest prestige in contemporary societies, and the lowest status groups in preindustrial societies have the lowest prestige in contemporary societies. Thus, insofar as Sjoberg's assertion of uniformity in the class structures of preindustrial

TABLE 5.8

The Occupational Hierarchy of Preindustrial Cities

The Preindustrial Occupational Hierarchy[a]	Matches to Standard Scale Categories[b]	Standard Scale Score
Upper class		
High political officials	Legislative Officials and Government Administrators – 020	64
High religious officials	High Church Official – 01411 (83) Clergyman – 01410 (60)	72
High educational officials	University and Higher Education Teachers – 0131	78
Landlords	Agricultural Landowner – 13003	65
Military leaders	High Armed Forces Officer – 10000 (73) Armed Forces Officer – 10001 (63)	68
Equivocal status		
Large merchants	General Managers – 0211	65
Lower class		
Lower government personnel	Government Executive Officials – 0310	55
Lower religious personnel	Other Religious Workers – 014 except 01410, 01411	46
Lower military personnel	Noncommissioned Officer – 10002 (44) Soldier – 10003 (39)	42
Prosperous merchants	Large Shop Owner – 04101	58
Master artisans	Independent Artisan – 09951	50
Small shopkeepers	Shopkeeper – 04100	42
Ordinary skilled workers	Skilled Worker – 09950	42
Unskilled laborers	Laborers – 0999	18
Peasants	Agricultural and Animal Husbandry Workers – 062	22

[a]Compiled from Sjoberg (1960:118–123). See text for details. Titles within brackets in left-hand columns have similar status.

[b]Matching title is followed by code number--see Appendix A. Where more than one Standard Scale title is matched to a preindustrial category, the scores are averaged; individual scores are given in parentheses.

cities is credible, we can infer from it a uniformity of occupational hierarchies throughout the urban world, past or present.

CONCLUSIONS

The concern of this chapter has been to evalute competing explanations for the worldwide similarity in occupational prestige hierarchies. Of the four theories of prestige determination outlined in Chapter 1, the first, a *pure cultural* theory that argues that prestige reflects specific cultural norms and values and hence will differ substantially from society to society, was rejected on the basis of the demonstration in the previous chapter of strong cross-cultural uniformity in prestige evaluations. The second, a *cultural diffusion* theory that argues that a Western pattern of occupational evaluation diffused throughout the world without a corresponding diffusion of a Western division of labor and organization of work roles, was rejected on the basis of a demonstration that not only prestige but other attributes of occupations—in particular, their relative educational requirements and income returns—are essentially invariant across contemporary societies. The third, a *structural diffusion* theory that argues that what was adopted from the West was not simply a pattern of occupational evaluation but a characteristic division of labor associated with industrialism, was rejected on the basis of a demonstration that occupational hierarchies of income and prestige are invariant over time as well as space, so that the same hierarchy characterizes preindustrial as well as industrial societies.

Having rejected these alternatives, we can conclude that the data favor the pure structural theory proposed in Chapter 1: In all complex societies, industrialized or not, a characteristic division of labor arises that creates intrinsic differences among occupational roles with respect to power; these in turn promote differences in privilege; and power and privilege create prestige. Since the same process operates in all complex societies, the resulting prestige hierarchy is relatively invariant in all such societies, past or present.

But this process does not create an *absolutely* invariant pattern of occupational evaluation. Within the constraints of the generic process it is possible that there are both systematic and idiosyncratic societal variations, and it is to a search for these that we now turn.

6

Prestige and Industrialization

In the previous chapter I attempted to account for the fundamental similarity of occupational prestige hierarchies around the world. In this and the following chapter I consider the converse question: How can we account for such intercountry differences in occupational evaluation as can be observed? To try to answer this question, two sorts of analysis are undertaken. First, in the present chapter the relationship between prestige and industrialization is examined, in an attempt to show that similarities with respect to level of industrialization give rise to similarities in occupational prestige evaluations. In Chapter 7, intercountry variations in the prestige of particular occupations are studied to see whether, and to what extent, patterns of prestige evaluation are affected by the idiosyncratic structural and cultural features of individual societies.

PRESTIGE SIMILARITY AND SOCIAL STRUCTURE

It must be remembered that in considering differences between countries in the evaluation of occupations we are operating within the context of very high general agreement in the basic pattern of occupational evaluation. The question is not what accounts for similarity or lack of similarity between countries in their prestige evaluations, but what accounts for differences in the *degree* of agreement? What determines the precise way in which occupations are hierarchically evaluated in particular countries? And what accounts for pairs of countries agreeing almost perfectly in the prestige they accord various occupations or being only in crude general agreement?

In the previous chapter it was shown that the prestige of occupations derives largely from the skill and training required to perform them and the income gained from doing them. Thus, as the socioeconomic characteristics of occupations change, their prestige ought to change accordingly. Hence, we must consider what macrosocial characteristics index variations in the way occupational systems are organized. A good candidate is the level of industrialization. Throughout the world, the fundamental trend in social and economic organization over the past century has been the pervasive move toward an industrial system. The pattern of social organization characterized by the factory system and the nation state—in short, by a high level of economic and political integration—that first developed in the Anglo-American countries during the nineteenth century, has been exported, to a greater or lesser extent, to most other nations throughout the world. Partly as a result of direct colonialization and partly as a consequence of economic hegemony, the Western pattern of industrial organization has come to be the dominant one throughout the world. Moreover, this is the pattern toward which countries generally are striving in their attempts to improve their national economic lot. Even such places as China, which violently reject the ideology of the West, are industrializing as rapidly as possible, following a basically Western pattern.

As countries adopt a Western mode of economic organization, they perforce adopt a Western pattern of division of labor. Occupational roles become much more specialized; new occupations are created and old ones are transformed to accomplish the new set of highly specialized and finely differentiated tasks characteristic of the modern mass-production factory system. Among the new occupational roles that are created as a concomitant of industrialization are, in the white-collar sector, a variety of managerial specialists, a large cadre of clerical workers, and some new technical specialists. In the blue-collar sector a host of specialized industrial workers come to take their place alongside traditional craftsmen. As nations grope their way toward modernization, importing new industries and the new occupational roles they require, it is likely that they will travel somewhat different paths to the same end, creating different sorts of industries and different sorts of jobs. Moreover, even where the same occupational roles exist it is very likely that they will be organized in somewhat different ways, the same tasks being performed by highly skilled personnel in some places and being distributed over a larger number of less skilled workers, each doing a limited piece of the task, in others. Similarly, the same jobs may be variously rewarded from place to place, depending on the demand for labor relative to the supply of skilled personnel. Thus, even where the same occupations exist in a number of countries, there are likely to be some differences in their location in the socioeconomic structure. In turn, these differences should give rise to differences in the way such occupations are perceived and evaluated with respect to prestige.

Although both white-collar and blue-collar positions are created in the process of industrialization, it is the blue-collar sector of the labor force that should be most responsive to changes in economic organization. Many—perhaps most—occupations in the white-collar sector are common to both traditional and modern societies. As I suggested in Chapter 1, specialized professionals to handle problems in religion, politics, health, and education exist everywhere where there are specialized occupational roles at all. Moreover, a bureaucratic administrative superstructure is a necessary component of any *national* politico-economic organization, and existed in all large political empires long before the industrial revolution. Thus, a similar complement of managerial and clerical roles will be found in both industrialized and nonindustrialized nations. Blue-collar occupations, by contrast, probably vary widely from country to country, depending upon the level of industrialization the country has attained. The presence or absence of various industries will determine whether or not some blue-collar jobs exist at all. And even where the same occupations exist, they are likely to be organized in radically different ways depending upon the productive complex in which they are embedded. One of the principal characteristics of advanced industrialization is the factory system—that is, the organization of production on a specialized, large-scale, mass-production basis. Thus, to be a shoemaker, for example, in a highly industrialized country probably means being a worker in a shoe factory, while in a country with production organized in traditional ways being a shoemaker means being an independent craftsman.

To sum up the discussion so far, differences among countries in the social organization of work created by the process of industrialization should give rise to differences in the exact amount of prestige accorded specific occupations. Three of the most important indicators of industrialization or modernization are (*1*) the extent to which a population is engaged in subsistence agriculture, (*2*) the extent to which members of the population receive advanced formal education, and (*3*) the general level of wealth of the society.

Percentage of Population in Agriculture. The proportion of the population engaged in agriculture is a particularly good indicator of the extent to which a country has industrialized because it is so strongly related to other crucial facets of social organization. High proportions of the economically active population in the agricultural sector tend to be characteristic of subsistence-level economies—most food is directly consumed by the producers, whose opportunities for personal mobility are circumscribed. Both the economic and political structure is organized essentially at the local level, without the network of interdependency characteristic of modern societies. Urbanization is limited, and the panoply of occupations present in urban, industrialized societies simply does not exist. In the absence of adequate data on the distribution of the labor force across occupational groups, the percentage of the labor force engaged in agriculture provides a good surrogate measure of the extent to which the economically active population is engaged in occupations characteristic of industrial societies.

Level of Education. Another good indicator of structural features related to the level of industrialization is the proportion of the population enrolled in secondary or higher education. An efficient way of imparting the skills necessary to perform the specialized tasks required by an industrialized economy is through a formal education system. In particular, the specialized technical and leadership skills demanded by complex industrialized economies tend to require advanced education, beyond the primary level. One of the requirements of modern industrial systems is a fluid supply of labor; job definitions tend to be standardized and occupational skills to be generalized in order to ensure the interchangeability of personnel in a given job and the adaptability of a given worker to a variety of jobs. Hence, the traditional apprenticeship system in which the apprentice was indentured to a particular master and learned only his master's way of doing things is no longer functional in complex industrial societies. As a result, the teaching responsibility of the individual master has been replaced by a formal apprenticeship system in conjunction with a formal educational system. This is true of professional as well as craft jobs. No longer in advanced industrial societies do lawyers read law in a law office; today lawyers are trained in law schools. In short, the expansion of secondary and higher education is a necessary concomitant of the adoption of a modern occupational structure.

GNP per Capita. Of the three basic indicators utilized here, the measure of societal wealth, gross national product per capita, is perhaps most closely tied to industrialization per se, if by industrialization is meant the use of inanimate energy in the production and distribution of goods (Davis, 1955:255); the correlation of GNP with various measures of energy consumption is extremely high (Ginsburg, 1961). Moreover, wealthier countries can allocate more resources to the production of specialized goods and services, which will tend to be reflected in the existence of large secondary and tertiary sectors of the economy and in an attendant shift in the occupational distribution of the labor force.

As a first approach to the question of whether prestige evaluations are affected by a country's level of industrialization, we can study the relationship between similarity to the United States in prestige evaluations and per capita GNP (GNP data are from Ginsburg, 1961: Table 3). On the basis of the foregoing discussion, industrialized countries would be expected to be more similar to the United States than would nonindustrialized countries, since the United States is the most highly industrialized country in the world. This is indeed the case, as can be seen from inspection of the scatterplot shown in Figure 6.1. Although the relationship is by no means perfect, there clearly is a positive association between per capita GNP and prestige similarity to the United States.

Actually, the scatterplot is instructive on a number of grounds. First, it makes abundantly clear the desirability of restricting the analysis of intercountry differences to those places for which good data are available (the 27 places scoring above 1 on the quality scale reported in Table 2.1). In the

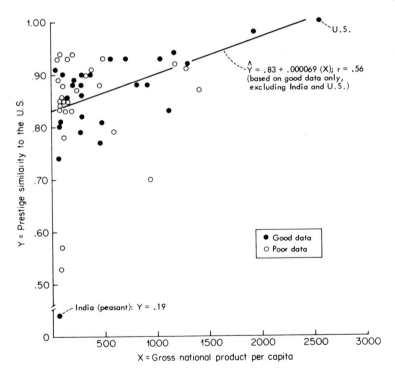

Figure 6.1. Scatter plot of relationship between gross national product per capita and prestige similarity to the United States for 54 places.

scatterplot, good data are shown as solid dots while poor data are shown as open circles; inspection of the scatterplot indicates that the dispersion of the prestige similarity scores is much greater for the poor data than for the good data. Obviously, while data from all 55 places (excluding the 5 data sets based on nonprestige criteria of evaluation) conform to a pattern of gross intersocietal similarity, somewhat greater precision is required when analyzing differences in the degree of similarity. For the 25 "good data" societies remaining after the United States and peasant India are excluded,[1] the correlation between per capita GNP and prestige similarity to the United States is .56, indicating a moderately strong relationship. The corresponding regression is given in the scatterplot. This line indicates that every $100 increase in per capita GNP increases the expected correlation with the United States by about two-thirds of a point. Countries with per capita GNP of $100 per year (for example, Mauritania and peasant Thailand) would be expected on the average to have prestige correlations with the United States of .84; those with per capita GNP of $1000 per year (for example, Denmark and West Germany) would be expected to have correlations averaging .90; and so on.[2]

The second point to be noted is that the scatter of points about the regression line is somewhat larger for the less industrialized countries, even ignoring India. Some of the countries with very low GNP have prestige structures as nearly similar to that of the United States as far more developed places, while others are much more dissimilar.[3] This pattern possibly reflects different paths to modernization being followed by various nonindustrialized places, and could perhaps provide a clue as to which nations are at a takeoff point with respect to industrial development (see

[1] The United States is, of course, omitted because it has a correlation of unity with itself and would have misleadingly inflated the GNP–prestige similarity correlation. Peasant India is omitted because it falls more than five standard deviations below the mean correlation with the United States, far lower than any other correlation, and would have seriously distorted the obtained results (see the discussion by Anscombe, 1968:15:178–181, on statistical outliers). Inclusion of peasant India drops the correlation a full 16 points, to .40, and noticeably alters the regression line. The correlation based on both good and poor data is even lower: $r = .29$, computed over the 53 foreign countries for which GNP data were available.

[2] Note that the GNP data are for 1955. While it would have been preferable to score each country with GNP for the year the prestige study was conducted, GNP data were not available on an annual basis. Moreover, we know from Chapter 3 that prestige hierarchies hardly change over time, at least in the short run, and it is probable that the rank order of nations with respect to GNP also remains essentially constant over the short run.

[3] Interestingly, Jackman (1975:40–42) finds a similar pattern with respect to the relationship between energy consumption per capita and various measures of economic inequality. Together, these results lend some modest support to the convergence hypothesis (Kerr et al., 1960).

Hodge, Treiman, and Rossi, 1966, for an argument to this effect). However, efforts to relate differences among nonindustrialized countries in the degree of prestige similarity to the United States to former colonial status proved unsuccessful; former colonies of highly industrialized European nations proved as diverse in their patterns of prestige similarity as those nations that had never experienced colonial rule, and were on the average no more like the United States. Obviously, further effort will be required to unravel the process by which some nations acquire Western patterns of occupational evaluation before attaining a commensurate level of industrial development.

In concluding this section, it can be noted that the relationship between per capita GNP and prestige similarity to the United States observed for all occupations holds up when the white-collar and blue-collar sectors are considered separately. The white-collar and blue-collar scatterplots, not shown here, are both quite similar to Figure 6.1. Moreover, the relationship between per capita GNP and prestige similarity to the United States is substantially stronger for blue-collar occupations than for white-collar occupations, as predicted in the preceding section. Excluding India and the United States, the correlation is .34 for the 24 places for which good white-collar data are available and .46 for the 22 places with good blue-collar data.[4] Thus, in sum, there is a moderately strong association between the level of industrialization of countries and their prestige similarity to the United States.[5]

Exactly why this is so is less than perfectly clear. Earlier in this chapter, I presented an argument suggesting that as countries industrialize the organi-

---

[4] Actually, while the results for all occupations are strongly affected by the inclusion of peasant India, the results for white- and blue-collar occupations considered separately are not affected at all. This is because peasant India is excluded from the white-collar computations altogether by virtue of having fewer than 10 white-collar occupations in common with the United States, and with respect to blue-collar ratings proves to be not particularly deviant relative to other countries. For all 53 countries, however, these correlations are .09 and .24, respectively, for white- and blue-collar occupations.

[5] When percentage of the labor force in agriculture is utilized in place of per capita GNP, exactly the same pattern of results emerges, and the correlations are even higher. For the 25 places with good data (excluding India and the United States), the correlations of prestige similarity to the United States with the percentage of the labor force engaged in agriculture are $-.60$ over all occupations, $-.29$ over white-collar occupations, and $-.53$ over blue-collar occupations. When peasant India is included, the correlations are, respectively, $-.49$, $-.29$, and $-.57$. And when all 55 countries are considered, the correlations are, respectively, $-.34$, $-.06$, and $-.37$. These results are particularly striking considering that the United States does not have the smallest agricultural labor force and hence is not a completely appropriate anchor point for this variable: 10% of the American labor force was engaged in agriculture in 1953, the year the data were compiled, compared to 5% of the British labor force and similar percentages in a number of other European countries (Ginsburg, 1961: Table 10).

zation of work changes and in particular the hierarchy of occupational requisites and perquisites changes as well, within the context of the general stability documented in Chapter 5. While data supporting this claim are extremely sparse, we do have available two bodies of pertinent evidence. First, in 1958 the International Labor Office (1958b) published estimates of the average hourly wages in 41 blue-collar occupations for a relatively large sample of countries. Such data are available for 27 of the countries for which we have prestige data. If the general thrust of my argument is correct, highly industrialized countries should exhibit wage structures—that is, a hierarchy of relative wages—more similar to that of the United States than those of relatively less industrialized places. Indeed, this turns out to be the case: The correlation between per capita GNP and wage similarity to the United States is .50, which is strikingly high considering the reduced range of occupations over which the wage similarity measure was computed. Second, the argument requires that the countries that are similar with respect to wage structures also be similar with respect to prestige structures, at least blue-collar prestige structures (note that this is a very general claim since the exact occupations entering the wage and prestige comparisons are somewhat different). This also proves to be the case, again using the United States as anchor point and considering only the good prestige data: The correlation between wage similarity to the United States and blue-collar prestige similarity to the United States is .40 for the 12 countries for which both measures are available. Again, the results are striking given the quality of the data and the level of abstraction at which we are operating—the number just reported is, after all, a correlation between two series of correlations, each of which itself is derived from the comparison of two series of mean values, which are in turn often based on data collected from poor and unrepresentative samples. That we get any systematic results at all is perhaps a tribute to the robustness of the basic phenomenon under investigation. Second, we can utilize the data on occupational hierarchies of education and income reported in Chapter 5 to provide a further test of the proposition that industrialized countries will be closer to the United States in their structures of occupational power and privilege than less industrialized societies (we do not have good prestige data for enough countries to relate similarity to the United States in hierarchies of power and privilege to similarity in prestige). In both cases, the data provide modest support for our expectations: The correlation between per capita GNP and similarity to the United States in occupational skill levels is .44 (computed over 14 countries), whereas the corresponding correlation involving per capita GNP and similarity in occupational income is .53 (computed over 10 countries).

PAIRWISE COMPARISONS

Thus far the analysis of societal variations in patterns of prestige evaluation has been restricted to consideration of the degree of similarity to the United States, largely for reasons of convenience of presentation. However, a much stronger test is possible, which makes much fuller use of the available data. If the theory proposed here is correct, it should be generally true that the more similar countries are with respect to industrial structure, the more similar they will be with respect to patterns of prestige evaluation.

To investigate this hypothesis, a regression procedure utilizing pairs of countries as observations was adopted. The analysis reported here was carried out at an earlier stage of the project, in 1967 (Treiman, 1968:78–91). At that time, data for 38 countries were available; for 25 of these places the data were judged to be of reasonably high quality. For these 25 countries, a new data set was defined with 300 ($= 25 \times 24/2$) observations consisting of all possible pairs of countries. The following variables were then constructed: T_{ij} = the correlation between the prestige scores for country i and the prestige scores for country j, computed over *all* occupations rated in both countries and transformed by Fisher's z;[6] W_{ij} = the transformed correlation between prestige scores for country i and for country j, computed over all *white-collar* occupations common to the two countries; and B_{ij} = the similarly defined correlations for *blue-collar* occupations. These constitute the dependent variables for this analysis.

I also constructed the following independent variables: A_{ij} = the absolute value of the difference between country i and country j in the percentage of the economically active population in agricultural occupations; E_{ij} = the absolute value of the difference between country i and country j in the square root of the percentage of the total population enrolled in postprimary schools; and G_{ij} = the absolute value of the difference between country i and country j in the square root of the gross national product per capita, in United States' dollars.[7] The square root transformations of E and G were used to make the distributions of these variables more nearly normal. Both the distribution over countries of GNP per capita and of proportion enrolled in secondary school are highly skewed to the right, with a

---

[6] Fisher's $z = \frac{1}{2} \, ln(1+r/1-r)$, is used to convert a distribution of rs into an approximately normal distribution on the assumption that they are all drawn from populations with the same correlation ρ. Although that assumption cannot be made here—if it could, the analysis being described would be pointless—the transformation still served in practice to convert a highly skewed distribution of rs into an approximately normal one (Walker and Lev, 1953:254).

[7] The data from which these three variables were constructed are from Ginsburg, 1961: Tables 10, 16, and 3, respectively.

very few countries exhibiting extremely high scores. Thus, not to have transformed the distributions would have resulted in extremely large difference scores between the economically and educationally most developed countries and virtually all other countries, and would have substantially distorted the distribution of difference scores.

Table 6.1 gives the correlations among the six variables under consideration here, together with the number of pairs of countries upon which each correlation is based (as with the analysis reported above, intercountry prestige correlations were computed only when a pair of countries had at least 10 occupational titles in common; moreover, for some countries information on social structural characteristics was not available). There are two basic points to be noted about the correlations presented in the table: First, there is a modest association between similarity with respect to social structural characteristics and similarity with respect to prestige evaluation, although perhaps only the correlations involving the agriculture variable are large enough to be of interest (the correlations are of course all negative, since the larger the difference between countries with respect to structural variables, the less the prestige similarity). Second, the correlations are substantially larger for blue-collar occupations than for either of the other two lines. The interpretation of this result is difficult, however. While it was predicted in the discussion above—the process of industrialization entails greater changes in the structure of blue-collar than of white-collar work, and hence should have greater consequence for the prestige evaluation of blue-collar occupations—it may arise simply from pecu-

TABLE 6.1
Correlations among Indicators of Prestige Similarity and
Indicators of Social Structural Similarity[a]

Variable	T	W	B	A	E	G
Prestige similarity (transformed correlations)						
Over all occupations (T)	_224_	.662	.784	-.305	-.235	-.172
Over white-collar occupations (W)	131	_131_	.645	-.285	-.150	-.198
Over blue-collar occupations (B)	51	46	_51_	-.604	-.421	-.456
Social structural difference scores						
Percentage in agriculture (A)	224	131	51	_253_	.489	.572
Square root percentage in post-primary school (E)	190	115	44	253	_300_	.430
Square root GNP/capita (G)	224	131	51	253	253	_300_

Source: See text for details on sources.

[a]Each correlation is based on observations present for both variables; upper triangle gives correlations, and diagonal and lower triangle give N's.

liarities in the countries for which data are available, since the blue-collar correlations are based on a much smaller number of pairs of countries than either the total or white-collar correlations. In sum, these results provide some evidence that prestige evaluations are affected by variations in generic aspects of social structure related to industrialization and that the evaluation of blue-collar jobs is particularly sensitive to such variations; but firm confirmation of this point must await the availability of more complete data.

While, indeed, a somewhat superior body of data is now available and is used for the bulk of the present analysis, the pairwise analysis reported above was not considered sufficiently instructive to repeat on the expanded data set, in part because it is almost certain that the same pattern of results would emerge and in part because these results do not really take us very far in understanding just what it is about industrial structure that leads to differences in occupational evaluations and which occupations in particular are affected by variations in the level of industrialization. Consideration of variations across countries in the prestige of particular occupations can perhaps provide a clue to some of these answers, and it is to such an analysis that we now turn.

SUMMARY

In this chapter I have shown that similarity between societies along dimensions associated with the level of industrialization gives rise to prestige similarity: More highly industrialized countries tend to be more similar to the United States than less industrialized places; and among pairs of countries the greater the similarity in level of industrialization the greater the similarity in prestige rankings. These patterns tend to be stronger with respect to the evaluation of manual occupations than of nonmanual occupations, probably reflecting the fact that the process of industrialization creates greater differences in the organization of manual than of nonmanual work.

7

Cross-Cultural Variations in Prestige Evaluations of Particular Occupations: Exceptions That Prove the Rule

A claim often advanced by students of particular cultures is that, even if it is true that occupational prestige hierarchies are generally similar across societies, the prestige of particular occupations will differ from place to place as a reflection of differences in cultural values or variations in the organization of work. For example, American professors are quick to assert their own low prestige compared to that enjoyed by their European counterparts, seeing in this a manifestation of antiintellectual American values.

Claims of this sort are readily tested with the data at hand. Since all the data have been converted to a common metric (see Chapter 8 for a description of the conversion procedure), we can directly compare the scores for "01310 University Professor" in the United States and, say, in Germany, a country known for its high regard for the professoriate (Ben-David and Sloczower, 1962:47–62). (These data, and those discussed in the remainder of the chapter are all to be found in Appendix D.) Clearly the self-deprecation of American academics is unwarranted—the prestige of professors in the eyes of the public is fully as high in the United States as in Germany. Indeed, the American score is marginally higher (78.3 in the United States compared to 76.7 in Germany), despite the fact that the title being evaluated in the United States was "college professor" while in Germany the title was "*universitatsprofessor*," which is understood, at least in educated circles, as referring to the holder of a chair in a university, roughly equivalent to our full professors. Lest the German datum appear anomalous, it should be noted that the mean score for "professor" in nine Western European countries is 77.1, just about the same as in the United States.

This chapter will be concerned with the analysis of a variety of similar hypotheses regarding societal differences in the evaluation of specific occupations or specific types of occupations. As will become evident, the thrust of the chapter is largely negative. For the most part, differences among countries in the prestige accorded specific occupations are unsystematic. And such systematic differences as can be found mainly reflect variations in the structural position of occupations in different societies—differences in power and privilege rather than in cultural norms. Thus they constitute exceptions that prove the rule. If, for example, an occupation has unusually high prestige in a society where, for particular historical reasons, it pays exceptionally well, the "exceptional" prestige of the occupation confirms the connection between privilege and prestige and thus lends support to the central argument of this book.

The paucity of systematic intersocietal variation in the prestige of specific occupations also provides additional support for the existence of a single generic worldwide occupational prestige hierarchy that is simply imperfectly measured in each country. Most of the intersocietal differences can be interpreted as reflecting measurement error rather than true differences in patterns of occupational evaluation. This view is reinforced by recognition that the matches of occupational titles from different societies are by no means perfect, so that part of the intersocietal variance in the prestige of any given occupation may simply reflect errors in matching titles. For example, the prestige of "07000 Foreman" is higher in Denmark than in Mauritania; but this may be due simply to the fact that the Danish title, "*formand pa fabrik*," describes a factory foreman while the Mauritanian title, "*chef d'equipe*," describes the boss of a gang of laborers, ordinarily a much less responsible position than that of a factory foreman. Difficulties such as these should caution us against being too quick to interpret intersocietal variations in particular scores as substantively meaningful. This is particularly true since—as necessarily follows from the very high average intercountry correlation—the intersocietal variances in the scores for individual occupations are relatively small. For all titles evaluated in more than one country, the average standard deviation of the scores across countries is 6.5. Keeping this in mind as a standard against which to interpret intercountry differences, let us turn to a review of the evidence for and against systematic cross-cultural differences in the prestige evaluation of particular occupations. First we consider hypotheses regarding cultural differences, then hypotheses regarding structural variations; we conclude with an inductive exercise designed to ensure that possible systematic societal variations are not overlooked due to a paucity of imagination.

CULTURAL VARIATIONS IN PRESTIGE EVALUATIONS

The cultures of the world vary in a variety of ways, ranging from patterns of dress to standards of honor: Some cultures value particular skills or traits that are ignored or disdained in other cultures; and particular objects or acts may be regarded as unclean or polluting in some cultures but not in others (Douglass, 1966). It follows, then, that those occupations that embody skills or talents or moral qualities that are highly valued in particular societies should be particularly highly regarded in those places, whereas those occupations that require dealing with polluted materials or performing unclean acts should be particularly disdained.

It has been claimed that a moral hierarchy, based solely upon the relative purity of persons or groups, may exist entirely independently of differences in power (Dumont, 1970:66). Be that as it may, it is unlikely that purely "ritual" differences between groups will determine their relative prestige standing in the society as a whole unless such differences are accompanied by differences in power and privilege as well. Indeed, it is not surprising that even in India, the case upon which Dumont bases his claim, there is a strong tendency for differences among castes in ritual purity to conform to differences in power and privilege (Bailey, 1957:266-267).

While it is possible to think of a variety of cultural differences in values that might be expected to give rise to differences in the prestige evaluation of particular occupations, hypotheses of this sort are peculiarly unrobust. The difficulty is that a negative finding is too easily explained away as due to the invalidity of the test of the hypothesis rather than as reflecting a true absence of differences in values. Nonetheless, several plausible hypotheses were examined. These by no means exhaust the possibilities in the data, and the reader who has a special interest in or knowledge about particular cultures is urged to utilize the data contained in Appendix D to carry out more extensive investigation of possible cultural differences in prestige evaluations.

It is noteworthy that of the several "cultural" hypotheses examined, the only ones for which support was found were those that entailed structural variations in the position of occupations in addition to cultural differences in values. Where only cultural differences were posited, the hypotheses uniformly failed. In particular:

1. Despite a special reverence for learning and scholarship among Jews

(Zborowski and Herzog, 1952), neither professors nor other teachers are more highly regarded in Israel than elsewhere, and neither, on the average, are members of the learned professions (science, medicine, and the law);

2.   Despite the fact that "dirty work" is said to be particularly disdained by Latin Americans (Beals, 1953:328; Lipset, 1967:19), street cleaners and garbage collectors are on the average, no more poorly regarded there than elsewhere;

3.   Despite the disdained position of merchants in the official class structures of traditional China and Japan (Yang, 1969:150–156; Bellah, 1957:24–25), neither shopkeepers in particular nor sales workers in general have lower prestige today in Taiwan or Japan than in other countries.

By contrast, the traditional low position of blacksmiths in West Africa (Vaughan, 1970:59) *is* reflected in a prestige deficit relative to other cultures. The prestige of "08310 Blacksmith" in Mauritania is 16.6 and in Nigeria (Bornu) is 24.5, compared to 32.7 in Uganda, an East African country, and an average of 39.5 in four non-African societies. However, in West Africa smiths are regarded as outcastes by other groups and practice strict endogamy. Hence, there is a clear structural basis for the low prestige of smiths in West African societies. In general, where occupations are restricted to or monopolized by outcaste groups or low-prestige ethnic groups, they can be expected to suffer in prestige. Of course, it is often unclear whether an occupation loses prestige because it comes to be performed by a low-status group or whether low-prestige occupations come to be dominated by low-status groups because their very lack of prestige reduces competition for them (cf. Hodge and Hodge, 1965; Taeuber, Taeuber, and Cain, 1966; and Treiman and Terrell, 1975c).

THE GLORIFICATION OF MANUAL WORK
IN SOCIALIST SOCIETY

A second, and particularly instructive, example of the connection between cultural norms and structural arrangements is to be found in the position of manual workers in Eastern Europe and the Soviet Union. A highly salient aspect of the official ideology of the Soviet bloc countries is the glorification of manual work, particularly skilled manual work (Parkin, 1969:356–360.) In various ways, ranging from public honor for superior work performance ("hero of the Soviet Union") to preferential opportunities for school enrollment, skilled manual work is recognized as especially valuable. Most critically, the importance of skilled manual work is recognized in the pay scales set by central authorities. In Eastern Europe and the Soviet Union the ratio of wages of manual workers to those of clerical workers appears to be substantially higher on the average than in Western Europe.[1] Moreover, as Parkin (1971:147) notes,

> the lower non-manual categories in socialist society could not be said to enjoy the same kinds of status, material, and social advantages over skilled or relatively well-paid manual workers as do their counterparts in capitalist society.... For example, office employees in socialist society are not generally accorded special privileges with regard to time-keeping, length of vacations, paid absenteeism, and the like. Nor can they expect to enjoy status advantages over shop floor workers in the way of separate canteens, entrances, lavatories, and so on, which serve to distinguish "staff" from "works" in the Western pattern.

Given the relative deprivation experienced by clerical workers in the socialist countries of Eastern Europe and the corresponding upgrading of skilled manual workers in these countries, we should expect a corresponding shift in the prestige of these two groups relative to other countries in the

---

[1] This assertion is surprisingly hard to document because of differences in the way earnings statistics are tabulated in Western and Eastern Europe. Nonetheless, sufficient information is available to permit a plausible inference. Computations from male labor force data for seven Western European countries yield an average ratio of the earnings of "clerical workers" to those of "skilled manual workers" of .99 (computed from United Nations, 1967: Table 5.16). In five Eastern European countries the average ratio of the earnings of "administrative and clerical personnel" to those of "manual workers" is .93 (computed from United Nations, 1967: Table 8.18). Considering that the Eastern European data include administrative workers, who are better paid than clerical workers in all countries, and also include semiskilled and unskilled workers as well as skilled workers, the lower ratio of nonmanual to manual wages for the Eastern European countries would appear to be definitive. But this conclusion would be premature, considering that the Western data are for males only whereas the Eastern European data include workers of both sexes. Since in most countries women earn two-thirds to three-fourths as much as men doing similar work (International Labour Office, 1969b: Tables 18–23, and 1974: Tables 7 and 8), the larger proportions of women in clerical than in manual work could account for the difference. Using data on the sex composition of the labor force drawn from the 1969 Year Book of Labour Statistics (International Labour Office, 1969b: Table 2B), I adjusted the earnings of "clerical and administrative workers" upward by a factor of 1.2 and the earnings of "manual workers" upward by a factor of 1.1 to estimate the relative earnings of the male labor force in these categories. Applying these adjustments to the earnings ratio of .93 reported above yields an adjusted ratio of 1.01, which is hardly larger than the corresponding ratio for Western Europe. Hence, our conclusion stands: The ratio of earnings of "clerical workers" to "skilled manual workers" in Western Europe is about the same as the ratio of earnings of "administrative and clerical workers" to all "manual workers" in Eastern Europe, and hence it can be inferred that the relative position of skilled manual workers compared to clerical workers in Eastern Europe is better than in the West. See also the documentation of reduced manual–nonmanual wage differentials in postwar Czechoslovakia (Kubat, 1963), Poland (Matejko, 1966), and Yugoslavia (Šefer, 1968).

world. We can test this hypothesis by computing, from the data in Appendix D, the average deviation from the Standard Scale scores of clerical and skilled manual occupational titles rated in Eastern European countries. If the hypothesis is true, the deviation for clerical occupations will be negative and that for skilled manual jobs will be positive, since the Standard Scale scores represent the worldwide average.

Table 7.1 presents the appropriate data. Because the 60 societies used in the previous analysis included only four Eastern European countries, and the data sets from two of these places utilized nonprestige criteria of evaluation, I supplemented these data sets with two acquired subsequently (described more fully in Chapter 8). For each of the six data sets, the mean deviations from the Standard Scale scores for clerical occupations and for skilled and semiskilled manual occupations were computed, and the difference of differences was calculated. Both skilled and semiskilled occupations were included because of the difficulty of distinguishing between the two groups in a consistent way. Although the pattern is not completely consistent, the main trend is clear—there is a pronounced tendency in Eastern Europe for clerical occupations to be downgraded in prestige and for manual occupations to be upgraded in prestige relative to the world as a whole.[2] Clearly, here is an instance in which an exception proves the rule. For the importance of this example is not that ideological differences lead to differential evaluations of occupational roles, but rather that differences in the *objective* position of manual and clerical jobs in communist and capitalist countries—in wages and working conditions, that is, in *privilege*—lead to differences in prestige. That differences in the material position of these groups in turn reflects ideological differences is not to be denied, but ideology matters little unless it is manifest in differential power or privilege.

Miners. A particularly striking manifestation of the relation between privilege and prestige as a reflection of ideology is shown in the situation of miners. Inspecting the prestige hierarchies of various countries, it will be observed that in Eastern Europe miners have strikingly high prestige compared to the rest of the world. But the high prestige of miners in socialist societies becomes entirely explicable when we note that their income is also strikingly high. In the three Eastern European countries for which we have

---

[2] Recall that the worldwide averages (the Standard Scale scores) are based, in part, on data from the socialist countries, so when comparing the average for these countries with the Standard Scale scores a part–whole comparison is involved. Were I to trouble to make an explicit comparison between the average scores for Eastern European and non-Eastern European countries the differences would be still larger, although not by much considering the small number of Eastern European countries.

TABLE 7.1

Estimate of Upgrading of Manual Work and Downgrading of
Routine Clerical Work in Eastern European Countries

Country and Study	Clerical Workers[a]		Production Workers[b]		Difference of Differences: Production Minus Clerical
	Mean Difference from Standard Scale	N[c]	Mean Difference from Standard Scale	N	
Czechoslovakia (ideal income)	-16.7	(2)	19.2	(6)	35.9
Czechoslovakia (prestige supplement)	7.5	(2)	6.4	(16)	-1.1
Poland (Warsaw)	-7.6	(6)	9.8	(11)	17.4
Poland (Łodz, supplement)	-2.6	(5)	5.8	(12)	8.4
USSR	-16.3	(5)	2.1	(28)	18.4
Yugoslavia	-4.2	(10)	4.0	(21)	8.2
Mean	-6.6		7.9		14.5

Sources: See Tables 2.1 and 8.4.

[a]Omits mail carriers and bus and tram conductors.

[b]Omits unskilled workers and self-employed workers.

[c]Number of occupations.

prestige ratings for miners,[3] the mean ratio of wages in mining to those in manufacturing is 1.6, while for 15 other countries for which both ratings of miners and adequate income data are available the mean ratio is 1.2.[4] Considering that, as we have seen above, the ratio of manual to nonmanual wages is generally higher in socialist than in capitalist countries, it is evident that the relative income position of miners is much higher in Eastern Europe than elsewhere; hence it is no surprise that the average prestige of miners is 25 points higher than in the West (54.6 in the 3 Eastern European countries compared to 29.6 as an average for 15 other countries). More generally, for these 18 countries the correlation between the prestige of miners and the wages of miners relative to manufacturing wages is .54, establishing once again the strong connection between privilege and prestige. Were adequate data available for other occupations that vary substantially in relative wages from country to country, no doubt similar associations could be established. But such an effort must await the improvement of comparative income statistics.

Taken together, these results go a long way toward explaining the relatively large deviation of the prestige hierarchies of Eastern European countries from the generic worldwide hierarchy, a topic we shall return to in the next chapter. But they also exhibit in a striking way the material underpinnings of ideology, the primacy of structure over culture. Marx would be pleased. The remaining examples of systematic societal variations in prestige evaluations likewise reflect variations in structural arrangements.

VARIATIONS IN THE STRUCTURAL BASES OF PRESTIGE

Office Clerks and Literacy.   Throughout this book I have argued that one of the main determinants of the prestige of occupations is how much

---

[3] Prestige ratings for "07110 Miner" are available for Poland and the USSR, and a rating of "ideal income" is available for Czechoslovakia. It is likely that the "ideal income" assigned to miners in Czechoslovakia was influenced by a perception of how hard the work is, since the rating was extraordinarily high, 80.1, on a par with high political officials in most countries. This result once again confirms the distinction between various dimensions of occupational hierarchy and the wisdom of excluding the Czech data from the main analysis. Accordingly, I substituted the score for "miner" derived from the supplementary Czech prestige study mentioned above. This score, 51.4, was essentially similar to those for Poland (58.2) and the USSR (54.1).

[4] These ratios were computed from International Labour Office, 1969: Tables 19-A and 20, supplemented by International Labour Office, 1960: Tables 16-A and 16-B and International Labour Office, 1952: Tables 17-A and 17-B. Where data for males and females had to be combined, weights were derived from International Labour Office, 1969b: Table 2-A.

skill their performance requires. In Chapter 5 I supported this claim by showing that there is a strong connection between education and prestige in all societies for which we have data. Here I approach the same hypothesis in another way, by relating the relative prestige of office clerks in various societies to the general level of literacy in the population. Office clerks are low-level clerical personnel whose sole qualification in most situations is simple literacy, the ability to read and write. Thus, the absolute level of skill required is fairly standardized across societies. But the *relative* skill of office clerks compared to other members of the labor force is highly variable from country to country. In countries where literacy is universal or nearly universal, literacy carries no special prestige. But in societies where most people are illiterate, literacy is a rare accomplishment and, hence, one held in high regard. Thus, those occupations requiring literacy as their main qualification should be most highly regarded in countries where literacy is least widespread. In particular, the prestige of "03930 Office Clerk" should be negatively correlated with the percentage of the population that is literate (Taylor and Hudson, 1972: Table 4.5). And this in fact proves to be the case. For the 34 countries for which data are available,[5] the correlation is $-.47$.

Garage Mechanics and Industrialization. A similar argument to the one developed with respect to office clerks holds for mechanics. The skills required of automobile mechanics are relatively standardized from place to place, but these skills are more common in some societies than in others. In highly industrialized countries a large fraction of the manual labor force works with machines of one sort or another, and for that matter so do many clerical and technical workers. In nonindustrialized countries there is relatively less reliance upon machinery. Indeed, the mechanized–non-mechanized distinction is the basis for one of the standard definitions of industrialization (Davis, 1955:255). Hence, in industrialized places automobile mechanics should be perceived as just another kind of skilled worker and accorded the same prestige as other skilled workers. But in nonindustrialized countries automobile mechanics, who tend to be among the most highly visible of craftsmen, should be accorded special prestige by virtue of their command of the mysteries of mechanization. To test this hypothesis, we correlate the prestige of "08430 Garage Mechanic" with the most salient measure of industrialization, energy consumption per capita (Taylor and Hudson, 1972: Table 5.7). For the 21 societies for which data

---

[5] Only data from the 55 societies for which we have prestige evaluations are considered here. The 5 data sets based on nonprestige criteria are excluded from this and all analysis in the remainder of the chapter.

are available the correlation is negative as expected: $r = -.45$; garage mechanics are indeed more highly regarded in less industrialized countries.[6]

Primary and Secondary Schoolteachers. Primary schoolteachers constitute a different sort of exception that proves the rule. Office clerks and automobile mechanics are more highly regarded in *less* industrialized countries because in such places the skills required to be a clerk or mechanic are relatively rare, so that the same level of qualification places one at a greater advantage in a less industrialized society. There are, however, some occupations in which the absolute level of qualification is itself affected by the type of society in which it is performed. Primary schoolteachers are a prime example. The mount of education necessary to qualify as a primary schoolteacher is highly variable across societies. In societies with a low level of education in the population, primary teachers often have little more than a primary education themselves. This was true in the nineteenth-century United States (Knight, 1951:312–313) and is true in such contemporary societies as Ghana (Ghana Census Office, 1964: Table 8), India (India Cabinet Secretariat, 1970: Table 7.1), and Brazil (Kimball, 1960:51–52). Because of this, it is hardly the case that the relative skill of primary teachers is greater in nonindustrialized places; rather, it is likely to be less, since in highly industrialized societies teachers are nearly always college trained (Mallinson, 1957: Chap. 7). Although, unfortunately, we have no data that bear directly on qualifications of primary teachers, we can use higher education enrollment rates as a surrogate measure. The assumption is that those countries that have relatively high proportions of the population enrolled in institutions of higher learning will have better educated primary school teachers than those that do not. Hence, we should expect a positive correlation between higher education enrollment rates (Taylor and Hudson, 1972: Table 4.4) and the prestige of primary teachers. The prestige of secondary school teachers, by contrast, would not be expected to vary with higher education enrollment rates because secondary education is elite education in almost all countries and hence everywhere requires highly trained staff. In order to test this pair of claims—that the prestige of primary school teachers should vary negatively with higher education enrollment rates while the prestige of secondary teachers should not vary systematically—we utilize those societies for which prestige ratings are available for both primary and secondary teachers. This strategy has the added advantage of avoiding a possible comparison between generic titles for "teachers" and titles referring specifically to "primary teachers." For

---

[6] If alternative measures of societal development are used the results are similar; see Table 7.2.

the 24 countries for which data are available, the correlations with higher education enrollment[7] are as hypothesized: .52 for "01330 Teacher, Primary Teacher" and − .07 for "01320 High School Teacher."

Large Farmers.   In general, owners and managers of large enterprises are more highly regarded than those who head smaller enterprises. This should be no surprise since they control more capital and exercise more power; their responsibilities are greater; and their incomes are higher. Farmers   are   no   exception.   "Large   farmers"   (*"hacendados,"* *"grossbauerin,"* "planters," *"zamindars,"* etc.) are on the average more highly regarded than "farmers" (*"gardejene," "cultivateurs," "bauerin,"* etc.). But among large farmers we would expect those in countries where there are extremely large estates to be more highly regarded than those where the average size of agricultural holdings is smaller. The argument goes as follows. The larger the size of the estate, the higher the prestige of the owner. Where farms vary substantially in size, larger ones will be more visible and hence large farmers will be identified in the public mind with the largest of the estates. Hence, the prestige of larger farmers should be positively correlated with the degree of inequality of the distribution of agricultural land. Once again, this proves to be the case. Using the Gini index as a measure of inequality in land holdings (Taylor and Hudson, 1972: Table 4.14), the correlation between the degree of inequality in agricultural land ownership and the prestige of "06111 Large Farmer" is .47, computed over 12 countries. Considering that titles referring to large farmers tended only to be rated in countries with substantial inequality in agricultural land—which accounts for the small number of cases—this correlation is at least suggestive if not definitive.

Clergyman.   Consideration of differences in the social organization of various religions leads to the expectation that Christian countries will accord higher prestige to religious functionaries than will non-Christian countries. In Christianity more than in most other major religions the clergyman stands as an intermediary between the deity and the individual worshipper. Even among Protestants, he is the leader of the congregation and an officer of God; he *ministers* to his flock in a manner quite uncharacteristic of non-Christian groups. Thus, the clergyman is a much more important element in the religious experience of Christians than of non-Christians—one goes to regular, scheduled services and sits listening, with greater or lesser participation, to the clergyman performing the ceremony;

---

[7] The rank among the world's nations was used rather than the actual enrollment per million population, in order to avoid an excessively skewed distribution.

by contrast, in most other religions worship does not depend upon the presence of a clergyman. Because the clergyman has a more important role in the religious life of his parishioners among Christians, his prestige should be correspondingly higher in such places. And indeed it is: The correlation between percentage Christian in the population (Taylor and Hudson, 1972: Table 4.16) and the prestige of "01410 Clergyman," computed over 40 countries, is .48.

Missionaries. For similar reasons Christian missionaries would be expected to be more highly regarded in Christian countries. And they are. The correlation between the percentage Christian in the population and the prestige of "01414 Missionary" is .62, computed over 11 places. As another perspective on the same phenomenon, we can note that the mean deviation from the Standard Scale score for "missionary" is 7.0 for 5 Western European countries while for the remaining places the mean deviation is -5.0, which can be interpreted as indicating a higher regard for missionaries among exporting than among importing countries.

Policemen and Civil Liberties. The role of policeman is structurally ambiguous. On the one hand, police are defenders of the public welfare and the moral order, and as such enjoy the prestige associated with the charismatic nature of their function (Shils, 1968). On the other hand, however, police may be (and often are) used as instruments of repression, defending the interests of the elite against those of the mass. As such, they may be resented and despised by the population subject to their authority. This strong bimodality in the perceptions of police no doubt accounts for the unusually large variance in the prestige accorded them. In most of the countries for which we have data, the variance in the prestige of police is substantially larger than average.

This same ambiguity in the role of police could also be expected to produce cross-cultural variation in their prestige. For if repressed subgroups within a society have less respect for police than do more favored subgroups, the same should be true for repressed populations in general. Hence, we would expect that in those countries with repressive regimes the prestige of "05820 Policeman" will be lower than in countries where civil liberties are carefully guarded. Testing this hypothesis requires that an adequate measure of national differences in repression by authority be found. *Faute de mieux* we make use of a press freedom index developed by the University of Missouri School of Journalism that was "designed to measure the freedom of a country's broadcasting and press systems to criticize their own local and national governments [Taylor and Hudson, 1972:21–22, Table 2.7]." Presumably, countries that permit criticism of the government will also protect the rights of individuals in other ways as well. In such countries the police should be regarded as defenders rather than repressors of the population, and hence should be accorded relatively higher prestige. This, indeed, proves to be the case. For the 39 societies for which data are available, the correlation between the Press Freedom Index and the prestige of "05820 Policeman" is .39.

Summary. One central conclusion emerges from our analysis so far in this chapter: Societal differences in the prestige of particular occupations reflect societal differences in their structural position. Occupations are particularly highly regarded where they exercise unusually great power (except in the case of policemen, where the power is considered illegitimate), entail scarce talent or skill, or are exceptionally well rewarded. In the absence of differential power or privilege, supposed cultural differences in values have no impact on the relative prestige position of occupations. In this sense, then, the apparent deviations from a generic worldwide prestige hierarchy confirm rather than confute the structural basis of prestige evaluations.

However, the occupations reviewed above constitute a small fraction of all occupations included in this study. Hence, to prevent a premature conclusion drawn on the basis of self-selected data, I turn now to an inductive exercise which involves the examination of cross-national variations in the prestige accorded each of the 50 occupations rated in at least 20 countries.

CROSS-CULTURAL VARIATIONS IN THE PRESTIGE
OF 50 COMMON OCCUPATIONS

Because the degree of industrialization of a nation's productive system determines in a fundamental way the organization of work and the character of the labor force, it is reasonable to focus the search for correlates of societal differences in the evaluation of particular occupations upon this factor. Many of the hypotheses explored earlier referred to societal features that vary as a concomitant of industrialization; here we investigate whether other occupations vary in the prestige they are accorded in industrialized and nonindustrialized countries.

To measure the tendency for the relative prestige of a given occupation to be systematically related to the degree of industrialization of the country in which it was evaluated, I simply computed the correlation over countries between the prestige score and various measures of level of industrialization. Because of the inductive character of this exercise—a fishing expedition if there ever was one—I thought it useful to minimize random variability ("noise") in the intercountry differences in the evaluation of particular occupations by restricting the scores entering the correlations to the 27 countries with good data. These correlations are shown in Table 7.2, together with the Standard Score and standard deviation of the Standard Score for each occupation and the number of countries in which the occupation was rated among the 27 countries with good data.

What can be said about the data reported here? Relatively little, as it turns out. It would be tempting to try to elucidate the observed pattern in light of the sorts of arguments offered above, but they do not admit of such interpretation. The difficulty is that while some of the coefficients appear to support the hypotheses outlined, other coefficients contradict them. For example, as would be expected from earlier analysis, the prestige of automobile mechanics and printers is higher in less industrialized countries—but the prestige of electricians is relatively unrelated to level of industrialization. Similarly, while office clerks are, as expected, more highly regarded in less industrialized places, the prestige of typist–stenographers and bookkeepers is unrelated to level of industrialization.

An inductive approach—inspecting those occupations strongly related to level of industrialization for a systematic pattern—succeeds no better. The following occupations are markedly more highly regarded in industrialized countries (the criterion is that at least one of the three coefficients is as large as .4 with appropriate sign): "physician," "pharmacist," "accountant," "lawyer," "building contractor," "insurance agent," "servant," "barber," "policeman," "foreman," "plumber." By contrast, the following occupations are markedly less highly regarded in industrialized countries, utilizing the same criterion: "civil servant, minor," "office clerk," "traveling salesman," "garage mechanic," "mechanic, repairman," "printer," "mason." It is not at all obvious what, if anything, the occupations constituting each of these groups have in common, nor how they are distinguished from the remaining occupations listed in Table 7.2. In view of this, the appropriate conclusion is that there is no systematic relationship between the characteristics of occupations and their tendency to be differentially evaluated in industrialized and nonindustrialized countries.

As still another approach, we examine those occupations (among the 50) that exhibit unusually large variation in the prestige they are accorded in different countries. Considering only those occupations with a standard deviation of 8.8 or greater (about the top fifth of the distribution), we have "accountant," "clergyman," "civil servant, minor," "bookkeeper," "mail carrier," "insurance agent," "policeman," "miner," "soldier." Once again there is nothing particularly distinctive about these occupations compared to the other 41. Of these, three ("clergyman," "policeman," and "miner")

TABLE 7.2

Selected Characteristics of 50 Common Occupations, Including Correlations of their Relative Standing across Countries with Three Indicators of Industrialization for the 27 Places for which Good Data are Available

Standard Scale Code	Standard Occupational Title	Standard Scale Score [a]	Standard Deviation of Standard Score [a]	Correlations of Prestige with			N [e]
				Agriculture [b]	Education [c]	GNP [d]	
00610	Physician	77.9	4.6	-.42	.07	.32	24
01310	University Professor	77.6	4.6	-.27	-.04	.20	20
01210	Lawyer, Trial Lawyer	70.6	7.2	-.57	.25	.32	20
02111	Head of Large Firm	70.4	4.7	.23	.00	-.35	17
00220	Engineer, Civil Engineer	70.3	7.3	-.38	.18	.08	17
02114	Banker	67.0	6.7	-.05	.17	.01	14
00410	Airline Pilot	66.5	5.0	.37	-.23	-.07	10
01320	High School Teacher	64.2	4.6	.15	.23	-.07	13
00670	Pharmacist	64.1	5.9	-.70	.38	.21	11
10001	Armed Forces Officer	63.2	6.5	.12	-.12	.01	15
01410	Clergyman	59.7	12.5	-.38	.21	.36	21
01610	Artist	57.2	7.8	-.07	.19	.07	10
01330	Teacher, Primary Teacher	57.0	7.3	-.10	.15	.22	25
01510	Journalist	54.9	6.7	.21	.18	-.06	15
01100	Accountant	54.6	9.1	-.80	.50	.57	12
03102	Civil Servant, Minor	53.6	11.3	.48	-.68	-.59	8
00710	Nurse	53.6	6.9	.23	.14	.38	13
02116	Building Contractor	53.4	6.6	-.42	.24	.15	10
01730	Actor	51.5	7.7	-.11	-.19	.16	9
03310	Bookkeeper	49.0	8.8	-.17	-.08	-.21	15
04321	Traveling Salesman	46.9	7.3	.63	-.62	-.36	14
06110	Farmer	46.8	7.4	-.04	.35	.03	17
08550	Electrician	44.5	7.4	.20	-.25	.06	11
04410	Insurance Agent	44.5	8.8	-.40	.10	.28	12
03930	Office Clerk	43.3	7.7	.39	-.29	-.61	20
08430	Garage Mechanic	42.9	6.4	.77	-.50	-.51	13
08490	Mechanic, Repairman	42.8	6.9	.34	-.41	-.39	9
04100	Shopkeeper	42.4	8.2	.01	.27	.14	23
09210	Printer	42.3	7.6	.59	-.86	-.25	9

TABLE 7.2 (Continued)

03210	Typist, Stenographer	41.6	7.0	-.14	-.22	-.05	12
05820	Policeman	39.8	9.0	-.30	.54	.41	24
07910	Tailor	39.5	5.3	-.35	.36	.24	17
07000	Foreman	39.3	8.3	-.44	.64	.51	15
10003	Soldier	38.7	11.0	.22	-.29	-.07	15
09540	Carpenter	37.2	5.8	-.01	-.07	.11	24
09510	Mason	34.1	5.8	.42	-.34	-.17	13
08710	Plumber	33.9	4.9	-.06	.26	.54	14
04510	Sales Clerk	33.6	6.1	.19	-.28	-.39	20
03700	Mail Carrier	32.8	9.5	-.08	.19	.28	14
09853	Driver, Truck Driver	32.6	5.6	.28	-.20	-.19	18
09852	Bus, Tram Driver	32.4	4.6	-.38	.08	.16	11
07110	Miner	31.5	9.2	.34	-.13	-.16	13
05700	Barber	30.4	6.9	-.40	.04	.51	14
08010	Shoemaker, Repairer	28.1	6.5	-.09	-.01	.25	14
05320	Waiter	23.2	3.9	-.27	-.02	-.25	15
06210	Farm Hand	22.9	6.5	-.02	.18	-.01	18
04521	Street Vendor, Peddler	21.9	7.0	.10	-.35	.04	13
05510	Janitor	21.0	4.5	.23	-.21	-.36	10
05400	Servant	17.2	5.8	-.60	.09	.50	12
09995	Street Sweeper	13.4	4.2	.12	-.31	-.18	10

aBased on 55 countries; see Chapter 8 for details.

bPercentage of the labor force engaged in agriculture.

cPercentage of the population enrolled in post-primary school.

dGross national product per capita.

eNumber of countries in which occupation was rated, among 27 for which good data are available.

have already been dealt with. Perhaps soldiers exhibit a high variance in prestige for the same reason policemen do—because they are sometimes regarded as defenders and sometimes regarded as oppressors—and this idea is lent some support by the fact that for the 25 countries (out of 55) where both policemen and soldiers were rated the correlation in their prestige is .53. Accountants, bookkeepers, and insurance agents may be unfamiliar in some societies and hence subject to unstable or fluctuating prestige evaluations; indeed, the higher evaluation of accountants and insurance agents in industrialized societies is consistent with this interpretation because lack of familiarity with the title would probably drive evaluations toward the mean, lowering the prestige of these occupations in countries where they are unfamiliar (since the prestige of bookkeepers is near the mean for all occupations, the evaluation of bookkeepers would not be subject to this effect). About minor civil servants and mail carriers nothing can be said. Hence, in sum there is very little additional information gained from inspection of those occupations with large intercountry variance in prestige. All in all, the attempt to discover interesting cross-cultural variations in prestige evaluations on an inductive basis cannot be said to be successful.

CONCLUSIONS

The conclusions of this chapter must be regarded as highly tentative. At best we have at hand some plausible speculations about inter-societal variations in the prestige of particular occupations. There seems to be no evidence of purely cultural differences in values giving rise to differences in the prestige accorded particular occupations or particular types of occupations. On the other hand, there does seem to be evidence that societal differences in the organization of work which create differences in the power and privilege associated with a particular occupation in different countries create corresponding differences in prestige. However, the inductive exercise that closed the chapter served to indicate how tenuous some of these conclusions are, because they do not apply to other occupations that on their face are little different from the occupations with respect to which specific hypotheses were tested. Hence, before the "findings" of this chapter can be accepted as firm conclusions, they must undergo rigorous testing under circumstances designed to permit their possible refutation.

IV

A STANDARD
INTERNATIONAL
OCCUPATIONAL PRESTIGE
SCALE

8

Developing the Scale

Throughout this book I have alluded to a scale that represents the generic worldwide occupational prestige hierarchy. This and the following chapter describe the development of the scale and discuss its potential uses. But these chapters have a substantive interest as well: Evidence confirming the validity of the scale serves to bolster the claim of a single worldwide prestige hierarchy; and a comparison of alternative occupational scaling procedures further clarifies the nature of the connection between power, privilege, and prestige.

THE NEED FOR A STANDARD INTERNATIONAL OCCUPATIONAL PRESTIGE SCALE

Sociological researchers are often faced with the problem of assessing the social standing of individuals, and sometimes have reason to be interested in occupational status in particular. It is widely recognized that the work men do plays a major role in determining their standing in the eyes of others and that the character of that work is importantly related to their life chances and life-style, to the way they view the world about them and to the way they behave in it. Thus most sociological researchers, and not only students of stratification, at one point or another have occasion to consider the relationship of occupational position to whatever other phenomena they are investigating.

Although it is possible to classify occupations in a variety of ways (see Hodge and Siegel, 1966, for a discussion of alternative bases of occupational classification), most sociological interest has focused on the hierarchical ordering of occupations with respect to prestige. Not only in the United States but in most foreign countries where the measurement of occupational status has been attempted, a prestige criterion has been implicitly or explicitly adopted (e.g., Moser and Hall, 1954; van Heek and Vercruijsse, 1958; Svalastoga, 1959:134ff.; Duncan, 1961:114–128; Blishen, 1958). However, despite reliance upon a common criterion for the construction of occupational status scales, genuine cross-national comparability has not been achieved. This has been a major deterrent to comparative research on occupational structure and on the relationship of occupational status to other aspects of social life.

The main reason for the noncomparability of actual scaling procedures is that researchers ordinarily have had to estimate the prestige of occupations from partial and incomplete data. With the exception of the United States (Siegel, Hodge, and Rossi, 1974) and Great Britain (Goldthorpe and Hope, 1974), actual prestige ratings have been available for only a small fraction of the occupational categories included in the detailed (three-digit) classification schemes typically utilized by national census bureaus. Thus, researchers wishing to categorize the labor force on the basis of occupational prestige have had to adopt some sort of estimation procedure to assign scores to those occupational categories for which no direct prestige ratings were available.[1]

A variety of procedures have been utilized. For example, in the United States Duncan (1961:114–128) estimated the prestige of occupations on the basis of the income and education of male incumbents, and Blishen (1958, 1967) did the same for Canadian data. Other researchers conducted surveys to obtain prestige data for a limited set of occupations but then relied on the judgments of experts to interpolate other titles among those explicitly rated (e.g., Glass and Hall, 1954:83; Svalastoga, 1959; van Tulder, 1962:13–20; see also the references cited in Duncan, 1961:110–112). Still other researchers did not make use of empirically derived prestige ratings at all but simply scaled occupations on the basis of their own judgments regarding the relative prestige of each occupation (Yauger and Lin, 1973:30; Kelley, 1971). And, in some cases, other criteria in addition to prestige, such as skill levels, size of establishment, and employment status, were taken into account in assigning occupation into broad groups that were known or assumed to be ordered with respect to prestige (e.g., Jelín de Balán, 1967:184–201; Cummings and Naoi, 1972).

Each of these approaches introduces substantial possibility of error. First, while a formal estimating procedure such as that utilized by Duncan and Blishen has much to be said for it, the result is in fact a socioeconomic status scale and not a prestige scale (which, of course, these authors recog-

---

[1] See Treiman (1975) for a more detailed examination of this problem.

nize full well). Although, as we have seen in Chapter 5, the prestige and socioeconomic status of occupations tend to be highly correlated, they are conceptually distinct. While for some purposes one might prefer a socioeconomic status scale to a prestige scale (as when one has no other information about the socioeconomic status of individuals), such a scale cannot be validly used as a substitute for a prestige scale, especially since the two sorts of scales produce somewhat different results. This issue will be discussed at greater length in the next chapter.

Second, procedures which require the interpolation of occupational titles among those for which prestige ratings are available are very unreliable, due to differences in the judgments of various coders (Duncan, 1961:113; Goldthorpe and Hope, 1974:7–9). Indeed, it was this problem that motivated Duncan to construct his scale.

Third, the ad hoc assignment of prestige scores to occupational titles on the basis of researchers' judgments depends upon the assumption that individual researchers can accurately estimate the average prestige evaluation made by the general public; but this is demonstrably false. Data from Yugoslavia (Hammel, 1970:6) and Costa Rica (Yauger and Lin, 1973) indicate only modest (on the order of .7) correlations between "expert" ratings and average ratings by population samples. Indeed, the experts prove to be no better than ordinary individuals in their ability to accurately predict the population means.

Fourth, when criteria other than prestige are introduced in assigning occupations to status categories, a distortion of an unknown degree is introduced. In particular, since (as we have seen in Chapter 5) the correlations between various attributes of occupations are by no means perfect, it is evident that the particular criteria used to hierarchically order occupations can produce substantial variation in the way individual occupations are classified.

Finally, reliance upon broad groups ordered with respect to prestige has three flaws. First, the specific occupations included in nominally similar gross categories are not always the same. For example, in Hungary salesclerks are considered to be manual workers, while in the United States they are considered to be nonmanual workers. Similarly, the U.S. Census occupational classification considers shopkeepers to be "managers, officials, and proprietors" while the International Standard Classification of Occupations considers shopkeepers to be "sales workers." Thus, mobility in and out of the sales category would have a very different meaning depending upon whether one used the United States' classification, the Hungarian classification, or the International Standard Classification. Many other examples of the same sort could be cited. Second, the same principles are not always used to aggregate detailed occupations into gross categories. But this can substantially affect the relationship of occupational status to other variables. For example, two studies of occupational mobility in Japan (Tominaga, 1969; and Cummings and Naoi, 1972) based on exactly the same data—the 1965 national mobility study—utilized different procedures for aggregating specific occupations into gross categories that were then assigned prestige scores drawn from Nisihira's Tokyo study (Nisihira, 1968). The result was a substantially different estimate of the correlation between father's and son's occupational prestige: Tominaga found a correlation of .33 while Cummings and Naoi found a correlation of .21. Clearly, the effect of scaling procedures is substantial. Third, even if a single way of aggregating detailed occupations into gross categories were uniformly adopted, the degree of overlap between categories with respect to the prestige of the included occupations would probably be so substantial as to virtually invalidate the use of the categories as a prestige scale. One way of seeing this is to inspect Figures 8.1a–8.1c, which show the mean, standard deviation, and range of prestige scores of occupations classified according to three schemes: the 1960 U.S. Census major groups, the major groups of the International Standard Classification of Occupations, and a classification of occupations as white-collar, blue-collar, or farm. It is evident that the overlap in prestige between categories is substantial. Moreover, the categories do not even form ordinal scales of prestige. Finally, comparison of Figures 8.1a and 8.1b lends further support to the point made earlier that nominally similar categories may not include the same occupations. Of 509 occupational titles classified according to these schemes, 34 fall into the "administrative and managerial" category of the ISCO while 73 fall into the "managerial, official, and proprietor" category of the United States Census classification; similar discrepancies can be noted throughout the schemes.

In sum, existing attempts in a number of countries to scale occupations on the basis of their prestige have failed to yield measurement procedures that may in any reasonable way be regarded as comparable. Thus, at the present time there is no way to make comparisons across countries with any degree of confidence in the validity of observed differences. Rather, we are forced to entertain the possibility that any apparent differences are as likely to reflect artifacts of measurement as true differences in social structure. Moreover, apparent similarities between societies may result from measurement procedures that mask true differences. In short, until a procedure is developed to scale occupations in a comparable way across countries, valid comparisons of occupational structure will be beyond our reach. And since the realities of research priorities effectively preclude the possibility that comprehensive occupational prestige scales will be developed separately for

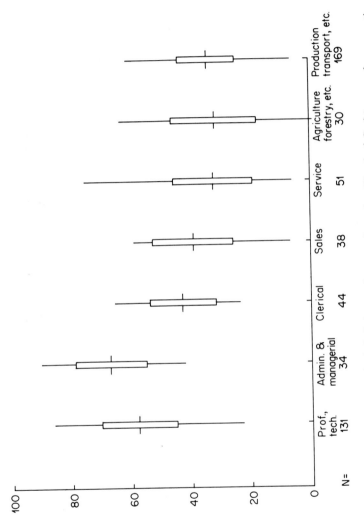

Figure 8.1A. Mean, standard deviation, and range of prestige (Standard Scale) scores for occupations classified according to the major groups of the International Standard Classification of Occupations (revised); *N*s are number of occupations in each category.

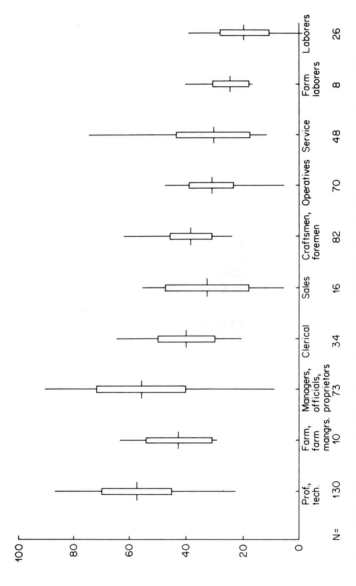

Figure 8.1B. Mean, standard deviation, and range of prestige (Standard Scale) scores for occupations classified according to the major groups of the 1960 U.S. Census classifications; *N*s are number of occupations in each category.

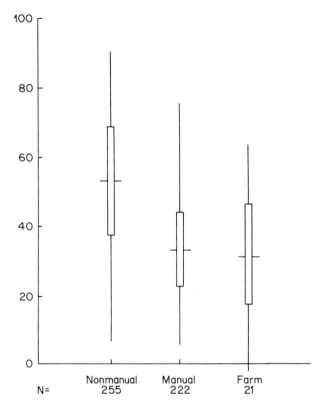

Figure 8.1C. Mean, standard deviation, and range of prestige (Standard Scale) scores for occupations classified as nonmanual, manual, or farm; *N*s are number of occupations in each category.

each country,[2] it would be desirable to have available a standardized occupational status scale that could be used to code occupations in any country, to enable cross-national comparisons uncontaminated by differences in scaling procedures.[3]

The obvious question regarding any such scale is the simple one of its validity. If, indeed, occupational status hierarchies differed substantially

---

[2] As indicated above, such scales are now available for the United States and Great Britain, and research is currently underway in Israel and Ireland that should yield similar scales for those countries. But there is no reason to be optimistic about the availability of such instruments for other nations.

[3] In fact, a standard international occupational prestige scale would be useful even if comprehensive prestige scales were widely available for individual countries, because then it would be possible to study the ways in which the prestige hierarchies of specific societies deviated from the worldwide average.

from country to country, any attempt to score occupations according to a status scale not specific to the society being studied would distort the realities of the local situation and thereby invalidate any attempted comparisons. However, we know from the analysis reported in Chapter 4 that occupational prestige hierarchies are essentially similar throughout the world—recall that the average intercountry occupational prestige correlation (computed over 55 countries) is .81. Thus, the question reduces to whether the distortion of the "true" situation for any given country that would result from use of a standard international scale is likely to be less than would result from use of alternative scaling procedures, such as those traditionally employed; the answer is affirmative. In the remainder of this chapter I will describe the construction of such a scale and present data pertinent to the assessment of its validity. In the following chapter I will discuss its potential uses, assess its relation to other measures of social status, and elaborate upon procedures for using it.

CONSTRUCTING THE SCALE

Recall from Chapter 3 that the basic data matrix consists of 509 rows, each representing a separately identified occupation, by 60 columns, each representing a separate place for which we have data. Each cell of the matrix is then a score for a specific occupation for a given country. Obviously, because not all occupations were rated in every country (indeed, the average number of occupations per place is 62, or about 12% of the total number of titles), the bulk of the cells in the matrix are blank. Moreover, the number of countries in which any given occupation appears varies enormously—some occupations are rated in a single country while at the other extreme primary schoolteachers are rated in 55 places; the average title is rated in approximately 7 places. The question was thus how to construct a set of standard scores on the basis of the available information.

As a first step, all scores were converted to a standard metric.[4] The basic procedure utilized was to convert each foreign data set to the United States' metric by equating the mean and standard deviation of all occupations rated in common in the United States and the given foreign country (Nunnally, 1967:108). That is, for occupation i in country j, a standard metric score, X'_{ij}, was computed by letting

$$X'_{ij} = \frac{s_{u_j}}{s_{j_u}} (X_{ij} - \bar{X}_{j_u}) + \bar{X}_{u_j}$$

[4] There are several ways to do this. Here I describe the procedure actually adopted. Appendix 8.1 to this chapter compares this procedure with the alternatives that were considered and rejected.

where X'_{ij} = the transformed prestige score for occupation i rated in country j,

s_{u_j} = the standard deviation of the United States' scores, for occupations rated in both the United States and country j,

s_{j_u} = the standard deviation of the country j scores, for occupations rated in both the United States and country j,

X_{ij} = the original metric prestige score for occupation i rated in country j,

$\bar{X}_{j_u}$ = the mean of the country j scores, for occupations rated in both country j and the United States,

$\bar{X}_{u_j}$ = the mean of the United States' scores for occupations rated in both country j and the United States.

This procedure yielded a set of scores for each country expressed in a standard metric with a range of roughly 0 to 100.[5]

The second step was to generate a summary score for each of the 509 occupations. This was done for each title by averaging all scores appearing in the given row of the matrix, excluding the five sets based on nonprestige criteria.[6] The scores thus derived are the basic scale scores; they are shown in the "occupation" column of Appendix A (the rightmost column).[7]

[5] Actually, although the United States metric has a theoretical range of 0 to 100, converted scores can fall outside this range. However, this occurred only 4 times out of a total of approximately 3700 rated titles.

[6] Utilizing all 60 places makes virtually no difference in the scale, since scale scores constructed for 60 places and for 55 places are almost perfectly correlated: $r = .9990$. Nonetheless, it seemed wise to omit the 5 countries with data based on nonprestige criteria to avoid any possible bias in the scale scores for particular occupations that happened to be rated in any of the 5 countries and in very few other places. Concern about this possibility stems from the fact that the average correlation of the scores in these 5 places with the Standard Scale (whatever version) is substantially below the average for the 55 remaining countries; in the version actually utilized, the 5-country average is .75, compared to .91 for the remaining 55 places. However, in the seven cases in which an occupation was rated *only* in one of the 5 omitted countries, the score for that country was used as an estimate of the Standard Scale score.

[7] Given the large differences between studies in the quality of the basic data, it appeared that it might be useful to weight the individual country scores used in the computation of each standard score proportionately to their quality. Accordingly, I constructed a weighted version of the Standard Scale, using as weights the data quality estimates presented in Table 2.1. Upon reflection, however, I rejected this alternative on the ground that it could only reinforce a bias already present in the data, the tendency for the Standard Scale scores to reflect more closely the prestige position of each occupation in industrialized countries than in nonindustrialized countries simply because the studies conducted in industrialized countries tend to contain more titles. However, as it turned out, this concern was pointless since weighting the data for quality made virtually no difference in the scale scores: The correlation between the two versions of the scale is .9986. For a discussion of the similarity of scales based on weighted and nonweighted averages see Nunnally (1967:278).

Scores for Aggregated Categories.   The final step was to produce scores for unit, minor, and major groups of the ISCO scheme. Recall from Chapter 2 that the category system utilized here is adapted from the revised edition of the *International Standard Classification of Occupations* (International Labor Office, 1969a). In this system occupations are classified in a nested set of four levels. With minor exceptions described in Chapter 2, the classification scheme utilized for the Standard Scale follows the ISCO scheme down to the unit group level. The fourth level consists of the specific occupations rated in the prestige studies. It is for the 509 lines at the "occupation" level that the standard scores just described were constructed.

To facilitate use of the Standard Scale, however, scores should be available for each of the higher levels of aggregation in the ISCO scheme. Often a researcher is not in the position to collect data on the entire detailed list of occupations, but must restrict himself to a more limited classification. Moreover, secondary analysts usually will be working with data that are already partially aggregated, and aggregated to different degrees for different parts of the Scale. Finally, censuses vary in their level of aggregation, with very detailed classifications corresponding to some sectors of the Scale and very gross categories corresponding to other sectors. Thus, if prestige scores are to be assigned to such data sets, the Scale must include scores at all levels of aggregation. The procedure utilized to develop such scores consisted of two separate steps: aggregation of individual occupations into unit groups, and aggregation of unit groups into minor and major groups.

Unit Groups.   Unit group scores ordinarily were derived simply by averaging the scores for the occupations included in the unit group. However, in a few cases occupations which I judged to be extremely atypical of the unit group were excluded from the computation of the average. Striking examples are "00411 Astronaut" in the unit group "0041 Aircraft Pilots, Navigators and Flight Engineers" and "01221 Supreme Court Justice" in the unit group "0122 Judges."[8]

In some cases, unit groups existed that included *no* occupations for which prestige ratings were available. In these cases, a score was assigned to each

---

[8] The reader should be aware that this represents a change from the practice followed in an earlier version of the Scale (Treiman, 1975). In that version, some occupations judged to be somewhat uncommon but not extremely rare were given a weight of .5 in computing the unit group score. However, subsequent work with the scale has made it evident that the use of half weights created various inconsistencies in the unit group scores, particularly with respect to craft occupations. Hence, in the present version of the Scale all occupational titles are either excluded or assigned full weight. The footnotes to Appendix A make the changes clear. See especially Appendix A footnotes 3, 27–29.

unit group on the basis of my judgment as to its similarity to categories for which prestige scores were available. Since the assignments are all designated by footnotes to the entries in Appendix A (as are the instances in which I excluded occupations from the unit group average), the reader can assess the quality of my judgments for himself.

Minor and Major Groups. The aggregation of unit groups into minor and major groups poses a special problem in view of the fact that although the prestige hierarchy remains relatively constant across time and space, the distribution of the labor force among occupations does not: typically, industrialization results in an upward shift in this distribution (Soares, 1966; Treiman, 1970). Hence, a set of minor and major group scores that accurately reflects the occupational distribution of any given country at any given time is likely to be somewhat inaccurate for other countries or other historical periods. For example, the prestige of "0985 Motor Vehicle Drivers" is nearly 10 points greater than that of "0986 Animal and Animal-Drawn Vehicle Drivers." Since both of these unit groups fall into the same minor group, "098 TRANSPORT EQUIPMENT OPERATORS," an estimate of the minor group prestige score that reflects differences between countries in the degree of mechanization of transportation would produce somewhat different minor group prestige scores for each country.

Fortunately, it proves to be the case that intercountry differences in occupational distributions have only a small effect on minor and major group scores; hence a single set of scores is appropriate for all countries, not only at the "occupation" level but at higher levels of aggregation as well.

The evidence supporting this claim is as follows: First, minor group scores based on a weighted average of unit group scores (with weights reflecting the proportion of the labor force in each unit group) for two countries varying widely in level of industrialization—the United States and India—are nearly identical (the correlation between the two sets of scores is .984).[9] Second, with one exception the weighted major group scores are virtually identical in the two countries (see Table 8.1). Sales workers as a class have substantially higher prestige in India than in the United States, reflecting the fact that they are mostly working proprietors in India and mostly shop assistants in the United States.

These results have substantive interest beyond their implications for the

---

[9] This correlation is based on 63 cases, although there are 84 minor groups in the Standard Scale classification. The discrepancy is due to the fact that some unit groups could not be adequately matched by occupational titles in the United States' and/or Indian census classifications. Where fewer than half of the unit groups in a particular minor group had matches in the census classification, no average score was computed for the minor group. This occurred 5 times for the United States, 16 times for India, and 10 times for both jointly.

TABLE 8.1

Standard Scale Scores for Major Occupation Groups--Selected Comparisons

ISCO Major Group	Percentage Distribution of Labor Force		Weighted Average Scores Based on Occupational Distribution		Unweighted Average of Unit Group Scores
	U.S.	India	U.S.	India	
Professional, technical, and related workers	11.6	1.7	58	58	56
Administrative and managerial workers	4.4	1.0	63	64	64
Clerical and related workers	15.0	1.7	40	42	43
Sales workers	12.0	3.7	37	43	41
Service workers	11.7	3.0	27	27	31
Agricultural, animal husbandry and forestry workers, fishermen and hunters	7.0	73.1	33	34	28
Production and related workers, transport equipment operators and laborers	38.3	15.9	33	32	35
Total	100.0	100.1	38.0	34.6	42.6
Size of labor force (000s)	(64,551)	(188,252)			

Sources: U.S. Census 1960 and India Census 1961 (U.S. Bureau of the Census, 1963; India Registrar General, 1965; International Labor Office, 1964).

validity of the Standard Scale, since they imply that the major transformation of the labor force that accompanies industrialization is a shift between different types of work—notably a shift out of agriculture and, within the nonagricultural sector, from manual to clerical, administrative, and professional work—rather than a shift in the distribution of personnel within gross categories. At the very least, what shifts do occur within major groups (or within minor groups, for that matter) do not seem to involve a general upgrading of the labor force to more prestigious jobs. In fact, there is some reason to suspect that industrialization results in increasing specialization of functions and, in particular, in an increase in the proportion of ancillary or supporting personnel. For example, while the number of doctors per capita is about three times as great in the United States as in India, the number of nurses per capita is more than 20 times as great, so that the ratio of nurses to doctors is much higher in the United States (United States Bureau of the Census, 1963:1–2; India Registrar General, 1965:94–95).

Despite these tendencies, however, the basic conclusion remains unaltered: the Standard Scale scores for minor and major groups are not substantially affected by national variations in the distribution of the labor force. This, however, still leaves us with the question of how best to derive scores for these groups. The alternatives I entertained were (1) to average the scores estimated for India and the United States or (2) to compute simple averages of unit group scores. As it turns out, these procedures yield nearly identical results for minor groups (the correlation between the two sets of derived scores is .981). Therefore, for most categories I used the simple averages, on the grounds that it was simpler to do so, that all the necessary information was available (which was not true for the India–United States matches), and that discrepancies between the Indian and/or U.S. Census classification and the Standard Scale classification themselves introduced additional error. However, for the four minor groups for which the discrepancy between the simple and weighted averages was more than five points, I substituted the India–United States averages for the unweighted averages. This was done because it was clear in each case that the bulk of the labor force in both countries fell into one or a few of the unit groups making up the minor group, so that unweighted averages would seriously distort the true score for the average individual falling into those minor groups. These groups were "006 MEDICAL, DENTAL, VETERINARY AND RELATED WORKERS," "061 FARMERS," "063 FORESTRY WORKERS," and "097 MATERIAL-HANDLING AND RELATED EQUIPMENT OPERATORS, DOCKERS AND FREIGHT HANDLERS."

To derive scores for major groups, I computed weighted averages of scores assigned to the detailed occupation lines of the United States and

Indian censuses and then simply averaged the two scores.[10] I did this in preference to simply averaging unit group lines because the latter procedure would have resulted in overestimates of several of the major group averages due to the fact that many relatively high-prestige categories include only small proportions of the labor force. The major group scores that would have resulted from a simple average of unit group lines are shown in Table 8.1, for purposes of comparison.

The relatively minor differences between the weighted and unweighted scores for minor and major groups is convenient in that a version of the Standard Scale that includes unweighted aggregate scores has been privately circulated. Also, a few errors in the occupation scores given in the prepublication version have been found and corrected. And, as mentioned in footnote 8, a decision not to use differential weights in computing unit group scores resulted in some changes in scores between the previously published version (Treiman, 1975) and the current version of the Scale. The results cited above suggest that users of previous versions of the Scale may be confident that their own analysis would be hardly affected by these alterations of the Scale scores. Nonetheless, the version presented here should be regarded as definitive.

PROPERTIES OF THE SCALE

To recapitulate, the Scale consists of prestige scores for 509 occupations, 288 unit groups, 84 minor groups, and 11 major groups (7 in the civilian labor force and 4 residual categories). The Scale has a range of 92 points, from "02010 Chief of State," with a score of 90, to "06291 Gatherer," with a score of -2. The mean scale score, computed over the 509 occupations, is 43.3 and the standard deviation is 16.9, with individual scores approximately normally distributed about the mean.[11]

---

[10] It was necessary to go back to the individual occupation lines to ensure that the entire labor force in each country was included in the computation of the averages.

[11] To some extent, the relatively high mean reflects the overrepresentation of titles in the "professional, technical, and related" major group (fully 26% of all titles fall into this category). But this is a generic feature of almost all detailed occupational classification schemes, and not simply an artifact of a preoccupation with high prestige occupations on the part of those who design occupational prestige studies. Twenty-eight per cent of the unit groups in the ISCO scheme (International Labor Office, 1969a), 28% of the titles in the United States Census 1960 detailed classification of occupations (U.S. Bureau of the Census, 1960a), and 18% of the titles in the British Census 1970 detailed classification of occupations (Great Britain Office of Population Censuses and Surveys, 1970) fall into the professional category. It is not clear whether the disproportionate detail in the classification of professional occupations reflects the greater ease of making distinctions in this sector, the greater importance of distinctions, or

As would be expected, the highest status positions are those at the top of the political, religious, and educational hierarchies. In addition to "chief of state," the titles with scores greater than 80 include, in order of their prestige, "02031 Ambassador," "02020 Leader of House," "01311 University President, Dean," "02021 Member, Upper House," "01411 High Church Official," "01221 Supreme Court Justice," and "02011 Provincial Governor." These are all really offices rather than occupations, with the exception of "high church official" and "university president or dean," and even these positions have so few incumbents in most countries as to effectively qualify as offices. Among more common occupations, those with the highest prestige include scientists, physicians, and professors. The only business occupation that scores as high is "02113 Banker, Large Bank." Contrary to popular academic opinion, businessmen are, in general, not as highly regarded as are professionals.

The lowest prestige occupations are mostly those that are illegal or illegitimate, although three marginal unskilled titles score very poorly as well. The occupations with Standard Scale scores less than 10 include "05999 Illegal Lottery Agent," "04525 Narcotics Peddler," "07780 Moonshiner," "04107 Smuggler," "09992 Contract Laborer," "06491 Hunter," and "06291 Gatherer." The first four clearly are illegitimate occupations and are accorded little respect by the populations they serve. The rating for "contract laborer" is based solely on the evaluation of the title "*ovambo kontrakwerker*" in South-West Africa; these are mostly young men imported to the capital from a native reserve to do unskilled labor and are regarded as a disreputable element by the local population (Kelley and Wade, 1975). Finally, "hunter" and "gatherer," which were rated exclusively in Peasant India, are subsistence occupations done on a part-time basis.

It is possible to get a sense of the generic prestige hierarchy by perusing Table 8.2, which contains a listing in rank order of one-twentieth of the occupations in the Standard Scale (all 509 occupations were listed in rank order and every 20th occupation was selected to form the table). What is striking about this list of occupations is that with the exception of the very top and the very bottom of the hierarchy there is no clear ordering of major occupational groups. High public officials and professionals top the list and unskilled workers monopolize the bottom, but throughout most of the range manual and nonmanual, sales and service, clerical and craft jobs are

---

simply the class-based biases of the designers of occupational classification schemes. But it does require us to be cautious about generalizing from the distribution of occupational titles to the prestige distribution of the labor force, even in countries like Great Britain and the United States. We will return to this issue in the following chapter.

TABLE 8.2
Standard Scale Scores for Every 20th Occupation in Rank Order[a]

Standard Scale Code and Occupation Title	Standard Scale Score
02010 Chief of State	90
05822 High Police Official	75
01924 Social Scientist (nec)	69
00230 Electrical Engineer	65
00790 Osteopath	62
02190 Businessman	58
04412 Stock Broker	56
01992 Fingerprint Expert	54
04221 Purchasing Agent	51
04411 Real Estate Agent	49
08431 Garage Operator	47
01630 Photographer	45
09830 Locomotive Engineer	43
09240 Metal Engraver	41
04222 Agricultural Buyer	39
01711 Jazz Musician	38
04520 Market Trader	36
08310 Blacksmith	34
03700 Mail Carrier	33
03311 Cashier	31
05512 Sexton	30
08491 Bicycle Repairman	28
05522 Chimney Sweep	25
05890 Watchman	22
09860 Animal Driver	18
09996 Garbage Collector	13

[a]The table was derived from a listing of Standard Scale scores expressed to three decimal places.

intermixed in no obvious order. So once again we have a confirmation of the point illustrated by Figures 8.1a–8.1c—the gross occupational categories conventionally used to categorize occupations do not do a very good job of differentiating occupations with respect to prestige. These classifications have many proper uses, but serving as surrogates for a prestige scale is not one of them.

The data in Table 8.2 serve to illustrate still another point alluded to above—the difficulty of accurately interpolating new occupational titles into a prestige ordering based on a small number of occupations. As an exercise, the reader is invited to try to guess the prestige of, say, "09540 Carpenter," "09210 Printer," "05700 Barber," "04510 Sales Clerk," and "01930 Social Worker." Having tried to interpolate these titles into the list in Table 8.2, check your answers by reference to Appendix A. Quite likely your error rate will be rather high, even if you divide the list in the table into four or five categories in the manner of Moser and Hall (1954) and try simply to place the titles in the appropriate category.

VALIDATING THE SCALE

We must now address the crucial question—how good is the Scale as a surrogate measure of the prestige hierarchy of any society? The answer is—very good. There are several bodies of evidence that support this claim.

Country–Standard Scale Correlations. First, the Standard Scale is extremely highly correlated with the prestige hierarchies of almost all the countries for which we have data. While this is hardly surprising, given the high average intercountry correlations and the method of scale construction, the magnitude of these correlations (shown in Table 8.3) is reassuring. The mean correlation with the Standard Scale is .91, computed over the 55 countries with pure prestige data. Moreover, the variance around this average is very low. Of the 55 countries, only 7 exhibit correlations with the Standard Scale smaller than .87.

However, objection may be raised to this evidence on the ground that the Standard Scale scores are averages of prestige scores from these same countries and that in consequence all the individual country–Standard Scale correlations are artificially inflated (McNemar, 1969:182). To assess the magnitude of such inflation, I constructed 55 versions of the Standard Scale, each time leaving out one country, and then computed the correlation between each set of individual country scores and the version of the Standard Scale omitting the scores for that country.[12] The resulting correlations are shown in the right-hand column of Table 8.3. Happily, these correlations are for the most part hardly attenuated at all: The mean correlation drops from .91 to .89, although the number of correlations less than .8 increases from 4 to 7 and the number of correlations between .8 and .9 increases from 9 to 15.

While most countries conform very closely to the generic occupational prestige hierarchy represented by the Standard Scale, there are several notable deviations. Thus, before accepting the Scale as a universally valid predictor of the prestige hierarchy in any country, we must assess the possibility that the Scale does not apply as well to some types of societies as to others. For example, nonindustrialized societies may conform less well to

---

[12] This is similar to a procedure recommended by Mosteller and Tukey (1968; see pp. 109–117, 133–160 for an excellent discussion of validation procedures.)

TABLE 8.3

Correlations of Individual Country Prestige Scores
with Standard Scale, and with Version of Standard
Scale Excluding Scores for Country in Correlation

Country		Standard Scale	Correlation with Standard Scale Excluding Scores for Country in Correlation
(1)	United States	.963	.933
(2)	Argentina	.923	.913
(3)	Australia	.960	.943
(4)	Belgium	.931	.922
(5)	Brazil (Açucena)	.881	.855
(6)	Brazil (Bezerros)	.936	.921
(7)	Brazil (São Paulo)	.909	.894
(8)	Canada	.962	.945
(9)	Ceylon	.884	.854
(10)	Chile	.957	.947
(11)	Congo (Kinshasa)	.770	.684
(12)	Costa Rica	.940	.928
(13)	Czechoslovakia	.610*	.610*
(14)	Denmark	.970	.960
(15)	France	.740	.722
(16)	French Guiana	.881	.865
(17)	Germany (West)	.916	.891
(18)	Ghana	.939	.928
(19)	Grenada	.672*	.672*
(20)	Great Britain	.956	.941
(21)	Guam	.913	.892
(22)	Guyana	.933	.910
(23)	India (Peasant)	.727	.579
(24)	India (University Students)	.971	.968
(25)	Indonesia (Java)	.927	.920
(26)	Indonesia (West Irian)	.894	.865
(27)	Iraq	.930	.919
(28)	Israel	.955	.945
(29)	Italy	.949	.943
(30)	Ivory Coast	.938	.926
(31)	Japan	.960	.939
(32)	Mauritania	.917	.888
(33)	Mexico	.920	.905
(34)	Netherlands	.936	.901
(35)	New Britain	.678	.624
(36)	New Zealand	.962	.954
(37)	Nigeria (Bornu)	.830*	.830*
(38)	Nigeria (Kano)	.833	.769
(39)	Norway	.902	.892
(40)	Pakistan	.947	.938
(41)	Philippines	.948	.941
(42)	Poland	.820	.793
(43)	Puerto Rico	.965	.955
(44)	Southern Rhodesia	.888	.843
(45)	South-West Africa	.900	.861
(46)	Spain	.899	.871
(47)	Surinam	.910	.881
(48)	Sweden	.842*	.842*

TABLE 8.3 *(Continued)*

(49)	Switzerland	.917	.880
(50)	Taiwan	.929	.922
(51)	Thailand (Peasant)	.875	.851
(52)	Thailand (Teachers' College. Students)	.924	.906
(53)	Thailand (University Students)	.934	.919
(54)	Turkey	.965	.948
(55)	Uganda	.950	.929
(56)	Union of South Africa	.920	.902
(57)	USSR	.837	.795
(58)	Uruguay	.926	.920
(59)	Yugoslavia	.809*	.809*
(60)	Zambia	.947	.939
Mean correlation (excludes*)		.910	.887

*Study used nonprestige criterion of occupational rating; hence, excluded from construction of Standard Scale Scores. Thus, correlation in second column is the same as that in first column.

the generic hierarchy than more industrialized places. Also, we saw in the previous chapter that the occupational prestige hierarchies of socialist bloc countries are somewhat deviant from those in the rest of the world. Figure 8.2 shows, for the 55 countries for which we have true prestige data, a scatterplot of the relationship between the level of industrialization (measured by per capita GNP rank)[13] and the degree of conformity to the Standard Scale (measured by the correlation between the individual country prestige hierarchy and the Standard Scale).[14] We also take advantage of this exercise to investigate the possibility that the uniformly high correlations with the Standard Scale result from the fact that prestige data for nonindustrialized countries tend to be based on student samples, which might exhibit more conformity to an emergent world pattern than would data for more representative samples from such countries; of course, this is unlikely given the results of the analysis reported in Chapter 3.

Inspection of the plot provides striking confirmation of the claim that the Standard Scale is a valid representation of the occupational prestige hierarchies for most countries in the world: Of the seven correlations falling below

[13] Recall from Chapter 6 that per capita GNP rank rather than the actual amount of GNP per capita is preferred in order to correct the extreme skewness of the distribution of per capita GNP among the countries of the world.

[14] The scatterplot presents the scores from the left-hand column of Table 8.2. Had we used the modified correlations presented in the right-hand column, the pattern would not have changed.

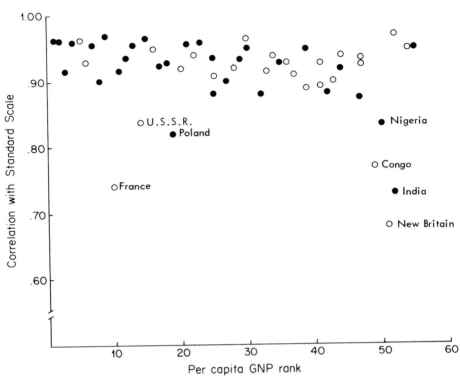

Figure 8.2. Scatterplot of relation between per capita GNP and correlation of individual country occupational prestige hierarchies with the Standard Scale (open circles indicate student samples and solid circles indicate nonstudent samples).

.87, six conform to a clear pattern. First, the two socialist bloc countries have noticeably lower-than-average correlations with the generic hierarchy (.82 and .84), which confirms that they have a somewhat different pattern of prestige evaluations than the rest of the world (see the more extended discussion of this point in Chapter 7). Second, four of the least economically developed places deviate substantially from the generic hierarchy, raising the possibility of genuine idiosyncracies in occupational evaluations in places far removed from the modern network of nation states. However, even for such places, the bulk of the available data conforms rather closely to the generic pattern. Thus, whereas data for Nigeria, Congo, peasant India, and New Britain deviate rather substantially from the Standard Scale, data for Brazil (Açucena), Mauritania, the Philippines, peasant Thailand, Uganda, and Zambia—all derived from samples more or less representative of the general population—conform about as closely to the Standard Scale as data from far more industrialized societies. In view of this, no definitive conclusion can be drawn regarding the validity of the Standard Scale to estimate the occupational prestige hierarchies of the least industrialized places in the world. Hence, it would be prudent to exercise considerable caution in utilizing the Scale in such places. Of course, it is probable that even in such places the Standard Scale is a better predictor of local prestige hierarchies than are ad hoc scales based on the judgments of individual researchers. Hence, unless a local prestige study is available, the Standard Scale is probably the most valid alternative.

One final coefficient remains to be considered—the unusually low correlation between the French occupational prestige data and the Standard Scale. I regard error in the French data to be the only tenable explanation for this. It is inconceivable that the French could be so perverse as to depart as radically from a worldwide prestige hierarchy as the data imply; and it is doubly inconceivable that such a radical cultural bias, if it existed, would not be shared by former French colonies. Yet the prestige hierarchies of French Guiana and Mauritania are in line with those for most other countries. The most likely explanations are either that some sort of error was made in tabulating the French data or, more likely, that the task was improperly administered to the sample of schoolboys from which ratings were obtained, resulting in peculiar responses. Clearly, here is an instance in which data being incompatible with theory, the prudent course is to keep the theory and ignore the data.

Apart from the deviations just discussed, there are no systematic societal variations in the degree of conformity to the generic hierarchy. First, there is no tendency for industrialization to engender convergence to a single pattern of occupational evaluation; indeed, there cannot be, given the extremely high agreement with the generic hierarchy in nonindustrialized countries. Second, there is no tendency for student respondents to conform either more or less closely to the generic hierarchy than do other sorts of respondents. In particular, students in nonindustrialized countries do not conform more closely to the generic hierarchy than do nonstudents from similar places. Thus, we need have no fear that the degree of worldwide consensus in occupational evaluation is overstated by reliance upon samples of students.

To sum up, with the possible exception of the least industrialized societies in the world, on the one hand, and the socialist bloc nations, on the other, the evidence just presented suggested that the Standard Scale scores will provide highly accurate estimates of the prestige of specific occupations in any nation in the world.

Cross-Validation. A second approach to assessing the validity of the Scale is to show that it accurately predicts prestige scores for data not used in forming the Scale. In one sense I have already shown this by presenting correlations with a set of scales constructed by omitting each country successively (the second column of Table 8.3). Here I carry the exercise one step further, making use of data which were located after the Scale was constructed. I assigned Standard Scale scores to each occupation in the new studies, following the procedures described in detail in the following chapter. Since the titles found in these studies were not used in constructing the Scale, many of them could be matched only approximately. But this is precisely the situation likely to be encountered by most users of the Scale. Thus, the correlations reported in Table 8.4 provide a test of the validity of the Scale under conditions closely approximating its actual use. Examining the data in the table, we have still another confirmation of the validity of the Scale. The average correlation with the Scale is .907, which is virtually identical to the average correlation reported in Table 8.3. Of equal interest is the fact that in two of the three cases where new studies were utilized for countries from which we already had data, the new correlations are actually higher. This is somewhat surprising, and can probably best be explained by the fact that the new studies are on the whole superior to those used in the body of the analysis.

Comparison with Alternative Scaling Procedures. As a final approach to validating the Scale, I show that it uniformly does a better job of predicting the prestige of occupations in individual countries than do occupational status scales developed specifically for those places. As we know from the discussion that opened this chapter, many researchers have developed occupational status scales that purport to score individuals on the basis of the

TABLE 8.4
Correlations with Standard Scale of Occupational Prestige
Data not Used in Constructing the Scale

Country and Source	Correlation with Standard Scale	Number of Occupations
Czechoslovakia (Kapr, 1969:386-387)	.842	65
Germany (Kleining and Moore, 1968:520-521)	.956	70
Italy (1974)[a]	.935	161
Poland (Słomczynski, 1972:109-111)	.894	42
Mean	.907	–

[a]Ratings of 164 occupations by urban respondents. Data supplied by Gerhard Kleining.

prestige of their occupations. However, because prestige scores typically are available for only a limited number of occupations in each place, researchers have had to estimate the prestige position of a large number of specific occupations in order to interpolate them into their scales. The result is that often so much error is introduced that the scales in question can only be said to provide rough approximations to the true occupational prestige hierarchy of the societies for which they were developed.

Under these circumstances, it is hardly surprising that the Standard Scale more closely approximates the true prestige hierarchies of individual countries than do available alternative scales. Table 8.5 presents data for 10 countries for which appropriate data were conveniently available. The table shows correlations between the Standard Scale and prestige data in each country, and also correlations between local prestige scales and other occupational status scales untilized in local occupational mobility studies.[15] If we compare the correlations, we find that in each of the 12 comparisons the Standard Scale is more closely correlated with the local prestige scale than is the scale used in the local stratification or mobility study. The average correlation of the local prestige scales with the Standard Scale is .94 while the average correlation of the local prestige scales with the alternative local scales is .84. Thus, insofar as one is interested in scaling occupations according to their prestige, one is actually better off using the Standard Scale than using the scales explicitly developed for use in each country. Not only is comparability across countries assured, but greater fidelity to the true prestige ordering of occupations in the local setting is assured as well.

This conclusion is, however, unsatisfactory in one respect. A major use of the Scale will be to assign occupational prestige scores to individuals in order to study the relationship between occupational status and other

---

[15] The careful reader will note that the correlations reported in Table 8.5 sometimes deviate slightly from the corresponding correlations reported in Table 8.3. Three factors account for this. First, titles representing non-labor-force categories (e.g., "person who lives off income from property") or high offices (e.g., "supreme court justice") were excluded from the comparison of alternative coding procedures because the interest here is in determining what procedure for coding ordinary occupations in a country's labor force best reproduces the country's occupational prestige hierarchy. Second, the correlations in Table 8.5 for the United States are computed over the categories of the 1960 Census detailed occupational classification, whereas those in Table 8.3 are, of course, based on the Standard Scale categories. Third, while the procedure in most countries was to assign the occupational titles appearing in the prestige study to the categories of the local scale, in Uganda and Costa Rica no criteria for interpolating into the local scale categories were available, but detailed occupational titles appearing in the local study were exhaustively listed. Thus, in these two cases I utilized for purposes of comparison only those titles for which I had fairly exact matches between the occupations appearing in the prestige study and the mobility study. Despite these differences, however, in no case does the correlation between the Standard Scale and the local prestige scale differ by more than .02 in the two tables.

TABLE 8.5

Comparison of Standard Scale and Alternative Status
Scales as Predictors of Local Occupational Prestige
Hierarchies for Selected Countries[a]

Country	Correlation of Local Prestige Scale with	
	Standard Scale	Alternative Local Status Scale
Argentina (Buenos Aires)	.95	.93
Australia	.96	.85
Brazil (São Paulo)	.93	.88
Chile (Santiago)	.97	.89
Costa Rica	.93	.72
Great Britain	.96	.92
Japan (Tominaga)	.95	.86
Japan (Cummings and Naoi)		.86
Mexico (Monterrey)	.91	.86
Uganda (Toro--Pearlman)	.94	.82
Uganda (Toro--Kelley)		.68
United States	.95	.86
Mean	.94	.84

[a]Sources of alternative local status scales are the following publications plus codebooks and unpublished materials from the studies referred to therein. For Argentina, Brazil, and Chile: Hutchinson, 1962; for Australia: Broom et al., 1966; for Costa Rica: Yauger and Lin, 1973; for Great Britain: Butler and Stokes, 1969; for Japan: Tominaga, 1969, and Cummings and Naoi, 1972; for Mexico: Balan et al., 1973; for Uganda: Kelley, 1971; and for the U.S.: Duncan, 1961. For more detail regarding sources, see Treiman, 1975.

phenomena. Thus, it would be useful to know how well the Scale does at predicting the occupational prestige of the average member of the labor force rather than simply, as above, the prestige of the average occupation. Errors of prediction obviously are far more serious when they affect large proportions of the labor force. For example, if the prestige of farmers is poorly estimated by the Standard Scale, the consequences would be far more severe in a country with 75% of the labor force in agriculture than in a country with 5% of the labor force in agriculture.

While data limitations preclude a definitive assessment of the Scale's adequacy for the prestige scoring of each country's labor force, one reassuring comparison is possible. Prestige scores are available for every occupation line in the U.S. Census 1960 detailed classification of occupations (Siegel, 1971:Table 5). And, of course, Standard Scale scores can be assigned to each of these lines (indeed, they are presented in Appendix C.3 as a convenience for readers). It is thus possible to compute a correlation between the United States' and Standard Scale scores both for the 295 lines[16] in the census classification and, by weighting each line by the size of the experienced civilian labor force[17] (U.S. Bureau of the Census, 1963:Table 1), for all individuals in the labor force. Insofar as the Standard Scale does a better job of predicting the prestige of occupations in the United States than of predicting the occupational prestige of individuals in the labor force, these two correlations will differ. Happily, they do not. Both correlations are .95. Thus, at least in the United States, errors of prediction are not concentrated in those occupations with large numbers of incumbents. Unfortunately, no similar comparison is possible for any other country since for no other country are there yet available data that permit the unambiguous assignment of prestige scores to every member of the labor force.[18] Still, for weighted correlations to differ much from the unweighted correlations reported above, the few occupations containing large fractions of the labor force would have to be very badly estimated.

Unfortunately, there is some indication that the Standard Scale does a poorer job of estimating the prestige of agricultural occupations in countries with high proportions of the labor force engaged in agriculture than in countries with a largely nonagricultural labor force. When we split countries into those with at least half and those with less than half of the labor force in agriculture, we discover that the intercountry variability in the prestige of both "06110 Farmer" and "06210 Farm Hand" is greater in the highly agricultural countries (the standard deviations for "farmer" are 11.8 and 7.1, with Ns of 18 for both groups; and the standard deviations for "farm hand" are 7.3 and 4.7, with Ns of 15 and 12, respectively). It is probable that this reflects the greater diversity of the agricultural labor force in highly agricultural societies, a diversity that is not adequately represented in the prestige data for these countries. Thus users of the Scale in agricultural counties should exercise considerable caution in the assignment of Scale scores to agricultural occupations, making sure to utilize those categories in the Scale that most closely represent the *true* nature of the agricultural jobs in these countries and discounting mere *nominal* similarity. Despite this potential source of error, however, it is unlikely that the overall accuracy of the Standard Scale would be much affected, even in highly agricultural countries.

[16] No score is available in the United States' data for "former member of the armed forces," but this is not properly an occupation in the experienced civilian labor force.

[17] If occupation lines are weighted by the size of the *male* rather than the *total* civilian labor force, the correlations and the conclusions remain virtually unchanged.

[18] When this was written, the Goldthorpe–Hope (1974) Scale for Great Britain was not yet available.

Limitations. A final word of caution is in order with respect to interpreting differences in Standard Scale scores. Sampling errors in the original studies from which scores are drawn, random variations in the particular occupations rated in various countries, and errors in classifying specific titles undoubtedly contribute a certain amount of error to the Standard Scale scores. In Appendix 8.2 to this chapter I have provided some computations pertinent to assessment of the magnitude of the measurement error likely to result from use of the Scale. The conclusion of that exercise is that while the Scale as a whole is highly reliable it is wise not to make too much of small differences between the scores for specific occupations. Standard Scale scores can be regarded as having an average standard error of about three points and hence differences of less than six points between the scores for individual occupations should not be regarded as meaningful.

SUMMARY

This chapter has been concerned with describing the development of a Standard International Occupational Prestige Scale (shown in Appendix A) and with documenting its validity for use in virtually any country in the world. The Scale provides prestige scores for the major, minor, and unit group categories of the revised *International Standard Classification of Occupations* and for a set of 509 specific occupational titles. In this chapter the Scale was shown to be a highly accurate predictor of the occupational prestige hierarchies of individual countries (the average correlation between Standard Scale and individual country scores is about .9) and to be substantially more accurate than alternative occupational scaling procedures currently in use. The next chapter will discuss potential uses of the scale, recommend practical procedures for its use, and compare it with competing occupational status scales such as Duncan's (1961) Socioeconomic Index.

Appendix 8.1

CONVERSION OF PRESTIGE DATA TO A STANDARD METRIC

This Appendix addresses the adequacy of the procedure utilized to convert the data for each country into a standard metric, since the averaging step in constructing the Standard Scale depends upon the assumption that scores for all countries actually are expressed in a common metric. Of three major possibilities, the procedure described in the body of the chapter appeared to be preferable, since it came closest to producing a common metric for all data. To make this point clear, let us review the other two possible procedures.[19]

The major alternative considered was to regress the United States' scores on each set of matching foreign scores and to use the resulting equations to transform all the scores for each foreign country. The basic difficulty with this procedure, however, is that the lower the correlation between two sets of scores, the flatter will be the regression slope relating them and hence the smaller will be the variance of the transformed values. Utilizing this procedure thus would have resulted in an inordinate reduction in the variance of the transformed (United States' metric) scores for countries with relatively low prestige correlations with the United States, and would have had the effect of pushing the high scores down and the low scores up. This, in turn, would have resulted in an artificial correlation between the relative prestige of given occupations in various countries and their level of industrialization, since nonindustrialized countries tend to exhibit lower prestige correlations with the United States (see Chapter 6). Occupations with generic low prestige would have seemed to have higher prestige in less industrialized places while occupations with generic high prestige would have appeared to have higher prestige in more industrialized countries. This artifact, of course, would have precluded the possibility of making systematic comparisons of the relative prestige of a given occupation in various countries. Accordingly, this procedure for converting the data into a common metric was rejected. (Actually, this procedure was the one initially utilized. It was the discovery of the artifactual correlation between the generic prestige of occupations and their tendency to be more highly regarded in industrialized countries that led me to seek an alternative.)

The third basic alternative involved simply converting all the data to standardized scores by subtracting the mean and dividing by the standard deviation of each distribution. However, this procedure, despite the advantage of simplicity, had the fatal weakness of throwing out the baby with the bath. The difficulty is that since the distribution of rated occupations differed from study to study, to equate the means and variances would in itself introduce an artifactual element. For example, consider a country in which mostly manual titles were rated and another study in which mostly nonmanual titles were rated. Computing z-scores for these two distributions could result in given occupations having substantially different transformed

[19] Thurstone's discriminant model was considered as still another a basis for deriving Standard Scale scores but was rejected on the ground that the procedure would not yield prestige scores for individual countries expressed in a common metric, thus precluding the possibility of comparing the prestige of specific occupations across countries (Nunnally, 1967:49–55).

scores in the two countries *even if the intercountry correlation over matching titles were unity.* The procedure actually utilized, which takes account of differences in the distributions of rated titles, and standardizes scores by equating the means and standard deviations of *matching titles,* is clearly to be preferred.

Some evidence of the superiority of the adopted procedure can be gained from a comparison of the ratios of the standard deviations of matching titles computed over all pairs of countries from data converted by two of the procedures described above, that which was ultimately utilized and the regression procedure which was ultimately rejected (the inferiority of the third procedure was so evident as not to warrant further analysis). To the extent that a transformation procedure based on conversion of all data sets to the United States' metric actually produced a common metric for all countries, all pairs of common distributions should have equal standard deviations. Thus, the mean ratio of standard deviations, computed over all pairs of countries, can be used as a measure of the comparability of the various distributions. Since, however, some ratios would be greater than unity and some less than unity, the mean was computed over all pairs of ratios so specified as to be always greater than or equal to one. That is, the quantities entering the computation of the mean are of the form s_i/s_j where s_i and s_j are the standard deviations of the occupations common to country i and country j with s_i greater than or equal to s_j. Using such quantities, the mean was computed over the 1770 ($= 60 \times 59/2$) pairs that can be formed from 60 countries. Computing these means for the data converted both by the rejected regression procedure and the procedure actually utilized, it is clear that the choice between procedures was correct: The mean ratio under the regression conversion procedure is 1.32:1; under the alternative it drops to 1.13:1. This result indicates that the conversion procedure adopted here produces a reasonably close approximation to a fully standardized scale. Had it been possible to compute the mean ratio only for those pairs of countries with at least 10 occupations in common among the 55 places with strict prestige data, the result no doubt would have been yet closer to unity—the stability of the variances being very low where only a few occupational titles enter into their computation.

Appendix 8.2

RELIABILITY AND ERRORS OF ESTIMATE

It is possible to get a numerical estimate of just how much error is likely to result from using the Standard Scale to estimate prestige scores for specific countries by adapting the domain-sampling model of psychometrics (Nunnally, 1967: Chapter 6). If we regard the set of ratings of a given occupation in various countries as constituting a random sample of all possible ratings of that occupation, then we can estimate the "true" score for the occupation by the mean of the individual country scores—which is, of course, precisely what we have done in constructing the Standard Scale. The reliability of a scale composed of scores estimated in this way is given by Nunnally (1967:193) as

$$r_{kk} = \frac{k\bar{r}_{ij}}{1 + (k - 1)\bar{r}_{ij}}$$

where r_{kk}, the reliability coefficient, is the expected correlation of one k-item test with other k-item tests drawn from the same domain; that is, r_{kk} is the expected correlation between occupational prestige scales each formed by averaging scores over k countries. Thus r_{kk} tells us how similar we could expect a scale to be that was formed by averaging scores from a set of countries different from those we actually used. The remaining term, $\bar{r}_{ij}$, is just the average inter-item correlation; or, in this case, the average intercountry correlation in occupational prestige ratings.

In the present case, of course, we have a problem because of the large amount of missing data. Suppose we had complete data. Then we would have 55 measurements for each occupation and an average correlation between measurements (between countries) of .81. These figures would yield

$$r_{kk} = \frac{55\,(.81)}{1 + (55 - 1)\,(.81)} = .9957$$

which implies an almost perfectly reliable scale. However, in fact the average occupation is rated in just under seven countries (precisely 6.95), so a more reasonable estimate of the reliability of the scale would be given by

$$r_{kk} = \frac{6.95\,(.81)}{1 + (6.95 - 1)\,(.81)} = .9674.$$

This is, of course, an extremely high coefficient, compared to conventional standards, and suggests that as a measure of a "true" occupational prestige hierarchy, the scale is nearly error-free. Specifically, the size of the reliability coefficient gives us great confidence that the scale is not importantly affected by accidents of inclusion or exclusion of particular titles from particular countries. Certainly, from a practical standpoint other sources of error—particularly those associated with the assignment of scale scores to occupations classified in other schemes—are likely to be far more serious. These will be treated in detail in the following chapter. Here it suffices to point out that if there were no other sources of error—that is, if the reliability coefficient estimated above could be taken as indicating the reliability of the scale in actual use—unreliability could be dismissed as negligible from the standpoint of its effect on the size of correlations between occupational prestige and other variables (see Nunnally, 1967:226, for further discussion of this point).

While the scale as a whole is highly reliable, it is of interest to know how much error can be expected in the scores estimated for each occupation. To see this, we estimate the standard error of measurement, given by (Nunnally, 1967:201)

$$\sigma_{meas.} = \sigma \, x \, (1 - r_{kk})^{1/2}$$

where σ_x is the standard deviation of the Standard Scale scores and the other terms are as described above. Substituting in the appropriate values, we have

$$\sigma_{meas.} = 16.9 \, (1 - .9674)^{1/2} = 3.05.$$

This tells us that the average standard error of the scale scores is just over three points. From this, of course, we can get a confidence interval, but first we have to make an adjustment for the fact that the observed scores are biased estimates of the true scores. The appropriate correction is (Nunnally, 1967:199):

$$x' = r_{kk} \, (x - \bar{x}) + \bar{x}.$$

Applying this formula to the Standard Scale scores, we note that for extreme values of the scale the true scores are a little more than one point closer to the mean than the observed scores. For example, where $x = 10$, $x' = 11.08$ and where $x = 80$, $x' = 78.8$ (the mean of the scale scores, $\bar{x}$, is 43.3). Thus, taking a confidence band as extending two standard errors around the true scores, we would have a confidence interval of an observed score of 10 extending from 5.0 to 17.2; a confidence band around an observed score of 45 extending from 38.8 to 51.0; and a confidence interval around an observed score of 80 extending from 72.7 to 84.9.

Of course, in some sense these estimates are misleading, in that they are based on the assumption that the scale is formed from 7 scores for each occupation and that the 7 sets of scores have an average correlation of .81. In fact, the number of scores available for each occupation range from 1 to 55 with an *average* of about 7 (actually 6.95), while the average inter-item correlation is based on the 1202 pairs of countries with at least 10 occupations in common, out of a potential total of 1485 ($= 55 \times 54/2$). How these deviations from the model affect the results is not clear, except that it is certain that some occupations are much more precisely estimated than others. One way of getting a sense of how the error of estimate varies for specific occupations is to compute the standard error of the mean, for samples of varying sizes. Noting that the average standard deviation of individual country scores around the Standard Scores for all occupations rated in more than one place (118 of the 509 occupations were rated in only one country) is 6.5, we can compute

$$s_{\bar{x}} = \frac{s_x}{(N-1)^{1/2}} = \frac{6.5}{(N-1)^{1/2}}$$

for Ns of varying size. For $N = 2$, $s_{\bar{x}} = 6.5$; for $N = 7$ (the number of places the average occupation was rated), $s_{\bar{x}} = 2.7$; for $N = 9$ (the number of places the average occupation was rated excluding those rated in only one place), $s_{\bar{x}} = 2.3$; for $N = 20$, $s_{\bar{x}} = 1.5$; for $N = 40$, $s_{\bar{x}} = 1.0$; for $N = 55$, $s_{\bar{x}} = .9$.

What can we conclude from all this? Mainly that while the Scale as a whole is highly reliable it is wise not to make too much of small differences between the scores for specific occupations. A good rule of thumb would be to regard differences of less than 6 points as representing chance fluctuation and only interpret differences of 6 points or more.

9

Using the Scale

While it is common to treat occupations as if they could be unambiguously and consistently ordered on some single "status" dimension that captures most of their important variability, this conception of occupational structure is more a reflection of our ignorance than of our understanding of social reality. In fact, occupations, perhaps more than any other social roles, are multifaceted. They vary in terms of the tasks they entail, the setting in which they are performed, the relations of authority they imply, the kind of commitment they require, the way they are remunerated, and in many other ways as well, only some portion of which is reflected in the prestige they are accorded, in their "socioeconomic status," or in any other single dimension. Moreover, these dimensions, while highly correlated, differ enough to prohibit treatment as interchangable indices, a point we will pursue below.

For these reasons, it is important for researchers who wish to study the relationship between occupational position and other phenomena to be very clear about what characteristics of occupations they wish to measure. For many purposes prestige may be the aspect of greatest interest, in which case the Standard Scale is clearly the instrument of choice. However, for other purposes a socioeconomic index, such as Duncan's, may be more useful; and for still other purposes a nominal classification by type of work (e.g., "occupation" categories in census classifications), by function (e.g., "industry" categories), by manner of remuneration (e.g., "class of worker" categories), or by still other characteristics may be optimal. The main point is that no single classification or scaling of occupations can tap all aspects of occupational differentiation. Thus, the fact that the Standard Scale is a standardized, cross-culturally valid instrument is not a sufficient basis for adopting it unthinkingly for use in any and all situations. The potential user should weigh the advantage of comparability to other research that use of a standardized instrument permits against the disadvantage of possible loss of precision in the representation of the unique features of his data or research problem. The choice among instruments will, of course, depend both upon the needs of the particular research and upon the availability of alternative schemes. Where more than one scale is available, a useful strategy is to code one's data in alternative ways and to compare the results obtained under the different codings. Often the discrepancies between the conclusions reached by alternative procedures yield additional insight regarding the substantive questions under consideration (for example, see Siegel's comparison of the prestige and socioeconomic status of occupations, 1971:193–249).

To provide a basis for intelligent choice among alternative occupational classification and coding schemes, the present chapter will discuss potential uses of the Standard Scale and will also describe practical procedures for its use. The chapter will conclude with a comparison of the Standard Scale and Duncan's (1961) Socioeconomic Index, the occupational status scale most widely utilized in contemporary American research. Not only will it be useful to researchers who are used to thinking about "occupational status" in terms of the Duncan index to know how the two scales are related, but the differences between them should be of substantive interest to students of stratification and mobility.

USES OF THE SCALE

There are three basic ways in which data on occupations can be used: to study the nature of occupational systems in their own right; to study the characteristics of particular occupations; and to classify individuals on the basis of their occupation. For all three purposes measures of prestige may be useful. Let us consider these one by one.

Occupational Structure.   Since the Standard Scale represents the worldwide average prestige hierarchy, it is possible to use it as a standard against which to compare the prestige hierarchies of particular societies. In earlier chapters I have made just such a use of the Scale, but the material presented in this book by no means exhausts the possibilities. Students of particular societies may wish to know just how closely the prestige hierarchy of the society they are studying corresponds to the worldwide norm. Furthermore, they may wish to know how intrasocietal variations in occupational evaluations are structured. For example, it is possible to show that Thai peasants from an isolated village conform somewhat less to the worldwide norm than do students and, moreover, that the discrepancies arise mostly in the evaluation of unfamiliar occupations. Another potential use of the Scale is to test propositions regarding societal differences in the evaluation of particular types of occupations. For example, Barber (1957:21) hypothesized that in consequence of differences in value systems, religious roles were more highly regarded and economically productive roles less highly regarded in traditional Hindu society than in the contemporary United States. However, he recognized that no definitive test of his hypothesis was possible at the time he wrote, suggesting that "for precise comparisons, we would need to have one index, for example an occupational prestige index, applicable to both societies." The Standard Scale is, of course, just such an index and could be used as a standard against which to measure the prestige of particular occupations in both societies. Analysis of this sort is uniquely possible with the Standard Scale and the data reported in Appendix D or other prestige data for individual countries.[1]

A second way the Standard Scale can be used in the comparative analysis of occupational structures is to study the prestige distribution of the labor force (Barber, 1957:87–89). Although the occupational prestige hierarchy is essentially invariant across time and space, the *shape* of the prestige distribution probably is not. As we know, the process of industrialization generally is accompanied by a shift from an agricultural to a nonagricultural labor force and a shift in the nonagricultural sector from manual to nonmanual work (Soares, 1966; Treiman, 1970). The implications for the prestige hierarchy are, however, not completely obvious. Since nonmanual workers generally have higher prestige than manual workers, we should expect an upward shift in the prestige distribution of the nonagricultural labor force in more industrialized countries. But mobility from farm to city often results in downward mobility with respect to prestige. Thus, as the labor force shifts away from agriculture, there may be a general shift downward in the prestige of the average worker. On the other hand, there may be an upward shift, and a lessening of inequality, in the urban prestige hierarchy. As yet we have a very poor idea of what implications, if any, the shape of the distribution has for the operation of a stratification system and the perceptions of its members; but we now have a basis for comparing distributions and hence a basis for beginning to think about such questions.[2]

---

[1] Of course, those who wish to compare other data with those reported in Appendix D will want to convert their data into the metric utilized here, following the procedure described in the previous chapter.

[2] Kazimierz Słomczynski and Lena Mistewicz at the University of Warsaw are currently engaged in a comparison of the occupational prestige distributions of a large number of societies that holds the promise of substantially enhancing our understanding of these issues.

A third use of the Scale in the analysis of occupational structures is as a surrogate for prestige scores in societies for which no prestige data exist. For example, suppose an historian wished to determine whether the occupational status hierarchy of some past society was similar to that of the contemporary world, and suppose his information were limited to assessments of the wealth possessed by incumbents of various occupations, a not infrequent occurrence (see Treiman, 1976). In such a case it would be possible to correlate his wealth data for occupations with Standard Scale scores to determine whether the degree of correspondence is similar to that for contemporary societies reported in Chapter 5. An affirmative result would permit a positive inference regarding the similarity of the occupational hierarchies. Analysis of this sort obviously is not limited to past societies.

Along the same lines, students of occupational structure who have need for a *socioeconomic* rather than a *prestige* scale for occupations may wish to use the Standard Scale as a criterion for combining indicators of socioeconomic status, much as Duncan did for the United States. Suppose data on the income and education levels of incumbents of various occupations, but no data on prestige, were available for a number of countries. Socioeconomic status scales could be constructed for each of these countries by regressing Standard Scale scores on the average education and average income of incumbents of each occupation, separately for each country. The resulting scores would then be directly comparable across countries, even if the coefficients of the estimating equations proved to be rather different.

Comparative Analysis of Specific Occupations.   Often students of occupations and professions will want to compare the relative prestige of a particular occupation in different countries, in the spirit of the analysis reported in Chapter 7. For example, it is often asserted that physicians in the Soviet Union have relatively low prestige because so many of them are women. However, the data presented in Appendix D allow us to dispel this illusion (the prestige of "*vrach*" in the USSR is 76.3, which is only 1.6 points below the Standard Scale score for "00610 Physician," an insignificant difference) and would allow us to test the implicit underlying hypothesis (that the prestige of physicians is negatively correlated with the proportion of female incumbents) if we had data on the sex composition of medicine for a sufficient number of the countries for which we have prestige data. This use of the scale is obviously equally valid for other occupations and is easy enough to accomplish, requiring only that the analyst pick out the appropriate scores from the data contained in Appendix D. Where data for enough countries exist, each country may be treated as an observation and the prestige scores correlated with other variables affecting the social organization of work.[3]

Measuring the Occupational Prestige of Individuals. A major use of the scale presumably will be to code detailed occupational descriptions in censuses and sample surveys in order to study the relationship between the occupational status of individuals and their other characteristics. In the previous chapter I argued at length for using a standardized occupational status scale in comparative analysis and so there is no further need to discuss the issue here. Suffice it to point to Treiman and Terrell (1975a), Lin and Yauger (1975), and Covello (1976) as examples of this sort of application of the scale.

PRACTICAL PROCEDURES FOR USING THE SCALE

There are two basic ways in which a researcher may wish to use the Standard Scale to assign prestige scores to occupations: (*1*) he may wish to code occupations de novo from interview schedules; or (*2*) he may wish to assign prestige scores to occupations already coded into some other classification scheme. We will consider these one at a time, but in either case the basic principle is the same: Each occupation being coded should be matched to the most detailed available category in the Scale, that is, the most detailed category that corresponds to the occupational description or occupation line being coded. Obviously, the coding requirements are the same regardless of whether the ultimate object is to assign prestige scores to occupations or occupational prestige scores to individuals, since in either case the problem is one of getting the correct score assigned to each occupation line or occupational description.

De Novo Coding. First consider de novo coding operations. Here the problem is to translate an occupational description written by a respondent or an interviewer into one of the categories of the Standard Scale. Since the Standard Scale classification is based on the *International Standard Classification of Occupations*, Revised Edition (International Labor Office,

---

[3] One reason for providing the raw data in Appendix D is that it leaves the analyst free to make his own decisions about how to effect whatever comparisons are of interest to him. For example, the United States' score matched to the Standard Scale category "00610 Physician" is an average of the scores for two titles, "physician" with a score of 81.5 and "psychiatrist" with a score of 74.9. For some purposes it is useful to combine the two titles, but for other purposes it may be desirable to separate them. The form of the data permits either possibility.

1969a), that volume is a useful aid in the coding task. Indeed, coding of occupations with Standard Scale scores should not be undertaken without it. The volume includes a combination dictionary and classification scheme and an alphabetical index of occupational titles. Using these materials, the appropriate unit group into which a particular occupation description falls can be found. Then turning to the Standard Scale (Appendix A), the coder can choose that occupation within the unit group that most closely matches the occupation description being coded. In the event that no individual occupation in the Standard Scale matches well, the unit group score would be used. In addition, Appendix B contains an alphabetical index to the titles in Appendix A so that it is possible to locate specific titles directly.

For example, suppose that the occupational description in the interview schedule reads "donkey winch operator." Consulting the alphabetical index in Appendix B, no entry would be found. But consulting the alphabetical index in the ISCO manual, the coder would discover an entry for "Donkey Engine Operator." Checking this entry in the dictionary classification he would find that it is included under the ISCO occupation "Winch Operator," which is part of unit group "9-73 Crane and Hoist Operators." Turning then to Appendix A he would discover that the Standard Scale includes two specific occupations under this unit group (0973): "Power Crane Operator" and "Drawbridge Tender." Since neither of these obviously matches "donkey winch operator," he would assign the unit group prestige score, 34, to this occupation.[4]

In addition to the prestige score, the Standard Scale classification code (on the left side of the occupation description) should be coded into the data.[5] This will enable the researcher to reclassify occupations at will if at

---

[4] In some cases it will not be possible to locate occupational titles in the Standard Scale or in the ISCO manual corresponding to the occupational description given on the interview schedule. In such cases, the coder should consult manuals such as the *1970 Census of Population Alphabetical Index of Industries and Occupations*, (United States Bureau of the Census, 1971a), and the *Dictionary of Occupational Titles 1965, Vol. I: Definitions of Titles* (United States Department of Labor, 1965). These volumes classify large numbers of highly specific occupational titles into occupational categories roughly corresponding to those of the ISCO unit group level. In addition, many foreign census bureaus publish similar indexes of occupational titles (e.g., Canada, Dominion Bureau of Statistics, 1961; Great Britain, Office of Population Censuses and Surveys, 1970). The potential user of the Standard Scale would be well advised to secure the appropriate volumes for each of the countries for which he has data.

[5] Recall from Chapter 2 that to facilitate data processing by computer, the format of the ·code numbers utilized in the ISCO manual is modified slightly. In particular, the first digit is expanded to two to permit numerical coding of occupations not in the labor force; and of course the ISCO scheme is only followed down to the unit group level, so the last digit for individual occupations does not correspond to anything in the ISCO manual. In addition, the hyphen separating the major group designation from the minor group designation is dropped and where a group is referred to by more than one digit, as in major group 0/1, only the first

some later point he wishes to do so. It would be unwise simply to code the prestige score because this would preclude knowing which occupation a particular score refers to (13 separate occupations have prestige scores of 34, for example). The cardinal principle in occupational coding (or, for that matter, in any coding of data for computer analysis) is to preserve as much information as possible in machine-readable form. It is far easier to recode and reclassify data by computer than to go back to the original source material and create a new data set. Ordinarily, the code for the most closely matching line in the Scale would be recoded along with the prestige score for this line. But no title exists in the Scale that corresponds closely to "donkey winch operator." Here two alternatives are possible. The four-digit unit group code, 0973, may be assigned. Alternatively, the coder may wish to expand the code by adding an extra occupation category, "09732 Donkey Winch Operator." The choice between these alternatives will necessarily depend upon the level of detail the researcher feels is required for his purposes. But in either event, the unit group prestige score would be assigned.

Recoding Existing Data.   Different problems arise in recoding data from other occupational coding schemes into the ISCO scheme. Ordinarily there will be little difficulty in locating at least roughly corresponding lines in the Standard Scale since few obscure or unusual titles will be included. However, because other coding schemes often include fewer categories than the ISCO scheme, it may be necessary to combine several lines in the Standard Scale classification to match a single line in the other scheme. In this case, the appropriate procedure is to carry out the aggregation that results in the closest match between the two schemes, and then to assign the average prestige score for the included Standard Scale lines to the corresponding occupation line in the other classification. For example, consider the category "Editors and Reporters" in the 1970 United States Census detailed occupational classification. Inspection of the specific occupations included under this heading in the *Classified Index of Industries and Occupations* (U.S. Bureau of the Census, 1971b:0–20) makes it clear that this category is best matched by an average of the Standard Scale scores for "01590 Journalist," "01591 Newspaper Editor," and "01592 Advertising Writer." The remaining occupation in the unit group "0159 Authors, Journalists, and Related Writers (nec)" is "01593 Public Relations Man," but this title closely matches another line in the U.S. Census classification,

---

digit is used to designate the group. Comparison of the ISCO manual format with the format of Appendix A should make the basic correspondence clear. However the correspondence is not perfect; see Chapter 2 for a discussion of two minor substantive modifications of the ISCO coding scheme.

"Public Relations Men and Publicity Writers." In making matches of this sort, it is necessary to be cautious about the possibility that a merely *nominal* correspondence exists between a line in the Standard Scale and a line in the classification to which Standard Scale scores are being assigned; the coder must determine what specific occupations are encompassed by a given category in the classification being scaled and make the closest match possible in light of this information. For example, the 1970 U.S. Census includes the category "Painters and Sculptors." At first glance, this would appear to closely match the Standard Scale unit group "0161 Sculptors, Painters, and Related Artists." However, inspection of the U.S. Classified Index indicates that commercial artists are included in U.S. Census category. Hence, the appropriate solution would be to assign to the United States' category an average of the scores for the Standard Scale unit groups 0161 and "0162 Commercial Artists and Designers."

One problem that arises frequently when Standard Scale scores are being assigned to occupations already classified according to some other coding scheme is that the other coding scheme lacks the detail of the Standard Scale. Sometimes there is nothing to be done but to assign a relatively highly aggregated Standard Scale score to the category, recognizing that some of the heterogeneity of the category is masked by the use of a single score. (Obviously, the heterogeneity would likewise be masked by the use of any other coding scheme, particularly those that assign occupations to a small number of categories.) But sometimes it is possible to overcome the limitations of existing occupation codes by utilizing additional information available for the individuals being coded, such as the size of farm or firm; the number of individuals supervised by managers or foremen; whether the individual is an owner, manager, or ordinary employee; and so on. Thus, for example, the extremely heterogeneous 1970 U.S. Census category, "Farmers (owners and tenants)," which corresponds to seven separate Standard Scale categories varying widely in prestige, could be subdivided were information available on whether the farmer was an owner or a tenant and how much land he owned.[6] Similarly, the 1960 U.S. Census category "Managers, Officials, and Proprietors (nec)," which encompasses Standard Scale titles in the administrative, sales, and service major groups, could be subdivided on the basis of industry and class of worker, information usually collected along with detailed occupation (in fact, published statistics of the

---

[6] Obviously, the amount of land owned is only useful if some sort of estimate is available as to what constitutes a "large farm," what constitutes an ordinary sized farm, and what constitutes a "small farm," since these are the categories of the Standard Scale. Still, an arbitrary tripartite division would seem to be preferable to assignment of a single prestige score to all farmers without regard to the size of their holdings.

United States Census Bureau ordinarily include these distinctions for managers).

Master Craftsmen, Journeymen, Apprentices, and Helpers. Sometimes occupational classifications make systematic distinctions between master craftsmen and journeymen, or between highly skilled and ordinary workers. Similarly, sometimes distinctions are made between fully qualified workers and apprentices, or between workers and their helpers. Because of the somewhat arbitrary nature of the data available for the construction of the Standard Scale, distinctions of this sort appear in the Scale for some occupations but not for others. But to make the distinction only where it happens to appear in the Scale would unduly distort the Scale scores for any society where such a distinction is common. Thus, a general solution to the scaling problem is offered here. Where specific scores for master craftsmen, apprentices, or helpers exist, they should be assigned. But where such scores do not exist, the average difference from the journeyman score should be assigned. For the 17 production process or service occupations for which a master-journeyman distinction appears in the Standard Scale—that is, for which prestige scores exist for both master craftsmen and journeymen performing the same craft—the average difference between the corresponding scores is 9 points. Hence, scores can be assigned to master craftsmen by adding 9 points to the corresponding scores for ordinary (journeymen) craftsmen. Similarly, for the 4 cases for which a distinction between journeymen and their helpers appears in the Scale, the average difference between the corresponding scores is 13 points. Hence, scores can be assigned to helpers by subtracting 13 points from the scores for journeymen. Finally, since the difference between the score for "apprentice" and the score for "skilled worker" is 5 points, scores can be assigned to apprentices by subtracting 5 points from the scores for journeymen.

Coding Reliability. A question of obvious concern to the potential user is how reliably his or her data can be coded with Standard Scale scores. Despite attempts to increase the ease and convenience of use, the Scale remains a rather formidable one, due to its length if for no other reason. To be sure, it requires no greater effort than the use of comparable scales, such as the Duncan scale. Nonetheless, it would be useful to assess the extent to which Standard Scale scores can be reliably assigned to specific occupation lines (de novo coding of interview schedules is a standard problem and has been adequately treated elsewhere, for example, Featherman, Sobel, and Dickens, 1975).

To do this, I had four data sets independently scored by two different coders. In all cases these were two- or three-digit codes used to classify occupations in sample surveys of general populations. One of the coders was experienced in working with the Standard Scale at the time this exercise was undertaken, and one was not. As a first step, the two coders assigned Standard Scale scores to three-digit census occupational classifications for Northern Ireland and Australia. Correlations computed between the two sets of scores were, respectively, .93 and .95, which compare favorably with the reliability coefficients ordinarily associated with coding procedures of this kind. Still, they were disappointingly low from my point of view. So the next step was to review coding procedures with the two coders, after which two additional data sets were coded—the 296-category 1960 Census classification for the United States and a 98-category classification for Monterrey, Mexico. Comparison of these pairs of scores yielded correlations of .98 and .99, respectively, which were reassuringly high. The lesson of this exercise would appear to be a cautionary one: High intercoder agreement in the prestige scoring of occupations by means of the Standard Scale appears to be readily obtainable, but requires that coders be adequately trained. In particular, analysis of errors made by the more naïve coder suggests that every effort should be made to ensure that coders are familiar with the scale before beginning coding. Second, "when in doubt, check it out!" Too often the naïve coder settled for a guess as to the appropriate code when a more careful reading of the ISCO manual or a more careful search of the Scale would have yielded the exactly correct category.

The above exercise, of course, only addresses the reliability of the assignment of prestige scores to occupational categories. Often, however, the question is not one of whether *occupations* can be reliably scored with respect to prestige but whether individual members of the labor force can be reliably scored with respect to the prestige of their occupation. Since some occupations encompassing relatively large proportions of the labor force are difficult to classify within the categories of the Standard Scale (farming occupations are a prime example, as was noted in the previous chapter), it is useful to assess the reliability of the assignment of occupational prestige scores to individual members of a labor force.

To do this, we utilized the scores created in the above exercises involving Northern Ireland and Australia to assign prestige scores to individuals on the basis of their current occupation. For samples of males age 25–64, the intercoder correlations were .91 and .96, respectively. Considering that these two data sets were coded by one naïve coder and one experienced coder, the resulting correlations are satisfactorily high. Were we to have repeated the exercise for the other two data sets, it is certain that the correlations over individuals would have been considerably higher.

Finally, we must consider the question of whether coding agreement between independent users of the scale can be expected to be as high as was obtained between two coders trained in the same "shop." Or rather, since this is surely not possible, is the loss of reliability likely to be large enough to cause concern? Interestingly, this problem is not often considered. But since the process of training coders is mainly one of institutionalizing conventions for handling ambiguous cases, it is almost necessarily the case that the judgments of coders who have been trained in different organizations or research groups will differ more than the judgments of coders trained by a single person or in a given organization. The result is that almost all published reports on intercoder reliability probably overstate the amount of agreement that could be expected of truly independent coders. In any event, one bit of evidence regarding the magnitude of the difference that is likely to result from truly independent coding stems from the fact that Professor David Featherman, of the University of Wisconsin, independently coded the 1960 U.S. Census detailed occupational titles with Standard Scale scores (these are the same United States categories as were coded in the exercise reported above). The correlation between Featherman's scores and the scores created by my research group (an amalgam of the scores assigned by my two coders) was .96 over the 296 occupational categories[7] and .97 over the entire United States' labor force in 1960. The small difference between the correlation of .98 obtained between my two trained coders and the correlation of .96 obtained between their reconciled scores and Featherman's codes is reassuring evidence—insofar as one case can be considered sufficient—that differences in interpretation of the meaning of occupational titles is not likely to be a major source of unreliability in the assignment of Standard Scale scores to other occupational classifications (recall that these coefficients reflect not only differences in judgment but also simple errors in score assignment).

Thus, in sum, we can have considerable confidence that Standard Scale scores can be reliably assigned to occupations and can reliably estimate the prestige of members of a nation's labor force, especially if care is taken to train coders for the task—a highly desirable procedure when any coding task is undertaken. Further, I recommend that each data set be coded twice by different coders and any discrepancies of sufficient magnitude (as large as, say, three points, which corresponds to one standard error of the Scale scores) be resolved by discussion and further examination of the ISCO

[7] For a number of managerial, operative, and laboring occupations Featherman had disaggregated the categories by making industry and class-of-worker distinctions, following the convention of the published reports of the U.S. Bureau of Census. In these cases we simply reaggregated the categories by taking weighted averages of the disaggregated scores, with weights proportional to the size of the labor force.

manual and the Standard Scale. In this way, the user can have full confidence that his or her own coding of data will not differ in any appreciable way from that which might have been made by others. This procedure is, in fact, one I have adopted in current comparative research on social mobility and social stratification.[8] It has proved feasible to execute and well worth the added effort.

Using the Appendixes.   We conclude this section by explicitly calling the reader's attention to the Appendixes to this volume.

Appendix A, which contains the Standard Scale itself, has already been discussed in the previous chapter and also, with respect to modifications of the *International Standard Classification of Occupations,* at the end of Chapter 3.

Appendix B is an alphabetical listing of all titles appearing in the Standard Scale, together with the modified ISCO codes used to identify each line. It is provided as an aid to locating occupational titles in the Scale.

Appendix C contains Standard Scale scores for the detailed occupation lines of the first edition of the *International Standard Classification of Occupations* as well as for the detailed occupational classifications utilized by the U.S. Bureau of the Census for the population censuses of 1950, 1960, and 1970. These scores are provided in recognition of the fact that many existing data sets contain occupational data coded according to one or another of these schemes and in realization that comparability is improved if a standardized set of scores for these codes is made publicly available.

Appendix D contains the basic data upon which the bulk of the analysis reported in this monograph is based. Occupational titles are presented for each country just as they appeared in the original study, together with translation into English where necessary. Because the data sets for some places were created by combining data from several studies, foreign language titles will sometimes be interspersed with English language titles. The titles are designated by the modified ISCO code numbers used to identify occupations in the Standard Scale. Each line includes, in addition, the

---

[8] In conjunction with this project, we have devoted additional attention to occupational coding procedures since this chapter was initially prepared. This has resulted in a set of coding rules designed to improve consistency in the treatment of ambiguous cases typically encountered when coding existing occupational classifications with Standard Scale scores. These rules are included here as Appendix 9.1 to this chapter, "Coding Rules for Assigning Standard Scale Scores." *Users of the Scale are strongly urged to closely consult this Appendix.* Our experience has shown that clear understanding of the rules laid out in the Appendix not only substantially improves coding reliability but also drastically reduces both the time spent coding and the frustration experienced by coders. Further, users of the Scale who have special coding problems not treated here may wish to contact me directly for suggestions as to how to resolve them.

prestige rating in the country in question, expressed in the United States' metric, and the difference between this score and the corresponding Standard Scale score. Thus, by skimming the right-hand column it is easy to locate those occupations for which prestige evaluations in particular countries differ substantially from the worldwide average. Sometimes it was necessary to combine several occupations rated in a given country in order to match a specific line in the Standard Scale. In this case, all component lines are shown, together with their own prestige scores expressed in the United States' metric (these are the scores in parentheses at the end of the titles). This makes it possible for the reader to assess for himself the effect of combining several lines to form a single prestige score, and to disaggregate them if necessary.

A NOMINAL CLASSIFICATION OF OCCUPATIONS

Although the major emphasis of this and the previous chapter has been on the development and utilization of a quantitative scale for measuring the prestige of specific occupations, there clearly are occasions when it would be desirable to classify occupations into a small number of distinct categories. The older tradition of mobility research, which focused on the analysis of patterns of movement between occupational categories, has been revived with improved procedures (e.g., Goodman, 1969; Hope, 1972; Singer and Spilerman, 1974; Hauser et al., 1975). Moreover, there often is reason to suspect that relations between occupational status and other aspects of social behavior are not linear or that, once a linear prestige component is removed, occupational groups continue to differ substantially (see Treiman, 1974: Table 2, for an example of this sort of situation involving the effect of father's occupation on son's education).

As was noted in the previous chapter, one of the major limitations of previous cross-national comparisons has been that nominally similar classification systems have proven, on close inspection, to be far from completely comparable. True comparability requires that the same occupational classification be utilized in all countries being compared. Specifically, this means that *exactly the same individual occupational titles* be assigned to a given category in all countries. For example, if shop keepers are defined as sales workers in one country, they cannot be defined as managers in another country. To ensure such comparability, a standardized occupational classification scheme is needed. But to be useful, such a classification must meet two criteria: It must be easy to apply, and it must conform to a theoretically meaningful division of the occupational structure.

To meet these demands, I propose a simple expansion of the major group categories of the ISCO. The obvious advantage of the ISCO scheme is the same one that led to its choice for the purpose of classifying the occupational prestige data upon which this book is based—it is the most widely utilized occupational classification scheme in the world. Moreover, the ISCO has a more sensible allocation of specific occupations to the various nonmanual categories than does, say, the U.S. Census classification scheme, which has an extremely heterogeneous managerial category encompassing everything from major corporation presidents to owners of newsstands. However, everything has its cost, and the allocation in the ISCO scheme of working proprietors to the sales and service categories and clerical supervisors to the clerical category introduces considerable heterogeneity into these groups. In addition, the ISCO scheme fails to distinguish manual workers by skill level, relying upon a single, very large, very heterogeneous category; it also fails to distinguish farm owners from farm laborers. Finally, the inclusion of professional and technical workers in a single category introduces excessive heterogeneity. The result is that, as we have seen (Figure 8.1a), the seven major groups of the ISCO classification do not do a very good job of differentiating occupations with respect to prestige: For the 497 civilian labor force occupations in the Standard Scale, the squared correlation ratio, η^2, of prestige on the major group categories is .52, indicating that only about half of the variance in the prestige of individual occupations is accounted for by the major groups.

To create a category scheme that would capture both differences in the type of work done, as represented by the ISCO major groups, and differences in prestige, the ISCO major group categories were divided into 14 subgroups on the basis of prestige. Each of the major groups except "Administrative and Managerial Workers" and "Production and Related Workers" was dichotomized at its mean on the Standard Scale. The administrative category was left whole because of the small number of occupations included in this category in most occupational classification schemes and the production process category was trichotomized because of its very large size.[9]

[9] If there is reason to include military personnel, two additional categories can be created by dichotomizing the armed forces category, putting commissioned officers in the high group and noncommissioned officers and soldiers in the low group. Also, in societies where the bulk of the labor force is in agriculture it may be useful to make still finer distinctions in the agricultural sector, by subdividing each of the two agricultural categories. A five category classification that captures the important variability in the social organization of agriculture can be created as follows (the prestige cutting points are given in parentheses): Large Farmers (≥ 60); Farmers and Farm Managers (47–59); Small Farmers and Farm Foremen (34–46); Tenant Farmers, Share Croppers, and Skilled Farm Workers (30–33); Farm Laborers (≤ 29). This classification also properly allocates forestry workers and fishermen.

The resulting classification scheme is shown in Table 9.1, which gives the mean and standard deviation of the Standard Scale scores for the occupations falling into each category, out of the 497 occupations remaining when the 12 non–labor force titles are omitted. It is evident that this procedure creates categories that are on the whole highly internally homogeneous with respect to prestige. As would be expected from the way the categories were constructed, most of the variance between individual occupations in prestige is accounted for by the 14 categories (η^2 = .82).

Before accepting this classification, however, we must assess its ability to differentiate individual members of a labor force rather than occupational categories. Here, we use the United States' 1970 labor force as an illustrative case. Table 9.2 gives the same information as Table 9.1 for the 426 categories in the 1970 U.S. Census occupational classification weighted by the number of incumbents of each occupation. Several points emerge from a comparison of the two tables. First, the classification scheme does an even better job of differentiating the United States' labor force with respect to prestige than of differentiating the occupations in the Standard Scale (the squared correlation ratio associated with Table 9.2 is .88). This is also manifest in the uniformly small within-category standard deviations; all the standard deviations in Table 9.2 are smaller than the corresponding standard deviations in Table 9.1 except that for low-prestige professionals. Second, the rank order of the means in the two tables is essentially the same. There are only two minor differences: In the United States' labor force low-prestige professionals outrank high-prestige clerical and sales workers and low-prestige clerical workers outrank medium-prestige production workers. Because of the essential similarity of the two tables and because we know from our comparison of data for the United States and India in the previous chapter that within major groups the prestige distribution of occupations is relatively invariant across societies, we can have full confidence in proposing this scheme as a standardized method of categorizing occupations for comparative purposes.[10]

One cautionary word is required, however. *This classification should not be utilized unless the data being aggregated are sufficiently detailed that Standard Scale scores can be assigned to them at the occupation level.* Paradoxically, valid utilization of a classificatory scheme of this sort places even greater demands upon the original data than the use of an interval scale. One difficulty with many census occupational classifications is their

[10] While it is possible to treat the categories in Table 9.1 as an ordinal scale, there is no necessary reason to do so. A useful alternative would be to derive a scale via canonical correlation procedures in the manner of Klatsky and Hodge (1971). And, of course, the main point of developing the Standard Classification is to permit purely nominal approaches, such as that exemplified by Hauser's application of Goodman's hierarchical models (Hauser *et al.*, 1975).

206

TABLE 9.1

A Standard International Classification of Occupations

Occupation Category and Prestige Cutting Point	Prestige		Occupation Titles	
	Mean	S.D.	Number	Percentage
(1) High-prestige professional and technical occupations ($\geq$58)	68.4	6.8	59	11.9
(2) Administrative and managerial occupations	67.1	11.8	34	6.8
(3) High-prestige clerical and related occupations ($\geq$41)	50.3	7.4	25	5.0
(4) High-prestige sales occupations ($\geq$40)	49.1	5.0	20	4.0
(5) Low-prestige professional and technical occupations (<58)	48.9	8.6	72	14.5
(6) High-prestige agricultural occupations ($\geq$34)	44.3	8.6	13	2.6
(7) High-prestige production and related occupations ($\geq$38)	43.6	4.8	62	12.5
(8) High-prestige service occupations ($\geq$27)	40.8	10.4	30	6.0
(9) Medium-prestige production and related occupations (26-37)	32.1	2.9	73	14.7
(10) Low-prestige clerical and related occupations (<41)	31.6	5.6	19	3.8
(11) Low-prestige sales occupations (<40)	28.1	11.0	18	3.6
(12) Low-prestige agricultural occupations (<34)	22.3	9.1	17	3.4
(13) Low-prestige service occupations (<27)	19.7	5.1	21	4.2
(14) Low-prestige production and related occupations (<26)	19.6	4.9	34	6.8
Total	43.2	16.8	497	99.8

TABLE 9.2

The 1970 U.S. Labor Force Classified According to the
International Standard Classification of Occupations $(N = 75,100,000)$ [a]

Occupation Category and Prestige Cutting Point	Prestige		Percentage of Labor Force
	Mean	S.D.	
(1) High-prestige professional and technical workers (>58)	65.4	6.7	6.0
(2) Administrative and managerial workers	57.2	5.2	5.8
(3) High-prestige clerical and related workers (≥41)	49.8	4.7	9.6
(4) High-prestige sales workers (≥40)	49.5	3.8	2.5
(5) Low-prestige professional and technical workers. (<58)	52.1	9.3	9.6
(6) High-prestige agricultural workers (≥34)	47.6	2.5	1.9
(7) High-prestige production and related workers (≥38)	41.4	2.8	9.8
(8) High-prestige service workers (≥27)	36.6	4.9	5.2
(9) Medium-prestige production and related workers (26–37)	32.7	2.8	19.9
(10) Low-prestige clerical and related workers (<44)	35.3	3.1	8.6
(11) Low-prestige sales workers (<40)	27.7	2.5	6.8
(12) Low-prestige agricultural workers (<34)	23.3	3.5	1.9
(13) Low-prestige service workers (<27)	23.4	3.0	7.6
(14) Low-prestige production and related workers (<26)	20.2	1.7	4.8
Total	39.8	13.1	100.0

Source: U.S. Bureau of the Census, 1973: Table 1. "Allocated" workers and former members of the armed forces are excluded.

207

tendency to include large and heterogeneous residual categories within major groups. These categories will often include occupations that would fall within both the high and low subgroups were more highly detailed data available. Because of this, placing the detailed title in either subgroup will have the effect of erroneously classifying a large number of workers. Thus, considerable noncomparability in the allocation of specific occupations to the 14 categories may be introduced in practice simply as a consequence of differences in the degree of detail retained in otherwise comparable occupational classifications. To avoid this sort of insidious noncomparability, it is best not to utilize the standardized classification at all unless one begins with occupational categories that are internally homogeneous with respect to prestige.

COMPARING THE STANDARD SCALE WITH DUNCAN'S SOCIOECONOMIC INDEX

Because Duncan's Socioeconomic Index of Occupations (Duncan, 1961) has become the most widely used occupational status scale in research carried out on American data, it is useful to compare it and the Standard Scale. Understanding how the two scales relate to each other and how each relates to other variables is necessary both to provide an intelligent basis for choice between them and to facilitate the integration of research results obtained with each scale.

Conceptually, the two scales are distinct, although not totally so. While the Standard Scale measures the relative *prestige* of occupations as popularly evaluated, the Duncan scale measures their *socioeconomic* status, that is, a combination of the education and income levels of incumbents. Although I have argued in previous chapters that the socioeconomic characteristics of occupations are the main determinants of their prestige, there are important and systematic discrepancies between the two which reflect the fact that prestige is determined by other factors as well. Duncan's scale recognizes the connection between socioeconomic status and prestige in the way it was created; the weights used in combining income and education were those that maximized the correlation of the scale scores with prestige. Because of this, Duncan's scores have often been treated as estimates of the relative prestige of occupations. But, in fact, the correlations between the Duncan scores and actual prestige scores are far from perfect when measured over occupations and even less perfect when occupations are weighted by the number of incumbents. Duncan, regressing prestige on the age-adjusted percentage of the male labor force in each occupation earning more than $3500 in 1949 and the percentage who were high school graduates in 1950 (for 45 occupations for which data were available), found a multiple correlation of .91, indicating that about 83% of the variance in the prestige of individual occupations can be attributed to a combination of the education and income of incumbents. A slightly lower correlation is obtained when Duncan scores are updated to correspond to the categories of the 1960 U.S. Census classification of occupations and are compared with prestige scores developed for each census line by Hodge, Siegel, and Rossi (reported in Siegel, 1971: Table 5); in this case the correlation is .87. Interestingly, this is almost identical to the correlation of .86 between Standard Scale scores and Duncan scores, likewise computed over the 296 categories of the 1960 U.S. Census detailed occupational classification. Moreover, when correlations are computed not over occupational titles but over all individuals in the labor force, the correlation with the Duncan scores drops somewhat, to .83 for the United States' prestige scores and .80 for the Standard Scale scores (the correlation between the United States' and Standard Scale scores, .95, is the same whether computed over individuals or over occupations). Thus, the Duncan scale cannot be considered an adequate substitute for prestige scores. If one wishes prestige scores developed specifically for the United States, Hodge–Siegel–Rossi scores are the obvious instrument of choice; and if one wishes to maximize cross-national comparability, the Standard Scale scores should be used.

It has been argued (Featherman, Jones, and Hauser, 1975) that prestige scores should be considered simply as fallible indicators of socioeconomic status. The basis of this claim is that when both prestige and Duncan scores are included in a causal analysis of status attainment and an underlying occupational status dimension is posited via confirmatory factor analysis procedures, the Duncan scores emerge as perfectly representing the underlying dimension while the prestige scores emerge as only imperfectly representing this dimension. I would argue that this result somewhat misrepresents the issue, since it arises as an artifact of the way the scales are constructed. Since the Duncan scale is based on summary measures of the education and income of the incumbents of each occupation, it is bound to be more highly correlated with these attributes of individuals than will a scale that is not devised in this way. And, indeed, it is true that Duncan scores tend to be more highly correlated with individual income and education than Standard Scale scores, as can be seen from inspection of the appropriate coefficients in Table 9.3. Thus, it *must* be the case that the Duncan scale will load more strongly on an underlying dimension representing occupational status when a criterion is the strength of correlation with educational attainment (income is not included in the model). There is a second difference between the two scales which exacerbates this difference. The Duncan scale typically produces higher correlations between fathers'

TABLE 9.3

Zero-order Correlations of Selected Variables with Standard, Duncan, and HSR Scale Scores, for Selected U.S. Samples

Sample and variables	Males			Females	
	Standard	Duncan	HSR	Standard	Duncan
White married women age 30-44 and their husbands (N = 689)[a]					
Years of school completed	.463	.520	--	.537	.582
Hours worked per year	.178	.120	--	.073	.006
Number of children under age 6	.041	.079	--	.039	.030
Number of children 6-18	-.039	-.035	--	-.045	-.016
Income last year	.324	.411	--	.234	.278
Percentage of years worked since school	--	--	--	.174	.160
Married adults, both spouses working (Male N = 164, female N = 202)[b]					
Subjective class identification[c]	.203	.234	--	.275	.309
Political party preference[d]	.107	.128	--	.148	.242
Liberalism[e]	.013	-.059	--	.054	-.002
Read a book in past six months?	.273	.227	--	.307	.313
Males age 25-64 (N = 636)[b]					
Father's years of school completed	.29	.35	.27	--	--
Father's occupation--same scale as son	.27	.38	.24	--	--
Father's occupation--standard scale	.27	.27	.26	--	--
Father's occupation--HSR scale	.25	.23	.24	--	--
Father's occupation--Duncan scale	.34	.38	.28	--	--
Years of school completed	.56	.58	.52	--	--
Family income last year	.36	.41	.33	--	--

[a] From "The Longitudinal Study of Labor Market Experience of Women." See Treiman and Terrell (1975b) for a more detailed description.

[b] From a survey conducted by the National Opinion Research Center in June 1965 (SRS 857), in conjunction with the project "Occupations and Social Stratification."

[c] A 5-point scale, ranging from "upper", scored 5, to "lower", scored 1.

[d] A 3-point scale: 1 = Republican, 2 = Independent, 3 = Democrat.

[e] A 3-point scale: 1 = Conservative, 2 = Neither, 3 = Liberal.

and sons' occupational status than the Standard Scale, mainly because of the difference in the prestige and socioeconomic status of farmers: "farmers (owners and tenants)" have average prestige but very low socioeconomic status. Typically, the sons of farmers who leave agriculture move into unskilled and semiskilled manual jobs, which have relatively low prestige. Thus, from a *prestige* standpoint, farmers' sons tend to experience downward mobility; however, in terms of socioeconomic status, they experience upward mobility. While this can hardly be considered an artifact—indeed, it could be argued that the move off the farm often is perceived as involving a tradeoff of prestige for economic opportunity—it does result in rather different father–son occupational status correlations depending upon which of the two scales is utilized, simply because about one-quarter of all men currently in the American labor force are the sons of farmers (Blau and Duncan, 1967:496); see Treiman (1975:198–199) for further discussion of this point.

In short, differences in the size of the correlations yielded by the two scales reflect both differences in the way the scales were constructed and true differences in the relationship of prestige and socioeconomic status to other attributes of individuals. Thus, the fact that the Duncan scale yields higher correlations does not of itself constitute a sufficient reason for utilizing it to score occupations. Furthermore, with the exception of intercorrelations among status variables, the Duncan scale does not yield higher correlations than the prestige scales. Table 9.3 gives correlations between each of three scales—the Duncan, Standard, and Hodge–Siegel–Rossi (HSR) scales (and sometimes just the Standard and Duncan scales)—and various other variables. Inspecting the coefficients in the table, it is evident that they are always of roughly comparable size and are sometimes larger when one scale is used and sometimes larger when another scale is used. Hence, from the standpoint of studying the relationship between occupational status and other areas of social life there is no obvious choice between the scales in terms of their predictive power. Once again it is evident that the choice among instruments must be made on conceptual grounds.

What, then, are appropriate criteria for choice between a prestige and socioeconomic scale of occupational status, or for that matter between a status scale and a nominal classification? I would suggest that in our present state of knowledge the answer is not at all obvious. We simply do not know enough about how people acquire jobs or how the sort of work they do affects their lives to be able definitively to decide among alternative occupational scaling schemes. In this circumstance, the best strategy is to code occupations in alternative ways and to investigate the differences in the results obtained. For example, on conceptual grounds it is reasonable to suppose that a socioeconomic index is a better indicator than a prestige index of the way occupations serve as *resources* that facilitate the transmission of advantage from one generation to the next or the conversion of one form of advantage into another. On the other hand, prestige, as a major occupational *reward*, may be a better indicator of "occupational attainment." Since the two sorts of indices are highly correlated, most occupations will have approximately equivalent prestige and socioeconomic status; but a substantial number will not. We need to investigate much more thoroughly what are the special properties of occupations with unusually high or unusually low prestige relative to socioeconomic status. We also need to understand better how both the prestige and socioeconomic status of occupations relate to their other attributes. There are, for instance, occupational differences in the physical and social organization of work; in knowledge, contacts, and exposure to opportunities of various kinds; and in values, attitudes, and norms. These differences cannot be accounted for simply by the prestige or socioeconomic status of occupations; but how these various attributes are related is yet far from clear.

Granted the desirability of studying the interrelations among occupational characteristics, it will nonetheless often be the case that a researcher whose primary interests lie elsewhere will wish to settle upon a single occupational status index without extensive deliberation in order to get on with his work. What help in making that decision can be offered here? For the researcher working on American data, there are two advantages to the Duncan index. First, since it is the most widely used occupational status scale at the present time, comparability to other United States' research is enhanced. Second, where no information but occupation is available regarding the socioeconomic status of individuals, the Duncan index is probably to be preferred precisely because—by virtue of the way it is constructed—it will capture more joint variance with education and income than would a prestige scale. However, this same attribute may be reason enough to eschew the Duncan scale when other information on the socioeconomic status of individuals is available, simply to avoid artificially inflated correlations.

The main reason for utilizing the Standard Scale even with A nerican data is that, as I have documented exhaustively in this book, the prestige hierarchy of occupations is essentially invariant in all populations, including subgroups within each society. Thus, for example, Standard Scale scores are valid representations of the prestige of occupations held by women and blacks in American society. Not only do women (Bose, 1973:49) and blacks (Siegel, 1970:160) evaluate occupations in the same way white males do, but identifying the sex of the incumbent makes no difference in the prestige accorded occupations by either males or females (Bose, 1973:49); there are no corresponding data for blacks (but see Rossi *et al.*, 1974:181–185, for indirect evidence supporting the claim of no racial difference). The socioeconomic structure of occupations, by contrast, differs substantially by sex and race. This is mainly because both women (Treiman and Terrell, 1975c:177) and blacks (Siegel, 1970:160) are paid substantially less than white males doing the same work. The result is that income is not nearly as important an aspect of occupational status for women and blacks as for white males. Because of this, use of the Duncan scale will misrepresent the average socioeconomic position of women and blacks in particular occupations (although not by a large degree given the generally high correlations among all these attributes). To base occupational status upon the socioeconomic characteristics of the dominant sector of the labor force (which is what use of the Duncan scale to assign scores to women or blacks amounts to) is implicitly to adopt an evaluative definition of status, in which case it is better to do so explicitly by utilizing a prestige scale to measure occupational status.

While both the HSR and Standard Scale are valid across subgroups within American society, the advantage of the Standard Scale is the one I have emphasized repeatedly in this and the previous chapter: It uniquely permits valid comparisons with data for other societies. Also, given the very high correlation between these two scales, the loss in precision in the representation of the unique aspects of American society is small enough to be more than offset by the gain in cross-cultural comparability created by use of the Standard Scale.

Even where a comprehensive and reliable occupational status scale is available for a given country, use of the Standard Scale is strongly to be encouraged simply to facilitate cross-national comparisons. Because of the very large expense involved in conducting sample surveys, it is unlikely that individual researchers will ordinarily be able to collect precisely comparable data for a large number of places. Rather, the ability to generalize about cross-national similarities and differences will no doubt continue to depend upon comparisons of data initially collected by a number of different researchers for diverse purposes. This circumstance makes it particularly important that each researcher code his data in a way that permits explicit cross-national comparisons. Routine coding of occupational data with Standard Scale scores, either as the primary coding scheme or as a supplement to a locally developed coding scheme such as Duncan's, would be a useful step in this direction.

SUMMARY

The main concern of this chapter has been to describe potential uses of the Standard Scale and practical procedures for exploiting it. Recognizing that occupation is a multidimensional concept, we have considered what can be learned from the analysis of a single dimension, prestige. The unique aspect of the Scale is that it is a cross-culturally valid index that represents a generic hierarchy of occupations common to virtually all societies. As such it can be used both as a standard against which to compare the idiosyncratic features of the prestige hierarchies of particular societies and as a standardized instrúment for the comparative study of the relationship between occupational status and other aspects of social life. Suggestions have been offered regarding the utility of the scale for the comparative study of occupational structures, the comparative study of the prestige of particular occupations, and the comparative study of the determinants, correlates, and consequences of occupational status as an attribute of individuals. Procedures for coding data with Standard Scale scores have been outlined and evidence offered that coding can be carried out with relative ease and high reliability. To accommodate the need for a standardized occupational *classification* scheme for use in cross-national comparisons, a 14-category classification was devised by subdividing ISCO major groups on the basis of prestige. Finally, an extended comparison was made between Duncan's Socioeconomic Index of Occupations and the Standard Scale.

Appendix 9.1

CODING RULES FOR ASSIGNING STANDARD SCALE SCORES[11]

These rules are intended to supplement the general coding instructions offered in Chapter 9. They derive from extensive experience in assigning Standard Scale scores to detailed (3-digit) occupational classifications used to code census and sample survey data in various countries. They have been developed inductively to cope with various difficulties which arose when carrying out coding tasks. Because these rules have now been through several revisions as we have gained additional experience, we are confident that they cover most of the situations researchers are likely to encounter when assigning Standard Scale scores to existing occupational classifications. We would not claim that they are in any sense easy to follow. However, there is a definite rationale underlying each rule, and they do, once mastered, substantially increase coding speed and reduce coder frustration, mainly by reducing the number of ambiguous cases requiring arbitrary decisions.

Since understanding the rules involves grasping the nature of the difficulties each is designed to deal with, we have tried to explain these and to give examples wherever possible. Rules are set out by separate problem areas (e.g., foremen, government employees, "not elsewhere classified" (nec) groups), so that users can consult them individually as coding problems arise.

[11] The rules described in this Appendix were devised by Jo Lea Gaddis, Patricia Roos, and J. L. P. Thompson. The text was drafted by Thompson.

1. FOLLOW THE ISCO CLASSIFICATION

The Standard Scale provides prestige scores for the categories of the *International Standard Classification of Occupations* (ISCO). To ensure coding reliability, follow the ISCO scheme *even when it leads you to assign apparently unsatisfactory prestige scores* to particular occupations in the classification being coded.

Example: Consider the category "347 Pearlers" in the 1961 Australian census occupational classification system (reported in Inter-University Consortium for Political Research, 1975:228). Reference work in the ISCO manual (International Labour Office, 1969a:147) places this title within unit group "0649 Fishermen, Hunters and Related Workers nec.," with a prestige score of 23. A plausible argument can be made that this is unsatisfactory, on the ground that the score of 23 is derived by averaging "06490 Whaler," with a score of 40, and "06491 Hunter," with a score of 6. The score for unit group "0641 Fishermen" might seem preferable to a score derived, in part, from the extremely deviant score for "hunter." Nonetheless, the score of 23 must stand. If we do not invariably accept the ISCO scheme, different coders will be free to make idiosyncratic assessments of which ISCO titles are inadequate, and to convince each other of what constitutes a "better" score; in short, individual coders would, in effect, be making up scores themselves, which would have the likely consequence of the same occupation being scored differently in different societies. Such an outcome would, of course, completely undercut the purpose of a standardized coding procedure.

2. MATCHING

a. Use the most specific Standard Scale category or categories that appear to make a match with the title being coded. If more than one Standard Scale category matches, compute the simple average of their scores. *Do not use weighted averages.*

Example: The United States title "671 Graders and Sorters, manufacturing" is scored as the average of "07321 Lumber Grader" and "07541 Cloth Grader." (N.B.: Averaging is treated in detail in Rule 4.)

b. In choosing matching categories, leave out Standard Scale titles that are obviously atypical.

Example: In the 1960 United States classification (U.S. Bureau of the Census, 1960a), the category "010 Actor" receives the score for the Standard Scale title "01730 Actor." It does *not* receive the average of the Standard Scale titles "01730 Actor" and "01731 Star Actor," even though inspection of the *Dictionary of Occupational Titles* (U.S. Department of Labor, 1965:4) makes it clear that U.S. category 010 does, in fact, include "leading man" and "leading lady," that is, "star actors." This is because on a common sense level we know that there are so few star actors that to simply average the scores for regular and star actors would produce an artificially inflated mean prestige score for actors as a whole. Since there is no reasonable basis for weighting the titles which fall within a category, extremely atypical titles are simply excluded.

c.   In choosing matching categories, choose on the basis of *substantive* rather than merely *nominal* correspondence between them.

> *Example:* Assume we are coding U.S. category "415 Cranemen, Derrickmen and Hoistmen." It might seem reasonable to give it the score for unit group "0973 Crane and Hoist operators" because of the close nominal correspondence of the two categories. However, it is essential to look at the specific titles in the Standard Scale which provide the score for 0973. Only if all of these titles are included within U.S. 415 can this unit group score be assigned to it. In fact the score for 0973 is based on the specific titles "09730 Power Crane Operator" and "09731 Drawbridge Tender" (see Appendix A), and drawbridge tenders fall within U.S. "860 Watchmen (Crossing) and Bridge Tenders," rather than U.S. 415 (we discover this by looking up "drawbridge tender" in the appropriate alphabetical index, U.S. Bureau of the Census, 1960a). We therefore cannot allow the score for "drawbridge tenders" to affect the score we give to U.S. 415. The correct procedure is to assign the score for "09730 Power Crane Operator," since this is the only occupation falling into U.S. 415 for which we have a prestige score.

d.   If there is no substantive match between the category to be coded and a specific Standard Scale title, use the next highest level of aggregation.

> *Example:* Assume that we are coding Philippines "431 Fishermen, Deep Sea" (University of the Philippines Population Institute, 1974: Annex 3). There is an ISCO occupational title of this name (see International Labour Office 1969a:145, 324), which falls into the unit group "0641 Fishermen." However, on consulting the Standard Scale we find that the only occupational titles for which it provides scores are "06410 Fisherman" and "06411 Fisherman With Own Boat," that is, no score is available for the specific title that we wish to code. Since there is no match, we proceed to the next highest level of aggregation and assign the unit group score.

e.   Note that the Standard Scale provides a score for every ISCO unit group. Recall also that under Rule 1 (on following the ISCO classification), we must assign these unit group scores to the titles which the ISCO locates within them, whether we like the match or not. Since ISCO unit groups are mutually exclusive and collectively exhaustive, this means that in general we will never have to rise to a higher level of aggregation than the unit group. The exceptions to this are:

i.   When the occupational classification being coded contains highly aggregated categories which correspond to standard scale minor groups.
Example: The 1961 Canadian census classification (Canada Dominion Bureau of Statistics, 1961) contains the title "17 Authors, Editors and Journalists," which corresponds to the Standard Scale minor group "015 AUTHORS, JOURNALISTS AND RELATED WORKERS."

ii.   When major or minor group codes of a classification used in coding a dataset have been assigned to individuals. See Rule 10 for how to proceed in this situation.

iii.   When categories exist for manual workers distinguished only by industry. See Rule 5.b.i. for how to proceed in this situation.

3. WORDING

Avoid getting hung up on the specific wording of the Standard Scale categories—they have to represent occupations in a diversity of countries.

Example: The rationale in developing the titles 05820 to 05823 is that "05820 Policeman" includes the "regular cop" (patrolmen, etc.). The title "05821 Police Officer" includes the upper stratum of policemen in two-tier law-enforcement systems such as are found in many countries but not in the United States. Therefore regular policemen in the United States, although often called "police officers," should be coded 05820, not 05821. (The title "05822 High Police Official" includes such occupations as "police chief" and "police commissioner"; "05823 Specialized Law Officer" includes "marshal," "sheriff," "detective," "secret service agent," etc.)

4. AVERAGING

a. In calculating averages, scores of .500 . . . are rounded to the nearest *even* number.

b. In averaging prestige scores, it is best to remain within one major group.

c. When it does become necessary to average prestige scores across major groups, assign the category being coded to the major group into which you would expect the majority of its members to fall.

Example: Assume that we are coding U.S. "642 Chainmen, Rodmen and Axmen: Surveying." This category includes not only "chainmen," "rodmen," and "axmen," who are laborers and therefore fall into ISCO major group 7, but also "surveyor's assistants," who are technical workers and therefore fall into ISCO major group 1 (see U.S. Bureau of the Census, 1960b:103; and International Labour Office, 1969a:315, 348). To obtain the prestige score the procedure is to average the appropriate occupational categories, which are "09990 Laborer" and "00330 Surveyor's Assistant." This is consistent with Rule 2.a., on matching. When we need to assign an ISCO major group code, as when utilizing the 14 category Standard Classification of Occupations, we assign the major group which we estimate to include the largest portion of the labor force in the category being coded. In the present case, we would assign the code for ISCO major group 7 rather than for ISCO major group 1 since we would expect U.S. category 642 to include more workers classified as "laborers" in the ISCO scheme than classified as "technical workers" in the ISCO scheme.

d. Do not use weighted averages in computing prestige scores. Either include a title and give it full weight, or exclude it under the typicality rule (Rule 2.b.).

5. LABORERS, FACTORY WORKERS, AND OTHER MANUAL WORKERS

Conventionally (although perhaps not invariably), the term "laborer" refers to an *unskilled* worker, the term "factory worker" refers to a *semiskilled* worker, and the term "worker in *X* industry" (e.g. "textile worker," "steel mill worker," or "chemical plant worker") refers to a *semiskilled* or *skilled* worker. We should, however, note that, although the prejudice is deeply entrenched among intellectuals and others, it is not true that laboring requires no skills. What laborers generally do not possess, and skilled and semiskilled workers in general do command, are *industry-specific* skills. In short, a laborer's job tends to be the same in terms of the demands, disadvantages, and symbolic and material rewards associated with it across different industries, whereas skilled and semiskilled workers experience much greater variation in all these respects. Our general coding strategy is, therefore, to take account of industry for skilled and semiskilled workers, but not in general for laborers. The ISCO is, fortunately, constructed in such a way as to permit this, since the minor groups 071 to 098 represent "industrial" sectors, and very few laborer titles are included within these sections. Almost all laborers fall into the unit group "0999 Laborers nec."

a. *Laborers.* All laborers receive the score for "09990 Laborer," except those matching one of the small number of specific laborer titles, viz. "08494 Unskilled Garage Worker," "09594 Construction Laborer nec," "09595 Unskilled Construction Laborer," or 09991 through 09997, the specific laborer titles within unit group 0999.

> *Example:* The Australian census classification includes such categories as "776 Labourers, Woodworking," "779 Labourers, Chemicals," and "784 Labourers, Commerce." These are all coded with the score for "09990 Laborer."

b. *Manual Workers Distinguished Only by Industry*

i. Where a category to be coded encompasses all workers in a particular industrial group, assign to it the minor group score for that industrial group, rather than trying to establish which particular occupational title(s) within the minor group make(s) the best match.

> *Example:* A title such as "workers in textiles" receives the score for the minor group "075 SPINNERS, WEAVERS, KNITTERS, DYERS and RELATED WORKERS," rather than the score for the specific occupation "07590 Textile Mill Worker." The reason for this is that since such a group of workers will generally cover a range of occupations, it is better to use the average of all the titles falling within that industrial group than to rely on the score for one single, and necessarily rather vague, title.

Rule ii indicates an important exception to Rule i:

ii. When a category to be coded refers to workers within a particular industrial group, but we have sufficient information to establish that it does not include all the titles within that industrial group, we should not assign to it the minor group score for that industry. Instead give it a score based on the pertinent subset of titles within the minor group.

> *Example:* If we were, as before, trying to code a category "workers in textiles," but happened to know that in the society in question the division of labor within this industry was largely limited to a distinction between weavers and dyers, we would assign the average of the scores of the specific titles "07540 Weaver" and "07650 Cloth Dyer" (as opposed to the score for the minor group "075 SPINNERS, WEAVERS, KNITTERS, DYERS and RELATED WORKERS").

> The "sufficient information," mentioned above might come from perusal of census volumes or monographic studies of the society.

iii. There exists in the Standard Scale a title "09970 Factory Worker." Use it only to code a title such as "factory worker(s)" or "factory workers in (an industry not explicitly covered by the standard scale)." The appropriate score to assign to factory workers who are explicitly identified as unskilled is that for "09991 Unskilled Factory Laborer."

A note on the problems in coding factory workers and laborers. In the above discussion, we have assumed that no problems arose in deciding whether or not the groups to be coded actually possessed industry-specific skills, that is, were either skilled or semiskilled workers as conventionally understood. Often there are such problems. Surveys may use different terminologies in distinguishing between these groups, or may not make the distinction at all; and some divide up workers in a typology whose logic is to an outsider completely incomprehensible on first inspection. The 1961 Australian census occupational classification is a case of the last type. It contains, for example, the titles "665 Electrical Workers nec," "668 Process Workers, Metal, Electric," and "669 Factory Workers, Metal, Electric." Here we must recognize that progress is impossible without an alphabetical or classified index from which we can infer the criteria used to distinguish electrical "process" from electrical "factory" workers, and "electrical workers nec." from both of these groups.

6. MASTER CRAFTSMEN, JOURNEYMEN, APPRENTICES, AND HELPERS

a. *Craftsmen.* In assigning scores to production process workers, an occupational title which includes both journeymen and master craftsmen should be given the score for journeymen only. It does *not* receive an average of journeyman and master craftsman scores, nor does it get a unit group score.

The reason for this is to ensure comparability. In many occupational classifications the *titles* refer only to journeymen, but master craftsmen are in fact routinely coded under these headings (this is the case in the U.S. Census). In other classifications journeymen and master craftsmen are also coded into the same categories but the "master craftsmen" designation *is* included in the occupational title. In the first sort of classification, Rule 2.b. (Typicality) requires that the journeyman score be assigned. Since the second system differs from the first solely in its convention for the naming of titles, and not in actual coding practices, the journeyman score should be assigned to it as well.

Example: An occupational title "plumbers and master plumbers" should be given the score of "08710 Plumber" rather than the unit group score "0871 Plumbers and Pipe Fitters." By this convention such a title will be assigned the same prestige score as U.S. "510 Plumbers and Pipe Fitters," which also includes master plumbers.

Note that this rule does not mean that we will never take account of the greater prestige of master craftsmen compared to journeymen. Where master craftsmen are coded under separate titles, they will routinely be assigned higher scores. These will be either the actual prestige scores for master craftsmen in a particular occupation, where these are available in the Standard Scale, or estimates produced by adding 9 to journeymen scores.

b. *Apprentices and Helpers.* For clarity, the above has referred only to the relationship between master craftsmen and journeymen scores. Exactly the same principles apply when prestige scores are assigned to the other modifiers ("apprentice," "helper"). Thus:

i. A title including journeymen and their apprentices and/or helpers receives the journeyman score.

ii. Where apprentices or helpers have separate titles, they get their own scores. If estimates are required, 13 is subtracted from the journeyman score for helpers and 5 for apprentices.

7. FOREMEN

Code all foremen titles with the score for "07000 Foreman." The rationale for this is twofold. First, there is no obvious way to take account of industrial distinctions which might affect the prestige of foremen. To do so would require much more information about the social organization of work, both as it varies across industries and as it varies across societies, than we ordinarily have at our disposal. Second, foremen of various types were combined in creating a score for 07000 in the Standard Scale; thus, this score is a good estimate of the average prestige of foremen in various industries.

Example: The 1961 Australian census classification distinguishes between various categories of foremen, e.g., "665 Foremen, Metal Working," "664 Foremen (Electrical), NEC," and "697 Foremen, Construction." All of these titles get the score for "07000 Foreman."

8. NEC GROUPS

Treat occupational categories which include "nec" in the title in exactly the same manner as other occupational categories.

In the interest of providing an exhaustive classification of occupations, most category schemes include a set of residual categories for occupations "not elsewhere classified." The ISCO, for example, includes "nec" categories at both the unit and minor group levels. At first glance, these categories would seem to require special treatment, both because the particular occupations designated as "not elsewhere classified" vary from country to country and because Standard Scale scores for unit group "nec" categories often are based on the scores for a small and heterogeneous set of occupational titles. For example, it might be argued that an occupational title falling within an ISCO unit group "nec" category should be assigned the minor group score because it would provide a better estimate of the prestige of that type of occupation than would a unit group score based on a very small number of occupational titles. However, consideration of this option led us to reject it, both on the ground that there is no basis for assuming that such scores would be more appropriate and because it would introduce inconsistency with our general coding procedures. Our general conclusion is, thus, do not be tempted to treat "nec" categories any differently from other occupational categories.

Example: The 1961 Australian title "347 Pearlers" receives the score of unit group "0649 Fishermen, Hunters and Related Workers nec." because it falls into this unit group and does not match any of the specific titles within it (see also Rules 1, 2.a., and 2.d.).

Example: The Philippine title "725 Leather-Products Makers nec" corresponds to the Standard Scale title "08030 Leather Worker," and so receives its score.

9. GOVERNMENT EMPLOYEES/CIVIL SERVANTS

Occupational classifications differ radically in their terminology and conventions for the classification of government workers. In the Standard Scale, the crucial distinction is a functional one between two minor groups.

The first minor group is "020 LEGISLATIVE OFFICIALS AND GOVERNMENT ADMINISTRATORS," which is included in major group "02 ADMINISTRATIVE AND MANAGERIAL WORKERS." Members of this group advise on government policy and direct the agencies which implement such policy (see International Labour Office, 1969a:94 for further detail).

The second minor group is "031 GOVERNMENT EXECUTIVE OFFICIALS," which is included in major group "03 CLERICAL AND RELATED WORKERS." The function of members of this group is to implement policy decisions, rather than advise on them or supervise the agencies which implement them (see International Labour Office, 1969a:100 for more detail).

This terminology can be very confusing, since in some classifications members of unit group 020 would be termed "executive officials" rather than "administrators," and members of unit group 031 called "administrators" rather than "executive officials." However, the functional distinction is fairly clear, and it is the one to bear in mind and always apply when coding.

The rules therefore are:

a.   When coding government titles, first assign them by function to the appropriate unit group, then assign them the scores of the occupations within their unit group that provide the best match, according to all the usual conventions.

We do not differentiate between federal, state, and local levels of government.

Translated into more substantive terms, minor group 020 consists of heads of government jurisdictions, members of legislatures, and the *heads* of government agencies (see unit groups 0201–0203 in the Standard Scale). All staff positions in government bureaucracies (i.e., all personnel below the position of department head) fall into minor group 031 (see unit group 0310).

Check your coding. Observe that in the Standard Scale many more titles are listed in minor group 020 than are listed in minor group 031. This is the phenomenon of "topheaviness"—the tendency for a more detailed breakdown of occupations to be provided in the Standard Scale at the higher levels of the prestige hierarchy. Do not be misled into assuming that the higher prestige groups contain more *individuals*: They do not. As regards government workers, we expect that in any society the combined total of heads of jurisdictions, legislators, and heads of government bodies will be much smaller in number than the total of government staff responsible to them. Accordingly, where you have any doubts as to whether or not you have assigned government workers to the correct minor group, check the frequency distributions: if you are dealing with a representative sample and the number of individuals you assign to minor group 020 is not considerably smaller than the number of individuals you assign to minor group 031, something is probably wrong. Reconsider.

b.   In classifications which do not distinguish government workers by function as described above, treat all government employees as falling into minor group 031.

This is an application of Rule 2.b., "Typicality." As noted above, there will be many more government workers in group 031 than in group 020. Therefore, simply averaging the scores of the two minor groups would artificially raise the prestige of government workers as a whole.

Example: The U.S. classification contains two codes for government workers, "260 Inspectors, Public Administration" and "270 Officials and Administrators (n.e.c.), Public Administration." Neither of these groups is distinguished by function in the way we have described above. They are therefore both treated as falling within minor group 031. U.S. 260 corresponds substantively to "03102 Government Inspector" and "03103 Customs Inspector," and so receives the average of the scores for these two titles. U.S. 270 does not include Standard Scale 03102 and 03103, but it includes all the other titles which fall into minor group 031, and so receives the average score of all the remaining titles in that group: "03100 Middle Rank Civil Servant," "03101 Civil Servant, Minor Civil Servant," and "03104 Tax Collector." We do not simply assign the unit group score to U.S. 270 because we have already used two titles within that unit group, 03102 and 03103, to classify U.S. 260. Because the unit group score is an average of the scores of its component occupational titles, we would, in effect, be assigning two different occupations in the U.S. classification with the same Standard Scale categories when it is clearly unwarranted.

10. CODING MINOR GROUPS USED TO CLASSIFY INDIVIDUALS

In most studies, only the lowest level (most detailed) occupational codes are used to classify individuals, and the higher levels of aggregation are used only to create summary statistics. For example, in the U.S. Census classification only detailed (3-digit) occupation codes are assigned to individuals; the major and minor group codes are never used.

However, in some studies, such as the 1973 Philippine National Demographic Survey, the more highly aggregated categories are assigned to individual respondents.

The easiest way to find out which procedure is followed in any dataset is to run a frequency distribution of all occupational variables (if they are not elsewhere available, e.g., from a codebook).

If you find that the more highly aggregated categories are not assigned to individuals, there is no need to assign Standard Scale scores to the major and minor group codes of the classification being coded. If you have reason to believe that the codes for aggregated categories have been assigned to individual respondents, then assign Standard Scale scores to these codes. The procedure is, as usual, to follow Rule 2, that is, code minor and/or major groups, as required, as if they were simply other occupational titles by making the best substantive matches to the categories of the Standard Scale.

11. UNCODABLE RESPONSES

Our convention is to code those not in the labor force, or for whom a "no answer" or "don't know" response is given, with a Standard Scale score of 99 and a major group code of 9; we find that this facilitates the subsequent treatment of these responses as missing data. However, in those few cases in which a legitimate occupation is given that we cannot allocate to one of the categories of the ISCO, we code the score for "12000 Unclassifiable Occupation."

V

CONCLUSION

10

Occupational Prestige and Social Structure

This book has been concerned with understanding why it is that occupational status structures are fundamentally similar in all complex societies. Starting with the observation that hierarchies of prestige are more or less invariant across societies, I have been able to show that this similarity extends to patterns of power and privilege as well, and have argued that prestige similarity derives from invariant features of social organization. In this chapter, I summarize the main results of the study, suggest where additional research is needed, and end with a discussion of the implications of the analysis for our understanding of the nature of social stratification.

SUMMARY OF THE ARGUMENT

In the first chapter, I proposed a structural theory of prestige determination that asserts that occupational prestige hierarchies are fundamentally invariant in all complex societies, past or present. In brief, the argument is that the functional imperatives faced by all societies together with limitations on possible organizational forms produce a similar complement of occupational roles in all complex societies. But occupational role differentiation inherently creates stratification, because occupations intrinsically differ with respect to their control over scarce resources—knowledge, authority, and property, all of which can be thought of as aspects of power. Differences in power engender differences in privilege; and differences in power and privilege create differences in prestige. Thus the fact that power differences among occupations are similar in all societies means that hierarchies of privilege and hence of prestige will also be similar in all societies.

To test this theory I amassed data on occupational hierarchies of power, privilege, and prestige for as many societies as possible. Data were only available for one measure of power (the relative educational attainments of incumbents of each occupation) and one measure of privilege (the average income of incumbents), and even these variables were available for only a limited number of societies. By contrast, data on prestige were available for 55 societies varying widely enough in economic and political structure to be regarded as collectively representative of the contemporary world. However, the prestige data had several potential weaknesses that had to be investigated before proceeding to the main analysis.

First, at the conceptual level, it has been questioned whether popular evaluations of the prestige of occupations produce ratings that conform to the classical sociological sense of prestige as a deference-entitlement. I argued that they do, on the basis of evidence showing that patterns of interpersonal association and interaction follow a prestige gradient. Second, many of the prestige studies available for analysis were based on specialized subsamples of the populations they purported to represent; in particular, many were based on samples of students, who might be expected to be rather deviant in their perceptions of the occupational prestige structure and, in nonindustrialized societies, rather more Westernized than the bulk of the population. However, in almost no society is there systematic subgroup variation in prestige ratings, which serves both to reinforce the conception of prestige as a manifestation of the *conscience collective* and to legitimate the use of data from unrepresentative samples to characterize entire societies. The only exception to the pattern of overwhelming societal consensus is the propensity in some nonindustrialized countries for regional variations to be about as great as variations across societies, reflecting the low level of sociocultural integration of such places. Third, some technical problems of effecting comparisons across studies initially designed without comparability in mind had to be solved, but these presented no great difficulty.

Having established the validity of the data, I then turned to a test of the structural theory and consideration of alternative theories of prestige determination and prestige similarity.

First, the fact that in all contemporary societies there is a very high degree of similarity in occupational prestige hierarchies (the average intersocietal correlation is .81) makes it possible to reject the hypothesis that prestige evaluations reflect idiosyncratic cultural values and norms. If prestige evaluations were mainly a manifestation of culturally specific norms, there should be far more cross-cultural variation than exists.

Moreover, we would expect subgroup variations in values—for example, class-based political ideologies and attitudes regarding the desirable features of jobs—to create corresponding variations in prestige evaluations. So the lack of subcultural variation in prestige rankings constitutes additional evidence against a cultural explanation. Finally, examination of societal differences in the prestige of specific occupations yields no systematic evidence of a connection between cultural values and prestige ratings. Thus the cultural hypothesis can be considered to be disconfirmed.

Second, the fact that not only prestige hierarchies but hierarchies of power and privilege (education and income) are fundamentally similar across societies makes it possible to reject the hypothesis that a Western prestige hierarchy diffused throughout the world without a corresponding structural transformation, but simply as a consequence of Euro-American hegemony and the development of mass communications. Industrialized and nonindustrialized countries in the contemporary world prove to have similar hierarchies of power and privilege as well as prestige. The relative educational attainments of incumbents of various occupations are nearly as highly correlated across countries as are prestige levels (the average intercorrelation among 15 countries is .76), and hierarchies of income are only slightly less correlated (the average intercorrelation among 11 countries is .65). Finally, in all societies for which we have data there is a close connection between occupational hierarchies of education, income, and prestige (the average education–income correlation is .77, the average education–prestige correlation is .72, and the average income–prestige correlation is .69). From this, we infer that occupational structures of power, privilege, and prestige are fundamentally similar in all contemporary societies.

However, this pattern could arise because a characteristic occupational structure associated with the industrial system has diffused throughout the contemporary world, even to countries which are not in other respects very far advanced along the road to industrialization. But data from past societies allow us to reject this hypothesis, since occupational hierarchies in past societies prove to be essentially the same as in contemporary societies. Occupational wealth hierarchies in six past societies, ranging from fifteenth-century Florence to late nineteenth-century London, exhibit a level of similarity fully as great as that among contemporary societies (the average correlation among the six past societies is .75), and the average correlation between occupational wealth levels in these societies and the generic occupational prestige hierarchy of the contemporary world is also .75. And data on "prestige" from fourteenth-century Nepal (caste rank) and fifteenth-century Florence (guild rank) are about as similar to the generic hierarchy as data from similar societies in the contemporary world.

Since the available data are consistent with the structural theory but not with any of the alternatives explored, we conclude tentatively that the structural theory is confirmed. That is, it appears to be the case that a similar configuration of occupational roles arises in all societies with an extensive division of labor, that some occupations are intrinsically more powerful than others, that powerful occupations come to enjoy the greatest privilege, and that powerful and privileged positions are accorded great respect everywhere; in short, the observed similarity in occupational prestige hierarchies in all complex societies appears to arise from inherent features of social organization.

LIMITATIONS OF THE ANALYSIS AND FUTURE RESEARCH NEEDS

A monograph of this sort necessarily leaves a trail of unanswered questions scattered through its pages. It is in the nature of secondary analysis to sometimes have the appearance of attempting to make silk purses out of sows' ears. This is especially true when bodies of data initially gathered under widely varying conditions for diverse purposes are brought together. Noncomparables are compared, conclusions are drawn from fragmentary data, gaping holes in the argument are ignored, and so on. Still, such an analysis is a useful endeavor, not only because some definitive answers can be reached but because the outcome provides guidance as to where effort should be concentrated in the collection of additional data and where subsequent research should be focused.

First, the main thesis of the book—the structural theory of prestige determination—needs to be more solidly grounded in empirical data. While the prestige data utilized here encompassed a fairly representative sample of contemporary societies, income and education data were available for a much more limited set of places. Just as the present analysis confirmed that the prestige similarity previously observed in a relatively limited set of societies is indeed characteristic of societies throughout the contemporary world, a task for the future is to verify the worldwide similarity in education and income hierarchies. Moreover, we need further verification of the claim of similarity in occupational status structures between past and present societies. This will require developing appropriate data for past societies. First, we need data on skill differences between occupations; these are totally lacking at present. One possibility would be to tabulate data on occupational differences in literacy rates from census or tax records. Prestige data for past societies are somewhat harder to come by, but with some ingenuity it might be possible to develop appropriate surrogates similar to those utilized here for Florence and Nepal. Given the conception of prestige as indicating institutionalized deference-entitlements, such indicators as marriage and residential patterns might prove useful in addition to the sort of protocol orderings I used. Finally, we need data on other aspects of power and privilege, for both past and present societies. In particular, we need to develop direct indicators of the authority and economic control entailed in occupational role performance.

Second, we must more carefully specify the exact nature of the connection between macrosocial aspects of social organization and variations in occupational status systems. While the main thrust of my argument has been that all complex societies have a fundamentally similar occupational status structure, I have also documented systematic differences across societies. Within the context of general similarity, variations in social organization associated with industrialization appear to affect occupational prestige structures. Highly industrialized countries tend to be more similar to the United States in their prestige hierarchies than less industrialized places, and the more similar societies are with respect to level of industrialization, the more similar they appear to be in their pattern of occupational prestige evaluations. Why this is so is not entirely evident, although there is limited evidence suggesting that—as would be expected from the structural theory of prestige determination—similarity in level of industrialization leads to similarity in hierarchies of occupational power and privilege, which in turn leads to similarity in prestige. Added support for the idea that industrialization creates changes in the organization of work that result in shifts in the prestige hierarchy is to be found in a comparison of the manual and nonmanual prestige hierarchies. Cross-national variations in the prestige of manual occupations are both larger and more systematic than variations in the prestige of nonmanual occupations; that is, variations in the prestige of manual occupations appear to be more closely linked to variations in levels of industrialization than is true of nonmanual occupations. This is as we would expect, since industrialization is likely to have a greater impact on the social organization of manual than of nonmanual work. Still, the evidence is very weak and the argument very sketchy. Much more work needs to be done in tracing out the exact ways in which macrosocial processes such as industrialization change the organization of work and how this in turn affects the prestige evaluation of particular occupations or classes of occupations. Given the theory of prestige determination advanced here, we would expect shifts in the organization of work to have their impact by affecting the relative power and privilege enjoyed by various occupations, and our examination of cross-national variations in the prestige of individual occupations yields some support for this idea, but not enough to forego additional analysis as better data become available. For example, we need to determine if there actually is a loss of skill when handicraftsmen responsible for a product from beginning to end are replaced by assembly-line workers each of whom is responsible only for a limited operation. Resolution of issues such as this will require the collection of additional and superior data on manual occupations, which have been relatively neglected in prestige studies to date.

Third, we must better specify the limits of generalizability of our results. I have claimed that occupational prestige hierarchies are fundamentally similar in all complex societies, and have shown that most of the societies studied here conform very closely to the generic worldwide prestige hierarchy represented by the Standard International Occupational Prestige Scale (the average correlation with the Scale is .91). However, there are two systematic exceptions to the dominant consensus. First, a few of the least industrialized societies considered here, including four in the contemporary world and the two past societies for which we have data, depart substantially from the generic hierarchy (with correlations ranging from .68 to .83). Second, the socialist societies of Eastern Europe (with correlations ranging from .82 to .89) are somewhat more deviant from the generic hierarchy than are other industrialized societies. Of course, both sets of societies still display considerable similarity to the generic hierarchy, but not the near-invariance implied by the theory. With respect to the Eastern European nations, the likelihood is that there are genuine deviations from the generic power and privilege hierarchies and hence deviations in the prestige hierarchy. We have documented the status inversion of skilled manual and routine nonmanual workers relative to the West, but additional work needs to be done to isolate other sources of variation. With respect to the least industrialized countries, inadequacies in the data provide at least as plausible an explanation as genuine differences in prestige evaluations, especially considering that other equally nonindustrialized societies conform somewhat more closely to the generic hierarchy. Still, we must consider the possibility that the generic occupational prestige structure of complex societies does not extend to societies at a very low level of sociocultural integration, especially outside major urban areas. To resolve this issue, additional data will be required; such data should include evaluations of large numbers of occupations by representative population samples that can be disaggregated to investigate subgroup variations in prestige ratings, especially regional and urban–rural variations.

Before concluding this section, it is important to emphasize what we have not shown in this analysis. In particular, we have been able to say nothing about the role of occupational prestige in determining the social standing of individuals. While we have established beyond doubt that people in all complex societies have similar perceptions regarding the relative prestige of occupations, it is not evident that the sort of work one does is an equally important determinant of individual status in all societies. In some societies wealth may play the dominant role, and in others ethnicity, and in still others different factors, such as family name. The fact is that very little is known about this topic, and it is an obvious line for further investigation.

We also have been able to say nothing about the role of occupational prestige in social interaction. Even in the United States, where the salience of occupation as a status attribute of individuals is well established, we do not know under what circumstances prestige is invoked, and with what success. For example, although the evidence is overwhelmingly clear that American professors are just as highly regarded as European professors in the eyes of the public, American professors uniformly complain about their lack of prestige. This cannot be accidental, but must reflect differences in day-to-day experience. Perhaps the fact that professors in particular and professionals in general constitute a much larger fraction of the labor force in the United States than in any European country accounts for the difference in self-perceptions. In the United States, professors must share the top with a great many others, while in Europe they crown the top of a much steeper pyramid.[1] Further, while occupational prestige may be a highly salient status attribute in the United States, status distinctions in general may be less salient. As Weber noted, writing about America at the turn of the century (1958:310):

> in a typical American club nobody would remember that the two members, for instance, who play billiards once stood in the relation of boss and clerk. Here equality of gentlemen prevailed absolutely. This was not always the case in the German–American clubs. When asking young German merchants in New York (with the best Hanseatic names) why they all strove to be admitted to an American club instead of the very nicely furnished German one, they answered that their (German–American) bosses would play billiards with them occasionally, however not without making them realize that they (the bosses) thought themselves to be "very nice" in doing so.

This sort of subtle distinction in deference patterns probably accounts for the apparent fact that people's feelings about the prestige hierarchy vary much more from group to group and from society to society than does the prestige hierarchy itself. Much more work needs to be done on the exact

---

[1] Recall that the method used to establish the extent of cross-cultural similarity in prestige hierarchies precludes assessment of the *absolute* difference in the prestige of an occupation in two countries, permitting only assessment of the difference *relative* to other occupations (because correlation coefficients are invariant with respect to linear transformations). This means that we have no way of deciding whether the prestige of professors is higher in an absolute sense in Europe than in the United States. We can only say that in both places professors stand in a nearly identical relationship to other occupations.

way prestige is translated into actual deference behavior in different societies.

ON THE INEVITABILITY OF STRATIFICATION AND THE DIGNITY OF WORK

What does this analysis tell us about the nature of stratification? Just this: Stratification is inevitable wherever there is differentiation. We have seen that occupational role differentation inherently creates differences in the control of socially valued resources, which in turn gives rise to differences in rewards. That is, there is an intrinsic connection between power, privilege, and prestige. Throughout history, all complex societies have been stratified, and there is no reason to believe that any future society will be different. Although there have been attempts to create classless societies, they have uniformly failed. The most notable current example is Communist China, which represents the greatest experiment at egalitarian social organization in history. But the Chinese case is notable not for its success but for its failure. The 25-year history of the Communist regime has been marked by constant and recurring tension between egalitarian social policies and attempts to improve productivity and efficiency, sloganized as the clash between "red" and "expert." For efficient social organization is necessarily inequalitarian, and the struggle the Chinese have faced is to prevent differentials in power required for efficient productivity from creating institutionalized differences in privilege. The conventional reading of the "cultural revolutions" is that they are devices to dismantle a reemerging stratification system (e.g., Funnell, 1968). Thus cultural revolutions can be expected to recur every five years or so until such time as the Chinese opt for efficiency in production. And at that point we can expect the development of an occupational status system not unlike those in other complex societies.

The concrete process by which stratification develops is very clearly illustrated by two examples, one from an Israeli kibbutz in which there was a deliberate effort to create a totally equalitarian social structure and another from feudal Europe.

Consider the Israeli case first, admirably described by Rosenfeld (1951). Rosenfeld argues that "The forty-year old history of the Israeli collectives reveals the process whereby social strata emerge out of an initially undifferentiated group of young adults living in an equalitarian and democratic system and bent on preventing the crystallization of fixed social strata [1951:766]." Starting from a system in which the ability to do manual work was highly valued, and in which work was assigned by committee and all administrative positions were filled by election—with a norm that both the unpleasant tasks and managerial roles should rotate—the tendency developed to identify particular individuals as "the best among the good workers" and to reelect them as managers for many successive terms. As Rosenfeld notes (1951:769):

> The collectives, as any pioneering society [one might argue, *any* society], suffer from a lack rather than abundance of men and women with talent, initiative and integrity; their scarcity puts them at a premium and gains them general recognition and high esteem. Thus there emerges a group of members whose personal status is so high that their reelection to important managerial positions is a matter of course, the benefit to the group in making best use of them being obvious to all. In the early years of settlement in Palestine, the formalities were observed more than now; managers would insist upon returning to "real, productive work" after a term in the office; but these periods of "productive work" grew shorter and shorter and the principle of turnover nowadays means, in reality, turnover within a given range of managerial positions. Simultaneously, the exigencies of managing a big enterprise and the scarcity of good managers made for a general shift in valuation from manual to "brainy" work.

At the same time, although the principle of equality of material rewards (pay, housing, etc.) continued to be strictly observed, in fact the perquisites of office served to make managerial roles considerably more gratifying than "rank-and-file" roles. As Rosenfeld notes (1951:772):

> managers and administrators often have a chance to leave the settlement and go to town on some errand; they enjoy a degree of freedom of movement and the pleasure of some petty cash which they can spend to see a show or to go to a cafe—pleasures which the rank and file are deprived of. On errands in town, the managers again experience the ego-expanding gratifications, as they represent their whole community in the dealings with banks, merchants and government agencies.
>
> These special life conditions tend to create a special "managerial Weltanschauung" among the upper stratum. They experience less of the strain and dependency and more of the pleasures of collective living.

What conclusions can we draw from this vignette? First, the need of the social system to cope with its environment in the most effective way resulted in ultimately abandoning an ideology of egalitarianism in favor of permanently assigning the most important jobs to the most competent people. Second—and it is no accident—managerial positions emerged as the most important jobs. It was apparently universally recognized that the survival or at least the success of the kibbutz depended crucially upon skilled administration and competent decision making. As we have seen, this is true everywhere. Third, those positions came to be regarded not only as *important* but as *prestigious,* in a process in which there was a shift from valuing the competence of particular individuals and *therefore* electing them as managers to valuing individuals *because* they were managers. Again, it is no accident that responsibility and skill should be highly regarded, and that positions that are regarded as requiring responsibility and skill should be prestigious. Finally, managerial positions, although not entailing any direct economic advantage, nonetheless offered greater gratification than other positions. Davis and Moore (1945:243) identify three classes of rewards associated with occupational roles: those that contribute to "sustenance and comfort," to "humor and diversion," and to "self-respect and ego-expansion." While managerial roles on the kibbutz apparently provided no greater sustenance and comfort than other roles, they clearly monopolized opportunities for both "humor and diversion" and "self-respect and ego-expansion."

Let us now consider another example of the way differentiation leads to stratification, this one involving the formation of a new stratum within an already stratified system. The rise of the "serf–knights" as a special class in medieval Europe is an especially interesting case, since it illustrates the way in which power begets privilege and power and privilege together ultimately beget prestige. As Bloch, in his classic treatise on feudal society describes the situation (1964:337):

> A powerful man does not live without servants, nor does he exercise authority without assistance. Even on the smallest manor a representative of the master was needed to direct the cultivation of the estate, to call for the labor services and see that they were properly carried out, to levy taxes, and to keep good order among the tenants. Frequently this *maire, bayle, Bauermeister* or "reeve" (as he was variously called according to the country) had assistance in his turn. It might be thought that such elementary duties would quite simply be exercised in rotation by the tenants, or even that the latter would be required to appoint temporary officials from among their own ranks. This was in fact a very common practice in England, but on the continent, as a rule, these functions—though also performed, as was natural, by the peasants—none the less constituted genuine offices, permanent and paid, and filled by men appointed by the lord alone.

In fact, the distinction between the English system of rotated office and the continental system of permanent appoitive office had enormous consequences, and was the key to the development of a special class of "serf–knights" on the continent. Again, here is Bloch (1964:338–9):

> Could the *maire,* the lord's steward, be described as a peasant? Undoubtedly he could—at the outset, at least, and sometimes to the end; but he was from the first a rich peasant who became progressively richer through his functions. For the lawful profits were already appreciable and still more so, doubtless, were the illicit ones. In this period, when the only effective authority was the one close at hand, it was only to be expected that the usurpations of rights which in practice made so many

great royal officials sovereigns on their own account, would be repeated at the lower end of the scale in the humble setting of the village . . . how much produce was improperly retained with a resulting loss to the lord's storehouse or his pocket? "An estate abandoned to serjeants, an estate lost," was a maxim of the wise Suger. How many taxes and labour services were extorted from the villeins for his own benefit by this petty rural tyrant; how many chickens taken from their poultry-yards; how many casks of wine claimed from their cellars, or cuts of bacon from their storehouses; how much weaving imposed on their wives! All these were often, in origin, simple gifts; but gifts which could scarcely be refused, and which custom as a rule very soon changed into obligations. What is more, this man of peasant birth was, in his own sphere, a master. In theory, no doubt, his orders were given in the name of one more powerful than himself; they were orders none the less. What is more, he was a judge. He presided, alone, over the peasant courts; and occasionally he sat on more serious cases by the side of the abbot or the baron. Among his other duties was that of marking out the boundaries of the fields in cases of dispute. What function was more calculated to inspire respect in peasant minds.

The upshot of all this was the rise in the status of these officials to a level often equalling that of the hereditary nobility. They lived, dressed, and acted "like noblemen." And, like parvenus everywhere, they did everything they could to secure a social status commensurate with their power and wealth, mostly by passing on their office to their sons and securing good marriages for their children. In time, the descendants of French *maires* came imperceptibly to be assimilated into the hereditary nobility; in Germany, where there were too many, the *Dienstmänner* first became defined as a class apart, "serf-knights," the lowest rung of the nobility, and only after a century and half acquired full noble status. "Here again . . . legal tradition had finally yielded to facts [Bloch, 1964:344]."

If stratification is inevitable, does this mean that social justice is a utopian fantasy? Not at all, although it requires concerted and continuous effort to forestall the rebirth of privilege, as the Chinese have discovered. Differences in power are inherent in the nature of occupational roles, but differences in privilege need not be the result. Although there will always be a strain in this direction, it is possible to organize social systems to reduce—perhaps eliminate—manifest differences in privilege, including the advantage that arises from superior social origins. For example, the elimination of property inheritance and the institutionalization of universal free education go a long way toward equalizing opportunity. By contrast, however, it will never be possible to eliminate differences in prestige, so in equalitarian societies status differences will come to play a more important role than class differences. Still, it is possible to design social systems so that all workers, no matter how lowly their station, take pride in their work and have a sense of dignity about it. The Chinese have apparently been quite successful in doing this, and so have the Danes, who treat every job as requiring specialized skills and run training courses for waitresses and domestic servants and the like as well as for more exalted occupations. A comparison of taxi drivers in New York and London further exemplifies the point. In both the United States and England taxi driving is a fairly low-status occupation. Yet, as every traveler knows, the difference in behavior and self-perception is enormous. New York City cab drivers, who can get a hack license if they can identify the location of the Empire State Building, Madison Square Garden, and a few other equally well known places, are bitter, sullen, and rude, in addition to being ignorant of the streets of the city. London cab drivers, who must pass a very rigorous geographical iden-tification test, take pride in their work; they are courteous, friendly, and knowledgable. Driving a cab in London is neither well paying nor pres-tigious, but London cabbies obviously feel a great deal better about their work than do their New York counterparts. Even given the inevitability of stratification there is no reason why social systems cannot be organized so that every worker, indeed, every citizen, has a sense of dignity and self-respect.

Appendix A

Standard International Occupational Prestige Scale

| | Prestige Score | | | |
Occupation	Major group	Minor group	Unit group	Occupa-tion
00 PROFESSIONAL, TECHNICAL AND RELATED WORKERS	58			
001 PHYSICAL SCIENTISTS AND RELATED TECHNICIANS		66		
0011 Chemists			69	
00110 Chemist				69
0012 Physicists			76	
00120 Physicist				76
0013 Physical Scientists n.e.c.			72	
00130 Scientist				78
00131 Geologist				67
00132 Astronomer				71
00133 Weatherman[1]				49
0014 Physical Science Technicians[2]			46	
002 ARCHITECTS, ENGINEERS AND RELATED TECHNICIANS		56		

This appendix is taken from Treiman (1975), with modifications.

Occupation	Prestige Score			
	Major group	Minor group	Unit group	Occupa-tion
0021 Architects and Town Planners			72	
00210 Architect				72
0022 Civil Engineers			70	
00220 Engineer, Civil Engineer				70
0023 Electrical and Electronics Engineers			65	
00230 Electrical Engineer				65
0024 Mechanical Engineers			66	
00240 Mechanical Engineer				66
0025 Chemical Engineers			66	
00250 Chemical Engineer				66
0026 Metallurgists			60	
00260 Metallurgist				60
0027 Mining Engineers			63	
00270 Mining Engineer				63
0028 Industrial Engineers			54	
00280 Industrial Engineer				54
0029 Engineers n.e.c.			55	
00290 Engineer n.e.c.				55
0031 Surveyors			58	
00310 Surveyor				58
0032 Draftsmen			55	
00320 Draftsman				55
00321 Tracer[3]				26
0033 Civil Engineering Technicians			39	
00330 Surveyor's Assistant				39
0034 Electrical and Electronics Engineering Technicians[2]			46	
0035 Mechanical Engineering Technicians[2]			46	
0036 Chemical Engineering Technicians[2]			46	
0037 Metallurgical Technicians[2]			46	
0038 Mining Technicians			54	
00380 Mining Technician				54
0039 Engineering Technicians n.e.c.			46	
00390 Engineer's Aide				46
004 AIRCRAFT AND SHIPS' OFFICERS		59		
0041 Aircraft Pilots, Navigators and Flight Engineers			66	
00410 Airline Pilot				66
00411 Astronaut[1]				80

	Prestige Score			
Occupation	Major group	Minor group	Unit group	Occupa- tion
0042 Ships' Deck Officers and Pilots			50	
00420 Ship's Officer				63
00421 Small Boat Officer [27]				36
0043 Ships' Engineers			60	
00430 Ship's Engineer				60
005 LIFE SCIENTISTS AND RELATED TECHNICIANS		61		
0051 Biologists, Zoologists and Related Scientists			69	
00510 Biologist				69
0052 Bacteriologists, Pharmacologists and Related Scientists			68	
00520 Medical Researcher				79
00521 Dairy Scientist				56
0053 Agronomists and Related Scientists			56	
00530 Agronomist				58
00531 Agricultural Agent				55
0054 Life Sciences Technicians			52	
00540 Medical Technician				58
00541 Agricultural Technician				47
006 MEDICAL, DENTAL, VETERINARY AND RELATED WORKERS[26]		60		
0061 Medical Doctors			78	
00610 Physician				78
00611 Chief Physician in Hospital[1]				80
0062 Medical Assistants			50	
00620 Medical Assistant				50
0063 Dentists			70	
00630 Dentist				70
0064 Dental Assistants[4]			44	
0065 Veterinarians			61	
00650 Veterinarian				61
0066 Veterinary Assistants[5]			48	
0067 Pharmacists			64	
00670 Pharmacist				64
0068 Pharmaceutical Assistants			44	
00680 Uncertified Pharmacist				44
0069 Dietitians and Public Health Nutritionists			52	
00690 Dietitian				52

	Prestige Score			
Occupation	Major group	Minor group	Unit group	Occupation
0071 Professional Nurses			54	
00710 Professional Nurse, Nurse				54
00711 Head Nurse[1]				58
0072 Nursing Personnel n.e.c.			44	
00720 Uncertified Nurse				44
0073 Professional Midwives			46	
00730 Professional Midwife, Midwife				46
0074 Midwifery Personnel n.e.c.[6]			42	
0075 Optometrists and Opticians			60	
00750 Optometrist				62
00751 Optician				57
0076 Physiotherapists and Occupational Therapists			51	
00760 Physiotherapist				67
00761 Occupational Therapist				57
00762 Masseur				30
0077 Medical X-Ray Technicians[7]			58	
0079 Medical, Dental, Veterinary and Related Workers n.e.c.			50	
00790 Osteopath				62
00791 Chiropractor				62
00792 Herbalist				29
00793 Sanitary Officer				48
008 STATISTICIANS, MATHEMATICIANS, SYSTEMS ANALYSTS AND RELATED TECHNICIANS	56			
0081 Statisticians			55	
00810 Statistician				55
0082 Mathematicians and Actuaries			69	
00820 Mathematician				69
0083 Systems Analysts[8]			51	
0084 Statistical and Mathematical Technicians			51	
00840 Computer Programmer				51
009 ECONOMISTS	60			
0090 Economists			60	
00900 Economist				60
011 ACCOUNTANTS	62			
0110 Accountants			62	
01100 Accountant				55
01101 Professional Accountant				68

	Prestige Score			
Occupation	Major group	Minor group	Unit group	Occupa-tion
012 JURISTS		73		
0121 Lawyers			73	
01210 Lawyer, Trial Lawyer				71
01211 Public Prosecutor				75
0122 Judges			76	
01220 Judge				78
01221 Supreme Court Justice[1]				82
01222 Local Court Judge				73
0129 Jurists n.e.c.			71	
01290 Non-Trial Lawyer				71
01291 Legal Advisor Without Degree[3]				52
013 TEACHERS		61		
0131 University and Higher Education Teachers			78	
01310 University Professor				78
01311 University President, Dean[1]				86
0132 Secondary Education Teachers			60	
01320 High School Teacher				64
01321 Middle School Teacher				57
0133 Primary Education Teachers			57	
01330 Teacher, Primary Teacher				57
0134 Pre-Primary Education Teachers			49	
01340 Pre-Primary Teacher				49
0135 Special Education Teachers[9]			62	
0139 Teachers n.e.c.			62	
01390 Vocational Teacher				57
01391 Principal, Primary Principal				66
01392 Education Officer				68
01393 Teacher's Aide				50
01394 Secondary School Principal				72
014 WORKERS IN RELIGION		46		
0141 Ministers of Religion and Related Members of Religious Orders			54	
01410 Clergyman				60
01411 High Church Official[1]				83
01412 Religious Reciter				46
01413 Evangelist				50
01414 Missionary				49
01415 Member of Religious Order				56
01416 Assistant Priest				61

	Prestige Score			
Occupation	Major group	Minor group	Unit group	Occupa-tion
0149 Workers in Religion n.e.c.			39	
01490 Religious Teacher				56
01491 Faith Healer				22
015 AUTHORS, JOURNALISTS AND RELATED WRITERS	58			
0151 Authors and Critics			62	
01510 Author				62
01511 Pulp Writer[1]				35
0159 Authors, Journalists and Related Writers n.e.c.			56	
01590 Journalist				55
01591 Newspaper Editor				65
01592 Advertising Writer				47
01593 Public Relations Man				57
016 SCULPTORS, PAINTERS, PHOTOGRAPHERS AND RELATED CREATIVE ARTISTS	51			
0161 Sculptors, Painters and Related Artists			57	
01610 Artist				57
0162 Commercial Artists and Designers			49	
01620 Commercial Artist				54
01621 Designer				56
01622 Window Display Artist				38
0163 Photographers and Cameramen			46	
01630 Photographer				45
01631 TV Cameraman				47
017 COMPOSERS AND PERFORMING ARTISTS	48			
0171 Composers, Musicians and Singers			45	
01710 Musician, Classical Musician				56
01711 Jazz Musician				38
01712 Musical Entertainer				32
01713 Music Teacher				53
0172 Choreographers and Dancers			40	
01720 Dancer				45
01721 Dancing Teacher				36
0173 Actors and Stage Directors			57	
01730 Actor				52
01731 Star Actor[1]				63
01732 Dramatic Director				62
0174 Producers, Performing Arts			68	
01740 Dramatic Producer				68

Occupation	Prestige Score			
	Major group	Minor group	Unit group	Occupa- tion
0175 Circus Performers[10]			33	
0179 Performing Artists n.e.c.			42	
01790 Radio, TV Announcer				50
01791 Entertainer				33
018 ATHLETES, SPORTSMEN AND RELATED WORKERS		49		
0180 Athletes, Sportsmen and Related Workers			49	
01800 Professional Athlete				48
01801 Coach, Manager				50
019 PROFESSIONAL, TECHNICAL AND RELATED WORKERS n.e.c.		57		
0191 Librarians, Archivists and Curators			54	
01910 Librarian				54
0192 Sociologists, Anthropologists and Related Scientists			68	
01920 Sociologist				67
01921 Psychologist				66
01922 Archeologist				69
01923 Historian				67
01924 Social Scientist n.e.c.				69
0193 Social Workers			52	
01930 Social Worker				56
01931 Group Worker				49
0194 Personnel and Occupational Specialists			56	
01940 Personnel Director				58
01941 Job Counselor				55
0195 Philologists, Translators and Interpreters			62	
01950 Translator				54
01951 Philologist				69
0199 Other Professional, Technical and Related Workers			51	
01990 Technician				58
01991 Diviner				37
01992 Fingerprint Expert				54
01993 Explorer				49
01994 Peace Corps Member				53
01995 Advertising Executive				57
02 ADMINISTRATIVE AND MANAGERIAL WORKERS	64			
020 LEGISLATIVE OFFICIALS AND GOVERN- MENT ADMINISTRATORS		64		

	Prestige Score			
Occupation	Major group	Minor group	Unit group	Occupation
0201 Heads of Government Jurisdictions			63	
02010 Chief of State[1]				90
02011 Provincial Governor[1]				82
02012 District Head				66
02013 Head, Large City				75
02014 Head, City or Small City				68
02015 Village Head				42
0202 Members of Legislative Bodies			64	
02020 Leader of House[1]				86
02021 Member Upper House[1]				85
02022 Member Lower House				72
02023 Member Provincial House				66
02024 Member Local Council				55
0203 High Administrative Officials			66	
02030 Government Minister[1]				79
02031 Ambassador[1]				87
02032 Diplomat				73
02033 High Civil Servant, Dept. Head				71
02034 Dept. Head, Provincial Government				74
02035 Dept. Head, Local Government				63
02036 Chief's Counselor				50
021 MANAGERS		63		
0211 General Managers			65	
02110 Member Board of Directors				75
02111 Head of Large Firm				70
02112 Head of Firm				63
02113 Head of Small Firm				52
02114 Banker				67
02115 Banker, Large Bank				76
02116 Building Contractor				53
0212 Production Managers (Except Farm)			64	
02120 Factory Manager				64
0219 Managers n.e.c.			60	
02190 Businessman				58
02191 Branch Manager				52
02192 Department Manager				60
02193 Department Manager, Large Firm				63
02194 Business Executive				67
02195 Politician, Party Official				63
02196 Union Official				50
02197 High Union Official				63

	Prestige Score			
Occupation	Major group	Minor group	Unit group	Occupa- tion
03 CLERICAL AND RELATED WORKERS	41			
030 CLERICAL SUPERVISORS		55		
0300 Clerical Supervisors			55	
03000 Office Manager				55
031 GOVERNMENT EXECUTIVE OFFICIALS		55		
0310 Government Executive Officials			55	
03100 Middle Rank Civil Servant				66
03101 Civil Servant, Minor Civil Servant				54
03102 Government Inspector				61
03103 Customs Inspector				44
03104 Tax Collector				52
032 STENOGRAPHERS, TYPISTS AND CARD- AND TAPE-PUNCHING MACHINE OPERATORS		46		
0321 Stenographers, Typists and Teletypists			48	
03210 Typist, Stenographer				42
03211 Secretary				53
0322 Card- and Tape-Punching Machine Operators			45	
03220 Keypunch Operator				45
033 BOOKKEEPERS, CASHIERS AND RELATED WORKERS		38		
0331 Bookkeepers and Cashiers			41	
03310 Bookkeeper				49
03311 Cashier				31
03312 Head Cashier[13]				65
03313 Bank Teller				48
03314 Post Office Clerk				39
03315 Ticket Seller				36
0339 Bookkeepers, Cashiers and Related Workers n.e.c.			34	
03390 Financial Clerk				42
03391 Bill Collector				27
034 COMPUTING MACHINE OPERATORS		49		
0341 Bookkeeping and Calculating Machine Operators[11]			45	
0342 Automatic Data-Processing Machine Operators			53	
03420 Computer Operator				53
035 TRANSPORT AND COMMUNICATIONS SUPERVISORS		50		
0351 Railway Station Masters			56	
03510 Railway Stationmaster				56
0352 Postmasters			58	
03520 Postmaster				58

	Prestige Score			
Occupation	Major group	Minor group	Unit group	Occupa-tion
0359 Transport and Communications Supervisors n.e.c.			37	
03590 Dispatcher, Expeditor				37
036 TRANSPORT CONDUCTORS		32		
0360 Transport Conductors			32	
03600 Railroad Conductor				39
03601 Bus, Streetcar Conductor				26
03602 Sleeping Car Porter				30
037 MAIL DISTRIBUTION CLERKS		30		
0370 Mail Distribution Clerks			30	
03700 Mail Carrier				33
03701 Office Boy, Messenger				26
038 TELEPHONE AND TELEGRAPH OPERATORS		44		
0380 Telephone and Telegraph Operators			44	
03800 Telephone Operator				38
03801 Telegraph Operator				45
03802 Radio Operator				49
039 CLERICAL AND RELATED WORKERS n.e.c.		38		
0391 Stock Clerks			30	
03910 Stockroom Attendant				32
03911 Shipping Clerk				29
0392 Material and Production Planning Clerks[1][2]			44	
0393 Correspondence and Reporting Clerks			44	
03930 Office Clerk				43
03931 Government Office Clerk				44
03932 Law Clerk[1]				59
0394 Receptionists and Travel Agency Clerks			34	
03940 Receptionist				38
03941 Transportation Agent				37
03942 Railway Baggageman				23
03943 Travel Agent				43
03944 Floor Walker				27
0395 Library and Filing Clerks			36	
03950 Library Assistant				41
03951 Filing Clerk				31
0399 Clerks n.e.c.			37	
03991 Proofreader				41
03992 Political Party Worker				48
03993 Meter Reader				21
04 SALES WORKERS	40			
040 MANAGERS (WHOLESALE AND RETAIL TRADE)		45		

Occupation	Prestige Score			
	Major group	Minor group	Unit group	Occupa-tion
0400 Managers (Wholesale and Retail Trade)			45	
04000 Retail Manager				47
04001 Service Station Manager				38
04002 Credit Manager				49
041 WORKING PROPRIETORS (WHOLESALE AND RETAIL TRADE)		48		
0410 Working Proprietors (Wholesale and Retail Trade)			48	
04100 Shop Keeper				42
04101 Large Shop Owner				58
04102 One-Man Stand Operator				38
04103 Automobile Dealer				44
04104 Broker				55
04105 Livestock Broker				40
04106 Wholesale Distributor				58
04107 Smuggler[1]				9
04108 Labor Contractor				49
042 SALES SUPERVISORS AND BUYERS		49		
0421 Sales Supervisors			52	
04210 Sales Manager				52
0422 Buyers			46	
04220 Buyer				49
04221 Purchasing Agent				51
04222 Agricultural Buyer				39
043 TECHNICAL SALESMAN, COMMERCIAL TRAVELLERS AND MANUFACTURERS' AGENTS		46		
0431 Technical Salesmen and Service Advisers			46	
04310 Sales Engineer				51
04311 Utility Co. Salesman				42
0432 Commercial Travellers and Manufacturers' Agents			47	
04320 Traveling Salesman				47
044 INSURANCE, REAL ESTATE, SECURITIES AND BUSINESS SERVICES SALESMEN AND AUCTIONEERS		46		
0441 Insurance, Real Estate and Securities Salesmen			50	
04410 Insurance Agent				44
04411 Real Estate Agent				49
04412 Stock Broker				56
0442 Business Services Salesmen			42	
04420 Advertising Salesman				42
0443 Auctioneers			45	
04430 Auctioneer				39

Occupation	Prestige Score			
	Major group	Minor group	Unit group	Occupa- tion
04431 Appraiser				48
04432 Insurance Claims Investigator				49
045 SALESMEN, SHOP ASSISTANTS AND RELATED WORKERS		28		
0451 Salesmen, Shop Assistants and Demonstrators			32	
04510 Sales Clerk				34
04511 Automobile Salesman				36
04512 Gas Station Attendant				25
04513 Model				36
04514 Sales Demonstrator				28
0452 Street Vendors, Canvassers and Newsvendors			24	
04520 Market Trader				36
04521 Street Vendor, Peddler				22
04522 Telephone Solicitor				26
04523 Newspaper Seller				14
04524 Routeman				24
04525 Narcotics Peddler[1]				6
049 SALES WORKERS n.e.c.		15		
0490 Sales Workers n.e.c.			15	
04900 Money Lender[16]				15
05 SERVICE WORKERS	27			
050 MANAGERS (CATERING AND LODGING SERVICES)		40		
0500 Managers (Catering and Lodging Services)			40	
05000 Bar Manager				32
05001 Hotel Manager[13]				53
05002 Apartment Manager				47
051 WORKING PROPRIETORS (CATERING AND LODGING SERVICES)		37		
0510 Working Proprietors (Catering and Lodging Services)			37	
05100 Restaurant Owner				48
05101 Lunchroom, Coffee Shop Operator				35
05102 Hotel Operator				46
05103 Boardinghouse Keeper				22
05104 Pub Keeper				33
052 HOUSEKEEPING AND RELATED SERVICE SUPERVISORS		37		
0520 Housekeeping and Related Service Supervisors			37	
05200 Steward				46
05201 Housekeeper				28

	Prestige Score			
Occupation	Major group	Minor group	Unit group	Occupa-tion
053 COOKS, WAITERS, BARTENDERS AND RELATED WORKERS	26			
0531 Cooks			31	
05310 Cook				31
05311 Master Cook[3]				38
05312 Cook's Helper [28]				22
0532 Waiters, Bartenders and Related Workers			21	
05320 Waiter				23
05321 Bartender				23
05322 Soda Fountain Clerk[29]				16
054 MAIDS AND RELATED HOUSEKEEPING SERVICE WORKERS n.e.c.	22			
0540 Maids and Related Housekeeping Service Workers n.e.c.			22	
05400 Servant				17
05401 Nursemaid				23
05402 Hotel Chambermaid				14
05403 Hotel Concierge				33
055 BUILDING CARETAKERS, CHARWORKERS, CLEANERS AND RELATED WORKERS	22			
0551 Building Caretakers			25	
05510 Janitor				21
05511 Concierge (Apartment House)				24
05512 Sexton				30
0552 Charworkers, Cleaners and Related Workers			20	
05520 Charworker				16
05521 Window Washer				19
05522 Chimney Sweep				25
056 LAUNDERERS, DRY-CLEANERS AND PRESSERS	22			
0560 Launderers, Dry-Cleaners and Pressers			22	
05600 Launderer				22
057 HAIRDRESSERS, BARBERS, BEAUTICIANS AND RELATED WORKERS	32			
0570 Hairdressers, Barbers, Beauticians and Related Workers			32	
05700 Barber				30
05701 Master Barber[3]				37
05702 Beautician				35
05703 Operator of Hairdressing Salon[3]				45
058 PROTECTIVE SERVICE WORKERS	35			
0581 Fire-Fighters			35	
05810 Fireman				35

Occupation	Prestige Score			
	Major group	Minor group	Unit group	Occupa-tion
0582 Police and Detectives			40	
05820 Policeman				40
05821 Police Officer[3]				60
05822 High Police Official[1]				75
05823 Specialized Law Officer[3]				52
0589 Protective Service Workers n.e.c.			30	
05890 Watchman				22
05891 Prison Guard				39
05892 Bailiff[1]				47
059 SERVICE WORKERS n.e.c.		31		
0591 Guides			29	
05910 Museum Attendant				29
0592 Undertakers and Embalmers			34	
05920 Undertaker				34
0599 Other Service Workers			29	
05990 Medical Attendant				42
05991 Entertainment Attendant				20
05992 Elevator Operator				24
05993 Hotel Bell Boy				14
05994 Doorkeeper				27
05995 Shoe Shiner				12
05996 Airline Stewardess				50
05997 Bookmaker				34
05998 Bell Captain in Hotel				41
05999 Illegal Lottery Agent[1]				6
06 AGRICULTURAL, ANIMAL HUSBANDRY AND FORESTRY WORKERS, FISHERMEN AND HUNTERS	34			
060 FARM MANAGERS AND SUPERVISORS		48		
0600 Farm Managers and Supervisors			48	
06000 Farm Manager				54
06001 Farm Foreman				41
061 FARMERS[26]		40		
0611 General Farmers			40	
06110 Farmer				47
06111 Large Farmer				63
06112 Small Farmer				38
06113 Tenant Farmer				30
06114 Share Cropper				32
06115 Collective Farmer				35
06116 Settler				39
06117 Unpaid Family Farm Worker				34

Occupation	Prestige Score			
	Major group	Minor group	Unit group	Occupation
0612 Specialized Farmers			55	
06120 Specialized Farmer				55
062 AGRICULTURAL AND ANIMAL HUSBANDRY WORKERS		22		
0621 General Farm Workers			20	
06210 Farm Hand				23
06211 Migrant Worker				18
0622 Field Crop and Vegetable Farm Workers			21	
06220 Field Crop Worker				21
0623 Orchard, Vineyard and Related Tree and Shrub Crop Workers			21	
06230 Palmwine Harvester				21
0624 Livestock Workers			26	
06240 Livestock Worker				26
0625 Dairy Farm Workers			23	
06250 Milker				23
0626 Poultry Farm Workers[14]			21	
0627 Nursery Workers and Gardeners			21	
06270 Gardener				21
0628 Farm Machinery Operators			31	
06280 Tractor Driver				31
0629 Agricultural and Animal Husbandry Workers n.e.c.			14	
06290 Skilled Farm Worker				30
06291 Gatherer				−2
063 FORESTRY WORKERS[26]		24		
0631 Loggers			18	
06310 Logger				19
06311 Whistle Punk				18
0632 Forestry Workers (Except Logging)			42	
06320 Forester				48
06321 Timber Cruiser				38
06322 Tree Surgeon				40
064 FISHERMEN, HUNTERS AND RELATED WORKERS		28		
0641 Fishermen			32	
06410 Fisherman				28
06411 Fisherman With Own Boat				37
0649 Fishermen, Hunters and Related Workers n.e.c.			23	
06490 Whaler				40
06491 Hunter				6

Occupation	Prestige Score			
	Major group	Minor group	Unit group	Occupation
07 PRODUCTION AND RELATED WORKERS, TRANSPORT EQUIPMENT OPERATORS AND LABORERS	32			
070 PRODUCTION SUPERVISORS AND GENERAL FOREMEN		46		
0700 Production Supervisors and General Foremen			46	
07000 Foreman				39
07001 Supervisor				52
071 MINERS, QUARRYMEN, WELL DRILLERS AND RELATED WORKERS		32		
0711 Miners and Quarrymen			34	
07110 Miner				32
07111 Specialized Mine Worker				36
07112 Quarry Worker				24
07113 Instructor in Mine				44
0712 Mineral and Stone Treaters[15]			32	
0713 Well Drillers, Borers and Related Workers			31	
07130 Oil Field Worker				31
072 METAL PROCESSERS		38		
0721 Metal Smelting, Converting and Refining Furnacemen			45	
07210 Steel Mill Worker				45
0722 Metal Rolling-Mill Workers			36	
07220 Rolling Mill Operator				36
0723 Metal Melters and Reheaters[15]			38	
0724 Metal Casters			33	
07240 Metal Caster				33
0725 Metal Moulders and Coremakers[15]			38	
0726 Metal Annealers, Temperers and Case-Hardeners[15]			38	
0727 Metal Drawers and Extruders[15]			38	
0728 Metal Platers and Coaters			28	
07280 Galvanizer[16]				28
0729 Metal Processers n.e.c.[15]			38	
073 WOOD PREPARATION WORKERS AND PAPER MAKERS		29		
0731 Wood Treaters[17]			29	

Occupation	Prestige Score			
	Major group	Minor group	Unit group	Occupa-tion
0732 Sawyers, Plywood Makers and Related Wood-Processing Workers			30	
07320 Sawyer in Saw Mill				30
07321 Lumber Grader				31
0733 Paper Pulp Preparers[18]			28	
0734 Paper Makers			28	
07340 Paper Maker				28
074 CHEMICAL PROCESSERS AND RELATED WORKERS	40			
0741 Crushers, Grinders and Mixers[19]			43	
0742 Cookers, Roasters and Related Heat-Treaters[19]			43	
0743 Filter and Separator Operators[19]			43	
0744 Still and Reactor Operators[19]			43	
0745 Petroleum-Refining Workers			37	
07450 Petroleum Worker				37
0749 Chemical Processers and Related Workers n.e.c.			30	
07490 Chemical Worker				43
07491 Charcoal Burner				16
075 SPINNERS, WEAVERS, KNITTERS, DYERS AND RELATED WORKERS		29		
0751 Fiber Preparers[15]			29	
0752 Spinners and Winders			34	
07520 Spinner				34
0753 Weaving- and Knitting-Machine Setters and Pattern-Card Preparers			30	
07530 Machine Loom Fixer, Operator				30
0754 Weavers and Related Workers			32	
07540 Weaver				30
07541 Cloth Grader				33
0755 Knitters			29	
07550 Knitting Machine Operator				29
0756 Bleachers, Dyers and Textile Product Finishers			25	
07560 Cloth Dyer				25
0759 Spinners, Weavers, Knitters, Dyers and Related Workers n.e.c.			26	
07590 Textile Mill Worker				26
076 TANNERS, FELLMONGERS AND PELT DRESSERS		22		
0761 Tanners and Fellmongers[20]			22	
0762 Pelt Dressers[20]			22	

	Prestige Score			
Occupation	Major group	Minor group	Unit group	Occupation
077 FOOD AND BEVERAGE PROCESSORS		34		
0771 Grain Millers and Related Workers			33	
07710 Grain Miller				33
07711 Grain Mill Owner-Operator[1]				42
0772 Sugar Processors and Refiners			45	
07720 Sugar Boiler				45
0773 Butchers and Meat Preparers			24	
07730 Butcher				31
07731 Packing House Butcher				18
07732 Master Butcher[3]				45
0774 Food Preservers			35	
07740 Cannery Worker				35
0775 Dairy Product Processers[15]			34	
0776 Bakers, Pastrycooks and Confectionery Makers			33	
07760 Baker				33
07761 Master Baker[3]				48
0777 Tea, Coffee and Cocoa Preparers[15]			34	
0778 Brewers, Wine and Beverage Makers[15]			34	
07780 Moonshiner[1]				6
0779 Food and Beverage Processers n.e.c.			34	
07790 Fish Butcher				34
078 TOBACCO PREPARERS AND TOBACCO PRODUCT MAKERS		34		
0781 Tobacco Preparers[15]			34	
0782 Cigar Makers			28	
07820 Cigar Maker				28
0783 Cigarette Makers[15]			34	
0789 Tobacco Preparers and Tobacco Product Makers n.e.c.			39	
07890 Tobacco Factory Worker				39
079 TAILORS, DRESSMAKERS, SEWERS, UPHOLSTERERS AND RELATED WORKERS		34		
0791 Tailors and Dressmakers			40	
07910 Tailor				40
07911 Custom Seamstress				39
0792 Fur Tailors and Related Workers			35	
07920 Fur Coat Tailor				35
0793 Milliners and Hatmakers			32	
07930 Milliner				32

Occupation	Prestige Score			
	Major group	Minor group	Unit group	Occupa-tion
0794 Patternmakers and Cutters			41	
07940 Garment Cutter				41
0795 Sewers and Embroiderers			26	
07950 Sewing Machine Operator				26
0796 Upholsterers and Related Workers			31	
07960 Upholsterer				31
0799 Tailors, Dressmakers, Sewers, Upholsterers and Related Workers n.e.c.[15]			34	
080 SHOEMAKERS AND LEATHER GOODS MAKERS		26		
0801 Shoemakers and Shoe Repairers			28	
08010 Shoemaker, Repairer				28
0802 Shoe Cutters, Lasters, Sewers and Related Workers[21]			28	
0803 Leather Goods Makers			22	
08030 Leather Worker				22
081 CABINETMAKERS AND RELATED WOODWORKERS		36		
0811 Cabinetmakers			40	
08110 Cabinetmaker				40
0812 Woodworking-Machine Operators[15]			36	
0819 Cabinetmakers and Related Woodworkers n.e.c.			31	
08190 Cooper				28
08191 Wood Vehicle Builder				34
082 STONE CUTTERS AND CARVERS		38		
0820 Stone Cutters and Carvers			38	
08200 Tombstone Carver				38
083 BLACKSMITHS, TOOLMAKERS AND MACHINE-TOOL OPERATORS		36		
0831 Blacksmiths, Hammersmiths and Forging-Press Operators			35	
08310 Blacksmith				34
08311 Forging-Press Operator				36
0832 Toolmakers, Metal Patternmakers and Metal Markers			40	
08320 Tool and Die Maker				40
08321 Metal Patternmaker				39
0833 Machine-Tool Setter-Operators			38	
08330 Machine Set-Up Man				40
08331 Turner				37
0834 Machine-Tool Operators			38	
08340 Machine Operator in Factory				38

Occupation	Prestige Score			
	Major group	Minor group	Unit group	Occupa-tion
0835 Metal Grinders, Polishers and Tool Sharpeners			27	
08350 Saw Sharpener				19
08351 Polishing Machine Operator				35
0839 Blacksmiths, Toolmakers and Machine-Tool Operators n.e.c.			40	
08390 Locksmith				40
084 MACHINERY FITTERS, MACHINE ASSEMBLERS AND PRECISION INSTRUMENT MAKERS (EXCEPT ELECTRICAL)	43			
0841 Machinery Fitters and Machine Assemblers			42	
08410 Machinist or Fitter				43
08411 Aircraft Worker				42
08412 Millwright[13]				40
0842 Watch, Clock and Precision Instrument Makers			47	
08420 Watch Maker, Repairman				40
08421 Fine Fitter				42
08422 Dental Mechanic[27]				60
0843 Motor Vehicle Mechanics			44	
08430 Garage Mechanic				43
08431 Garage Operator[3]				47
0844 Aircraft Engine Mechanics			50	
08440 Airplane Mechanic				50
0849 Machinery Fitters, Machine Assemblers and Precision Instrument Makers (Except Electrical) n.e.c.			30	
08490 Mechanic, Repairman				43
08491 Bicycle Repairman				28
08492 Mechanic's Helper				31
08493 Assembly Line Worker				30
08494 Unskilled Garage Worker				18
085 ELECTRICAL FITTERS AND RELATED ELECTRICAL AND ELECTRONICS WORKERS	41			
0851 Electrical Fitters			38	
08510 Electrical Fitter				38
0852 Electronics Fitters[22]			48	
0853 Electrical and Electronic Equipment Assemblers			48	
08530 Electronic Assembler				48
0854 Radio and Television Repairmen			42	
08540 Radio, TV Repairman				42
0855 Electrical Wiremen			44	
08550 Electrician				44
08551 Master Electrician (Own Shop)[3]				48

Occupation	Prestige Score			
	Major group	Minor group	Unit group	Occupation
0856 Telephone and Telegraph Installers			35	
08560 Telephone Installer				35
0857 Electric Linemen and Cable Jointers			36	
08570 Power Lineman				36
0859 Electrical Fitters and Related Electrical and Electronics Workers n.e.c.[15]			40	
086 BROADCASTING STATION AND SOUND EQUIPMENT OPERATORS AND CINEMA PROJECTIONISTS	44			
0861 Broadcasting Station Operators			53	
08610 Broadcasting Station Operator				53
0862 Sound Equipment Operators and Cinema Projectionists			34	
08620 Motion Picture Projectionist				34
087 PLUMBERS, WELDERS, SHEET METAL AND STRUCTURAL METAL PREPARERS AND ERECTORS	38			
0871 Plumbers and Pipe Fitters			34	
08710 Plumber				34
08711 Master Plumber (Own Business)[3]				45
0872 Welders and Flame-Cutters			39	
08720 Welder				39
0873 Sheet-Metal Workers			34	
08730 Sheet-Metal Worker				36
08731 Copper, Tin Smith				32
08732 Boilermaker				31
08733 Vehicle Body Builder				36
0874 Structural Metal Preparers and Erectors			44	
08740 Structural Steel Worker				44
088 JEWELRY AND PRECIOUS METAL WORKERS	43			
0880 Jewelry and Precious Metal Workers			43	
08800 Jeweler, Goldsmith				43
08801 Master Jeweler, Goldsmith[3]				57
089 GLASS FORMERS, POTTERS AND RELATED WORKERS	31			
0891 Glass Formers, Cutters, Grinders and Finishers			37	
08910 Lens Grinder				41
08911 Glass Blower				33
0892 Potters and Related Clay and Abrasive Formers			25	
08920 Potter				25
0893 Glass and Ceramics Kilnmen[15]			31	
0894 Glass Engravers and Etchers[15]			31	

Occupation	Prestige Score			
	Major group	Minor group	Unit group	Occupa-tion
0895 Glass and Ceramics Painters and Decorators[15]			31	
0899 Glass Formers, Potters and Related Workers n.e.c.[15]			31	
090 RUBBER AND PLASTICS PRODUCT MAKERS		30		
0901 Rubber and Plastics Product Makers (Except Tire Makers and Tire Vulcanizers)[23]			30	
0902 Tire Makers and Vulcanizers[23]			30	
091 PAPER AND PAPERBOARD PRODUCTS MAKERS		28		
0910 Paper and Paperboard Products Makers[18]			28	
092 PRINTERS AND RELATED WORKERS		41		
0921 Compositors and Typesetters			42	
09210 Printer				42
09211 Master Printer[3]				51
0922 Printing Pressmen			41	
09220 Printing Pressman				41
0923 Stereotypers and Electrotypers[15]			41	
0924 Printing Engravers (Except Photoengravers)			41	
09240 Metal Engraver				41
0925 Photoengravers			46	
09250 Photoengraver				46
0926 Bookbinders and Related Workers			32	
09260 Bookbinder				32
0927 Photographic Darkroom Workers			36	
09270 Photograph Developer				36
0929 Printers and Related Workers n.e.c.			52	
09290 Graphics Printer				52
093 PAINTERS		30		
0931 Painters, Construction			31	
09310 Building Painter				31
09311 Master Building Painter[3]				39
0939 Painters n.e.c.			29	
09390 Automobile Painter				29
094 PRODUCTION AND RELATED WORKERS n.e.c.		31		
0941 Musical Instrument Makers and Tuners			33	
09410 Piano Tuner				33
0942 Basketry Weavers and Brush Makers			21	
09420 Basketweaver				21
0943 Non-Metallic Mineral Product Makers[23]			30	

	Prestige Score			
Occupation	Major group	Minor group	Unit group	Occupa-tion
0949 Other Production and Related Workers			41	
09490 Quality Checker				39
09491 Ivory Carver				33
09492 Taxidermist				50
09493 Calabash Maker[13]				23
095 BRICKLAYERS, CARPENTERS AND OTHER CONSTRUCTION WORKERS	31			
0951 Bricklayers, Stonemasons and Tile Setters			34	
09510 Mason				34
0952 Reinforced-Concreters, Cement Finishers and Terrazzo Workers			34	
09520 Cement Finisher				34
0953 Roofers			31	
09530 Roofer				31
0954 Carpenters, Joiners and Parquetry Workers			37	
09540 Carpenter				37
09541 Master Carpenter[3]				48
09542 Carpenter's Helper[28]				23
0955 Plasterers			31	
09550 Plasterer				31
09551 Master Plasterer[3]				39
0956 Insulators			28	
09560 Insulation Installer				28
0957 Glaziers			26	
09570 Glazier				26
0959 Construction Workers n.e.c.			28	
09590 Paperhanger				24
09591 Master Paperhanger[3]				38
09592 Maintenance Man				28
09593 Skilled Construction Worker				46
09594 Construction Laborer n.e.c.				26
09595 Unskilled Construction Laborer				15
09596 House Builder[13]				36
096 STATIONARY ENGINE AND RELATED EQUIPMENT OPERATORS	38			
0961 Power-Generating Machinery Operators			42	
09610 Power Station Operator				42
0969 Stationary Engine and Related Equipment Operators n.e.c.			34	
09690 Stationary Engineer				34

	Prestige Score			
Occupation	Major group	Minor group	Unit group	Occupa-tion
097 MATERIAL-HANDLING AND RELATED EQUIPMENT OPERATORS, DOCKERS AND FREIGHT HANDLERS[26]		22		
0971 Dockers and Freight Handlers			20	
09710 Longshoreman				21
09711 Warehouse Hand				20
09712 Porter				17
09713 Railway, Airport Porter				18
09714 Packer				22
0972 Riggers and Cable Splicers[24]			32	
0973 Crane and Hoist Operators			32	
09730 Power Crane Operator				39
09731 Drawbridge Tender [27]				25
0974 Earth-Moving and Related Machinery Operators			32	
09740 Road Machinery Operator				32
0979 Material-Handling Equipment Operators n.e.c.[15]			28	
098 TRANSPORT EQUIPMENT OPERATORS		28		
0981 Ships' Deck Ratings, Barge Crews and Boatmen			29	
09810 Seaman				35
09811 Boatman				23
0982 Ships' Engine-Room Ratings			25	
09820 Ship's Engine-Room Hand				25
0983 Railway Engine Drivers and Firemen			34	
09830 Locomotive Engineer				43
09831 Locomotive Fireman				33
09832 Ore Train Motorman in Mine				27
0984 Railway Brakemen, Signalmen and Shunters			29	
09840 Railway Switchman, Brakeman				29
0985 Motor Vehicle Drivers			31	
09850 Taxi Driver				28
09851 Bus, Tram Driver				32
09852 Driver, Truck Driver				33
09853 Small Transport Operator				39
09854 Truck Driver's Helper				15
09855 Driving Teacher				41
0986 Animal and Animal-Drawn Vehicle Drivers			22	
09860 Animal Driver				18
09861 Wagoneer				26
0989 Transport Equipment Operators n.e.c.			24	
09890 Pedal-Vehicle Driver				17
09891 Railway Crossing Guard				30

	Prestige Score			
Occupation	Major group	Minor group	Unit group	Occupation
099 MANUAL WORKERS n.e.c.		32		
0995 Skilled Workers n.e.c.			46	
09950 Skilled Worker				42
09951 Independent Artisan				50
0997 Semi-Skilled Workers n.e.c.			33	
09970 Factory Worker				29
09971 Apprentice				37
0999 Laborers n.e.c.			18	
09990 Laborer				19
09991 Unskilled Factory Laborer				18
09992 Contract Laborer				8
09993 Itinerant Worker				20
09994 Railway Track Worker				33
09995 Street Sweeper				13
09996 Garbage Collector				13
09997 Road Construction Laborer				20
10 MEMBERS OF THE ARMED FORCES	42			
100 MEMBERS OF THE ARMED FORCES		42		
1000 Members of the Armed Forces			42	
10000 High Armed Forces Officer[1]				73
10001 Armed Forces Officer[3]				63
10002 Non-Commissioned Officer				44
10003 Soldier				39
11 NEW WORKERS SEEKING EMPLOYMENT[25]	32			
110 NEW WORKERS SEEKING EMPLOYMENT[25]		32		
1100 New Workers Seeking Employment			32	
11000 New Worker Seeking Employment				32
12 UNCLASSIFIABLE OCCUPATIONS	40			
120 UNCLASSIFIABLE OCCUPATIONS		40		
1200 Unclassifiable Occupations			40	
12000 Unclassifiable Occupation				40
13 NOT IN LABOR FORCE	41			
130 NOT IN LABOR FORCE		41		
1300 Not in Labor Force			41	
13000 Lives Off Stock-Bond Income				55
13001 Lives Off Income from Property				57
13002 Lives Off Inheritance Income				48
13003 Agricultural Land Owner				65
13004 Lives Off Social Security				30
13005 Lives From Public Assistance				16
13006 Beggar				15

[1]Excluded from unit group average score.

[2]Score is average of 00330 Surveyor's Assistant, 00380 Mining Technician, and 00390 Engineer's Aide.

[3]Excluded from unit group average score. Assigned weight of .5 in previous version of the scale (Treiman, 1975).

[4]Score borrowed from 00720 Uncertified Nurse.

[5]Score borrowed from average of 00541 Agricultural Technician and 00620 Medical Assistant (half weighted).

[6]Score borrowed from 05990 Medical Attendant.

[7]Score borrowed from 00540 Medical Technician.

[8]Score borrowed from 00840 Computer Programmer.

[9]Score borrowed from unit group 0139 "Teachers n.e.c."

[10]Score borrowed from 01791 Entertainer.

[11]Score borrowed from 03220 Keypunch Operator.

[12]Score borrowed from unit group 0393 "Correspondence and Reporting Clerks."

[13]Excluded from unit group average since title was only rated in countries utilizing nonprestige criteria of evaluation. Score is from alternative version of scale based on all 60 places.

[14]Score borrowed from average of all other unit groups in minor group 062 "Agricultural and Animal Husbandry Workers" except 0628 "Farm Machinery Operators."

[15]Score borrowed from average of all unit groups in same minor group undesignated by footnotes.

[16]Occupation occurs only in countries utilizing nonprestige criteria, hence score is from alternative version of scale. Occupation score used for unit group score since no other occupations occur in unit group. This unit group score is excluded from any further aggregation.

[17]Score borrowed from average of unit groups 0732 "Sawyers, Plywood Makers. . ." and 0734 "Paper Makers."

[18]Score borrowed from 07340 Paper Maker.

[19]Score borrowed from 07490 Chemical Worker.

[20]Score borrowed from 08030 Leather Worker.

[21]Score borrowed from 08010 Shoemaker, Repairer.

[22]Score borrowed from 08530 Electronic Assembler.

[23]Score borrowed from unit group 0749 "Chemical Processers and Related Workers n.e.c.

[24]Score borrowed from unit group 0973 "Crane and Hoist Operators."

[25]Score borrowed from average score for major group 07 "Production and Related Workers. . . ."

[26]Weighted average of unit group scores. Weights derived from the occupational distributions of India and the U.S. See Chapter 8 for details.

[27]Weighted .5 when computing unit group score in previous version of scale (Treiman, 1975); given full weight in current version.

[28]Excluded from unit group average; included in unit group average in previous version of scale (Treiman, 1975).

[29]Code changed from 05313 in previous version of scale (Treiman, 1975); unit group averages for 0530 and 0531 modified in consequence.

Appendix B

Alphabetical Index to Standard Scale

This index shows in alphabetical order all of the titles appearing in the Standard Scale (Appendix A). Occupation lines are shown in upper- and lower-case roman letters followed by a five-digit code; unit lines are in upper- and lowercase italic letters followed by a four-digit code; minor group lines are in uppercase roman letters followed by a three-digit code; and major group lines are in uppercase italic letters followed by a two-digit code.

The index is intended as an aid to locating occupational titles in the Standard Scale. But since the same title may have different meanings in different countries and sometimes even within a country, the user should be sure that the title he is coding is correctly identified within the ISCO classification. Use of the dictionary contained within International Standard Classification of Occupations (ILO, 1969) will greatly facilitate correct mapping of occupational titles in other studies into the categories of the Standard Scale.

Accountant, 01100
Accountants, 0110
ACCOUNTANTS, 011
Actor, 01730
Actors and Stage Directors, 0173
ADMINISTRATIVE AND MANAGERIAL WORKERS, 02
Advertising Executive, 01995
Advertising Salesman, 04420
Advertising Writer, 01592
Agricultural Agent, 00531
AGRICULTURAL AND ANIMAL HUSBANDRY WORKERS, 062
Agricultural and Animal Husbandry Workers (nec) 0629
AGRICULTURAL, ANIMAL HUSBANDRY AND FORESTRY WORKERS, FISHERMAN AND HUNTERS, 06
Agricultural Buyer, 04222
Agricultural Land Owner, 13003
Agricultural Technician, 00541
Agronomist, 00530
Agronomists and Related Scientists, 0053
AIRCRAFT AND SHIPS' OFFICERS, 004
Aircraft Engine Mechanics, 0844
Aircraft Pilots, Navigators and Flight Engineers, 0041
Aircraft Worker, 08411
Airline Pilot, 00410
Airline Stewardess, 05996
Airplane Mechanic, 08440
Ambassador, 02031
Animal and Animal-Drawn Vehicle Drivers, 0986
Animal Driver, 09860
Apartment Manager, 05002
Appraiser, 04431
Apprentice, 09971
Archeologist, 01922
Architect, 00210
Architects and Town Planners, 0021
ARCHITECTS, ENGINEERS AND RELATED TECHNICIANS, 002
Armed Forces Officer, 10001
Artist, 01610
Assembly Line Worker, 08493
Assistant Priest, 01416
Astronaut, 00411
Astronomer, 00132
ATHLETES, SPORTSMEN AND RELATED WORKERS, 018
Athletes, Sportsmen and Related Workers, 0180
Auctioneer, 04430
Auctioneers, 0443
Author, 01510
Authors and Critics, 0151
AUTHORS, JOURNALISTS, AND RELATED WRITERS, 015
Authors, Journalists, and Related Writers (nec), 0159
Automatic Data-Processing Machine Operators, 0342
Automobile Dealer, 04103
Automobile Painter, 09390
Automobile Salesman, 04511
Bacteriologists, Pharmacologists, and Related Scientists, 0052
Bailiff, 05892
Baker, 07760

Bakers, Pastrycooks and Confectionery Makers, 0776
Bank Teller, 03314
Banker, 02114
Banker, Large Bank, 02115
Bar Manager, 05000
Barber, 05700
Bartender, 05322
Basketry Weavers and Brush Makers, 0942
Basketweaver, 09420
Beautician, 05702
Beggar, 13006
Bell Captain in Hotel, 05998
Bicycle Repairman, 08491
Bill Collector, 03391
Biologist, 00510
Biologists, Zoologists and Related Scientists, 0051
Blacksmith, 08310
Blacksmiths, Hammersmiths, and Forging-Press Operators, 0831
BLACKSMITHS, TOOLMAKERS, AND MACHINE-TOOL OPERATORS, 083
Blacksmiths, Toolmakers, and Machine-Tool Operators(nec), 0839
Bleachers, Dyers, and Textile Product Finishers, 0756
Boardinghouse Keeper, 05103
Boatman, 09811
Boilermaker, 08732
Bookbinder, 09260
Bookbinders and Related Workers, 0926
Bookkeeper, 03310
Bookkeepers and Cashiers, 0331
BOOKKEEPERS, CASHIERS, AND RELATED WORKERS, 033
*Bookkeepers, Cashiers, and Related Workers(nec),*0339
Bookkeeping and Calculating Machine Operators, 0341
Bookmaker, 05997
Branch Manager, 02191
Brewers, Wine and Beverage Makers, 0778
BRICKLAYERS, CARPENTERS AND OTHER CONSTRUCTION WORKERS, 095
Bricklayers, Stonemasons, and Tile Setters, 0951
BROADCASTING STATION AND SOUND EQUIPMENT OPERATORS AND CINEMA PROJECTIONISTS
086
Broadcasting Station Operator, 08610
Broadcasting Station Operators, 0861
Broker, 04104
Building Caretakers, 0551
BUILDING CARETAKERS, CHARWORKERS, CLEANERS, AND RELATED WORKERS, 055
Building Contractor, 02116
Building Painter, 09310
Bus, Streetcar Conductor, 03601
Bus, Tram Driver, 09852
Business Executive, 02194
Business Services Salesmen, 0442
Businessman, 02190
Butcher, 07730
Butchers and Meat Preparers, 0773
Buyer, 04220
Buyers, 0422
Cabinet Maker, 08110
Cabinetmakers, 0811

CABINETMAKERS AND RELATED WOODWORKERS, 081
Cabinetmakers and Related Woodworkers, (nec), 0819
Calabash Maker, 09493
Card- and Tape-Punching Machine Operators, 0322
Carpenter, 09540
Carpenter's Helper, 09542
Carpenters, Joiners, and Parquetry Workers, 0954
Cashier, 03312
Cement Finisher, 09520
Charcoal Burner, 07491
Charworker, 05520
Charworkers, Cleaners, and Related Workers, 0552
Chemical Engineer, 00250
Chemical Engineering Technicians, 0036
Chemical Engineers, 0025
CHEMICAL PROCESSORS AND RELATED WORKERS, 074
Chemical Processors and Related Workers, (nec), 0749
Chemical Worker, (nec), 07490
Chemist, 00110
Chemists, 0011
Chief of State, 02010
Chief Physician in Hospital, 00611
Chief's Counselor, 02036
Chimney Sweep, 05523
Chiropractor, 00791
Choreographers and Dancers, 0172
Cigar Maker, 07820
Cigar Makers, 0782
Cigarette Makers, 0783
Circus Performers, 0175
Civil Engineering Technicians, 0033
Civil Engineers, 0022
Civil Servant, Minor Civil Servant, 03102
Clergyman, 01410
CLERICAL AND RELATED WORKERS, 03
CLERICAL AND RELATED WORKERS, (NEC), 039
CLERICAL SUPERVISORS, 030
Clerical Supervisors, 0300
Clerks, (nec), 0399
Cloth Dyer, 07560
Cloth Grader, 04541
Coach, Manager, 01801
Collective Farmer, 06115
Commercial Artist, 01620
Commercial Artists and Designers, 0162
Commercial Travelers and Manufacturers' Agents, 0432
COMPOSERS AND PERFORMING ARTISTS, 017
Composers, Musicians, and Singers, 0171
Compositors and Typesetters, 0921
Computer Programmer, 00840
COMPUTING MACHINE OPERATORS, 034
Computer Operator, 03420
Concierge (Apartment House), 05511
Construction Laborer, (nec), 09595
Construction Workers, (nec), 0959
Contract Laborer, 09992

Cook, 05310
Cook's Helper, 05312
Cookers, Roasters, and Related Heat-Treaters, 0742
Cooks, 0531
COOKS, WAITERS, BARTENDERS, AND RELATED WORKERS, 053
Cooper, 08190
Coppersmith, Tinsmith, 08731
Correspondence and Reporting Clerks, 0393
Crane and Hoist Operators, 0973
Credit Manager, 04002
Crushers, Grinders and Mixers, 0741
Custom Seamstress, 07912
Customs Officer, 03104
Dairy Farm Workers, 0625
Dairy Product Processors, 0775
Dairy Scientist, 00521
Dancer, 01720
Dancing Teacher, 01721
Dental Assistants, 0064
Dental Mechanic, 08423
Dentist, 00630
Dentists, 0063
Department Manager, 02192
Department Manager, Large Firm, 02193
Department Head, Local Government, 02035
Department Head, Provincial Government, 02034
Designer, 01621
Dietician, 00690
Dieticians and Public Health Nutritionists, 0069
Diplomat, 02032
Dispatcher or Expeditor, 03590
District Head, 02012
Diviner, 01991
Dockers and Freight Handlers, 0971
Doorkeeper, 05994
Draftsman, 00320
Dramatic Director, 01732
Dramatic Producer, 01740
Draughtsmen, 0032
Drawbridge Tender, 09731
Driver, Truck Driver, 09853
Driving Teacher, 09856
Earth-Moving and Related Machinery Operators, 0974
Economist, 00900
ECONOMISTS, 009
Economists, 0090
Education Officer, 01392
Electric Linemen and Cable Jointers, 0857
Electrical and Electronic Equipment Assemblers, 0853
Electrical and Electronics Engineers, 0023
Electrical and Electronics Engineering Technicians, 0034
Electrical Engineer, 00230
Electrical Fitter, 08510
Electrical Fitters, 0851
ELECTRICAL FITTERS AND RELATED ELECTRICAL AND ELECTRONICS WORKERS, 085
Electrical Fitters and Related Electrical and Electronics Workers, nec, 0859

Electrical Wiremen, 0855
Electrician, 08550
Electronic Assembler, 08530
Electronics Fitters, 0852
Elevator Operator, 05992
Engineer, (nec), 00290
Engineer, Civil Engineer, 00220
Engineer's Aide, 00390
Engineering Technicians, (nec), 0039
Engineers, (nec), 0029
Entertainer, 01791
Entertainment Attendant, 05991
Evangelist, 01413
Explorer, 01993
Factory Manager, 02120
Factory Worker, 09970
Faith Healer, 01491
Farm Foreman, 06001
Farm Hand, 06210
Farm Machinery Operators, 0628
Farm Manager, 06000
FARM MANAGERS AND SUPERVISORS, 060
Farm Managers and Supervisors, 0060
Farmer, 06110
FARMERS, 061
Fiber Preparers, 0751
Field Crop and Vegetable Farm Workers, 0622
Field Crop Worker, 06220
Filing Clerk, 03951
Filter and Separator Operators, 0743
Financial Clerk, 03390
Fine Fitter, 08422
Fingerprint Expert, 01992
Fire-Fighters, 0581
Fireman, 05810
Fisherman, 06410
Fisherman with own Boat, 06411
Fishermen, 0641
FISHERMEN, HUNTERS, AND RELATED WORKERS, 064
Fishermen, Hunters and Related Workers, (nec), 0649
Floor Walker, 03944
FOOD AND BEVERAGE·PROCESSORS, 077
Food and Beverage Processors, (nec) 0779
Food Preservers, 07740
Food Preservers, 0774
Food, Beverage Processors, (nec), 07790
Foreman, 07000
Forester, 06320
FORESTRY WORKERS, 063
Forestry Workers (except logging), 0632
Forging-Press Operator, 08311
Fur Coat Tailor, 07920
Fur Tailors and Related Workers, 0792
Garbage Collector, 09996
Garage Mechanic, 08430
Garage Operator, 08431

Gardener, 06270
Garment Cutter, 07940
Gas Station Attendant, 04512
Gatherer, 06292
General Farm Workers, 0621
General Farmers, 0611
General Managers, 0211
Geologist,·00131
Glass and Ceramics Kilnmen, 0893
Glass and Ceramics Painters and Decorators, 0895
Glass Blower, 08911
Glass Engravers and Etchers, 0894
Glass Formers, Cutters, Grinders, and Finishers, 0891
GLASS FORMERS, POTTERS AND RELATED WORKERS, 089
Glass Formers, Potters, and Related Workers, (nec), 0899
Glazier, 09570
GOVERNMENT EXECUTIVE OFFICIALS, 031
Government Executive Officials, 0310
Government Inspector, 03103
Government Minister, 02030
Government Office Clerk, 03931
Grain Mill Owner - Operator, 07711
Grain Miller, 07710
Grain Millers and Related Workers, 0771
Group Worker, 01931
Guides, 0591
HAIRDRESSERS, BARBERS, BEAUTICIANS, AND RELATED WORKERS, 057
Hairdressers, Barbers, Beauticians, and Related Workers, 0570
Head Cashier, 03313
Head Nurse, 00711
Head of Firm, 02112
Head of Large Firm, 02111
Head of Small Firm, 02113
Head, City or Small City, 02014
Head, Large City, 02013
Heads of Governmental Jurisdictions, 0201
Herbalist, 00792
High Administrative Officials, 0203
High Armed Forces Officer, 1000
High Church Official, 01411
High Civil Servant, Department Head, 02033
High Police Official, 05822
High School Teacher, 01320
High Union Official, 02198
Historian, 01923
Hotel Manager, 05001
Hotel Bellboy, 05993
Hotel Chambermaid, 05402
Hotel Concierge, 05403
Hotel Operator, 05102
House Builder, 09597
Housekeeper, 05201
HOUSEKEEPING AND RELATED SERVICE SUPERVISORS, 052
Housekeeping and Related Service Supervisors, 0520
Hunter, 06491
Illegal Lottery Agent, 05999

Independant Artisan, 09951
Industrial Engineer, 00280
Industrial Engineers, 0028
Instructor in Mine, 07113
Insulation Installer, 09560
Insulators, 0956
Insurance Agent, 04410
Insurance Claims Investigator, 04432
Insurance, Real Estate and Securities Salesmen, 0441
INSURANCE, REAL ESTATE, SECURITIES, AND BUSINESS SERVICES SALESMEN AND
 AUCTIONEERS, 044
Itinerant Worker, 09993
Ivory Carver, 09491
Janitor, 05510
Jazz Musician, 01711
Jeweler, Goldsmith, 08800
JEWELERY AND PRECIOUS METAL WORKERS, 088
Jewelery and Precious Metal Workers, 0880
Job Counselor, 01941
Journalist, 01590
Judge, 01220
Judges, 0122
JURISTS, 012
Jurists, (nec), 0129
Keypunch Operator, 03220
Knitters, 0755
Knitting Machine Operator, 07550
Labor Contractor, 04108
Laborer, 09990
LABORERS, (NEC), 099
Laborers, (nec), 0999
Large Farmer, 06111
Large Shop Owner, 04101
Launderer, 05600
LAUNDERERS, DRY-CLEANERS, AND PRESSERS, 056
Launderers, Dry-Cleaners, and Pressers, 0560
Law Clerk, 03932
Lawyer, Trial Lawyer, 01210
Lawyers, 0121
Leader of House, 02020
Leather Goods Maker, 08030
Leather Goods Makers, 0803
Legal Advisor Without Degree, 01291
LEGISLATIVE OFFICIALS AND GOVERNMENT ADMINISTRATORS, 020
Lens Grinder, 08910
Librarian, 01910
Librarians, Archivists, and Curators, 0191
Library and Filing Clerks, 0395
Library Assistant, 03950
Life Sciences Technicians, 0054
LIFE SCIENTISTS AND RELATED TECHNICIANS, 005
Lives from Public Assistance, 13005
Lives off Income from Property, 13001
Lives off Inheritance Income, 13002
Lives off Social Security, 13004
Lives off Stock-Bond Income, 13000

Livestock Broker, 04105
Livestock Worker, 06240
Livestock Workers, 0624
Local Court Judge, 01222
Locksmith, 08390
Locomotive Engineer, 09830
Locomotive Fireman, 09831
Logger, 06310
Logging Machinery Operator, 06311
Longshoreman, 09710
Lumber Grader, 07321
Lunchroom, Coffee Shop Operator, 05101
Machine Loom Fixer, Operator, 07530
Machine Operator in Factory, 08340
Machine Set-Up Man, 08330
Machine-Tool Operators, 0834
Machine-Tool Setter-Operators, 0833
Machinery Fitters and Machine Assemblers, 0841
MACHINERY FITTERS, MACHINE ASSEMBLERS AND PRECISION INSTRUMENT MAKERS
 (EXCEPT ELECTRICAL), 084
Machinery Fitters, Machine Assemblers and Precision Instrument Makers
 (except electrical), (nec), 0849
Machinist or Fitter, 08410
MAIDS AND RELATED HOUSEKEEPING SERVICE WORKERS, (NEC), 054
Maids and Related Housekeeping Service Workers, (nec), 0540
Mail Carrier, 03700
MAIL DISTRIBUTION CLERKS, 037
Maintenance Man, 09593
MANAGERS, 021
MANAGERS (CATERING AND LODGING SERVICES), 050
Managers (Catering and Lodging Services), 0500
MANAGERS (WHOLESALE AND RETAIL TRADE), 040
Managers (Wholesale and Retail Trade), 0400
Managers, (nec), 0219
Market Trader, 04520
Mason, 09510
Masseur, 00762
Master Baker, 07761
Master Barber, 05701
Master Building Painter, 09311
Master Butcher, 07732
Master Carpenter, 09541
Master Cook, 05311
Master Electrician (Own Shop), 08551
Master Jeweler, Goldsmith, 08801
Master Paperhanger, 09591
Master Plasterer, 09551
Master Plumber (Own Business), 08711
Master Printer, 09211
Material and Production Planning Clerks, 0392
MATERIAL-HANDLING AND RELATED EQUIPMENT OPERATORS, DOCKERS AND FREIGHT
 HANDLERS, 097
Material-Handling Equipment Operators, (nec), 0979
Mathematician, 00820
Mathematicians and Actuaries, 0082

Mechanic, Repairman, 08490
Mechanic's Helper, 08492
Mechanical Engineer, 00240
Mechanical Engineering Technicians, 0035
Mechanical Engineers, 0024
Medical Assistant, 00620
Medical Assistants, 0062
Medical Attendant, 05990
Medical Doctors, 0061
Medical Researcher, 00520
Medical Technician, 00540
Medical X-ray Technicians, 0077
MEDICAL, DENTAL, VETERINARY, AND RELATED WORKERS, 006
Medical, Dental, Veterinary, and Related Workers, (nec), 0079
Member, Board of Directors, 02110
Member, Local Council, 02024
Member, Lower House, 02022
Member of Religious Order, 01415
Member of Provincial House, 02023
Member of Upper House, 02021
MEMBERS OF THE ARMED FORCES, 10
Members of Legislative Bodies, 0202
Metal Annealers, Temperers, and Case-Hardeners, 0726
Metal Caster, 07240
Metal Casters, 0724
Metal Drawers and Extruders, 0727
Metal Engraver, 09240
Metal Grinders, Polishers, and Tool Sharpeners, 0835
Metal Melters and Reheaters, 0723
Metal Moulders and Coremakers, 0725
Metal Patternmaker, 08321
Metal Plater or Coater, 07280
Metal Platers and Coaters, 0728
METAL PROCESSORS, 072
Metal Processors, (nec), 0729
Metal Rolling-Mill Workers, 0722
Metal Smelting, Converting, and Refining Furnacemen, 0721
Metallurgical Technicians, 0037
Metallurgist, 00260
Metallurgists, 0026
Meteorologist, 00133
Meter Reader, 03994
Middle Rank Civil Servant, 03101
Middle School Teacher, 01321
Midwifery Personnel, (nec), 0074
Migrant Worker, 06211
Milker, 06250
Milliner, 07930
Milliners and Hatmakers, 0793
Millwright, 08412
Miner, 07110
Mineral and Stone Treaters, 0712
Miners and Quarrymen, 0711
MINERS, QUARRYMEN, WELL DRILLERS, AND RELATED WORKERS, 071
Mining Engineer, 00270
Mining Engineers, 0027

Peace Corps Member, 01994
Pedal-Vehicle Driver, 09890
Pelt Dressers, 0762
Performing Artists, (nec), 0179
Personnel and Occupational Specialists, 0194
Personnel Director, 01940
Petroleum Refining Worker, 07450
Petroleum Refining Workers, 0745
Pharmaceutical Assistants, 0068
Pharmacist, 00670
Pharmacists, 0067
Philologist, 01951
Philologists, Translators, and Interpreters, 0195
Photoengraver, 09250
Photoengravers, 0925
Photograph Developer, 09270
Photographer, 01630
Photographers and Cameramen, 0163
Photographic Darkroom Workers, 0927
Physical Science Technicians, 0014
PHYSICAL SCIENTISTS AND RELATED TECHNICIANS, 001
Physical Scientists, (nec), 0013
Physician, 00610
Physicist, 00120
Physicists, 0012
Physiotherapist, 00760
Physiotherapists and Occupational Therapists, 0076
Piano Tuner, 09410
Plasterer, 09550
Plasterers, 0955
Plumber, 08710
Plumbers and Pipe Fitters, 0871
PLUMBERS, WELDERS, SHEET METAL AND STRUCTURAL METAL PREPARERS AND ERECTORS, 087
Police Officer, 05821
Policeman, 05820
Policemen and Detectives, 0582
Polishing Machine Operator, 08351
Political Party Worker, 03992
Politician, Party Official, 02196
Porter, 09712
Post Office Clerk, 03315
Postmaster, 03520
Postmasters, 0352
Potter, 08920
Potters and Related Clay and Abrasive Formers, 0892
Poultry Farm Workers, 0626
Power Crane Operator, 09730
Power Lineman, 08570
Power Station Operator, 09610
Power-Generating Machinery Operators, 0961
Pre-Primary Education Teachers, 0134
Pre-Primary Teacher, 01340
Primary Education Teachers, 0133
Principal, Primary Principal, 01391
Printer, 09210

PRINTERS AND RELATED WORKERS, 092
Printers and Related Workers, (nec), 0929
Printing Engravers (Except Photoengravers), 0924
Printing Pressman, 09220
Printing Pressmen, 0922
Printing Worker, (nec), 09290
Prison Guard, 05891
Producers, Performing Arts, 0174
PRODUCTION AND RELATED WORKERS, (NEC), 094
PRODUCTION AND RELATED WORKERS, TRANSPORT EQUIPMENT OPERATORS AND LABORERS,07
Production Managers (except Farm), 0212
PRODUCTION SUPERVISORS AND GENERAL FOREMEN, 070
Production Supervisors and General Foremen, 0700
Professional Accountant, 01101
Professional Athlete, 01800
Professional Midwife, Midwife, 00730
Professional Midwives, 0073
Professional Nurse, Nurse, 00710
Professional Nurses, 0071
PROFESSIONAL, TECHNICAL, AND RELATED WORKERS, 00
PROFESSIONAL, TECHNICAL, AND RELATED WORKERS, (NEC), 019
Proofreader, 03991
PROTECTIVE SERVICE WORKERS, 058
Protective Service Workers, (nec), 0589
Provincial Governor, 02011
Psychologist, 01921
Pub Keeper, 05104
Public Prosecutor, 01211
Public Relations Man, 01593
Pulp Writer, 01551
Purchasing Agent, 04221
Quality Checker, 09490
Quarry Worker, 07112
Radio and Television Repairmen, 0854
Radio Operator, 03802
Radio, TV Announcer, 01790
Radio, TV Repairman, 08540
Railroad Conductor, 03600
Railway Baggagemen, 03942
Railway Brakemen, Signalmen, and Shunters, 0984
Railway Crossing Guard, 09891
Railway Engine Drivers and Firemen, 0983
Railway Stationmaster, 03510
Railway Stationmasters, 0351
Railway Switchman, Brakeman, 09840
Railway Track Worker, 09994
Railway, Airport Porter, 09713
Real Estate Agent, 04411
Receptionist, 03940
Receptionists and Travel Agency Clerks, 0394
Reinforced-Concreters, Cement Finishers and Terrazzo Workers, 0952
Religious Reciter, 01412
Religious Teacher, 01490
Restaurant Owner, 05100
Retail Manager, 04000
Riggers and Cable Splicers, 0972

Road Construction Laborer, 09998
Road Machinery Operator, 09740
Rolling Mill Operator, 07220
Roofer, 09530
Roofers, 0953
Routeman, 04525
RUBBER AND PLASTICS PRODUCT MAKERS, 090
Rubber and Plastics Product Makers (except Tire Makers and Tire Vulcanizers), 0901
Sales Clerk, 04510
Sales Demonstrator, 04514
Sales Engineer, 04310
Sales Manager, 04210
Sales Supervisors, 0421
SALES SUPERVISORS AND BUYERS, 042
SALES WORKERS, 04
SALES WORKERS, (NEC), 049
Sales Workers, (nec), 0490
Salesman, Shop Assistants, and Demonstrators, 0451
SALESMEN, SHOP ASSISTANTS, AND RELATED WORKERS, 045
Sanitary Officer, 00794
Saw Sharpener, 08350
Sawyer in Saw Mill, 07320
Sawyers, Plywood Makers, and Related Wood-Processing Workers, 0732
Scientist, 00130
Sculptors, Painters, and Related Artists, 0161
SCULPTORS, PAINTERS, PHOTOGRAPHERS, AND RELATED CREATIVE ARTISTS, 016
Seaman, 09810
Secondary Education Teachers, 0132
Secondary School Principal, 01394
Secretary, 03211
Semiskilled Workers, (nec), 0997
Servant, 05400
Service Station Manager, 04001
SERVICE WORKERS, 05
SERVICE WORKERS, (NEC), 059
Settler, 06116
Sewers and Embroiderers, 0795
Sewing Machine Operator, 07950
Sexton, 05512
Sharecropper, 06114
Sheet Metal Worker, 08730
Sheet Metal Workers, 0873
Ship's Engine-Room Hand, 09820
Ship's Engineer, 00430
Ship's Officer, 00420
Shipping Clerk, 03911
Ship's Deck Officers and Pilots, 0042
Ship's Deck Ratings, Barge Crews, and Boatmen, 0981
Ships' Engine-Room Ratings, 0982
Ships' Engineers, 0043
Shoe Cutters, Lasters, Sewers, and Related Workers, 0802
Shoe Shiner, 05995
Shoemaker, Repairer, 08010
SHOEMAKERS AND LEATHER GOODS MAKERS, 080
Shoemakers and Shoe Repairers, 0801

Shopkeeper, 04100
Skilled Construction Worker, 09594
Skilled Worker, 09950
Skilled Workers, (nec), 0995
Sleeping Car Porter, 03602
Small Boat Officer, 00421
Small Farmer, 06112
Small Transport Operator, 09854
Smuggler, 04107
Social Scientist, (nec), 01924
Social Worker, 01930
Social Workers, 0193
Sociologist, 01920
Sociologists, Anthropologists, and Related Scientists, 0192
Soda Fountain Clerk, 05314
Soldier, 10003
Sound Equipment Operators and Cinema Projectionists, 0862
Special Education Teachers, 0135
Specialized Farmer, 06120
Specialized Farmers, 0612
Specialized Agricultural Worker, (nec), 06290
Specialized Law Officer, 05823
Specialized Mine Worker, 07111
Spinner, 07520
Spinners and Winders, 0752
SPINNERS, WEAVERS, KNITTERS, DYERS, AND RELATED WORKERS, 075
Spinners, Weavers, Knitters, Dyers, and Related Workers, (nec), 0759
Star Actor, 01731
STATIONARY ENGINE AND RELATED EQUIPMENT OPERATORS, 096
Stationary Engine and Related Equipment Operators, (nec), 0969
Stationary Engineer, 09690
Statistical and Mathematical Technicians, 0084
Statistician, 00810
Statisticians, 0081
STATISTICIANS, MATHEMATICIANS, SYSTEMS ANALYSTS, AND RELATED TECHNICIANS, 008
Steel Mill Worker, 07210
STENOGRAPHERS, TYPISTS, AND CARD- AND TAPE-PUNCHING OPERATORS, 032
Stenographers, Typists, and Teletypists, 0321
Stereotypers and Electrotypers, 0923
Steward, 05200
Still and Reactor Operators, 0744
Stockbroker, 04412
Stock Clerks, 0391
Stockroom Attendant, 03910
STONE CUTTERS AND CARVERS, 082
Stone Cutters and Carvers, 0820
Street Sweeper, 09995
Street Vendor, Peddler, 04521
Street Vendors, Canvassers, and News Vendors, 0452
Structural Metal Preparers and Erectors, 0874
Structural Steel Worker, 08740
Sugar Processors and Refiners, 0772
Sugar Boiler, 07720
Supervisor, 07001
Supreme Court Justice, 01221
Surveyor, 00310

Surveyor's Assistant, 00330
Surveyors, 0031
Systems Analysts, 0083
Tailor, 07910
Tailors and Dressmakers, 0791
TAILORS, DRESSMAKERS, SEWERS, UPHOLSTERERS, AND RELATED WORKERS, 079
Tailors, Dressmakers, Sewers, Upholsterers, and Related Workers, 0799
Tanners and Fellmongers, 0761
TANNERS, FELLMONGERS, AND PELT DRESSERS, 076
Tax Collector, 03105
Taxi Driver, 09851
Taxidermist, 09492
Tea, Coffee, and Cocoa Preparers, 0777
Teacher, Primary Teacher, 01330
Teacher's Aide, 01393
TEACHERS, 013
Teachers, (nec), 0139
Technical Salesmen and Service Advisors, 0431
TECHNICAL SALESMEN, COMMERCIAL TRAVELERS, AND MANUFACTURERS' AGENTS, 043
Technician, 01990
Telegraph Operator, 03801
Telephone and Telegraph Installers, 0856
TELEPHONE AND TELEGRAPH OPERATORS, 038
Telephone and Telegraph Operators, 0380
Telephone Installer, 08560
Telephone Operator, 03800
Telephone Solicitor, 04523
Tenant Farmer, 06113
Textile Mill Worker, 07590
Ticket Seller, 03316
Timber Cruiser, 06321
Tire Makers and Vulcanizers, 0902
Tobacco Preparers, 0781
TOBACCO PREPARERS AND TOBACCO PRODUCT MAKERS, 078
Tobacco Preparers and Tobacco Product Makers, (nec), 0789
Tobacco Worker, (nec), 07890
Tombstone Carver, 08200
Tool and Die Maker, 08320
Toolmakers, Metal Patternmakers and Metal Markers, 0832
Tracer, 00321
Tractor Driver, 06280
Translator, 01950
TRANSPORT AND COMMUNICATIONS SUPERVISORS, 035
Transport and Communications Supervisors, (nec), 0359
TRANSPORT CONDUCTORS, 036
Transport Conductors, 0360
TRANSPORT EQUIPMENT OPERATORS, 098
Transport Equipment Operators, (nec), 0989
Transportation Agent, 03941
Travel Agent, 03943
Traveling Salesman, 04321
Tree Surgeon, 06322
Truck Driver's Helper, 09855
Turner, 08331
TV Cameraman, 01631
Typist, Stenographer, 03210

Uncertified Nurse, 00720
Uncertified Pharmacist, 00680
Unclassifiable Occupation, 12000
UNCLASSIFIABLE OCCUPATIONS, 12
UNCLASSIFIABLE OCCUPATIONS, 120
Unclassifiable Occupations, 1200
Undertaker, 05920
Undertakers and Embalmers, 0592
Union Official, 02197
University Administrator, 01311
University and Higher Education Teachers, 0131
University Professor, 01310
Unpaid Family Farm Worker, 06117
Unskilled Construction Laborer, 09596
Unskilled Factory Laborer, 09991
Unskilled Garage Worker, 08494
Upholsterer, 07960
Upholsterers and Related Workers, 0796
Utility Company Salesman, 04311
Vehicle Body Builder, 08733
Veterinarians, 0065
Veterinary Assistants, 0066
Village Head, 02015
Vocational Teacher, 01390
Wagoneer, 09861
Waiter, 05320
Waiters, Bartenders, and Related Workers, 0532
Warehouse Hand, 09711
Watch Maker, Repairman, 08420
Watch, Clock, and Precision Instrument Makers, 0842
Watchman, 05890
Weaver, 07540
Weavers and Related Workers, 0754
Weaving- and Knitting-Machine Setters and Pattern-Card Preparers, 0753
Welder, 08720
Welders and Flame-Cutters, 0872
Well Drillers, Borers, and Related Workers, 0713
Whaler, 06490
Wholesale Distributor, 04106
Window Display Artist, 01622
Window Washer, 05522
WOOD PREPARATION WORKERS AND PAPER MAKERS, 073
Wood Treaters, 0731
Wood Vehicle Builder, 09543
Woodworking-Machine Operators, 0812
WORKERS IN RELIGION, 014
Workers in Religion, nec, 0149
WORKING PROPRIETORS (CATERING AND LODGING SERVICES), 051
Working Proprietors (Catering and Lodging Services), 0510
WORKING PROPRIETORS (WHOLESALE AND RETAIL TRADE), 041
Working Proprietors (Wholesale and Retail Trade), 0410

Appendix C

Standard Scale Scores for Other Occupational Classifications

STANDARD SCALE SCORES FOR ISCO FIRST EDITION

Since many compilations of occupational data, particularly those generated in the 1960 round of national censuses, utilize classifications based on the first edition of the *International Standard Classification of Occupations* (International Labour Office, 1958a), Standard Scale scores are presented for the categories of this classification as a convenience to research workers.

The scores were generated by a two-step procedure. Like the revised ISCO, upon which the Standard Scale was based, the first edition of the ISCO is a nested scheme of major, minor, and unit groups. Thus, the first step was to create scores for the unit groups. This was done by utilizing the conversation table provided in the revised edition (International Labour Office, 1969a:289–307) to allocate each "occupation" line in the Standard Scale to a unit group in the first edition of the ISCO. All the scores for occupation lines matching each first edition unit group were then simply averaged, omitting scores for highly atypical titles just as was done in creating unit group scores for the Standard Scale.

To derive scores for minor and major groups, the same procedure was followed as in the Standard Scale. Both simple and weighted averages of unit group scores were computed, the weighted averages based on the labor force distributions of Sweden and India (two countries chosen as examples of the least and most industrialized nations of the world). With the exception of two minor groups, "0–6 Teachers," and "2–9 Other Clerical Workers," the weighted and unweighted averages were very close and hence the unweighted averages were utilized for the sake of simplicity, just as in the derivation of minor group scores for the Standard Scale. The major group scores, however, were derived from the weighted unit group scores, again just as with the Standard Scale.

Appendix C.1

Standard Scale Scores for the International Standard Classification
of Occupations (first edition, 1958)

Major, Minor, and Unit Groups	Major	Minor	Unit
MAJOR GROUP 0: PROFESSIONAL, TECHNICAL, AND RELATED WORKERS	58		
0-0 Architects, Engineers, and Surveyors		64	
0-01 Architects			72
0-02 Engineers			62
0-03 Surveyors			58
0-1 Chemists, Physicists, Geologists, and Other Physical Scientists		72	
0-11 Chemists			69
0-12 Physicists			76
0-19 Physical Scientists Not Elsewhere Classified			72
0-2 Biologists, Veterinarians, Agronomists, and Related Scientists		62	
0-21 Veterinarians			61
0-22 Biologists and Animal Scientists Not Elsewhere Classified			68
0-23 Agronomists, Silviculturists and Horticultural Scientists			56
0-3 Physicians, Surgeons, and Dentists		74	
0-31 Physicians and Surgeons			78
0-32 Dentists			70
0-4 Nurses and Midwives		48	
0-41 Nurses, Professional			54
0-42 Midwives			46
0-49 Nurses Not Elsewhere Classified			44
0-5 Professional Medical Workers Not Elsewhere Classified and Medical Technicians		57	
0-51 Pharmacists			64
0-52 Optometrists			62
0-53 Medical Technicians			50
0-59 Professional Medical Workers Not Elsewhere Classified			51

Appendix C.1 (Continued)

Major, Minor, and Unit Groups	Major	Minor	Unit
0-6 Teachers		60	
0-61 University Teachers			78
0-69 Teachers Not Elsewhere Classified			59
0-7 Clergy and Related Members of Religious Orders		50	
0-71 Clergy and Related Members of Religious Orders			50
0-8 Jurists		70	
0-81 Jurists			70
0-9 Artists, Writers and Related Workers		50	
0-91 Painters, Sculptors and Related Creative Artists			51
0-92 Authors, Journalists, and Related Writers			54
0-93 Actors, Musicians, Dancers, and Related Workers			46
0-X Draftsmen, and Science and Engineering Technicians Not Elsewhere Classified		52	
0-X1 Draftsmen			55
0-X9 Science and Engineering Technicians Not Elsewhere Classified and Laboratory Assistants			48
0-Y Other Professional, Technical, and Related Workers		57	
0-Y1 Accountants, Professional			62
0-Y2 Social Workers			52
0-Y3 Librarians and Archivists			54
0-Y4 Economists, Actuaries, and Statisticians			58
0-Y9 Professional, Technical, and Related Workers Not Elsewhere Classified			59
MAJOR GROUP 1: ADMINISTRATIVE, EXECUTIVE AND MANAGERIAL WORKERS	55		
1-0 Administrators and Executive Officials, Government		55	
1-01 Administrators and Executive Officials, Government			55
1-1 Directors, Managers and Working Proprietors		55	
1-11 Directors, Managers and Working Proprietors, Mining and Quarrying, Manufacturing, Construction, Electricity, Gas, Water and Sanitary Services			59

Code	Occupation	Major	Sub	Unit
1-12	Directors and Managers, Wholesale and Retail Trade			45
1-13	Directors, Managers and Working Proprietors, Banks and Other Financial Institutions, Insurance and Real Estate			64
1-14	Directors, Managers and Working Proprietors, Transport, Storage and Communication			60
1-15	Directors, Managers and Working Proprietors, Service Industries			48
1-19	Directors, Managers and Working Proprietors Not Elsewhere Classified			52
	MAJOR GROUP 2: CLERICAL WORKERS	40		
2-0	Bookkeepers and Cashiers		41	
2-01	Bookkeepers and Cashiers			41
2-1	Stenographers and Typists		48	
2-11	Stenographers and Typists			48
2-9	Other Clerical Workers		39	
2-91	Office-Machine Operators			49
2-99	Clerical Workers Not Elsewhere Classified			38
	MAJOR GROUP 3: SALES WORKERS	42		
3-0	Working Proprietors, Wholesale and Retail Trade		48	
3-01	Working Proprietors, Wholesale Trade			50
3-02	Working Proprietors, Retail Trade			46
3-1	Insurance and Real Estate Salesmen, Salesmen of Securities and Services, and Auctioneers		47	
3-11	Insurance and Real Estate Salesmen, Salesmen of Securities and Services, and Auctioneers			47
3-2	Commercial Travelers and Manufacturers' Agents		47	
3-21	Commercial Travelers and Manufacturers' Agents			47
3-3	Salesmen, Shop Assistants, and Related Workers		34	
3-31	Salesmen and Shop Assistants			35
3-32	Street Vendors, Canvassers, and Newsvendors			24
3-39	Salesmen, Shop Assistants, and Related Workers Not Elsewhere Classified			42

Appendix C.1 (Continued)

Major, Minor, and Unit Groups	Major	Minor	Unit
MAJOR GROUP 4: FARMERS, FISHERMEN, HUNTERS, LOGGERS, AND RELATED WORKERS	35		
4-0 Farmers and Farm Managers		43	
4-01 Farmers and Farm Managers			43
4-1 Farm Workers Not Elsewhere Classified		23	
4-11 Farm Workers Not Elsewhere Classified			23
4-2 Hunters and Related Workers		6	
4-21 Hunters and Related Workers			6
4-3 Fishermen and Related Workers		35	
4-31 Fishermen and Related Workers			35
4-4 Loggers and Other Forestry Workers		30	
4-41 Loggers and Other Forestry Workers			30
MAJOR GROUP 5: MINERS, QUARRYMEN AND RELATED WORKERS	32		
5-0 Miners and Quarrymen		34	
5-01 Miners and Quarrymen			34
5-1 Well Drillers and Related Workers		31	
5-11 Well Drillers and Related Workers			31
5-2 Mineral Treaters		32	
5-21 Mineral Treaters			32
5-9 Miners, Quarrymen and Related Workers Not Elsewhere Classified		27	
5-99 Miners, Quarrymen and Related Workers Not Elsewhere Classified			27
MAJOR GROUP 6: WORKERS IN TRANSPORT AND COMMUNICATION OCCUPATIONS	32		
6-0 Deck Officers, Engineer Officers, and Pilots, Ship		55	
6-01 Deck Officers and Pilots, ship			50
6-02 Engineer Officers, Ship			60

284

Appendix C.1 (Continued)

Major, Minor, and Unit Groups	Major	Minor	Unit
MAJOR GROUP 7/8: CRAFTSMEN, PRODUCTION-PROCESS WORKERS, AND LABORERS NOT ELSEWHERE CLASSIFIED	31		
7-0 Spinners, Weavers, Knitters, Dyers, and Related Workers		30	
7-01 Fiber Preparers			29
7-02 Spinners and Winders, Textile			34
7-03 Weavers, Loom Fixers, and Loom Preparers			30
7-04 Knitters and Knitting Machine Setters			29
7-05 Pattern-Card Preparers			30
7-06 Bleachers, Dyers and Finishers of Textiles			25
7-09 Textile Fabric and Related Product Makers Not Elsewhere Classified			30
7-1 Tailors, Cutters, Furriers, and Related Workers		34	
7-11 Tailors, Dressmakers, and Garment Makers			40
7-12 Fur Tailors and Related Workers			35
7-13 Milliners and Hatmakers			32
7-14 Upholsterers and Related Workers			31
7-15 Patternmakers, Markers, and Cutters (Textile Products, Leather Garments, and Gloves)			41
7-16 Sewers and Embroiderers (Textile and Fur Products, Leather Garments, and Gloves)			26
7-19 Apparel and Related Product Makers Not Elsewhere Classified			34
7-2 Leather Cutters, Lasters, and Sewers (except Gloves and Garments) and Related Workers		25	
7-21 Shoemakers and Shoe Repairers			28
7-22 Cutters, Lasters, Sewers (Footwear), and Related Workers			28
7-23 Harness and Saddle Makers			22
7-29 Leather-Product Makers Not Elsewhere Classified			22
7-3 Furnacemen, Rollers, Drawers, Molders, and Related Metal Making and Treating Workers		38	
7-31 Furnacemen, Metal			45
7-32 Annealers, Temperers, and Related Heat Treaters			38

Code		Description		
7-33		Rolling-Mill Operators, Metal		36
7-34		Blacksmiths, Hammersmiths, and Forgemen		35
7-35		Molders and Coremakers		33
7-36		Metal Drawers and Extruders		38
7-39		Metal Making and Treating Workers Not Elsewhere Classified		38
7-4	45	Precision-Instrument Makers, Watchmakers, Jewelers, and Related Workers		
7-41		Precision-Instrument Makers, Watch and Clock Makers, and Repairmen		50
7-42		Jewelers, Goldsmiths, and Silversmiths		43
7-43		Jewelery Engravers		43
7-5	36	Toolmakers, Machinists, Plumbers, Welders, Platers, and Related Workers		
7-50		Fitter-Machinists, Toolmakers, and Machine Tool Setters		39
7-51		Machine-Tool Operators		38
7-52		Fitter-Assemblers and Machine Erectors (except Electrical and Precision-Instrument Fitter-Assemblers)		42
7-53		Mechanics-Repairmen (except Electrical and Precision-Instrument Repairmen)		39
7-54		Sheet-Metal Workers		35
7-55		Plumbers and Pipe Fitters		34
7-56		Welders and Flame Cutters		39
7-57		Metal-Plate and Structural-Metal Workers		38
7-58		Electro-Platers, Dip Platers and Related Workers		28
7-59		Metal Workers Not Elsewhere Classified		31
7-6	39	Electricians and Related Electrical and Electronics Workers		
7-61		Electricians, Electrical Repairmen, and Related Electrical Workers		43
7-62		Electrical and Electronics Fitters		38
7-63		Mechanics-Repairmen, Radio and Television		42
7-64		Installers and Repairmen, Telephone and Telegraph		35
7-65		Linemen and Cable Jointers		36
7-69		Electrical and Electronics Workers Not Elsewhere Classified		41
7-7	34	Carpenters, Joiners, Cabinetmakers, Coopers, and Related Workers		
7-71		Carpenters and Joiners		37
7-72		Cabinetmakers		40
7-73		Sawyers and Woodworking Machine Setters and Operators		30
7-79		Woodworkers Not Elsewhere Classified		31

Major, Minor, and Unit Groups	Major	Minor	Unit
7-8 Painters and Paperhangers		28	
7-81 Painters and Paperhangers, Construction and Maintenance			28
7-82 Painters (except Construction and Maintenance)			29
7-9 Bricklayers, Plasterers, and Construction Workers Not Elsewhere Classified		30	
7-91 Bricklayers, Stonemasons, and Tile Setters			34
7-92 Plasterers			31
7-93 Cement Finishers and Terrazzo Workers			34
7-94 Insulation Appliers			28
7-95 Glaziers			26
7-99 Construction Workers Not Elsewhere Classified			29
8-0 Compositors, Pressmen, Engravers, Bookbinders, and Related Workers		42	
8-01 Compositors and Typesetters			42
8-02 Pressmen, Printing			41
8-03 Stereotypers and Electrotypers			41
8-04 Engravers, Printing (except Photo-Engravers)			41
8-05 Photo-Engravers			46
8-06 Bookbinders and Related Workers			32
8-09 Printing Workers Not Elsewhere Classified			52
8-1 Potters, Kilnmen, Glass and Clay Formers, and Related Workers		31	
8-11 Glass Formers, Cutters, Grinders, and Finishers			37
8-12 Potters and Related Clay and Abrasive Formers			25
8-13 Furnacemen and Kilnmen, Glass and Ceramics			31
8-14 Decorators, Glass and Ceramics			31
8-19 Glass and Ceramics Workers Not Elsewhere Classified			31
8-2 Millers, Bakers, Brewmasters and Related Food and Beverage Workers		32	
8-21 Millers, Grain and Related Products			33
8-22 Bakers and Pastrycooks			33
8-23 Sugar and Chocolate Confectionery Makers			33
8-24 Brewers, Wine Makers and Related Workers			34

Appendix C.1 (Continued)

Major, Minor, and Unit Groups	Major	Minor	Unit
8-73 Riggers and Cable Splicers			32
8-74 Operators of Earth-Moving and Other Construction Machinery Not Elsewhere Classified			32
8-75 Material-Handling Equipment Operators			28
8-76 Oilers and Greasers (Stationary Engines, Motor Vehicles, and Related Equipment)			18
8-8 Longshoremen and Related Freight Handlers		19	
8-81 Longshoremen and Related Freight Handlers			19
8-9 Laborers Not Elsewhere Classified		18	
8-99 Laborers Not Elsewhere Classified			18
MAJOR GROUP 9: SERVICE, SPORT AND RECREATION WORKERS	27		
9-0 Fire Fighters, Policemen, Guards and Related Workers		35	
9-01 Fire Fighters and Related Workers			35
9-02 Policemen and Detectives			40
9-09 Guards and Related Workers Not Elsewhere Classified			30
9-1 Housekeepers, Cooks, Maids and Related Workers		30	
9-11 Housekeepers, Housekeeping Stewards, and Matrons			37
9-12 Cooks			31
9-19 Maids, Valets, and Related Service Workers Not Elsewhere Classified			22
9-2 Waiters, Bartenders, and Related Workers		21	
9-21 Waiters, Bartenders, and Related Workers			21
9-3 Building Caretakers, Cleaners, and Related Workers		22	
9-31 Building Caretakers			25
9-32 Charworkers, Cleaners, and Related Workers			20
9-4 Barbers, Hairdressers, Beauticians, and Related Workers		32	
9-41 Barbers, Hairdressers, Beauticians, and Related Workers			32
9-5 Launderers, Dry Cleaners and Pressers		22	
9-51 Launderers, Dry Cleaners and Pressers			22

STANDARD SCALE SCORES FOR
UNITED STATES CENSUSES

Appendices C.2, C.3, and C.4 give Standard Scale scores for the detailed occupation lines in the United States Census Bureau's 1950, 1960, and 1970 occupational classifications (United States Bureau of the Census, 1950, 1960, 1971a). These are provided as a convenience to research workers who may wish to assign Standard Scale scores to data initially coded with the three-digit codes of the United States Census classifications.

The procedure for creating these scores was the same in each case. Each line in the detailed Census classification was matched to the line(s) from the Standard Scale that provided the closest fit. Ordinarily, matches were made to the "occupation" lines but where no precisely corresponding "occupation" line was available, the match was made to the best fitting "unit group" line or the best fitting combination of lines. The score (or average score) from the Standard Scale was then assigned to the Unted States Census category.

Scores for the major groups in the United States Census classification were then derived by computing a weighted average of the scores for the detailed occupation lines, the weights corresponding to the proportion of the total labor force in each category. The use of the total labor force rather than the male labor force was based on the desirability of creating a scale that can be used to assign occupational prestige scores to both men and women. As was indicated in Chapters 2 and 9, there is substantial evidence that the prestige of occupations is not affected by the sex of incumbents.

Standard Scale Scores for the 1950 U. S. Census
Detailed Occupational Classification

Occupation Code		Standard Scale Score
	PROFESSIONAL, TECHNICAL, AND KINDRED WORKERS[1]	59
000	Accountants and auditors	62
001	Actors and actresses	52
002	Airplane pilots and navigators	66
003	Architects	72
004	Artists and art teachers	56
005	Athletes	48
006	Authors	62
007	Chemists	69
008	Chiropractors	62
009	Clergymen	60
	College presidents, professors, and instructors (nec)	
010	College presidents and deans	86
012	Professors and instructors, agricultural sciences	78
013	Professors and instructors, biological sciences	78
014	Professors and instructors, chemistry	78
015	Professors and instructors, economics	78
016	Professors and instructors, engineering	78
017	Professors and instructors, geology and geophysics	78
018	Professors and instructors, mathematics	78
019	Professors and instructors, medical sciences	78
023	Professors and instructors, physics	78
024	Professors and instructors, psychology	78
025	Professors and instructors, statistics	78
026	Professors and instructors, natural sciences (nec)	78
027	Professors and instructors, social sciences (nec)	78
028	Professors and instructors, nonscientific subjects	78
029	Professors and instructors, subject not specified	78
031	Dancers and dancing teachers	40
032	Dentists	70
033	Designers	56
034	Dietitians and nutritionists	52
035	Draftsmen	55
036	Editors and reporters	56
041	Engineers, aeronautical	66
042	Engineers, chemical	66
043	Engineers, civil	70
044	Engineers, electrical	65
045	Engineers, industrial	54
046	Engineers, mechanical	66
047	Engineers, metallurgical, and metallurgists	60
048	Engineers, mining	63
049	Engineers (nec)	55
051	Entertainers (nec)	33
052	Farm and home management advisers	53
053	Foresters and conservationists	42
054	Funeral directors and embalmers	34
055	Lawyers and judges	73
056	Librarians	54

057	Musicians and music teachers	45
	Natural scientists (nec)	
061	Agricultural scientists	58
062	Biological scientists	68
063	Geologists and geophysicists	67
067	Mathematicians	69
068	Physicists	76
069	Miscellaneous natural scientists	72
058	Nurses, professional	54
059	Nurses, student professional	49
070	Optometrists	62
071	Osteopaths	62
072	Personnel and labor relations workers	56
073	Pharmacists	64
074	Photographers	46
075	Physicians and surgeons	78
076	Radio operators	49
077	Recreation and group workers	49
078	Religious workers	51
079	Social and welfare workers, except group	56
	Social scientists	
081	Economists	60
082	Psychologists	66
083	Statisticians and actuaries	58
084	Miscellaneous social scientists	68
091	Sports instructors and officials	50
092	Surveyors	58
093	Teachers	58
094	Technicians, medical and dental	53
095	Technicians, testing	58
096	Technicians (nec)	58
097	Therapists and healers (nec)	44
098	Veterinarians	61
099	Professional, technical, and kindred workers (nec)	59

	FARMERS AND FARM MANAGERS	40
100	Farmers (owners and tenants)	40
123	Farm managers	54

	MANAGERS, OFFICIALS, AND PROPRIETORS, EXCEPT FARM	52
200	Buyers and department heads, store	48
201	Buyers and shippers, farm products	39
203	Conductors, railroad	39
204	Credit men	49
205	Floormen and floor managers, store	52
210	Inspectors, public administration	52
230	Managers and superintendents, building	47
240	Officers, pilots, pursers, and engineers, ship	50
250	Officials and administrators (nec), public administration	60
260	Officials, lodge, society, union, etc.	50
270	Postmasters	58
280	Purchasing agents and buyers (nec)	50
290	Managers, officials, and proprietors (nec)	52

	CLERICAL AND KINDRED WORKERS	43
300	Agents (nec)	43

301	Attendants and assistants, library	41
302	Attendants, physician's and dentist's office	42
304	Baggagemen, transportation	23
305	Bank tellers	48
310	Bookkeepers	49
320	Cashiers	31
321	Collectors, bill and account	27
322	Dispatchers and starters, vehicle	37
325	Express messengers and railway mail clerks	30
335	Mail carriers	33
340	Messengers and office boys	26
341	Office machine operators	46
342	Shipping and receiving clerks	29
350	Stenographers, typists, and secretaries	48
360	Telegraph messengers	26
365	Telegraph operators	45
370	Telephone operators	38
380	Ticket, station, and express agents	36
390	Clerical and kindred workers (nec)	43
	SALES WORKERS	38
400	Advertising agents and salesmen	42
410	Auctioneers	39
420	Demonstrators	28
430	Hucksters and peddlers	22
450	Insurance agents and brokers	44
460	Newsboys	14
470	Real estate agents and brokers	49
480	Stock and bond salesmen	56
490	Salesmen and sales clerks (nec)	38
	CRAFTSMEN, FOREMEN, AND KINDRED WORKERS	39
500	Bakers	33
501	Blacksmiths	34
502	Bookbinders	32
503	Boilermakers	31
504	Brickmasons, stonemasons, and tile setters	34
505	Cabinetmakers	40
510	Carpenters	37
511	Cement and concrete finishers	34
512	Compositors and typesetters	42
513	Cranemen, derrickmen, and hoistmen	39
514	Decorators and window dressers	38
515	Electricians	44
520	Electrotypers and sterotypers	41
521	Engravers, except photoengravers	36
522	Excavating, grading, and road machinery operators	32
523	Foreman (nec)	39
524	Forgemen and hammermen	36
525	Furriers	35
530	Glaziers	26
531	Heat treaters, annealers, and temperers	38
532	Inspectors, scalers, and graders, log and lumber	31
533	Inspectors (nec)	39
534	Jewelers, watchmakers, goldsmiths, and silversmiths	42

535	Jobsetters, metal	40
540	Linemen and servicemen, telegraph, telephone, and power	36
541	Locomotive engineers	43
542	Locomotive firemen	33
543	Loom fixers	30
544	Machinists	43
545	Mechanics and repairmen, airplane	50
550	Mechanics and repairmen, automobile	43
551	Mechanics and repairmen, office machine	43
552	Mechanics and repairmen, radio and television	42
553	Mechanics and repairmen, railroad and car shop	43
554	Mechanics and repairmen, (nec)	43
555	Millers, grain, flour, feed, etc.	33
560	Millwrights	40
561	Molders, metal	38
562	Motion picture projectionists	34
563	Opticians and lens grinders and polishers	49
564	Painters, construction and maintenance	31
565	Paperhangers	24
570	Pattern and model makers, except paper	39
571	Photoengravers and lithographers	46
572	Piano and organ tuners and repairmen	33
573	Plasterers	31
574	Plumbers and pipe fitters	34
575	Pressmen and plate printers, printing	41
580	Rollers and roll hands, metal	36
581	Roofers and slaters	31
582	Shoemakers and repairers, except factory	28
583	Stationary engineers	34
584	Stone cutters and stone carvers	38
585	Structural metal workers	44
590	Tailors and tailoresses	40
591	Tinsmiths, coppersmiths, and sheet metal workers	34
592	Tool makers, and die makers and setters	40
593	Upholsterers	31
594	Craftsmen and kindred workers (nec)	39
595	Members of the armed forces	39

OPERATIVES AND KINDRED WORKERS[2]

		30
600	Apprentice auto mechanics	38
601	Apprentice bricklayers and masons	29
602	Apprentice carpenters	32
603	Apprentice electricians	39
604	Apprentice machinists and toolmakers	36
605	Apprentice·mechanics, except auto	38
610	Apprentice plumbers and pipe fitters	29
611	Apprentices, building trades (nec)	23
612	Apprentices, metalworking trades (nec)	37
613	Apprentices, printing trades	36
614	Apprentices, other specified trades	37
615	Apprentices, trade not specified	37
620	Asbestos and insulation workers	28
621	Attendants, auto service and parking	24
622	Blasters and powdermen	34
623	Boatmen, canalmen, and lock keepers	23

624	Brakemen, railroad	29
625	Bus drivers	32
630	Chainmen, rodmen, and axmen, surveying	20
631	Conductors, bus and street railway	26
632	Deliverymen and routemen	24
633	Dressmakers and seamstresses, except factory	39
634	Dyers	25
635	Filers, grinders, and polishers, metal	27
640	Fruit, nut, and vegetable graders and packers, except factory	34
641	Furnacemen, smeltermen, and pourers	45
642	Heaters, metal	38
643	Laundry and dry cleaning operatives	22
644	Meatcutters, except slaughter and packinghouse	31
645	Milliners	32
650	Mine operatives and laborers	32
660	Motormen, mine, factory, logging camp, etc.	27
661	Motormen, street, subway, and elevated railway	32
662	Oilers and greasers, except auto	30
670	Painters, except construction and maintenance	29
671	Photographic process workers	36
672	Power station operators	42
673	Sailors and deck hands	35
674	Sawyers	30
675	Spinners, textile	34
680	Stationary firemen	34
681	Switchmen, railroad	29
682	Taxicab drivers and chauffeurs	28
683	Truck and tractor drivers	32
684	Weavers, textile	30
685	Welders and flame-cutters	39
690	Operatives and kindred workers (nec)	30

	PRIVATE HOUSEHOLD WORKERS	19
700	Housekeepers, private household	28
710	Laundresses, private household	22
720	Private household workers (nec)	17

	SERVICE WORKERS, EXCEPT PRIVATE HOUSEHOLD	29
730	Attendants, hospital and other institution	42
731	Attendants, professional and personal service (nec)	29
732	Attendants, recreation and amusement	20
740	Barbers, beauticians, and manicurists	32
750	Bartenders	23
751	Bootblacks	12
752	Boarding and lodging house keepers	22
753	Charwomen and cleaners	20
754	Cooks, except private household	31
760	Counter and fountain workers	16
761	Elevator operators	24
762	Firemen, fire protection	35
763	Guards, watchmen, and doorkeepers	30
764	Housekeepers and stewards, except private household	37
770	Janitors and sextons	26

771	Marshals and constables	52
772	Midwives	46
773	Policemen and detectives	40
780	Porters	24
781	Practical nurses	44
782	Sheriffs and bailiffs	50
783	Ushers, recreation and amusement	20
784	Waiters and waitresses	23
785	Watchmen (crossing) and bridge tenders	28
790	Service workers, except private household (nec)	29

FARM LABORERS AND FOREMEN — 25

810	Farm foremen	41
820	Farm laborers, wage workers	22
830	Farm laborers, unpaid family workers	34
840	Farm service laborers, self-employed	31

LABORERS EXCEPT FARM AND MINE[2] — 20

910	Fishermen and oystermen	32
920	Garage laborers and car washers and greasers	18
930	Gardeners, except farm, and groundskeepers	21
940	Longshoremen and stevedores	21
950	Lumbermen, raftsmen, and woodchoppers	18
960	Teamsters	22
970	Laborers (nec)	20

995   OCCUPATION NOT REPORTED

[1] Each major group score is the weighted average of all occupation lines within the major group, weighted by the total 1950 experienced civilian labor force.

[2] Mine laborers are included in the major group "Operatives and kindred workers."

Standard Scale Scores for the 1960 U. S. Census
Detailed Occupational Classification

Occu-pation Code		Standard Scale Score
	PROFESSIONAL, TECHNICAL, AND KINDRED WORKERS[1]	59
000	Accountants and auditors	62
010	Actors and actresses	52
012	Airplane pilots and navigators	66
013	Architects	72
014	Artists and art teachers	56
015	Athletes	48
020	Authors	62
021	Chemists	69
022	Chiropractors	62
023	Clergymen	60
	College presidents, professors, and instructors (nec)	
030	College presidents and deans	86
031	Professors and instructors, agricultural sciences	78
032	Professors and instructors, biological sciences	78
034	Professors and instructors, chemistry	78
035	Professors and instructors, economics	78
040	Professors and instructors, engineering	78
041	Professors and instructors, geology and geophysics	78
042	Professors and instructors, mathematics	78
043	Professors and instructors, medical sciences	78
045	Professors and instructors, physics	78
050	Professors and instructors, psychology	78
051	Professors and instructors, statistics	78
052	Professors and instructors, natural sciences (nec)	78
053	Professors and instructors, social sciences (nec)	78
054	Professors and instructors, nonscientific subjects	78
060	Professors and instructors, subject not specified	78
070	Dancers and dancing teachers	40
071	Dentists	70
072	Designers	56
073	Dietitians and nutritionists	52
074	Draftsmen	55
075	Editors and reporters	56
080	Engineers, aeronautical	66
081	Engineers, chemical	66
082	Engineers, civil	70
083	Engineers, electrical	65
084	Engineers, industrial	54
085	Engineers, mechanical	66
090	Engineers, metallurgical, and metallurgists	60
091	Engineers, mining	63
092	Engineers, sales	51
093	Engineers (nec)	55
101	Entertainers (nec)	33
102	Farm and home management advisers	53

103	Foresters and conservationists	42
104	Funeral directors and embalmers	34
105	Lawyers and judges	73
111	Librarians	54
120	Musicians and music teachers	45
	Natural scientists (nec)	
130	Agricultural scientists	58
131	Biological scientists	68
134	Geologists and geophysicists	67
135	Mathematicians	69
140	Physicists	76
145	Miscellaneous natural scientists	72
150	Nurses, professional	54
151	Nurses, student professional	49
152	Optometrists	62
153	Osteopaths	62
154	Personnel and labor relations workers	56
160	Pharmacists	64
161	Photographers	46
162	Physicians and surgeons	78
163	Public relations men and publicity writers	57
164	Radio operators	49
165	Recreation and group workers	49
170	Religious workers	51
171	Social and welfare workers, except group	56
	Social scientists	
172	Economists	60
173	Psychologists	66
174	Statisticians and actuaries	58
175	Miscellaneous social scientists	68
180	Sports instructors and officials	50
181	Surveyors	58
182	Teachers, elementary schools	57
183	Teachers, secondary schools	60
184	Teachers (nec)	60
185	Technicians, medical and dental	53
190	Technicians, electrical and electronic	46
191	Technicians, other engineering and physical sciences	46
192	Technicians (nec)	58
193	Therapists and healers (nec)	44
194	Veterinarians	61
195	Professional, technical, and kindred workers (nec)	59
N(200)	FARMERS AND FARM MANAGERS	40
	Farmers (owners and tenants)	40
222	Farm managers	54
	MANAGERS, OFFICIALS, AND PROPRIETORS, EXCEPT FARM	52
250	Buyers and department heads, store	48
251	Buyers and shippers, farm products	39
252	Conductors, railroad	39

253	Credit men	49
254	Floormen and floor managers, store	52
260	Inspectors, public administration	52
262	Managers and superintendents, building	47
265	Officers, pilots, pursers, and engineers, ship	50
270	Officials and administrators (nec), public administration	60
275	Officials, lodge, society, union, etc.	50
280	Postmasters	58
285	Purchasing agents and buyers (nec)	50
R(290)	Managers, officials, and proprietors (nec)	52

	CLERICAL AND KINDRED WORKERS	43
301	Agents (nec)	43
302	Attendants and assistants, library	41
303	Attendants, physician's and dentist's office	42
304	Baggagemen, transportation	23
305	Bank tellers	48
310	Bookkeepers	49
312	Cashiers	31
313	Collectors, bill and account	27
314	Dispatchers and starters, vehicle	37
315	Express messengers and railway mail clerks	30
320	File clerks	31
321	Insurance adjusters, examiners, and investigators	49
323	Mail carriers	33
324	Messengers and office boys	26
325	Office machine operators	46
333	Payroll and timekeeping clerks	34
340	Postal clerks	39
341	Receptionists	38
Z(342)	Secretaries	53
343	Shipping and receiving clerks	29
345	Stenographers	42
350	Stock clerks and storekeepers	32
351	Telegraph messengers	26
352	Telegraph operators	45
353	Telephone operators	38
354	Ticket, station, and express agents	36
360	Typists	42
Y(370)	Clerical and kindred workers (nec)	43

	SALES WORKERS	38
380	Advertising agents and salesmen	42
381	Auctioneers	39
382	Demonstrators	28
383	Hucksters and peddlers	22
385	Insurance agents, brokers, and underwriters	44
390	Newsboys	14
393	Real estate agents and brokers	49
395	Stock and bond salesmen	56
S(396)	Salesmen and sales clerks (nec)	38

	CRAFTSMEN, FOREMEN, AND KINDRED WORKERS	39
401	Bakers	33

402	Blacksmiths	34
403	Boilermakers	31
404	Bookbinders	32
405	Brickmasons, stonemasons, and tile setters	34
410	Cabinetmakers	40
Q(411)	Carpenters	37
413	Cement and concrete finishers	34
414	Compositors and typesetters	42
415	Cranemen, derrickmen, and hoistmen	39
420	Decorators and window dressers	38
421	Electricians	44
423	Electrotypers and sterotypers	41
424	Engravers, except photoengravers	36
425	Excavating, grading, and road machinery operators	32
430	Foremen (nec)	39
431	Forgemen and hammermen	36
432	Furriers	35
434	Glaziers	26
435	Heat treaters, annealers, and temperers	38
444	Inspectors, scalers, and graders, log and lumber	31
450	Inspectors (nec)	39
451	Jewelers, watchmakers, goldsmiths, and silversmiths	42
452	Job setters, metal	40
453	Linemen and servicemen, telegraph, telephone, and power	36
454	Locomotive engineers	43
460	Locomotive firemen	33
461	Loom fixers	30
465	Machinists	43
470	Mechanics and repairmen, air conditioning, heating and refrigeration	42
471	Mechanics and repairmen, airplane	50
472	Mechanics and repairmen, automobile	43
473	Mechanics and repairmen, office machine	43
474	Mechanics and repairmen, radio and television	42
475	Mechanics and repairmen, railroad and car shop	43
480	Mechanics and repairmen (nec)	43
490	Millers, grain, flour, feed, etc.	33
491	Millwrights	40
492	Molders, metal	38
493	Motion picture projectionists	34
494	Opticians, and lens grinders and polishers	49
495	Painters, construction and maintenance	31
501	Paperhangers	24
502	Pattern and model makers, except paper	39
503	Photoengravers and lithographers	46
504	Piano and organ tuners and repairmen	33
505	Plasterers	31
510	Plumbers and pipe fitters	34
512	Pressmen and plate printers, printing	41
513	Rollers and roll hands, metal	36
514	Roofers and slaters	31
515	Shoemakers and repairers, except factory	28
520	Stationary engineers	34
521	Stone cutters and stone carvers	38
523	Structural metal workers	44

524	Tailors and tailoresses	40
525	Tinsmiths, coppersmiths, and sheet metal workers	34
530	Toolmakers, and die makers and setters	40
535	Upholsterers	31
545	Craftsmen and kindred workers (nec)	39
555	Members of the armed forces	39
	OPERATIVES AND KINDRED WORKERS	30
601	Apprentice auto mechanics	38
602	Apprentice bricklayers and masons	29
603	Apprentice carpenters	32
604	Apprentice electricians	39
605	Apprentice machinists and toolmakers	36
610	Apprentice mechanics, except auto	38
612	Apprentice plumbers and pipe fitters	29
613	Apprentices, building trades (nec)	23
614	Apprentices, metalworking trades (nec)	37
615	Apprentices, printing trades	36
620	Apprentices, other specified trades	37
621	Apprentices, trade not specified	37
630	Asbestos and insulation workers	28
631	Assemblers	30
632	Attendants, auto service and parking	24
634	Blasters and powdermen	34
635	Boatmen, canalmen, and lock keepers	23
640	Brakemen, railroad	29
641	Bus drivers	32
642	Chainmen, rodmen, and axmen, surveying	20
643	Checkers, examiners, and inspectors, manufacturing	39
645	Conductors, bus and street railway	26
650	Deliverymen and routemen	24
651	Dressmakers and seamstresses, except factory	39
652	Dyers	25
653	Filers, grinders, and polishers, metal	27
654	Fruit, nut, and vegetable graders and packers, except factory	34
670	Furnacemen, smeltermen, and pourers	45
671	Graders and sorters, manufacturing	33
672	Heaters, metal	38
673	Knitters, loopers, and toppers, textile	29
674	Laundry and dry cleaning operatives	22
675	Meat cutters, except slaughter and packing house	31
680	Milliners	32
685	Mine operatives and laborers (nec)	32
690	Motormen, mine, factory, logging camp, etc.	27
691	Motormen, street, subway, and elevated railway	32
692	Oilers and greasers, except auto	30
693	Packers and wrappers (nec)	22
694	Painters, except construction and maintenance	29
695	Photographic process workers	36
701	Power station operators	42
703	Sailors and deck hands	35
704	Sawyers	30
705	Sewers and stitchers, manufacturing	26
710	Spinners, textile	34

712	Stationary firemen	34
713	Switchmen, railroad	29
714	Taxicab drivers and chauffeurs	28
T(725)	Truck and tractor drivers	32
720	Weavers, textile	30
721	Welders and flame-cutters	39
W(725)	Operatives and kindred workers (nec)	30

PRIVATE HOUSEHOLD WORKERS — 19

801	Babysitters, private household	23
802	Housekeepers, private household	28
803	Laundresses, private household	22
P(804)	Private household workers (nec)	17

SERVICE WORKERS, EXCEPT PRIVATE HOUSEHOLD — 29

810	Attendants, hospital and other institutions	42
812	Attendants, professional and personal service (nec)	29
813	Attendants, recreation and amusement	20
814	Barbers	30
815	Bartenders	23
820	Bootblacks	12
821	Boarding and lodging house keepers	22
823	Chambermaids and maids, except private household	14
824	Charwomen and cleaners	20
825	Cooks, except private household	31
830	Counter and fountain workers	16
831	Elevator operators	24
832	Housekeepers and stewards, except private household	37
834	Janitors and sextons	26
835	Kitchen workers (nec), except private household	22
840	Midwives	46
841	Porters	24
842	Practical nurses	44
843	Hairdressers and cosmetologists	35
	Protective service workers	
850	Firemen, fire protection	35
851	Guards, watchmen, and doorkeepers	30
852	Marshals and constables	52
853	Policemen and detectives	40
854	Sheriffs and bailiffs	50
860	Watchmen (crossing) and bridge tenders	28
874	Ushers, recreation and amusement	20
875	Waiters and waitresses	23
890	Service workers, except private household	29

FARM LABORERS AND FOREMEN — 25

901	Farm foremen	41
U(902)	Farm laborers, wage workers	22
V(903)	Farm laborers, unpaid family workers	34
905	Farm service laborers, self-employed	31

LABORERS, EXCEPT FARM AND MINE[2] — 20

960	Carpenters' helpers, except logging and mining	23

962	Fishermen and oystermen	32
963	Garage laborers, and car washers and greasers	18
964	Gardeners, except farm, and groundskeepers	21
965	Longshoremen and stevedores	21
970	Lumbermen, raftsmen, and woodchoppers	18
971	Teamsters	22
972	Truck drivers' helpers	15
973	Warehousemen (nec)	20
X(985)	Laborers (nec)	20
995	OCCUPATION NOT REPORTED	

[1]Each major group score is the weighted average of all occupation lines within the group, weighted by the total 1960 experienced civilian labor force.

[2]Mine laborers are included in the major group "Operatives and kindred workers."

Standard Scale Scores for the 1970 U.S. Census
Detailed Occupational Classification

Occu- pation Code		Standard Scale Score
	PROFESSIONAL, TECHNICAL, AND KINDRED WORKERS[1]	59
001	Accountants	62
002	Architects	72
	Computer specialists	
003	Computer programmers	51
004	Computer systems analysts	51
005	Computer specialists (nec)	51
	Engineers	
006	Aeronautical and astronautical engineers	66
010	Chemical engineers	66
011	Civil engineers	70
012	Electrical and electronic engineers	65
013	Industrial engineers	54
014	Mechanical engineers	66
015	Metallurgical and materials engineers	60
020	Mining engineers	63
021	Petroleum engineers	63
022	Sales engineers	51
023	Engineers (nec)	55
024	Farm management advisors	55
025	Foresters and conservationists	42
026	Home management advisors	51
	Lawyers and judges	
030	Judges	76
031	Lawyers	72
	Librarians, archivists, and curators	
032	Librarians	54
033	Archivists and curators	54
	Mathematical specialists	
034	Actuaries	69
035	Mathematicians	69
036	Statisticians	55
	Life and physical scientists	
042	Agricultural scientists	58
043	Atmospheric and space scientists	72
044	Biological scientists	68
045	Chemists	69
051	Geologists	67
052	Marine scientists	69
053	Physicists and astronomers	74
054	Life and physical scientists (nec)	72
055	Operations and systems researchers and analysts	60
056	Personnel and labor relations workers	58
	Physicians, dentists, and related practitioners	
061	Chiropractors	62
062	Dentists	70
063	Optometrists	62
064	Pharmacists	64
065	Physicians, medical and osteopathic	78
071	Podiatrists	50

072	Veterinarians	61
073	Health practitioners (nec)	50
	Nurses, dietitians, and therapists	
074	Dietitians	52
075	Registered nurses	54
076	Therapists	62
	Health technologists and technicians	
080	Clinical laboratory technologists and technicians	58
081	Dental hygienists	44
082	Health record technologists and technicians	50
083	Radiologic technologists and technicians	58
084	Therapy assistants	42
085	Health technologists and technicians (nec)	50
	Religious workers	
086	Clergymen	60
090	Religious workers (nec)	46
	Social scientists	
091	Economists	60
092	Political scientists	69
093	Psychologists	66
094	Sociologists	67
095	Urban and regional planners	72
096	Social scientists (nec)	68
	Social and recreation workers	
100	Social workers	56
101	Recreation workers	49
	Teachers, college and university	
102	Agriculture teachers	78
103	Atmospheric, earth, marine, and space teachers	78
104	Biology teachers	78
105	Chemistry teachers	78
110	Physics teachers	78
111	Engineering teachers	78
112	Mathematics teachers	78
113	Health specialties teachers	78
114	Psychology teachers	78
115	Business and commerce teachers	78
116	Economics teachers	78
120	History teachers	78
121	Sociology teachers	78
122	Social science teachers (nec)	78
123	Art, drama, and music teachers	78
124	Coaches and physical education teachers	78
125	Education teachers	78
126	English teachers	78
130	Foreign language teachers	78
131	Home economics teachers	78
132	Law teachers	78
133	Theology teachers	78
134	Trade, industrial, and technical teachers	78
135	Miscellaneous teachers, college and university	78
140	Teachers, college and university, subject not specified	78
	Teachers, except college and university	
141	Adult education teachers	62
N(142)	Elementary school teachers	57
143	Prekindergarten and kindergarten teachers	49

144	Secondary school teachers	60
145	Teachers, except college and university (nec)	60
	Engineering and science technicians	
150	Agriculture and biological technicians, except health	47
151	Chemical technicians	46
152	Draftsmen	55
153	Electrical and electronic engineering technicians	46
154	Industrial engineering technicians	46
155	Mechanical engineering technicians	46
156	Mathematical technicians	51
161	Surveyors	58
162	Engineering and science technicians (nec)	46
	Technicians, except health, and engineering and science	
163	Airplane pilots	66
164	Air traffic controllers	37
165	Embalmers	34
170	Flight engineers	66
171	Radio operators	49
172	Tool programmers, numerical control	58
173	Technicians (nec)	58
174	Vocational and educational counselors	55
	Writers, artists, and entertainers	
175	Actors	52
180	Athletes and kindred workers	49
181	Authors	62
182	Dancers	45
183	Designers	56
184	Editors and reporters	56
185	Musicians and composers	45
190	Painters and sculptors	56
191	Photographers	46
192	Public relations men and publicity writers	57
193	Radio and television announcers	50
194	Writers, artists, and entertainers (nec)	43
195	Research workers, not specified	58
	MANAGERS AND ADMINISTRATORS, EXCEPT FARM	53
201	Assessors, controllers, and treasurers; local public administration	63
202	Bank officers and financial managers	67
203	Buyers and shippers, farm products	39
205	Buyers, wholesale and retail trade	49
210	Credit men	49
211	Funeral directors	34
212	Health administrators	60
213	Construction inspectors, public administration	61
215	Inspectors, except construction, public administration	52
216	Managers and superintendents, building	47
220	Office managers (nec)	55
221	Officers, pilots, and pursers; ship	50
222	Officials and administrators; public administration (nec)	60
223	Officials of lodges, societies, and unions	56
224	Postmasters and mail superintendents	58
225	Purchasing agents and buyers (nec)	50
226	Railroad conductors	39
230	Restaurant, cafeteria, and bar managers	37

231	Sales managers and department heads, retail trade	50
233	Sales managers, except retail trade	52
235	School administrators, college	86
240	School administrators, elementary and secondary	69
245	Managers and administrators (nec)	52

	SALES WORKERS	39
260	Advertising agents and salesmen	42
261	Auctioneers	39
262	Demonstrators	28
264	Hucksters and peddlers	22
265	Insurance agents, brokers, and underwriters	44
266	Newsboys	14
270	Real estate agents and brokers	49
271	Stock and bond salesmen	56
280	Salesmen and sales clerks (nec)[2]	38
281	Sales representatives, manufacturing industries (Ind. 107-399)	47
282	Sales representatives, wholesale trade (Ind. 017-058, 507-599)	47
283	Sales clerks, retail trade (Ind. 608-699 except 618, 639, 649, 667, 668, 688)	34
284	Salesmen, retail trade (Ind. 607, 618, 639, 649, 667, 668,688)	36
285	Salesmen of services and construction (Ind. 067-073, 407-499, 707-947)	42

	CLERICAL AND KINDRED WORKERS	42
301	Bank tellers	48
303	Billing clerks	34
P(305)	Bookkeepers	49
310	Cashiers	31
311	Clerical assistants, social welfare	44
312	Clerical supervisors (nec)	55
313	Collectors, bill and account	27
314	Counter clerks, except food	37
315	Dispatchers and starters, vehicle	37
320	Enumerators and interviewers	37
321	Estimators and investigators (nec)	34
323	Expediters and production controllers	40
325	File clerks	31
326	Insurance adjusters, examiners, and investigators	49
330	Library attendants and assistants	41
331	Mail carriers, post office	33
332	Mail handlers, except post office	26
333	Messengers and office boys	26
334	Meter readers, utilities	21
	Office machine operators	
341	Bookkeeping and billing machine operators	45
342	Calculating machine operators	45
343	Computer and peripheral equipment operators	53
344	Duplicating machine operators	37
345	Key punch operators	45
350	Tabulating machine operators	53
355	Office machine operators (nec)	37

360	Payroll and timekeeping clerks	34
361	Postal clerks	39
362	Proofreaders	41
363	Real estate appraisers	48
364	Receptionists	38
	Secretaries	
370	Secretaries, legal	53
371	Secretaries, medical	53
Q(372)	Secretaries (nec)	53
374	Shipping and receiving clerks	29
375	Statistical clerks	37
376	Stenographers	42
381	Stock clerks and storekeepers	32
382	Teacher aides, except school monitors	50
383	Telegraph messengers	26
384	Telegraph operators	45
385	Telephone operators	38
390	Ticket, station, and express agents	32
391	Typists	42
392	Weighers	30
394	Miscellaneous clerical workers	42
395	Not specified clerical workers	43
	CRAFTSMEN AND KINDRED WORKERS	39
401	Automobile accessories installers	30
402	Bakers	33
403	Blacksmiths	34
404	Boilermakers	31
405	Bookbinders	32
410	Brickmasons and stonemasons	34
411	Brickmasons and stonemasons, apprentices	29
412	Bulldozers operators	32
413	Cabinetmakers	40
R(415)	Carpenters	37
416	Carpenter apprentices	32
420	Carpet installers	28
421	Cement and concrete finishers	34
422	Compositors and typesetters	42
423	Printing trades apprentices, except pressmen	35
424	Cranemen, derrickmen, and hoistmen	39
425	Decorators and window dressers	38
426	Dental laboratory technicians	60
430	Electricians	44
431	Electrician apprentices	39
433	Electric power linemen and cablemen	36
434	Electrotypers and stereotypers	41
435	Engravers, except photoengravers	36
436	Excavating, grading, and road machine operators; except bulldozer	32
440	Floor layers, except tile setters	37
441	Foreman (nec)	39
442	Forgemen and hammermen	36
443	Furniture and wood finishers	31
444	Furriers	35
445	Glaziers	26

446	Heat treaters, annealers, and temperers	38
450	Inspectors, scalers, and graders; log and lumber	31
452	Inspectors (nec)	39
453	Jewelers and watchmakers	42
454	Job and die setters, metal	40
455	Locomotive engineers	43
456	Locomotive firemen	33
461	Machinists	43
462	Machinist apprentices	38
	Mechanics and repairmen	
470	Air conditioning, heating, and refrigeration	42
471	Aircraft	50
472	Automobile body repairmen	36
S(473)	Automobile mechanics	43
474	Automobile mechanic apprentices	38
475	Data processing machine repairmen	48
480	Farm implement	43
481	Heavy equipment mechanics, including diesel	43
482	Household appliance and accessory installers and mechanics	44
483	Loom fixers	30
484	Office machine	43
485	Radio and television	42
486	Railroad and car shop	43
491	Mechanic, except auto, apprentices	38
492	Miscellaneous machanics and repairmen	43
495	Not specified mechanics and repairmen	43
501	Millers; grain, flour, and feed	33
502	Millwrights	40
503	Molders, metal	38
504	Molder apprentices	33
505	Motion picture projectionists	34
506	Opticians, and lens grinders and polishers	49
510	Painters, construction and maintenance	31
511	Painter apprentices	26
512	Paperhangers	24
514	Pattern and model makers, except paper	39
515	Photoengravers and lithographers	46
516	Piano and organ tuners and repairmen	33
520	Plasterers	31
521	Plasterer apprentices	26
522	Plumbers and pipe fitters	34
523	Plumber and pipe fitter apprentices	29
525	Power station operators	42
530	Pressmen and plate printers, printing	41
531	Pressman apprentices	36
533	Rollers and finishers, metal	36
534	Roofers and slaters	31
535	Sheetmetal workers and tinsmiths	34
536	Sheetmetal apprentices	29
540	Shipfitters	44
542	Shoe repairmen	28
543	Sign painters and letterers	29
545	Stationary engineers	34
546	Stone cutters and stone carvers	38
550	Structural metal craftsmen	44
551	Tailors	40

552	Telephone installers and repairmen	35
554	Telephone linemen and splicers	36
560	Tile setters	34
561	Tool and die makers	40
562	Tool and die maker apprentices	35
563	Upholsterers	31
571	Specified craft apprentices (nec)	37
572	Not specified apprentices	37
575	Craftsmen and kindred workers (nec)	39
580	Former members of the Armed Forces	39
	OPERATIVES, EXCEPT TRANSPORT	32
601	Asbestos and insulation workers	28
T(602)	Assemblers	30
603	Blasters and powdermen	34
604	Bottling and canning operatives	35
605	Chainmen, rodmen, and axmen; surveying	20
610	Checkers, examiners, and inspectors; manufacturing	39
611	Clothing ironers and pressers	22
612	Cutting operatives (nec)	32
613	Dressmakers and seamstresses, except factory	39
614	Drillers, earth	32
615	Dry wall installers and lathers	31
620	Dyers	25
621	Filers, polishers, sanders, and buffers	27
622	Furnacemen, smeltermen, and pourers	45
623	Garage workers and gas station attendants	22
624	Graders and sorters, manufacturing	33
625	Produce graders and packers, except factory and farm	34
626	Heaters, metal	38
630	Laundry and dry cleaning operatives (nec)	22
631	Meat cutters and butchers, except manufacturing	31
633	Meat cutters and butchers, manufacturing	18
634	Meat wrappers, retail trade	20
635	Metal platers	28
636	Milliners	32
640	Mine operatives (nec)	32
641	Mixing operatives	32
642	Oilers and greasers, except auto	30
643	Packers and wrappers, except meat and produce	22
644	Painters, manufactured articles	29
645	Photographic process workers	36
	Precision machine operatives	
650	Drill press operatives	38
651	Grinding machine operatives	38
652	Lathe and milling machine operatives	38
653	Precision machine operatives (nec)	38
656	Punch and stamping press operatives	40
660	Riveters and fasteners	44
661	Sailors and deckhands	35
662	Sawyers	30
663	Sewers and stitchers	26
664	Shoemaking machine operatives	28
665	Solderers	39
666	Stationary firemen	34

	Textile operatives	
670	Carding, lapping, and combing operatives	29
671	Knitters, loopers, and toppers	29
672	Spinners, twisters, and winders	34
673	Weavers	30
674	Textile operatives (nec)	26
680	Welders and flame-cutters	39
681	Winding operatives (nec)	32
690	Machine operatives, miscellaneous specified	38
692	Machine operatives, not specified	38
694	Miscellaneous operatives	32
695	Not specified operatives	29

	TRANSPORT EQUIPMENT OPERATIVES	30
701	Boatmen and canalmen	23
703	Bus drivers	32
704	Conductors and motormen, urban rail transit	29
705	Deliverymen and routemen	24
706	Fork lift and tow motor operatives	28
710	Motormen; mine, factory, logging camp, etc.	27
711	Parking attendants	24
712	Railroad brakemen	29
713	Railroad switchmen	29
714	Taxicab drivers and chauffeurs	28
U(715)	Truck drivers	33

	LABORERS, EXCEPT FARM	21
740	Animal caretakers, except farm	26
750	Carpenters' helpers	23
V(751)	Construction laborers, except carpenters' helpers	26
752	Fishermen and oystermen	32
753	Freight and material handlers	20
754	Garbage collectors	13
755	Gardeners and groundskeepers, except farm	21
760	Longshoremen and stevedores	21
761	Lumbermen, raftsmen, and woodchoppers	18
762	Stock handlers	20
763	Teamsters	22
764	Vehicle washers and equipment cleaners	19
770	Warehousemen (nec)	20
780	Miscellaneous laborers	21
785	Not specified laborers	19

	FARMERS AND FARM MANAGERS	41
W(801)	Farmers (owners and tenants)	40
802	Farm managers	54

	FARM LABORERS AND FARM FOREMEN	24
821	Farm foremen	41
822	Farm laborers, wage workers	22
823	Farm laborers, unpaid family workers	34
824	Farm service laborers, self-employed	31

	SERVICE WORKERS, EXCEPT PRIVATE HOUSEHOLD	29

Cleaning service workers

901	Chambermaids and maids, except private household	14
902	Cleaners and charwomen	20
X(903)	Janitors and sextons	26
	Food service workers	
910	Bartenders	23
911	Busboys	21
912	Cooks, except private household	31
913	Dishwashers	18
914	Food counter and fountain workers	16
Y(915)	Waiters	23
916	Food service workers (nec), except private household	22
	Health service workers	
921	Dental assistants	44
922	Health aides, except nursing	42
923	Health trainees	49
924	Lay midwives	42
925	Nursing aides, orderlies, and attendants	42
926	Practical nurses	44
	Personal service workers	
931	Airline stewardesses	50
932	Attendants, recreation and amusement	20
933	Attendants, personal service (nec)	29
934	Baggage porters and bellhops	16
935	Barbers	30
940	Boarding and lodging house keepers	22
941	Bootblacks	12
942	Child care workers, except private household	42
943	Elevator operators	24
944	Hairdressers and cosmetologists	35
945	Personal service apprentices	27
950	Housekeepers, except private household	28
952	School monitors	50
953	Ushers, recreation and amusement	20
954	Welfare service aides	45
	Protective service workers	
960	Crossing guards and bridge tenders	28
961	Firemen, fire protection	35
962	Guards and watchmen	30
963	Marshals and constables	52
964	Policemen and detectives	40
965	Sheriffs and bailiffs	50

	PRIVATE HOUSEHOLD WORKERS	20
980	Child care workers, private household	23
981	Cooks, private household	31
982	Housekeepers, private household	28
983	Laundresses, private household	22
Z(984)	Maids and servants, private household	17

995	OCCUPATION NOT REPORTED[3]	

	ALLOCATION CATEGORIES[4]	
196	Professional, technical, and kindred workers--allocated	59
246	Managers and administrators, except farm--allocated	53
296	Sales workers--allocated	39

396	Clerical and kindred workers--allocated	42
586	Craftsmen and kindred workers--allocated	39
696	Operatives, except transport--allocated	32
726	Transport equipment operatives--allocated	30
796	Laborers, except farm--allocated	21
806	Farmers and farm managers--allocated	41
846	Farm laborers and farm foremen--allocated	24
976	Service workers, except private household--allocated	29
986	Private household workers--allocated	20

[1]Each major group score is the weighted average of all occupation lines within the group, weighted by the total 1970 experienced civilian labor force.

[2]Category "280 Salesmen and sales clerks, (nec)" was subdivided in the Census into five occupation groups dependent on industry. The industry codes are shown in parentheses.

[3]This code is used to identify not reported occupations in surveys where the not reported cases are not allocated.

[4]Those returns from the population census which do not have an occupation entry are allocated among the major occupation groups during computer processing. These cases are labeled with the code for the "allocation" category to which they are assigned.

Appendix D

Occupational Prestige Scores for Each Country

PROFESSIONAL, TECHNICAL AND RELATED WORKERS

ISCO NO.	OCCUPATION TITLE	PRESTIGE SCORE	SCORE MINUS STD. SCORE
00110	CHEMIST	68.8	-0.3
00120	NUCLEAR PHYSICIST (80.8)	77.3	0.8
	PHYSICIST (73.8)		
00130	SCIENTIST (80.8)	79.8	1.5
	GOVERNMENT SCIENTIST (78.9)		
00131	GEOLOGIST	67.2	-0.2
00133	WEATHERMAN	48.6	0.0
00210	ARCHITECT	70.5	-1.3
00220	CIVIL ENGINEER (67.8)	67.4	-2.9
	ENGINEER (67.1)		
00230	ELECTRICAL ENGINEER	69.4	4.1
00240	AERONAUTICAL ENGINEER (71.1)	66.7	0.3
	MECHANICAL ENGINEER (62.3)		
00250	CHEMICAL ENGINEER	67.3	0.9
00260	METALLURGIST	55.8	-4.3
00270	MINING ENGINEER	61.6	-1.2
00280	PRODUCTION EFFICIENCY EXPERT	54.4	0.0
00310	SURVEYOR	53.3	-4.6
00320	DRAFTSMAN	56.1	1.2
00330	SURVEYOR'S ASSISTANT	39.4	0.0
00390	ENGINEER'S AIDE	45.5	0.0
00410	AIRLINE PILOT	70.1	3.6
00411	ASTRONAUT	79.8	0.0
00420	SHIP'S CAPTAIN	59.9	-3.3
00421	CANAL BARGE PILOT	36.8	0.9
00510	BIOLOGIST	67.7	-1.0
00521	DAIRY SCIENTIST	55.8	0.0
00531	COUNTY AGRICULTURAL AGENT	53.9	-0.9
00540	MEDICAL OR DENTAL TECHNICIAN	61.0	3.0
00541	MILK TESTER	31.6	-15.1
00610	PHYSICIAN (81.5)	78.2	0.3
	PSYCHIATRIST (74.9)		

Code	Occupation		
00630	DENTIST	73.5	3.0
00650	VETERINARIAN	59.7	-1.7
00670	DRUGGIST	60.7	-3.4
00690	DIETICIAN IN A HOSPITAL	52.1	0.0
00710	REGISTERED NURSE	61.5	7.9
00720	STUDENT NURSE	45.1	1.1
00730	MIDWIFE	23.3	-23.2
00750	OPTOMETRIST	62.0	-0.0
00751	OPTICIAN	61.6	4.3
00761	OCCUPATIONAL THERAPIST	57.1	0.0
00762	MASSEUR	30.5	0.0
00790	OSTEOPATH	61.9	0.0
00791	CHIROPRACTOR	60.0	-2.5
00793	PUBLIC HEALTH ANALYST	62.0	14.4
00810	STATISTICIAN	55.4	0.2
00820	MATHEMATICIAN	65.0	-4.1
00840	COMPUTER PROGRAMMER	51.3	0.1
00900	ECONOMIST	56.8	-3.7
01100	ACCOUNTANT	56.7	-2.1
01101	ACCOUNTANT FOR A LARGE BUSINESS	61.7	-6.7
01210	LAWYER	75.7	5.1
01220	FEDERAL COURT JUDGE	83.4	5.7
01221	U.S. SUPREME COURT JUSTICE (77.3)	84.5	2.5
01222	JUSTICE OF A MUNICIPAL COURT	75.4	2.2
	COUNTY JUDGE (73.5)		
01310	COLLEGE PROFESSOR	78.3	0.7
01311	COLLEGE OR UNIVERSITY PRESIDENT	82.4	-3.8
01320	HIGH SCHOOL TEACHER (63.3)	63.1	-1.1
01330	INSTRUCTOR IN PUBLIC SCHOOLS	61.7	4.7
	PUBLIC SCHOOL TEACHER (61.7)		
	PUBLIC GRADE SCHOOL TEACHER (60.1)		
01392	SCHOOL SUPERINTENDENT	67.4	-0.2
01410	PRIEST (73.2)	70.5	10.8
	MINISTER (71.8)		
	CLERGYMAN (69.0)		
	RABBI (68.0)		
01413	EVANGELIST	51.3	1.2
01490	RELIGIOUS EDUCATION DIRECTOR	59.7	3.5
01491	FAITH HEALER	22.4	0.0
01510	AUTHOR (62.6)	59.8	-1.9
	AUTHOR OF NOVELS (57.0)		
01590	JOURNALIST (58.8)	51.6	-3.3

ISCO NO.	OCCUPATION TITLE	PRESTIGE SCORE	SCORE MINUS STD. SCORE
	UNITED STATES		
01592	NEWSPAPER COLUMNIST (49.5)	48.2	0.8
01593	REPORTER ON A DAILY NEWSPAPER (46.6)	56.7	-0.4
	ADVERTISING COPYWRITER	57.0	-0.2
01610	PUBLIC RELATIONS MAN		
	ARTIST WHO PAINTS PICTURES THAT ARE EXHIBITED IN GALLERIES (57.0)		
01620	SCULPTOR (57.0)	54.5	0.1
01621	COMMERCIAL ARTIST	58.1	2.2
	DESIGNER (58.5)		
	FASHION DESIGNER (57.8)		
01622	WINDOW DISPLAY ARTIST	37.4	-0.4
01630	PHOTOGRAPHER	40.5	-4.6
01631	TELEVISION CAMERA MAN	47.6	0.8
01710	MUSICIAN IN A SYMPHONY ORCHESTRA (59.0)	55.0	-1.0
	MUSICIAN (51.1)		
01711	JAZZ MUSICIAN	37.2	-0.9
01712	SINGER IN A NIGHT CLUB	25.9	-5.6
01720	BALLET DANCER	42.9	-1.9
01721	DANCING TEACHER	32.3	-3.9
01730	ACTOR OR ACTRESS	55.0	3.5
01731	TV STAR	63.0	0.3
01732	TV DIRECTOR	59.9	-2.3
01790	TV ANNOUNCER (54.2)	44.5	-5.8
	RADIO ANNOUNCER (45.2)		
01800	DISK JOCKEY (34.2)		
01801	PROFESSIONAL ATHLETE	51.4	2.9
	ATHLETIC COACH	53.2	2.8
01910	PROFESSIONALLY TRAINED LIBRARIAN	54.6	0.1
01920	SOCIOLOGIST	65.0	-2.4
01921	PSYCHOLOGIST	71.4	5.4
01924	SOCIAL SCIENTIST	66.2	-2.6
01930	PSYCHIATRIC SOCIAL WORKER (57.2)	52.4	-3.9
	SOCIAL WORKER (50.3)		
	WELFARE WORKER FOR A CITY GOVERNMENT (49.7)		
01931	SOCIAL WORKER (55.2)	48.5	-0.3
	YMCA DIRECTOR (55.2)		
	PLAYGROUND DIRECTOR (41.9)		

Code	Occupation		
01940	PERSONNEL DIRECTOR	57.8	-0.7
01941	JOB COUNSELOR	54.2	-0.6
01990	TECHNICIAN	56.5	-1.7
01992	FINGERPRINT EXPERT	53.6	0.0
01994	PEACE CORPS MEMBER	52.6	0.0
01995	ADVERTISING EXECUTIVE	59.8	3.0

ADMINISTRATIVE AND MANAGERIAL WORKERS

Code	Occupation		
02011	STATE GOVERNOR	84.9	3.0
02013	MAYOR OF A LARGE CITY	75.1	-0.1
02014	CITY MANAGER	65.6	-2.7
02021	MEMBER OF THE U.S. SENATE	88.4	3.4
02022	MEMBER OF THE U.S. HOUSE OF REPRESENTATIVES	85.5	13.3
02030	MEMBER OF A CITY COUNCIL	59.4	4.4
02031	MEMBER OF THE PRESIDENT'S CABINET	88.9	10.2
02032	AMBASSADOR TO A FOREIGN COUNTRY	80.7	-6.4
02033	DIPLOMAT IN THE U.S. FOREIGN SERVICE	75.3	2.1
02034	DEPARTMENT HEAD IN THE FEDERAL GOVERNMENT	84.6	13.5
02035	DEPARTMENT HEAD IN THE STATE GOVERNMENT	79.5	5.6
02110	DEPARTMENT HEAD IN A CITY GOVERNMENT	69.9	6.8
02111	MEMBER OF THE BOARD OF DIRECTORS OF A LARGE CORPORATION	71.8	-3.3
	OWNER OF A MANUFACTURING PLANT (65.2)	62.6	-7.8
02112	OWNER OF A FACTORY THAT EMPLOYS ABOUT 100 PEOPLE (60.1)		
	A MANAGER (52.1)		
	GENERAL MANAGER OF A MOVING AND STORAGE COMPANY (47.4)	49.8	-13.0
02113	MANAGER OF A REAL ESTATE OFFICE	53.2	0.9
02114	BANKER	72.0	5.0
02116	BUILDING CONTRACTOR	58.7	5.3
02120	GENERAL MANAGER OF A MANUFACTURING PLANT	63.9	-0.3
02190	BUSINESSMAN	57.7	-0.3
02191	GENERAL MANAGER OF A TELEPHONE COMPANY BRANCH OFFICE	61.2	9.4
02196	LOCAL OFFICIAL OF A LABOR UNION	41.2	-8.3
02197	OFFICIAL OF AN INTERNATIONAL LABOR UNION	55.4	-7.4

CLERICAL AND RELATED WORKERS

Code	Occupation		
03103	CUSTOMS INSPECTOR	43.3	-1.1
03104	TAX COLLECTOR	44.4	-7.2
03210	STENOGRAPHER (43.3)	42.3	0.7
03211	TYPIST (41.3)		
	SECRETARY	45.8	-7.2

ISCO NO.	OCCUPATION TITLE UNITED STATES	PRESTIGE SCORE	SCORE MINUS STD. SCORE
03220	IBM KEYPUNCH OPERATOR	44.9	-0.3
03310	BOOKKEEPER	47.6	-1.4
03311	CASHIER IN A SUPERMARKET	30.9	-0.3
03313	BANK TELLER	49.5	1.9
03314	POST OFFICE CLERK	43.0	4.0
03390	PAYROLL CLERK	41.3	-0.8
03391	BILL COLLECTOR	25.9	-1.1
03420	COMPUTER TECHNICIAN	57.0	4.3
03520	POSTMASTER	58.1	-0.2
03590	TRUCK DISPATCHER	33.5	-3.4
03600	RAILROAD CONDUCTOR	40.9	2.3
03601	STREETCAR CONDUCTOR	28.0	2.0
03700	MAILMAN (44.7)	40.7	7.9
	MAIL CARRIER (39.9)		
03701	RAILWAY MAIL CLERK (37.6)	24.4	-1.4
	TELEGRAPH MESSENGER (29.8)		
	OFFICE BOY (19.1)		
03800	TELEPHONE OPERATOR	40.4	2.0
03801	TELEGRAPH OPERATOR	43.5	-1.8
03802	RADIO OPERATOR	42.8	-6.4
03910	STOCKROOM ATTENDANT	23.4	-8.7
03911	SHIPPING CLERK	29.2	-0.2
03930	CLERK IN AN OFFICE (35.8)	33.5	-9.8
	CLERK FOR A CITY BUS COMPANY (31.3)		
03932	LAW CLERK	50.8	-8.0
03940	RECEPTIONIST	39.4	1.5
03941	RAILROAD TICKET AGENT	35.4	-1.2
03942	RAILWAY BAGGAGEMAN	23.2	0.0
03943	TRAVEL AGENT	42.5	-0.9
03944	FLOOR WALKER IN A DEPARTMENT STORE	27.4	0.0
03950	LIBRARY ASSISTANT	41.3	0.0
03951	FILE CLERK	30.3	-0.5
03991	NEWSPAPER PROOFREADER	41.4	0.0

SALES WORKERS

Code	Occupation		
04000	MANAGER OF A SUPERMARKET (47.4)	43.4	-3.2
	RETAIL LUMBER YARD MANAGER (41.6)		
	MANAGER OF A SMALL STORE IN A CITY (41.2)		
04001	CREDIT MANAGER	37.1	-1.2
04002	SERVICE STATION MANAGER	48.8	0.0
C4100	OWNER OF A FOOD STORE	46.1	3.7
04103	AUTOMOBILE DEALER	43.5	0.0
04106	WHOLESALE DISTRIBUTER	44.5	-13.9
04220	MERCHANDISE BUYER FOR A DEPARTMENT STORE	50.0	0.7
04221	PURCHASING AGENT	47.9	-3.1
04222	FARM PRODUCE BUYER	40.9	1.6
04310	SALES ENGINEER	50.6	0.0
04320	MANUFACTURER'S REPRESENTATIVE (49.1)	43.5	-3.4
	TRAVELING SALESMAN (41.5)		
	TRAVELING SALESMAN FOR A WHOLESALE CONCERN (39.9)		
04410	INSURANCE AGENT	46.8	2.3
04411	REAL ESTATE AGENT	44.0	-5.0
04412	STOCK AND BONDS SALESMAN	50.6	-5.1
04420	ADVERTISING SALESMAN	42.2	0.0
04430	AUCTIONEER	31.9	-7.3
04432	INSURANCE CLAIMS INVESTIGATOR	47.7	-1.5
04510	CLERK IN A STORE (28.0)	27.5	-6.1
	SALES CLERK IN A STORE (27.1)		
04511	USED CAR SALESMAN	30.6	-5.2
04512	FILLING STATION ATTENDANT	21.6	-3.7
04514	HOME PRODUCTS DEMONSTRATOR	28.3	0.0
04521	DOOR-TO-DOOR SALESMAN	21.7	-0.2
04522	TELEPHONE SOLICITOR	26.0	-0.2
04523	NEWSPAPER DELIVERY BOY (15.8)	15.3	1.3
	NEWSPAPER PEDDLER (14.9)		
04524	MILK ROUTEMAN	28.0	3.9

SERVICE WORKERS

Code	Occupation		
05002	APARTMENT BUILDING MANAGER	38.3	-8.3
05100	RESTAURANT OWNER	46.4	-1.4
05101	OWNER-OPERATOR OF A LUNCH STAND (36.1)	33.5	-1.4
	LUNCHROOM OPERATOR (30.9)		
C5102	MOTEL OWNER	45.4	-1.0
05103	BOARDINGHOUSE KEEPER	22.1	0.0

ISCO NO.	OCCUPATION TITLE	PRESTIGE SCORE	SCORE MINUS STD. SCORE
	UNITED STATES		
05201	HOUSEKEEPER IN A PRIVATE HOME	24.9	-3.3
05310	COOK IN A RESTAURANT	26.0	-4.9
05312	SALAD MAKER IN A HOTEL KITCHEN	21.8	-0.7
05313	SODA FOUNTAIN CLERK (16.5)	15.3	-1.0
	SODA JERK (14.1)		
05320	RESTAURANT WAITER (20.9)	20.3	-3.0
	WAITRESS IN A RESTAURANT (19.6)		
05321	BARTENDER	19.9	-3.3
05400	BUTLER	21.7	4.5
05401	PROFESSIONAL BABYSITTER	23.2	0.4
05402	HOTEL CHAMBERMAID	13.6	0.0
05510	JANITOR	16.1	-4.9
05520	CLEANING WOMAN IN PRIVATE HOMES (14.4)	13.4	-3.1
	OFFICE CLEANER (12.4)		
05600	WORKER IN A DRY CLEANING OR LAUNDRY PLANT (19.0)	18.0	-4.1
	LAUNDRESS (17.6)		
	CLOTHES PRESSER IN A LAUNDRY (17.4)		
05700	BARBER	37.9	7.5
05702	BEAUTY OPERATOR	33.2	-1.6
05810	FIREMAN	43.8	8.5
05820	POLICEMAN	47.8	8.0
05823	SECRET SERVICE AGENT (67.8)	56.2	4.5
	COUNTY SHERIFF (55.0)		
	TOWN MARSHAL (45.8)		
05890	NIGHT WATCHMAN	21.9	-0.1
05920	FUNERAL DIRECTOR (53.4)	52.1	18.5
	UNDERTAKER (50.9)		
05990	OFFICE NURSE IN A DENTIST'S OFFICE (47.8)	42.0	0.4
	FIRST AID NURSE (41.9)		
	HOSPITAL ATTENDANT (36.3)		
05991	THEATRE USHER (14.9)	14.6	-5.4
	ATTENDANT IN AN ICE SKATING RINK (14.7)		
	HAT CHECK GIRL (14.1)		
05992	ELEVATOR OPERATOR IN A BUILDING	20.9	-3.4
05993	BELLBOY IN A HOTEL	14.4	0.0

Code	Occupation		
05995	SHOESHINER	9.3	-2.9
05996	AIRLINE STEWARDESS	47.8	-2.3

AGRICULTURAL, ANIMAL HUSBANDRY AND FORESTRY WORKERS, FISHERMEN AND HUNTERS

Code	Occupation		
06000	FARM SUPERINTENDENT	43.7	-10.6
06001	FARM FOREMAN	35.0	-5.8
06110	FARM OWNER AND OPERATOR	43.7	-3.4
06113	TENANT FARMER	21.5	-8.0
06114	SHARE CROPPER	14.9	-16.6
06210	FARM LABORER	21.4	-1.5
06211	MIGRANT WORKER	13.7	-4.4
06270	GARDENER	22.5	1.1
06310	LUMBERJACK (26.9)	26.3	7.1
	LOGGER (25.8)		
06320	PROFESSIONALLY TRAINED FORESTER	53.9	6.4
06322	TREE SURGEON	40.1	0.0
06411	FISHERMAN WHO OWNS HIS OWN BOAT	30.2	-7.1

PRODUCTION AND RELATED WORKERS, TRANSPORT EQUIPMENT OPERATORS AND LABORERS

Code	Occupation		
07000	CONSTRUCTION FOREMAN (46.1)	45.6	6.3
	FOREMAN IN A FACTORY (45.1)		
07001	SUPERINTENDENT OF A CONSTRUCTION JOB	51.1	-1.0
07110	IRON MINER (28.3)	26.8	-4.7
	COAL MINER (25.2)		
07111	DYNAMITE BLASTER	32.1	-3.9
07112	QUARRY WORKER	23.4	-1.1
07130	OILFIELD WORKER	28.4	-2.7
07210	STEEL MILL WORKER	34.7	-10.6
07220	ROLLING MILL OPERATOR IN A METAL SHOP	36.0	0.0
07240	METAL CASTER IN A FOUNDRY	32.9	0.0
07320	SAW MILL OPERATOR (30.8)	29.3	-1.3
	BAND SAW OPERATOR (27.7)		
07321	LUMBER GRADER	31.3	0.0
07340	PAPER MAKING MACHINE TENDER	25.7	-2.3
07530	LOOM FIXER IN A TEXTILE MILL	30.4	0.0
07540	LOOM OPERATOR	24.9	-5.5
07541	CLOTH GRADER IN A TEXTILE MILL	32.9	0.0
07550	KNITTING MACHINE OPERATOR	29.4	0.0
07560	CLOTH DYER	25.0	-0.1
07590	TEXTILE MILL WORKER	28.8	2.7

ISCO NO.	OCCUPATION TITLE	PRESTIGE SCORE	SCORE MINUS STD. SCORE
	UNITED STATES		
07710	FLOUR MILLER	25.2	-7.7
07730	BUTCHER IN A STORE	32.1	0.8
07731	WORKER IN A MEAT PACKING PLANT	24.1	6.0
07760	BAKER	34.2	1.0
07910	TAILOR	41.2	1.7
07911	CUSTOM SEAMSTRESS	31.7	-7.7
07920	FUR COAT TAILOR	34.7	0.0
07930	MILLINER	33.4	1.1
07950	SEWING MACHINE OPERATOR	24.9	-1.4
07960	UPHOLSTERER	30.3	-0.5
08010	PROPRIETOR OF A SHOE REPAIR SHOP	32.8	4.6
08110	CABINET MAKER	38.6	-1.8
08200	TOMBSTONE CARVER	32.6	-5.9
08311	FORGE OPERATOR IN A STEEL MILL	35.5	0.0
08320	TOOL AND DIE MAKER	42.0	1.7
08321	PATTERNMAKER IN A METAL SHOP	39.1	0.0
08330	MACHINE SET-UP MAN IN A FACTORY	40.3	0.1
08340	MACHINE OPERATOR IN A FACTORY	31.6	-6.6
08350	SAW SHARPENER	18.7	-0.6
08410	TRAINED MACHINIST (52.4)	47.8	4.5
	MACHINIST (43.3)		
08411	AIRCRAFT WORKER	41.9	0.1
08430	AUTOMOBILE REPAIRMAN (36.7)	35.8	-7.1
	GARAGE MECHANIC (34.9)		
08431	OWNER OF A FILLING STATION AND GARAGE	39.2	-8.1
08440	AIRPLANE MECHANIC	48.2	-1.4
08490	MECHANIC (38.8)	34.5	-8.4
	LOCOMOTIVE REPAIRMAN (37.2)		
	AIR CONDITIONING MECHANIC (37.0)		
	CASH REGISTER REPAIRMAN (33.9)		
	REPAIRMAN (30.9)		
	OPERATOR OF A FIXIT SHOP (29.0)		
08493	AUTOMOBILE WORKER (30.8)	28.9	-0.9
	ASSEMBLY LINE WORKER (27.1)		
08494	GREASE MONKEY IN A SERVICE STATION	16.3	-1.5

Code	Occupation		
08530	PRODUCTION WORKER IN THE ELECTRONICS INDUSTRY	47.1	-0.6
08540	TV REPAIRMAN	35.0	-7.0
08550	ELECTRICIAN	49.2	4.7
08560	TELEPHONE INSTALLER	38.6	3.9
08570	POWER LINEMAN	39.9	3.6
08620	MOTION PICTURE PROJECTIONIST	33.9	0.0
08710	PLUMBER	40.6	6.7
08720	WELDER	40.1	0.9
08730	SHEET METAL WORKER	36.8	1.3
08732	BOILERMAKER	30.7	0.0
08740	CONSTRUCTION RIVETER	35.5	-8.1
08800	JEWELRY REPAIRMAN	37.3	-5.7
08910	LENS GRINDER	41.2	0.0
09210	TYPESETTER	38.0	-4.3
09211	OWNER-OPERATOR OF A PRINTING SHOP	52.4	1.7
09220	PRINTING PRESS OPERATOR	40.2	-0.4
09240	METAL ENGRAVER	41.2	0.0
09250	PHOTOENGRAVER	40.3	-5.9
09260	BOOKBINDING MACHINE OPERATOR	31.3	-1.2
09270	PHOTOGRAPH DEVELOPER	35.9	0.0
09310	HOUSE PAINTER	29.8	-1.2
09390	AUTOMOBILE PAINTER	29.0	0.0
09410	PIANO TUNER	32.0	-1.4
09490	QUALITY CHECKER IN A MANUFACTURING PLANT	36.2	-3.2
09510	BRICKLAYER	35.7	1.6
09520	CEMENT FINISHER	31.6	-2.8
09530	ROOFER	31.2	0.0
09540	CARPENTER (42.5) HOUSE CARPENTER (37.3)	39.9	2.7
09542	CARPENTER'S HELPER	22.9	0.3
09550	PLASTERER	33.2	2.3
09560	ROCK WOOL INSULATION INSTALLER	28.4	0.0
09570	WINDOW GLASS INSTALLER	25.5	0.0
09590	PAPER HANGER	24.3	0.0
09592	MAINTENANCE MAN	28.0	0.0
09594	SKILLED CRAFTSMAN IN A CONSTRUCTION CREW	49.6	4.1
09610	CONSTRUCTION LABORER	26.2	0.6
09690	ELECTRIC POWER STATION ATTENDANT PUMP-HOUSE ENGINEER (35.0) STEAM BOILER FIREMAN (32.5)	38.8	-3.7
09710	LONGSHOREMAN (26.9) DOCK WORKER (21.9)	33.8	-0.2
		24.4	3.2

ISCO NO.	OCCUPATION TITLE	PRESTIGE SCORE	SCORE MINUS STD. SCORE
	UNITED STATES		
09711	WAREHOUSE HAND	20.2	-0.2
09713	RAILROAD PORTER	20.2	2.1
09714	PACKER IN A WHOLESALE VEGETABLE MARKET (21.5)	20.4	-1.8
09730	FRUIT PACKER IN A CANNERY (19.4)	38.8	0.2
09731	POWER CRANE OPERATOR	23.5	-1.7
09740	DRAWBRIDGE TENDER	32.6	0.8
09810	STEAM ROLLER OPERATOR	33.7	-1.0
09820	MERCHANT SEAMAN	24.2	-1.2
09830	MACHINE OILER	50.8	8.1
	RAILROAD ENGINEER (53.9)		
09831	LOCOMOTIVE ENGINEER (47.7)	36.2	3.1
09832	LOCOMOTIVE FIREMAN	27.2	0.0
09840	ORE TRAIN MOTORMAN (34.7)	33.8	4.9
	RAILROAD BRAKEMAN (32.8)		
	RAILROAD SWITCHMAN		
09850	TAXICAB DRIVER	22.0	-5.8
09851	BUS DRIVER (32.4)	30.2	-2.2
	STREETCAR MOTORMAN (28.0)		
09852	TRAILER TRUCK DRIVER (32.1)	31.7	-0.9
	TRUCK DRIVER (31.3)		
09854	TRUCK DRIVER'S HELPER	20.0	4.8
09855	DRIVING SCHOOL TEACHER	43.1	1.7
09860	MULE TEAM DRIVER	12.2	-5.9
09950	SKILLED CRAFTSMAN IN A FACTORY (45.8)	45.1	3.3
	SKILLED CRAFTSMAN IN A METAL WORKING SHOP (44.4)		
09570	SEMI-SKILLED WORKER (31.4)	30.4	1.2
	FACTORY WORKER (29.4)		
09971	APPRENTICE TO A MASTER CRAFTSMAN	40.8	4.2
09991	UNSKILLED WORKER IN A FACTORY	15.0	-3.1
09994	RAILROAD SECTION HAND	22.2	-11.1
09995	STREET SWEEPER	10.6	-2.8
09996	GARBAGE COLLECTOR	12.6	-0.1

MEMBERS OF THE ARMED FORCES

10000	COLONEL IN THE ARMY	70.8	-2.1
10001	CAPTAIN IN THE REGULAR ARMY	63.3	0.1
10002	CORPORAL IN THE REGULAR ARMY	34.9	-8.7
10003	ENLISTED MAN IN THE ARMY	40.3	1.6

SOURCES OF LIVELIHOOD OTHER THAN LABOR FORCE ACTIVITY

13000	SOMEONE WHO LIVES OFF STOCKS AND BONDS	55.2	0.5
13001	SOMEONE WHO LIVES OFF PROPERTY HOLDINGS	43.8	-13.3
13002	SOMEONE WHO LIVES OFF INHERITED WEALTH	42.8	-5.2
13004	SOMEONE WHO LIVES OFF HIS SOCIAL SECURITY PENSION	30.5	0.0
13005	SOMEONE ON PUBLIC ASSISTANCE	25.1	8.9

ISCO NO.	OCCUPATION TITLE	PRESTIGE SCORE	SCORE MINUS STD. SCORE
	ARGENTINA		
PROFESSIONAL, TECHNICAL AND RELATED WORKERS			
00610	MEDICO/PHYSICIAN	76.4	-1.5
01101	CONTADOR PUBLICO NACIONAL/CERTIFIED PUBLIC ACCOUNTANT	68.9	0.5
01210	ABOGADO EN PEQUENA CIUDAD/LAWYER IN A SMALL CITY	66.9	-3.7
01330	MAESTRO PRIMARIO/PRIMARY SCHOOL TEACHER	58.2	1.1
01590	PERIODISTA (REPORTER)/JOURNALIST	55.1	0.2
ADMINISTRATIVE AND MANAGERIAL WORKERS			
02111	DIRECTOR DE SOCIEDAD ANONIMA/DIRECTOR OF A CORPORATION	75.7	5.2
02112	GERENTE DE EMPRESA (IMPORT. MEDIA)/MANAGER OF AN AVERAGE SIZE ENTERPRISE	67.4	4.7
03100	JEFE DE OFICINA (REPARTICION PUBLICA)/OFFICE MANAGER, GOVT AGENCY	51.7	-14.0
CLERICAL AND RELATED WORKERS			
03700	CARTERO/MAILMAN	28.0	-4.9
03930	EMPLEADO DE ESCRITORIO/OFFICE EMPLOYEE	45.8	2.5
SALES WORKERS			
04102	PROPIETARIO QUIOSCO (DARIOS, REVISTAS)/PROPRIETOR OF A STAND WHICH SELLS NEWSPAPERS AND MAGAZINES	31.7	-5.9
04210	JEFE DE VENTAS/SALES MANAGER	55.8	3.4
04320	VIAJANTE DE COMERCIO/TRAVELING SALESMAN	48.7	1.8
04410	AGENTE DE SEGUROS/INSURANCE AGENT	50.3	5.8
04510	VENDEDOR DE TIENDA/SHOP CLERK	36.5	2.9
SERVICE WORKERS			
05311	JEFE DE COCINA/HEAD COOK	35.1	-2.5
05320	MOZO DE CAFE O BAR/WAITER IN A CAFE OR BAR	25.8	2.6
05820	AGENTE DE POLICIA/POLICEMAN	29.7	-10.1

AGRICULTURAL, ANIMAL HUSBANDRY AND FORESTRY WORKERS, FISHERMEN AND HUNTERS

Code	Description		
06111	ESTANCIERO/LARGE RANCHER	69.1	5.7
06112	AGRICULTOR (PROPIETARIO PEQUENO CAMPO)/SMALL FARMER (OWNER OF A LITTLE LAND)	50.3	12.6
06210	PEON DE CAMPO/AGRICULTURAL LABORER	19.2	-3.7
06280	TRACTORISTA (TRABAJO RURAL)/TRACTOR DRIVER	32.8	1.9

PRODUCTION AND RELATED WORKERS, TRANSPORT EQUIPMENT OPERATORS AND LABORERS

Code	Description		
08710	PLOMERO/PLUMBER	31.9	-2.0
09510	ALBANIL (OFICIAL)/MASON (JOURNEYMAN)	33.7	-0.4
09540	CARPINTERO/CARPENTER	34.9	-2.3
09710	ESTIBADOR/LONGSHOREMAN	19.2	-2.0
09713	CHANGADOR (EN ESTACION DEL F.C.)/PORTER IN A RAILROAD STATION	16.5	-1.6
09950	OBRERO MECANICO ESPECIALIZADO/SKILLED MECHANIC	45.8	4.0
09995	BARRENDERO/STREET SWEEPER	17.2	3.8

MEMBERS OF THE ARMED FORCES

Code	Description		
10001	OFICIAL FUERZAS ARMADAS/OFFICER IN THE ARMED FORCES	58.3	-4.9

ISCO NO.	OCCUPATION TITLE	PRESTIGE SCORE	SCORE MINUS STD. SCORE
	AUSTRALIA		
	PROFESSIONAL, TECHNICAL AND RELATED WORKERS		
00110	INDUSTRIAL CHEMIST	66.8	-2.4
00210	ARCHITECT	77.9	6.1
00220	ENGINEER, PROFESSIONAL	74.8	4.4
00310	SURVEYOR	63.2	5.3
00410	AIRLINE PILOT, INTERNATIONAL AIRLINE	63.2	-3.3
00610	DOCTOR	81.2	3.3
00630	DENTIST	75.9	5.4
00650	VETERINARY SURGEON	73.3	11.9
00670	CHEMIST, PHARMACEUTICAL	64.4	0.3
00710	TRAINED NURSE	57.2	3.6
00711	MATRON, LARGE HOSPITAL	63.2	5.2
00750	OPTOMETRIST	62.0	0.0
00760	PHYSIOTHERAPIST	65.9	-1.3
01100	ACCOUNTANT, TO A BUSINESS	63.4	8.8
01101	REGISTERED PUBLIC ACCOUNTANT	70.5	2.1
01210	BARRISTER	77.4	6.7
01221	JUDGE OF SUPREME COURT	83.3	1.3
01290	SOLICITOR	78.5	7.8
01310	UNIVERSITY PROFESSOR (81.1)	77.6	-0.0
	UNIVERSITY LECTURER (74.1)		
01320	SECONDARY SCHOOL TEACHER	61.6	-2.6
01330	PRIMARY SCHOOL TEACHER	52.7	-4.4
01391	SCHOOL PRINCIPAL	71.4	5.8
01410	CLERGYMAN WITH UNIVERSITY DEGREE (76.1)	67.4	7.7
	CLERGYMAN, SOME UNIVERSITY TRAINING, BUT NOT A DEGREE (67.1)		
	CLERGYMAN, NO UNIVERSITY TRAINING (59.0)		
01590	NEWS REPORTER	50.0	-5.0
01591	NEWSPAPER EDITOR	68.5	3.5
01622	WINDOW DRESSER, LARGE BUSINESS	36.1	-1.8
01710	MUSICIAN, IN A SYMPHONY ORCHESTRA	53.8	-2.3
01790	RADIO ANNOUNCER	51.6	1.2
01800	JOCKEY	30.5	-18.0

Code	Occupation		
01801	TRAINER, RACEHORSE	35.8	-14.6
01910	TRAINED LIBRARIAN	58.4	3.9
01930	SOCIAL WORKER	56.1	-0.2

ADMINISTRATIVE AND MANAGERIAL WORKERS

Code	Occupation		
02013	MAYOR, LARGE CITY	73.8	-1.4
02030	CABINET MEMBER IN FEDERAL GOVERNMENT	79.7	1.0
02032	DIPLOMAT IN THE AUSTRALIAN FOREIGN SERVICE	80.9	7.7
02033	DEPARTMENTAL HEAD, IN GOVERNMENT SERVICE	67.2	-3.9
02110	DIRECTOR, LARGE FINANCIAL OR INDUSTRIAL ENTERPRISE (77.2)	78.1	3.1
02111	OWNER, BUSINESS VALUED AT MORE THAN 50,000 POUNDS (77.2)	73.1	2.6
	MANAGER, LARGE FINANCIAL OR INDUSTRIAL ENTERPRISE (71.8)		
	COMPANY MANAGER, LARGE BUSINESS (70.2)		
02112	OWNER, BUSINESS, VALUED AT 15,000 TO 50,000 POUNDS (70.8)	67.5	4.7
	OWNER BUSINESS, VALUED AT 7,500 TO 15,000 POUNDS (64.1)		
02113	OWNER, BUSINESS, VALUED AT 1500 TO 7500 POUNDS (55.1)	50.1	-2.2
	OWNER, BUSINESS, VALUED AT LESS THAN 1500 POUNDS (45.1)		
02115	BANK MANAGER, LARGE BANK	70.3	-5.9
02116	JOBBING MASTER BUILDER	49.4	-4.0
02120	WORKS MANAGER, LARGE BUSINESS	63.2	-1.0
02192	DEPARTMENTAL MANAGER, GENERAL	59.2	-1.2
02193	DEPARTMENTAL MANAGER, LARGE BUSINESS	64.6	1.4
02196	TRADE UNION SECRETARY	47.9	-1.6

CLERICAL AND RELATED WORKERS

Code	Occupation		
03000	OFFICE MANAGER, GENERAL	61.9	7.3
03210	STENOGRAPHER	44.8	3.2
03211	PRIVATE SECRETARY, TO EXECUTIVE	54.9	1.9
03310	BOOKKEEPER	45.0	-4.0
03313	BANK CLERK OR TELLER	45.5	-2.1
03314	POST OFFICE CLERK	35.3	-3.7
03520	POSTMASTER	51.7	-6.6
03600	RAILWAY CONDUCTOR	28.1	-10.5
03601	TRAM CONDUCTOR OR DRIVER	28.4	2.4
03700	POSTMAN	21.9	-10.9
03800	TELEPHONE OPERATOR	34.2	-4.2
03910	STOREMAN	28.2	-3.9
03930	ROUTINE OFFICE CLERK	35.4	-7.9
03931	GOVERNMENT OFFICE CLERK	41.0	-3.3
03940	RECEPTIONIST, TO A DENTIST	37.3	-0.6

ISCO NO.	OCCUPATION TITLE AUSTRALIA	PRESTIGE SCORE	SCORE MINUS STD. SCORE
03993	METER READER, GAS OR ELECTRICITY	20.7	0.0
SALES WORKERS			
04210	SALES MANAGER, LARGE BUSINESS	62.3	9.9
04320	COMMERCIAL TRAVELLER	41.0	-5.9
04410	INSURANCE AGENT	44.0	-0.5
04411	REAL ESTATE AGENT (49.5)	48.7	-0.4
	LAND AGENT (47.9)		
04412	STOCKBROKER	60.9	5.1
04430	AUCTIONEER	39.6	0.5
04510	SALESMAN, BOOKSTORE (36.0)	32.1	-1.6
	SALESMAN, FURNITURE STORE (34.7)		
	SALESMAN, DEPARTMENT STORE (33.2)		
	SHOP ASSISTANT (29.4)		
	SALES PERSON, CHAIN STORE (27.1)		
04511	MOTOR CAR SALESMAN	37.8	2.0
04512	PETROL STATION ATTENDANT	24.8	-0.5
04524	MILK DELIVERY MAN	24.8	0.7
SERVICE WORKERS			
05000	BAR MANAGER	34.3	1.8
05104	PUBLICAN	40.4	7.7
05201	HOUSEKEEPER	29.2	1.0
05310	COOK, RESTAURANT	30.6	-0.3
05313	MILK-BAR ATTENDANT	17.2	1.0
05320	WAITER IN A RESTAURANT	19.6	-3.7
05321	BARMAN (20.9)	20.5	-2.7
	BARMAID (20.1)		
05400	DOMESTIC WORKER	22.2	5.0
05510	JANITOR	20.7	-0.3
05520	CHARWOMAN	19.5	3.0
05521	WINDOW CLEANER	14.8	-3.8
05600	CLOTHES-PRESSER IN A LAUNDRY OR DRY-CLEANER'S	19.6	-2.5

Code	Occupation		
05700	BARBER	34.9	4.5
05702	BEAUTY OPERATOR	35.2	0.4
05810	FIREMAN	33.1	-2.2
05820	POLICEMAN	43.5	3.7
05890	NIGHTWATCHMAN	21.8	-0.1
05920	UNDERTAKER	38.9	5.3
05991	USHER IN A CINEMA	18.4	-1.6
05996	AIR HOSTESS	49.1	-1.0
05997	BOOKMAKER	33.7	0.0

AGRICULTURAL, ANIMAL HUSBANDRY AND FORESTRY WORKERS, FISHERMEN AND HUNTERS

Code	Occupation		
06000	FARM MANAGER, SUPERVISES PROPERTY	54.2	-0.0
06110	FARMER, ACTIVELY OPERATES OWN LAND WITH HIRED HELP (54.6)	54.1	7.1
06111	FARMER, OWNER, OPERATES LAND WITH FAMILY (53.7)	64.7	1.3
	LARGE FARM OWNER, SUPERVISES WORK ON OWN LAND, BUT SELDOM WORKS ACTIVELY ON IT	42.3	12.8
06113	FARMER, TENANT, OPERATES LAND WITH FAMILY (46.6)	49.5	10.3
	FARMER, TENANT, OWNS NO CAPITAL, ANIMALS OR MACHINERY (38.0)	58.5	3.6
06116	SQUATTER (68.7)		
06120	GRAZIER (68.7)		
	SHEEP FARMER, WELL ESTABLISHED (62.1)	28.3	5.4
	DAIRY FARMER, WELL ESTABLISHED (57.5)	20.2	2.1
	SHAREMILKER, OWNS CATTLE OR MACHINERY (45.9)		
06210	FARM LABOURER, ESTABLISHED		
06211	FARM LABOURER, MIGRATORY (20.5)	21.8	0.5
	LABOURER, SEASONAL (19.9)	26.0	0.4
06220	CANE CUTTER		
06240	SHEARER (29.6)		
	JACKAROO (26.8)		
	DROVER (25.5)		
	SHEPHERD (22.0)		
06411	FISHERMAN WHO OWNS OWN BOAT	27.8	-9.5

PRODUCTION AND RELATED WORKERS, TRANSPORT EQUIPMENT OPERATORS AND LABORERS

Code	Occupation		
07000	INDUSTRIAL FOREMAN	45.9	6.6
07110	MINER	27.3	-4.2
07730	BUTCHER, WAGES	33.9	-2.5
07760	BAKER AND PASTRYCOOK	31.4	-1.8
07910	TAILOR	37.3	-2.2
07911	DRESSMAKER	36.1	-3.3

OCCUPATION TITLE

ISCO NO.	OCCUPATION TITLE	PRESTIGE SCORE	SCORE MINUS STD. SCORE
	AUSTRALIA		
07960	UPHOLSTERER	31.4	0.5
08010	BOOT REPAIRER	26.6	-1.5
08340	MACHINIST	31.0	-7.2
08410	FITTER	36.4	-7.0
08420	WATCHMAKER, OWN BUSINESS	51.3	11.5
08430	MOTOR MECHANIC, WAGES	36.9	-6.0
08550	ELECTRICIAN, WAGES	38.9	-5.6
08551	ELECTRICIAN, OWN BUSINESS	52.1	4.0
08560	TELEPHONE REPAIRMAN	34.9	0.2
08711	PLUMBER, OWN BUSINESS	48.2	3.3
09210	PRINTER, WAGES	36.5	-5.8
09310	PAINTER, WAGES	34.2	3.1
09410	PIANO TUNER	32.5	-0.8
09510	BRICK LAYER	32.8	-1.3
09540	CARPENTER, WAGES	36.5	-0.7
09541	CARPENTER, OWN BUSINESS	48.9	0.7
09550	PLASTERER, WAGES	34.5	3.6
09594	BUILDING CONSTRUCTICN WORKER	30.3	4.7
09710	WARF LABOURER	20.5	-0.8
09713	RAILWAY ECRTER	22.1	3.9
09714	PACKER	21.6	-0.7
09830	ENGINE DRIVER OR FIREMAN	32.4	-10.3
09831	ENGINE DRIVER OR FIREMAN	32.4	-0.7
09840	RAILWAY SHUNTER	23.3	-5.5
09850	TAXI DRIVER	29.9	2.1
09851	BUS DRIVER	29.6	-2.8
09852	LORRY OR TRUCK DRIVER	25.9	-6.7
09853	CARRIER OR HAULIER	30.7	-8.7
09970	FACTORY OPERATIVE	27.9	-1.3
09990	LABOURER, UNSKILLED	19.1	-0.8
09993	ITINERANT WORKER	21.3	0.8
09995	ROADSWEEPER	19.1	5.7
09996	GARBAGE COLLECTOR	13.7	1.0

MEMBERS OF THE ARMED FORCES

   10001   CAPTAIN, IN THE PERMANENT ARMY   61.0   -2.2

SOURCES OF LIVELIHOOD OTHER THAN LABOR FORCE ACTIVITY

   13003   GENTLEMAN FARMER, WELL ESTABLISHED, DOES NOT SUPERVISE
           DIRECTLY THE WORK ON HIS PROPERTY (67.4)   65.8   0.7
          GENTLEMAN FARMER, REASONABLY WELL ESTABLISHED DOES NOT SUPERVISE
           DIRECTLY THE WORK ON HIS PROPERTY (64.2)

ISCO NO.	OCCUPATION TITLE	PRESTIGE SCORE	SCORE MINUS STD. SCORE
	BELGIUM		
	PROFESSIONAL, TECHNICAL AND RELATED WORKERS		
00610	PHYSICIAN	81.4	3.5
01210	LAWYER	71.2	0.5
01310	UNIVERSITY PROFESSOR	79.3	1.6
01330	ELEMENTARY SCHOOL TEACHER	65.3	8.3
01391	SCHOOL PRINCIPAL	66.4	0.8
01410	CLERGYMAN	66.2	6.6
01414	MISSIONARY	69.6	20.5
01510	AUTHOR	64.6	2.9
01610	ARTIST	65.0	7.9
01730	ACTOR	63.8	12.3
	ADMINISTRATIVE AND MANAGERIAL WORKERS		
02114	BANKER	58.0	-9.0
02190	BUSINESSMAN	59.0	1.0
02195	POLITICIAN	61.4	-1.3
	CLERICAL AND RELATED WORKERS		
03101	CIVIL SERVICE EMPLOYEE	51.6	-2.1
03310	BOOKKEEPER	51.0	2.1
03700	MAIL CARRIER	39.5	6.6
	SALES WORKERS		
04100	GROCER	33.3	-9.2
	SERVICE WORKERS		
05510	JANITOR	23.7	2.7
05700	BARBER	32.6	2.2
05820	POLICEMAN	46.5	6.7

AGRICULTURAL, ANIMAL HUSBANDRY AND FORESTRY WORKERS, FISHERMEN AND HUNTERS

06110   FARMER   39.7   -7.4

PRODUCTION AND RELATED WORKERS, TRANSPORT EQUIPMENT OPERATORS AND LABORERS

07110   COAL MINER   38.3   6.8
07730   BUTCHER   34.6   3.3
07910   TAILOR   40.0   0.6
08010   SHOEMAKER   28.3   0.2
08550   ELECTRICIAN   49.4   4.8
08710   PLUMBER   29.5   -4.4
09210   TYPOGRAPHER   46.7   4.4
09540   CARPENTER   39.2   2.0
09852   TRUCK DRIVER   32.4   -0.2

MEMBERS OF THE ARMED FORCES

10003   SOLDIER   39.9   1.1

339

ISCO NO.	OCCUPATION TITLE	PRESTIGE SCORE	SCORE MINUS STD. SCORE
	BRAZIL-ACUCENA		
	PROFESSICNAL, TECHNICAL AND RELATED WORKERS		
00110	QUIMICO/CHEMIST	54.9	-14.2
00531	EXTENCICNISTA/COUNTY AGRICULTURAL AGENT	49.2	-5.6
00670	FARMACEUTICO-DONO DE FARMACIA/OWNER-OPERATOR OF A PHARMACY	60.6	-3.5
00810	AGENTE DE ESTATISTICA/COUNTY STATISTICS AGENT	57.8	-2.5
00900	ECONOMISTA/ECONOMIST	41.4	-19.2
01211	PROMOTOR PUBLICO/PUBLIC PROSECUTOR	74.2	-1.2
01221	JUIZ DE SUPREMC TRIBUNAL/SUPREME COURT JUSTICE	81.6	-0.4
01290	TABELIAC/NCN-TRIAL LAWYER	48.9	-21.8
01310	PRCFESSOR DE UNIVERSIDADE/UNIVERSITY PROFESSOR	68.1	-9.5
01330	PROFESSORA DE FRIMARIA/PRIMARY SCHOOL TEACHER (FEMALE)	67.7	10.7
01510	ESCRITOR DE ROMANCES/AUTHOR OF NOVELS	53.1	-8.6
01610	ARTISTA QUE FINTA QUADROS QUE SAO MOSTRADOS EM GALERIAS/ARTIST WHO PAINTS PICTURES THAT ARE EXHIBITED IN GALLERIES	40.3	-16.9
01921	PSICOLOGO/PSYCHOLOGIST	57.8	-8.2
01930	ASSISTENTE SOCIAL DE UMA CIDADE/WELFARE WORKER, CITY GOVERNMENT	60.3	4.0
	ADMINISTRATIVE AND MANAGERIAL WORKERS		
02014	PREFEITO/MAYOR	70.6	2.3
02030	MINISTRO DO GOVERNO/MINISTER IN GOVERNMENT	78.9	0.1
02032	DIPLCMATA/DIFLCMAT	61.7	-11.5
02034	CHEFE DE UM DEPARTAMENTO DO GOVERNO ESTADUAL/HEAD OF A DEPARTMENT IN A STATE GCVERNMENT	73.1	-0.9
02111	DIRETOR DE UMA GRANDE COMPANHIA/HEAD OF A LARGE COMPANY	70.6	0.2
02114	BANQUEIRC-DONO CU DIRETOR DE UM BANCO/BANKER (72.7)	71.8	4.8
	GERENTE DE BANCO/BANK MANAGER (70.9)		
02194	TESOURERO DE UMA COMPANHIA GRANDE/TREASURER OF A LARGE COMPANY	75.9	9.3
02197	DIRETOR DE UM SINDICATO INTERNACIONAL/OFFICIAL OF AN INTERNATIONAL LABOR UNION	71.3	8.5

CLERICAL AND RELATED WORKERS

Code	Description		
03310	GUARDA LIVROS/BOOKKEEPER	41.7	-7.2
03311	CAIXEIRO DC LOJA/CASHIER IN A STORE	27.8	-3.4
03510	CHEFE DE ESTACAO DE ESTRADA DE FERRO/STATIONMASTER	65.6	9.5
03600	CHEFE DE TREM/RAILROAD CONDUCTOR	68.1	29.5
03801	TELEGRAFISTA/TELEGRAPH OPERATOR	42.8	-2.5

SALES WORKERS

Code	Description		
04000	GERENTE DE UMA PEQUENA LOJA NA CIDADE/MANAGER OF A SMALL STORE IN THE CITY	49.2	2.6
04100	DONO DE QUITANDA/SMALL MERCHANT	26.4	-16.0
04102	DONO DE BANCA DE JORNAIS E REVISTAS/OWNER, NEWSPAPER STAND	40.3	2.6
04320	REPRESENTANTE DE FIRMA CCMERCIAL/REPRESENTATIVE	63.8	16.9
04521	FEIRANTE/VENDOR	26.0	4.1
04524	LEITEIRO-ENTREGADOR DE LEITE/MILK ROUTE MAN	21.4	-2.7

SERVICE WORKERS

Code	Description		
05102	DCNO DE HOTEL/HOTEL KEEPER	49.6	3.2
05321	PESSOA QUE PREPARA E SERVE BEBIDAS NO BALCAO DE UM RESTAURANTE/ BARTENDER	32.8	9.6
05820	POLICIA/POLICEMAN	41.7	1.9
05821	DELEGADO DE POLICIA/POLICE OFFICIAL	46.0	-13.7
05890	VIGIA NOTURNO/NIGHT WATCHMAN	28.9	6.9

AGRICULTURAL, ANIMAL HUSBANDRY AND FORESTRY WORKERS, FISHERMEN AND HUNTERS

Code	Description		
06000	ADMINISTRADOR DE UMA GRANDE FAZENDA/MANAGER OF A LARGE FARM	53.5	-0.8
06111	GRANDE FAZENDEIRO/LARGE FARMER	65.2	1.9
06112	SITIANTE/SMALL FARMER	37.4	-0.2
06114	TERCEIRO/SHARECROPPER WHO GIVES 1/3 CF CROP TO LANDLORD (25.7)	23.4	-8.2
06116	MEIEIRO/SHARECROPPER WHO GIVES 1/2 OF CROP TO LANDLORD (21.1)		
06210	COLONO/SETTLER	31.0	-8.2
	MORADOR ASSALARIADO NUMA FAZENDA/RESIDENT FARM WAGE WORKER (27.1)	18.2	-4.7
06240	PEAO/FARM HAND (9.3)		
06250	VAQUEIRO/COWBOY	23.6	-2.1
06290	RETIREIRO/MILKER	28.9	5.5
06310	EMPRETEIRO PARA UM SERVICO NUMA FAZENDA/SKILLED FARM WORKER	32.5	2.2
	LENHADOR/LOGGER (18.9)	17.1	-2.1
	LENHEIRO/WOODCUTTER (15.4)		

341

BRAZIL-ACUCENA

ISCO NO.	OCCUPATION TITLE	PRESTIGE SCORE	SCORE MINUS STD. SCORE
	PRODUCTION AND RELATED WORKERS, TRANSPORT EQUIPMENT OPERATORS AND LABORERS		
07000	FEITOR OU CAPATAZ/FOREMAN	31.4	-7.9
07760	PADEIRO/BAKER	31.0	-2.1
07910	ALFAIATE/TAILOR	32.5	-7.0
08010	SAPATEIRO/SHOEMAKER	26.4	-1.7
08430	MECANICO DE AUTOMOVEIS/AUTO MECHANIC	59.2	16.3
09211	PESSOA QUE TEM E OPERA UMA PEQUENA TIPOGRAFIA/OWNER-OPERATOR OF A PRINTING SHOP	35.7	-15.0
09510	PEDREIRO/MASON	49.9	15.8
09540	CARPINTEIRO/CARPENTER	37.8	0.6
09713	CARREGADOR DE MALAS DE ESTACAO/LUGGAGE HANDLER IN RAILWAY STATION	10.0	-8.1
09840	TRABALHADOR NA LINHA DO TREM/WORKER ON A RAILWAY	27.8	-1.0
09860	TROPEIRO/MULETEER	15.0	-3.1
09861	DONO DE CHARRETE DE ALUGUEL/OWNER OF A TWO-WHEELED HORSE CARRIAGE WHICH IS AVAILABLE FOR HIRE	27.5	1.0
09990	DIARISTA/DAY LABORER	19.3	0.2
09994	FERROVIARIO/RAILROAD SECTION HAND	51.7	18.5
09996	LIXEIRO/GARBAGE COLLECTOR	13.2	0.5
	MEMBERS OF THE ARMED FORCES		
10000	GENERAL DO EXERCITO/ARMY GENERAL	79.5	6.6
10001	OFICIAL DE EXERCITO/ARMY OFFICER	65.6	2.4
10002	CABO DO EXERCITO/CORPORAL IN THE ARMY	53.8	10.3
10003	SOLDADO/SOLDIER	31.0	-7.7

PROFESSIONAL, TECHNICAL AND RELATED WORKERS

Code	Description		
00110	QUIMICO/CHEMIST	70.6	1.4
00531	EXTENCICNISTA/CCUNTY AGRICULTURAL AGENT	44.5	-10.4
00610	MEDICO/PHYSICIAN	75.2	-2.7
00670	FARMACEUTICO-DONO DE FARMACIA/OWNER-OPERATOR OF A PHARMACY	56.1	-8.1
00810	AGENTE DE ESTATISTICA/COUNTY STATISTICS AGENT	52.6	-2.7
00900	ECONOMISTA/ECONOMIST	59.3	-1.2
C1210	ADVOGADO/LAWYER	73.3	-2.6
C1211	PRCMOTOR PUBLICO/PUBLIC PROSECUTCR	74.4	-1.0
C1221	JUIZ DE SUPREMO TRIBUNAL/SUPREME COURT JUSTICE	84.6	-2.6
C1290	TABELIAO/NON-TRIAL LAWYER	64.1	-6.5
C1310	PROFESSOR DE UNIVERSIDADE/UNIVERSITY PROFESSOR	72.2	-5.4
C1320	PRCFESSCRA SECUNDARIA/SECONDARY SCHOOL TEACHER	59.6	-4.6
C1330	PROFESSCRA DE PRIMARIA/PRIMARY SCHOOL TEACHER (FEMALE)	59.6	2.5
C1410.	PADRE/PRIEST	76.8	17.1
C1510	ESCRITOR DE RCMANCES/AUTHOR OF NOVELS	47.7	-14.0
C1610	ARTISTA QUE PINTA QUADROS QUE SAO MOSTRADOS EM GALERIAS/ARTIST WHO PAINTS PICTURES THAT ARE EXHIBITED IN GALLERIES	47.7	-9.5
C1921	PSICOLOGO/PSYCHOLOGIST	61.2	-4.8
C1930	ASSISTENTE SOCIAL DE UMA CIDADE/WELFARE WORKER, CITY GOVERNMENT	60.4	4.1

ADMINISTRATIVE AND MANAGERIAL WORKERS

Code	Description		
02014	FREFEITO/MAYOR	64.4	-3.9
02030	MINISTRO DO GOVERNO/MINISTER IN GOVERNMENT	78.7	-0.1
02032	DIPLOMATA/DIPLOMAT	64.1	-9.1
02034	CHEFE DE UM DEPARTAMENTO DO GOVERNO ESTALUAL/HEAD OF A DEPARTMENT IN A STATE GOVERNMENT	71.7	-2.3
02111	DIRETOR DE UMA GRANDE COMPANHIA/HEAD OF A LARGE COMPANY	71.4	1.0
02114	BANQUEIRO-DCNO CU DIRETOR DE UM BANCO/BANKER (72.5) GERENTE DE BANCO/BANK MANAGER (71.9)	72.2	5.2
02194	TESOURERC DE UMA COMPANHIA GRANDE/TREASURER OF A LARGE CCMPANY	74.1	7.4
02197	DIRETOR DE UM SINDICATO INTERNACIONAL/OFFICIAL OF AN INTERNATIONAL LABOR UNION	66.0	3.3

343

ISCO NO.	OCCUPATION TITLE	PRESTIGE SCORE	SCORE MINUS STD. SCORE
	BRAZIL-BEZERROS		
	CLERICAL AND RELATED WORKERS		
03310	GUARDA LIVROS/BOOKKEEPER	53.6	4.7
03311	CAIXEIRO DO LOJA/CASHIER IN A STORE	29.4	-1.8
03511	CHEFE DE ESTACAO DE ESTRADA DE FERRO/STATIONMASTER	51.8	-4.3
03600	CHEFE DE TREM/RAILROAD CONDUCTOR	44.5	5.9
03801	TELEGRAFISTA/TELEGRAPH OPERATOR	44.5	-0.8
	SALES WORKERS		
04000	GERENTE DE UMA PEQUENA LOJA NA CIDADE/MANAGER OF A SMALL STORE IN THE CITY	47.4	0.8
04100	DONO DE QUITANDA/SMALL MERCHANT	23.8	-18.7
04102	DONO DE BANCA DE JORNAIS E REVISTAS/OWNER, NEWSPAPER STAND	42.9	5.2
04320	REPRESENTANTE DE FIRMA COMERCIAL/REPRESENTATIVE	61.4	14.5
04521	FEIRANTE/VENDOR	23.2	1.3
04524	LEITERIRO-ENTREGADOR DE LEITE/MILK ROUTE MAN	17.6	-6.5
	SERVICE WORKERS		
05102	DONO DE HOTEL/HOTEL KEEPER	42.1	-4.3
05321	PESSOA QUE PREPARA E SERVE BEBIDAS NO BALCAO DE UM RESTAURANTE/ BARTENDER	30.5	7.3
05820	POLICIA/POLICEMAN	42.6	2.8
05821	DELEGADO DE POLICIA/POLICE OFFICIAL	53.9	-5.8
05890	VIGIA NCTURNO/NIGHT WATCHMAN	23.0	1.0
	AGRICULTURAL, ANIMAL HUSBANDRY AND FORESTRY WORKERS, FISHERMEN AND HUNTERS		
06000	ADMINISTRADOR DE UMA GRANDE FAZENDA/MANAGER OF A LARGE FARM	49.1	-5.2
06111	GRANDE FAZENDEIRO/LARGE FARMER	60.1	-3.3
06112	SITIANTE/SMALL FARMER	40.2	2.5
06113	TERCEIRO/SHARECROPPER WHO GIVES 1/3 OF CROP TO LANDLORD (45.0)	35.9	4.3
06114	MEIEIRO/SHARECROPPER WHO GIVES 1/2 OF CROP TO LANDLORD (26.7)		

344

Code	Description		
06116	COLONO/SETTLER	36.4	-2.8
06210	PEAO/FARM HAND (24.6)	23.4	0.4
	MORADOR ASSALARIADO NUMA FAZENDA/RESIDENT FARM WAGE WORKER (22.2)		
06240	VAQUEIRO/COWBOY	27.0	-1.4
06250	RETIREIRO/MILKER	13.8	-9.6
06290	EMPRETEIRO PARA UM SERVICO NUMA FAZENDA/SKILLED FARM WORKER	28.1	-2.2
06310	LENHEIRO/WOODCUTTER	17.6	-1.6

PRODUCTION AND RELATED WORKERS, TRANSPORT EQUIPMENT OPERATORS AND LABORERS

Code	Description		
07000	FEITOR OU CAPATAZ/FOREMAN	34.3	-5.0
07760	PADEIRO/BAKER	31.3	-1.9
07910	ALFAIATE/TAILOR	35.1	-4.4
08010	SAPATEIRO/SHOEMAKER	24.9	-3.3
08430	MECANICO DE AUTOMOVEIS/AUTO MECHANIC	53.1	10.2
09211	PESSOA QUE TEM E OPERA UMA PEQUENA TIPOGRAFIA/OWNER-OPERATOR OF A PRINTING SHOP	49.6	-1.1
09510	PEDREIRO/MASON	42.1	8.0
09540	CARPINTEIRO/CARPENTER	34.5	-2.7
09713	CARREGADOR DE MALAS DE ESTACAO/LUGGAGE HANDLER IN RAILWAY STATION	10.6	-7.5
09840	TRABALHADOR NA LINHA DO TREM/WORKER ON A RAILWAY	22.7	-6.1
09860	TECPEIRO/MULETEER	30.2	12.1
09861	DONO DE CHARRETE DE ALUGUEL/OWNER OF A TWO-WHEELED HORSE CARRIAGE WHICH IS AVAILABLE FOR HIRE	31.6	5.1
09990	DIARISTA/DAY LABORER	17.9	-1.3
09994	FERROVIARIO/RAILROAD SECTION HAND	47.7	14.5
09996	LIXEIRO/GARBAGE COLLECTOR	10.1	-2.6

MEMBERS OF THE ARMED FORCES

Code	Description		
10000	GENERAL DO EXERCITO/ARMY GENERAL	84.8	11.9
10001	OFICIAL DE EXERCITO/ARMY OFFICER	76.8	13.5
10002	CABO DO EXERCITO/CORPORAL IN THE ARMY	50.4	6.8
10003	SOLDADO/SOLDIER	25.1	-13.6

BRAZIL-SAO PAOLO

PROFESSIONAL, TECHNICAL AND RELATED WORKERS

ISCO NO.	OCCUPATION TITLE	PRESTIGE SCORE	SCORE MINUS STD. SCORE
00610	MEDICO/PHYSICIAN	72.7	-5.2
01100	CONTADOR/ACCOUNTANT	53.9	-0.7
01210	ADVOGADO/LAWYER	70.0	-0.6
01330	PROFESSOR PRIMARIO/PRIMARY SCHOOL TEACHER	57.8	0.8
01410	PADRE/PRIEST	68.1	8.4
01590	JORNALISTA/JOURNALIST	63.9	9.0

ADMINISTRATIVE AND MANAGERIAL WORKERS

ISCO NO.	OCCUPATION TITLE	PRESTIGE SCORE	SCORE MINUS STD. SCORE
02111	DIRETOR SUPT. DE COMPANHIA/COMPANY DIRECTOR	65.9	-4.5
02112	GERENTE COMERCIAL DE FIRMA/BUSINESS MANAGER	59.8	-3.0
02116	EMPREITEIRO/CONTRACTOR	41.2	-12.2
02120	GERENTE DE FABRICA/FACTORY MANAGER	59.5	-4.7

CLERICAL AND RELATED WORKERS

ISCO NO.	OCCUPATION TITLE	PRESTIGE SCORE	SCORE MINUS STD. SCORE
03100	FUNCIONARIO PUBLICO DE PADRAO MEDIO/MIDDLE GRADE CIVIL SERVANT	51.4	-14.3
03590	DESPACHANTE/DISPATCHER OR EXPEDITOR	44.7	7.8
03600	CONDUCTOR DE TRENS/RAILROAD CONDUCTOR	27.6	-11.0
C3930	ESCRITURARIO/OFFICE CLERK	46.4	3.1

SALES WORKERS

ISCO NO.	OCCUPATION TITLE	PRESTIGE SCORE	SCORE MINUS STD. SCORE
04100	DONO DE PEQUENO ESTABELECIMENTO COMERCIAL/SMALL SHOPKEEPER	51.7	9.2
04320	VIAJANTE COMERCIAL/TRAVELING SALESMAN	45.3	-1.6
04510	BALCONISTA/SHOP CLERK	33.5	-0.1

SERVICE WORKERS

ISCO NO.	OCCUPATION TITLE	PRESTIGE SCORE	SCORE MINUS STD. SCORE
05311	COSINHEIRO-REST. DE 1A CLASSE/CHEF	30.0	-7.6
05320	GARCON/WAITER	26.7	3.5
05820	GUARDA CIVIL/POLICEMAN	35.5	-4.3

346

AGRICULTURAL, ANIMAL HUSBANDRY AND FORESTRY WORKERS, FISHERMEN AND HUNTERS

06111	FAZENDEIRO/LARGE FARMER	63.5	0.1
06112	SITIANTE/SMALL FARMER	42.0	4.4
06210	TRABALHADOR AGRICOLA/AGRICULTURAL LABOURER	25.6	2.7
06280	TRATORISTA/TRACTOR DRIVER	28.9	-2.0

PRODUCTION AND RELATED WORKERS, TRANSPORT EQUIPMENT OPERATORS AND LABORERS

08490	MECANICO/MECHANIC	35.0	-7.8
09510	PEDREIRO/MASON	23.7	-10.4
09540	CARPINTEIRO/CARPENTER	30.0	-7.2
09710	ESTIVADOR/LONGSHOREMAN	17.7	-3.5
09852	MOTORISTA/DRIVER	33.3	0.7
09996	LIXEIRO/GARBAGE COLLECTOR	13.6	0.9

CANADA

PROFESSIONAL, TECHNICAL AND RELATED WORKERS

ISCO NO.	OCCUPATION TITLE	PRESTIGE SCORE	SCORE MINUS STD. SCORE
00110	CHEMIST	69.8	0.6
00120	PHYSICIST	73.6	-2.8
00210	ARCHITECT	74.1	2.3
00220	CIVIL ENGINEER	69.4	-0.9
00270	MINING ENGINEER	65.3	2.6
00310	SURVEYOR	58.9	1.0
00320	DRAUGHTSMAN	57.0	2.1
00380	MINE SAFETY ANALYST	54.3	0.0
00410	AIRLINE PILOT	62.8	-3.7
00420	SHIP'S PILOT	56.7	-6.5
00510	BIOLOGIST	68.9	0.2
00540	MEDICAL OR DENTAL TECHNICIAN	64.1	6.1
00610	PHYSICIAN	82.7	4.8
00650	VETERINARIAN	63.4	2.7
00670	DRUGGIST	65.8	1.7
00710	REGISTERED NURSE	61.5	7.9
00760	PHYSIOTHERAPIST	68.4	1.3
00791	CHIROPRACTOR	65.0	2.5
00820	MATHEMATICIAN	69.0	-0.0
00840	COMPUTER PROGRAMMER	51.2	-0.1
00900	ECONOMIST	59.0	-0.1
01100	ACCOUNTANT	60.2	-1.5
01210	LAWYER	78.1	5.7
01222	COUNTY COURT JUDGE	78.3	7.4
01310	UNIVERSITY PROFESSOR	80.2	5.1
01320	HIGH SCHOOL TEACHER	62.8	2.6
01330	PUBLIC GRADE SCHOOL TEACHER	56.7	-1.4
01410	CATHOLIC PRIEST (69.1)	66.8	-0.4
	PROTESTANT MINISTER (64.4)		7.1
01510	AUTHOR	61.6	-0.2
01590	JOURNALIST	57.9	-2.9
01592	ADVERTISING COPYWRITER	46.6	-0.8

01593	PUBLIC RELATIONS MAN	57.5	0.4
01610	SCULPTOR	54.1	-3.1
01620	COMMERCIAL ARTIST	54.4	-0.1
01631	TV CAMERAMAN	46.0	-0.8
01710	MUSICIAN IN A SYMPHONY ORCHESTRA (53.3)	51.4	-4.7
	MUSICIAN (49.6)		
01711	JAZZ MUSICIAN	39.0	0.9
01720	BALLET DANCER	46.7	1.9
01731	TV STAR	62.3	-0.3
01732	TV DIRECTOR	59.0	-3.2
01790	TV ANNOUNCER (54.8)	45.5	-4.9
	DISC JOCKEY (36.3)		
01800	PROFESSIONAL ATHLETE	51.5	3.0
01910	PROFESSIONALLY TRAINED LIBRARIAN	55.2	0.7
01921	PSYCHOLOGIST	71.1	5.1
01930	SOCIAL WORKER	52.4	-3.9
01931	YMCA DIRECTOR (55.3)	48.1	-0.8
	PLAYGROUND DIRECTOR (40.8)		
01941	JOB COUNSELOR	55.4	0.6
01990	RESEARCH TECHNICIAN	63.5	5.3
01995	ADVERTISING EXECUTIVE	53.7	-3.0

ADMINISTRATIVE AND MANAGERIAL WORKERS

02011	PROVINCIAL PREMIER	85.2	3.3
02013	MAYOR OF A LARGE CITY	75.3	0.6
02021	MEMBER OF THE CANADIAN SENATE	81.7	-3.4
02022	MEMBER OF THE CANADIAN HOUSE OF COMMONS	80.4	8.3
02024	MEMBER OF CITY COUNCIL	59.8	4.8
02030	MEMBER OF THE CANADIAN CABINET	79.0	0.3
02035	DEPARTMENTAL HEAD IN A CITY GOVERNMENT	67.7	4.6
02111	OWNER OF A MANUFACTURING PLANT	65.9	-4.5
02113	MANAGER OF A REAL ESTATE OFFICE	55.4	3.1
02114	BANK MANAGER	67.3	0.3
02116	BUILDING CONTRACTOR	53.7	0.4
02120	GENERAL MANAGER OF A MANUFACTURING PLANT	65.6	1.4
02196	TRADE UNION BUSINESS AGENT	46.8	-2.7

CLERICAL AND RELATED WORKERS

03100	ADMINISTRATIVE OFFICER IN FEDERAL CIVIL SERVICE	65.3	-0.4
03210	STENOGRAPHER (43.8)	41.9	0.3

CANADA

ISCO NO.	OCCUPATION TITLE	PRESTIGE SCORE	SCORE MINUS STD. SCORE
03220	TYPIST (39.9)	45.4	0.3
03310	IBM KEYPUNCH OPERATOR	47.0	-1.9
03311	BOOKKEEPER	29.8	-1.5
03313	CASHIER IN A SUPERMARKET	40.3	-7.3
03314	BANK TELLER	35.5	-3.5
03391	POST OFFICE CLERK	28.2	1.1
03590	BILL COLLECTOR	30.8	-6.1
03600	TRUCK DISPATCHER	43.2	4.6
03700	RAILROAD CONDUCTOR	34.5	1.6
03800	MAILMAN	36.4	-2.0
03910	TELEPHONE OPERATOR	24.8	-7.3
03911	STOCKROOM ATTENDANT	29.6	0.2
03930	SHIPPING CLERK	34.0	-9.3
03940	CLERK IN AN OFFICE	36.9	-0.9
03941	RECEPTIONIST	34.1	-2.5
03943	RAILROAD TICKET AGENT	44.4	0.9
03951	TRAVEL AGENT	31.3	0.5
03951	FILE CLERK		

SALES WORKERS

ISCO NO.	OCCUPATION TITLE	PRESTIGE SCORE	SCORE MINUS STD. SCORE
04000	MANAGER OF A SUPERMARKET	50.0	3.3
04001	SERVICE STATION MANAGER	39.6	1.2
04100	OWNER OF A FOOD STORE	45.5	3.1
04106	WHOLESALE DISTRIBUTOR	45.6	-12.8
04220	MERCHANDISE BUYER FOR A DEPARTMENT STORE	48.6	-0.7
04221	GOVERNMENT PURCHASING AGENT	54.0	3.1
04222	LIVESTOCK BUYER	37.8	-1.6
04320	MANUFACTURER'S REPRESENTATIVE (49.6)	44.0	-2.9
	TRAVELLING SALESMAN (38.3)		
04410	INSURANCE AGENT	45.0	0.5
04411	REAL ESTATE AGENT	44.9	-4.2
04432	INSURANCE CLAIMS INVESTIGATOR	48.6	-0.6
04510	SALES CLERK IN A STORE	25.4	-8.2
04511	USED CAR SALESMAN	29.9	-5.9

Code	Occupation		
04512	FILLING STATION ATTENDANT	22.4	-2.9
04522	TELEPHONE SOLICITOR	25.6	-0.2
04523	NEWSPAPER PEDDLER	14.4	0.3

SERVICE WORKERS

Code	Occupation		
05101	LUNCHROOM OPERATOR	30.2	-4.7
05102	MOTEL OWNER	49.1	2.7
05201	HOUSEKEEPER IN A PRIVATE HOME	27.6	-0.6
05310	COOK IN A RESTAURANT	28.4	-2.4
05320	WAITRESS IN A RESTAURANT	19.2	-4.1
05321	BARTENDER	19.5	-3.8
05401	PROFESSIONAL BABYSITTER	24.8	2.0
05510	JANITOR	16.7	-4.3
05600	WORKER IN A DRY CLEANING OR LAUNDRY PLANT (20.0) LAUNDRESS (18.6)	19.3	-2.8
05700	BARBER	37.5	7.1
05702	BEAUTY OPERATOR	33.6	-1.2
05810	FIREFIGHTER	41.5	6.1
05820	POLICEMAN	49.1	9.3
05910	MUSEUM ATTENDANT	29.1	0.0
05920	FUNERAL DIRECTOR	52.2	18.6
05990	HOSPITAL ATTENDANT	33.3	-8.3
05992	ELEVATOR OPERATOR IN A BUILDING	19.4	-4.9
05996	AIR HOSTESS	54.2	4.1

AGRICULTURAL, ANIMAL HUSBANDRY AND FORESTRY WORKERS, FISHERMEN AND HUNTERS

Code	Occupation		
06110	FARM OWNER AND OPERATOR	42.0	-5.1
06112	PART-TIME FARMER	24.1	-13.6
06120	DAIRY FARMER (42.1) COMMERCIAL FARMER (40.0) HOG FARMER (31.5)	37.9	-17.1
06210	FARM LABOURER	20.7	-2.2
06310	LOGGER	23.9	4.7
06311	WHISTLE PUNK	17.8	0.0
06320	PROFESSIONALLY TRAINED FORESTER	57.0	9.5
06321	TIMBER CRUISER	38.4	0.0
06410	TROLLER (22.7) COD FISHERMAN (22.5)	22.6	-5.0

ISCO NO.	OCCUPATION TITLE	PRESTIGE SCORE	SCORE MINUS STD. SCORE
	CANADA		
PRODUCTION AND RELATED WORKERS, TRANSPORT EQUIPMENT OPERATORS AND LABORERS			
07000	CONSTRUCTION FOREMAN (48.6)	48.5	9.2
07001	FOREMAN IN A FACTORY (48.4)	51.3	-0.9
07110	SUPERINTENDENT OF A CONSTRUCTION JOB	26.5	-5.0
07111	COAL MINER	36.3	0.3
	DIAMOND DRILLER (42.4)		
07112	MUCKING MACHINE OPERATOR (30.1)		
	QUARRY WORKER	25.6	1.1
07130	OIL FIELD WORKER	33.7	2.7
07210	STEEL MILL WORKER	32.8	-12.6
07320	SAW MILL OPERATOR	35.3	4.9
07340	PAPER MAKING MACHINE TENDER	30.2	2.3
07540	LCOM OPERATOR	31.8	1.4
07590	TEXTILE MILL WORKER	27.6	1.5
07730	BUTCHER IN A STORE	33.2	1.9
07731	WORKER IN A MEAT PACKING PLANT	24.2	6.1
07760	BAKER	37.1	3.9
07911	CUSTOM SEAMSTRESS	31.9	-7.5
07950	SEWING MACHINE OPERATOR	27.0	0.8
08320	TOOL AND DIE MAKER	40.5	0.2
08330	MACHINE SET-UP MAN IN A FACTORY	40.1	-0.1
08340	MACHINE OPERATOR IN A FACTORY	33.3	-4.9
08350	SAW SHARPENER	19.9	-0.6
08410	MACHINIST	42.1	-1.2
08411	AIRCRAFT WORKER	41.6	-0.1
08430	AUTOMOBILE REPAIRMAN	36.4	-6.6
08440	AIRPLANE MECHANIC	47.9	-1.7
08493	AUTOMOBIF WORKER (34.3)	30.7	-0.9
	ASSEMBLY LINE WORKER (27.0)		
08530	PRODUCTION WORKER IN THE ELECTRONICS INDUSTRY	48.3	0.6
08540	TV REPAIRMAN	35.5	-6.5
08550	ELECTRICIAN	47.8	3.3
08570	POWER LINEMAN	39.0	2.7

Code	Occupation		
08710	PLUMBER	40.6	6.7
08720	WELDER	39.9	0.6
08730	SHEET METAL WORKER	34.3	-1.3
09210	TYPESETTER	40.2	-2.1
09220	NEWSPAPER PRESSMAN	41.0	0.4
09260	BOOK BINDER	33.6	1.2
09310	HOUSE PAINTER	28.6	-2.4
09510	BRICKLAYER	34.6	0.5
09540	HOUSE CARPENTER	37.1	-0.1
09542	CARPENTER'S HELPER	22.2	-0.3
09594	CONSTRUCTION LABORER	25.4	-0.2
09690	PUMPHOUSE ENGINEER (37.1)	34.2	0.2
09710	STEAM BOILER FIREMAN (31.4)		
09711	LONGSHOREMAN	25.0	3.8
09714	WAREHOUSE HAND	20.5	0.2
09730	FRUIT PACKER IN A CANNERY	22.3	0.0
09740	POWER CRANE OPERATOR	38.3	-0.2
09820	STEAM ROLLER OPERATOR	30.8	-1.0
09830	OILER ON A SHIP	26.5	1.1
09840	LOCOMOTIVE ENGINEER	46.6	3.9
09850	RAILROAD BRAKEMAN	35.4	6.6
09851	TAXICAB DRIVER	24.1	-3.7
09852	BUS DRIVER	34.3	1.9
09855	TRAILER TRUCK DRIVER	31.4	-1.2
09971	DRIVING INSTRUCTOR	39.7	-1.7
09994	APPRENTICE TO A MASTER CRAFTSMAN	32.4	-4.2
	RAILROAD SECTION HAND	26.2	-7.1
C9996	GARBAGE COLLECTOR	14.4	1.7

MEMBERS OF THE ARMED FORCES

Code	Occupation		
10000	COLONEL IN THE ARMY	67.2	-5.7
10003	PRIVATE IN THE ARMY	27.2	-11.5

SOURCES OF LIVELIHOOD OTHER THAN LABOR FORCE ACTIVITY

Code	Occupation		
13000	SOMEONE WHO LIVES OFF STOCKS AND BONDS	54.1	-0.5
13001	SOMEONE WHO LIVES OFF PROPERTY HOLDINGS	46.4	-10.7
13002	SOMEONE WHO LIVES OFF INHERITED WEALTH	43.6	-4.4
13005	SOMEONE WHO LIVES ON RELIEF	7.3	-8.9

ISCO NO.	OCCUPATION TITLE	PRESTIGE SCORE	SCORE MINUS STD. SCORE
	CEYLON		
	PROFESSIONAL, TECHNICAL AND RELATED WORKERS		
00530	TEA RESEARCH WORKER	66.6	8.8
00610	GOVERNMENT DOCTOR	85.3	7.4
00670	APOTHECARY	51.1	-13.0
00793	SANITARY INSPECTOR	47.9	0.4
01101	CHIEF ACCOUNTANT	74.4	6.0
01220	JUDGE	82.2	4.5
01222	STIPENDIARY MAGISTRATE	77.5	4.3
01320	TEACHER IN ENGLISH SCHOOL	58.9	-5.3
01330	TEACHER IN VERNACULAR SCHOOL	49.5	-7.5
01392	EDUCATION OFFICER OF A PROVINCE (80.7)	72.9	5.3
	INSPECTOR OF SCHOOLS (65.1)		
01394	PRINCIPAL, GOVERNMENT CENTRAL SCHOOL	68.2	-4.0
01950	GOVERNMENT TRANSLATOR	46.4	-7.6
01990	ASSISTANT GOVERNMENT ANALYST	69.8	11.5
	ADMINISTRATIVE AND MANAGERIAL WORKERS		
02022	MEMBER OF PARLIAMENT	72.9	0.7
	CLERICAL AND RELATED WORKERS		
03100	REGISTRAR OF LANDS	62.0	-3.8
03101	CIVIL SERVANT (MEMBER OF CEYLON CIVIL SERVICE)	83.8	30.1
03102	INCOME TAX ASSESSOR (71.3)	56.8	-4.4
	INSPECTOR, VALUATIONS DEPARTMENT (55.7)		
	FOOD INSPECTOR (43.3)		
03510	RAILWAY STATIONMASTER	54.2	-1.9
03520	POSTMASTER	63.5	5.2
03600	RAILWAY GUARD, GOVERNMENT RAILWAY	44.8	6.2
03700	POSTMAN	32.4	-0.5
03701	"PEON"/MESSENGER, OFFICE BOY	33.9	8.1
03800	TELEPHONE OPERATOR (SWITCHBOARD)	40.2	1.8

03931 GOVERNMENT CLERK	52.6	8.3

SERVICE WORKERS

05820 POLICE CONSTABLE	37.0	-2.8
05821 INSPECTOR OF POLICE	60.4	0.7
05822 SUPERINTENDENT OF POLICE (79.1)	77.5	2.3
ASSISTANT SUPERINTENDENT OF POLICE (76.0)		
05890 WATCHER (CARETAKER)	30.8	8.8
05891 PRISON GUARD	41.7	2.6
05990 HOSPITAL ATTENDANT	35.5	-6.1

PRODUCTION AND RELATED WORKERS, TRANSPORT EQUIPMENT OPERATORS AND LABORERS

09830 ENGINE DRIVER, GOVERNMENT RAILWAY	57.3	14.6
09840 RAILWAY SIGNALMAN	38.6	9.8
09990 LABOURER (COOLIE)	29.3	10.1

ISCO NO.	OCCUPATION TITLE	PRESTIGE SCORE	SCORE MINUS STD. SCORE
	CHILE		
	PROFESSIONAL, TECHNICAL AND RELATED WORKERS		
00130	INVESTIGADOR CIENTIFICO/SCIENTIST	77.0	-1.4
00210	ARQUITECTO/ARCHITECT	75.9	4.1
00220	INGENIERO/ENGINEER	77.0	6.7
00410	PILOTO COMERCIAL/COMMERCIAL AIRLINE PILOT	62.1	-4.4
00610	MEDICO/PHYSICIAN	78.1	0.2
00620	PRACTICANTE/MEDICAL ASSISTANT	47.2	-2.8
00630	DENTISTA/DENTIST	70.6	0.1
00670	QUIMICO-FARMACEUTICO/PHARMACIST	66.4	2.2
00710	ENFERMA/NURSE	55.7	2.1
00900	ECONOMISTA/ECONOMIST	66.4	5.8
01100	CONTADOR/ACCOUNTANT	56.8	2.2
01210	ABOGADO/LAWYER	69.5	-1.1
01220	JUEZ/JUDGE	71.7	-6.0
01310	PROFESOR UNIVERSITARIO/UNIVERSITY PROFESSOR	73.8	-3.8
01320	PROFESOR SECUNDARIO/SECONDARY SCHOOL TEACHER	57.8	-6.3
01330	PROFESOR PRIMARIO/PRIMARY SCHOOL TEACHER	50.4	-6.6
01410	SACERDOTE/PRIEST	64.2	4.6
01510	ESCRITOR/WRITER	66.4	4.6
01590	NEWSPAPER REPORTER	55.7	0.8
01610	PINTOR O ESCULTOR/PAINTER OR SCULPTOR	62.1	4.9
01710	MUSICO DE ORQUESTA SINFONICA/MUSICIAN IN SYMPHONY ORCHESTRA	63.2	7.1
01790	LOCUTOR DE RADIO/RADIO ANNOUNCER	51.5	1.1
01791	ARTISTA DE CLUB NOCTURNO/NIGHT CLUB ENTERTAINER	34.4	1.7
01920	SOCIOLOGO/SOCIOLOGIST	67.4	-0.0
01921	PSICOLOGO/PSYCHOLOGIST	67.4	1.5
01930	VISITADORA SOCIAL/SOCIAL WORKER	56.8	0.5
	ADMINISTRATIVE AND MANAGERIAL WORKERS		
02022	DIPUTADO/REPRESENTATIVE TO LEGISLATURE	71.7	-0.5
02030	MINISTER OF STATE (77.0) MINISTRO DE LA CORTE DE JUSTICIA/ATTORNEY GENERAL (75.9)	76.5	-2.3

356

Code	Occupation		
02032	DIPLOMATICO/DIPLOMAT	80.2	7.0
02033	INTENDENTE/HIGH PUBLIC ADMINISTRATOR	71.7	0.6
02111	INDUSTRIAL/INDUSTRIALIST (68.5)	68.5	-1.9
	DIRECTOR DE COMPANIA/DIRECTOR OF A COMPANY (68.5)		
02112	GERENTE DE COMPANIA/COMPANY MANAGER	73.8	11.1
02114	BANQUERO/BANKER	69.5	2.6
02116	CONSTRUCTOR/BUILDING CONTRACTOR	63.2	9.8
02194	VICEPRESIDENTE FISCAL/LEGAL VICE PRESIDENT	67.4	0.8
02196	DIRIGENTE SINDICAL/LABOR UNION OFFICIAL	50.4	0.9

CLERICAL AND RELATED WORKERS

Code	Occupation		
03210	SECRETARIA DACTILOGRAFA/SECRETARY TYPIST	48.3	6.7
03313	EMPLEADO BANCARIO/BANK EMPLOYEE	55.7	8.1
03500	OFICIAL DE LAS FF. AA./STATE RAILWAY OFFICIAL	56.3	0.7
03600	CONDUCTOR DE TREN/RAILROAD CONDUCTOR	33.4	-5.2
03700	CARTERO/MAILMAN	27.0	-5.8
03910	ALMACENERO/WAREHOUSE CLERK	41.9	9.8
03930	EMLEADO PARTICULAR/EMPLOYEE IN PRIVATE FIRM	49.3	6.0
03931	EMPLEADO SEMI-FISCAL/GOVERNMENT CLERK	46.1	1.8

SALES WORKERS

Code	Occupation		
04100	DUENO DE LIBRERIA/OWNER OF BOOKSTORE (47.2)	37.6	-4.8
	DUENO DE TIENDA O PAQUETERIA/SHOPKEEPER (44.0)		
	LIQUOR STORE OWNER (21.7)		
04104	COMISIONISTA O CORREDOR/COMMISSION MERCHANT OR BROKER	54.7	0.0
04320	VENDEDOR VIAJERO/TRAVELING SALESMAN	41.9	-5.0
04410	AGENTE DE SEGUROS/INSURANCE AGENT	50.4	5.9
04510	EMPLEADO DE TIENDA COMERCIAL/SHOE CLERK	45.1	11.4
04523	SUPLEMENTERO/NEWSPAPER SELLER	12.1	-1.9
04524	LECHERO/MILKMAN	23.8	-0.3

SERVICE WORKERS

Code	Occupation		
05102	HOTELERO/HOTEL KEEPER	51.5	5.1
05200	MAYORDOMO/STEWARD	38.7	-7.5
05320	GARZON/WAITER	28.1	4.8
05400	EMPLEADO DOMESTICO/DOMESTIC SERVANT	16.4	-0.8
05600	LAVANDERA/LAUNDRESS	16.4	-5.7
05700	PELUQUERO/BARBER	32.3	1.9
05702	PEINADORA/HAIRDRESSER	35.5	0.7

357

ISCO NO.	OCCUPATION TITLE	PRESTIGE SCORE	SCORE MINUS STD. SCORE
	CHILE		
05820	POLICEMAN (37.6)		
	CARABINERO/POLICEMAN (34.4)	36.0	-3.8
05990	PERSONAL AUXILIAR DE HOSPITAL/HOSPITAL ORDERLY	45.1	3.5
	AGRICULTURAL, ANIMAL HUSBANDRY AND FORESTRY WORKERS, FISHERMEN AND HUNTERS		
06000	ADMINISTRADOR DE FUNDO/AGRICULTURAL ESTATE MANAGER	55.7	1.4
06111	HACENDADO/AGRICULTURAL ESTATE OWNER	68.5	5.1
06210	PEON DE FUNDO/AGRICULTURAL LABORER	13.2	-9.8
06270	JARDINERO/GARDENER	24.9	3.5
06410	PESCADOR DE CALETA/FISHERMAN	18.5	-9.1
	PRODUCTION AND RELATED WORKERS, TRANSPORT EQUIPMENT OPERATORS AND LABORERS		
07000	CAPATAZ/FOREMAN	39.8	0.5
07110	MINERO/MINER	25.9	-5.5
07320	OBRERO DE INDUSTRIA MADERERA/WORKER IN LUMBER INDUSTRY	31.3	0.0
07450	OBRERO DE INDUSTRIA PETROLERA/WORKER IN PETROLEUM INDUSTRY	36.6	0.0
07910	SASTRE/TAILOR	43.0	3.5
07911	MODISTA/DRESSMAKER	44.0	4.6
08010	ZAPATERO (REMENDON)/SHOE REPAIRER	17.4	-10.7
08430	MECANICO DE AUTOMOVILES/AUTO MECHANIC	40.8	-2.1
08490	MECANICO DE INDUSTRIA/INDUSTRIAL MECHANIC (51.5) MECANICO DE PRECISION/PRECISION MECHANIC (48.3)	49.9	7.0
08550	ELECTRICISTA/ELECTRICIAN	41.9	-2.6
08610	TECNICO EN RADIO/RADIO TECHNICIAN	51.5	-1.3
08710	GASFITER/GAS-PIPE FITTER	21.7	-12.2
08801	DUEÑO DE JOYERIA O RELOJERIA/OWNER OF JEWELERY OR WATCH STORE	66.0	2.9
09540	CARPINTERO/CARPENTER	25.9	-11.3
09550	ESTUCADOR/PLASTERER	23.8	-7.1
09710	ESTIBADOR/LONGSHOREMAN	23.8	2.6
09810	MARINERO/SEAMAN	28.1	-6.7
09851	CHOFER DE TROLLEY-BUS/TROLLEY-BUS DRIVER	34.4	2.0
09852	CHOFER DE CAMION/TRUCK DRIVER	31.3	-1.3
09970	OBRERO DE FABRICA/FACTORY WORKER	25.9	-3.3

09990	JORNALERO O PECN/CASUAL LABORER	14.2	-4.9
09994	OBRERO FERROVIARIO/RAILWAY WCRKER	28.1	-5.2
09995	BARRENDERO/STREET SWEPPER	11.0	-2.3

MEMBERS OF THE ARMED FORCES

10001	ARMED FORCES OFFICER	63.2	-0.1

UNCLASSIFIABLE CCCUEATICNS

12000	DUENA DF CASA/HOUSEWIFE	62.1	22.2

ISCO NO.	OCCUPATION TITLE	PRESTIGE SCORE	SCORE MINUS STD. SCORE
	CONGO (ZAIRE)		
	PROFESSIONAL, TECHNICAL AND RELATED WORKERS		
00541	ASSISTANT AGRONOME/ASSISTANT AGRONOMIST	52.5	5.8
00620	ASSISTANT MEDICAL/MEDICAL ASSISTANT	58.9	8.9
00710	INFIRMIER/MALE NURSE	53.3	-0.3
01330	INSTITUTEUR/PRIMARY SCHOOL TEACHER	56.8	-0.2
	CLERICAL AND RELATED WORKERS		
03600	CONDUCTEUR DE TRAIN/RAILROAD CONDUCTOR	35.3	-3.3
03701	PLANTON/OFFICE BOY	21.6	-4.2
03802	OPERATEUR DE RADIO/RADIO OPERATOR	46.6	-2.6
03930	CLERC/OFFICE CLERK	52.3	9.0
	SALES WORKERS		
04100	COMMERCANT/MERCHANT	45.4	3.0
04210	"CAPITA" VENDEUR/HEAD SALESMAN	31.9	-20.6
04521	DEBITANT DE MALOFU/PALM WINE RETAILER	22.2	0.2
	SERVICE WORKERS		
05102	HOTELIER/HOTEL KEEPER	35.3	-11.1
05400	BOY/HOUSE BOY	22.3	5.1
05820	POLICIER/POLICEMAN	27.9	-11.9
	AGRICULTURAL, ANIMAL HUSBANDRY AND FORESTRY WORKERS, FISHERMEN AND HUNTERS		
06110	CULTIVATEUR/FARMER	35.8	-11.3
06230	RECOLTEUR DE VIN DE PALME/PALM-WINE HARVESTER	20.8	0.0
06410	PECHEUR/FISHERMAN	28.4	0.8

PRODUCTION AND RELATED WORKERS, TRANSPORT EQUIPMENT OPERATORS AND LABORERS

Code	Occupation		
07000	"CAPITA" DE TRAVAILLEURS/LABOURERS' FOREMAN	31.3	-8.0
07910	TAILLEUR/TAILOR	39.8	0.3
08010	CORDONNIER/SHOEMAKER	36.9	8.7
08490	MECANICIEN/MECHANIC	49.9	7.0
09210	TYPOGRAPHE/TYPOGRAPHER	36.5	-5.8
09491	IVOIRIER/IVORY WORKER	32.7	0.0
09510	MACON/MASON	39.3	5.2
09540	MENUISIER/JOINER	48.1	10.9
09852	CHAUFFEUR/DRIVER	37.6	5.0
09990	TRAVAILLEUR ORDINAIRE/UNSKILLED LABOURER	20.8	1.7

MEMBERS OF THE ARMED FORCES

Code	Occupation		
10003	SOLDAT/SOLDIER	35.1	-3.6

COSTA RICA

PROFESSIONAL, TECHNICAL AND RELATED WORKERS

ISCO NO.	OCCUPATION TITLE	PRESTIGE SCORE	SCORE MINUS STD. SCORE
00110	CHEMIST	73.7	4.5
00120	NUCLEAR PHYSICIST	75.1	-1.4
00130	SCIENTIST	82.2	3.8
00210	ARCHITECT	76.5	4.7
00220	CIVIL ENGINEER	78.4	8.1
00410	PILOT OF A COMMERCIAL AIRLINE	70.8	4.3
00510	BIOLOGIST	72.2	3.5
00531	AGRICULTURAL AGENT	55.1	0.3
00610	DOCTOR	84.8	6.9
00630	DENTIST	66.0	-4.5

CLERICAL AND RELATED WORKERS

ISCO NO.	OCCUPATION TITLE	PRESTIGE SCORE	SCORE MINUS STD. SCORE
01100	ACCOUNTANT (BOOK TENDER)	63.9	14.3

PROFESSIONAL, TECHNICAL AND RELATED WORKERS

ISCO NO.	OCCUPATION TITLE	PRESTIGE SCORE	SCORE MINUS STD. SCORE
01101	ACCOUNTANT (BOOK TENDER) FOR A LARGE BUSINESS	66.0	-2.4
01210	LAWYER	77.9	7.3
01221	JUDGE OF THE SUPREME COURT OF JUSTICE	66.3	-15.7
01222	JUSTICE OF A MUNICIPIO/COUNTY JUDGE	58.4	-14.8
01310	UNIVERSITY PROFESSOR	79.1	1.5
01330	MAESTRO DE ESCUELA/SCHOOL TEACHER	57.2	0.2
01410	MINISTER OR PRIEST	60.8	1.1
01510	AUTHOR OF NOVELS	54.1	-7.6
01590	REPORTER OF A DAILY NEWSPAPER (51.3) COLUMNIST OF A PERIODICAL (48.9)	50.1	-4.8
01610	PAINTER OF PICTURES	55.1	-2.1
01710	MUSICIAN IN A SYMPHONY ORCHESTRA	56.0	-0.0
01712	SINGER IN A NIGHT CLUB	40.8	9.3
01790	RADIO ANNOUNCER	45.3	-5.0
01920	SOCIOLOGIST	69.8	2.4

Code	Occupation		
01921	PSYCHOLOGIST	72.0	6.0
01930	SOCIAL WORKER FOR LOCAL GOVERNMENT	59.4	3.1
01931	DIRECTOR OF A PLAYGROUND	47.5	-1.4

ADMINISTRATIVE AND MANAGERIAL WORKERS

Code	Occupation		
02011	GOVERNOR OF THE STATE	76.0	-5.9
02013	PRESIDENT OF A LARGE CITY	78.9	3.6
02022	DEPUTY OF THE NATIONAL CONGRESS	75.3	3.2
02030	MEMBER OF THE CABINET OF THE NATIONAL GOVERNMENT	70.8	-7.9
02032	DIPLOMAT IN THE FOREIGN SERVICE	78.6	5.4
02034	DIRECTOR OF A DEPARTMENT OF THE GOVERNMENT OF THE STATE	71.5	-2.4
02110	MEMBER OF THE GROUP (JUNTA) OF THE DIRECTORS OF A LARGE CORPORATION	64.1	-10.9
02111	OWNER OF A FACTORY THAT EMPLOYS 100 MEN	67.5	-3.0
02114	BANKER	74.4	7.4
02116	BUILDING CONTRACTOR	56.3	2.9
02196	LOCAL OFFICIAL OF A LABOR UNION	48.9	-0.6
02197	OFFICIAL OF AN INTERNATIONAL LABOR UNION (SINDICATO)	59.4	-3.4

CLERICAL AND RELATED WORKERS

Code	Occupation		
03600	CONDUCTOR OF THE RAILROAD	45.8	7.2
03700	MAILMAN	24.9	-8.0

SALES WORKERS

Code	Occupation		
04000	MANAGER OF A SMALL STORE IN THE CITY	43.0	-3.7
04320	TRAVELLING SALESMAN FOR A LARGE CORPORATION	44.6	-2.3
04410	INSURANCE AGENT	59.9	15.3
04510	CLERK IN A STORE	31.5	-2.1
04512	EMPLOYEE OF A GASOLINE STATION	31.3	6.0
04521	REFRESHMENT VENDOR	16.1	-5.9
04524	MILK DELIVERY MAN	16.8	-7.3

SERVICE WORKERS

Code	Occupation		
05101	OWNER AND OPERATOR OF A LUNCH STAND	39.9	5.0
05320	RESTARANT WAITER	23.2	-0.0
05511	CONSERGE/APARTMENT "SUPER"	29.9	5.4
05600	PRESSER IN A LAUNDRY	23.2	1.1
05700	BARBER	27.7	-2.7
05820	POLICEMAN	19.4	-20.4

ISCO NO.	OCCUPATION TITLE	PRESTIGE SCORE	SCORE MINUS STD. SCORE
	COSTA RICA		
05890	NIGHT WATCHMAN	17.5	-4.5
05920	DIRECTOR OF A FUNERAL AGENCY	40.3	6.7
05995	SHOESHINER	-1.3	-13.5
	AGRICULTURAL, ANIMAL HUSBANDRY AND FORESTRY WORKERS, FISHERMEN AND HUNTERS		
06116	COLONO/SETTLER	39.9	0.7
06210	RURAL LABORER	23.0	0.0
06310	LENADOR/LOGGER	16.8	-2.4
	PRODUCTION AND RELATED WORKERS, TRANSPORT EQUIPMENT OPERATORS AND LABORERS		
07110	MINER	37.7	6.3
08340	MACHINIST IN A FACTORY	43.9	5.7
08410	MECANICO DE PAICER/MACHINIST	48.9	5.6
08430	MECHANIC, AUTOMOBILE	53.0	10.0
08550	ELECTRICIAN	44.9	0.3
08710	PLUMBER	34.2	0.3
09211	OWNER AND OPERATOR OF A PRINTING SHOP	68.4	17.7
09540	CARPENTER	23.2	-14.0
09710	DOCK WORKER	29.9	8.6
09830	MAQUINISTA/LOCOMOTIVE ENGINEER	42.7	0.1
09850	CHAUFFER OF A TAXI	30.6	2.8
09851	DRIVER OF A STREETCAR OR OF AN URBAN BUS	33.2	0.8
09852	TRUCK DRIVER	33.0	0.4
09994	RAILROAD LABORER	36.5	3.3
09995	PUBLIC SWEEPER	10.6	-2.8
09996	GARBAGE COLLECTOR	5.6	-7.1
	MEMBERS OF THE ARMED FORCES		
10001	CAPTAIN IN THE ARMY	58.0	-5.3
10002	SERGEANT IN THE ARMY	49.9	6.3

CZECHOSLOVAKIA

PROFESSIONAL, TECHNICAL AND RELATED WORKERS

Code	Occupation		
00130	SCIENTIFIC WORKER	84.6	6.2
00210	ARCHITECT	68.6	-3.2
00220	ENGINEER-DESIGNER	78.1	7.7
00530	AGRONOMIST	50.5	-7.3
00610	PHYSICIAN	82.6	4.7
00710	NURSE	34.0	-19.6
01100	ACCOUNTANT	42.6	-12.0
01220	JUDGE	60.3	-17.4
01310	UNIVERSITY TEACHER	78.0	0.4
01320	HIGH SCHOOL TEACHER	55.3	-8.8
01410	CLERGYMAN	27.2	-32.5
01510	WRITER	57.8	-3.9
01590	JOURNALIST	49.7	-5.3
01730	ACTOR	51.9	0.4

ADMINISTRATIVE AND MANAGERIAL WORKERS

02030	MINISTER	100.2	21.5

CLERICAL AND RELATED WORKERS

03930	CORRESPONDENT/CORRESPONDENCE CLERK	22.7	-20.7
03992	NATIONAL COMMITTEE WORKER	35.5	-12.7

SALES WORKERS

04510	SALESMAN	30.6	-3.1

SERVICE WORKERS

05520	CHARWOMAN	17.0	0.5
05820	POLICEMAN (PUBLIC SECURITY)	42.9	3.1

ISCO NO.	OCCUPATION TITLE	PRESTIGE SCORE	SCORE MINUS STD. SCORE
	CZECHOSLOVAKIA		
	AGRICULTURAL, ANIMAL HUSBANDRY AND FORESTRY WORKERS, FISHERMEN AND HUNTERS		
06115	CO-OPERATIVE FARMER	41.3	6.7
	PRODUCTION AND RELATED WORKERS, TRANSPORT EQUIPMENT OPERATORS AND LABORERS		
07000	FACTORY FOREMAN	56.0	16.7
07110	MINER	80.1	48.7
07910	TAILOR	35.8	-3.7
08331	LATHE TURNER	49.9	13.4
09510	BRICKLAYER	53.1	19.0
09595	DIGGER	43.3	28.1
09830	ENGINE-DRIVER	63.9	21.3
09995	SEWAGE CLEANER	42.4	29.0
	MEMBERS OF THE ARMED FORCES		
10001	REGULAR OFFICER	45.7	-17.5

PROFESSIONAL, TECHNICAL AND RELATED WORKERS

Code	Occupation		
00210	ARKITEKT/ARCHITECT	66.4	-5.4
00220	CIVILINGENIOE/CIVIL ENGINEER	71.1	0.8
00420	SKIBSKAPTAJN/SHIP'S CAPTAIN	66.0	2.9
00531	LANDBRUGSKONSULENT/AGRICULTURAL CONSULTANT	54.0	-0.9
00610	LAEGE/PHYSICIAN	75.4	-2.5
00611	OVERLAEGE/PHYSICIAN IN CHIEF, LARGE HOSPITAL	83.6	3.1
00670	APOTEKER/PHARMACIST	74.6	10.5
01100	REVISOR/ACCOUNTANT	55.3	0.8
01210	LANDSRETSSAGFORER/LAWYER, DISTRICT COURT	71.5	0.8
01221	HOJESTERTSPRAESIDENT/PRESIDENT, SUPREME COURT	84.5	2.5
01310	PROFESSOR/UNIVERSITY PROFESSOR	83.4	5.8
01320	LEKTOR/ACADEMIC HIGH SCHOOL TEACHER	70.9	6.7
01330	LAERER/PRIMARY SCHOOL TEACHER	58.4	1.4
01391	SKOLEBESTYRER/PRIMARY SCHOOL PRINCIPAL	61.2	-4.4
01410	SOGNEPRAEST/MINISTER, NATIONAL CHURCH	65.5	5.8
01411	BISKOP/BISHOP, NATIONAL CHURCH (87.9)	83.0	0.0
	PROVOST/DEAN, NATIONAL CHURCH (78.1)		
01590	JOURNALIST/JOURNALIST	47.0	-8.0
01591	RELAKTOR/EDITOR	61.0	-4.0
01710	MUSIKER I DET KGL. KAPEL/MUSICIAN IN ROYAL ORCHESTRA	55.7	-0.4
01730	SKUESPILLER/ACTOR	47.5	-4.0
01990	VIDENSKABELIG ASSISTENT/RESEARCH ASSISTANT	58.6	0.4

ADMINISTRATIVE AND MANAGERIAL WORKERS

Code	Occupation		
02010	STATSMINISTER/PRIME MINISTER	89.0	-1.1
02022	FOLKETINGSMAND/MEMBER OF PARLIAMENT	65.5	-6.7
02031	AMBASSADOR/AMBASSADOR	91.0	3.9
02033	DEPARTEMENTCHEF/ADMINISTRATIVE HEAD OF MINISTRY (86.1)	80.0	8.8
	KONTORCHEF I MINISTERIUM/DIVISION-CHIEF IN A MINISTRY (73.8)		
02111	DIREKTOB/MANAGING DIRECTOR (76.4)	70.0	-0.4
	SKRIBSREDER/SHIP OWNER (75.4)		
	FABRIKANT/MANUFACTURER (58.2)		
02114	BANKFULDMAEGTIG/CONFIDENTIAL CLERK IN A BANK	60.8	-6.2
02192	KONTORCHEF I PRIVAT FIRMA/DEPARTMENT HEAD IN A PRIVATE FIRM	64.1	3.6

ISCO NO.	OCCUPATION TITLE	PRESTIGE SCORE	SCORE MINUS STD. SCORE
	DENMARK		
	CLERICAL AND RELATED WORKERS		
03100	SEKRETAER I MINISTERIUM/PROFESSIONAL ASSISTANT IN A MINISTRY	62.9	-2.8
03103	TOLDASSISTENT/JUNIOR CUSTOMS OFFICIAL	45.0	0.6
03310	BOGHOLDER/BOOKKEEPER	51.0	2.1
03520	POSTMESTE/POSTMASTER	60.8	2.5
03601	SPORVOGNSKONDUKTOR/STREETCAR CONDUCTOR	30.0	4.0
03700	POSTBUD/MAILMAN	29.6	-3.2
03801	TELEGRAFIST/TELEGRAPH OPERATOR	45.2	-0.1
C3930	KONTORASSISTENT/OFFICE CLERK	36.8	-6.5
	SALES WORKERS		
04100	VIKTUALIEHANDLER/DELICATESSEN OWNER	40.3	-2.1
04106	GROSSER/WHOLESALER	60.4	2.0
04320	REPRAESENTANT/REPRESENTATIVE	37.0	-9.9
04510	EKSPEDIENT/SHOP CLERK	33.1	-0.5
	SERVICE WORKERS		
05102	HOTELEJER/HOTEL KEEPER	54.4	8.0
05320	TJENER/WAITER	27.5	4.2
05400	HUSASSISTENT/MAID	24.4	7.2
05701	BARBER-CG FRISCRMESTER (BARBER, SELF EMPLOYED)	40.7	4.2
05820	POLITIBETJENT/POLICEMAN	41.5	1.7
05822	POLITIMESTER/CHIEF OF POLICE	72.9	-2.3
05994	MINISTERIALETJENT/DOORKEEPER IN A MINISTRY (37.0)	32.4	5.4
05995	PORTNER/DOORKEEPER IN A LARGE BUILDING (27.9)	21.0	8.8
	SKOPUDSER/SHOESHINER		
	AGRICULTURAL, ANIMAL HUSBANDRY AND FORESTRY WORKERS, FISHERMEN AND HUNTERS		
06110	GARDEJER/FARMER	47.3	0.3
06112	HUSMAND/SMALL HOLDER	27.9	-9.8

Code	Occupation		
06210	LANDARBEJDER/AGRICULTURAL LABORER	23.6	0.6
06240	FODERMESTER/ANIMAL HUSBANDRYMAN	26.1	0.5
06410	FISKER/FISHERMAN	28.8	1.3

PRODUCTION AND RELATED WORKERS, TRANSPORT EQUIPMENT OPERATORS AND LABORERS

Code	Occupation		
07000	FORMAND PA FABRIK/FACTORY FOREMAN	39.7	0.4
07761	BAGERMESTER/MASTER BAKER	46.0	-2.2
08801	GULDSMEDEMESTER/MASTER-GOLDSMITH	53.4	-3.7
09210	TYPOGRAF/TYPOGRAPHER	37.2	-5.1
09211	BOGTRYKKER/MASTER PRINTER, PRINT SHOP OWNER	50.3	-0.4
09540	SNEDKERSVEND/JOINER	29.4	-7.8
09830	LOKOMITIVFORER/LOCOMOTIVE ENGINEER	41.9	-0.8
09852	CHAUFFOR/DRIVER	26.5	-6.1
09970	FABRIKSARBEJDER/FACTORY WORKER	24.4	-4.9
09990	ARBEJDSMAND/UNSKILLED LABORER	23.4	4.3

MEMBERS OF THE ARMED FORCES

Code	Occupation		
10000	OBERST /COLONEL	74.6	1.7
10001	KAPTAJN IN HAEREN/CAPTAIN IN ARMY	67.6	4.4

UNCLASSIFIABLE OCCUPATIONS

Code	Occupation		
12000	GREVE ARB. S. KONTORASSISTENT/COUNT, WORKS AS A CLERK	48.3	8.4

SOURCES OF LIVELIHOOD OTHER THAN LABOR FORCE ACTIVITY

Code	Occupation		
13003	GODSEJER/LANDOWNER	69.5	4.4

ISCO NO.	OCCUPATION TITLE	PRESTIGE SCORE	SCORE MINUS STD. SCORE
	FRANCE		
	PROFESSIONAL, TECHNICAL AND RELATED WORKERS		
00610	PHYSICIAN	75.8	-2.1
01210	LAWYER	67.6	-3.1
01310	UNIVERSITY PROFESSOR	73.1	-4.5
01330	ELEMENTARY SCHOOL TEACHER	67.5	10.5
01391	SCHOOL PRINCIPAL	70.8	5.2
01410	CLERGYMAN	20.8	-38.9
01414	MISSIONARY	35.2	-13.9
01510	AUTHOR	58.0	-3.7
01610	ARTIST	65.3	8.1
01730	ACTOR	61.7	10.2
	ADMINISTRATIVE AND MANAGERIAL WORKERS		
02114	BANKER	64.4	-2.6
02190	BUSINESSMAN	60.4	2.4
02195	POLITICIAN	50.4	-12.3
	CLERICAL AND RELATED WORKERS		
03101	CIVIL SERVICE EMPLOYEE	55.3	1.7
03310	BOOKKEEPER	62.4	13.4
03700	MAIL CARRIER	40.0	7.2
	SALES WORKERS		
04100	GROCER	37.9	-4.5
	SERVICE WORKERS		
05510	JANITOR	18.5	-2.5
05700	BARBER	38.9	8.5
05820	POLICEMAN	57.9	18.1

AGRICULTURAL, ANIMAL HUSBANDRY AND FORESTRY WORKERS, FISHERMEN AND HUNTERS

06110	FARMER	31.7	-15.4

PRODUCTION AND RELATED WORKERS, TRANSPORT EQUIPMENT OPERATORS AND LABORERS

07110	COAL MINER	35.0	3.6
07730	BUTCHER	38.3	7.0
07910	TAILOR	40.3	0.8
08010	SHOEMAKER	22.4	-5.8
08550	ELECTRICIAN	60.6	16.1
08710	PLUMBER	37.9	4.1
09210	TYPOGRAPHER	52.2	9.9
09540	CARPENTER	42.4	5.2
09852	TRUCK DRIVER	47.4	14.8

MEMBERS OF THE ARMED FORCES

10003	SOLDIER	40.1	1.4

ISCO NO.	OCCUPATION TITLE	PRESTIGE SCORE	SCORE MINUS STD. SCORE

FRENCH GUIANA

PROFESSIONAL, TECHNICAL AND RELATED WORKERS

ISCO NO.	OCCUPATION TITLE	PRESTIGE SCORE	SCORE MINUS STD. SCORE
00131	GEOLOGIST	68.4	1.0
00220	ENGINEER	68.4	-2.0
00410	PILOT	66.5	0.0
00530	AGRICULTURIST	61.5	3.7
00610	DOCTOR	72.7	-5.2
00630	DENTIST	70.2	-0.3
00670	PHARMACIST	64.6	0.5
00710	NURSE	55.9	2.4
00793	SANITARY OFFICER	38.5	-9.0
01100	ACCOUNTANT	54.1	-0.5
01210	LAWYER	65.9	-4.8
01330	TEACHER	63.4	6.4
01590	JOURNALIST	61.5	6.6
01710	MUSICIAN	42.9	-13.2

ADMINISTRATIVE AND MANAGERIAL WORKERS

ISCO NO.	OCCUPATION TITLE	PRESTIGE SCORE	SCORE MINUS STD. SCORE
02190	BUSINESSMAN	59.0	1.1

CLERICAL AND RELATED WORKERS

ISCO NO.	OCCUPATION TITLE	PRESTIGE SCORE	SCORE MINUS STD. SCORE
03100	ADMINISTRATOR	72.7	7.0
03101	CIVIL SERVANT	55.3	1.7
03210	TYPIST	54.1	12.5
03211	SECRETARY	51.0	-2.0
03310	BOOKKEEPER	45.4	-3.6
03700	POSTMAN	46.6	13.8
03701	MESSENGER	24.9	-0.9
03930	CLERK	44.1	0.8

SALES WORKERS

Code	Occupation		
04100	SHOPKEEPER	55.9	13.5
04510	SALESMAN	39.8	6.2

SERVICE WORKERS

Code	Occupation		
05400	DOMESTIC	16.8	-0.4
05600	LAUNDERER	37.3	15.2
05700	BARBER	24.3	-6.1
05702	HAIRDRESSER	32.3	-2.5
05820	POLICEMAN	5C.3	10.5
05890	WATCHMAN	16.8	-5.2
05892	BAILIFF	48.5	1.1
05996	STEWARDESS	52.3	2.7

AGRICULTURAL, ANIMAL HUSBANDRY AND FORESTRY WORKERS, FISHERMEN AND HUNTERS

Code	Occupation		
06110	FARMER	19.9	-27.2
06310	LOG CUTTER	24.3	5.1
06410	FISHERMAN	20.5	-7.1

PRODUCTION AND RELATED WORKERS, TRANSPORT EQUIPMENT CPERATORS AND LABORERS

Code	Occupation		
07110	GOLD MINER	32.3	0.9
07730	BUTCHER	23.C	-8.3
07760	BAKER	40.4	7.2
07910	TAILOR	37.3	-2.2
07911	SEAMSTRESS	40.4	1.0
08420	WATCH REPAIRER	19.9	-19.8
08490	MECHANIC	39.2	-3.7
08550	ELECTRICIAN	40.4	-4.1
08720	WELDER	39.2	-0.1
08800	JEWELLER	36.7	-6.3
09210	PRINTER	57.2	14.9
09510	MASON	38.5	4.4
09540	JOINER (38.5)		
	CARPENTER (38.5)	38.5	1.4
09712	PORTER	16.8	-0.0
09810	SAILOR	19.9	-14.8
09852	CHAUFFEUR	38.5	5.9
09990	LABORER	16.8	-2.3

ISCO　　　　OCCUPATION TITLE　　　　　　　　　　　　　　　　　　PRESTIGE　　SCORE MINUS
NO.　　　　　　　　　　　　　　　　　　　　　　　　　　　　　　　　SCORE　　STD. SCORE

FRENCH GUIANA

MEMBERS OF THE ARMED FORCES

10001　MILITARY OFFICER　　　　　　　　　　　　　　　　　　　　64.6　　　　1.4

374

PROFESSIONAL, TECHNICAL AND RELATED WORKERS

Code	Occupation		
00220	CIVIL ENGINEER	67.9	-2.4
00230	ELEKTROINGENIEUR/ELECTRICAL ENGINEER	62.7	-2.6
00320	TECHNISCHER ZEICHNER/DRAFTSMAN	46.9	-8.1
00540	MED. TECH. ASSISTENTIN/MEDICAL TECHNICIAN (FEMALE)	55.7	-2.3
00610	ARZT/PHYSICIAN	75.0	-2.9
00670	APOTHEKER/PHARMACIST	66.2	-2.1
00710	KRANKENSCHWESTER/NURSE	53.9	0.3
01210	LAWYER	73.2	-2.6
01310	UNIVERSITAITAISPROFESSOR/UNIVERSITY PROFESSOR	76.7	-0.9
01320	STUDIENRAT/HIGH SCHOOL TEACHER	69.7	5.5
01321	OBEELEHRER/MIDDLE SCHOOL TEACHER	64.4	7.4
01330	VOLKSSCHULLEHRER/PRIMARY SCHOOL TEACHER	59.2	2.1
01392	SUPERINTENDENT OF SCHOOLS	64.4	-3.2
01410	PFARRER (PASTOR)/CLERGYMAN	69.7	10.0
01414	FOREIGN MISSIONARY	60.9	11.8
01511	SCHRIFTSTELLER (VERFASSER VCN 50-PFENNIG-ROMANEN)/WRITER OF CHEAP NOVELS	34.6	0.0
01590	AUSLANDSKORRESPONDENTIN/FOREIGN CORRESPONDENT (FEMALE)	60.9	6.0
01710	OPERNSANGER/OPERA SINGER	53.9	-2.2
01712	MUSIKER IN EINER TANZKAPELLE/MUSICIAN IN A DANCE BAND	31.1	-0.4
01713	KLAVIERIEHERIN/PIANO TEACHER (FEMALE)	52.1	-0.9
01930	FURSORGERIN/SOCIAL WORKER (FEMALE)	60.9	4.7

ADMINISTRATIVE AND MANAGERIAL WORKERS

Code	Occupation		
02033	REGIERUNGSRAT (HOHERER BEAMTER)/HIGH CIVIL SERVANT	71.5	0.3
02111	FAERIKBESITZER/FACTORY OWNER	67.9	-2.5
02114	BANKER	71.5	4.5
02120	FABRIKDIREKTOR (Z.B. GIESSEREIDIREKTOR)/FACTORY MANAGER	73.2	9.0

CLERICAL AND RELATED WORKERS

Code	Occupation		
03100	STADTINSPEKTOR/MUNICIPAL OFFICIAL--MIDDLE LEVEL	66.2	0.4
03101	OBERSEKRETAR/MINOR CIVIL SERVANT	48.6	-5.0
03210	STENOTYPISTIN/STENOGRAPHER (FEMALE)	41.6	0.0

ISCO NO.	OCCUPATION TITLE	PRESTIGE SCORE	SCORE MINUS STD. SCORE
	GERMANY (WEST)		
03310	BUCHHALTER/BOOKKEEPER (53.9)	50.4	1.4
	BUCHHALTERIN/BOOKKEEPER (FEMALE) (48.6)		
	BANKANGESTELLTER (BUCHHALTER)/BANK EMPLOYEE (BOOKKEEPER (48.6)		
03314	POSTBEAMTER (SCHALTERBEAMTER)/POST OFFICE CLERK	39.8	0.8
03601	SCHAFFNER (STRASSENBAHN, BUS)/STREETCAR CR BUS CONDUCTOR	27.6	1.5
03700	MAIL CARRIER	22.3	-10.6
03701	BOTE (BÜROBOTE)/OFFICE MESSENGER	18.3	-7.0
SALES WORKERS			
04100	LADENBESITZER/SHOPKEEPER (39.8)	49.2	6.8
	KOLONIALWARENHÄNDLER (EIGENES GESCHÄFT, 2 VERKÄUFER)/GROCER WITH TWO EMPLOYEES (53.9)		
	TEXTILKAUFMANN (INHABER EINES HERREN- UND DAMEN WÄSCHEGESCHÄFTS, 1 VERKÄUFER)/OWNER OF CLOTHING STORE WITH ONE EMPLOYE (53.9)		
04320	VERTRETER/REPRESENTATIVE	38.1	-8.8
04410	VERSICHERUNGSAGENT (VERTRETER)/INSURANCE AGENT	41.6	-2.9
04510	VERKAUFER IM LEBENSMITTELGESCHAFT/GROCERY STORE CLERK (31.1)	26.7	-7.0
	VERKAUFERIN IM WARENHAUS/DEPARTMENT STORE SALESWOMAN (27.6)		
	VERKAUFERIN IM SCHLACHTERLADEN/SALESGIRL IN A BUTCHER SHOP (27.6)		
	VERKAUFERIN/SALES WOMAN (20.5)		
04513	MANNEQUIN/MODEL	36.3	0.0
04521	VORKNECHT/PEDDLER (29.3)	24.9	3.0
	AMBULANTER HÄNDLER (Z.B. SPEISEEISVERKÄUFER)/STREET VENDOR,E.G. ICE CREAM PEDDLER (20.5)		
SERVICE WORKERS			
05310	KOCHIN/COOK (FEMALE)	36.3	5.5
05320	KELLNER/WAITER	27.6	4.3
05510	JANITOR	25.8	4.8
05520	REINMACHEFRAU/CHARWOMAN	17.0	0.5
05700	BARBER	15.3	-15.1
05702	FRISEUSE/HAIRDRESSER (FEMALE)	34.6	-0.2

Code	Title		
05703	FRISURMEISTER (EIGENES GESCHAFT, 1 GEHILFE)/OPERATOR OF A HAIR-DRESSING SALON, WITH ONE EMPLOYEE	50.4	5.1
05990	KRANKENPFLEGER/MEDICAL ORDERLY	27.6	-14.1

AGRICULTURAL, ANIMAL HUSBANDRY AND FORESTRY WORKERS, FISHERMEN AND HUNTERS

Code	Title		
06000	MEIEREIVERWALTER/DAIRY MANAGER	53.9	-0.4
06110	BAUER (MITTELGROSSER BETRIEB)/FARMER (MIDDLE SIZED FARM)	57.4	10.3
06111	GROSSBAUER (100 HA.)/LARGE FARMER (100 HECTARES)	67.9	4.6
06112	KLEINER BAUER/SMALL FARMER	34.6	-3.1
06113	PACHTER/TENANT FARMER, HIGH LEVEL (59.2)	50.4	20.9
06210	KATNER/TENANT FARMER, LOW LEVEL (41.6)	18.8	-4.2
06250	LANDARBEITER/AGRICULTURAL LABORER MELKER, VERH./MILKER	27.6	4.1

PRODUCTION AND RELATED WORKERS, TRANSPORT EQUIPMENT OPERATORS AND LABORERS

Code	Title		
07000	WERKMEISTER/FOREMAN	48.6	9.3
07110	COAL MINER	31.1	-0.4
07540	TUCHWEBER/WEAVER	34.6	4.2
07732	FLEISCHERMEISTER, SELBST./BUTCHER WITH HIS OWN SHOP (55.7) FLEISCHEPMEISTER (ANGESTELLT IN EINER WURSTFABRIK)/MASTER BUTCHER IN A SAUSAGE FACTORY (45.1)	50.4	5.2
07761	BACKERMEISTER/MASTER BAKER	55.7	7.4
07910	SCHNEIDERMEISTER (EIGENES GESCHAFT, OHNE GEHILFEN)/TAILOR WITH HIS OWN WORKSHOP BUT NO EMPLOYES	45.1	5.6
08110	TISCHLERMEISTER (ANGESTELLT IN EINER MOBELFABRIK)/MASTER CARPENTER IN FURNITURE FACTORY	46.9	6.5
08310	SCHMIED (LAND)/RURAL BLACKSMITH	50.4	15.9
08340	MASCHINENSCHLOSSER (GESELLE)/MACHINE OPERATOR IN A FACTORY	36.3	-1.9
08410	MACHINIST	43.4	0.0
08431	AUTOSCHLOSSER (EIGENE WERKSTATT, 2 GEHILFE)/GARAGE OPERATOR WITH TWO HELPERS	53.9	6.6
08550	ELECTRICIAN	46.9	2.3
08710	PLUMBER	36.3	2.5
09510	MAURER (GESELLE)/MASON	31.1	-3.0
09541	TISCHLERMEISTER, SELBST./SELF EMPLOYED MASTER CARPENTER	55.7	7.5
09595	DITCH DIGGER (13.5) HOD CARRIER (10.0)	11.7	-3.5
09810	SEEMAN/SEAMAN	25.8	-8.9
09830	LOKFUHRER/LOCOMOTIVE ENGINEER	48.6	6.0
09851	POSTSCHAFFNER/DRIVER FOR THE GOVERNMENT BUS LINE	41.6	9.2

ISCO NO.	OCCUPATION TITLE	PRESTIGE SCORE	SCORE MINUS STD. SCORE
	GERMANY (WEST)		
09852	TRUCK DRIVER	34.6	2.0
09950	INDUSTRIEIFACHARBEITER (Z.B.SCHLOSSER, DREHER USW.)/SKILLED INDUSTRIAL WORKER (E.G. METAL WORKER, LATHE OPERATOR ETC.) (41.6)	38.1	-3.7
	GERLERNTER ARBEITER/SKILLED WORKER (34.6)		
09951	HANDWERKER/SELF EMPLOYED ARTISAN	53.9	4.2
09970	FABRIKARBEITERIN/FACTORY GIRL	22.3	-7.0
C9990	UNGELERNTER ARBEITER/UNSKILLED LABORER	17.0	-2.1
09994	BAHNARBEITER/RAILROAD WORKER	24.0	-9.2
MEMBERS OF THE ARMED FORCES			
10001	MAJOR (ACTIV)/MAJOR IN THE ARMED FORCES	59.2	-4.1
10002	UNTEROFFIZIER (ACTIV)/NON-COMMISSIONED OFFICER	29.3	-14.3
10003	SOLDIER	18.8	-20.0
SOURCES OF LIVELIHOOD OTHER THAN LABOR FORCE ACTIVITY			
13003	GUTSBESITZER/LANDOWNER	71.5	6.3

PROFESSIONAL, TECHNICAL AND RELATED WORKERS

Code	Occupation		
00610	DOCTOR	92.6	4.7
00710	NURSE	54.3	0.7
01210	LAWYER	76.3	5.7
01310	UNIVERSITY LECTURER	81.8	4.2
01320	SECONDARY-SCHOOL TEACHER	64.8	0.7
01321	MIDDLE-SCHOOL TEACHER	46.6	-10.4
01330	PRIMARY-SCHOOL TEACHER	41.9	-15.1
01410	CLERGYMAN	64.6	5.0
01510	AUTHOR	66.4	4.6
01730	ACTOR	50.3	-1.2

ADMINISTRATIVE AND MANAGERIAL WORKERS

Code	Occupation		
02012	CHIEF	67.9	2.1
02036	CHIEF'S COUNSELLOR	50.1	0.0
02190	BUSINESSMAN	56.2	-1.7

CLERICAL AND RELATED WORKERS

Code	Occupation		
03930	OFFICE WORKER	47.4	4.1
03931	GOVERNMENT CLERK	52.2	7.9
03992	POLITICAL PARTY WORKER	52.4	4.2

SALES WORKERS

Code	Occupation		
04510	SHOP ASSISTANT	31.3	-2.3
04520	PETTY TRADER	34.8	-1.3

SERVICE WORKERS

Code	Occupation		
05820	POLICEMAN	47.8	8.0

ISCO NO.	OCCUPATION TITLE	PRESTIGE SCORE	SCORE MINUS STD. SCORE
	GHANA		
	AGRICULTURAL, ANIMAL HUSBANDRY AND FORESTRY WORKERS, FISHERMEN AND HUNTERS		
06110	FARMER	47.6	0.5
06210	FARM LABORER	18.5	-4.4
	PRODUCTION AND RELATED WORKERS, TRANSPORT EQUIPMENT OPERATORS AND LABORERS		
08430	MOTOR CAR MECHANIC	35.4	-7.6
09540	CARPENTER	30.6	-6.6
09995	STREET CLEANER	13.4	-0.0
	MEMBERS OF THE ARMED FORCES		
10003	SOLDIER	50.9	12.1

380

PROFESSIONAL, TECHNICAL AND RELATED WORKERS

Code	Occupation		
00610	DOCTOR	70.2	-7.7
00620	DISPENSER	43.8	-6.1
00630	DENTIST	69.7	-0.8
00670	PHARMACIST	45.4	-18.7
00710	NURSE	44.5	-9.1
01100	ACCOUNTANT	69.2	14.6
01210	JUDGE, BARRISTER	71.7	1.0
01220	JUDGE, BARRISTER	71.7	-6.0
01290	SOLICITOR, ATTORNEY	60.9	-9.7
01391	HEAD TEACHER, PRIMARY SCHOOL	39.8	-25.7
01394	HEAD TEACHER, SECONDARY SCHOOL	62.9	-9.3
01410	PRIEST	74.2	14.5

ADMINISTRATIVE AND MANAGERIAL WORKERS

Code	Occupation		
02110	DIRECTOR	76.2	1.1
02112	COMMERCIAL MANAGER	61.9	-0.8
02113	AERATED WATER MANUFACTURER	30.1	-22.2
02116	BUILDING CONTRACTOR	61.4	8.0

CLERICAL AND RELATED WORKERS

Code	Occupation		
03100	WAGE-EMPLOYED EXECUTIVE IN GOVERNMENT AND AGRICULTURE (63.2) GOVERNMENT-EMPLOYED EXECUTIVE (62.7)	62.9	-2.8
03101	GOVERNMENT SUBORDINATE & TECHNICAL, EXCEPT TYPISTS & CLERKS	41.6	-12.1
03210	TYPIST, COMMERCIAL (59.7) TYPIST, GOVERNMENT (40.7)	50.2	8.6
03930	CLERK, COMMERCIAL	46.7	3.4
03931	CLERK, GOVERNMENT	47.9	3.6

SALES WORKERS

Code	Occupation		
04000	WAGE-EMPLOYED SHOPKEEPER	43.8	-2.8
04100	OWN-ACCOUNT SHOPKEEPER	24.9	-17.6
04101	MERCHANT	54.7	-3.8

ISCO NO.	OCCUPATION TITLE	PRESTIGE SCORE	SCORE MINUS STD. SCORE
	GRENADA		
04104	COMMISSION AGENT	61.1	6.5
04106	PRODUCE DEALER	42.3	-16.1
04430	AUCTIONEER	53.2	14.0
	SERVICE WORKERS		
05001	HOTELIER, MANAGER	53.2	0.0
05102	HOTEL PROPRIETOR	58.8	12.4
	AGRICULTURAL, ANIMAL HUSBANDRY AND FORESTRY WORKERS, FISHERMEN AND HUNTERS		
06000	MANAGER, ESTATE	63.9	9.6
06001	OVERSEER	35.7	-5.1
06110	OWN-ACCOUNT PROPRIETOR (AGRICULTURAL)	34.9	-12.2
06111	PLANTER	67.2	3.8
	PRODUCTION AND RELATED WORKERS, TRANSPORT EQUIPMENT OPERATORS AND LABORERS		
08431	GARAGE PROPRIETOR	39.1	-8.2
08490	MECHANIC	37.4	-5.4
09951	CRAFTSMAN	31.1	-18.6

PROFESSIONAL, TECHNICAL AND RELATED WORKERS

Code	Occupation		
00110	RESEARCH CHEMIST	71.8	2.6
00120	PHYSICIST	68.0	-8.4
00220	ENGINEER	59.5	-10.8
00510	BIOLOGIST	62.8	-5.9
00610	MEDICAL OFFICER OF HEALTH	79.8	1.9
01101	CHARTERED ACCOUNTANT	75.5	7.1
01290	SOLICITOR (COUNTRY PRACTICE)	77.1	6.4
01320	TEACHER (OTHER THAN SCIENCE) (63.3)	62.3	-1.9
	SCIENCE TEACHER (61.2)		
01330	ELEMENTARY SCHOOL TEACHER (ASSISTANT)	54.4	-2.6
01410	MINISTER (NONCONFORMIST)	67.5	7.9
01590	NEWS REPORTER	52.9	-2.1
01921	PSYCHOLOGIST	60.9	-5.1
01930	SOCIAL WORKER	57.5	1.2
01940	PERSONNEL MANAGER	59.2	0.6

ADMINISTRATIVE AND MANAGERIAL WORKERS

Code	Occupation		
02110	COMPANY DIRECTOR	79.4	4.4
02112	BUSINESS MANAGER (10-99 HANDS)	67.9	5.1
02114	BANKER	65.0	-2.0
02116	JOBBING MASTER BUILDER	52.9	-0.5
02120	WORKS MANAGER (INDUSTRIAL)	67.2	3.0
02194	INSURANCE EXECUTIVE	57.5	-9.1

CLERICAL AND RELATED WORKERS

Code	Occupation		
03100	CIVIL SERVANT (EXECUTIVE GRADE)	68.2	2.5
03930	CLERK (ROUTINE)	43.2	-0.1

SALES WORKERS

Code	Occupation		
04102	NEWS AGENT AND TOBACCONIST (ONE-MAN SHOP)	43.9	6.2
04320	COMMERCIAL TRAVELLER	49.3	2.4
04410	INSURANCE AGENT (INDUSTRIAL)	45.1	0.5

ISCO NO.	OCCUPATION TITLE	PRESTIGE SCORE	SCORE MINUS STD. SCORE
	GREAT BRITAIN		
04510	SHOP ASSISTANT (DRAPERY STORE)	34.0	0.4
	SERVICE WORKERS		
05311	CHEF (HOTEL)	47.8	10.2
05321	BARMAN	19.4	-3.9
05820	POLICEMAN	43.0	3.2
	AGRICULTURAL, ANIMAL HUSBANDRY AND FORESTRY WORKERS, FISHERMEN AND HUNTERS		
06111	FARMER (OVER 100 ACRES)	64.5	1.1
06210	AGRICULTURAL LABOURER	19.9	-3.1
06280	TRACTOR DRIVER (AGRICULTURAL)	27.5	-3.4
	PRODUCTION AND RELATED WORKERS, TRANSPORT EQUIPMENT OPERATORS AND LABORERS		
07110	COAL HEWER	25.7	-5.8
08510	FITTER (ELECTRICAL ENGINEERING)	38.1	0.0
09510	BRICKLAYER	31.6	-2.5
09540	CARPENTER	36.9	-0.3
09710	DOCK LABOURER	16.8	-4.4
09713	RAILWAY PORTER	19.9	1.7
09861	CARTER	18.5	-8.0
09995	ROAD SWEEPER	14.8	1.4

384

PROFESSIONAL, TECHNICAL AND RELATED WORKERS

Code	Occupation		
00220	CIVIL ENGINEER	69.9	-0.4
00610	PHYSICIAN	77.7	-0.2
01210	LAWYER	72.5	1.9
01330	ELEMENTARY SCHOOL TEACHER	67.3	10.3
01392	SUPERINTENDENT OF SCHOOLS	75.1	7.5
01410	PRIEST	57.0	-2.7
01414	FOREIGN MISSIONARY	49.2	0.1
01415	NUN	38.8	-17.4

ADMINISTRATIVE AND MANAGERIAL WORKERS

Code	Occupation		
02114	BANKER	62.1	-4.8

SALES WORKERS

Code	Occupation		
04100	GROCER	36.2	-6.3
04410	INSURANCE AGENT	54.4	9.8

SERVICE WORKERS

Code	Occupation		
05510	JANITOR	23.2	2.2
05700	BARBER	31.0	0.6

AGRICULTURAL, ANIMAL HUSBANDRY AND FORESTRY WORKERS, FISHERMEN AND HUNTERS

Code	Occupation		
06110	FARMER	46.6	-0.5

PRODUCTION AND RELATED WORKERS, TRANSPORT EQUIPMENT OPERATORS AND LABORERS

Code	Occupation		
08410	MACHINIST	51.8	8.4
08550	ELECTRICIAN	59.6	15.0
08710	PLUMBER	33.6	-0.3
09543	CARPENTER	44.0	6.8
09595	DITCH DIGGER	25.8	10.6
09852	TRUCK DRIVER	28.4	-4.2

ISCO NO.	OCCUPATION TITLE	PRESTIGE SCORE	SCORE MINUS STD. SCORE
	GUAM		
MEMBERS OF THE ARMED FORCES			
10001	AIR FORCE CAPTAIN	64.7	1.5
10003	SAILOR	41.4	2.6

PROFESSIONAL, TECHNICAL AND RELATED WORKERS

00220	ROAD ENGINEER IN A MINISTRY OF WORKS AND HYDRAULICS	62.3	-8.0
00610	DOCTOR	79.7	1.8
00710	SICK NURSE AND DISPENSER	55.1	1.5
01222	MAGISTRATE	73.9	0.6
01310	UNIVERSITY PROFESSOR	78.7	1.1
01391	HEADMASTER OF A PRIMARY SCHOOL	63.7	-1.9
01394	MASTER AT QUEENS COLLEGE	73.6	1.4

ADMINISTRATIVE AND MANAGERIAL WORKERS

02015	VILLAGE OVERSEER	44.6	2.7
02033	HEAD OF GOVERNMENT DEPARTMENT	72.7	1.6

CLERICAL AND RELATED WORKERS

03101	SENIOR CLERK IN CIVIL SERVICE	59.1	5.5
03310	BOOKKEEPER ON A SUGAR ESTATE	49.1	0.2
03313	BANK CLERK	52.3	4.7
03520	POSTMASTER IN COUNTRY POST OFFICE	59.2	0.9

SALES WORKERS

04100	OWNER OF A SMALL GROCERY AND PARLOUR	33.5	-8.9
04101	OWNER-MANAGER OF A LARGE DRY GOODS STORE	64.1	5.6
04410	INSURANCE SALESMAN	39.5	-5.0
04510	MALE STORE CLERK IN FOGARTY'S	29.9	-3.8
04521	HUCKSTER	17.9	-4.0

SERVICE WORKERS

05104	RUM SHOP PROPRIETOR	42.6	9.9
05320	WAITER IN HOTEL	19.0	-4.2
05820	POLICE CONSTABLE	34.0	-5.8
05821	POLICE INSPECTOR	60.9	1.2

ISCO NO.	OCCUPATION TITLE	PRESTIGE SCORE	SCORE MINUS STD. SCORE
	GUYANA		
	AGRICULTURAL, ANIMAL HUSBANDRY AND FORESTRY WORKERS, FISHERMEN AND HUNTERS		
06000	GENERAL MANAGER OF A SUGAR ESTATE	69.6	15.4
06001	FIELD FOREMAN ON SUGAR ESTATE	33.7	-7.1
06110	RICE AND PROVISION FARMER OF ABOUT 15 ACRES	34.4	-12.7
06111	RICE FARMER OF ABOUT 100 ACRES	55.8	-7.5
06220	CANECUTTER	17.8	-3.5
06410	FISHERMAN	23.2	-4.4
	PRODUCTION AND RELATED WORKERS, TRANSPORT EQUIPMENT OPERATORS AND LABORERS		
07000	OVERSEER OF A ROAD GANG	42.8	3.5
07110	PORK KNOCKER	23.2	-8.2
07320	SAW MILL MACHINE OPERATOR	33.0	2.4
07720	SUGAR BOILER	50.7	5.3
07910	TAILOR WORKING ON HIS OWN ACCOUNT	37.4	-2.0
08340	MACHINE OPERATOR IN A FACTORY	47.4	9.2
08410	SKILLED FITTER AND WELDER IN INDUSTRIAL FIRM	52.6	9.2
08430	GARAGE MECHANIC	42.8	-0.1
08720	SKILLED FITTER AND WELDER IN INDUSTRIAL FIRM	52.6	13.3
09540	CARPENTER	46.0	8.8
09710	STEVEDORE	23.3	2.0
09810	SEAMAN	25.4	-9.3
09850	OWNER-DRIVER OF HIRE CAR	30.4	2.6

PROFESSIONAL, TECHNICAL AND RELATED WORKERS

01330	TEACHER (40.0)	45.2	-11.8
01410	PRIEST (40.0)	26.4	-33.3
	GURDWARA PRIEST (12.7)		

CLERICAL AND RELATED WORKERS

03701	PEON/OFFICE BOY	30.8	5.0
03930	CLERK	41.2	-2.1

SALES WORKERS

04100	SHOPKEEPER (42.8)	42.6	0.2
04524	GROCER (42.4) MILKMAN	42.4	18.3

SERVICE WORKERS

05102	HOTELKEEPER	43.2	-3.2
C5600	WASHERMAN	17.5	-4.6
05700	FARBER	9.9	-20.5
05890	WATCHMAN	22.3	0.4

AGRICULTURAL, ANIMAL HUSBANDRY AND FORESTRY WORKERS, FISHERMEN AND HUNTERS

06110	OWNER CULTIVATOR	58.5	11.4
06111	PLANTATION OWNER	61.7	-1.7
06113	TENANT CULTIVATOR	52.4	23.0
06114	SHARE CROPPER	52.0	20.5
06210	AGRICULTURAL LABOURER	30.4	7.4
06270	GARDENER	18.7	-2.6
06291	FIREWOOD GATHERER (-3.7)	-1.5	0.0
	HONEY GATHERER (0.7)		
06491	HUNTER	6.3	0.0

389

ISCO NO.	OCCUPATION TITLE	PRESTIGE SCORE	SCORE MINUS STD. SCORE
	INDIA-PEASANT		
	PRODUCTION AND RELATED WORKERS, TRANSPORT EQUIPMENT OPERATORS AND LABORERS		
07540	WEAVER	29.6	-0.9
07590	MILL WORKER	25.6	-0.5
07910	TAILOR	29.6	-9.9
08010	COBBLER	7.9	-20.2
08310	BLACKSMITH	30.4	-4.2
08490	MECHANIC	58.1	15.2
08800	GOLDSMITH	35.2	-7.8
08920	POTTER	16.3	-8.8
09420	LEAF-PLATER	13.1	-7.9
09540	CARPENTER	33.2	-4.0
09712	WATER-CARRIER	14.7	-2.1
09990	LABOURER	10.3	-8.8
09995	SWEEPER	17.5	4.1
	MEMBERS OF THE ARMED FORCES		
10003	MILITARY-JAWAN	31.6	-7.2

INDIA—UNIVERSITY STUDENT

PROFESSIONAL, TECHNICAL AND RELATED WORKERS

00610	DOCTOR	75.5	-2.4
01101	CHARTERED ACCOUNTANT	67.2	-1.2
01210	LAWYER	69.3	-1.4
01330	PRIMARY SCHOOL TEACHER	52.5	-4.5
01410	PRIEST	66.1	6.4
01590	NEWSPAPER REPORTER	55.5	0.5

ADMINISTRATIVE AND MANAGERIAL WORKERS

02110	COMPANY DIRECTOR	74.3	-0.7
02120	WORKS MANAGER	64.4	0.3
02194	BUSINESS EXECUTIVE	71.6	4.9

CLERICAL AND RELATED WORKERS

03100	GOVERNMENT OFFICIAL	66.5	0.8
03930	OFFICE CLERK	44.7	1.4

SALES WORKERS

04100	STATIONERY DEALER	44.9	2.5
04108	LABOUR CONTRACTOR	48.6	0.0
04320	SALES REPRESENTATIVE	52.5	5.6
04410	INSURANCE AGENT	54.3	9.8
04510	SHOP ASSISTANT	49.1	6.5

SERVICE WORKERS

05102	HOTEL KEEPER	45.8	-0.6
05320	WAITER	18.7	-4.5
05820	POLICE CONSTABLE	40.5	0.7

ISCO NO.	OCCUPATION TITLE	PRESTIGE SCORE	SCORE MINUS STD. SCORE

INDIA-UNIVERSITY STUDENT

AGRICULTURAL, ANIMAL HUSBANDRY AND FORESTRY WORKERS, FISHERMEN AND HUNTERS

| 06110 | OWNER CULTIVATOR | 55.9 | 8.9 |
| 06210 | AGRICULTURAL LABOURER | 25.6 | 2.7 |

PRODUCTION AND RELATED WORKERS, TRANSPORT EQUIPMENT OPERATORS AND LABORERS

07590	MILL HAND	22.4	-3.7
08410	FITTER	32.0	-11.3
09510	MASON	28.1	-6.0
09540	CARPENTER	33.2	-4.0
09710	DOCK WORKER	23.1	1.8
09713	RAILWAY COOLI	14.8	-3.3
09850	TAXI DRIVER	27.4	-0.3
09851	BUS DRIVER	29.5	-2.9
09995	SWEEPER	12.3	-1.1

INDONESIA-JAVA

PROFESSIONAL, TECHNICAL AND RELATED WORKERS

Code	Occupation		
00220	ENGINEER (CHEMICAL, CIVIL, ARCHITECTURAL)	82.2	11.8
00410	AIRLINE PILOT, SHIP OFFICER	62.5	-4.0
00420	AIRLINE PILOT, SHIP OFFICER	62.5	-0.7
00610	PHYSICIAN	86.6	8.7
00710	NURSE, MIDWIFE	40.5	-13.0
00730	NURSE, MIDWIFE	40.5	-5.9
01210	LAWYER	80.0	9.3
01310	COLLEGE PROFESSOR	84.4	6.7
01320	HIGH SCHOOL TEACHER	60.3	-3.9
01330	ELEMENTARY SCHOOL TEACHER	42.7	-14.3
01510	ARTIST, PIANIST, AUTHOR	55.8	-5.8
01590	NEWSPAPER REPORTER	58.1	3.1
01610	ARTIST, PIANIST, AUTHOR	55.9	-1.3
01710	ARTIST, PIANIST, AUTHOR	55.9	-0.2
01712	ACTOR, SINGER	38.4	6.9
01730	ACTOR, SINGER	38.4	-13.2

ADMINISTRATIVE AND MANAGERIAL WORKERS

Code	Occupation		
02022	MEMBER:PEOPLE'S REPRESENTATIVE COUNCIL	77.9	5.6
02033	HEAD OF GOVERNMENT DEPARTMENT	75.6	4.5
02111	HEAD OF A NATIONAL INDUSTRY (71.2) DIRECTOR OF A PRIVATE CORPORATION (66.8)	62.0	-1.4

CLERICAL AND RELATED WORKERS

Code	Occupation		
03100	EMBASSY EMPLOYEE	69.0	3.3
03701	LABORER (SERVANT, MESSENGER, JANITOR)	25.2	-0.6
03930	OFFICE EMPLOYEE IN INDUSTRY	49.3	6.0
03931	GOVERNMENT OFFICE WORKER	47.1	2.8

SALES WORKERS

Code	Occupation		
04100	SMALL BUSINESSMAN	51.5	9.1

ISCO NO.	OCCUPATION TITLE	PRESTIGE SCORE	SCORE MINUS STD. SCORE
	INDONESIA-JAVA		
SERVICE WORKERS			
05101	OWNER-OPERATOR CF LUNCH STAND	31.8	-3.1
05400	LABORER (SERVANT, MESSENGER, JANITOR)	25.2	8.0
05510	LABORER (SERVANT, MESSENGER, JANITOR)	25.2	4.2
05820	COMMON POLICEMAN	29.6	-10.2
05821	POLICE OFFICER	64.6	5.0
AGRICULTURAL, ANIMAL HUSBANDRY AND FORESTRY WORKERS, FISHERMEN AND HUNTERS			
06110	FARM OWNER AND OPERATOR	53.7	6.6
PRODUCTION AND RELATED WORKERS, TRANSPORT EQUIPMENT OPERATORS AND LABORERS			
08410	MACHINIST, ELECTRICIAN	36.2	-7.2
08550	MACHINIST, ELECTRICIAN	36.2	-8.4
09852	AUTO OR TRUCK DRIVER	27.4	-5.2
09890	BICYCLE RICKSHAW DRIVER	23.0	6.3
MEMBERS OF THE ARMED FORCES			
10001	MILITARY OFFICER	73.4	10.2
10002	NONCOMMISSIONED MILITARY OFFICER	44.9	1.4
10003	MILITARY ENLISTED MAN	34.0	-4.8

PROFESSIONAL, TECHNICAL AND RELATED WORKERS

00420	CAPTAIN OF A SHIP	58.8	-4.3
00710	NURSE (SPECIAL CERTIFICATE)	52.8	-0.8
00720	VILLAGE NURSE	43.0	-1.1
01330	VILLAGE TEACHER (48.8)	43.0	-9.0
	TEACHER TOWN ELEMENTARY SCHOOL (47.2)		
01410	PROTESTANT MINISTER	61.7	2.1
01413	EVANGELIST-TEACHER	45.4	-4.7
01415	CATHOLIC BROTHER OR SISTER	47.2	-8.9

ADMINISTRATIVE AND MANAGERIAL WORKERS

02012	DISTRICT HEAD	55.3	-10.5
02015	VILLAGE HEAD	29.6	-12.3
02023	NEW GUINEA COUNCIL MEMBER	70.0	4.3
02195	COMMITTEE MEMBER POLITICAL PARTY	59.7	-3.0
02196	COMMITTEE MEMBER TRADE UNION (PROTESTANT OR CATHOLIC)	54.6	5.1

CLERICAL AND RELATED WORKERS

03101	ASSISTANT DISTRICT OFFICER	61.1	7.4
03103	CUSTOMS OFFICIAL	52.6	8.2
03210	TYPIST	37.6	-4.0
03930	OFFICE CLERK	47.7	4.3

SALES WORKERS

04100	TRADESMAN (39.6)	37.3	-5.1
	SHOPKEEPER (35.0)		

SERVICE WORKERS

05400	DOMESTIC SERVANT	5.3	-11.9
05510	JANITOR	24.0	3.0
05820	POLICEMAN	48.6	8.8
05891	JAIL GUARD	36.5	-2.6

ISCO NO.	OCCUPATION TITLE	PRESTIGE SCORE	SCORE MINUS STD. SCORE
	INDONESIA-WEST IRIAN		
	AGRICULTURAL, ANIMAL HUSBANDRY AND FORESTRY WORKERS, FISHERMEN AND HUNTERS		
06120	INDEPENDENT GARDENER (CACAO)	45.7	-9.3
06310	WOODCUTTER	16.9	-2.3
	PRODUCTION AND RELATED WORKERS, TRANSPORT EQUIPMENT OPERATORS AND LABORERS		
07001	TECHNICAL SUPERVISOR	55.0	2.9
08490	MECHANIC	48.6	5.7
08550	ELECTRICIAN	43.0	-1.5
09710	DOCK WORKER	27.6	6.3
09740	BULLDOZER OPERATOR	34.1	2.3
09810	SAILOR	32.5	-2.2
09851	BUS DRIVER	36.5	4.1
09997	ROADWORKER	21.3	1.2
	MEMBERS OF THE ARMED FORCES		
10003	MEMBER PAP. VOL. CORPS	52.8	14.1

PROFESSIONAL, TECHNICAL AND RELATED WORKERS

Code	Occupation		
00220	ENGINEER	79.8	9.4
00610	DOCTOR	82.4	4.5
00650	VET	61.9	0.5
00670	PHARMACIST	72.0	7.9
00710	NURSE	37.1	-16.4
01100	ACCOUNTANT	52.6	-1.9
01210	LAWYER	66.7	-3.9
01220	JUDGE	78.5	0.8
01310	PROFESSOR	82.7	0.0
01320	HIGH SCHOOL TEACHER	63.7	5.0
01330	ELEMENTARY SCHOOL TEACHER	53.0	-0.5
01410	RELIGIOUS LEADER	59.1	-4.0
01591	NEWSPAPER EDITOR	61.2	-0.6
01930	SOCIAL WORKER	57.1	-3.8
			0.9

ADMINISTRATIVE AND MANAGERIAL WORKERS

Code	Occupation		
02111	GENERAL DIRECTOR	78.7	8.3
02113	GRAIN SHED OWNER	52.0	-0.3
02116	CONTRACTOR	62.9	9.5

CLERICAL AND RELATED WORKERS

Code	Occupation		
03211	SECRETARY	56.7	3.7
03700	MAILMAN	29.6	-3.2
03930	CLERK	38.8	-4.6

SALES WORKERS

Code	Occupation		
04100	STORE OWNER (43.4)	38.5	-4.0
	GROCER (33.6)		
04101	MERCHANT	63.1	9.6
04411	REAL ESTATE AGENT	41.3	-7.7
C4510	SPICE SALESMAN (35.4)	34.3	0.7
	SALESPERSON (33.2)		

ISCO NO.	OCCUPATION TITLE	PRESTIGE SCORE	SCORE MINUS STD. SCORE
	IRAQ		
04521	SIDEWALK SHISHKEBAB MAN	24.6	2.6
04523	NEWSPAPER BOY	25.7	11.6
SERVICE WORKERS			
05100	RESTAURANT OWNER	46.3	-1.5
05101	COFFEE SHOP OWNER	38.5	3.6
05320	WAITER	22.1	-1.1
05510	CUSTODIAN	22.2	1.2
05600	DRY CLEANER	31.9	9.8
05700	BARBER	34.8	4.4
05810	FIREMAN	29.6	-5.7
05820	POLICEMAN	25.8	-14.0
05890	NIGHT GUARD	23.6	1.6
05995	SHOE-SHINE BOY	21.5	9.3
AGRICULTURAL, ANIMAL HUSBANDRY AND FORESTRY WORKERS, FISHERMEN AND HUNTERS			
06110	FARMER	27.7	-19.4
PRODUCTION AND RELATED WORKERS, TRANSPORT EQUIPMENT OPERATORS AND LABORERS			
07000	CONSTRUCTION FOREMAN	34.9	-4.3
07540	WEAVER	27.0	-3.4
07730	BUTCHER	36.2	4.9
07760	BAKER	30.2	-3.0
07910	TAILOR	44.3	4.8
08420	WATCH REPAIRMAN	39.5	-0.3
08490	MECHANIC	45.1	2.3
08540	RADIO/TV REPAIRMAN	38.6	-3.4
08550	ELECTRICAL WORKER	32.5	-12.0
08570	PHONE LINEMAN	29.9	-6.4
08710	PLUMBER	26.5	-7.4
08720	WELDER	29.4	-9.8
09310	HOUSE PAINTER	31.7	0.7

398

09540	CARPENTER	38.8	1.6
09594	CONSTRUCTION WORKER	28.7	3.1
09595	SEWER WORKER	20.5	5.3
09712	PORTER	21.2	4.3
09850	TAXI DRIVER	28.9	1.2
09995	SWEEPER	21.4	8.0
09996	GARBAGEMAN	21.0	8.3

MEMBERS OF THE ARMED FORCES

| 10001 | ARMY OFFICER | 68.3 | 5.1 |
| 10003 | SOLDIER | 27.2 | -11.5 |

SOURCES OF LIVELIHOOD OTHER THAN LABOR FORCE ACTIVITY

| 13001 | LAND OWNER | 68.3 | 11.2 |

ISCO NO.	OCCUPATION TITLE	PRESTIGE SCORE	SCORE MINUS STD. SCORE
	ISRAEL		

PROFESSIONAL, TECHNICAL AND RELATED WORKERS

ISCO NO.	OCCUPATION TITLE	PRESTIGE SCORE	SCORE MINUS STD. SCORE
00130	SCIENTIST	83.6	5.2
00220	ENGINEER	72.7	2.4
00410	FLIGHT OFFICER	74.9	8.4
00610	PHYSICIAN	79.3	1.4
01210	LAWYER	63.4	-2.3
01310	UNIVERSITY PROFESSOR	81.0	3.4
01320	HIGH SCHOOL TEACHER	66.2	2.0
01330	ELEMENTARY SCHOOL TEACHER	63.0	6.0
01391	SCHOOL PRINCIPAL	69.6	4.0
01410	RABBI (55.3)	52.0	-7.6
01414	CLERGYMAN (48.7)	41.6	-7.5
01510	MISSIONARY	70.6	8.9
01610	AUTHOR	57.5	0.3
01710	ARTIST, PAINTER, MUSICIAN	57.5	1.4
01730	ARTIST, PAINTER, MUSICIAN	57.5	6.0
01800	ACTOR	53.2	4.7
	ATHLETE		

ADMINISTRATIVE AND MANAGERIAL WORKERS

ISCO NO.	OCCUPATION TITLE	PRESTIGE SCORE	SCORE MINUS STD. SCORE
02022	MEMBER OF PARLIAMENT	77.1	4.9
02032	DIPLOMAT	81.4	8.2
02111	INDUSTRIALIST	59.7	-10.7
02114	BANKER	64.0	-2.9
02195	POLITICIAN	76.4	13.7

CLERICAL AND RELATED WORKERS

ISCO NO.	OCCUPATION TITLE	PRESTIGE SCORE	SCORE MINUS STD. SCORE
03101	PUBLIC SERVANT	51.0	-2.7
03310	BOOKKEEPER	60.5	11.5
03700	MAIL CARRIER	28.2	-4.6
03930	CLERK IN A PRIVATE FIRM	44.5	1.1

03992 PARTY FUNCTIONARY   46.6   -1.6

SALES WORKERS

04100 GROCER   35.3   -6.7
04101 TRADER, BUSINESSMAN   48.8   -9.7

SERVICE WORKERS

05320 WAITER   29.2   6.0
05510 JANITOR   17.5   -3.5
05700 BARBER   30.2   -0.2
05820 POLICEMAN   43.8   4.0
05991 USHER, MOVIE   27.1   7.1

AGRICULTURAL, ANIMAL HUSBANDRY AND FORESTRY WORKERS, FISHERMEN AND HUNTERS

06110 FARMER IN MOSHAVA (PRIVATE OWNERSHIP)   42.3   -4.8
06115 MEMBER OF A KIBBUTZ (COLLECTIVE SETTLEMENT) (35.8)   34.7   0.0
       MEMBER OF A MOSHAV (COOPERATIVE SETTLEMENT) (33.6)

PRODUCTION AND RELATED WORKERS, TRANSPORT EQUIPMENT OPERATORS AND LABORERS

07110 COAL MINER   27.5   -4.0
07730 BUTCHER   27.2   -4.1
07910 TAILOR   37.6   -1.9
08010 SHOEMAKER   28.3   0.1
08390 LOCKSMITH   37.9   -2.2
08490 MECHANIC   40.1   -2.7
08550 ELECTRICIAN   47.3   2.8
08710 PLUMBER   31.5   -2.8
09210 TYPOGRAPHER   40.9   -2.4
09540 CARPENTER   39.6   -1.4
09852 DRIVER   31.4   -1.2

MEMBERS OF THE ARMED FORCES

10001 ARMY OFFICER   61.9   -1.4
10003 SOLDIER   45.1   6.3

ISCO NO.	OCCUPATION TITLE	PRESTIGE SCORE	SCORE MINUS STD. SCORE
	ITALY		
PROFESSIONAL, TECHNICAL AND RELATED WORKERS		
00610	PHYSICIAN	79.0	1.1
01210	LAWYER	71.9	1.3
01310	UNIVERSITY PROFESSOR	77.7	0.1
01330	ELEMENTARY SCHOOL TEACHER	61.9	4.8
01391	SCHOOL PRINCIPAL	70.9	5.3
01410	CLERGYMAN	65.4	5.8
01414	MISSIONARY	64.1	15.0
01510	AUTHOR	71.0	9.3
01610	ARTIST	63.2	6.1
01730	ACTOR	58.7	7.2
ADMINISTRATIVE AND MANAGERIAL WORKERS		
02114	BANKER	65.2	-1.8
02190	BUSINESSMAN	56.9	-1.1
02195	POLITICIAN	70.9	8.2
CLERICAL AND RELATED WORKERS		
03101	CIVIL SERVICE EMPLOYEE	60.5	6.9
03310	BOOKKEEPER	51.2	2.2
03700	MAIL CARRIER	31.2	-1.6
SALES WORKERS		
04100	GROCER	38.1	-4.3
SERVICE WORKERS		
05510	JANITOR	25.0	3.9
05700	BARBER	29.4	-1.0
05820	POLICEMAN	50.1	10.3

AGRICULTURAL, ANIMAL HUSBANDRY AND FORESTRY WORKERS, FISHERMEN AND HUNTERS

| C6110 | FARMER | 39.4 | -7.7 |

PRODUCTION AND RELATED WORKERS, TRANSPORT EQUIPMENT OPERATORS AND LABORERS

07110	COAL MINER	31.5	0.0
07730	BUTCHER	36.6	5.2
07910	TAILOR	41.7	2.3
08010	SHOEMAKER	29.8	1.7
08550	ELECTRICIAN	42.2	-2.3
08710	PLUMBER	35.9	2.1
09210	TYPOGRAPHER	46.4	4.1
09540	CARPENTER	35.4	-1.8
09852	TRUCK DRIVER	30.4	-2.2

MEMBERS OF THE ARMED FORCES

| 10003 | SOLDIER | 53.0 | 14.2 |

403

ISCO NO.	OCCUPATION TITLE	PRESTIGE SCORE	SCORE MINUS STD. SCORE
	IVORY COAST		
	PROFESSIONAL, TECHNICAL AND RELATED WORKERS		
00220	INGENIEUR/ENGINEER	80.5	10.2
00610	MEDECIN/PHYSICIAN	76.5	-1.4
00710	INFIRMIER/MALE NURSE	49.0	-4.6
01210	AVOCAT/LAWYER	69.8	-0.8
01310	PROFESSEUR D'UNIVERSITE/UNIVERSITY PROFESSOR	80.0	2.3
01320	PROFESSEUR DE LYCEE/SECONDARY SCHOOL TEACHER, LYCEE (68.9)	66.5	2.3
	PROFESSEUR DE COLLEGE/SECONDARY SCHOOL TEACHER, COLLEGE (64.0)		
01330	INSTITUTEUR/PRIMARY SCHOOL TEACHER	52.1	-4.9
01410	ECCLESIASTIQUE/CLERGYMAN	62.0	2.4
01712	GRIOT/MINSTREL	17.3	-14.2
01790	SPEAKER DE LA RADIO/RADIO ANNOUNCER	56.6	6.2
	ADMINISTRATIVE AND MANAGERIAL WORKERS		
02012	CHEF COUTUMIER/CHIEF	48.3	-17.5
	CLERICAL AND RELATED WORKERS		
03313	EMPLOYE DE BANQUE/BANK CLERK	52.1	4.5
03931	COMMIS D'ADMINISTRATION/GOVERNMENT CLERK	47.7	3.4
	SALES WORKERS		
04510	VENDEUR/SALESMAN	29.4	-4.2
04521	COLPORTEUR/PEDLER	17.8	-4.1
	SERVICE WORKERS		
05820	AGENT DE POLICE/POLICEMAN	47.5	7.7

AGRICULTURAL, ANIMAL HUSBANDRY AND FORESTRY WORKERS, FISHERMEN AND HUNTERS

06110	PLANTEUR/FARMER	46.5	-0.6
06210	MANOEUVRE AGRICOLE/AGRICULTURAL LABORER	28.5	5.6

PRODUCTION AND RELATED WORKERS, TRANSPORT EQUIPMENT OPERATORS AND LABORERS

08430	MECANICIEN AUTOMOBILE/AUTO MECHANIC	45.5	2.6
08550	ELECTRICIEN/ELECTRICIAN	51.2	6.6
09540	MENUISIER/JOINER	32.7	-4.5
09853	COMMERCANT-TRANSPORTEUR/TRANSPORT PROPRIETOR	40.8	1.4
09996	BOUEUR/GARBAGE COLLECTOR	16.0	3.4

MEMBERS OF THE ARMED FORCES

10003	GARDE REPUBLICAIN/SOLDIER	38.8	0.1

ISCO NO.	OCCUPATION TITLE	PRESTIGE SCORE	SCORE MINUS STD. SCORE
	JAPAN		
	PROFESSIONAL, TECHNICAL AND RELATED WORKERS		
00120	ATOMIC PHYSICIST (83.6)	83.6	7.1
	PHYSICIST (83.5)		
00220	CIVIL ENGINEER	62.6	-7.8
00230	ELECTRICAL ENGINEER	64.8	-0.5
00240	MECHANICAL ENGINEER	62.5	-4.0
00270	MINING ENGINEER	59.0	-3.8
00410	AIRLINE PILOT	65.5	-1.0
00420	CAPTAIN OF A LARGE MERCHANT SHIP	65.5	2.3
00510	BOTONIST	74.4	5.6
00520	CANCER RESEARCHER	78.2	-0.6
00610	PHYSICIAN (73.0)	69.9	-7.9
	CETHCMOLOGIST (66.8)		
00611	DIRECTOR OF A LARGE HOSPITAL (CHIEF PHYSICIAN)	83.5	3.0
00710	NURSE	48.8	-4.7
00900	ECONOMIST	79.0	18.5
01210	LAWYER	70.6	-0.0
01220	JUDGE	82.6	4.9
01221	PRESIDENT OF THE SUPREME COURT	87.1	5.1
01222	LOCAL COURT JUDGE	75.8	2.6
01311	UNIVERSITY PROFESSOR	79.7	2.1
01311	RECTOR AT THE UNIVERSITY OF TOKYO	89.1	2.8
01330	ELEMENTARY SCHOOL TEACHER	56.0	-1.0
01410	PRIEST IN A BUDDHIST TEMPLE	51.5	-8.2
01510	NOVELIST	60.9	-0.8
01590	NEWSPAPER REPORTER	57.0	2.1
01710	COMPOSER	63.8	7.7
01730	ACTOR (49.8)	45.2	-6.3
	MOVIE PERFORMER (40.6)		
01732	CINEMA DIRECTOR	62.4	0.1
01790	TELEVISICN ANNOUNCER	59.1	8.7
01801	MANAGER OF A PROFESSIONAL BASEBALL TEAM	62.8	12.4

ADMINISTRATIVE AND MANAGERIAL WORKERS

Code	Occupation		
02010	PRIME MINISTER	91.2	1.1
02011	PREFECT	80.2	-1.7
02020	PRESIDENT OF THE DIET	86.1	0.0
02022	MEMBER OF THE DIET	78.9	6.8
02030	MINISTER OF STATE	86.1	7.4
02033	DEPARTMENT HEAD IN A GOVERNMENT AGENCY	60.1	-11.0
02035	DEPARTMENT HEAD IN A MUNICIPAL OFFICE	56.0	-7.1
02111	PRESIDENT OF A LARGE COMPANY	79.1	8.7
02112	OWNER OF A MEDIUM OR SMALL FACTORY	59.9	-2.9
02192	DEPARTMENT HEAD IN A PRIVATE COMPANY	57.5	-3.0
02193	DEPARTMENT HEAD IN A LARGE COMPANY	62.4	-0.7
02194	OFFICER OF A LARGE COMPANY (73.4)	71.5	4.8
	CORPORATION EXECUTIVE (69.6)		
02196	UNION LEADER	56.0	6.5
02197	SECRETARY GENERAL OF A LARGE LABOR UNION	59.4	-3.3

CLERICAL AND RELATED WORKERS

Code	Occupation		
03211	PRIVATE SECRETARY	50.8	-2.2
03602	SLEEPING CAR PORTER	30.5	0.0
03930	OFFICE EMPLOYEE IN A LARGE COMPANY (45.4)	43.5	0.1
	OFFICE WORKER IN A PRIVATE COMPANY (43.8)		
	OFFICE EMPLOYEE IN A LARGE SPINNING MILL (41.2)		
03931	OFFICE WORKER IN A GOVERNMENT OFFICE	46.0	1.7
03941	AIRLINE OFFICE EMPLOYEE (42.9)	40.3	3.7
	OFFICE EMPLOYEE IN THE TOKYO CENTRAL RAILROAD STATION (41.2)		
	RAILROAD STATION OFFICE EMPLOYEE (36.9)		

SALES WORKERS

Code	Occupation		
04100	SHOPKEEPER (41.5)	38.8	-3.7
	OWNER OF A GREEN GROCERY SHOP (36.0)		
04410	INSURANCE AGENT	29.7	-14.9
04510	DEPARTMENT STORE SALESMAN (34.0)	29.7	-3.9
	SHOP CLERK (31.0)		
	SUPERMARKET SALES CLERK (29.2)		
	SALESMAN IN A BOOKSTORE (28.6)		
	HARDWARE STORE CLERK (28.6)		
	SALES CLERK IN GREEN GROCERY (26.8)		
04511	AUTOMOBILE SALESMAN	41.5	5.8

ISCO NO.	OCCUPATION TITLE	PRESTIGE SCORE	SCORE MINUS STD. SCORE
	JAPAN		
04512	FILLING STATION ATTENTANT	28.0	2.8
04521	PEDDLER (17.6)	17.4	-4.5
	STREETSTALL KEEPER (17.2)		
	SERVICE WORKERS		
05102	HOTEL KEEPER	44.9	-1.5
05403	HEAD CLERK IN A JAPANESE STYLE INN	28.5	-4.3
05700	BARBER	30.2	-0.2
05702	HAIR DRESSER	39.4	4.6
05703	OPERATOR OF A HAIR DRESSING SALON	39.5	-5.8
05820	POLICEMAN	45.6	5.8
05995	SHOE SHINER	11.7	-0.6
05998	BELL CAPTAIN IN A HOTEL	40.7	0.0
	AGRICULTURAL, ANIMAL HUSBANDRY AND FORESTRY WORKERS, FISHERMEN AND HUNTERS		
06110	FARM OWNER (36.2)	36.1	-11.0
	HEAD OF A FAMILY FARM (36.0)		
06113	TENANT FARMER	21.5	-8.0
06117	UNPAID FAMILY FARM WORKER	33.5	0.0
06210	AGRICULTURAL LABORER	23.0	0.1
06410	FISHERMAN	28.1	0.6
06411	OPERATOR OF A FISHING BOAT	53.9	16.6
06490	HARPOONER ON A WHALEBOAT	40.0	0.0
	PRODUCTION AND RELATED WORKERS, TRANSPORT EQUIPMENT OPERATORS AND LABORERS		
07110	GOLD MINER (22.9)	19.7	-11.8
	COAL MINER (16.5)		
07491	CHARCOAL MAKER	16.5	0.0
07520	SPINNER IN A LARGE MILL (31.3)	30.5	-3.0
	TEXTILE SPINNING MACHINE OPERATOR (29.8)		
07760	WORKER IN A MACARONI FACTORY (29.7)	26.9	-6.2
	WORKER IN A BREAD BAKERY (26.3)		

07910	WORKER IN A UDON (JAPANESE NOODLE) FACTORY (24.9)	38.2	-1.3
08110	TAILOR	39.5	-0.9
08331	FURNITURE MAKER	31.2	-5.4
08430	TURNER	37.0	-6.0
08431	AUTOMOBILE REPAIRMAN	46.2	-1.0
09210	OPERATOR OF A SERVICE STATION	28.8	-13.5
09540	PRINTER	36.8	-0.4
09541	CARPENTER	44.4	-3.8
09594	MASTER CARPENTER	17.8	-7.8
09610	CONSTRUCTION LABOURER	46.3	3.7
	GENERATOR OPERATOR IN A NEW AND POWERFUL STEAM POWER PLANT (48.1)		
	GENERATOR OPERATOR IN A STEAM POWER PLANT (44.5)		
09712	PORTER	19.5	2.7
09830	ENGINEER ON NEW TOKAIDO LINE (44.5)	43.4	0.7
	STEAM LOCOMOTIVE ENGINEER (43.2)		
	ELECTRIC TRAIN ENGINEER (42.4)		
09851	BUS DRIVER	28.8	-3.6
09852	DRIVER (34.6)	32.2	-0.4
	DRIVER OF A MAIL TRUCK (32.5)		
	DRIVER OF A GARBAGE TRUCK (29.4)		
09997	ROAD WORKER	19.9	-0.2
	MEMBERS OF THE ARMED FORCES		
10003	AIR FORCE ENLISTED MAN (39.4)	39.1	0.4
	ARMY ENLISTED MAN (38.9)		

TSCO NO.	OCCUPATION TITLE	PRESTIGE SCORE	SCORE MINUS STD. SCORE

MAURITANIA

PROFESSIONAL, TECHNICAL AND RELATED WORKERS

TSCO NO.	OCCUPATION TITLE	PRESTIGE SCORE	SCORE MINUS STD. SCORE
00321	TIREUR DE PLAN/TRACER OF PLANS:ROUTINE DRAFTSMAN	26.2	0.0
00610	MEDECIN/PHYSICIAN	66.3	-11.6
01330	INSTITUTEUR/PRIMARY SCHOOL TEACHER	59.4	2.4
01391	DIRECTEUR ECOLE PRIMAIRE/PRIMARY SCHOOL PRINCIPAL	62.2	-3.4
01393	MONITEUR D'ENSEIGNEMENT/TEACHER'S AIDE	42.8	-7.1

ADMINISTRATIVE AND MANAGERIAL WORKERS

TSCO NO.	OCCUPATION TITLE	PRESTIGE SCORE	SCORE MINUS STD. SCORE
02030	MINISTRE/MINISTER OF STATE	69.1	-9.7
02111	DIRECTEUR ENTREPRISE PILOTE/HEAD OF A "MODEL ENTERPRISE"	69.1	-1.4
02112	DIRECTEUR ENTREPRISE SECONDAIRE/HEAD OF AN ENTERPRISE OF SECONDARY IMPORTANCE	64.9	2.2
02193	CHEF DE SERVICE GRANDE ENTREPRISE/DEPT. HEAD IN LARGE COMPANY	62.2	-1.0

CLERICAL AND RELATED WORKERS

TSCO NO.	OCCUPATION TITLE	PRESTIGE SCORE	SCORE MINUS STD. SCORE
03103	DOUANIER/CUSTOMS OFFICIAL	49.7	5.3
03210	DACTYLOGRAPHE/TYPIST	52.5	10.9
03211	SECRETAIRE/SECRETARY	56.6	3.6
03310	AIDE-COMPTABLE/ASSISTANT ACCOUNTANT	51.1	2.1
03701	PLANTON DE BUREAU/OFFICE BOY	20.7	-5.1
03802	OPERATEUR RADIO/RADIO OPERATOR	59.4	10.2
03910	MAGASINIER/WAREHOUSE CLERK	41.4	9.4
03930	COMMIS AUX ECRITURES/OFFICE CLERK	45.6	2.2
03931	COMMIS D'ADMINISTRATION/GOVERNMENT CLERK	53.9	9.6

SALES WORKERS

TSCO NO.	OCCUPATION TITLE	PRESTIGE SCORE	SCORE MINUS STD. SCORE
04100	COMMERCANT (PETITE BOUTIQUE)/SMALL SHOP KEEPER	27.6	-14.8
04101	COMMERCANT-TRANSPORTEUR/SHOP OWNER-TRANSPORT OPERATOR:OWNS SHOPS AND TRUCKS	55.2	-3.3

SERVICE WORKERS

Code	Occupation		Value
05312	BOY-CUISINIER DE RESTAURANT/COOK'S HELPER IN A RESTAURANT		20.7	-1.8
05400	BOY-CUISINIER DE FAMILLE/COOK IN PRIVATE HOUSEHOLD		15.2	-2.0
05820	GENDARME AUXILIARE/POLICEMAN (58.0)		44.9	5.1
	GOUMIER/TRADITIONAL POLICEMAN (31.8)			
05890	GARDIEN (AVEC FUSIL)/WATCHMAN WITH GUN (23.5)		20.0	-2.0
	GARDIEN (SANS FUSIL)/WATCHMAN WITHOUT GUN (16.6)			

PRODUCTION AND RELATED WORKERS, TRANSPORT EQUIPMENT OPERATORS AND LABORERS

Code	Occupation	Value	
07000	CHEF D'EQUIPE/GANG BOSS	27.6	-11.7
08310	FORGERON/BLACKSMITH	16.6	-18.0
08331	TOURNEUR/LATHE OPERATOR	37.3	0.7
08410	AJUSTEUR/FITTER	40.1	-3.3
08430	CHAUFFEUR-MECANICIEN/DRIVER-MECHANIC	48.0	4.0
08490	MECANICIEN/MECHANIC	48.3	5.5
08492	AIDE-MECANICIEN/MECHANIC'S HELPER	33.1	1.8
08494	MANOEUVRE (DANS UN GARAGE)/UNSKILLED GARAGE LABORER	19.3	1.5
08550	ELECTRICIEN/ELECTRICIAN	44.2	-0.3
08720	SOUDEUR/WELDER	38.7	-0.6
09310	PEINTRE/BUILDING PAINTER	30.4	-0.7
09540	MENUISIER/JOINER	34.5	-2.7
09594	MANOEUVRE DE CHANTIER/CONSTRUCTION LABORER	13.8	-11.8
09840	AIGUILLEUR/RAILWAY WORKER:SWITCHMAN, BRAKEMAN, ETC.	24.9	-3.9
09852	CHAUFFEUR/DRIVER	35.9	3.3

MEMBERS OF THE ARMED FORCES

Code	Occupation	Value	
10000	COMMANDANT DE CERCLE/COMMANDER OF AN ARMY UNIT	66.3	-6.6

ISCO NO.	OCCUPATION TITLE	PRESTIGE SCORE	SCORE MINUS STD. SCORE
	MEXICO		
	PROFESSIONAL, TECHNICAL AND RELATED WORKERS		
00210	ARCHITECT	77.5	5.7
00220	ENGINEER	76.8	6.4
00610	DOCTOR	80.8	2.0
00670	PHARMACIST	60.8	-3.3
00710	NURSE	56.7	3.1
01210	LAWYER	70.1	-0.6
01310	UNIVERSITY PROFESSOR	79.6	2.0
01330	SCHOOL TEACHER	74.5	17.5
01410	PRIEST (54.3)	51.7	-7.9
	MINISTER (49.2)		
01730	TV OR RADIO ACTOR	49.4	-2.2
01930	SOCIAL WORKER	62.2	6.0
	ADMINISTRATIVE AND MANAGERIAL WORKERS		
02022	CONGRESSMAN	60.1	-12.0
	CLERICAL AND RELATED WORKERS		
03100	GOVERNMENT OFFICIAL	56.7	-9.1
03315	AGENT FOR LOTTERY TICKETS	30.7	-5.1
03700	POSTMAN	49.6	16.8
03930	OFFICE WORKER	50.4	7.1
	SALES WORKERS		
04100	SMALL RETAIL MERCHANT	44.7	2.3
04107	CONTRABAND DEALER	8.8	0.0
04320	TRAVELING SALESMAN	51.9	5.0
04512	GASOLINE STATION ATTENDANT	25.3	0.0
04521	PRODUCE PEDDLER	47.3	25.4

SERVICE WORKERS

05101	SMALL RESTAURANT OWNER	31.9	-3.0
05320	RESTAURANT WAITER	20.4	-2.9
05400	DOMESTIC SERVANT	12.7	-4.5
05403	HOTEL WORKER	31.7	-1.1
05510	JANITOR	19.3	-1.7
05700	BARBER	31.2	0.8
05820	POLICEMAN	27.6	-18.3
05995	BOOTBLACK	10.0	-2.2

AGRICULTURAL, ANIMAL HUSBANDRY AND FORESTRY WORKERS, FISHERMEN AND HUNTERS

06110	FARMER	51.5	4.4
06113	FARM TENANT	36.3	6.8
06120	CATTLEMAN	54.8	-0.2
06410	FISHERMAN	27.9	0.3

PRODUCTION AND RELATED WORKERS, TRANSPORT EQUIPMENT OPERATORS AND LABORERS

07780	'MOONSHINER'	7.4	1.5
07910	TAILOR	40.2	0.7
07911	DRESSMAKER WHO WORKS AT HOME	36.3	-3.0
08010	COBBLER	26.9	-1.3
08430	AUTOMOBILE MECHANIC	41.1	-1.8
09540	CARPENTER	33.8	-3.4
09594	CONSTRUCTION WORKER	20.3	-5.3
09710	STEVEDORE	17.9	-3.3
09850	TAXI DRIVER	24.6	-3.1
09851	BUS DRIVER	34.5	2.1
09852	TRUCK DRIVER	29.0	-3.6
09970	FACTORY WORKER	39.7	10.4
09995	STREET CLEANER	9.5	-3.9
09997	ROAD WORKER	36.2	16.1

MEMBERS OF THE ARMED FORCES

10001	OFFICER IN ARMED FORCES	56.6	-6.6
10003	SOLDIER	22.2	-16.6

ISCO NO.	OCCUPATION TITLE	PRESTIGE SCORE	SCORE MINUS STD. SCORE
	NETHERLANDS		
	PROFESSIONAL, TECHNICAL AND RELATED WORKERS		
00210	ARCHITECT/ARCHITECT	67.9	-3.9
00220	INGENIEUR/ENGINEER	75.8	5.5
00320	TEKENAAR, TECHNISCH/DRAFTSMAN	56.1	1.1
00410	PILOOT/AIRPLANE PILOT	56.2	-10.3
00420	KAPITEIN GROTE VAART/SHIP'S CAPTAIN (77.2)	69.8	6.6
	GEZAGVOERDER GROTE VAART/SHIP'S CAPTAIN (73.3)		
	STUURMAN GROTE VAART/SHIP'S PILOT (58.9)		
00421	SCHIPPER ZELFSTANDIG/SELF EMPLOYED SKIPPER (37.2)	35.0	-0.9
	SCHIPPER BINNENVAART/BOAT SKIPPER (36.3)		
	SCHIPPER/SKIPPER (31.4)		
00430	MACHINIST GROTE VAART/SHIP'S ENGINEER	60.0	0.0
00540	ANALIST/MEDICAL TECHNICIAN	51.1	-6.8
00541	MELKCONTROLEUR/MILK TESTER	35.2	-11.5
00610	ARTS/PHYSICIAN	78.7	-0.8
00611	DIRECTEUR VAN EEN ZIEKENHUIS/DIRECTOR OF A HOSPITAL (79.5)	74.4	-6.1
	DIRECTRESS VAN EEN ZIEKENHUIS/HOSPITAL DIRECTOR (FEMALE) (69.2)		
00630	TANDARTS/DENTIST	72.4	1.9
00650	VEEARTS/VETERINARIAN	72.4	11.0
00670	APOTHEKER/PHARMICIST	73.2	9.1
00680	APOTHEKERASSISTENT/PHARMACIST (EMPLOYEE)	49.8	5.3
00710	VERPLEEGSTER/NURSE	41.1	-12.4
00711	HOOFDVERPLEEGSTER/HEAD NURSE	52.8	-5.2
00730	VROEDVROW, VERIOSKUNDIGE/MIDWIFE	51.1	4.7
00751	ZELFSTANDIGE AMBACHTSBEROEPEN:OPTICIEN/OPTICIAN	52.9	-4.3
01100	ACCOUNTANT/ACCOUNTANT	62.6	8.1
01101	ACCOUNTANT (AC. GEVORMDEN DAARMEDE GELIJK TE STELLEN) / ACCOUNTANT WITH UNIVERSITY TRAINING OR EQUIVALENT	73.3	4.9
01210	ADVOCAAT/LAWYER	73.5	2.8
01220	RECHTER/JUDGE	78.1	0.4
01290	NOTARIS/NON-TRIAL LAWYER	74.0	3.4
01291	RECHTSKUNDIG ADVISEUR (GEEN ACADEMICUS)/LEGAL ADIVSOR (WITHOUT ACADEMIC DEGREE)	51.7	0.0

414

Code	Occupation		
01310	HOOGLERAAR/UNIVERSITY PROFESSOR	80.6	3.0
01320	LERAAR H.B.S.-GYMNASIUM/HIGH SCHOOL TEACHER	69.2	5.0
01330	ONDERWIJZER L.O./PRIMARY SCHOOL TEACHER	57.6	0.6
01390	LERAAR AMBACHTSSCHOOL/TRADE SCHOOL TEACHER	62.0	5.1
01391	HOOFDONDERWIJZER/PRIMARY SCHOOL PRINCIPAL	58.4	-7.2
01410	RABBIJN/RABBI (73.2)	69.9	10.2
	PREDIKANT/PROTESTANT MINISTER (70.2)		
	PASTOOR/CATHOLIC PRIEST (69.1)		
	GEESTELIJKE/CLERGYMAN (67.2)		
01416	KAPELAAN/ASSISTANT PRIEST	61.1	0.0
01490	GODSDIENSTONDERWIJZER/RELIGION TEACHER	50.6	-5.6
01590	JOURNALIST/JOURNALIST	56.6	1.7
01610	KUNSTSCHILDER/PAINTER	45.5	-11.7
01621	TEKENAAR-CONSTRUCTEUR/INDUSTRIAL DESIGNER	55.2	-0.7
01622	ETALEUR/WINDOW DRESSER	40.0	2.2
01630	PHOTOGRAAF (ZELFSTANDIG)/SELF-EMPLOYED PHOTOGRAPHER	44.1	-1.0
01710	OPERA- EN CONCERTZANGER/OPERA AND CONCERT SINGER (58.9)	57.2	1.1
01712	TOONKUNSTENAAR/MUSICIAN (55.4)	24.0	-7.5
01713	MUZIKANT STRIJKJE/MUSICIAN IN A STRING BAND	54.0	0.9
01721	MUZIEKLERAAR/MUSIC TEACHER	40.0	3.9
01730	DANSLERAAR/DANCING TEACHER	53.1	1.5
01791	TONEELSPELER/ACTOR	40.9	8.1
01801	VARIETE-ARTIST/VARIETY ARTIST	48.0	-2.4
01910	GYMNASTIEKLERAAR/PHYSICAL EDUCATION TEACHER (49.5)	51.8	-2.7
	SPORTLERAAR/PHYSICAL EDUCATION TEACHER (46.5)		
	BIBLIOTHECARIS/HEAD LIBRARIAN (62.0)		
	ASSISTENT BIBLIOTHEEK OF LEESZAAL/LIBRARIAN IN PUBLIC LIBRARY (41.7)		
01930	SOCIAAL WERKSTER/SOCIAL WORKER	50.9	-5.4
01990	HOGER TECHNISCH PERSONEEL (M.T.S. OPLEIDING)/HIGHER TECHNICAL PERSONNEL (TECHNICAL HIGH SCHOOL EDUCATION) (56.5)	55.3	-2.9
	ASSISTANT M.T.S./TECHNICIAN (MIDDLE TECHNICAL SCHOOL) (54.1)		

ADMINISTRATIVE AND MANAGERIAL WORKERS

Code	Occupation		
02013	BURGEMEESTER VAN GROTE GEMEENTE (B.V. GRONINGEN, ARNHEM, TILBURG, HAARLEM)/MAYOR OF A LARGE CITY	78.1	2.9
02014	BURGEMEESTER KLEINE GEMEENTE (MINDER DAN 10,000 INWONERS)/MAYOR OF A SMALL CITY (FEWER THAN 10,000 INHABITANTS)	71.0	2.7
02033	OVERHEIDSPERSONEEL HOGERE AMBTENAAR (B.V. LEIDER VAN EEN BEPAALDE DIENST/HIGH CIVIL SERVANT (HEAD OF A DEPARTMENT)	60.7	-10.4
02111	EIGENAAR GROTE BEDRIJVEN/OWNER OF A LARGE ENTERPRISE (82.0)	71.2	0.8

ISCO NO.	OCCUPATION TITLE	PRESTIGE SCORE	SCORE MINUS STD. SCORE
	NETHERLANDS		
	ZELFSTANDIGE LEIDERS VAN GROTE ONDERNEMINGEN/OWNER OF A LARGE ENTERPRISE (78.1)		
	HOOFD VAN EEN ZIEKENFONDS/HEAD OF A MEDICAL INSURANCE FUND (51.4)		
	BEDRIJFSLEIDER GROTE ONDERNEMING/COMPANY MANAGER OF A LARGE ENTERPRISE (72.4)		
	DIRECTOR GROTE ONDERNEMING (B.V. MET 500 MAN PERSONEEL)/HEAD OF A LARGE COMPANY (WITH MORE THAN 500 EMPLCYEES) (72.4)		
02112	DIRECTOR KLEINE ONDERNEMING (B.V. MET 50 MAN PERSONEEL) GEEN MIDDENSTANDS-BEDRIJF/HEAD OF A SMALL INDUSTRIAL FIRM	62.6	-0.1
02113	ZELFSTANDIGE LEIDERS VAN KLEINERE ONDERNEMINGEN/OWNER OF A SMALL ENTERPRISE (55.9)	53.3	0.9
	BEDRIJFSLEIDER KLEINE ONDERNEMING/COMPANY MANAGER OF A SMALL ENTERPRISE (50.6)		
02114	BANKDIRECTOR/BANK PRESIDENT	77.6	10.6
02116	AANNEMER/CONTRACTOR	54.4	1.1
02191	FILIAALHOUDER/BRANCH MANAGER	42.4	-9.4
02194	PROCURATIEHOUDER/CONFIDENTIAL CLERK	60.2	-6.5

CLERICAL AND RELATED WORKERS

ISCO NO.	OCCUPATION TITLE	PRESTIGE SCORE	SCORE MINUS STD. SCORE
03000	AFDELINGSCHEF OP EEN KANTOOR/OFFICE MANAGER	50.9	-3.8
03100	SECRETARIS VAN GROTE GEMEENTE/TOWN CLERK OF A LARGE CITY (69.1)	58.4	-7.3
	OVERHEIDSPERSONEEL, MIDDELBARE AMBTENAAR (B.V.COMMIES TER SECRETARIE/MIDDLE GRADE CIVIL SERVANT (CFFICIAL IN TOWN HALL) (53.3)		
	SECRETARIS VAN KLEINE GEMEENTE/TOWN CLERK OF A SMALL CITY (52.8)		
03101	OVERHEIDSPERSONNEL -AMBTENAREN/PUBLIC SERVANT	47.4	-6.2
03102	INSPECTEUR DER BELASTINGEN/TAX INSPECTOR (65.1)	63.3	2.2
03104	INSPECTEUR DER P.T.T./PCSTAL INSPECTOR (61.5)	58.8	7.2
	CNTVANGER DER DIR. BELASTIGEN/COLLECTOR OF DIRECT TAXES	33.0	-8.6
03210	TYPIST/TYPIST	50.6	1.6
0331C	BOEKHOUDER/BOOKKEEPER	43.0	0.8
03390	CALCULATOR/COSTING CLERK (45.2)		
	BELASTINGKOMMIES/TAX CLERK (40.7)		
03510	STATIONCHEF/STATIONMASTER	57.7	1.6
03600	CONDUCTOR TREIN/RAILROAD CONDUCTOR	31.7	-6.9

Code	Occupation		
03700	POSTBODE/MAILMAN	28.3	-4.6
03701	BODE (STADHUIS ETC.)/PORTER IN A GOVERNMENT BUILDING (28.3)	22.2	-3.6
	LOOPKNECHT, BESTELLER/OFFICE MESSENGER (16.1)		
03800	TELEFONIST/TELEPHONE OPERATOR	39.2	0.8
03801	MARCONIST/TELEGRAPH OR CABLE OPERATOR (49.1)	45.4	0.1
	TELEGRAFIST/TELEGRAPH OPERATOR (41.7)		
03802	RADIOTELEGRAFIST/RADIO OPERATOR ON SHIP	47.8	-1.3
03910	MAGAZIJNBEDIENDE/WAREHOUSE CLERK	26.5	-5.6
03930	KANTOORPERSONEEL (GEEN OVERHEID) ONDERGESCHIKT/OFFICE CLERK	34.7	-8.6
03931	OVERHEIDSPERSONEEL LAGERE AMBTENAREN (B.V. SCHRIJVER TER SECRETARIE)/GOVERNMENT CLERK	42.9	-1.4
03932	CANDIDAAT-NOTARIS/LAW CLERK	66.8	8.0

SALES WORKERS

Code	Occupation		
04000	WINKELCHEF/SHOE MANAGER	43.6	-3.0
04100	ZELFSTANDIGE DETAILHANDELSBEROEPEN:DROGISTERIJEN/DRYSALTER (DEALER IN CHEMICALS, PRESERVED FOODS, ETC.) (50.9)	42.3	-0.2
	ZELFSTANDIGE DETAILHANDELSBEROEPEN:BOEKEN/BOOKSTORE OWNER (48.1)		
	ZELFSTANDIGE DETAILHANDELSBEROEPEN:MUZIEKINSTRUMENTEN/MUSICAL INSTRUMENT SHOP OWNER (46.1)		
	ZELFSTANDIGE DETAILHANDELSBEROEPEN:MANUFACTUREN/HABADASHER (45.8)		
	ZELFSTANDIGE DETAILHANDELSBEROEPEN:SCHOENEN/SHOE STORE OWNER (43.9)		
	ZELFSTANDIGE DETAILHANDELSBEROEPEN:KANTOORBEHOEFTEN/STATIONERY STORE OWNER (43.5)		
	ZELFSTANDIGE DETAILHANDELSBEROEPEN:ZUIVELPRODUCTEN/DAIRY SHOP OWNER (42.9)		
	ZELFSTANDIGE DETAILHANDELSBEROEPEN:IJZERWAREN/HARDWARE STORE OWNER (42.9)		
	ZELFSTANDIGE DETAILHANDELSBEROEPEN:KRUIDENIERSWAREN/GROCER (42.5)		
	KLEINE WINKELIER/SMALL SHOPKEEPER (42.2)		
	ZELFSTANDIGE DETAILHANDELSBEROEPEN:HUISHOUDELIJKE ARTIKELEN/HOUSEWARES STORE OWNER (42.1)		
	ZELFSTANDIGE DETAILHANDELSBEROEPEN:AARDAPPELEN,GROENTE EN FRUIT/GREEN GROCER (39.6)		
	ZELFSTANDIGE DETAILHANDELSBEROEPEN:BLOEMEN/FLOWER SHOP OWNER (39.6)		
	ZELFSTANDIGE DETAILHANDELSBEROEPEN:BRANDSTOFFEN/RETAIL FUEL DEALER (38.8)		
	ZELFSTANDIGE DETAILHANDELSBEROEPEN:TWEEDEHANDS GOEDEREN/JUNK STORE OWNER (25.2)		
04101	GROTE WINKELIER/LARGE SHOP OWNER	56.5	-2.0
04102	ZELFSTANDIGE DETAILHANDELSBEROEPEN:TABAK/TOBACCONIST	33.6	-4.1
04104	MAKELAAR/BROKER	54.6	-0.0
04105	VEEKOOPMAN/LIVESTOCK BROKER	38.3	-1.7
04106	IMPORTEUR/IMPORTER (60.2)	56.4	-2.0

NETHERLANDS

ISCO NO.	OCCUPATION TITLE	PRESTIGE SCORE	SCORE MINUS STD. SCORE
04320	GROSSIER/WHOLESALER (52.6)		
	VERTEGENWOORDIGER/REPRESENTATIVE (38.7)	37.4	-9.5
	HANDELSREIZIGER/TRAVELING SALESMAN (36.1)		
04410	VERZEKERINGSAGENT/INSURANCE AGENT	35.2	-9.3
04430	VEILINGMEESTER/AUCTIONEER	45.9	6.8
04431	EXPERT-TAXATEUR/APPRAISER	47.6	0.0
04432	VERZEKERINGSINSPECTEUR/INSURANCE INSPECTOR	51.4	2.2
04510	WINKELBEDIENDE/SHOP CLERK	24.3	-9.4
04521	VENTER/STREET CART VENDOR (24.4)	22.9	1.0
	MARKTKOOPMAN ZON DER WINKEL/MARKET SELLER WITHOUT SHOP (21.4)		

SERVICE WORKERS

ISCO NO.	OCCUPATION TITLE	PRESTIGE SCORE	SCORE MINUS STD. SCORE
05100	EIGENAAR VAN EEN RESTAURANT/OWNER OF A RESTAURANT	50.6	2.8
05101	CAFEHOUDER/CAFE OPERATOR	27.6	-7.3
05102	HOTELHOUDER/HOTEL KEEPER	56.3	10.0
05200	HOFMEESTER/SHIP'S STEWARD	49.4	3.2
05310	KOK/COOK	33.9	3.0
05312	BUFFET- EN KEUKENPERSONEEL (BEHALVE KOK)/KITCHEN WORKERS EXCEPT COCKS	25.0	2.5
05320	SERVEERSTER/WAITRESS (24.7)	23.4	0.2
	KELLNER/WAITER (22.1)		
05400	HUISPERSONEEL/SERVANT	25.2	8.0
05511	CONCIERGE/APARTMENT "SUPER"	26.9	2.4
05512	KOSTER/SEXTON	29.5	0.0
05521	ZELFSTANDIG AMBACHTSMAN:GLAZENWASSER/SELF EMPLOYED WINDOW WASHER	22.4	3.8
05522	SCHOORSTEENVEGER/CHIMNEY SWEEP	24.7	0.0
05600	STRIJKSTER/CLOTHES PRESSER IN A LAUNDRY	24.7	2.6
05701	EIGENAAR VAN EEN HERENKAPPERSZAAK/OWNER OF A BARBERSHOP	43.3	6.8
05703	EIGENAAR VAN EEN DAMESKAPSALON/OPERATOR OF A HAIRDRESSING SALON	46.1	0.8
05820	POLITIEAGENT/POLICEMAN	38.3	-1.6
05821	INSPECTEUR VAN POLITIE/POLICE INSPECTOR	59.6	-0.0
05823	RECHERCHEUR/DETECTIVE	50.2	-1.6
05892	DEURWARDER/BAILIFF	51.1	3.8
05920	BEGRAFENISONDERNEMER/UNDERTAKER	44.7	11.1

AGRICULTURAL, ANIMAL HUSBANDRY AND FORESTRY WORKERS, FISHERMEN AND HUNTERS

Code	Description		
06110	LANDBOUWER, MIDDELGROOT (MET PERSONEEL)/MIDDLE SIZED FARMER WITH HIRED HELP	50.4	3.4
06111	LANDBOUWER, GROOT (ALEEN LEIDINGGEVEND)/LARGE FARMER, SUPERVISES WORK BUT DOES NOT WORK HIMSELF	55.7	-7.7
06112	LANDBOUWER, KLEIN (ZONDER PERSONEEL)/SMALL FARMER WITHOUT HELP	37.3	-0.4
06120	TUINDER/INTENSIVE HORTICULTURALIST	39.4	-15.6
06210	ARBEIDER, LAND- OF TUINBOUW/AGRICULTURAL LABORER	27.0	4.1
06270	TUINMAN/GARDENER	28.0	6.6
06410	VISSER/FISHERMAN	29.3	1.8

PRODUCTION AND RELATED WORKERS, TRANSPORT EQUIPMENT OPERATORS AND LABORERS

Code	Description		
07000	VAKBAAS/CRAFT FOREMAN (48.0) FABRIEKSBAAS/FACTORY FOREMAN (45.0) MAGAZIJNCHEF/WAREHOUSE FOREMAN (40.9) ONDERBAAS/UNDER-FOREMAN (29.1)	40.7	1.4
07001	OPZICHTER/SUPERVISOR	45.9	-6.2
07540	WEVER/WEAVER	28.5	-1.9
07732	ZELFSTANDIGE AMBACHTSBEROEPEN:SLAGER/BUTCHERSHOP OWNER	40.0	-5.2
07761	ZELFSTANDIGE AMBACHTSBEROEPEN:BANKETBAKKER/BAKER WITH OWN BUSINESS	43.1	-5.2
C7790	ZELFSTANDIGE DETAILHANDELSBEROEPEN:VIS/FISH STORE OWNER	34.3	0.0
07820	ARBEIDER, GEOEFEND, SIGARENMAKER/CIGAR MAKER	28.4	0.0
07910	ZELFSTANDIG AMEACHTSMAN:KLEERMAKER/SELF EMPLOYED TAILOR	43.7	4.3
07911	HUISNAAISTER/SEAMSTRESS	30.0	-9.3
07930	HOEDENMODISTE/MILLINER	31.1	-1.1
07940	COUPEUR (ONZELFSTANDIG)/CUTTER IN A GARMENT SHOP	41.4	0.0
07950	CONFECTIENAAISTER/SEWING MACHINE OPERATOR	26.9	0.6
08010	ZELFSTANDIG AMBACHTSMAN:SCHOENHERSTELLER/SELF EMPLOYED SHOEMAKER	33.9	5.7
08110	ZELFSTANDIGE AMBACHTSBEROEPEN:MEUBELMAKER/CABINET MAKER, OWN SHOP	42.8	2.4
08320	ZELFSTANDIGE AMBACHTSBEROEPEN:SMID/BLACKSMITH,OWN SHOP	39.8	5.2
08320	INSTRUMENTMAKER (GESCHOOLD)/TOOL AND DIE MAKER	38.9	-1.4
08340	MACHINIST OPFABRIEK/MACHINE OPERATOR IN A FACTORY	39.1	0.9
08410	ARBEIDER, GESCHOOLD, MACHINEBANKWERKER/MACHINIST	37.8	-5.5
08420	ZELFSTANDIGE AMBACHTSBEROEPEN:UURWERKMAKER/SELF-EMPLOYED WATCHMAKER	48.7	8.9
08421	FIJNBANKWERKER/FINE FITTER	37.2	-5.3
08430	AUTOMONTEUR (GESCHOOLD)/AUTO MECHANIC	36.9	-6.0
08431	ZELFSTANDIGE AMBACHTSBEROEPEN:AUTOMOBIELREPARATEUR/GARAGE OPERATOR	43.2	-4.1
08490	MONTEUR/MECHANIC	39.4	-3.5

ISCO NO.	OCCUPATION TITLE	PRESTIGE SCORE	SCORE MINUS STD. SCORE
	NETHERLANDS		
08491	ZELFSTANDIGE AMBACHTSBEROEPEN:RIJWIELHERSTELLER/OPERATOR OF A BICYCLE REPAIR SHOP (34.0)	30.0	2.5
	RIJWIELHERSTELLER (GEOFEND) /BICYCLE REPAIRMAN (26.1)	33.5	-11.1
08550	ELECTRICIEN/ELECTRICIAN		
08551	ZELFSTANDIGE AMBACHTSBEROEPEN:ELECTRICIEN/SELF-EMPLOYED ELECTRICIAN	43.6	-4.5
08711	ZELFSTANDIG AMEACHTSMAN:LOODGIETER/SELF-EMPLOYED PLUMBER	39.4	-5.6
08800	GOUD- ZILVER- EN KUNSTMID/GOLD, SILVER AND ARTSMITH	50.3	7.4
08911	GLASINSTRUMENTMAKER/GLASS INSTRUMENT MAKER (36.6)	32.8	0.0
	GLASBLAZER/GLASS BLOWER (29.1)	39.1	0.0
09311	ZELFSTANDIGE AMBACHTSBEROEPEN:SCHILDER/SELF-EMPLOYED HOUSE PAINTER	35.5	2.2
09410	PIANOSTEMMER/PIANO TUNER	29.6	-4.5
09510	METSELAAR/MASON	34.7	0.3
09520	BETON- EN CEMENTWERKER (GESCHOOLD)/SKILLED CEMENT WORKER	32.1	-5.1
09540	TIMMERMAN/CARPENTER	43.3	-4.9
09541	EIGENAAR VAN EEN TIMMERMANSWERKPLAATS/OWNER OF A CARPENTRY SHOP	38.9	0.0
09551	ZELFSTANDIG AMEACHTSMAN:STUCADOOR/SELF-EMPLOYED PLASTERER		
09591	ZELFSTANDIGE AMBACHTSBEROEPEN:BEHANGER, STOFFERDER/SELF-EMPLOYED WALL PAPERER AND UPHOLSTERER	38.4	0.0
09594	BOUWVAKERBEIDER/CONSTRUCTION LABORER	30.4	4.8
09710	ARBEIDER, ONGESCHOOLD, HAVENARBEIDER/UNSKILLED DOCK WORKER	18.4	-2.9
09731	BRUG- EN SLUISWACHTER/BRIDGE AND LOCK TENDER	26.9	1.7
09740	BAGGERPERSONEEL/DREDGE OPERATOR	25.2	-6.6
09810	MATROOS KOOPVAARDIJ/MERCHANT SEAMAN	25.4	-9.4
09820	STOKER/FIREMAN ON A SHIP	25.5	0.1
09830	MACHINIST N.S./LOCOMOTIVE ENGINEER (42.5)	40.6	-2.0
	TREINMACHINIST/LOCOMOTIVE ENGINEER (41.7)		
	WAGENVOERDER (ELECTR. TREIN ETC.)/ELECTRIC TRAIN ENGINEER (37.7)		
09852	CHAUFFEUR/DRIVER	28.4	-4.2
09853	EIGENAAR EXPEDITE-ONDERNEMING/OWNER,SMALL TRANSPORT FIRM	47.0	7.6
09861	VOERMAN/WAGONEER	20.3	-6.1
09891	BLCK- EN SEINHUISWACHTER N.S./RAILWAY CROSSING GUARD	30.3	0.0
09950	ARBEIDER:GESCHCOLD--INDUSTRIE/SKILLED INDUSTRIAL WORKER	37.4	-4.2
09951	AMBACHTSMAN ZELFSTANDIG/SELF EMPLOYED ARTISAN	45.5	-4.2
C9970	ARBEIDER:GEOFEND-INDUSTRIE/SEMI-SKILLED INDUSTRIAL WORKER	27.2	-2.1

09991	ARBEIDER:LOS-INDUSTRIE/UNSKILLED INDUSTRIAL WORKER	16.5	-1.6
09994	WEGWERKER N.S./RAILWAY WORKER	25.2	-8.0
09995	STRAATREINIGER/STREET SWEEPER	16.7	3.4
09997	STRAATMAKER/STREET MAKER	26.1	6.0

MEMBERS OF THE ARMED FORCES

10000	HOOFD- OF OPPEROFFICIER, KOLONEL OF GENERAAL/HIGH MILITARY OFFICER	68.5	-4.4
10001	BEROEPSMILITAIR-OFFICIER/MILITARY OFFICER (62.5)	60.1	-3.1
	SUBALTERN OFFICIER, KAPITEIN OF LUITENANT/CAPTAIN OR LIEUTENANT (57.7)		
10002	ONDEROFFICIER(BEROEPS-)SERGEANT/NON-COMMISSIONED OFFICER(SERGEANT)	41.5	-2.0
10003	BEROEPSSOLDAAT/ENLISTED MAN IN THE ARMED FORCES (26.6)	23.1	-15.6
	BEROEPSMILITAIR--MINDERE/ENLISTED MAN IN THE ARMED FORCES (19.6)		

UNCLASSIFIABLE OCCUPATIONS

| 12000 | HULPASSISTENT/ASSISTANT'S ASSISTANT (E.G. IN AN OFFICE) (40.4) | 31.8 | -8.1 |
| | OVERHEIDSPERSONEEL WERKLIEDEN/BLUE COLLAR PUBLIC EMPLOYEE (23.2) | | |

ISCO NO.	OCCUPATION TITLE	PRESTIGE SCORE	SCORE MINUS STD. SCORE
	NEW BRITAIN		
PROFESSIONAL, TECHNICAL AND RELATED WORKERS			
00541	AGRICULTURAL ASSISTANT	52.3	5.6
01330	PRIMARY SCHOOL TEACHER	51.7	-5.3
01391	HEADMASTER, PRIMARY SCHOOL	53.1	-12.5
01393	EDUCATIONAL ASSISTANT	57.1	7.1
01410	NATIVE MINISTER, PRIEST	58.5	-1.2
ADMINISTRATIVE AND MANAGERIAL WORKERS			
02116	BUILDING CONTRACTOR	46.3	-7.1
CLERICAL AND RELATED WORKERS			
03701	ADMINISTRATION MESSENGER	50.1	24.3
03800	TELEPHONIST	45.9	7.5
03931	L.G. COUNCIL CLERK	50.7	6.4
SALES WORKERS			
04100	STOREKEEPER	32.4	-10.0
04510	SHOP ASSISTANT	30.6	-3.0
04512	PETROL PUMP ATTENDANT	26.8	1.5
SERVICE WORKERS			
05320	HOTEL WAITER	18.8	-4.4
05400	DOMESTIC	16.2	-1.0
05820	NATIVE POLICEMAN (38.6)	38.2	-1.6
	POLICE CLERK (37.8)		
05990	MEDICAL ORDERLY	52.7	11.0

AGRICULTURAL, ANIMAL HUSBANDRY AND FORESTRY WORKERS, FISHERMEN AND HUNTERS

Code	Occupation		
06120	COPRA PRODUCER/DRIED COCONUT MEAT (52.9)	52.2	-2.8
	COCOA GROWER (51.5)		

PRODUCTION AND RELATED WORKERS, TRANSPORT EQUIPMENT OPERATORS AND LABORERS

Code	Occupation		
07000	BOSS BOY OF LABOUR LINE	15.0	-24.3
08430	GARAGE MECHANIC	47.5	4.5
08550	ELECTRICIAN	50.7	6.1
08710	PLUMBER	41.5	7.6
09310	PAINTER	27.6	-3.4
09540	CARPENTER	55.7	18.5
09810	SEAMAN	37.4	2.7
09850	TAXI DRIVER	24.2	-3.6
09852	LORRY DRIVER	22.6	-10.0
09853	TRUCK OWNER-OPERATOR	37.0	-2.4
09597	ROADWORKER	40.1	20.0

ISCO NO.	OCCUPATION TITLE	PRESTIGE SCORE	SCORE MINUS STD. SCORE
	NEW ZEALAND		
PROFESSIONAL, TECHNICAL AND RELATED WORKERS			
00130	SCIENTIST	74.8	-3.6
00220	ENGINEER, PROFESSIONAL	72.6	2.3
00610	DOCTOR	82.6	4.7
00630	DENTIST	74.6	4.1
00710	TRAINED NURSE	56.0	2.4
01100	ACCOUNTANT IC A BUSINESS	60.5	5.9
01101	REGISTERED PUBLIC ACCOUNTANT	70.0	2.5
01290	SOLICITOR	80.6	10.0
01310	UNIVERSITY TEACHER	73.5	-4.2
01320	SECONDARY SCHOOL TEACHER	62.4	-1.8
01330	PRIMARY SCHOOL TEACHER	51.4	-5.6
01391	SCHOOL PRINCIPAL	73.0	7.5
01410	CLERGYMAN WITH UNIVERSITY DEGREE (74.8)	68.2	8.6
	CLERGYMAN, SOME UNIVERSITY TRAINING, BUT NOT A DEGREE (68.4)		
	CLERGYMAN, NO UNIVERSITY TRAINING (61.5)		
01590	NEWS REPORTER	48.6	-6.3
01591	NEWSPAPER EDITCR	68.5	3.6
01790	RADIO ANNOUNCER	49.8	-0.5
01910	TRAINED LIBRARIAN	52.6	-1.9
01930	SOCIAL WORKER	54.0	-2.2
ADMINISTRATIVE AND MANAGERIAL WORKERS			
02014	MAYOR	69.8	1.6
02033	DEPARTMENTAL HEAD IN GOVERNMENT SERVICE	72.9	1.8
02110	DIRECTOR LARGE FINANCIAL OR INDUSTRIAL ENTERPRISE	80.8	5.8
02111	OWNER LARGE BUSINESS VALUED AT L25,000 OR OVER (82.7)	75.9	5.5
	MANAGER, LARGE FINANCIAL OR INDUSTRIAL ENTERPRISE (72.7)		
	COMPANY MANAGER OF A LARGE BUSINESS (72.3)		
02112	OWNER, BUSINESS, VALUED AT L10,000 TO L25,000 (73.0)	68.8	6.1
	OWNER, BUSINESS, VALUED AT L5,000 TO L10,000 (64.6)		
02113	OWNER, BUSINESS VALUED AT L1,000 TO L5,000 (54.1)	51.4	-0.9

Code	Occupation		
	OWNER, BUSINESS VALUED AT LESS THAN I1,000 (48.6)		
02114	BANKER	64.8	-2.2
02116	JOBBING MASTER BUILDER	48.9	-4.5
02120	WORKS MANAGER, LARGE BUSINESS	60.6	-3.6
02192	DEPARTMENTAL MANAGER, GENERAL	61.2	0.7
02193	DEPARTMENTAL MANAGER, LARGE BUSINESS	63.4	0.3

CLERICAL AND RELATED WORKERS

Code	Occupation		
03000	OFFICE MANAGER, GENERAL	60.0	5.3
03210	STENOGRAPHER	41.9	0.3
03211	PRIVATE SECRETARY, TO EXECUTIVE	58.3	5.3
03310	BOCKKEEPER	43.4	-5.6
03313	BANK TELLER OR CLERK	45.3	-2.3
03314	POST OFFICE CLERK	38.5	-0.5
03520	POSTMASTER	56.6	-1.8
03600	RAILWAY CONDUCTOR	26.7	-11.9
03601	TRAM CONDUCTOR OR MOTORMAN	27.1	1.1
03800	TELEPHONE OPERATOR	31.0	-7.5
03910	STOREMAN	29.9	-2.2
03930	ROUTINE OFFICE CLERK	39.0	-4.4
03931	GOVERNMENT OFFICE CLERK	42.6	-1.7

SALES WORKERS

Code	Occupation		
04000	MANAGER OF STORE	49.8	3.2
04102	NEWS AGENT AND BOCKSELLER (ONE MAN SHOP)	44.9	7.2
04210	SALES MANAGER, LARGE BUSINESS	59.8	7.4
04320	COMMERCIAL TRAVELLER	45.3	-1.6
04410	INSURANCE AGENT	47.8	3.2
04411	REAL ESTATE AGENT (54.4)	53.5	4.5
	LAND AGENT (52.7)		
04510	SALESMAN, BOCKSTORE (38.0)	33.7	0.0
	SALESMAN, FURNITURE STORE (37.4)		
	SALESMAN, DEPARTMENT STORE (36.6)		
	SHOP ASSISTANT (31.0)		
	SALES PERSON, WOOLWORTH'S (25.3)		
04511	MOTOR CAR SALESMAN	39.0	3.2
04512	PETROL STATION ATTENDANT	26.9	1.6
04524	MILK DELIVERYMAN	21.2	-3.0

ISCO NO.	OCCUPATION TITLE	PRESTIGE SCORE	SCORE MINUS STD. SCORE

NEW ZEALAND

SERVICE WORKERS

ISCO NO.	OCCUPATION TITLE	PRESTIGE SCORE	SCORE MINUS STD. SCORE
05000	BAR MANAGER	30.6	-1.8
05201	HOUSEKEEPER	31.1	-2.9
05310	COOK, RESTAURANT	29.4	-1.5
05320	WAITRESS	21.2	-2.1
05321	BARMAN	20.2	-3.1
05400	DOMESTIC WORKER	23.8	6.6
05510	JANITOR	19.4	-1.6
05520	CHARWOMAN	17.5	1.1
05700	BARBER	35.0	4.6
05702	BEAUTY OPERATOR	34.4	-0.4
05810	FIREMAN	35.1	-0.2
05820	POLICEMAN	41.7	1.9
05890	NIGHT WATCHMAN	18.8	-3.2

AGRICULTURAL, ANIMAL HUSBANDRY AND FORESTRY WORKERS, FISHERMEN AND HUNTERS

ISCO NO.	OCCUPATION TITLE	PRESTIGE SCORE	SCORE MINUS STD. SCORE
06000	FARM MANAGER, SUPERVISES PROPERTY	54.5	0.2
06110	FARM OWNER, ACTIVELY OPERATES LAND WITH HELP (59.3)	56.9	9.8
06111	FARMER, OWNER, OPERATES LAND WITH FAMILY (54.5) LARGE FARM OWNER, SUPERVISES WORK ON OWN LAND BUT SELDOM WORKS ACTIVELY ON IT	70.7	7.4
06113	FARMER TENANT, OPERATES LAND WITH FAMILY (46.0) FARMER, TENANT, OWNS NO CAPITAL, CATTLE OR MACHINERY (33.2)	42.1	12.7
06120	SHEEP FARMER, WELL ESTABLISHED (67.0) DAIRY FARMER, WELL ESTABLISHED (61.1) SHAREMILKER, OWNS CATTLE OR MACHINERY (46.3)	58.1	3.1
06210	FARM LABOURER, ESTABLISHED	29.7	6.8
06211	LABOURER, SEASONAL (21.0) FARM LABOURER, MIGRATORY (19.9)	20.4	2.3
06240	SHEPHERD	25.9	0.3
06280	TRACTOR DRIVER	27.1	-3.8

PRODUCTION AND RELATED WORKERS, TRANSPORT EQUIPMENT OPERATORS AND LABORERS

Code	Occupation		
07000	INDUSTRIAL FOREMAN	45.9	6.6
07110	MINER	27.2	-4.3
07730	BUTCHER, WAGES	30.8	-0.5
08340	MACHINIST	31.4	-6.8
08410	FITTER	33.0	-10.3
08420	WATCHMAKER, OWN BUSINESS	50.9	11.2
08430	MOTOR MECHANIC, WAGES	34.4	-8.6
08550	ELECTRICIAN, WAGES	35.9	-8.6
08551	ELECTRICIAN, OWN BUSINESS	48.6	0.5
08560	TELEPHONE REPAIRMAN	30.6	-4.1
08711	PLUMBER, OWN BUSINESS	47.2	2.3
09210	PRINTER, WAGES	34.7	-7.6
09310	PAINTER, WAGES	31.3	0.2
09510	BRICKLAYER	30.1	-4.?
09540	CARPENTER, WAGES	32.0	-5.1
09541	CARPENTER, OWN BUSINESS	48.6	0.5
09550	PLASTERER, WAGES	31.3	0.4
09594	BUILDING CONSTRUCTION WORKER	30.4	4.8
09710	WHARF LABOURER	18.0	-3.3
09713	RAILWAY PORTER	19.1	0.9
09714	PACKER	24.8	2.5
09830	ENGINE DRIVER OR FIREMAN	30.7	-11.0
09831	ENGINE DRIVER OR FIREMAN	30.7	-2.4
09840	RAILWAY SHUNTER	23.9	-4.9
09850	TAXI DRIVER	29.3	1.5
09851	BUS DRIVER	29.3	-3.1
09852	LORRY DRIVER	25.8	-6.8
09853	CARRIER	31.1	-8.3
09970	FACTORY OPERATIVE	27.1	-2.1
09990	LABOURER, UNSKILLED	17.9	-1.2
09993	MIGRANT WORKER	19.7	-0.8
09995	ROAD SWEEPER	17.5	4.2

SOURCES OF LIVELIHOOD OTHER THAN LABOR FORCE ACTIVITY

| 13003 | GENTLEMAN FARMER (WELL ESTABLISHED, DOES NOT SUPERVISE DIRECTLY THE WORK ON HIS PROPERTY) (76.7) | 73.8 | 8.7 |
| | GENTLEMAN FARMER (REASONABLY WELL ESTABLISHED, DOES NOT SUPERVISE DIRECTLY THE WORK ON HIS PROPERTY) (70.9) | | |

427

ISCO NO.	OCCUPATION TITLE	PRESTIGE SCORE	SCORE MINUS STD. SCORE
	NIGERIA-BORNU		
	PROFESSIONAL, TECHNICAL AND RELATED WORKERS		
00220	ENGINEER	60.5	-9.8
00531	AGRICULTURAL OFFICER	72.5	17.6
00610	MEDICAL OFFICER	70.2	-7.7
00710	MALE NURSE	51.5	-2.1
01220	ALKALAI (MUSLIM JUDGE)	62.8	-14.9
01490	KORANIC MALLAM/KORANIC TEACHER	74.6	18.4
01590	JOURNALIST	55.5	0.5
01712	DRUMMER-ENTERTAINER	16.7	-14.8
01790	RADIO ANNOUNCER	57.0	6.6
	ADMINISTRATIVE AND MANAGERIAL WORKERS		
02011	SHEHU OF BORNU (80.9)	79.4	-2.6
	WAZIRI OF BORNU (77.8)		
02012	DISTRICT OFFICER (79.7)	69.7	3.9
	DISTRICT HEAD (AJIA) (67.9)		
02015	KAIGAMA (A DISTRICT HEAD TODAY, TRADITIONALLY A HIGH STATUS TITLE) (61.4)	44.9	3.0
	RURAL VILLAGE HEAD—SALARIED (52.2)		
	RURAL HAMLET HEAD—UNSALARIED (37.5)	77.1	11.4
02023	MEMBER OF NORTHERN HOUSE OF ASSEMBLY	43.5	-11.5
02024	MEMBER OF NATIVE AUTHORITY COUNCIL	55.6	-7.1
02112	EUROPEAN COMPANY MANAGER	58.1	-8.9
02114	BANK MANAGER	40.0	-13.4
02116	BUILDING CONTRACTOR		
	CLERICAL AND RELATED WORKERS		
03100	GOVERNMENT SERVICE (74.8)	71.7	6.0
	NATIVE AUTHORITY (70.3)		
	CHIEF SCRIBE OF THE CAPITAL CITY OF MAIDUGURI (SALARIED) (70.2)		
03313	BANK CLERK	60.7	13.1
03930	CLERK IN A EUROPEAN TRADING COMPANY	58.7	15.3

SALES WORKERS

Code	Occupation		
04100	OWNER OF A RETAIL STORE	54.2	11.8
04101	TRADER WITH CREDIT FROM EUROPEAN COMPANIES	54.1	-4.4
04222	SCALE MAN (CASH CROP BUYER IN BUSH)	38.5	-0.9
04520	TRADITIONAL TRADER	43.7	7.5
04521	SMALL RETAILER AT ROADSIDE TABLE SELLING SUNDRIES (37.2)	29.4	7.4
	SELLER OF CHARMS (31.4)		
	KOLA-NUT SELLER (29.3)		
	PETTY BROKER (19.6)		
04990	MONEYLENDER	15.3	0.0

SERVICE WORKERS

Code	Occupation		
05102	HOTEL OWNER	49.6	3.3
05700	BARBER	24.2	-6.2

AGRICULTURAL, ANIMAL HUSBANDRY AND FORESTRY WORKERS, FISHERMEN AND HUNTERS

Code	Occupation		
06110	FARMER	56.7	9.6
06491	HUNTER	29.3	23.0

PRODUCTION AND RELATED WORKERS, TRANSPORT EQUIPMENT OPERATORS AND LABORERS

Code	Occupation		
07540	WEAVER	23.9	-6.5
07730	BUTCHER	16.4	-14.9
07910	TAILOR ON SEWING MACHINE	39.4	-0.1
07930	HATMAKER	27.6	-4.7
08010	SHOEMAKER	27.7	-0.4
08310	BLACKSMITH	24.5	-10.0
08490	MECHANIC	46.3	3.4
09493	CALABASH MAKER	23.0	0.0
09540	CARPENTER	40.0	2.8
09596	MUDHOUSE BUILDING (TRADITIONAL)	35.5	0.0
09852	TRUCK DRIVER	49.2	16.6
09853	TRUCK OWNER	41.9	2.4
09990	LABORER	25.3	6.2

UNCLASSIFIABLE OCCUPATIONS

Code	Occupation		
12000	KACHELLA SHEHUBE (TRADITIONAL TITLE, UNSALARIED JOB TODAY) (40.0)	32.4	-7.4
	HORSED SERVANT (TRADITIONAL POLITICAL POSITION UNSALARIED) (29.7)		

NIGERIA-BORNU

SHEHU'S SLAVE--UNSALARIED (27.6)

PROFESSIONAL, TECHNICAL AND RELATED WORKERS

Code	Occupation		
00610	DOCTORS	76.6	-1.3
01210	LAWYERS	74.0	3.3
01330	PRIMARY SCHOOL TEACHERS	54.4	-2.6
01490	MALLAMS/KORANIC TEACHERS	64.6	8.4
01712	PRAISE-SINGERS AND DRUMMERS	16.5	-15.0

ADMINISTRATIVE AND MANAGERIAL WORKERS

Code	Occupation		
02116	BUILDING CONTRACTORS	41.0	-12.4

CLERICAL AND RELATED WORKERS

Code	Occupation		
03100	GOVERNMENT AND NATIVE-AUTHORITY OFFICIALS	88.1	22.4
03930	OFFICE CLERKS	55.1	11.8

SALES WORKERS

Code	Occupation		
04510	STORE CLERKS	54.3	20.7
04520	MARKET TRADERS	46.5	10.3

SERVICE WORKERS

Code	Occupation		
05820	POLICEMAN	39.7	-0.2

AGRICULTURAL, ANIMAL HUSBANDRY AND FORESTRY WORKERS, FISHERMEN AND HUNTERS

Code	Occupation		
06110	FARM OWNERS	35.9	-11.2

PRODUCTION AND RELATED WORKERS, TRANSPORT EQUIPMENT OPERATORS AND LABORERS

Code	Occupation		
07730	BUTCHERS	24.1	-7.2
07910	TAILORS	37.9	-1.6
08030	LEATHERWORKERS	21.6	0.0
09970	FACTORY WORKERS	42.1	12.9

ISCO NO.	OCCUPATION TITLE	PRESTIGE SCORE	SCORE MINUS STD. SCORE
	NORWAY		

PROFESSIONAL, TECHNICAL AND RELATED WORKERS

ISCO NO.	OCCUPATION TITLE	PRESTIGE SCORE	SCORE MINUS STD. SCORE
00210	ARKITEKT/ARCHITECT	67.9	-3.9
00220	SIVILINGENIOR/CIVIL ENGINEER	67.9	-2.4
00420	KAPTEIN/SHIP'S CAPTAIN	66.2	3.0
00610	PHYSICIAN	75.7	-2.2
01100	REVISOR/ACCOUNTANT	62.2	7.6
01210	LAWYER	69.4	-1.3
01310	UNIVERSITY PROFESSOR	74.5	-3.1
01330	ELEMENTARY SCHOOL TEACHER	58.4	1.4
01391	SCHOOL PRINCIPAL	70.9	5.3
01410	CLERGYMAN	58.3	-1.4
01414	MISSIONARY	50.7	1.6
01510	AUTHOR	54.7	-7.0
01591	REDAKTOR/EDITOR	73.1	8.1
01610	ARTIST	47.5	-9.7
01730	ACTOR	47.9	-3.6

ADMINISTRATIVE AND MANAGERIAL WORKERS

ISCO NO.	OCCUPATION TITLE	PRESTIGE SCORE	SCORE MINUS STD. SCORE
02111	SKIPSREDER/SHIP OWNER	76.5	6.1
02174	BANKER	55.8	-11.2
02190	BUSINESSMAN	57.0	-0.0
02195	POLITICIAN	54.6	-8.1

CLERICAL AND RELATED WORKERS

ISCO NO.	OCCUPATION TITLE	PRESTIGE SCORE	SCORE MINUS STD. SCORE
03101	CIVIL SERVICE EMPLOYEE	53.2	-0.5
03310	BOOKKEEPER	46.3	-2.7
03590	EKSPEDITOR/EXPEDITOR	38.5	1.6
03700	MAIL CARRIER	27.6	-5.2

SALES WORKERS

Code	Occupation		
04100	GROCER	41.9	-0.5
04106	GROSSERER/WHOLESALER	68.8	10.4
04320	SALGSREPRESENTANT/REPRESENTATIVE	55.3	8.5

SERVICE WORKERS

Code	Occupation		
05510	JANITOR	30.1	9.1
057CC	BARBER	31.8	1.4
05820	POLICEMAN	52.1	12.3

AGRICULTURAL, ANIMAL HUSBANDRY AND FORESTRY WORKERS, FISHERMEN AND HUNTERS

Code	Occupation		
06110	FARMER	49.7	2.7

PRODUCTION AND RELATED WORKERS, TRANSPORT EQUIPMENT OPERATORS AND LABORERS

Code	Occupation		
07110	COAL MINER	26.4	-5.1
07730	BUTCHER	28.6	-2.7
07910	TAILOR	35.2	-4.3
08010	SHOEMAKER	24.3	-3.8
08550	ELECTRICIAN	50.9	6.4
08710	PLUMBER	37.2	3.4
08801	GULLSMEDMESTER/MASTER GOLDSMITH	57.9	0.8
09210	TYPOGRAPHER	41.2	-1.0
09211	BOKTRYKKER/MASTER PRINTER, BOOK SHOE OWNER	44.5	-6.2
09540	CARPENTER	41.1	3.0
09852	TRUCK DRIVER	33.2	0.6
09970	FAERIKKARBEIDER/FACTORY WORKER	28.5	-0.8
09990	ARBEIDER/LAEGRER	27.6	8.5

MEMBERS OF THE ARMED FORCES

Code	Occupation		
10003	SOLDIER	66.4	27.7

ISCO NO.	OCCUPATION TITLE	PRESTIGE SCORE	SCORE MINUS STD. SCORE
	PAKISTAN		
	PROFESSIONAL, TECHNICAL AND RELATED WORKERS		
00210	ARCHITECT	70.2	-1.6
00220	CIVIL ENGINEER	70.2	-0.1
00410	AIRPLANE PILOT	71.4	4.9
00610	PHYSICIAN	82.7	4.8
00710	NURSE	53.3	-0.3
01100	ACCOUNTANT	60.0	5.5
01210	LAWYER	63.0	-2.7
01221	HIGH COURT JUDGE	87.2	5.2
01310	PROFESSOR	78.2	0.5
01311	VICE CHANCELLOR CF A UNIVERSITY	87.2	1.0
01330	TEACHER	56.7	-0.4
01394	HEAD OF A COLLEGE	79.3	7.1
01410	MAULVI/RELIGIOUS LEADER (34.0)	30.0	-29.6
	IMAM/LEADER OF MOSLEM CONGREGATION (26.1)		
01590	JOURNALIST	70.2	15.3
01591	EDITOR OF A CAILY NEWSPAPER	77.0	12.0
01630	PHOTOGRAPHER	52.1	7.0
C1790	RADIO ARTIST	46.5	-3.9
01791	NIGHTCLUB ENTERTAINER	34.0	1.3
	ADMINISTRATIVE AND MANAGERIAL WORKERS		
02011	GOVERNOR OF A WING	87.2	5.3
02030	CENTRAL GOVERNMENT MINISTER	82.7	4.0
02031	AMBASSADCR	89.5	2.4
02033	HIGH GOVERNMENT OFFICIAL--GAZETTED CSP	77.0	5.9
02111	OWNER OF A FACTORY EMPLOYING MORE THAN 100 PERSONS	71.4	1.0
02112	MANAGER OF A PRIVATE BUSINESS	65.7	3.0
02114	BANKER	66.8	-0.1
02116	BUILDING CONTRACTOR	52.1	-1.2

434

CLERICAL AND RELATED WORKERS

03210	STENOGRAPHER	43.1	-1.5
03601	TEAM CONDUCTOR	23.8	-2.2
03700	MAIL CARRIER	28.3	-4.5
03701	BEARER/ORDERLY	22.7	-3.1
03931	MINOR GOVT CLERK	30.6	-13.7

SALES WORKERS

04100	OWNER OF A SMALL SHOP	49.9	7.4
04410	INSURANCE AGENT	40.8	-3.7
04510	SHOP ASSISTANT	35.1	1.5

SERVICE WORKERS

05520	BHANGI/CLEANING PERSON	18.2	1.7
05600	DHOBI/LAUNDERER	23.8	1.7
05820	POLICEMAN	29.5	-10.3
05994	CHOWKIDAR/DOORMAN	21.6	-5.4
05995	SHOE SHINER	18.2	5.9
05996	AIRLINE HOSTESS	41.0	-8.2

AGRICULTURAL, ANIMAL HUSBANDRY AND FORESTRY WORKERS, FISHERMEN AND HUNTERS

06110	SMALL LANDOWNER	52.1	5.0
06111	ZAMINDAR/AGRICULTURAL LAND OWNER	56.7	-6.7
06210	FARM LABORER	32.9	9.9

PRODUCTION AND RELATED WORKERS, TRANSPORT EQUIPMENT OPERATORS AND LABORERS

07910	TAILOR	37.4	-2.1
08430	AUTO MECHANIC	43.1	0.1
08550	ELECTRICIAN	41.9	-2.6
09540	CARPENTER	35.1	-2.0
09830	RAILROAD ENGINEER	38.5	-4.1
09850	TAXI DRIVER	31.7	4.0

MEMBERS OF THE ARMED FORCES

10001	CAPTAIN IN THE ARMY	71.4	8.1

ISCO NO.	OCCUPATION TITLE	PRESTIGE SCORE	SCORE MINUS STD. SCORE
	PHILIPPINES		
	PROFESSIONAL, TECHNICAL AND RELATED WORKERS		
00220	ENGINEER	71.5	1.2
00610	PHYSICIAN	78.9	1.0
00710	NURSE	61.7	8.1
00730	MIDWIFE	51.9	5.5
01210	LAWYER	74.0	3.3
01310	UNIVERSITY PROFESSOR	69.1	-8.6
01321	INTERMEDIATE SCHOOL TEACHER	59.3	-2.2
01330	ELEMENTARY SCHOOL TEACHER	54.4	-2.6
01392	SUPERINTENDENT OF SCHOOLS	66.6	-1.0
01410	PRIEST	66.6	7.0
01414	FOREIGN MISSIONARY	64.2	15.1
01510	AUTHOR	61.7	0.0
01610	PROFESSIONAL ARTIST	56.8	-0.3
01730	MOVIE ARTIST	49.5	-2.0
	ADMINISTRATIVE AND MANAGERIAL WORKERS		
02022	CONGRESSMAN	76.4	4.3
02112	MANAGER OF A BUSINESS COMPANY	64.2	1.4
02113	SMALL FACTORY OWNER	44.6	-7.7
02114	BANKER	59.1	2.1
02194	CORPORATION EXECUTIVE	66.6	-0.0
02196	LABOR UNION LEADER	49.5	-0.0
	CLERICAL AND RELATED WORKERS		
03211	PRIVATE SECRETARY	47.0	-5.9
03700	MAIL CARRIER	25.0	-7.8
03930	OFFICE CLERK	49.5	6.2
03931	GOVERNMENT CLERK	49.5	5.2

436

SALES WORKERS

Code	Occupation		
04100	OWNER OF A SARI-SARI STORE (44.6)	40.5	-1.9
	GROCER (44.6)		
	STOREKEEPER (32.4)		
04320	TRAVELLING SALESMAN	49.5	2.6
04410	INSURANCE AGENT	54.4	9.9
04510	DEPARTMENT STORE SALES CLERK (42.1)	38.9	5.3
	SALESMAN (39.7)		
	SMALL STORE SALES CLERK (34.8)		
04512	GASOLINE-STATION ATTENDANT	15.2	-10.1
04521	PRODUCE PEDDLER	10.3	-11.6

SERVICE WORKERS

Code	Occupation		
05400	DOMESTIC SERVANT	7.9	-9.3
05510	JANITOR	17.7	-3.4
05700	BARBER	20.1	-10.3
05702	BEAUTICIAN	37.3	2.5
05820	POLICEMAN	47.0	7.2

AGRICULTURAL, ANIMAL HUSBANDRY AND FORESTRY WORKERS, FISHERMEN AND HUNTERS

Code	Occupation		
06110	FARMER	54.4	7.3
06113	FARM TENANT	29.9	0.5
06210	FARM LABORER	37.3	14.3
06220	SUGAR-CANE PLANTATION WORKER	22.6	1.2
06410	FISHERMAN	34.8	7.2

PRODUCTION AND RELATED WORKERS, TRANSPORT EQUIPMENT OPERATORS AND LABORERS

Code	Occupation		
07110	COAL MINER	37.3	5.8
07910	TAILOR	37.3	-2.2
08410	MACHINIST	51.9	8.6
08550	ELECTRICIAN	42.1	-2.4
08710	PLUMBER	29.9	-4.0
09540	CARPENTER	32.4	-4.8
09594	CONSTRUCTION WORKER	27.5	1.9
09595	HOD CARRIER (20.1)	16.4	1.2
	DITCH DIGGER (12.8)		
09850	BUS OR JEEPNEY DRIVER	20.1	-7.7
09851	MOTORMAN (BUSDRIVER) (34.8)	27.5	-4.9

ISCO NO.	OCCUPATION TITLE	PRESTIGE SCORE	SCORE MINUS STD. SCORE
	PHILIPPINES		
09852	BUS OR JEEPNEY DRIVER (20.1)	27.5	-5.1
09950	TRUCK DRIVER	42.1	0.3
C9970	SKILLED FACTORY WORKER	25.0	-4.2
09991	FACTORY WORKER	22.6	4.5
09997	UNSKILLED FACTORY WORKER	12.8	-7.3
	ROAD REPAIRMAN		

MEMBERS OF THE ARMED FORCES

| 10001 | OFFICER IN THE ARMED FORCES | 61.7 | -1.5 |
| 10003 | ENLISTED MAN IN THE ARMED FORCES | 44.6 | 5.9 |

PROFESSIONAL, TECHNICAL AND RELATED WORKERS

Code	Occupation		
00240	MECHANICAL ENGINEER	71.4	4.9
00410	AIRPLANE PILOT	70.0	3.5
00530	AGRONOMIST	66.3	8.4
00610	DOCTOR	80.5	2.6
00710	NURSE	55.3	1.7
01100	ACCOUNTANT	51.0	-3.6
01210	LAWYER, ATTORNEY	66.3	-4.4
01310	UNIVERSITY PROFESSOR	86.4	8.8
01330	TEACHER	73.2	16.2
01391	SCHOOL PRINCIPAL	70.3	4.7
01410	PRIEST (56.1)	51.1	-8.6
01414	CLERGYMAN (46.1)		
01510	MISSIONARY	44.5	-4.6
01590	AUTHOR	66.0	4.3
01610	JOURNALIST	62.0	7.0
01730	ARTIST	66.3	9.1
	ACTOR	66.3	14.7

ADMINISTRATIVE AND MANAGERIAL WORKERS

Code	Occupation		
02030	MINISTER OF THE NATIONAL GOVERNMENT	63.6	-15.1
02114	BANKER	48.8	-18.2
02190	BUSINESSMAN	50.2	-7.8
02195	POLITICIAN	64.6	1.9

CLERICAL AND RELATED WORKERS

Code	Occupation		
03000	OFFICE SUPERVISOR	44.8	-9.8
03101	CIVIL SERVICE EMPLOYEE	53.9	0.3
03210	TYPIST	25.2	-16.4
03310	BOOKKEEPER	50.4	1.5
03600	RAILWAY CONDUCTOR	33.8	-4.8
03700	MAIL CARRIER	45.9	13.0
03930	OFFICE CLERK	27.1	-16.2

ISCO NO.	OCCUPATION TITLE	PRESTIGE SCORE	SCORE MINUS STD. SCORE
	POLAND		
SALES WORKERS			
04100	SHOPKEEPER (48.3)	43.8	1.4
	GROCER (39.4)		
04510	SALES CLERK	22.8	-10.8
SERVICE WORKERS			
05510	JANITOR	29.0	7.9
05520	CLEANING WOMAN	9.6	-6.8
05700	BARBER	34.9	4.5
05820	POLICEMAN	33.0	-6.8
AGRICULTURAL, ANIMAL HUSBANDRY AND FORESTRY WORKERS, FISHERMEN AND HUNTERS			
06112	SMALL FARMER	51.2	13.6
06210	UNSKILLED FARM LABORER ON A STATE FARM	7.5	-15.4
PRODUCTION AND RELATED WORKERS, TRANSPORT EQUIPMENT OPERATORS AND LABORERS			
07000	FACTORY FOREMAN	51.2	11.9
07110	COAL MINER	58.2	26.7
07210	SKILLED STEEL-MILL WORKER	60.6	15.3
07730	BUTCHER	33.5	2.2
07910	TAILOR WITH HIS OWN WORKSHOP	46.7	7.2
08010	SHOEMAKER	34.3	6.2
08390	LOCKSMITH WITH HIS OWN WORKSHOP	45.9	5.7
08410	MACHINIST	51.8	8.4
08550	ELECTRICIAN	58.2	13.7
08710	PLUMBER	39.7	5.8
09210	TYPOGRAPHER	47.2	4.9
09540	CARPENTER	38.1	0.9
09595	UNSKILLED CONSTRUCTION LABORER	13.1	-2.1
09852	TRUCK DRIVER	44.0	11.4

440

MEMBERS OF THE ARMED FORCES

| 10001 | ARMY OFFICER | 44.3 | -19.0 |
| 10003 | SOLDIER | 42.1 | 3.4 |

441

ISCO NO.	OCCUPATION TITLE	PRESTIGE SCORE	SCORE MINUS STD. SCORE
	PUERTO RICO		
PROFESSIONAL, TECHNICAL AND RELATED WORKERS		
00210	ARCHITECT	70.1	-1.7
00220	ENGINEER—ROAD AND PUBLIC WORKS	73.0	2.7
00610	PHYSICIAN	76.0	-1.9
00670	DRUGGIST	64.3	0.2
00710	NURSE	55.5	2.0
01210	LAWYER	74.5	3.9
01310	PROFESSOR AT THE UNIVERSITY	71.6	-6.0
01330	SCHOOL TEACHER	61.4	4.4
01410	PRIEST (65.7)	61.4	1.7
	REVEREND—PROTESTANT (57.0)		
01790	ENTERTAINER ON ISLAND TV OR RADIO	52.6	2.2
01930	SOCIAL WORKER	59.9	3.6
ADMINISTRATIVE AND MANAGERIAL WORKERS		
02022	CONGRESSMAN	67.2	-4.9
02194	ADMINISTRATOR IN A "FOMENTO" FACTORY	58.5	-8.2
02196	UNION LEADER	46.8	-2.7
CLERICAL AND RELATED WORKERS		
03100	OFFICIAL IN INSULAR GOVERNMENT	68.7	2.9
03315	AGENT FOR LOTTERY TICKETS	40.9	5.1
03700	POSTMAN	48.2	15.4
03930	OFFICE WORKER	54.1	10.7
SALES WORKERS		
04100	RETAIL MERCHANT—SMALL	45.3	2.9
04102	"KIOSKO" OWNER	26.4	-11.3
04510	SALESMAN	42.4	8.8
04512	GASOLINE-STATION ATTENDANT	19.1	-6.2

Code	Occupation		
04521	PRODUCE PEDDLER	13.2	-8.7

SERVICE WORKERS

Code	Occupation		
05101	"FONDA" OWNER/SMALL WORKING CLASS RESTAURANT OWNER	33.7	-1.2
05320	RESTAURANT WAITER	22.0	-1.3
05400	DOMESTIC SERVANT	10.3	-6.9
05403	HOTEL WORKER	38.0	5.3
05700	BARBER	32.2	1.8
05820	POLICEMAN	51.2	11.4
05995	BOOTBLACK	7.4	-4.8
05999	"BOLITERO"/NUMBERS RUNNER	5.9	0.0

AGRICULTURAL, ANIMAL HUSBANDRY AND FORESTRY WORKERS, FISHERMEN AND HUNTERS

Code	Occupation		
06110	FARMER	49.7	2.6
06113	FARM TENANT	30.7	1.3
06220	SUGAR-CANE PLANTATION WORKER	11.8	-9.6
06410	FISHERMAN	17.6	-10.0

PRODUCTION AND RELATED WORKERS, TRANSPORT EQUIPMENT OPERATORS AND LABORERS

Code	Occupation		
07780	"MOONSHINER"	4.5	-1.5
07911	DRESSMAKER WHO WORKS AT HOME	36.6	-2.8
08010	COBBLER	20.5	-7.6
08430	AUTOMOBILE MECHANIC	43.9	0.9
09540	CARPENTER	39.5	2.3
09594	CONSTRUCTION WORKER	24.9	-0.7
09710	STEVEDORE	16.1	-5.1
09850	"PUBLICO" DRIVER/TAXI DRIVER	23.4	-4.3
09851	BUS-DRIVER	29.3	-3.1
09970	FACTORY WORKER	27.8	-1.4
09995	STREET CLEANER	8.9	-4.5
09997	ROAD REPAIRMAN	14.7	-5.4

MEMBERS OF THE ARMED FORCES

Code	Occupation		
10001	OFFICER IN THE ARMED FORCES	62.8	-0.4
10003	ENLISTED MAN IN THE ARMED FORCES	35.1	-3.6

ISCO NO.	OCCUPATION TITLE	PRESTIGE SCORE	SCORE MINUS STD. SCORE

SOUTHERN RHODESIA

PROFESSIONAL, TECHNICAL AND RELATED WORKERS

ISCO NO.	OCCUPATION TITLE	PRESTIGE SCORE	SCORE MINUS STD. SCORE
00610	MEDICAL OFFICER	62.9	-14.9
00793	HEALTH DEMONSTRATOR	51.4	3.8
01210	LAWYER	68.0	-2.6
01320	SECONDARY SCHOOL TEACHER	65.7	1.5
01330	PRIMARY SCHOOL TEACHER	51.0	-6.0
01391	HEADMASTER	62.0	-3.6
01392	SCHOOL INSPECTOR	66.9	-0.8
01410	PRIEST (60.6)	60.2	0.5
	AFRICAN MINISTER OF RELIGION (59.8)		
01413	PREACHER	48.3	-1.9
01590	REPORTER	41.6	-13.4
01591	NEWSPAPER EDITOR	53.0	-12.0
01790	RADIO ANNOUNCER	54.7	4.3
01930	AFRICAN WELFARE OFFICER	51.8	-4.5
01990	LABORATORY ASSISTANT	48.8	-9.4
01991	DIVINER	36.9	0.0

ADMINISTRATIVE AND MANAGERIAL WORKERS

ISCO NO.	OCCUPATION TITLE	PRESTIGE SCORE	SCORE MINUS STD. SCORE
02196	TRADE UNION BRANCH SECRETARY	50.0	0.5

CLERICAL AND RELATED WORKERS

ISCO NO.	OCCUPATION TITLE	PRESTIGE SCORE	SCORE MINUS STD. SCORE
03000	SENIOR CLERK	58.8	4.2
03210	TYPIST	51.4	9.8
03601	BUS CONDUCTOR	25.3	-0.7
03701	OFFICE MESSENGER (31.0)	30.6	4.8
	NAT. COM. MESSENGER (30.2)		
03910	STOREKEEPER	40.6	8.5

SALES WORKERS

Code	Occupation		
04512	PETROL PUMP BOY	21.0	-4.3
04520	MARKET SELLER	22.6	-13.5
04521	PEDLAR	17.1	-4.8
04523	NEWSPAPER BOY	15.9	1.9
04525	DAGGA BOY/MARIJUANA PEDDLER	6.5	0.0

SERVICE WORKERS

Code	Occupation		
05310	COOK	18.9	-12.0
05320	HOTEL WAITER	20.2	-3.0
05400	DOMESTIC SERVANT	23.8	6.6
05820	AFRICAN CONSTABLE	42.2	2.4
05821	AFRICAN POLICE INSPECTOR	53.5	-6.1
05990	MEDICAL ORDERLY	52.6	10.9
05992	LIFT OPERATOR	32.6	8.3

AGRICULTURAL, ANIMAL HUSBANDRY AND FORESTRY WORKERS, FISHERMEN AND HUNTERS

Code	Occupation		
06270	GARDEN BOY	8.5	-12.9
06310	WOOD CUTTER	10.8	-8.4

PRODUCTION AND RELATED WORKERS, TRANSPORT EQUIPMENT OPERATORS AND LABORERS

Code	Occupation		
07000	FOREMAN	35.9	-3.4
08010	SHOEMAKER	29.3	1.1
08430	GARAGE MECHANIC	49.4	6.5
08540	RADIO MECHANIC	54.7	12.7
08710	PLUMBER	34.9	1.1
09310	PAINTER	34.9	3.9
09510	BRICKLAYER	27.3	-6.8
09540	CARPENTER	43.6	6.4
09713	STATION BOY (RAILWAYS)	25.9	7.8
09850	TAXI DRIVER	39.8	12.1
09851	BUS DRIVER	41.2	8.8
09852	LORRY DRIVER	34.7	2.1
09853	BUS OWNER	53.9	14.5
09854	LORRY BOY	10.4	-4.8
09995	SWEEPER OF SAN. LANES	5.2	-8.2
09996	SCAVENGER	3.0	-9.7
09997	ROAD REPAIRER	12.0	-8.1

ISCO NO.	OCCUPATION TITLE	PRESTIGE SCORE	SCORE MINUS STD. SCORE
	SOUTHERN RHODESIA		
	MEMBERS OF THE ARMED FORCES		
10002	SERGEANT IN ARMY	54.7	11.1
	UNCLASSIFIABLE OCCUPATIONS		
12000	TEA BOY	11.8	-28.1

SOUTH WEST AFRICA (NAMIBIA)

PROFESSIONAL, TECHNICAL AND RELATED WORKERS

Code	Description		
00710	VERSLEEGSTERS/NURSE	58.1	4.5
01330	ONDERWYSER/MALE PRIMARY SCHOOL TEACHER (65.3)	62.3	5.3
	ONDERWYSERESSE/FEMALE PRIMARY SCHOOL TEACHER (59.3)		
01392	SKOOLINSPEKTEUR/SCHOOL INSPECTOR	62.3	-5.3
01410	PREDIKANTE/CLERGYMAN	64.8	5.1
01413	EVANGELISTE/EVANGELIST	55.6	5.4
01630	FOTOGRAWE/PHOTOGRAPHER	28.9	-16.2
01712	SANGER/SINGER, MALE (48.6)	48.4	16.8
	MUSIKANTE/MUSICIAN (PROBABLY WITH A BAND) (48.4)		
	SANGSTER/SINGER, FEMALE (48.1)		

ADMINISTRATIVE AND MANAGERIAL WORKERS

Code	Description		
02024	LID VAN DIE ADVIESRAAD/ADVISORY BOARD MEMBER	45.9	-9.2
02116	BOUER/BUILDING CONTRACTOR	50.6	-2.8

CLERICAL AND RELATED WORKERS

Code	Description		
03314	POSKANTOORWERKER/POST OFFICE WORKER	38.4	-0.6
03701	POSBODES/MESSENGER	21.4	-4.4
03931	MUNISPAIELKLERKE/MUNICIPAL CLERK	38.1	-6.2

SALES WORKERS

Code	Description		
04100	WINKELEINAAR/SHOP KEEPER	52.8	10.4
04510	WINKELKLERK (M)/MALE SHOP CLERK (34.6)	34.5	0.9
	WINKELKLERK (V)/FEMALE SHOP CLERK (34.4)		
04512	PATROLJOGGIES/GAS STATION ATTENDENT	20.4	-4.9
04521	SMOUS/RETAIL TRAVELING SALESMAN (DRIVES FROM PLACE TO PLACE IN BUSH PEDDLING WARES FROM TRUNK OF CAR) (27.9)	20.8	-1.1
	SHEBEEN/WOMAN WHO MAKES AND SELLS BEER (13.7)		
04523	KOERANTVERKOPERS/NEWSPAPER SELLER	0.7	-13.3

447

ISCO NO.	OCCUPATION TITLE	PRESTIGE SCORE	SCORE MINUS STD. SCORE
	SOUTH WEST AFRICA (NAMIBIA)		
SERVICE WORKERS			
05101	KAFEEENAARK/CAFE OWNER	42.1	7.2
05310	KOK (V)/FEMALE COOK (25.7)	18.4	-12.4
	KOK (M)/MALE COOK (11.2)		
05320	KAFEMEISIE/WAITRESS (25.9)	19.1	-4.2
	TAFELBEDIENDE/WAITER (12.2)		
05400	HUISBEDIENDE/SERVANT	17.2	-0.0
05401	BABA-OPPASTERS/NANNY FOR EUROPEAN CHILDREN	20.4	-2.4
05520	SKOONMAKSTER/CLEANING WOMAN (22.2)	20.1	3.6
	SKOONMAAKER/CLEANING MAN (17.9)		
05600	WASVROUE/WASHERWOMAN	21.7	-0.4
05700	HAARKAPPERS/BARBER	29.4	-1.0
05820	POLISIE (MUNISIPALIE)/AFRICAN MUNICIPAL POLICEMAN	34.1	-5.7
AGRICULTURAL, ANIMAL HUSBANDRY AND FORESTRY WORKERS, FISHERMEN AND HUNTERS			
06270	TUINIERS/GARDENER	20.2	-1.2
PRODUCTION AND RELATED WORKERS, TRANSPORT EQUIPMENT OPERATORS AND LABORERS			
07110	MUNWERKER/MINES	26.9	-4.6
07910	KLEREMAKER/TAILOR	41.6	2.1
07911	KLEREMAKSTER/SEAMSTRESS	47.9	8.5
08010	SKOENMAKER/SHOEMAKER	25.2	-3.0
08430	MOTOREGMAKER/AUTO MECHANIC	43.9	0.9
09540	SKRYNWERKER/CARPENTER	48.8	11.7
09850	HUURMOTORGESTUURDER/TAXI DRIVER	33.6	5.9
09851	BUSBESTUURDER/BUS DRIVER	33.9	1.5
09852	MOTORBESTUURDER/DRIVER	35.4	2.8
09970	FABRIEKWERKER/FACTORY WORKER	37.6	8.4
09990	ARBEIDER/LABORER	21.2	2.1
09992	OVAMBO KONTRAKWERKER/CONTRACT LABORER FROM OVAMBOLAND	7.7	0.0

448

SPAIN

PROFESSIONAL, TECHNICAL AND RELATED WORKERS

Code	Occupation	Value	Value
00210	ARQUITECTO/ARCHITECT	75.8	4.1
00220	INGENIERO CAMINOS/HIGHWAY ENGINEER	77.4	7.1
00410	PILOTO IBERIA/PILOT FOR IBERIAN AIRLINES	68.1	1.6
00541	PERITO AGRICOLA/AGRICULTURAL TECHNICIAN	62.0	15.2
00610	MEDICO/PHYSICIAN	74.3	-3.6
00620	PRACTICANTE/MEDICAL ASSISTANT	40.3	-9.6
00650	VETERINARIO/VETERINARIAN	55.8	-5.6
01100	CONTABLE/ACCOUNTANT	45.0	-9.6
01210	PROCURADOR EN CORTES/LAWYER	69.7	-1.0
01211	ABOGADO DEL ESTADO/STATE PROSECUTOR	75.8	0.5
01221	MAGISTRADO T.S./SUPREME COURT JUSTICE	78.9	-3.1
01290	NOTARIO/NON-TRIAL LAWYER	69.7	-0.9
01310	CATEDRATICO/UNIVERSITY PROFESSOR	72.8	-4.9
01330	MAESTRO NACIONAL/PUBLIC SCHOOL TEACHER	41.9	-15.1
01410	SACERDOTE/PRIEST	66.6	6.9
01800	FUTBOLISTA (P.S.)/PROFESSIONAL SOCCER PLAYER	55.8	7.3

ADMINISTRATIVE AND MANAGERIAL WORKERS

Code	Occupation	Value	Value
02011	GOBERNADOR/PROVINCIAL GOVERNOR	82.0	0.1
02013	ALCALDE CAPITAL/MAYOR OF THE CAPITAL CITY	69.7	-5.6
02030	MINISTRO/GOVERNMENT MINISTER	83.6	4.9
02111	EMPRESARIO (100TR.)/BUSINESSMAN WITH 100 EMPLOYEES	69.7	-0.7
02112	EMPRESARIO (40TR.)/BUSINESSMAN WITH 40 EMPLOYEES	51.1	-11.6
02115	PRESIDENTE GRAN BANCO/HEAD OF A LARGE BANK	82.0	5.9
02197	JEFE PROV. SINDICATOS/REGIONAL HEAD OF LABOR UNION	65.0	2.3

CLERICAL AND RELATED WORKERS

Code	Occupation	Value	Value
03210	MECANOGRAFIA/TYPIST	35.7	-5.9
03700	CARTERO/MAILMAN	11.0	-21.8

449

ISCO NO.	OCCUPATION TITLE	PRESTIGE SCORE	SCORE MINUS STD. SCORE
	SPAIN		
	SALES WORKERS		
04100	PROPIETARIO TIENDA TEJIDOS/OWNER OF A FABRIC SHOP	58.9	16.4
04510	DEPENDIENTE BUEN COMERCIO/SHOP CLERK	32.6	-1.0
	AGRICULTURAL, ANIMAL HUSBANDRY AND FORESTRY WORKERS, FISHERMEN AND HUNTERS		
06120	PROPIETARIO OLIVARES/OLIVE FARMER	68.1	13.1
06280	TRACTORISTA/TRACTOR DRIVER	24.9	-6.0
	PRODUCTION AND RELATED WORKERS, TRANSPORT EQUIPMENT OPERATORS AND LABORERS		
07111	MINERO ESPECIALISTA/SPECIALIZED MINE WORKER	38.8	2.8
08331	TORNERO/LATHE OPERATOR	40.3	3.8
08340	MAQUINA BENFE/MACHINE OPERATOR	35.7	-2.5
08440	MECANICO AVIACION/AIRPLANE MECHANIC	52.7	3.1
08550	ELECTRICISTA/ELECTRICIAN	35.7	-8.8
09595	PEON ALBANIL/HOD CARRIER	-6.0	-21.2
09810	MARINO MERCANTE/MERCHANT SEAMAN	55.8	21.0
09851	CONDUCTOR AUTOB./BUS DRIVER	21.8	-10.6
	MEMBERS OF THE ARMED FORCES		
10000	COMANDANTE EJERCITO/ARMY COMMANDER	65.0	-7.9
	SOURCES OF LIVELIHOOD OTHER THAN LABOR FORCE ACTIVITY		
13001	TITULO VIVE RENTA/PROPERTY OWNER	60.4	3.3

PROFESSIONAL, TECHNICAL AND RELATED WORKERS

00131	GEOLOGIST	67.3	-0.1
00210	ARCHITECT	64.8	-7.0
00220	ENGINEER	62.9	-7.4
00310	SURVEYOR	56.1	-1.8
00320	DRAUGHTSMAN	58.6	3.7
00410	PILOT	69.1	2.7
00530	AGRICULTURIST	58.0	0.2
00610	DOCTOR	73.5	-4.4
00630	DENTIST	67.3	-3.2
00670	PHARMACIST	64.2	0.1
00710	NURSE	58.0	4.4
00793	SANITARY OFFICER	38.2	-9.4
01100	ACCOUNTANT	61.1	6.5
01210	LAWYER	64.8	-5.8
01330	TEACHER	58.6	1.6
01410	CLERGYMAN	66.7	7.0
01590	JOURNALIST	58.6	3.7
01630	PHOTOGRAPHER	36.3	-8.8
01710	MUSICIAN	54.9	-1.2
01990	TECHNICIAN	62.3	4.1

ADMINISTRATIVE AND MANAGERIAL WORKERS

02116	CONTRACTOR	51.8	-1.6
02190	BUSINESSMAN	62.3	4.4

CLERICAL AND RELATED WORKERS

03100	ADMINISTRATOR	73.5	7.7
03101	CIVIL SERVANT	59.8	6.2
03211	SECRETARY	53.7	0.7
03310	BOOKKEEPER	57.4	8.4
03311	CASHIER	38.2	7.0
03510	STATIONMASTER	50.6	-5.5
03600	TRAIN CONDUCTOR	36.3	-2.3

ISCO NO.	OCCUPATION TITLE	SURINAM PRESTIGE SCORE	SCORE MINUS STD. SCORE
03700	POSTMAN	42.5	9.7
03701	MESSENGER	22.7	-3.1
03930	CLERK	53.7	10.3
SALES WORKERS			
04100	SHOPKEEPER	33.9	-8.6
04411	REALTOR	51.8	2.8
04510	SALESMAN	37.6	3.9
04521	HUCKSTER	20.2	-1.7
SERVICE WORKERS			
05400	DOMESTIC	17.8	0.6
05600	LAUNDERER	24.0	1.9
05700	BARBER	20.9	-9.5
05702	HAIRDRESSER	33.2	-1.6
05820	POLICEMAN	56.1	16.3
05890	WATCHMAN	17.8	-4.2
05892	BAILIFF	42.5	-4.9
05996	STEWARDESS	54.9	4.8
AGRICULTURAL, ANIMAL HUSBANDRY AND FORESTRY WORKERS, FISHERMEN AND HUNTERS			
06001	OVERSEER	53.7	12.9
06110	FARMER	24.0	-23.1
06310	LOG CUTTER	21.5	-2.3
06320	RANGER	31.4	-16.1
06410	FISHERMAN	20.2	-7.3
PRODUCTION AND RELATED WORKERS, TRANSPORT EQUIPMENT OPERATORS AND LABORERS			
07000	FOREMAN	41.9	2.6
07001	SUPERVISOR	57.4	5.2
07720	SUGAR BOILER	40.0	-5.3

452

Code	Occupation		
07730	BUTCHER	26.4	-4.9
07760	BAKER	35.1	1.9
07910	TAILOR	38.2	-1.3
07911	SEAMSTRESS	38.2	-1.2
08190	COOPER	28.3	-0.0
08420	WATCH REPAIRER	29.5	-10.2
08422	DENTAL MECHANIC	60.5	0.0
08490	MECHANIC	35.1	-7.7
08550	ELECTRICIAN	33.9	-10.7
08770	PLUMBER	33.9	-0.0
08720	WELDER	35.1	-4.1
08800	JEWELLER	40.0	-2.9
09210	PRINTER	56.8	14.5
09210	PAINTER	36.3	5.3
09510	MASON	33.9	-0.2
09540	CARPENTER (38.2)	36.9	-0.2
09543	JOINER (35.7)	33.9	0.0
09710	BOAT BUILDER	25.8	4.6
09712	STEVEDORE	17.8	0.9
09740	PORTER	36.3	4.5
09810	DRAGLINE OPERATOR	39.4	4.7
09852	SAILOR	37.6	5.0
09990	CHAUFFEUR	17.8	-1.4
09994	LABORER	37.6	4.3
	PLATE LAYER/RAILWAY TRACK LAYER		

MEMBERS OF THE ARMED FORCES

Code	Occupation		
10001	MILITARY OFFICER	68.5	5.3

ISCO NO.	OCCUPATION TITLE	PRESTIGE SCORE	SCORE MINUS STD. SCORE
	SWEDEN		
PROFESSIONAL, TECHNICAL AND RELATED WORKERS			
00420	SJOKAPTEN/SHIP'S CAPTAIN	56.3	-6.9
00670	APOTEKARE/PHARMACIST	64.7	0.6
01100	REVISOR/ACCOUNTANT	50.7	-3.9
01310	PROFESSOR/UNIVERSITY PROFESSOR	75.9	-1.7
01320	LARARE, LAROVERK/HIGH SCHOOL TEACHER	64.7	0.5
01330	LARARE, FOLKSKOLA/PRIMARY SCHOOL TEACHER	64.7	7.7
01730	SKADESPELARE/ACTOR	33.8	-17.7
ADMINISTRATIVE AND MANAGERIAL WORKERS			
02111	VERKSTALLANDE DIREKTOR/COMPANY DIRECTOR (73.1)	68.9	-1.5
	SKEPPSREDARE/SHIP OWNER (64.7)		
CLERICAL AND RELATED WORKERS			
03312	KAMRER/HEAD CASHIER	64.7	0.0
03700	BREVBARARE/MAILMAN	28.2	-4.6
SALES WORKERS			
04100	SPECERIHANDLARE, EGEN/GROCER, SHOP OWNER	59.1	16.6
04320	HANDELSRESANDE/TRAVELLING SALESMAN	33.8	-13.1
04510	AFFARSBITRADE/SHOP CLERK	36.6	3.0
SERVICE WORKERS			
05320	KYPARE/WAITER	31.0	7.8
05701	FRISORMASTARE, EGEN/BARBER, INDEPENDENT OR EMPLOYER	53.5	16.9
05820	POLISKONSTAPEL/POLICEMAN	39.4	-0.4
05995	SKOPUTSARE/SHOE SHINER	0.2	-12.1

PRODUCTION AND RELATED WORKERS, TRANSPORT EQUIPMENT OPERATORS AND LABORERS

07910	SKRADDARE EJ EGEN/TAILOR, EMPLOYEE	28.2	-11.3
08800	GULDSMED, EJ EGEN/GOLDSMITH, EMPLOYEE	53.5	10.5
09210	TYPOGRAF/TYPOGRAFHER	39.4	-2.9
09541	SNICKARE, EGEN/CARPENTER, INDEPENDENT OR EMPLOYER	53.5	5.3
09594	BYGGNADSARBETARE/BUILDING LABOURER	36.6	11.0
09850	DROSKAGARE/TAXI DRIVER	39.4	11.7

MEMBERS OF THE ARMED FORCES

10000	OVERSTE/COLONEL IN THE ARMED FORCES	61.9	-11.1
10002	UNDEROFFICER I FORSVARET/NON-COMMISSIONED OFFICER	36.6	-6.9

	SWITZERLAND		
	PROFESSIONAL, TECHNICAL AND RELATED WORKERS		
00110	CHIMISTE/CHEMIST	68.6	-0.6
00120	PHYSICIEN/PHYSICIST	78.1	1.6
00130	HOMME DE SCIENCE/SCIENTIST	76.3	-2.1
00132	ASTRONOME/ASTRONOMER	71.2	0.0
00210	ARCHITECTE/ARCHITECT	69.4	-2.4
00220	INGENIEUR/ENGINEER	74.6	4.3
00410	PILOTE/AIRPLANE PILOT (66.8)	67.7	1.2
00510	BIOLOGISTE/BIOLOGIST	64.3	-4.5
00530	NATURALISTE/NATURALIST (61.7)	46.1	-11.7
00610	HORTICULTEUR/HORTICULTURIST	75.5	-2.4
00630	MEDECIN/PHYSICIAN	67.7	-2.8
00650	DENTISTE/DENTIST	64.3	2.9
00670	VETERINAIRE/VETERINARIAN	59.9	-4.2
00820	PHARMACIEN/PHARMACIST	65.1	-3.9
00900	MATHEMATICIEN/MATHEMATICIAN (71.2)		
	GEOMETRE/GEOMETRICIAN (59.1)		
	ECONOMISTE/ECONOMIST	65.1	4.6
01100	COMPTABLE/ACCOUNTANT	41.8	-12.8
01101	CHEF COMPTABLE/CHIEF ACCOUNTANT	53.0	-15.4
01210	AVOCAT/LAWYER	70.3	-0.4
01320	PROFESSEUR DU COLLEGE/HIGH SCHOOL TEACHER	64.3	0.1
01330	INSTITUTEUR/PRIMARY SCHOOL TEACHER	55.6	-1.4
01394	DOYEN DU COLLEGE/DEAN OF A HIGH SCHOOL	57.7	-4.5
01410	PASTEUR/PROTESTANT MINISTER	66.0	6.3
01590	JOURNALISTE/JOURNALIST	61.7	6.7
01610	PEINTRE (ARTISTE)/PAINTER (ARTIST)	62.5	5.4
01621	DECORATEUR/DECORATOR (56.5)	54.3	-1.6
	DESSINATEUR/DESIGNER (52.2)		
01710	COMPOSITEUR (MUSICIEN)/COMPOSER (MUSICIAN) (66.8)	63.0	6.9
	MUSICIEN/MUSICIAN (59.1)		
01730	ACTEUR DE CINEMA/MOVIE ACTOR	56.5	5.0
01732	METTEUR EN SCENE/STAGE OR CINEMA PRODUCER OR DIRECTOR	67.7	5.5

Code	Occupation		
01740	METTEUR EN SCENE/STAGE OR CINEMA PRODUCER OR DIRECTOR	67.7	0.0
01801	PROFESSEUR DE SPORT/SPORTS INSTRUCTOR	52.2	1.8
01922	ARCHEOLOGUE/ARCHEOLOGIST	69.4	0.0
01923	HISTORIEN/HISTORIAN	68.6	1.3
01924	PHILOSOPHE/PHILOSOPHER	70.3	1.5
01940	CHEF DE PERSONNEL/PERSONNEL DIRECTOR	60.8	2.3
01950	INTERPRETE/INTERPRETER	61.7	7.6
01990	TECHNICIEN/TECHNICIAN	58.2	-0.0

ADMINISTRATIVE AND MANAGERIAL WORKERS

Code	Occupation		
02032	DIPLOMATE/DIPLOMAT (65.1)	63.4	-9.8
	FONCTIONAIRE INTERNATIONAL/INTERNATIONAL FUNCTIONARY (61.7)		
02033	CONSEILLER FEDERAL (MINISTRE)/FEDERAL COUNSELLOR IN A MINISTRY	78.9	7.8
02111	DIRECTEUR/HEAD OF A FIRM (72.9)	67.1	-3.3
	INDUSTRIEL/INDUSTRIALIST (69.4)		
	FABRICANT/MANUFACTURER (59.1)		
02112	FONDE DE POUVOIR/BUSINESS MANAGER	56.5	-6.3
02116	ENTREPRENEUR/CONTRACTOR	56.5	3.1
02190	HOMME D'AFFAIRES/BUSINESSMAN	60.8	2.9

CLERICAL AND RELATED WORKERS

Code	Occupation		
03100	ADMINISTRATEUR/ADMINISTRATOR	56.5	-9.3
03103	DOUANIER/CUSTOMS OFFICIAL	31.5	-13.0
03210	DACTYLOGRAPHE/TYPIST	34.9	-6.7
03313	EMPLOYEE DE BANQUE/BANK CLERK (FEMALE)	40.1	-7.5
03314	EMPLOYE PTT/POSTAL EMPLOYEE	29.7	-9.3
03601	CONTROLEUR DE TRAM/STREETCAR CONDUCTOR	22.8	-3.2
03930	EMPLOYE DE BUREAU/OFFICE EMPLOYEE	40.1	-3.2
03931	EMPLOYE D'ETAT (FONCTIONAIRE)/GOVERNMENT CLERK	40.1	-4.2

SALES WORKERS

Code	Occupation		
04100	PATRON DE MAGASIN DE CONFECTION/OWNER OF A CLOTHING STORE (54.8)	51.3	8.9
	DROGUISTE/DRYSALTER (DEALER IN CHEMICALS, PRESERVED FOOD, ETC.) (47.9)		
04106	NEGOCIANT/WHOLESALER	49.6	-8.8
04320	REPRESENTANT/REPRESENTATIVE (42.7)	42.2	-4.7
	VOYAGEUR DE COMMERCE/TRAVELING SALESMAN (41.8)		
04410	AGENT D'ASSURANCE/INSURANCE AGENT	47.9	3.3
04411	REGISSEUR (GERANT D'IMMEUBLES)/REAL ESTATE AGENT	59.1	10.0
04510	VENDEUR/SALESMAN	36.6	3.0

ISCO NO.	OCCUPATION TITLE	PRESTIGE SCORE	SCORE MINUS STD. SCORE
	SWITZERLAND		
04512	EMPLOYE DE GARAGE/GARAGE EMPLOYEE	34.0	8.8
04524	LIVREUR/DELIVERYMAN	21.1	-3.0
SERVICE WORKERS			
05200	STEWARD/STEWARD	50.4	4.3
05310	CUISINIER/COOK	32.3	1.4
05320	GARCON DE CAFE/WAITER	28.0	4.8
05511	CONCIERGE/APARTMENT "SUPER"	16.8	-7.7
05702	COIFFEUR/HAIRDRESSER	34.0	-0.8
05810	POMPIER/FIREMAN	28.9	-6.5
05820	GENDARME/POLICEMAN	33.2	-6.6
05823	DETECTIVE/DETECTIVE	48.7	-2.9
AGRICULTURAL, ANIMAL HUSBANDRY AND FORESTRY WORKERS, FISHERMEN AND HUNTERS			
06110	AGRICULTEUR/FARMER	44.4	-2.7
06120	MARIACHER/MARKET GARDENER	34.9	-20.1
C6270	JARDINIER/GARDENER	39.2	17.8
PRODUCTION AND RELATED WORKERS, TRANSPORT EQUIPMENT OPERATORS AND LABORERS			
07000	CONTREMAITRE (INDUSTRIE)/INDUSTRIAL FOREMAN (47.0) CONTREMAITRE (MASON)/BRICKLAYER'S FOREMAN (39.2)	43.1	3.8
07730	BOUCHER/BUTCHER	32.3	1.0
07760	BOULANGER/BAKER OF BREAD	34.0	0.9
07910	COUTURIER/DRESS TAILOR	23.7	-15.8
C8200	MARBRIER/MONUMENT MASON	44.4	5.9
08331	TOURNEUR (POLISSEUR)/LATHE OPERATOR	35.8	-0.8
08390	SERRURIER/LOCKSMITH	36.6	-3.5
08420	HORLOGER/CLOCK, WATCH MAKER	37.5	-2.3
08431	GARAGISTE/GARAGE OPERATOR	54.8	7.5
C8490	MECANICIEN/MECHANIC (40.9) REPARATEUR/REPAIRMAN (39.2)	40.1	-2.7
08540	RADIO-ELECTRICIEN/RADIO REPAIRMAN	46.1	4.1

Code	Occupation		
08550	ELECTRICIEN/ELECTRICIAN	40.9	-3.6
08710	PLOMBIER/PLUMBER	31.5	-2.4
08731	FERBLANTIER/TINSMITH	39.2	7.0
08733	CARROSSIER/AUTO BODY BUILDER	32.3	-4.2
08800	BIJOUTIER/JEWELER	54.8	11.8
09210	TYPOGRAPHE/TYPOGRAPHER	40.1	-2.2
09211	IMPRIMEUR/PRINTER	53.9	3.2
09250	PHOTOGRAVEUR/PHOTOENGRAVER	52.2	5.9
09290	GRAPHISTE/GRAPHIC PRINTER	52.2	0.0
09310	PEINTRE (EN BATIMENT)/PAINTER OF BUILDINGS	36.6	-0.4
09490	CONTROLEUR DE FABRICATION/FACTORY INSPECTOR	42.7	3.2
09492	TAXIDERME/TAXIDERMIST	49.6	0.0
09510	CARRELEUR/TILE LAYER (38.4)	33.2	-0.9
	MACON/MASON (28.0)		
09540	CHARPENTIER/CARPENTER	34.9	-2.3
09594	MANOEVRE (BATIMENT)/CONSTRUCTION LABORER	18.5	-7.1
09830	CONDUCTEUR DE LOCOMOTIVE/LOCOMOTIVE ENGINEER	32.3	-10.3
09850	CHAUFFEUR DE TAXI/TAXI DRIVER	22.8	-5.0
09970	OUVRIER D'USINE/FACTORY WORKER	28.0	-1.2

UNCLASSIFIABLE OCCUPATIONS

| 12000 | EMPLOYE T.V./T.V. EMPLOYEE | 47.9 | 8.0 |

ISCO NO. | OCCUPATION TITLE | PRESTIGE SCORE | SCORE MINUS STD. SCORE

TAIWAN

ISCO NO.	OCCUPATION TITLE	PRESTIGE SCORE	SCORE MINUS STD. SCORE
PROFESSIONAL, TECHNICAL AND RELATED WORKERS			
00110	CHEMIST	69.5	0.4
00220	CIVIL ENGINEER	69.5	-0.8
00610	PHYSICIAN	79.2	1.3
01100	ACCOUNTANT	52.3	-2.3
01211	PUBLIC PROSECUTOR	77.0	1.6
01310	UNIVERSITY PROFESSOR	80.4	2.7
01321	MIDDLE SCHOOL TEACHER	57.9	0.9
01392	SUPERVISOR IN BOARD OF EDUCATION	65.7	-1.9
01410	TAOIST PRIEST	28.7	-31.0
01590	NEWSPAPER REPORTER	60.1	5.2
ADMINISTRATIVE AND MANAGERIAL WORKERS			
02111	FACTORY OWNER-MANAGER	71.7	1.3
02112	GENERAL MANAGER OF A COMPANY	64.1	1.4
02116	BUILDING CONTRACTOR	62.5	9.2
02194	EXECUTIVE SECRETARY OF A COMPANY	63.1	-3.5
CLERICAL AND RELATED WORKERS			
03930	CLERK	48.3	5.0
03992	POLITICAL PARTY WORKER	50.9	2.7
SALES WORKERS			
04100	RETAIL MERCHANT (SMALLER SCALE)	46.1	3.7
04101	SHOP OWNER (LARGE SCALE)	60.9	2.4
04510	SHOP CLERK	36.1	2.5
04521	STREET VENDOR	25.5	3.5

SERVICE WORKERS

05400	SERVANT	19.9	2.7
05510	JANITOR	22.9	1.8
05700	BARBER	29.3	-1.1
05820	POLICEMAN	45.5	5.7

AGRICULTURAL, ANIMAL HUSBANDRY AND FORESTRY WORKERS, FISHERMEN AND HUNTERS

06110	OWNER-CULTIVATOR	46.5	-0.6
06210	FARM LABORER	22.1	-0.9

PRODUCTION AND RELATED WORKERS, TRANSPORT EQUIPMENT OPERATORS AND LABORERS

07000	FACTORY FOREMAN	45.9	6.6
08490	REPAIRMAN	28.5	-14.4
09540	CARPENTER	32.5	-4.7
09852	DRIVER	39.5	6.9
09890	PEDICAB DRIVER	22.7	6.0
09950	SKILLED LABORER IN A FACTORY	42.3	0.5
09990	UNSKILLED LABORER (E.G. COOLIE)	18.3	-0.9
09996	RUBBISH COLLECTOR	15.4	2.8

MEMBERS OF THE ARMED FORCES

10001	ARMY CAPTAIN	52.5	-10.7
10002	ARMY CORPORAL	32.7	-10.9

461

TSCO NO.	OCCUPATION TITLE	PRESTIGE SCORE	SCORE MINUS STD. SCORE

THAILAND-PEASANT

PROFESSIONAL, TECHNICAL AND RELATED WORKERS

TSCO NO.	OCCUPATION TITLE	PRESTIGE SCORE	SCORE MINUS STD. SCORE
00220	CIVIL ENGINEER	51.4	-19.0
00410	AIRPLANE PILOT	70.4	3.9
00610	PHYSICIAN WITH M.D.	72.5	-5.4
00620	DISTRICT DOCTOR	52.6	2.6
00650	VETERINARIAN	47.1	-14.2
00670	CERTIFIED PHARMACIST	55.4	-8.7
00680	DRUGSTORE OWNER-OPERATOR	45.9	1.5
00710	NURSE IN A HOSPITAL OR CLINIC	59.5	5.9
00730	MIDWIFE	52.8	6.3
01100	ACCOUNTANT	48.1	-6.5
01210	LAWYER	35.2	-35.4
01220	PROVINCIAL COURT JUDGE	79.4	1.7
01310	UNIVERSITY PROFESSOR	78.2	0.6
01320	INSTRUCTOR IN TEACHERS' TRAINING COLLEGE	74.9	10.7
01330	TEACHER	59.0	-2.0
01414	CHRISTIAN MISSIONARY	20.0	-29.0
01415	BUDDHIST MONK	67.8	11.6
01590	JOURNALIST	48.8	-6.2
01630	PHOTOGRAPHER	54.0	8.9
01730	MOVIE SPEAKER	46.6	-4.9
01790	RADIO ANNOUNCER	46.6	-3.7
01791	NATIVE STYLE ENTERTAINER	27.2	-5.6
01993	EXPLORER	45.0	-4.3

ADMINISTRATIVE AND MANAGERIAL WORKERS

TSCO NO.	OCCUPATION TITLE	PRESTIGE SCORE	SCORE MINUS STD. SCORE
02011	PROVINCIAL GOVERNOR	85.1	3.2
02012	DISTRICT CHIEF	77.0	11.3
02015	VILLAGE CHIEF	42.4	0.5
02022	REPRESENTATIVE IN LOWER HOUSE	61.8	-10.3
02035	DIVISION CHIEF IN A DISTRICT OFFICE	66.4	3.2
02113	OWNER OF A RICE MILL (61.4)	55.1	2.7

ICE FACTORY OWNER (48.8)

Code	Occupation		
02114	BANKER	70.4	3.4
02120	TOBACCO FACTORY MANAGER	53.3	-10.4

CLERICAL AND RELATED WORKERS

Code	Occupation		
03210	TYPIST	45.0	3.4
03310	ACCOUNTING CLERK	47.6	-1.4
03314	POST OFFICE CLERK	52.6	13.6
03601	BUS INSPECTOR AND TICKET TAKER	21.2	-4.8
03801	TELEGRAPH OPERATOR	56.1	10.9
03930	CLERK	51.4	8.1
03931	CLERK IN A GOVERNMENT OFFICE	46.6	2.3

SALES WORKERS

Code	Occupation		
04100	OWNER OF A YARD GOODS STORE	49.3	6.8
04101	DEPARTMENT STORE OWNER-MANAGER	59.7	1.2
04106	IMPORT-EXPORT COMPANY OWNER	62.3	3.9
04410	LIFE INSURANCE SALESMAN	23.4	-21.2
04510	SALESMAN IN A STORE	27.4	-6.2
04512	GAS STATION ATTENDANT	33.3	8.1
04521	SELLER OF FRESH FOOD IN MARKETPLACE (33.1)	20.8	-1.1
	FOOD PEDDLER (16.0)		
	PEDDLER WITH A CART (13.4)		

SERVICE WORKERS

Code	Occupation		
05101	COFFEEHOUSE OWNER-OPERATOR	40.0	5.1
05310	RESTAURANT COOK	43.6	12.7
05320	RESTAURANT WAITER	17.0	-6.3
05400	SERVANT	8.9	-8.3
05510	JANITOR	21.5	-0.4
05600	LAUNDRYWOMAN	11.0	-11.1
05700	FULL-TIME BARBER	31.0	0.6
05820	POLICE PRIVATE	45.0	5.2
05821	MIDDLE RANKING POLICE OFFICER	72.3	12.6
05890	NIGHT WATCHMAN	29.3	7.3
05920	UNDERTAKER	15.1	-18.6

ISCO NO.	OCCUPATION TITLE	PRESTIGE SCORE	SCORE MINUS STD. SCORE
	THAILAND-PEASANT		
	AGRICULTURAL, ANIMAL HUSBANDRY AND FORESTRY WORKERS, FISHERMEN AND HUNTERS		
06110	FARMER	51.2	4.1
06113	TENANT FARMER	4.1	-25.3
06120	OWNER OF A MACHINE OPERATED RICE FARM	67.5	12.5
06210	AGRICULTURAL LABORER	12.7	-10.3
06280	TRACTOR DRIVER	40.7	9.8
06310	LOGGER	11.0	-8.2
06410	FISHERMAN	31.0	3.4
	PRODUCTION AND RELATED WORKERS, TRANSPORT EQUIPMENT OPERATORS AND LABORERS		
07110	TIN MINER	26.7	-4.8
07320	SAWYER OR LABORER IN A SAW MILL	34.8	4.2
07560	TEXTILE DYER	22.7	-2.4
07710	RICE MILL WORKER	41.9	9.0
07711	OWNER OF A SMALL RICE MILL	40.7	-1.4
07731	SLAUGHTER HOUSE BUTCHER	13.6	-4.4
07740	CANNED FOOD FACTORY WORKER	37.9	2.6
07890	TOBACCO FACTORY WORKER	38.8	-0.4
07910	TAILOR OF DRESS MAKER	41.9	2.4
07911	TAILOR OR DRESS MAKER	41.9	2.5
08010	SHOEMAKER	34.8	6.6
08340	MACHINE OPERATOR	48.3	10.1
08490	MECHANIC	45.5	2.6
08550	ELECTRICIAN	48.5	4.0
08710	PLUMBER	35.7	1.8
08731	METAL SMITH	26.0	-6.2
08733	BUS BODY BUILDER	40.2	3.8
08800	JEWELER AND GOLDSMITH	33.6	-9.4
08920	POTTER	23.6	-1.6
09210	PRINTER	50.7	8.4
09310	BUILDING PAINTER	28.4	-2.7
09420	BASKET WEAVER	18.9	-2.1

464

Code		Value 1	Value 2
09510	BRICK LAYER AND CEMENT WORKER	37.6	3.5
09520	BRICK LAYER AND CEMENT WORKER	37.6	3.2
09540	CARPENTER	37.9	0.7
09594	CONSTRUCTION LABORER	31.9	6.3
09710	LONGSHOREMAN	18.1	-3.1
09811	GONDOLIER	29.1	5.8
09830	LOCOMOTIVE ENGINEER	48.5	5.9
09851	BUS DRIVER	32.2	-0.3
09852	TRUCK DRIVER	29.1	-3.5
09890	PEDICAB DRIVER	7.2	-9.5
09991	UNSKILLED FACTORY WORKER	21.2	3.1
09995	STREET CLEANER	14.3	1.0
09997	ROAD WORKER	16.5	-3.6

MEMBERS OF THE ARMED FORCES

Code		Value 1	Value 2
10001	MIDDLE RANKING ARMY OFFICER	68.5	5.2
10003	LOW RANKING ARMY OFFICER OR ARMY PRIVATE	55.4	16.7

SOURCES OF LIVELIHOOD OTHER THAN LABOR FORCE ACTIVITY

Code		Value 1	Value 2
13001	LANDLORD	57.1	0.0
13002	LEGATEE WHO DOES NOT HAVE TO WORK	56.4	8.4
13003	AGRICULTURAL LAND OWNER	61.6	-3.5

ISCO NO.	OCCUPATION TITLE	PRESTIGE SCORE	SCORE MINUS STD. SCORE
	THAILAND-TCHRS COL STUDENT		
	PROFESSIONAL, TECHNICAL AND RELATED WORKERS		
00220	CIVIL ENGINEER	54.4	-15.9
00410	AIRPLANE PILOT	66.0	-0.5
00610	PHYSICIAN WITH M.D.	78.8	0.9
00620	DISTRICT DOCTOR	55.6	5.7
00650	VETERINARIAN	65.3	3.9
00670	CERTIFIED PHARMACIST	66.7	2.6
00680	DRUGSTORE OWNER-OPERATOR	36.7	-7.8
00710	NURSE IN A HOSPITAL OR CLINIC	63.3	9.7
00730	MIDWIFE	58.6	12.1
01100	ACCOUNTANT	55.6	1.1
01210	LAWYER	60.6	-10.1
01220	PROVINCIAL COURT JUDGE	75.6	-2.1
01310	UNIVERSITY PROFESSOR	80.3	2.7
01320	INSTRUCTOR IN TEACHERS' TRAINING COLLEGE	69.2	5.0
01330	TEACHER	62.1	5.0
01414	CHRISTIAN MISSIONARY	39.9	-9.2
01415	BUDDHIST MONK	62.3	6.1
01590	JOURNALIST	51.0	-4.0
01630	PHOTOGRAPHER	52.2	7.0
01730	MOVIE SPEAKER	45.3	-6.2
01790	RADIO ANNOUNCER	50.7	0.3
01791	NATIVE STYLE ENTERTAINER	31.5	-1.2
01993	EXPLORER	50.2	1.0
	ADMINISTRATIVE AND MANAGERIAL WORKERS		
02011	PROVINCIAL GOVERNOR	79.3	-2.6
02012	DISTRICT CHIEF	74.4	8.6
02015	VILLAGE CHIEF	45.0	3.1
02022	REPRESENTATIVE IN LOWER HOUSE	58.8	-13.3
02035	DIVISION CHIEF IN A DISTRICT OFFICE	60.3	-2.8
02113	OWNER OF A RICE MILL (56.1)	53.7	1.3

ICE FACTORY OWNER (51.2)

Code	Occupation		
02114	BANKER	69.2	2.2
02120	TOBACCO FACTORY MANAGER	61.3	-2.9

CLERICAL AND RELATED WORKERS

Code	Occupation		
03210	TYPIST	38.4	-3.2
03310	ACCOUNTING CLERK	41.8	-7.1
03314	POST OFFICE CLERK	40.4	1.3
03601	BUS INSPECTOR AND TICKET TAKER	25.1	-0.9
03801	TELEGRAPH OPERATOR	47.5	2.2
03930	CLERK	35.4	-7.9
03931	CLERK IN A GOVERNMENT OFFICE	37.1	-7.2

SALES WORKERS

Code	Occupation		
04100	OWNER OF A YARD GOODS STORE	46.3	3.8
04101	DEPARTMENT STORE OWNER-MANAGER	63.3	4.8
04106	IMPORT-EXPORT COMPANY OWNER	68.2	9.8
04410	LIFE INSURANCE SALESMAN	39.4	-5.1
04510	SALESMAN IN A STORE	32.5	-1.2
04512	GAS STATION ATTENDANT	30.5	5.2
04521	SELLER OF FRESH FOOD IN MARKETPLACE (34.4)	23.8	1.9
	PEDDLER WITH A CART (22.8)		
	FOOD PEDDLER (14.2)		

SERVICE WORKERS

Code	Occupation		
05101	COFFEEHOUSE OWNER-OPERATOR	35.7	0.8
05310	RESTAURANT COOK	37.6	6.8
05320	RESTAURANT WAITER	21.1	-2.1
05400	SERVANT	10.3	-6.9
05510	JANITOR	15.9	-5.1
05600	LAUNDRYWOMAN	17.7	-4.4
05700	FULL-TIME BARBER	35.2	4.8
05820	POLICE PRIVATE	34.4	-5.4
05821	MIDDLE RANKING POLICE OFFICER	69.7	10.0
05890	NIGHT WATCHMAN	19.6	-2.4
05920	UNDERTAKER	6.8	-26.8

ISCO NO.	OCCUPATION TITLE	PRESTIGE SCORE	SCORE MINUS STD. SCORE
	THAILAND--TCHRS COL STUDENT		
	AGRICULTURAL, ANIMAL HUSBANDRY AND FORESTRY WORKERS, FISHERMEN AND HUNTERS		
06110	FARMER	56.4	9.3
06113	TENANT FARMER	4.1	-25.3
06120	OWNER OF A MACHINE OPERATED RICE FARM	70.9	15.9
06210	AGRICULTURAL LABORER	25.3	2.4
06280	TRACTOR DRIVER	32.7	1.8
06310	LOGGER	16.4	-2.8
06410	FISHERMAN	39.9	12.3
	PRODUCTION AND RELATED WORKERS, TRANSPORT EQUIPMENT OPERATORS AND LABORERS		
07110	TIN MINER	34.4	3.0
07320	SAWYER OR LABORER IN A SAW MILL	26.8	-3.8
07560	TEXTILE DYER	24.6	-0.5
07710	RICE MILL WORKER	34.9	2.0
07711	OWNER OF A SMALL RICE MILL	39.1	-3.0
07731	SLAUGHTER HOUSE BUTCHER	12.2	-5.8
07740	CANNED FOOD FACTORY WORKER	35.9	0.7
07890	TOBACCO FACTORY WORKER	38.1	-1.1
07910	TAILOR OR DRESS MAKER	45.8	6.3
07911	TAILOR OR DRESS MAKER	45.8	6.4
08010	SHOEMAKER	31.0	2.8
08340	MACHINE OPERATOR	45.3	7.1
08490	MECHANIC	47.8	4.9
08550	ELECTRICIAN	44.5	-0.0
08710	PLUMBER	30.7	-3.1
08731	METAL SMITH	34.9	2.7
08733	BUS BODY BUILDER	40.1	3.6
08800	JEWELER AND GOLDSMITH	50.7	7.8
08920	POTTER	30.2	5.1
09210	PRINTER	46.8	4.5
09310	BUILDING PAINTER	33.0	1.9
09420	BASKET WEAVER	26.5	5.6

Code	Occupation		
09510	BRICK LAYER AND CEMENT WORKER	40.4	6.3
09520	BRICK LAYER AND CEMENT WORKER	40.4	6.0
09540	CARPENTER	39.4	2.2
09594	CONSTRUCTION LABORER	32.7	7.1
09710	LONGSHOREMAN	18.9	-2.3
09811	GONDOLIER	23.1	-0.2
09830	LOCOMOTIVE ENGINEER	49.7	7.1
09851	BUS DRIVER	35.4	3.0
09852	TRUCK DRIVER	29.8	-2.9
09890	PEDICAB DRIVER	15.2	-1.5
09991	UNSKILLED FACTORY WORKER	13.5	-4.6
09995	STREET CLEANER	7.8	-5.6
09997	ROAD WORKER	8.3	-11.8

MEMBERS OF THE ARMED FORCES

Code			
10001	MIDDLE RANKING ARMY OFFICER	65.3	2.0
10003	LOW RANKING ARMY OFFICER OR ARMY PRIVATE	35.4	-3.3

SOURCES OF LIVELIHOOD OTHER THAN LABOR FORCE ACTIVITY

Code			
13001	LANDLORD	53.4	-3.7
13002	LEGATEE WHO DOES NOT HAVE TO WORK	38.1	-9.9
13003	AGRICULTURAL LAND OWNER	56.9	-8.3

ISCO NO.	OCCUPATION TITLE	PRESTIGE SCORE	SCORE MINUS STD. SCORE

THAILAND—UNIVERSITY STUDENT

PROFESSIONAL, TECHNICAL AND RELATED WORKERS

ISCO NO.	OCCUPATION TITLE	PRESTIGE SCORE	SCORE MINUS STD. SCORE
00220	CIVIL ENGINEER	65.3	-5.1
00410	AIRPLANE PILOT	67.3	0.9
00610	PHYSICIAN WITH M.D.	79.7	1.8
00620	DISTRICT DOCTOR	54.6	4.6
00650	VETERINARIAN	61.7	0.4
00670	CERTIFIED PHARMACIST	65.6	1.5
00680	DRUGSTORE OWNER-OPERATOR	45.4	1.0
00710	NURSE IN A HOSPITAL OR CLINIC	52.9	-0.7
00730	MIDWIFE	46.9	0.4
01100	ACCOUNTANT	59.3	4.7
01210	LAWYER	66.6	-4.1
01220	PROVINCIAL COURT JUDGE	75.4	-2.3
01310	UNIVERSITY PROFESSOR	80.1	2.4
01320	INSTRUCTOR IN TEACHERS' TRAINING COLLEGE	60.2	-4.0
01330	TEACHER	58.9	1.9
01414	CHRISTIAN MISSIONARY	49.0	-0.1
01415	BUDDHIST MONK	64.7	8.6
01590	JOURNALIST	55.5	0.6
01630	PHOTOGRAPHER	54.6	9.4
01730	MOVIE SPEAKER	39.8	-11.7
01790	RADIO ANNOUNCER	50.8	0.5
01791	NATIVE STYLE ENTERTAINER	28.4	-4.3
01993	EXPLORER	52.5	3.3

ADMINISTRATIVE AND MANAGERIAL WORKERS

ISCO NO.	OCCUPATION TITLE	PRESTIGE SCORE	SCORE MINUS STD. SCORE
02011	PROVINCIAL GOVERNOR	79.5	-2.4
02012	DISTRICT CHIEF	70.5	4.8
02015	VILLAGE CHIEF	49.0	7.1
02022	REPRESENTATIVE IN LOWER HOUSE	63.0	-9.1
02035	DIVISION CHIEF IN A DISTRICT OFFICE	58.5	-4.6
02113	OWNER OF A RICE MILL (55.5)	54.6	2.3

02114	ICE FACTORY OWNER (53.7)		
02114	BANKER	78.9	12.0
02120	TOBACCO FACTORY MANAGER	73.3	9.1

CLERICAL AND RELATED WORKERS

03210	TYPIST	35.5	-6.1
03310	ACCOUNTING CLERK	37.0	-12.0
03314	POST OFFICE CLERK	33.2	-5.8
03601	BUS INSPECTOR AND TICKET TAKER	20.9	-5.1
03801	TELEGRAPH OPERATOR	37.2	-8.1
03930	CLERK	30.8	-12.5
03931	CLERK IN A GOVERNMENT OFFICE	32.5	-11.8

SALES WORKERS

04100	OWNER OF A YARD GOODS STORE	51.0	8.6
04101	DEPARTMENT STORE OWNER-MANAGER	69.2	10.7
04106	IMPORT-EXPORT COMPANY OWNER	68.8	10.4
04410	LIFE INSURANCE SALESMAN	40.5	-4.0
04510	SALESMAN IN A STORE	35.1	1.5
04512	GAS STATION ATTENDANT	31.4	6.1
04521	SELLER OF FRESH FOOD IN MARKETPLACE (28.9)	23.7	1.7
	PEDDLER WITH A CART (23.5)		
	FOOD PEDDLER (18.6)		

SERVICE WORKERS

05101	COFFEEHOUSE OWNER-OPERATOR	42.2	7.3
05310	RESTAURANT COOK	42.6	11.7
05320	RESTAURANT WAITER	27.8	4.6
05400	SERVANT	17.9	0.7
05510	JANITOR	14.1	-6.9
05600	LAUNDRYWOMAN	24.1	2.0
05700	FULL-TIME BARBER	37.2	6.8
05820	POLICE PRIVATE	27.8	-12.0
05821	MIDDLE RANKING POLICE OFFICER	66.0	6.3
05890	NIGHT WATCHMAN	21.1	-0.9
05920	UNDERTAKER	18.8	-14.8

ISCO NO.	OCCUPATION TITLE	PRESTIGE SCORE	SCORE MINUS STD. SCORE

THAILAND-UNIVERSITY STUDENT

AGRICULTURAL, ANIMAL HUSBANDRY AND FORESTRY WORKERS, FISHERMEN AND HUNTERS

ISCO NO.	OCCUPATION TITLE	PRESTIGE SCORE	SCORE MINUS STD. SCORE
06110	FARMER	59.5	12.4
06113	TENANT FARMER	18.1	-11.4
06120	OWNER OF A MACHINE OPERATED RICE FARM	71.8	16.8
06210	AGRICULTURAL LABORER	27.8	4.9
06280	TRACTOR DRIVER	27.2	-3.6
06310	LOGGER	19.8	0.6
06410	FISHERMAN	38.7	11.1

PRODUCTION AND RELATED WORKERS, TRANSPORT EQUIPMENT OPERATORS AND LABORERS

ISCO NO.	OCCUPATION TITLE	PRESTIGE SCORE	SCORE MINUS STD. SCORE
07110	TIN MINER	24.3	-7.2
07320	SAWYER OR LABORER IN A SAW MILL	23.5	-7.0
07560	TEXTILE DYER	28.0	2.9
07710	RICE MILL WORKER	29.7	-3.2
07711	OWNER OF A SMALL RICE MILL	46.5	4.4
07731	SLAUGHTER HOUSE BUTCHER	16.2	-1.9
07740	CANNED FOOD FACTORY WORKER	31.9	-3.3
07890	TOBACCO FACTORY WORKER	40.7	1.5
07910	TAILOR OR DRESS MAKER	52.3	12.9
07911	TAILOR OR DRESS MAKER	52.3	13.0
08010	SHOEMAKER	28.9	0.8
08340	MACHINE OPERATOR	42.2	4.0
08490	MECHANIC	43.2	0.3
08550	ELECTRICIAN	40.0	-4.5
08710	PLUMBER	27.4	-6.4
08731	METAL SMITH	30.1	-2.1
08733	BUS BODY BUILDER	33.2	-3.2
08800	JEWELER AND GOLDSMITH	48.0	5.1
08920	POTTER	30.4	5.3
09210	PRINTER	37.2	-5.1
09310	BUILDING PAINTER	32.5	1.5
09420	BASKET WEAVER	25.4	4.4

09510	BRICK LAYER AND CEMENT WORKER	27.6	-6.5
09520	BRICK LAYER AND CEMENT WORKER	27.6	-6.8
09540	CARPENTER	37.9	0.7
09594	CONSTRUCTION LABORER	25.2	-0.4
09710	LONGSHOREMAN	19.0	-2.2
09811	GONDOLIER	17.7	-5.6
09830	LOCOMOTIVE ENGINEER	35.5	-7.2
09851	BUS DRIVER	31.0	-1.4
09852	TRUCK DRIVER	25.4	-7.2
09890	PEDICAB DRIVER	15.4	-1.3
09991	UNSKILLED FACTORY WORKER	19.9	-1.8
09995	STREET CLEANER	12.3	-1.1
09997	ROAD WORKER	13.0	-7.1

MEMBERS OF THE ARMED FORCES

| 10001 | MIDDLE RANKING ARMY OFFICER | 63.4 | 0.2 |
| 10003 | LOW RANKING ARMY OFFICER OR ARMY PRIVATE | 34.0 | -4.7 |

SOURCES OF LIVELIHOOD OTHER THAN LABOR FORCE ACTIVITY

13001	LANDLORD	62.5	5.4
13002	LEGATEE WHO DOES NOT HAVE TO WORK	59.1	11.1
13003	AGRICULTURAL LAND OWNER	63.2	-1.9

ISCO NO.	OCCUPATION TITLE	PRESTIGE SCORE	SCORE MINUS STD. SCORE

TURKEY

PROFESSIONAL, TECHNICAL AND RELATED WORKERS

ISCO NO.	OCCUPATION TITLE	PRESTIGE SCORE	SCORE MINUS STD. SCORE
00130	FEN ADAMI/SCIENTIST	75.0	-3.4
00220	MUHENDIS/ENGINEER	78.3	8.0
00610	DOKTOR/PHYSICIAN	81.6	3.7
00630	DISCI/DENTIST	66.9	-3.6
00650	VETERINER/VETERINARIAN	59.9	-1.4
00670	ECZACI/PHARMACIST	69.6	5.5
01100	MUHASIP/ACCOUNTANT	51.3	-3.3
01210	AVUKAT/LAWYER	76.4	5.8
01220	HAKIM/JUDGE	78.0	0.3
01310	UNIVERSITE PROFESORU/UNIVERSITY PROFESSOR	80.6	3.0
01320	LISE OGRETMEN/HIGH SCHOOL TEACHER	70.3	6.1
01330	KOY OGRETMENI/VILLAGE SCHOOL TEACHER	59.6	2.6
01410	IMAM/LEADER OF MOSLEM CONGREGATION	47.1	-12.5
01412	HAFIZ/RELIGIOUS RECITER	45.7	0.0
01490	HOCA/RELIGIOUS TEACHER	50.0	-6.2
01510	MUHARRIR/PROFESSIONAL WRITER	67.6	5.9
01590	GAZETECI/JOURNALIST	58.5	3.5
01610	RESSAM/PAINTER	57.1	-0.1
01710	KONSER PIYANIST/CONCERT PIANIST	57.1	1.0
01730	TEATRO ARTISTI/DRAMATIC ACTOR	46.3	-5.2

ADMINISTRATIVE AND MANAGERIAL WORKERS

ISCO NO.	OCCUPATION TITLE	PRESTIGE SCORE	SCORE MINUS STD. SCORE
02011	VALI/CHIEF PROVINCIAL ADMINISTRATOR	79.7	-2.2
02012	KAYMAKAM/CHIEF COUNTY ADMINISTRATOR	70.7	4.9
02015	KOY MUHTARI/VILLAGE HEADMAN	44.6	2.7
02022	MEBUS/MEMBER OF PARLIAMENT	80.3	8.2
02030	VEKIL/CABINET MINISTER	79.3	0.6
02111	FABRIKATOR/MANUFACTURER	71.8	1.4
02114	BANKA MUDURU/BANK DIRECTOR	70.2	3.2
02195	POLITIKACI/POLITICIAN	61.2	-1.5

CLERICAL AND RELATED WORKERS

Code	Occupation		
03101	MEMUR/CIVIL SERVANT	54.7	1.1
03102	MUFETTIS/OFFICIAL INSPECTOR	69.1	8.0
03211	SEKRETER/SECRETARY	55.1	2.2

SALES WORKERS

Code	Occupation		
04100	BAKKAL/GROCER (43.8)	31.4	-11.0
	KUCUK DUKKANCI/SHOP KEEPER (34.5)		
	ESKURBACI/USED CLOTHING DEALER (15.9)		
04101	BUYUK DUKKANCI/RETAILER, LARGE STORE	52.3	-6.2
04521	SOKAK SATICISI/STREET VENDOR	18.9	-3.1

SERVICE WORKERS

Code	Occupation		
05101	KREAPCI/SMALL SHORT-ORDER RESTAURANT PROPRIETOR	26.5	-8.4
05104	MEYHANECI/TAVERN KEEPER	15.2	-17.6
05320	GARSON/WAITER	22.0	-1.3
05400	HIZMETCI/SERVANT	12.0	-5.2
05510	KAPICI/JANITOR	14.0	-7.1
C5700	BERBEB/EARBER	36.2	5.8

AGRICULTURAL, ANIMAL HUSBANDRY AND FORESTRY WORKERS, FISHERMEN AND HUNTERS

Code	Occupation		
06112	KOYLU CIFTCI/VILLAGE FARMER, PEASANT	43.4	5.8
06240	COBAN/SHEPHERD	16.5	-9.1
0627C	BAHCEVAN/GARDENER	29.1	7.7
06410	BALIKCI/FISHERMAN	28.1	0.5

PRODUCTION AND RELATED WORKERS, TRANSPORT EQUIPMENT OPERATORS AND LABORERS

Code	Occupation		
07730	KASAP/BUTCHER	32.0	0.7
07910	TERZI/TAILOR	44.4	4.9
08010	KUNDURACI/SHOEMAKER	36.8	8.7
08420	SAATCI/WATCH REPAIRMAN AND MAKER	43.6	3.8
08430	OTOMOBIL TAMIRCISI/AUTO MECHANIC	41.8	-1.4
08731	BAKIRCI/COPPERSMITH	30.7	-1.4
09310	BINA BOYACISI/HOUSE PAINTER	29.7	-1.4
09540	MARANGOZ/CARPENTER	40.4	3.2
09712	HAMMAL/PORTER	11.1	-5.7
09810	GEMICI/SEAMAN	42.5	7.8

ISCO NO.	OCCUPATION TITLE	PRESTIGE SCORE	SCORE MINUS STD. SCORE
	TURKEY		
09852	SOFOR/DRIVER	33.4	0.8
09860	DEVECI/CAMEL DRIVER	15.0	-3.1
MEMBERS OF THE ARMED FORCES			
10000	ALBAY/COLONEL	79.6	6.6
10001	TEGMEN/LIEUTENANT	66.3	3.0
10003	ER/SOLDIER, PRIVATE	50.6	11.8
SOURCES OF LIVELIHOOD OTHER THAN LABOR FORCE ACTIVITY			
13003	CIFTLIK SAHIBI/AGRICULTURAL LANDLORD	58.8	-6.3
13006	DILENCI/BEGGAR	9.6	-5.0

PROFESSIONAL, TECHNICAL AND RELATED WORKERS

Code	Occupation		
00531	AGRICULTURAL OFFICER	72.4	17.6
00610	DOCTOR	84.5	6.6
00710	MALE NURSE	47.5	-9.1
00793	SANITARY INSPECTOR	47.3	-0.2
01210	LAWYER	80.7	10.0
01220	JUDGE (BUGANDA GOVERNMENT)	70.0	-7.7
01310	UNIVERSITY LECTURER	81.7	4.0
01320	SECONDARY SCHOOL TEACHER	61.6	-2.6
01330	PRIMARY SCHOOL TEACHER	45.3	-11.7
01390	AGRICULTURAL INSTRUCTOR	51.7	-5.1
01410	ROMAN CATHOLIC PRIEST (69.2)	66.7	7.0
01590	CLERGYMAN (ANGLICAN CHURCH) (64.2)	40.5	-14.4
01591	NEWSPAPER REPORTER	57.6	-7.4
01630	EDITOR OF A NEWSPAPER (LUGUANDA NEWSPAPER)	43.5	-1.6
01712	PHOTOGRAPHER (SELF-EMPLOYED)	41.2	9.7
	BAND MASTER (44.5)		
	DANCE BAND MUSICIAN (37.9)		
01790	RADIO ANNOUNCER	49.7	-0.6
01990	LABORATORY ASSISTANT	50.9	-7.3

ADMINISTRATIVE AND MANAGERIAL WORKERS

Code	Occupation		
02012	SAZA CHIEF (BUGANDA)/COUNTY CHIEF (69.6)	62.1	-3.7
	GAMBOLOLA CHIEF (BUGANDA)/SUB COUNTY CHIEF (54.6)		
02015	MULUKA CHIEF (BUGANDA)/PARISH CHIEF	38.1	-3.8
02022	MEMBER OF THE LEGCO (NATIONAL LEGISLATURE)	73.8	1.7
02023	MEMBER OF LUKIKO (BUGANDA LEGISLATURE)	61.4	-4.3
02030	MINISTER IN H.H. THE KABAKA'S GOVERNMENT	85.3	6.6
02110	DIRECTOR OF COMPANIES	76.8	1.8
02116	BUILDING CONTRACTOR	58.4	5.0
02195	POLITICAL PARTY LEADER	65.2	2.5

ISCO NO.	OCCUPATION TITLE	PRESTIGE SCORE	SCORE MINUS STD. SCORE
	UGANDA		
	CLERICAL AND RELATED WORKERS		
03101	ASSISTANT COMMUNITY DEVELOPMENT OFFICER	58.8	5.1
03102	LABOUR INSPECTOR	55.4	-5.8
03210	TYPIST	43.7	2.1
03310	ACCOUNTS CLERK	51.1	2.2
03314	POST OFFICE WORKER (BEHIND THE COUNTER)	42.7	3.7
03601	BUS CONDUCTOR	31.9	5.9
03701	OFFICE BOY	16.6	-9.2
03800	TELEPHONE OPERATOR	40.1	1.7
03930	CLERK	44.5	1.2
	SALES WORKERS		
04100	SHOPKEEPER (45.3)	44.2	1.8
	PROPRIETOR OF BAR AND SMALL SHOP (43.1)		
04105	CATTLE TRADER	41.7	1.7
04106	WHOLESALE MERCHANT	59.2	0.8
04311	PETROL COMPANY SALESMAN	41.7	0.0
04510	SHOP ASSISTANT (IN A LARGE SHOP IN KAMPALA) (41.1)	33.3	-0.4
	SHOP ASSISTANT (IN A SMALL VILLAGE DUKA) (25.4)		
04512	PETROL PUMP ATTENDANT	18.6	-6.7
04521	FISH SELLER (25.2)	19.7	-2.3
	MATOKE (BANANA) SELLER (AT THE MARKET) (24.8)		
	CHARCOAL SELLER (15.6)		
	WATER SELLER (SELLING WATER BY THE DEBE/CAN) (13.0)		
04523	NEWSPAPER SELLER (ON THE STREET)	14.2	0.1
	SERVICE WORKERS		
05002	HOUSING ESTATE MANAGER	55.0	8.3
05102	HOTEL KEEPER	39.1	-7.3
05320	HOTEL WAITER (LARGE HOTEL IN KAMPALA)	27.3	4.0
05400	COOK-HOUSEBOY	16.6	-0.6

Code	Occupation		
05600	DHOBI/LAUNDERER-SELF EMPLOYED	23.4	1.3
05701	BARBER (SELF-EMPLOYED)	25.6	-10.9
05820	POLICEMAN (PROT. GOVT.) (41.5)	36.7	-3.1
05821	POLICEMAN (BUGANDA GOVERNMENT) (31.9)	57.5	-2.2
	POLICE OFFICER (RANK OF INSPECTO) (65.2)		
	POLICE SERGEANT (49.7)		
05890	WATCHMAN	18.6	-3.4
05990	MEDICAL ORDERLY	38.9	-2.7

AGRICULTURAL, ANIMAL HUSBANDRY AND FORESTRY WORKERS, FISHERMEN AND HUNTERS

Code	Occupation		
06110	FARMER (EMPLOYS 2 TO 3 PORTERS)	42.7	-4.4
06111	FARMER (EMPLOYING A LARGE NUMBER OF PORTERS)	69.0	5.6
06112	FARMER (EMPLOYING NO PORTERS)	25.8	-11.8
06270	SHAMBA-BOY/GARDENER	11.0	-10.4
06410	FISHERMAN	31.3	3.7

PRODUCTION AND RELATED WORKERS, TRANSPORT EQUIPMENT OPERATORS AND LABORERS

Code	Occupation		
07000	LABOURERS' FOREMAN	34.9	-4.4
07730	MEAT SELLER	29.5	-1.9
07910	TAILOR (SELF-EMPLOYED)	38.5	-1.0
08010	SHOE REPAIRER (SELF-EMPLOYED)	29.7	1.5
08310	BLACKSMITH	32.7	-1.8
08420	WATCH REPAIRER (SELF-EMPLOYED)	36.9	-2.9
08430	GARAGE MECHANIC	38.9	-4.0
08431	PROPRIETOR OF PETROL STAND	46.3	-0.9
08491	BICYCLE REPAIRER (SELF-EMPLOYED)	25.0	-2.5
08492	LEARNER MECHANIC	29.5	-1.8
08550	ELECTRICIAN	54.0	9.4
09310	HOUSE PAINTER	26.4	-4.6
09510	BRICKLAYER	33.3	-0.8
09540	CARPENTER	41.5	4.3
09850	TAXI DRIVER	29.1	1.3
09851	BUS DRIVER	33.9	1.5
09852	LORRY DRIVER	27.9	-4.7
09853	TRANSPORT CONTRACTOR (OWNING ONE LORRY)	42.3	-2.9
09990	PORTER/UNSKILLED LABORER	13.4	-5.7
09995	SANITARY SWEEPER	14.2	0.8

ISCO NO.	OCCUPATION TITLE	PRESTIGE SCORE	SCORE MINUS STD. SCORE
	UGANDA		
	MEMBERS OF THE ARMED FORCES		
10003	SOLDIER (K.A.R.)	43.1	4.4
	SOURCES OF LIVELIHOOD OTHER THAN LABOR FORCE ACTIVITY		
13001	LANDOWNER (WITH MANY TENANTS)	64.8	7.7

PROFESSIONAL, TECHNICAL AND RELATED WORKERS

06610	DOCTOR	80.4	2.5
00710	NURSE	60.5	7.0
00792	HERBALIST	28.8	0.0
01210	LAWYER	76.4	5.8
01310	UNIVERSITY LECTURER	72.4	-5.2
01330	TEACHER	64.5	7.5
01410	MINISTER OF RELIGION	68.5	8.8
01610	ARTIST	56.6	-0.6
01930	SOCIAL WORKER	44.7	-11.6

CLERICAL AND RELATED WORKERS

03101	CIVIL SERVANT	36.7	-16.9
03930	CLERK	52.6	9.3

SALES WORKERS

04520	TRADER	40.7	4.6

AGRICULTURAL, ANIMAL HUSBANDRY AND FORESTRY WORKERS, FISHERMEN AND HUNTERS

06110	FARMER	48.6	1.6

PRODUCTION AND RELATED WORKERS, TRANSPORT EQUIPMENT OPERATORS AND LABORERS

09540	CARPENTER	32.8	-4.4
09970	FACTORY WORKER	24.8	-4.4
09990	LABORER	20.9	1.8

ISCO NO.	OCCUPATION TITLE	PRESTIGE SCORE	SCORE MINUS STD. SCORE
	U.S.S.R.		
	PROFESSIONAL, TECHNICAL AND RELATED WORKERS		
00110	NAUCHNYI RABOTNIKI V OBLASTI: KHIMII/CHEMIST	77.1	7.9
00120	NAUCHNYI RABOTNIKI V OBLASTI: FIZIKI/PHYSICIST	79.5	3.0
00131	NAUCHNYI RABOTNIKI V OBLASTI: GEOLOGI/GEOLOGIST (70.7)	66.8	-0.6
	INZHENER GEOLOG/GEOLOGICAL ENGINEER (62.8)		
00220	INZHENER-STROITEL'/CONSTRUCTION ENGINEER	65.2	-5.2
00230	INZHENER-RADIOTEKHNIK/RADIO ENGINEER (56.8)	64.4	-0.9
	INZHENER-ELEKTRIK/ELECTRICAL ENGINEER (63.6)		
	INZHENER-SVIAZIST/COMMUNICATIONS ENGINEER (62.9)		
00240	INZHENER-MASHINOSTROITEL'/MECHANICAL ENGINEER	65.2	-1.3
00250	INZHENER-KHIMIK/CHEMICAL ENGINEER (67.6)	65.6	-0.9
	INZHENER-NEFTIANIK/OIL ENGINEER (63.6)		
00260	INZHENEF-METALLURG/METALLURGICAL ENGINEER	64.4	4.3
00270	GORNYI INZHENER/MINING ENGINEER	65.2	2.4
00290	INZHENER-TRANSPORTNIK/TRANSPORTATION ENGINEER (60.4)	55.2	0.0
	INZHENER-TEKSTIL'SHCHIK/TEXTILE ENGINEER (55.6)		
	INZHENER-SHVEINIK/SEWING INDUSTRY ENGINEER (53.3)		
	INZHENER-PISHCHEVIK/FOOD ENGINEER (51.7)		
00410	LETCHIK/AIRPLANE PILOT	69.9	3.5
00510	NAUCHNYI RABOTNIKI V OBLASTI: BIOLOGII/BIOLOGIST	70.7	2.0
00520	NAUCHNYI RABOTNIKI V OBLASTI: MEDITSINY/MEDICAL RESEARCHER	79.5	0.6
00530	AGRONOM/AGRONOMIST	48.5	-9.3
00610	VRACH/PHYSICIAN	76.3	-1.6
00620	MEDSESTRA, FEL'DSHER/NURSE, MEDICAL ASSISTANT	40.6	-9.4
00650	VRACH-VETERINAR/VETERINARIAN	51.7	-9.7
00710	MEDSESTRA, FEL'DSHER/NURSE, MEDICAL ASSISTANT	40.6	-13.0
00820	NAUCHNYI RABOTNIKI V OBLASTI: MATEMATIKI/MATHEMATICIAN	77.1	8.0
00900	EKONOMIKO-MATEMATICHESKIE ISSLEDOVANIIA/MATHEMATICAL ECONOMIC RESEARCHER (68.3)		
	NAUCHNYI RABOTNIKI V OBLASTI:EKONOMIKI/ECONOMIST (66.0)	57.2	-3.3
	EKONOMIST, PLANOVIK/ECONOMIST, PLANNER (37.4)		
01100	BUKHGALTER, SCHETOVOD/BOOKKEEPER, ACCOUNTANT	22.3	-32.3
01310	PREPODAVATEL' VYSSHIKH SHKOL/HIGHER EDUCATION INSTRUCTOR	66.8	-10.9

01320	PREPODAVATEL' SREDNIKH SHKOL/SECONDARY SCHOOL TEACHER	56.4	-7.7
01330	UCHITEL' NACHAL'NYKH SHKCL/PRIMARY SCHOOL TEACHER	51.7	-5.3
01340	VOSPITATEL' DETSADA/EDUCATOR IN CHILD-CARE INSTITUTION	49.3	0.0
01510	RABCTNIK LITERATURY I ISKUSSTVA/LITERARY AND ARTISTIC PERSONNEL	70.7	9.0
01610	RABOTNIK LITERATURY I ISKUSSTVA/LITERARY AND ARTISTIC PERSONNEL	70.7	13.6
01923	NAUCHNYI RABOTNIKI V OBLASTI: ISTORI/HISTORIAN	66.0	-1.3
01924	NAUCHNYI RABOTNIKI V OBLASTI: FILOSOFI/PHILOSOPHER	69.9	1.1
01951	NAUCHNYI RABOTNIKI V OBLASTI: FILOLOGI/PHILOLOGIST	69.1	0.0

CLERICAL AND RELATED WORKERS

03101	RABOTNIK KOMMUNAL'NYKH PREDPRIIATII/COMMUNAL FUNCTIONARY	25.5	-28.2
03310	BUKHGALTER, SCHETOVOD/BOOKKEEPER, ACCOUNTANT	22.3	-26.7
03420	OPERATOF NA-AVTOMATOV OBORUDOVANIYA/AUTOMATIC EQUIPMENT OPERATOR	48.5	-4.3
03700	POCHTAL'CN/MAILMAN	38.2	5.3
03930	DELCPROIZVODITEL'/OFFICE WORKER	26.3	-17.1
03992	KUL'TPROSVETRABOTNIK/CULTURAL AND INFORMAL EDUCATION WORKER	42.9	-5.3

SALES WORKERS

| 04510 | PRODAVETS/SALESMAN | 29.4 | -4.2 |

SERVICE WORKERS

| 05310 | POVAR, OFITSIANT/COOK, WAITER | 31.0 | 0.2 |
| 05320 | FOVAR, OFITSIANT/CCOK, WAITER | 31.0 | 7.8 |

AGRICULTURAL, ANIMAL HUSBANDRY AND FORESTRY WORKERS, FISHERMEN AND HUNTERS

06220	RABOTNIK POLEVODSTVA/FIELD CROP PERSONNEL	32.6	11.3
06240	RABOTNIK ZHIVOTNOVODSTVA/LIVE STOCK RAISING PERSONNEL	34.2	8.6
06280	TRAKTORIST, KCMBAINER/TRACTOR OR COMBINE OPERATOR	36.6	5.7
06310	RABOCHII LESOZAGOTOVOK/LOGGER	29.4	10.2
06320	LESOVOD/FORESTER	47.7	0.2

PRODUCTION AND RELATED WORKERS, TRANSPORT EQUIPMENT OPERATORS AND LABORERS

07110	SHAKHTER/MINER	54.1	22.6
07210	STALEVAR/STEEL FCUNDER	53.3	7.9
07490	RABOCHII-KHIMIK/CHEMICAL WORKER	42.9	0.0
07520	TKACH, PRIADIL'SHCHIK/WEAVER,SPINNER	36.6	3.0
07540	TKACH, FRIADIL'SHCHIK/WEAVER, SPINNER	36.6	6.2

ISCO NO.	OCCUPATION TITLE U.S.S.R.	PRESTIGE SCORE	SCORE MINUS STD. SCORE
07910	PORTNOI, SHBEIA/TAILOR, SEAMSTRESS	38.2	-1.3
07911	PORTNOI, SHBEIA/TAILOR, SEAMSTRESS	38.2	-1.2
08010	OBUVSHCHIK/SHOE WORKER	35.0	-6.9
08110	STCLIAR, PLOTNIK/CARPFNTER, CABINETMAKER	34.2	-6.2
08310	KUZNETS/BLACKSMITH	37.4	-2.9
08320	SLESAR'-INSTRUMENTAL'SHCHIK/TOOL AND DIE MAKER	39.8	-0.5
08331	TCKAR/LATHE OPERATOR	38.2	-1.6
08340	FREZEROVSHCHIK/MILLING MACHINE OPERATOR (37.4)	36.3	-1.9
	KARUCEL'SHCHIK/VERTICAL TURRET LATHE CPEFATOR (35.8)		
	RASTOCHNIK/BORING MACHINE OPERATOR (35.8)		
08351	SHILFOBSHCHIK/POLISHING MACHINE OPER.TOR	35.0	0.0
08410	SLESAR'-REMONTNIK/MACHINIST-REPAIRMAN	44.5	1.2
08421	NALADCHIK AVTCMATOV/AUTOMATIC EQUIPMENT SETUP AND REPAIRMAN	47.7	5.3
08490	MOTOFIST/MOTER OPERATOR (42.9)	42.9	0.1
	MEKHANIK/MECHANIC (42.9)		
08550	ELEKTROMCNTER/ELECTRICIAN	38.2	-6.4
08610	RADIOTEKHNIK/RADIO TECHNICIAN	54.1	1.3
08720	ELEKTRO-I GAZOSVARSHCHIK/ELECTRIC AND GAS WELDER	39.0	-0.3
08740	SUDOSTROITEL'/SHIP BUILDER	51.7	8.1
09210	POLIGRAFIST/PRINTER	35.0	-7.3
09310	MALIAR/BUILDING PAINTER	28.6	-2.4
09510	KAMENSHCHIK, SHTUKATUR/BRICK LAYER, PLASTERER	31.8	-2.3
09540	STOLIAR, PLOTNIK/CARPENTER, CABINETMAKER	34.2	-3.0
09550	KAMENSHCHIK, SHTUKATUR/BRICK LAYER, PLASTERER	31.8	-0.9
09593	STEOTTEL'-MONTAZHNIK/BUILDING ERECTOR	41.4	-4.1
09810	RABOTNIK MORSKOVO I RECHNOI FLOTA/WORKER IN SEA OR RIVER INDUSTRY	50.9	16.1
09830	MASHINIST TEPLOVOZA/LOCOMOTIVE ENGINEER	42.9	0.3
09852	SHOFER/DRIVER	45.3	12.7

MEMBERS OF THE ARMED FORCES

10001	VOENNYI/MILITARY CAREERIST	60.4	-2.8

UNCLASSIFIABLE OCCUPATIONS

12000   RABOTNIK-ZHELEZNODOROCZHNOVO/RAILROAD PERSONNEL   37.4   -2.5

ISCO NO.	OCCUPATION TITLE	PRESTIGE SCORE	SCORE MINUS STD. SCORE
	URUGUAY		
	PROFESSIONAL, TECHNICAL AND RELATED WORKERS		
00410	AVIADOR/AIRPLANE PILOT	55.0	-11.5
00610	MEDICO/PHYSICIAN	77.0	-0.8
01100	CONTADOR/ACCOUNTANT	57.4	2.9
01210	ABOGADO/LAWYER	74.6	3.9
01290	ESCRIBANO/NON-TRIAL LAWYER	72.1	1.5
01330	MAESTRO/PUBLIC SCHOOL TEACHER	67.2	10.2
01410	SACERDOTE/PRIEST	62.3	2.7
01590	PERIODISTA/JOURNALIST	47.6	-7.3
	ADMINISTRATIVE AND MANAGERIAL WORKERS		
02112	GERENTE DE CAMPANIA COMERCIAL/MANAGER OF A BUSINESS FIRM	59.9	-2.9
02114	GERENTE DE BANCO/BANKER	64.8	-2.2
	CLERICAL AND RELATED WORKERS		
03101	EMPLEADO PUBLICO/CIVIL SERVANT	52.5	-1.1
	SALES WORKERS		
04100	PEQUENO COMERCIANTE/SMALL BUSINESSMAN	50.1	7.7
04320	VIAJERO COMERCIAL/TRAVELING SALESMAN	45.2	-1.7
	SERVICE WORKERS		
05310	COCINERO/COOK	23.1	-7.7
05320	MOZO DE CAFE/CAFE WAITER	25.6	2.3
05820	GUARDIA CIVIL (POLICIA)/POLICEMAN	28.0	-11.8

AGRICULTURAL, ANIMAL HUSBANDRY AND FORESTRY WORKERS, FISHERMEN AND HUNTERS			
06111	ESTANCIERO/LARGE RANCHER	69.7	6.3
06210	PEON/AGRICULTURAL LABORER	15.8	-7.2
06280	TRACTORISTA/TRACTOR DRIVER	30.5	-0.4
PRODUCTION AND RELATED WORKERS, TRANSPORT EQUIPMENT OPERATORS AND LABORERS			
08340	MAQUINISTA/MACHINE OPERATOR	32.0	-5.3
08490	MECANICO/MECHANIC	42.7	-0.1
09210	IMPRESOR/PRINTER	37.8	-4.5
09540	CARPINTERO/CARPENTER	40.3	3.1
09595	PICAPEDRERO/STONE BREAKER	20.7	5.5
09713	CHANGADOR/RAILWAY STATION PORTER	18.2	0.1
09852	CHOFER/DRIVER	35.4	2.8

ISCO NO.	OCCUPATION TITLE	PRESTIGE SCORE	SCORE MINUS STD. SCORE
	YUGOSLAVIA		

PROFESSIONAL, TECHNICAL AND RELATED WORKERS

ISCO NO.	OCCUPATION TITLE	PRESTIGE SCORE	SCORE MINUS STD. SCORE
00210	ARCHITECT, 4 YEARS COLLEGE	69.4	-2.4
00220	CIVIL ENGINEER, 4 YEARS COLLEGE	70.0	-0.4
00240	MECHANICAL ENGINEER, 4 YEARS COLLEGE	72.2	5.7
00270	MINING ENGINEER, 4 YEARS COLLEGE	63.3	0.6
00290	AGRICULTURAL ENGINEER, 4 YEARS COLLEGE	66.6	11.4
00320	TECHNICAL DRAFTSMAN, HIGH SCHOOL	38.0	-16.9
00380	MINING TECHNICIAN, HIGH SCHOOL	50.1	-4.2
00540	MEDICAL TECHNICIAN, HIGH SCHOOL	54.0	-4.0
00541	AGRICULTURAL TECHNICIAN, 2 YEARS COLLEGE (61.1)	56.2	9.5
	AGRICULTURAL TECHNICIAN, HIGH SCHOOL (51.2)		
00610	MEDICAL DOCTOR	71.1	-6.8
00650	VETERINARIAN, 2 YEARS COLLEGE	61.7	0.3
00900	ECONOMIST, 4 YEARS COLLEGE (66.1)	58.4	-2.1
	ECONOMIST, HIGH SCHOOL (50.7)		
01100	ACCOUNTANT, HIGH SCHOOL	41.3	-13.3
01210	LAWYER, 4 YEARS COLLEGE	68.8	-1.8
01310	UNIVERSITY PROFESSOR WITH PH.D.	71.6	-6.0
01320	HIGH SCHOOL TEACHER, 4 YEARS COLLEGE (64.4)	61.4	-2.8
	HIGH SCHOOL TEACHER, 2 YEARS COLLEGE (58.4)		
01330	ELEMENTARY SCHOOL TEACHER, HIGH SCHOOL DIPLOMA	43.5	-13.5
01410	PRIEST, 4 YEARS COLLEGE	39.1	-20.6
01610	ARTIST, 4 YEARS COLLEGE	68.3	11.1
01730	ACTOR, 4 YEARS COLLEGE	67.2	15.7
01800	PROFESSIONAL ATHLETE	59.5	11.0

ADMINISTRATIVE AND MANAGERIAL WORKERS

ISCO NO.	OCCUPATION TITLE	PRESTIGE SCORE	SCORE MINUS STD. SCORE
02111	ADMINISTRATIVE DIRECTOR, 4 YEARS COLLEGE (70.5)	69.1	-1.3
	ADMINISTRATIVE DIRECTOR, 2 YEARS COLLEGE (67.7)		
02192	ADMINISTRATIVE HEAD OF DEPARTMENT, 4 YEARS COLLEGE (62.2)	57.8	-2.7
	ADMINISTRATIVE HEAD OF DEPARTMENT, HIGH SCHOOL (53.4)		

CLERICAL AND RELATED WORKERS

Code	Description		
03210	CLERK-TYPIST, ELEMENTARY SCHOOL	27.0	-14.6
03310	BOOKKEEPER, HIGH SCHOOL (49.0)	41.0	-7.9
	BOOKKEEPER, ELEMENTARY SCHOOL (33.0)		
03313	BANK CLERK, HIGH SCHOOL (52.9)	44.1	-3.6
	BANK CLERK, ELEMENTARY SCHOOL (35.2)		
03314	POSTAL CLERK, HIGH SCHOOL (35.8)	29.7	-9.3
	POSTAL CLERK, UNSKILLED (23.7)		
03390	BUDGET CLERK, ELEMENTARY SCHOOL	29.2	-13.0
03590	DISPATCHER, ELEMENTARY SCHOOL	27.5	-9.3
03701	MESSENGER, ELEMENTARY SCHOOL	19.8	-6.0
03910	CONTROL CLERK, HIGH SCHOOL	46.3	14.2
03930	CLERK, 4 YEARS COLLEGE (60.0)	48.5	5.1
	BUSINESS OFFICE CLERK, HIGH SCHOOL (51.8)		
	CLERK, HIGH SCHOOL (44.6)		
	BUSINESS OFFICE CLERK, ELEMENTARY SCHOOL (37.4)		
03941	RAILWAY CLERK, HIGH SCHOOL	38.5	1.9

SALES WORKERS

Code	Description		
04210	COMMERCIAL SPECIALIST, 4 YEARS COLLEGE	65.5	13.1
04510	SALESMAN, 2 YEARS COLLEGE (60.6)	37.9	4.3
	SALESMAN, HIGH SCHOOL (49.6)		
	SALESMAN, ELEMENTARY SCHOOL (31.4)		
	SALES CLERK, ELEMENTARY SCHOOL (26.4)		
	SALES CLERK, UNSKILLED (21.5)		

SERVICE WORKERS

Code	Description		
05320	WAITER, SKILLED	43.0	19.7
05702	HAIRDRESSER, SKILLED	48.5	13.7
05820	POLICEMAN, SKILLED	24.8	-15.0

AGRICULTURAL, ANIMAL HUSBANDRY AND FORESTRY WORKERS, FISHERMEN AND HUNTERS

Code	Description		
06112	PEASANT, SMALL-HOLDER WITH GOOD LAND	44.1	6.4
06210	LANDLESS PEASANT	20.4	-2.6
06280	TRACTOR DRIVER, SKILLED	28.1	-2.8
06320	FORESTER, ELEMENTARY SCHOOL	29.7	-17.8

ISCO NO.	OCCUPATION TITLE	PRESTIGE SCORE	SCORE MINUS STD. SCORE
	YUGOSLAVIA		
	PRODUCTION AND RELATED WORKERS, TRANSPORT EQUIPMENT OPERATORS AND LABORERS		
07280	GALVANIZER, SKILLED (31.9)	28.1	0.0
	GALVANIZER, SEMI-SKILLED (24.2)		
07730	BUTCHER, SKILLED	39.6	8.3
07910	TAILOR,SKILLED (41.9)	33.9	-5.6
	VILLAGE TAILOR, SKILLED (25.9)		
08010	SHOEMAKER, SKILLED	34.1	6.0
08310	BLACKSMITH, SKILLED	25.3	-9.2
08320	TOOL-AND-DIE MAKER, HIGHLY SKILLED (55.6)	51.2	10.9
	TOOL-AND-DIE MAKER, SKILLED (46.8)		
08331	LATHE OPERATOR, HIGHLY SKILLED (55.1)	47.9	11.4
	LATHE OPERATOR, SKILLED (40.8)		
08340	METAL TRIMMER, SKILLED (47.4)	33.6	-4.6
	BORING-TOOL OPERATOR, SKILLED (33.6)		
	METAL TRIMMER, SEMI-SKILLED (30.8)		
	BORING-TOOL OPERATOR, SEMISKILLED (22.6)		
08390	LOCKSMITH, SKILLED (45.2)	37.7	-2.4
	LOCKSMITH, SEMI-SKILLED (30.3)		
08410	MACHINIST, SKILLED	47.9	4.6
08412	INSTALLER, SKILLED	40.2	0.0
08420	WATCHMAKER AND REPAIRMAN, SKILLED	52.3	12.6
08430	AUTO MECHANIC, HIGHLY SKILLED (63.9)	60.0	17.1
	AUTO MECHANIC, SKILLED (56.2)		
08440	AIRCRAFT MECHANIC, HIGHLY SKILLED (62.8)	58.7	9.1
	AIRCRAFT MECHANIC, SKILLED (54.5)		
08490	MACHINE TECHNICIAN, HIGH SCHOOL	57.8	15.0
08550	ELECTRICIAN, HIGHLY SKILLED (56.7)	51.2	6.7
	ELECTRICIAN, SKILLED (45.7)		
08731	TINSMITH, SKILLED (35.2)	29.2	-3.0
	COPPERSMITH, SKILLED (23.1)		
09510	MASON, SKILLED	32.5	-1.6
09540	CARPENTER, SKILLED	36.9	-0.3
09593	CONSTRUCTION TECHNICIAN, HIGH SCHOOL	58.9	13.5

Code	Occupation		
09595	MASON, UNSKILLED	20.9	5.7
09712	PORTER, UNSKILLED	17.6	0.8
09820	STOKER, HIGHLY SKILLED (34.7)	25.3	-0.1
	STOKER, SKILLED (22.0)		
	STOKER, SEMI-SKILLED (19.3)		
09830	RAILWAY ENGINEER, SKILLED	28.6	-14.0
09852	DRIVER, SKILLED	42.4	9.8
09990	MACHINE CLEANER, UNSKILLED	18.2	-1.0
09994	RAILWAY WORKER, UNSKILLED	18.7	-14.5

MEMBERS OF THE ARMED FORCES

10001	MILITARY OFFICER, 4 YEARS COLLEGE (65.0)	61.1	-2.1
	ARMY OFFICER, 2 YEARS MILITARY ACADEMY (57.3)		

ISCO NO.	OCCUPATION TITLE	PRESTIGE SCORE	SCORE MINUS STD. SCORE
	ZAMBIA		
	PROFESSIONAL, TECHNICAL AND RELATED WORKERS		
01320	SECONDARY SCHOOL TEACHER	62.1	-2.1
01330	PRIMARY SCHOOL TEACHER	50.9	-6.1
01391	HEADMASTER	59.8	-5.7
01392	AFRICAN EDUCATION OFFICER	67.1	-0.5
01410	AFRICAN MINISTER OF RELIGION	62.8	3.1
01930	AFRICAN WELFARE OFFICER	59.8	3.6
01931	SOCIAL ORGANIZER (MINE)	51.4	2.5
01940	AFRICAN PERSONNEL OFFICER	56.4	-2.1
	ADMINISTRATIVE AND MANAGERIAL WORKERS		
02196	T.U. BRANCH SECRETARY	52.3	2.8
	CLERICAL AND RELATED WORKERS		
03000	SENIOR CLERK (MINE)	51.4	-3.2
03101	SENIOR CLERK (BOMA)/GOVERNMENT	50.2	-3.4
03210	TYPIST	41.1	-0.5
03701	BOMA MESSENGER/GOVERNMENT MESSENGER (28.3)	26.2	0.4
	OFFICE MESSENGER (24.0)		
	SALES WORKERS		
04100	SHOP OWNER	53.4	11.0
04512	PETROL PUMP BOY	24.2	1.0
04521	FISH SELLER	30.4	8.5
	SERVICE WORKERS		
05320	HOTEL WAITER	22.2	-1.0
05400	DOMESTIC SERVANT	20.4	3.2
05820	AFRICAN CONSTABLE	27.9	-11.9

492

Code	Occupation		
05821	AFRICAN POLICE INSPECTOR	51.6	-8.1
05990	MEDICAL ORDERLY	47.1	5.4

AGRICULTURAL, ANIMAL HUSBANDRY AND FORESTRY WORKERS, FISHERMEN AND HUNTERS

Code	Occupation		
06270	GARDEN BOY	11.7	-9.7
06310	WOOD CUTTER	16.9	-2.3

PRODUCTION AND RELATED WORKERS, TRANSPORT EQUIPMENT OPERATORS AND LABORERS

Code	Occupation		
07000	BOSS BOY (MINE) (43.6)	39.4	0.1
07111	CONTRACTOR'S-CAPITAO (35.2) SUB-DEVELOPMENT CLEANER (39.5) PIPE LAYER (MINE) (37.9) MACHINE BOY (33.1)	36.9	0.9
07113	UNDERGROUND INSTRUCTOR	43.9	0.0
08010	SHOEMAKER	31.5	3.4
08430	GARAGE MECHANIC	43.9	0.9
08710	PLUMBER	36.6	2.7
09310	PAINTER	33.6	2.6
09510	BRICKLAYER	38.6	4.5
09540	CARPENTER	42.3	5.1
09595	TRENCH DIGGER	19.5	4.2
09713	STATION BOY	22.2	4.1
09852	LORRY DRIVER	33.4	0.8
09853	BUS OWNER	53.2	13.8
09996	SCAVENGER	13.5	0.9
09997	ROAD WORKER	20.4	0.3

References

Aberle, D. F., A. K. Cohen, A. K. Davis, M. J. Levy, Jr., and F. X. Sutton
  1950 "The functional prerequisites of a society." Ethics 60 (January):100–111.
Achebe, C.
  1969 Arrow of God. New York: Doubleday (Anchor Books).
Alzobaie, A. J., and M. A. A. El-Ghannam
  1968 "Iraqi student perceptions of occupations." Sociology and Social Research 52 (April):231–236.
Anscombe, F. J.
  1968 "Statistical analysis, special problems of: I. Outliers." Pp. 15:178–182 in David L. Sills (ed.), International Encyclopedia of the Social Sciences. New York: Macmillan.
Armer, M. J.
  1968 "Intersociety and intrasociety correlations of occupational prestige." American Journal of Sociology 74 (July):28–36.
Bailey, F. G.
  1957 Caste and the Economic Frontier: A Village in Highland Orissa. Manchester: Manchester University Press.
Balán, J., H. L. Browning, and E. Jelín
  1973 Man in a Developing Society: Geographic and Social Mobility in Monterrey, Mexico. Austin: University of Texas Press.
Barber, B.
  1957 Social Stratification: A Comparative Analysis of Structure and Process. New York: Harcourt, Brace & World.
Barilari, F., and J. Oxley
  1966 "Evaluación del prestigio de 90 ocupaciones por una muestra de estudiantes Chilenos." Acta Psiquiatrica y Psicologica de América Latina 12:39–50.
Beals, R. L.
  1953 "Social stratification in Latin America." American Journal of Sociology 58 (January):327–339.
Bellah, R. N.
  1957 Tokugawa Religion: The Values of Pre-industrial Japan. Glencoe, Illinois: Free Press.
Ben-David, J., and A. Sloczower
  1962 "Universities and academic systems in modern societies." Archives Européennes de Sociologie 3(No. 1):45–84.
Berle, A. A., Jr., and G. C. Means
  1933 The Modern Corporation and Private Property. New York: Macmillan.
Beveridge, A.
  1974 "Economic independence, indigenization, and the African businessman." African Studies Review 17(December):477–490.

Blau, P M.
  1973 The Organization of Academic Work. New York: Wiley.
Blau, P. M., and O. D. Duncan
  1967 The American Occupational Structure. New York: Wiley.
Blishen, B. R.
  1958 "The construction and use of an occupational class scale." Canadian Journal of Eco-
        nomics and Political Science 24 (November):519–531.
  1967 "A socio-economic index for occupations in Canada." Canadian Review of
        Sociology and Anthropology 4 (February):41–53.
Bloch, M.
  1964 Feudal Society. Volume II: Social Classes and Political Organization. Chicago:
        University of Chicago Press (Phoenix).
Blumin, S.
  1969 "Mobility and change in ante-bellum Philadelphia." Pp. 165–208 in Stephan
        Thernstrom and Richard Sennett (eds.), Nineteenth Century Cities. New Haven:
        Yale University Press.
Bolte, K. M.
  1959 Sozialer Aufstief und Abstieg: Eine Untersuchung Uber Berufsprestige und
        Berufsmobilitat. Stuttgart: Ferdinand Enke Verlag.
Bone, L.
  1962 Secondary Education in the Guianas. Chicago: University of Chicago, Comparative
        Education Center.
Bonis, J.
  1964 "Echelle de prestige social en Mauritanie." Sociologie de Travail 6 (October–
        December):381–393.
Booth, C. (ed.)
  1889 Labour and Life of the People. Volume I: East London. London: Williams and
        Norgate.
  1895 Life and Labour of the People in London. Volumes V–VIII: Population Classified by
        Trades. London: Macmillan.
Bose, C. E.
  1973 Jobs and Gender: Sex and Occupational Prestige. Baltimore: Johns Hopkins
        University, Center for Metropolitan Planning and Research.
Brenner, V., and M. Hrouda
  1969 "Science and college education in the prestige of profession." Unpublished paper,
        Prague. Published German version: "Wissenschaft und hochschubildung im prestige
        der berufe." Soziale Welt 20 (1969):11–27.
Broom, L., F. L. Jones, and J. Zubrzycki
  1966 "Five measures of social rank in Australia." Paper given at the Sixth World
        Congress of Sociology, Evian, France.
Brown, E. H. P., and S. V. Hopkins
  1955 "Seven centuries of building wages." Economica 22 (August):195–206.
Butcher, H. J., and H. B. Pont
  1968 "Opinions about careers among Scottish secondary school children of high ability."
        British Journal of Educational Psychology 38 (November):272–279.
Butler, D., and D. Stokes
  1969 Political Change in Britain: Forces Shaping Electoral Change. New York: St.
        Martin's Press.
Canada Dominion Bureau of Statistics
  1961 Occupational Classification Manual Census of Canada 1961. Ottawa: Queen's
        Printer and Controller of Stationery (April).

1963a 1961 Census of Canada. Volume III, Part I: Labour Force: Occupations. Ottawa: Department of Public Printing and Stationery.

1963b 1961 Census of Canada. Volume III, Part 3: Wage Earners: Earnings and Employment. Ottawa: Department of Public Printing and Stationery.

Cancian, F.

1965 Economics and Prestige in a Maya Community: The Religious Cargo System in Zinacantan. Stanford: Stanford University Press.

Carlsson, G.

1958 Social Mobility and Class Structure. Lund, Sweden: C. W. K. Gleerup.

Carter, R. E., and O. Sepulveda

1964 "Occupational prestige in Santiago, Chile." American Behavioral Scientist 8 (September):20–24.

Castaldi, C.

1956 "Nota sóbra a hierarquia de prestígio das ocupacoes, segundo um grupo de emigrantes italianos e seus descendentes na cidade de São Paulo." Educacão e Ciências Sociais 1 (December):109–124.

Castillo, G. T.

1962 "Occupation evaluation in the Philippines." Philippine Sociological Review 10 (July–October):147–157.

Ceylon Department of Census and Statistics

1962 Census of Ceylon: 1953. Volume IV, Part 2, Section 8(A)—Income. Colombo: The Government Press.

Clignet, R., and P. Foster

1966 The Fortunate Few: A Study of Secondary Schools and Students in the Ivory Coast. Evanston, Illinois: Northwestern University Press.

Cohen, R.

1970 "Social stratification in Bornu." Pp. 225–267 in Arthur Tuden and Leonard Plotnicov (eds.), Social Stratification in Africa. New York: Free Press.

Congalton, A. A.

1962 Social Standing of Occupations in Sydney. Studies in Sociology No. 2. Kensington, Australia: University of New South Wales, School of Sociology.

1965 "Methodology of research into occupational prestige: reply to Allingham." Australian and New Zealand Journal of Sociology 1 (October):121–131.

Congalton, A. A., and R. J. Havighurst

1954 "Status ranking of occupations in New Zealand." Australian Journal of Psychology 6 (June):10–15.

Cooper, J. G., D. Brown, and B. Santos

1962 "The social status of occupations in Micronesia." Personnel and Guidance Journal 41 (November):267–269.

Costa Rica Direccion General de Estadistica y Censos

1966 Censo de Poblacion: 1963. San Jose: Seccion de Publicaciones.

Counts, G. S.

1925 "The social status of occupations: a problem in vocational guidance." School Review 33 (January):16–27.

Covello, V. T.

1976 "The process of status attainment in contemporary societies: a cross-national comparison." Unpublished Ph.D. dissertation, Columbia University.

Cucullu de Murmis, C. G.

1961 Estudio sobre el Prestigio de las Ocupaciones. Buenos Aires: University of Buenos Aires, Department of Sociology.

Cummings, W. K., and A. Naoi
   1972   "Education and mobility: an international comparison with special reference to
           Japan and the United States." Paper given at the annual meetings of the American
           Sociological Association, New Orleans (August).

Davis, K.
   1955   "Social and demographic aspects of economic development in India." Pp. 263–315 in
           Simon Kuznets, Wilbert E. Moore, and Joseph J. Spengler (eds.), Economic Growth:
           Brazil, India, Japan. Durham: Duke University Press.

Davis, K., and W. E. Moore
   1945   "Some principles of stratification." American Sociological Review 10 (April):242–
           249.

de Miguel, A.
   1967   "El prestigio de ocupaciones entre los jovenes espanoles." Anales de Sociologia 2
           (June):50–65.

Douglass, M.
   1966   Purity and Danger: A Comparative Study of Concepts of Pollution and Taboo.
           London: Routledge.

D'Souza, V. S.
   1962   "Social grading of occupations in India." Sociological Review. New series 10
           (July):145–159.
   1964   "Social grading of village occupations." Journal of the Gujarat Research Society 26
           (January):33–44.

Dumont, L.
   1970   Homo Hierarchicus: An Essay on the Caste System. Chicago: University of Chicago
           Press.

Duncan, O. D.
   1961   "A socioeconomic index for all occupations." Pp. 109–138 in Albert J. Reiss, Jr.
           (ed.), Occupations and Social Status. New York: Free Press of Glencoe.

Duncan, O. D., and J. W. Artis
   1951   "Some problems of stratification research." Rural Sociology 16 (March):17–29.

Duncan, O. D., and B. Duncan
   1955   "Residential distribution and occupational stratification." American Journal of
           Sociology 60 (March):493–503.

Durkheim, E.
   1933   The Division of Labor in Society. Tr. George Simpson. Glencoe, Illinois: Free Press.

Eister, A. W.
   1965   "Evaluations of selected jobs and occupations by university students in a developing
           country: Pakistan." Social Forces 49 (December):66–73.

Epstein, A. L.
   1967   "Occupational prestige on the Gazelle peninsula, New Britain." Australian and New
           Zealand Journal of Sociology 3 (October):111–121.

Erman, A.
   1894   Life in Ancient Egypt. H. M. Tirard (Tr.). New York: Benjamin Blom. [Reissued
           1969.]

Featherman, D. L., F. L. Jones, and R. M. Hauser
   1975   "Assumptions of social mobility research in the U.S.: the case of occupational
           status." Social Science Research 4 (December):329–360.

Featherman, D. L., M. Sobel, and D. Dickens
   1975   A Manual for Coding Occupations and Industries into Detailed 1970 Categories and
           a Listing of 1970-Basis Duncan Socioeconomic and NORC Prestige Scores.

Madison: University of Wisconsin, Center for Demography and Ecology Working Paper No. 75-1.

Firth, R.
1929 Primitive Economics of the New Zealand Maori. New York: E. P. Dutton.

Forster, R. E. (ed.)
1969 European Society in the 18th Century. New York: Walker and Co.

Foster, P.
1965 Education and Social Change in Ghana. Chicago: University of Chicago Press.

Funnell, V. C.
1968 "Social stratification." Problems of Communism 27 (March–April):14–21.

Geiger, H. K.
1968 The Family in Soviet Russia. Cambridge: Harvard University Press.

Ghana Census Office
1964 1960 Population Census of Ghana. Volume IV: Economic Characteristics of Local Authorities, Regions and Total Country. Accra: Census Office.

Ginsburg, N.
1961 Atlas of Economic Development. Chicago: University of Chicago Press.

Glass, D. V., and J. R. Hall
1954 "A description of a sample inquiry into social mobility in Great Britain." Pp. 79–97 in D. V. Glass (ed.), Social Mobility in Britain. London: Routledge and Kegan Paul.

Goldthorpe, J. H., and K. Hope
1972 "Occupational grading and occupational prestige." Pp. 19–80 in Keith Hope (ed.), The Analysis of Social Mobility: Methods and Approaches. Oxford Studies in Social Mobility Working Papers 1. Oxford: Clarendon Press.
1974 The Social Grading of Occupations: A New Approach and Scale. Oxford: Clarendon Press.

Goodman, L.
1969 "How to ransack social mobility tables and other kinds of cross-classification tables." American Journal of Sociology 75 (July):1–40.

Graham, S., and D. Beckles
1968 "The prestige ranking of occupations: problems of method and interpretation suggested by a study in Guyana." Social and Economic Studies 17 (December):367–380.

Great Britain Office of Population Censuses and Surveys
1970 Classification of Occupations 1970. London: Her Majesty's Stationery Office.

Great Britain General Register Office
1956 Census 1951: England and Wales. General Tables. London: Her Majesty's Stationery Office.

Green, T. L.
1953 "Ceylon." Pp. 484–502 in R. K. Hall (ed.), The Year Book of Education 1953. London: Evans Bros.

Gulliksen, H.
1964 "Intercultural studies of attitudes." Pp. 61–108 in Norman Frederiksen and Harold Gulliksen (eds.), Contributions to Mathematical Psychology. New York: Holt, Rinehart & Winston.

Gunn, B.
1964 "Children's conceptions of occupational prestige." Personnel and Guidance Journal 42 (February):558–563.

Haller, A. O., and D. M. Lewis
1966 "The hypothesis of intersocietal similarity in occupational prestige hierarchies." American Journal of Sociology 72 (September):210–216.

Haller, A. O., D. B. Holsinger, and H. U. Saraiva
   1972   "Variations in occupational prestige hierarchies: Brazilian data." American Journal
          of Sociology 77 (March):941–956.
Halmos, P. (ed.)
   1964   The Development of Industrial Societies: Papers read at the Nottingham Conference
          of the British Sociological Association, April, 1961. The Sociological Review
          Monograph No. 8. Keele: University of Keele.
Hammel, E. A.
   1970   "The ethnographer's dilemma: occupational prestige in Belgrade." Unpublished
          paper, University of California, Berkeley, Department of Anthropology.
Hashmi, S. S., M. R. Khan, and K. J. Kroti
   1964   The People of Karachi: Data from a Survey. Statistical Papers No. 2 (June).
          Karachi: Pakistan Institute of Development Economics.
Hauser, R. M., J. N. Koffel, H. P. Travis, and P. J. Dickinson
   1975   "Temporal changes in occupational mobility: evidence for men in the United States."
          American Sociological Review 40 (June):279–297.
Helling, G.
   n.d.   "Changing attitudes toward occupational status and prestige in Turkey." Unpublished
          paper, University of Omaha.
Hicks, R. E.
   1967   "Similarities and differences in occupational prestige ratings: a comparative study of
          two cultural groups in Zambia." African Social Research 3 (June):206–227.
   1969   "The relationship of sex to occupational prestige in an African country." Personnel
          and Guidance Journal 47 (March):665–668.
Hodge, P. L., and R. W. Hodge
   1964   "What ever happened to the nuclear physicist?" Paper given at the annual meetings
          of the American Sociological Association, Montreal (August).
Hodge, R. W., and P. L. Hodge
   1965   "Occupational assimilation as a competitive process." American Journal of Soci-
          ology 71 (November):249–264.
Hodge, R. W., and P. M. Siegel
   1965   "Selective perception of occupational prestige." Unpublished paper, National
          Opinion Research Center, Chicago (January).
   1966   "The classification of occupations: some problems of sociological interpretation."
          Paper given at the annual meetings of the American Statistical Association, Los
          Angeles (August).
Hodge, R. W., P. M. Siegel, and P. H. Rossi
   1964   "Occupational prestige in the United States, 1925–63." American Journal of
          Sociology 70 (November):286–302.
Hodge, R. W., D. J. Treiman, and P. H. Rossi
   1966   "A comparative study of occupational prestige." Pp. 309–321 in Reinhard Bendix
          and Seymour Martin Lipset (eds.), Class, Status, and Power: Social Stratification in
          Comparative Perspective. Second Edition. New York: Free Press.
Hope, K. (ed.)
   1972   The Analysis of Social Mobility: Methods and Approaches. Oxford Studies in Social
          Mobility Working Papers 1. Oxford: Clarendon.
Horowitz, M. A., M. Zymelman, and I. L. Herrnstadt
   1966   Manpower Requirements for Planning: An International Comparison Approach.
          Boston: Northeastern University, Department of Economics.

Hughes, J. R. T.
  1968 "Industrialization: Economic aspects." Pp. 7:252–263 in David L. Sills (ed.), International Encyclopedia of the Social Sciences. New York: Macmillan.
Hutchinson, B.
  1957 "The social grading of occupations in Brazil." British Journal of Sociology 8 (June):176–189.
  1962 "Social mobility in Buenos Aires, Montevideo, and Sao Pãulo: a preliminary comparison." American Latina 5 (October–December):3–19.
Hyman, H. H.
  1953 "The value systems of different classes: a social psychological contribution to the analysis of stratification." Pp. 426–442 in Reinhard Bendix and Seymour Martin Lipset (eds.), Class, Status and Power: A Reader in Social Stratification. Glencoe, Illinois: Free Press.
India Cabinet Secretariat
  1970 The National Sample Survey. Nineteenth Round: July 1964–June 1965. No. 163. Tables with Notes on Urban Labor Force. Delhi: Government of India Press.
India Registrar General
  1965 Census of India 1961. Volume I: India. Part II-B(ii): General Economic Tables. Delhi: Government of India Press.
Inkeles, A.
  1960 "Industrial man: the relation of status to experience, perception, and value." American Journal of Sociology 66 (July):1–31.
Inkeles, A., and P. H. Rossi
  1956 "National comparisons of occupational prestige." American Journal of Sociology 61 (January):329–339.
International Labour Office
  1952 Year Book of Labour Statistics 1951–52. Geneva: International Labour Office.
  1958a International Standard Classification of Occupations. Geneva: International Labour Office.
  1958b Year Book of Labour Statistics 1958. Geneva: International Labour Office.
  1960 Year Book of Labour Statistics 1960. Geneva: International Labour Office.
  1964 Year Book of Labour Statistics 1964. Geneva: International Labour Office.
  1969a International Standard Classification of Occupations. Revised Edition 1968. Geneva: International Labour Office.
  1969b Year Book of Labour Statistics 1969. Geneva: International Labour Office.
  1974 Bulletin of Labour Statistics, 1974 1st Quarter. Geneva: International Labour Office.
Inter-University Consortium for Political Research
  1975 Australian National Political Attitudes. Wave I: September–November, 1967. Ann Arbor: University of Michigan, Inter-University Consortium for Political Research.
Israel Central Bureau of Statistics
  n.d. Population and Housing Census: 1961. Jerusalem: Central Bureau of Statistics.
Jackman, R. W.
  1975 Politics and Social Equality: A Comparative Analysis. New York: Wiley.
Japan Bureau of Statistics
  1963 1960 Population Census of Japan. Volume II: One Per Cent Sample Tabulation. Part I: Age, Marital Status, Nationality, and Fertility. Tokyo: Office of the Prime Minister.
Japan Sociological Society Research Committee
  1954 "Social stratification in six large cities of Japan." Pp. 414–431 in Transactions of the

Second World Congress of Sociology. Volume II. London: International Sociological Association.

Jelín de Balán, E.
1967   "Fuerza de trabajo." Pp. 161–202 in Movilidad Social, Migracion y Fecundidad en Monterrey Metropolitano. Monterrey, Mexico: Universidad de Nuevo Leon, Centro de Investigaciones Economicas.

Kapr, J.
1969   "Obecná struktura prestiže povolání v Československu." Pp. 377–400 in Pavel Machonin (ed.), Československá Společnost: Sociologická Analýza Sociální Stratifikace. Bratislava: Epocha.

Katz, M.
1971   "Data on changes in household and occupational structure, 1851–1861." The Canadian Social History Project Interim Report No. 3. Toronto: Ontario Institute for Studies in Education.

Kelley, J.
1971   "Social mobility in traditional society: the Toro of Uganda." Unpublished Ph.D. dissertation, University of California, Berkeley.

Kelley, J., and W. Pendleton
1975   "Structure, culture and occupational prestige: data from sub-Saharan Africa." American Journal of Sociology. Forthcoming.

Kerr, C., J. T. Dunlop, F. H. Harbison, and C. A. Myers
1960   Industrialism and Industrial Man: The Problems of Labor and Management in Economic Growth. Cambridge: Harvard University Press.

Kimball, S. T.
1960   "Primary education in Brazil." Comparative Education Review 4 (June):49–54.

Kimberly, J. C.
1970   "The emergence and stabilization of stratification in simple and complex social systems." Pp. 73–101 in Edward O. Laumann (ed.), Social Stratification: Research and Theory for the 1970s. Indianapolis: Bobbs-Merrill.

Klatzky, S. R.
1970   Patterns of Contact with Relatives. Washington, D.C.: American Sociological Association (Rose Monograph Series).

Klatzky, S., and R. W. Hodge
1971   "A canonical correlation analysis of occupational mobility." Journal of the American Statistical Association 66 (March):16–22.

Kleining, G.
1973   "Die legitimation der ungleichheit." Pp. 303–326 in René König (ed.), Soziologie: Sprache Bezug zur Praxis Verhältnis zu Anderen Wissenschaften. Opladen: Westdeutscher Verlag.

Kleining, G., and H. Moore
1968   "Soziale selbsteinstufung (SSE): ein instrument zur messung sozialer schichten." Kölner Zeitschrift für Soziologie und Sozial-Psychologie 20 (September):502–552.

Knight, E. W.
1951   Education in the United States. Third Revised Edition. Boston: Ginn.

Koppel, M. H.
1964   "Occupational stratification in an emerging society." Caribbean Studies 3 (January):3–16.

Kubat, D.
1963   "Social mobility in Czechoslovakia." American Sociological Review 28 (April):203–212.

Kuiper, G.
1954 Mobiliteit in de Sociale en Beroepshierarchie. Utrecht: Van Gorcum.
Kunde, T. A., and R. V. Dawes
1959 "Comparative study of occupational prestige in three western cultures." Personnel and Guidance Journal 37 (January):350–352.
Kuper, L.
1965 An African Bourgeoisie. New Haven: Yale University Press.
Laumann, E. O.
1965 "Subjective social distance and urban occupational stratification." American Journal of Sociology 71 (July):26–36.
1966 Prestige and Association in an Urban Community: An Analysis of an Urban Stratification System. Indianapolis: Bobbs-Merrill.
1973 Bonds of Pluralism: The Form and Substance of Urban Social Networks. New York: Wiley.
Laumann, E. O., and R. Senter
1976 "Subjective social distance, occupational stratification, and forms of status and class consciousness: a cross-national replication and extension." American Journal of Sociology 81 (May):1304–1338.
Lenski, G. E.
1966 Power and Privilege: A Theory of Social Stratification. New York: McGraw-Hill.
Leik, R. K., S. A. Leik, B. Morton, R. B. Beardsley, and M. E. Hardy.
1975 "The emergence and change of stratification in social exchange systems." Social Science Research 4 (March):17–40.
Lewis, D. M., and A. O. Haller
1964 "Rural–urban differences in pre-industrial and industrial evaluations of occupations by Japanese adolescent boys." Rural Sociology 29 (September):324–329.
Lieberson, S.
1970 Language and Ethnic Relations in Canada. New York: Wiley.
Lin, N., and D. Yauger
1975 "The process of occupational status achievement: a preliminary cross-national comparison." American Journal of Sociology 81 (November):543–562.
Lipset, S. M.
1967 "Values, education, and entrepreneurship." Pp. 3–60 in Seymour Martin Lipset and Aldo Solari (eds.), Elites in Latin America. New York: Oxford University Press (Galaxy).
Lissak, M.
1964 "Haribud hahevrati bayishuv uvamedina." Molad 22 (November):493–502.
1965 "Patterns of change in ideology and class structure in Israel." Jewish Journal of Sociology 7 (June):46–62.
Main, J. T.
1965 The Social Structure of Revolutionary America. Princeton: Princeton University Press.
Mallinson, V.
1957 An Introduction to the Study of Comparative Education. Melbourne: William Heinemann.
Marsh, R. M.
1970 "Evolution and revolution: two types of change in China's system of social stratification." Pp. 149–172 in Leonard Plotnicov and Arthur Tuden (eds.), Essays in Comparative Social Stratification. Pittsburgh: University of Pittsburgh Press.

Matejko, A.
  1966 "Status incongruence in the Polish intelligentsia." Social Research 33 (Winter):611–
         638.
Mayntz, R.
  1956 "Gedanken und ergebnisse zur empirischen feststellung sozialer schichten." In Kolner
         Zeitschrift für Soziologie und Sozialpsychologie, Sonderheft I: Soziologie der
         Gemeinde.
McNemar, Q.
  1969 Psychological Statistics. Fourth Edition. New York: John Wiley & Sons.
Means, P. A.
  1936 Ancient Civilizations of the Andes. New York: Charles Scribner's Sons.
Mitchell, J. C.
  1966 "Aspects of occupational prestige in a plural society." Pp. 256–271 in P. C. Lloyd
         (ed.), The New Elites of Tropical Africa. London: Oxford University Press.
Mitchell, J. C., and A. L. Epstein
  1959 "Occupational prestige and social status among urban Africans in Northern
         Rhodesia." Africa 29:22–40.
Mitchell, J. C., and S. H. Irvine
  1966 "Social position and the grading of occupations." Rhodes–Livingstone Journal 38
         (January):42–54.
Moser, C. A., and J. R. Hall
  1954 "The social grading of occupations." Pp. 29–50 in D. V. Glass (ed.), Social Mobility
         in Britain. London: Routledge and Kegan Paul.
Mosteller, F., and J. W. Tukey
  1968 "Data analysis, including statistics." Pp. 80–203 in Gardner Lindzey and Elliot
         Aronson (eds.), The Handbook of Social Psychology. Second Edition. Volume 2:
         Research Methods. Reading, Massachusetts: Addison-Wesley.
Murdock, G. P.
  1937 "Comparative data on the division of labor by sex." Social Forces 15 (May):551–553.
New Zealand Department of Statistics
  1964 New Zealand Population Census: 1961. Volume V: Incomes. Wellington: Department
         of Statistics.
Nisihira, S.
  1968 "Le prestige social des différentes professions: l'evaluation populaire au Japon."
         Revue Francaise de Sociologie 9 (October–December):548–557.
Nunnally, J. C.
  1967 Psychometric Theory. New York: McGraw-Hill.
Onions, C. T. (ed.)
  1955 The Oxford Universal Dictionary on Historical Principles. Third Edition Revised
         with Addenda. Oxford: Clarendon.
Øyen, Ø.
  1964 "Notat vedrørende sammenlignbarheten av skalaer for yrkesprestisje." Sociologiske
         Meddelelser 9:147–150.
Parkin, F.
  1969 "Class stratification in socialist societies." British Journal of Sociology 20 (De-
         cember):355–375.
  1971 Class Inequality and Political Order: Social Stratification in Capitalist and Com-
         munist Countries. New York: Praeger.
Parsons, T.
  1954 "A revised analytical approach to the theory of social stratification." Pp. 386–439 in
         Essays in Sociological Theory. Revised Edition. Glencoe, Illinois: Free Press.

Pineo, P. C., and J. Porter
1967 "Occupational prestige in Canada." Canadian Review of Sociology and Anthropology 4 (February):24–40.

Rama, C. M.
1960 Las Clases Sociales en el Uruguay. Montevideo: Ediciones Nuestro Tiempo.

Ramsey, C. E., and R. J. Smith
1960 "Japanese and American perceptions of occupations." American Journal of Sociology 65 (March):475–482.

Ray, V. F.
1933 The Sanpoil and Nespelem: Salishan Peoples of Northeastern Washington. University of Washington Publications in Anthropology 5, December, 1932. Seattle: University of Washington Press.

Reiss, A. J., Jr.
1961 Occupations and Social Status. New York: Free Press of Glencoe.

Rosenfeld, E.
1951 "Social stratification in a 'classless' society." American Sociological Review 16 (December):766–774.

Rossi, P. H., W. A. Sampson, C. E. Bose, G. Jasso, and J. Passel
1974 "Measuring household social standing." Social Science Research 3 (September):169–190.

Sarapata, A.
1963 "Iustrum pretium." Polish Sociological Bulletin 1 (January–March):41–56.

Sarapata, A., and W. Wesołowski
1961 "The evaluation of occupations by Warsaw inhabitants." American Journal of Sociology 66 (May):581–591.

Šefer, B.
1968 "Income distribution in Yugoslavia." International Labour Review 97 (April):371–389.

Shepard, R. N., A. K. Romney, and S. B. Nerlove (eds.)
1972 Multidimensional Scaling: Theory and Applications in the Behavioral Sciences. Volume 1: Theory. New York: Seminar Press.

Shils, E.
1968 "Deference." Pp. 104–132 in J. A. Jackson (ed.), Social Stratification. Sociological Studies 1. Cambridge: Cambridge University Press.

Siegel, P. M.
1967 "The prestige of occupations and the social standing of people." Unpublished Ph.D. dissertation proposal, University of Chicago.
1970 "Occupational prestige in the Negro subculture." Pp. 156–171 in Edward O. Laumann (ed.), Social Stratification: Research and Theory for the 1970s. Indianapolis: Bobbs-Merrill.
1971 "Prestige in the American occupational structure." Unpublished Ph.D. dissertation, University of Chicago.

Siegel, P. M., R. W. Hodge, and P. H. Rossi.
1974 Occupational Prestige in the United States. New York: Academic Press. Forthcoming.

Simmons, D. D.
1962 "Children's rankings of occupational prestige." Personnel and Guidance Journal 41 (December):332–336.

Singer, B., and S. Spilerman
1974 "Social mobility models for heterogeneous populations." Pp. 356–402 in Herbert L. Costner (ed.), Sociological Methodology 1973–1974. San Francisco: Jossey-Bass.

Singh, H.
  1967 "Social grading of castes and occupations in an Indian village." Indian Journal of
        Social Work 27 (January):381–386.
Sjoberg, G.
  1960 The Preindustrial City: Past and Present. Glencoe, Illinois: Free Press.
Słomczynski, K.
  1972 Zróżnicowanie Społeczno-Zawodowe I Jego Korelaty: z Badań Nad Ludnościa
        Miejska W Latach 1964–1967. Warsaw: Zakład Narodowy Imienia Ossolińskich,
        Wydawnictwo Polskiej Akademii Nauk.
Smith, M. G.
  1965 Stratification in Grenada. Berkeley: University of California Press.
Soares, G. A. D.
  1966 "Economic development and class structure." Pp. 190–199 in Reinhard Bendix and
        Seymour Martin Lipset (eds.), Class, Status, and Power: Social Stratification in
        Comparative Perspective. Second Edition. New York: Free Press.
Staley, E.
  1906 The Guilds of Florence. London: Methuen.
Stewart, A., K. Prandy, and R. M. Blackburn
  1973 "Measuring the class structure." Nature 245 (October 26):415–417.
Surinam Algemeen Bureau voor de Statistiek
  1962 Bedrijfs- En Beroepsstelling 1961. Geheel Suriname. Paramaribo: Ministerie van
        Algemene Zaken (September).
Svalastoga, K.
  1959 Prestige, Class, and Mobility. Copenhagen: Gyldendale.
Sweden Statistiska Centralbyrån
  1965 Folkräkningen, 1960. Volume XI: Urvalsbearbetning: Familjer, Inkomst, Inrikes
        Omflyttning och Näringsgrensvaxling. Stockholm: Statistiska Centralbyrån.
Taeuber, A. F., K. E. Taeuber, and G. G. Cain
  1966 "Occupational assimilation and the competitive process: a reanalysis." American
        Journal of Sociology 72 (November):273–285.
Taiwan Labor Force Survey Research Institute
  1968 Manpower Requirements Survey Report. Taipei: Council for International Economic
        Cooperation and Development.
Taiwan Provincial Government, Department of Reconstruction
  1969 Report of Taiwan Labour Statistics. Taipei: Taiwan Provincial Government.
Taylor, C. L., and M. C. Hudson
  1972 World Handbook of Political and Social Indicators. Second Edition. New Haven:
        Yale University Press.
Thomas, R. M. and Soeparman
  1963 "Occupational prestige: Indonesia and America." Personnel and Guidance Journal
        41 (January):430–434.
Tiryakian, E.
  1958 "The prestige evaluation of occupations in an underdeveloped country: the Philip-
        pines." American Journal of Sociology 63 (January):390–399.
Tobi, E. J., and A. W. Luyckx
  1950 Herkomst en Toekomst van de Middenstander. Amsterdam: A. J. G. Strengholt.
Tofigh, F.
  1964 Du Choix des Professions. Geneva: Librarie Droz.
Tominaga, K.
  1969 "Trend analysis of social stratification and social mobility in contemporary Japan."
        Developing Economies 7 (December):471–498.

Treiman, D. J.
1968 "Occupational prestige and social structure: a cross-national comparison." Unpublished Ph.D. dissertation, University of Chicago.
1970 "Industrialization and social stratification." Pp. 207–234 in Edward O. Laumann (ed.), Social Stratification: Research and Theory for the 1970s. Indianapolis: Bobbs-Merrill.
1974 "Problems of occupational classification for comparative socioeconomic analysis." Paper given at the Workshop on Census Measurement of Socioeconomic Status, East–West Population Institute, Honolulu (December 9–13).
1975 "Problems of concept and measurement in the comparative study of occupational mobility." Social Science Research 4 (September):183–230.
1976 "A standard occupational prestige scale for use with historical data." Journal of Interdisciplinary History 7 (Autumn):283–304.

Treiman, D. J., and K. Terrell
1975a "The process of status attainment in the United States and Great Britain." American Journal of Sociology 81 (November):563–583.
1975b "Sex and the process of status attainment: a comparison of working women and men." American Sociological Review 40 (April):174–200.
1975c "Women, work, and wages—trends in the female occupational structure since 1940." Pp. 157–199 in Kenneth C. Land and Seymour Spilerman (eds.), Social Indicator Models. New York: Russell Sage.

Treiman, D. J., T. Lux, and R. W. Hodge
1969 "Rural–urban differences in occupational prestige evaluations in Thailand." Paper given at the Behavioral Science Workshop, Graduate School of Business, University of Chicago (April).

Udy, S.
1959 The Organization of Work: A Comparative Analysis of Production among Nonindustrial Peoples. New Haven: HRAF Press.

USSR Tsentral'noye Statistichyeskoye Oopravlyeniye
1962 Itogi Vsesoyooznoi Perepisi Naseleniya 1959 Goda. SSSR (Svodnii Tom). Moscow: Gosstatizdat.

United Nations Secretariat of the Economic Commission for Europe
1967 Incomes in Postwar Europe: A Study of Policies, Growth and Distribution. Economic Survey of Europe in 1965 Part 2. Geneva: United Nations.

United States Bureau of the Census
1950 1950 Census of Population Alphabetical Index of Occupations and Industries (Revised Edition). Washington, D.C.: U.S. Government Printing Office.
1960a 1960 Census of Population Alphabetical Index of Occupations and Industries (Revised edition). Washington, D.C.: U.S. Government Printing Office.
1960b 1960 Census of Population Classified Index of Occupations and Industries. Washington, D.C.: U.S. Government Printing Office.
1963 U.S. Census of Population: 1960. Subject Reports. Final Report PC(2)–7A. Occupational Characteristics. Washington, D.C.: U.S. Government Printing Office.
1971a 1970 Census of Population Alphabetical Index of Industries and Occupations. Washington, D.C.: U.S. Government Printing Office.
1971b 1970 Census of Population Classified Index of Industries and Occupations. Washington, D.C.: U.S. Government Printing Office.
1973 Census of Population: 1970. Subject Reports. Final Report PC(2)–7A. Occupational Characteristics. Washington, D.C.: U.S. Government Printing Office.

United States Department of Labor
 1965   Dictionary of Occupational Titles 1965. Volume I: Definitions of Titles. Washington,
        D.C.: U.S. Government Printing Office.
University of the Philippines Population Institute
 1974   1973 National Demographic Survey. Manila: University of the Philippines, Popula-
        tion Institute.
Van Der Veur, P. W.
 1966   "Occupational prestige among secondary school students in West New Guinea (West
        Irian)." Australian and New Zealand Journal of Sociology 2 (October):107–110.
van Heek, F.
 1945   Stijging en Daling op de Maatschappelijke Ladder. Leiden: E. J. Brill.
van Heek, F., and E. V. W. Vercruijsse
 1958   "De Nederlandse beroepsprestige-stratificatie." Pp. 11–48 in F. van Heek, E. V. W.
        Vercruijsse, H. M. in 't Veld-Langeveld, G. Kuiper, A. van Braam, and B. Korstanje,
        Sociale Stijging en Daling in Nederland. Volume I. Leiden: H. E. Stenfert Kroese.
van Hulten, I. E.
 1953   Stijging en Daling in een Modern Grotbedrijf. Leiden: H. E. Stenfert Kroese.
van Tulder, J. J. M.
 1962   De Beroepsmobiliteit in Nederland van 1919 tot 1954: een Sociaal-Statistische
        Studie. Leiden: H. E. Stenfert Kroese.
Vaughan, J. H., Jr.
 1970   "Caste systems in the Western Sudan." Pp. 59–92 in Arthur Tuden and Leonard
        Plotnicov (eds.), Social Stratification in Africa. New York: Free Press.
Veblen, T.
 1919   The Theory of the Leisure Class: An Economic Study of Institutions. New York: B.
        W. Huebsch.
Vellekoop, C.
 1966   "The meanings of occupational prestige and the semantic differential." Australian
        and New Zealand Journal of Sociology 2 (April):45–49.
Vodzinskaia, V. V.
 1969   "O sotsial'noi obuslovlennosti vybora professii." Pp. 39–61 in G. V. Osipov and Ia.
        Shchepanskii (eds.), Sotsial'nye Problemy Truda i Proizvadstva. Moscow: Misl.
Walker, H. M., and J. Lev
 1953   Statistical Inference. New York: Holt, Rinehart & Winston.
Warner, W. L.
 1960   Social Class in America: A Manual of Procedure for the Measurement of Social
        Status. New York: Harper (Torchbooks).
Weber, M.
 1947   The Theory of Social and Economic Organization. Edited and translated by Talcott
        Parsons. Glencoe, Illinois: Free Press.
 1958   From Max Weber: Essays in Sociology. Translated, edited, and with an introduction
        by H. H. Gerth and C. Wright Mills. New York: Oxford (Galaxy).
Wilkerson, S. K.
 1967   "Occupational prestige in Mexico as perceived by college students." Human Mosaic
        2 (Fall):56–64.
Wright, D. (ed.)
 1958   History of Nepal. Tr. Munshi Shew Shunker Singh and Pandit Sri Gunanand. Cal-
        cutta: Susil Gupta (India) Private Ltd. (First published by Cambridge University
        Press, 1877.)

Wurzbacher, G.
1954 Das Dorf im Spannungsfeld Industrieller Entwicklung. Stuttgart: Ferdinand Enke Verlag.
Xydias, N.
1956 "Prestiges des professions." Pp. 489–500 in Daryll Forde (ed.), Aspects Sociaux de L'industrialisation et de L'urbanisation en Afrique au Sud du Sahara. Paris: UNESCO.
Yang, M. M. C.
1969 Chinese Social Structure: A Historical Study. Taipei: Eurasia Book Co.
Yauger, D., and N. Lin
1973 Economic Development and Occupational Stratification: A Preliminary Cross-National Comparison. Albany: State University of New York, Department of Sociology, International Center for Social Research Monograph No. 003.
Yugoslavia Savezni Zavod Za Statistiku
1965 Statistički Godišnajak SFRJ: 1965. Belgrad Savezni Zavod Za Statistiku.
Zambia Office of National Development and Planning
1966 Manpower Report; A Report and Statistical Handbook of Manpower, Education, Training, and Zambinisation, 1965–1966. Lusaka: Government Printer.
Zborowski, M., and E. Herzog
1952 Life IS with People: The Culture of the Shtetl. New York: Schocken Books.

Index

A
B 7
C 8
D 9
E 0
F 1
G 2
H 3
I 4
J 5